T0314221

MACHINE LEARNING
FOR BUSINESS ANALYTICS

MACHINE LEARNING
FOR BUSINESS ANALYTICS

Concepts, Techniques and Applications in RapidMiner

GALIT SHMUELI
National Tsing Hua University

PETER C. BRUCE
statistics.com

AMIT V. DEOKAR
University of Massachusetts Lowell

NITIN R. PATEL
Cytel, Inc.

WILEY

This edition first published 2023
© 2023 John Wiley & Sons, Inc.

The right of Galit Shmueli, Peter C. Bruce, Amit V. Deokar, and Nitin R. Patel to be identified as the authors of this work has been asserted in accordance with law.

Registered Office
John Wiley & Sons, Inc., 111 River Street, Hoboken, NJ 07030, USA

For details of our global editorial offices, customer services, and more information about Wiley products visit us at www.wiley.com.

Wiley also publishes its books in a variety of electronic formats and by print-on-demand. Some content that appears in standard print versions of this book may not be available in other formats.

Library of Congress Cataloging-in-Publication Data Applied for:

Hardback: 9781119828792

Cover Design: Wiley
Cover Image: © Eakarat Buanoi/Getty Images

Set in 11.5/14.5pt BemboStd by Straive, Chennai, India
Printed and bound by CPI Group (UK) Ltd, Croydon, CR0 4YY

C9781119828792_090223

To our families

Boaz and Noa

Liz, Lisa, and Allison

Aparna, Aditi, Anuja, Ajit, Aai, and Baba

Tehmi, Arjun, and in memory of Aneesh

Contents

<u>PART I **PRELIMINARIES**</u>

PART II DATA EXPLORATION AND DIMENSION REDUCTION

CHAPTER 3 Data Visualization 63

PART IV   PREDICTION AND CLASSIFICATION METHODS

CHAPTER 6   Multiple Linear Regression   163

CHAPTER 7 k-Nearest Neighbors (k-NN)   189

CHAPTER 8   The Naive Bayes Classifier   209

CHAPTER 9 **Classification and Regression Trees**   229

CHAPTER 10 **Logistic Regression**   269

CHAPTER 13 Generating, Comparing, and Combining Multiple Models

359

PART V INTERVENTION AND USER FEEDBACK

CHAPTER 14 Interventions: Experiments, Uplift Models, and Reinforcement Learning

387

PART VI   MINING RELATIONSHIPS AMONG RECORDS

CHAPTER 15   Association Rules and Collaborative Filtering   409

CHAPTER 16   Cluster Analysis   445

CHAPTER 22 **Responsible Data Science**   617

PART IX CASES

CHAPTER 23 Cases   647

Foreword by Ravi Bapna

Converting data into an asset is the new business imperative facing modern managers. Each day the gap between what analytics capabilities make possible and companies' absorptive capacity of creating value from such capabilities increases. In many ways, data is the new gold—and mining this gold to create business value in today's context of a highly networked and digital society requires a skillset that we haven't traditionally delivered in business or statistics or engineering programs on their own. For those businesses and organizations that feel overwhelmed by today's big data, the phrase *you ain't seen nothing yet* comes to mind. Yesterday's three major sources of big data—the 20+ years of investment in enterprise systems (ERP, CRM, SCM, etc.), the 3 billion plus people on the online social grid, and the close to 5 billion people carrying increasingly sophisticated mobile devices—are going to be dwarfed by tomorrow's smarter physical ecosystems fueled by the Internet of Things (IoT) movement.

The idea that we can use sensors to connect physical objects such as homes, automobiles, roads, and even garbage bins and streetlights to digitally optimized systems of governance goes hand in glove with bigger data and the need for deeper analytical capabilities. We are not far away from a smart refrigerator sensing that you are short on, say, eggs, populating your grocery store's mobile app's shopping list, and arranging a Task Rabbit to do a grocery run for you. Or the refrigerator negotiating a deal with an Uber driver to deliver an evening meal to you. Nor are we far away from sensors embedded in roads and vehicles that can compute traffic congestion, track roadway wear and tear, record vehicle use, and factor these into dynamic usage-based pricing, insurance rates, and even taxation. This brave new world is going to be fueled by analytics and the ability to harness data for competitive advantage.

Business Analytics is an emerging discipline that is going to help us ride this new wave. This new Business Analytics discipline requires individuals who are grounded in the fundamentals of business such that they know the right questions to ask; who have the ability to harness, store, and optimally process vast datasets from a variety of structured and unstructured sources; and who can then use an array of techniques from machine learning and statistics to uncover new insights for decision-making. Such individuals are a rare commodity today, but their creation has been the focus of this book for a decade now. This book's forte is that it relies on explaining the core set of concepts required for today's business analytics professionals using real-world data-rich cases in a hands-on manner, without sacrificing academic rigor. It provides a modern-day foundation for Business Analytics, the notion of linking the x's to the y's of interest in a predictive sense. I say this with the confidence of someone who was probably the first adopter of the zeroth edition of this book (Spring 2006 at the Indian School of Business).

After the publication of the R and Python editions, the new RapidMiner edition is an important addition. RapidMiner is gaining in popularity among analytics professionals as it is a non-programming environment that lowers the barriers for managers to adopt analytics. The new addition also covers causal analytics as experimentation (often called A/B testing in the industry), which is now becoming mainstream in the tech companies. Further, the authors have added a new chapter on Responsible Data Science, a new part on AutoML, more on deep learning and beefed up deep learning examples in the text mining and forecasting chapters. These updates make this new edition "state of the art" with respect to modern business analytics and AI.

I look forward to using the book in multiple fora, in executive education, in MBA classrooms, in MS-Business Analytics programs, and in Data Science bootcamps. I trust you will too!

RAVI BAPNA
Carlson School of Management, University of Minnesota, 2022

Preface to the RapidMiner Edition

This textbook first appeared in early 2007 and has been used by numerous students and practitioners and in many courses, including our own experience teaching this material both online and in person for more than 15 years. The first edition, based on the Excel add-in Analytic Solver Data Mining (previously XLMiner), was followed by two more Analytic Solver editions, a JMP edition, an R edition, a Python edition, and now this RapidMiner edition, with its companion website, www.dataminingbook.com.

This new RapidMiner edition relies on the open source machine learning platform *RapidMiner Studio* (generally called *RapidMiner*), which offers both free and commercially-licensed versions. We present output from RapidMiner, as well as the processes used to produce that output. We show the specification of the appropriate operators from RapidMiner and some of its key extensions. Unlike computer science- or statistics-oriented textbooks, the focus in this book is on machine learning concepts and how to implement the associated algorithms in RapidMiner. We assume a familiarity with the fundamentals of data analysis and statistics. Basic knowledge of Python can be helpful for a few chapters.

For this RapidMiner edition, a new co-author, Amit Deokar comes on board bringing both expertise teaching business analytics courses using RapidMiner and extensive data science experience in working with businesses on research and consulting projects. In addition to providing RapidMiner guidance, and RapidMiner process and output screenshots, this edition also incorporates updates and new material based on feedback from instructors teaching MBA, MS, undergraduate, diploma, and executive courses, and from their students.

Importantly, this edition includes several new topics:

- A dedicated section on *deep learning* in Chapter 11, with additional deep learning examples in text mining (Chapter 21) and time series forecasting (Chapter 19).

- A new chapter on *Responsible Data Science* (Chapter 22) covering topics of fairness, transparency, model cards and datasheets, legal considerations, and more, with an illustrative example.

- The *Performance Evaluation* exposition in Chapter 5 was expanded to include further metrics (precision and recall, F1, AUC) and the SMOTE oversampling method.
- A new chapter on *Generating, Comparing, and Combining Multiple Models* (Chapter 13) that covers AutoML, explaining model predictions, and ensembles.
- A new chapter dedicated to *Interventions and User Feedback* (Chapter 14), that covers A/B tests, uplift modeling, and reinforcement learning.
- A new case (Loan Approval) that touches on regulatory and ethical issues.

A note about the book's title: The first two editions of the book used the title *Data Mining for Business Intelligence*. *Business intelligence* today refers mainly to reporting and data visualization ("what is happening now"), while *business analytics* has taken over the "advanced analytics," which include predictive analytics and data mining. Later editions were therefore renamed *Data Mining for Business Analytics*. However, the recent AI transformation has made the term *machine learning* more popularly associated with the methods in this textbook. In this new edition, we therefore use the updated terms *Machine Learning* and *Business Analytics*.

Since the appearance of the (Analytic Solver-based) second edition, the landscape of the courses using the textbook has greatly expanded: whereas initially the book was used mainly in semester-long elective MBA-level courses, it is now used in a variety of courses in business analytics degrees and certificate programs, ranging from undergraduate programs to postgraduate and executive education programs. Courses in such programs also vary in their duration and coverage. In many cases, this textbook is used across multiple courses. The book is designed to continue supporting the general "predictive analytics", "data mining", or "machine learning" course as well as supporting a set of courses in dedicated business analytics programs.

A general "business analytics," "predictive analytics," or "machine learning" course, common in MBA and undergraduate programs as a one-semester elective, would cover Parts I–III, and choose a subset of methods from Parts IV and V. Instructors can choose to use cases as team assignments, class discussions, or projects. For a two-semester course, Part VII might be considered, and we recommend introducing Part VIII (Data Analytics).

For a set of courses in a dedicated business analytics program, here are a few courses that have been using our book:

Predictive Analytics—Supervised Learning: In a dedicated business analytics program, the topic of predictive analytics is typically instructed across a set of courses. The first course would cover Parts I–III, and instructors typically choose a subset of methods from Part IV according to the course length. We recommend including Part VIII: Data Analytics.

Predictive Analytics—Unsupervised Learning: This course introduces data exploration and visualization, dimension reduction, mining relationships, and clustering (Parts II and VI). If this course follows the Predictive Analytics: Supervised Learning course, then it is useful to examine examples and approaches that integrate unsupervised and supervised learning, such as Part VIII on Data Analytics.

Forecasting analytics: A dedicated course on time series forecasting would rely on Part VI.

Advanced analytics: A course that integrates the learnings from predictive analytics (supervised and unsupervised learning) can focus on Part VIII: Data Analytics, where social network analytics and text mining are introduced, and responsible data science is discussed. Such a course might also include Chapter 13, Generating, Comparing, and Combining Multiple Models and AutoML from Part IV, as well as Part V, which covers experiments, uplift modeling, and reinforcement learning. Some instructors choose to use the cases (Chapter 23) in such a course.

In all courses, we strongly recommend including a project component, where data are either collected by students according to their interest or provided by the instructor (e.g., from the many machine learning competition datasets available). From our experience and other instructors' experience, such projects enhance the learning and provide students with an excellent opportunity to understand the strengths of machine learning and the challenges that arise in the process.

GALIT SHMUELI, PETER C. BRUCE, AMIT V. DEOKAR, AND NITIN R. PATEL
2022

Acknowledgments

We thank the many people who assisted us in improving the book from its inception as *Data Mining for Business Intelligence* in 2006 (using XLMiner, now Analytic Solver), its reincarnation as *Data Mining for Business Analytics*, and now *Machine Learning for Business Analytics*, including translations in Chinese and Korean and versions supporting Analytic Solver Data Mining, R, Python, SAS JMP, and now RapidMiner.

Anthony Babinec, who has been using earlier editions of this book for years in his data mining courses at Statistics.com, provided us with detailed and expert corrections. Dan Toy and John Elder IV greeted our project with early enthusiasm and provided detailed and useful comments on initial drafts. Ravi Bapna, who used an early draft in a data mining course at the Indian School of Business and later at University of Minnesota, has provided invaluable comments and helpful suggestions since the book's start.

Many of the instructors, teaching assistants, and students using earlier editions of the book have contributed invaluable feedback both directly and indirectly, through fruitful discussions, learning journeys, and interesting machine learning projects that have helped shape and improve the book. These include MBA students from the University of Maryland, MIT, the Indian School of Business, National Tsing Hua University, University of Massachusetts Lowell, and Statistics.com. Instructors from many universities and teaching programs, too numerous to list, have supported and helped improve the book since its inception. Scott Nestler has been a helpful friend of this book project from the beginning.

Kuber Deokar, instructional operations supervisor at Statistics.com, has been unstinting in his assistance, support, and detailed attention. We also thank Anuja Kulkarni, assistant teacher at Statistics.com. Valerie Troiano has shepherded many instructors and students through the Statistics.com courses that have helped nurture the development of these books.

Colleagues and family members have been providing ongoing feedback and assistance with this book project. Vijay Kamble at UIC and Travis Greene at NTHU have provided valuable help with the section on reinforcement learning. Boaz Shmueli and Raquelle Azran gave detailed editorial comments and suggestions on the first two editions; Bruce McCullough and Adam Hughes did the same for the first edition. Noa Shmueli provided careful proofs of the third edition. Ran Shenberger offered design tips. Che Lin and Boaz Shmueli provided feedback on deep learning. Ken Strasma, founder of the microtargeting firm HaystaqDNA and director of targeting for the 2004 Kerry campaign and the 2008 Obama campaign, provided the scenario and data for the section on uplift modeling. We also thank Jen Golbeck, director of the Social Intelligence Lab at the University of Maryland and author of *Analyzing the Social Web*, whose book inspired our presentation in the chapter on social network analytics. Inbal Yahav and Peter Gedeck, co-authors of the R and Python editions, helped improve the social network analytics and text mining chapters. Randall Pruim contributed extensively to the chapter on visualization. Inbal Yahav, co-author of the R edition, helped improve the social network analytics and text mining chapters.

Marietta Tretter at Texas A&M shared comments and thoughts on the time series chapters, and Stephen Few and Ben Shneiderman provided feedback and suggestions on the data visualization chapter and overall design tips.

Susan Palocsay and Mia Stephens have provided suggestions and feedback on numerous occasions, as have Margret Bjarnadottir and Mohammad Salehan. We also thank Catherine Plaisant at the University of Maryland's Human–Computer Interaction Lab, who helped out in a major way by contributing exercises and illustrations to the data visualization chapter. Gregory Piatetsky-Shapiro, founder of KDNuggets.com, has been generous with his time and counsel in the early years of this project.

We thank colleagues at the MIT Sloan School of Management for their support during the formative stage of this book—Dimitris Bertsimas, James Orlin, Robert Freund, Roy Welsch, Gordon Kaufmann, and Gabriel Bitran. As teaching assistants for the data mining course at Sloan, Adam Mersereau gave detailed comments on the notes and cases that were the genesis of this book, Romy Shioda helped with the preparation of several cases and exercises used here, and Mahesh Kumar helped with the material on clustering.

Colleagues at the University of Maryland's Smith School of Business: Shrivardhan Lele, Wolfgang Jank, and Paul Zantek provided practical advice and comments. We thank Robert Windle and University of Maryland MBA students Timothy Roach, Pablo Macouzet, and Nathan Birckhead for invaluable datasets. We also thank MBA students Rob Whitener and Daniel Curtis for the heatmap and map charts.

We are grateful to colleagues at UMass Lowell's Manning School of Business for their encouragement and support in developing data analytics courses at the undergraduate and graduate levels that led to the development of this edition: Luvai Motiwalla, Harry Zhu, Thomas Sloan, Bob Li, and Sandra Richtermeyer.

We also thank Michael Goul (late), Dan Power (late), Ramesh Sharda, Babita Gupta, Ashish Gupta, Uday Kulkarni, and Haya Ajjan from the Association for Information System's Decision Support and Analytics (SIGDSA) community for ideas and advice that helped the development of the book.

Anand Bodapati provided both data and advice. Jake Hofman from Microsoft Research and Sharad Borle assisted with data access. Suresh Ankolekar and Mayank Shah helped develop several cases and provided valuable pedagogical comments. Vinni Bhandari helped write the Charles Book Club case.

We would like to thank Marvin Zelen, L. J. Wei, and Cyrus Mehta at Harvard, as well as Anil Gore at Pune University, for thought-provoking discussions on the relationship between statistics and machine learning. Our thanks to Richard Larson of the Engineering Systems Division, MIT, for sparking many stimulating ideas on the role of machine learning in modeling complex systems. Over two decades ago, they helped us develop a balanced philosophical perspective on the emerging field of machine learning.

Our thanks to Scott Genzer at RapidMiner, Inc., for insightful discussions and help. We are appreciative of the vibrant online RapidMiner Community for being an extremely helpful resource. We also thank Ingo Mierswa, the Founder of RapidMiner, for his encouragement and support.

Lastly, we thank the folks at Wiley for the 15-year successful journey of this book. Steve Quigley at Wiley showed confidence in this book from the beginning and helped us navigate through the publishing process with great speed. Curt Hinrichs' vision, tips, and encouragement helped bring this book to the starting gate. Brett Kurzman has taken over the reins and is now shepherding the project with the help of Kavya Ramu and Sarah Lemore. Sarah Keegan, Mindy Okura-Marszycki, Jon Gurstelle, Kathleen Santoloci, and Katrina Maceda greatly assisted us in pushing ahead and finalizing earlier editions. We are also especially grateful to Amy Hendrickson, who assisted with typesetting and making this book beautiful.

Preliminaries

CHAPTER 1

Introduction

1.1 WHAT IS BUSINESS ANALYTICS?

Business analytics (BA) is the practice and art of bringing quantitative data to bear on decision making. The term means different things to different organizations.

Consider the role of analytics in helping newspapers survive the transition to a digital world. One tabloid newspaper with a working-class readership in Britain had launched a web version of the paper and did tests on its home page to determine which images produced more hits: cats, dogs, or monkeys. This simple application, for this company, was considered analytics. By contrast, the *Washington Post* has a highly influential audience that is of interest to big defense contractors: it is perhaps the only newspaper where you routinely see advertisements for aircraft carriers. In the digital environment, the *Post* can track readers by time of day, location, and user subscription information. In this fashion, the display of the aircraft carrier advertisement in the online paper may be focused on a very small group of individuals—say, the members of the House and Senate Armed Services Committees who will be voting on the Pentagon's budget.

Business analytics, or more generically, *analytics*, includes a range of data analysis methods. Many powerful applications involve little more than counting, rule checking, and basic arithmetic. For some organizations, this is what is meant by analytics.

The next level of business analytics, now termed *business intelligence* (BI), refers to data visualization and reporting for understanding "what happened and what is happening." This is done by use of charts, tables, and dashboards to display, examine, and explore data. BI, which earlier consisted mainly of generating static reports, has evolved into more user-friendly and effective tools and

Machine Learning for Business Analytics: Concepts, Techniques and Applications in RapidMiner, First Edition.
Galit Shmueli, Peter C. Bruce, Amit V. Deokar, and Nitin R. Patel.

practices, such as creating interactive dashboards that allow the user not only to access real-time data but also to directly interact with it. Effective dashboards are those that tie directly into company data and give managers a tool to quickly see what might not readily be apparent in a large complex database. One such tool for industrial operations managers displays customer orders in a single two-dimensional display, using color and bubble size as added variables, showing customer name, type of product, size of order, and length of time to produce.

Business analytics now typically includes BI as well as sophisticated data analysis methods, such as statistical models and machine learning algorithms used for exploring data, quantifying and explaining relationships between measurements, and predicting new records. Methods like regression models are used to describe and quantify "on average" relationships (e.g., between advertising and sales), to predict new records (e.g., whether a new patient will react positively to a medication), and to forecast future values (e.g., next week's web traffic).

Readers familiar with earlier editions of this book might have noticed that the book title changed from *Data Mining for Business Intelligence* to *Data Mining for Business Analytics* and, finally, in this edition to *Machine Learning for Business Analytics*. The change reflects the more recent term BA, which overtook the earlier term BI to denote advanced analytics. Today, BI is used to refer to data visualization and reporting. The change from *data mining* to *machine learning* reflects today's common use of *machine learning* to refer to algorithms that learn from data. This book uses primarily the term *machine learning*.

WHO USES PREDICTIVE ANALYTICS?

The widespread adoption of predictive analytics, coupled with the accelerating availability of data, has increased organizations' capabilities throughout the economy. A few examples are as follows:

Credit scoring: One long-established use of predictive modeling techniques for business prediction is credit scoring. A credit score is not some arbitrary judgment of credit-worthiness; it is based mainly on a predictive model that uses prior data to predict repayment behavior.

Future purchases: A controversial example is Target's use of predictive modeling to classify sales prospects as "pregnant" or "not-pregnant." Those classified as pregnant could then be sent sales promotions at an early stage of pregnancy, giving Target a head start on a significant purchase stream.

Tax evasion: The US Internal Revenue Service found it was 25 times more likely to find tax evasion when enforcement activity was based on predictive models, allowing agents to focus on the most likely tax cheats (Siegel, 2013).

The business analytics toolkit also includes statistical experiments, the most common of which is known to marketers as A/B testing. These are often used for pricing decisions:

- Orbitz, the travel site, found that it could price hotel options higher for Mac users than Windows users.
- Staples online store found it could charge more for staplers if a customer lived far from a Staples store.

Beware the organizational setting where analytics is a solution in search of a problem: a manager, knowing that business analytics and machine learning are hot areas, decides that her organization must deploy them too, to capture that hidden value that must be lurking somewhere. Successful use of analytics and machine learning requires both an understanding of the business context where value is to be captured and an understanding of exactly what the machine learning methods do.

1.2 What Is Machine Learning?

In this book, machine learning (or data mining) refers to business analytics methods that go beyond counts, descriptive techniques, reporting, and methods based on business rules. While we do introduce data visualization, which is commonly the first step into more advanced analytics, the book focuses mostly on the more advanced data analytics tools. Specifically, it includes statistical and machine learning methods that inform decision making, often in automated fashion. Prediction is typically an important component, often at the individual level. Rather than "what is the relationship between advertising and sales," we might be interested in "what specific advertisement, or recommended product, should be shown to a given online shopper at this moment?" Or, we might be interested in clustering customers into different "personas" that receive different marketing treatment and then assigning each new prospect to one of these personas.

The era of big data has accelerated the use of machine learning. Machine learning algorithms, with their power and automaticity, have the ability to cope with huge amounts of data and extract value.

1.3 Machine Learning, AI, and Related Terms

The field of analytics is growing rapidly, both in terms of the breadth of applications and in terms of the number of organizations using advanced analytics. As a result, there is considerable overlap and inconsistency of definitions. Terms have also changed over time.

The older term *data mining* means different things to different people. To the general public, it may have a general, somewhat hazy and pejorative meaning of digging through vast stores of (often personal) data in search of something interesting. *Data mining*, as it refers to analytic techniques, has largely been superseded by the term *machine learning*. Other terms that organizations use are *predictive analytics*, *predictive modeling*, and most recently *machine learning* and *artificial intelligence (AI)*.

Many practitioners, particularly those from the IT and computer science communities, use the term *AI* to refer to all the methods discussed in this book. AI originally referred to the general capability of a machine to act like a human, and, in its earlier days, existed mainly in the realm of science fiction and the unrealized ambitions of computer scientists. More recently, it has come to encompass the methods of statistical and machine learning discussed in this book, as the primary enablers of that grand vision, and sometimes the term is used loosely to mean the same thing as *machine learning*. More broadly, it includes generative capabilities such as the creation of images, audio, and video.

Statistical Modeling vs. Machine Learning

A variety of techniques for exploring data and building models have been around for a long time in the world of statistics: linear regression, logistic regression, discriminant analysis, and principal components analysis, for example. However, the core tenets of classical statistics—computing is difficult and data are scarce—do not apply in machine learning applications where both data and computing power are plentiful.

This gives rise to Daryl Pregibon's description of "data mining" (in the sense of machine learning) as "statistics at scale and speed" (Pregibon, 1999). Another major difference between the fields of statistics and machine learning is the focus in statistics on inference from a sample to the population regarding an "average effect"—for example, "a \$1 price increase will reduce average demand by 2 boxes." In contrast, the focus in machine learning is on predicting individual records—"the predicted demand for person i given a \$1 price increase is 1 box, while for person j it is 3 boxes." The emphasis that classical statistics places on inference (determining whether a pattern or interesting result might have happened by chance in our sample) is absent from machine learning. Note also that the term *inference* is often used in the machine learning community to refer to the process of using a model to make predictions for new data, also called *scoring*, in contrast to its meaning in the statistical community.

In comparison with statistics, machine learning deals with large datasets in an open-ended fashion, making it impossible to put the strict limits around the question being addressed that classical statistical inference would require.

As a result, the general approach to machine learning is vulnerable to the danger of *overfitting*, where a model is fit so closely to the available sample of data that it describes not merely structural characteristics of the data but random peculiarities as well. In engineering terms, the model is fitting the noise, not just the signal.

In this book, we use the term *machine learning algorithm* to refer to methods that learn directly from data, especially local patterns, often in layered or iterative fashion. In contrast, we use *statistical models* to refer to methods that apply global structure to the data that can be written as a simple mathematical equation. A simple example is a linear regression model (statistical) vs. a k-nearest neighbors algorithm (machine learning). A given record would be treated by linear regression in accord with an overall linear equation that applies to *all* the records. In k-nearest neighbors, that record would be classified in accord with the values of a small number of nearby records.

1.4 BIG DATA

Machine learning and big data go hand in hand. *Big data* is a relative term—data today are big by reference to the past and to the methods and devices available to deal with them. The challenge big data presents is often characterized by the four V's—volume, velocity, variety, and veracity. *Volume* refers to the amount of data. *Velocity* refers to the flow rate—the speed at which it is being generated and changed. *Variety* refers to the different types of data being generated (time stamps, location, numbers, text, images, etc.). *Veracity* refers to the fact that data is being generated by organic distributed processes (e.g., millions of people signing up for services or free downloads) and not subject to the controls or quality checks that apply to data collected for a study.

Most large organizations face both the challenge and the opportunity of big data because most routine data processes now generate data that can be stored and, possibly, analyzed. The scale can be visualized by comparing the data in a traditional statistical analysis (e.g., 15 variables and 5000 records) to the Walmart database. If you consider the traditional statistical study to be the size of a period at the end of a sentence, then the Walmart database is the size of a football field. Moreover, that probably does not include other data associated with Walmart—social media data, for example, which comes in the form of unstructured text.

If the analytical challenge is substantial, so can be the reward:

- OKCupid, the online dating site, uses statistical models with their data to predict what forms of message content are most likely to produce a response.

- Telenor, a Norwegian mobile phone service company, was able to reduce subscriber turnover 37% by using models to predict which customers were most likely to leave and then lavishing attention on them.

- Allstate, the insurance company, tripled the accuracy of predicting injury liability in auto claims by incorporating more information about vehicle type.

The examples above are from Eric Siegel's book *Predictive Analytics* (2013, Wiley).

Some extremely valuable tasks were not even feasible before the era of big data. Consider web searches, the technology on which Google was built. In early days, a search for "Ricky Ricardo Little Red Riding Hood" would have yielded various links to the *I Love Lucy* TV show, other links to Ricardo's career as a band leader, and links to the children's story of Little Red Riding Hood. Only once the Google database had accumulated sufficient data (including records of what users clicked on) would the search yield, in the top position, links to the specific *I Love Lucy* episode in which Ricky enacts, in a comic mixture of Spanish and English, Little Red Riding Hood for his infant son.

1.5 DATA SCIENCE

The ubiquity, size, value, and importance of big data has given rise to a new profession: the *data scientist*. *Data science* is a mix of skills in the areas of statistics, machine learning, math, programming, business, and IT. The term itself is thus broader than the other concepts we discussed above, and it is a rare individual who combines deep skills in all the constituent areas. In their book *Analyzing the Analyzers* (Harris et al., 2013), the authors describe the skillsets of most data scientists as resembling a "T"—deep in one area (the vertical bar of the T) and shallower in other areas (the top of the T).

At a large data science conference session (Strata-Hadoop World, October 2014), most attendees felt that programming was an essential skill, though there was a sizable minority who felt otherwise. Also, although big data is the motivating power behind the growth of data science, most data scientists do not actually spend most of their time working with terabyte-size or larger data.

Data of the terabyte or larger size would be involved at the deployment stage of a model. There are manifold challenges at that stage, most of them IT and programming issues related to data handling and tying together different components of a system. Much work must precede that phase. It is that earlier piloting and prototyping phase on which this book focuses—developing the statistical and machine learning models that will eventually be plugged into a deployed system. What methods do you use with what sorts of data and problems? How do the methods work? What are their requirements, their strengths, their weaknesses? How do you assess their performance?

1.6 WHY ARE THERE SO MANY DIFFERENT METHODS?

As can be seen in this book or any other resource on machine learning, there are many different methods for prediction and classification. You might ask yourself why they coexist and whether some are better than others. The answer is that each method has advantages and disadvantages. The usefulness of a method can depend on factors such as the size of the dataset, the types of patterns that exist in the data, whether the data meet some underlying assumptions of the method, how noisy the data are, and the particular goal of the analysis. A small illustration is shown in Figure 1.1, where the goal is to find a combination of *household income level* and *household lot size* that separates owners (solid circles) from nonowners (hollow circles) of riding mowers. The first method (left panel) looks only for horizontal and vertical lines to separate owners from nonowners; the second method (right panel) looks for a single diagonal line.

FIGURE 1.1   **TWO METHODS FOR SEPARATING OWNERS FROM NONOWNERS**

Different methods can lead to different results, and their performance can vary. It is therefore customary in machine learning to apply several different methods (and perhaps their combination) and select the one that appears most useful for the goal at hand.

1.7 TERMINOLOGY AND NOTATION

Because of the hybrid parentry of data science, its practitioners often use multiple terms to refer to the same thing. For example, in the machine learning and artificial intelligence fields, the variable being predicted is the *output variable* or *target variable.* A categorical target variable is often called a *label*. To a statistician or social scientist, the variable being predicted is the *dependent variable* or the *response.* Here is a summary of terms used:

Algorithm   A specific procedure used to implement a particular machine learning technique: classification tree, discriminant analysis, and the like.

Attribute   Any measurement on the records, including both the input (X) variables and the output (Y) variable.

Binary attribute   A variable that takes on two discrete values (e.g., *fraud* and *non-fraud* transactions); also called *binominal attribute.*

Case   See **Record**.

Categorical attribute   See **Nominal attribute**.

Class label   See **Label**.

Confidence   A performance measure in association rules of the type "IF A and B are purchased, THEN C is also purchased." Confidence is the conditional probability that C will be purchased IF A and B are purchased.

Confidence   In classification problems, it is used to denote the probability of belonging to a certain class.

Confidence   Also has a broader meaning in statistics (*confidence interval*), concerning the degree of error in an estimate that results from selecting one sample as opposed to another.

Dependent variable   See **Target attribute**.

Estimation   See **Prediction**.

Example   See **Record**.

Feature   See **Attribute**. The term *feature* is also used in the context of selecting attributes (*feature selection*) or generating new attributes (*feature generation*) through some mechanism. More broadly, this process is called *feature engineering.* This usage is adopted in certain RapidMiner operator names.

Holdout data   (or **holdout set**) The portion of the data used only at the end of the model building and selection process to assess how well the final model might perform on new data; also called *test set.*

Inference   In statistics, the process of accounting for chance variation when making estimates or drawing conclusions based on samples; in machine learning, the term often refers to the process of using a model to make predictions for new data (see *Score*).

Input variable   See **Attribute**.

Label   A nominal (categorical) attribute being predicted in supervised learning.

Model   An algorithm as applied to a dataset, complete with its settings (many of the algorithms have parameters that the user can adjust).

Nominal attribute A variable that takes on one of several fixed values, for example, a flight could be on-time, delayed, or canceled; also called *categorical variable* or *polynominal attribute*.

Numerical attribute A variable that takes on numeric (integer or real) values; also called *numerical variable*.

Observation See **Record**.

Outcome variable See **Target attribute**.

Output variable See **Target attribute**.

$P\ (A|B)$ The conditional probability of event A occurring given that event B has occurred. Read as "the probability that A will occur given that B has occurred."

Positive class The class of interest in a binary target attribute (e.g., *purchasers* in the target attribute *purchase/no purchase*); the positive class need not be favorable.

Prediction The prediction of the numerical value of a continuous output variable; also called *estimation*.

Predictor A variable, usually denoted by X, used as an input into a predictive model. Also called a *feature*, *input variable*, *independent variable*, or, from a database perspective, a *field*.

Record The unit of analysis on which the measurements are taken (a customer, a transaction, etc.); also called *example, instance, case, observation, sample, pattern*, or *row*. In spreadsheets, each row typically represents a record; each column, a variable. Note that the use of the term "sample" here is different from its usual meaning in statistics, where it refers to a collection of observations.

Profile A set of measurements on an observation (e.g., the height, weight, and age of a person).

Response See **Target attribute**.

Sample In the statistical community, "sample" means a collection of observations. In the machine learning community, "sample" means a single observation.

Score A predicted value or class. *Scoring new data* means using a model developed with training data to predict output values in new data.

Success class See **Positive class**.

Supervised learning The process of providing an algorithm (logistic regression, classification tree, etc.) with records in which an output variable of interest is known and the algorithm "learns" how to predict this value for new records where the output is unknown.

Target attribute   A variable, usually denoted by Y, which is the variable being predicted in supervised learning; also called *dependent variable, output variable, target variable*, or *outcome variable*.

Test data   (or **test set**) A sample of data not used in fitting a model, but instead used to assess the performance of that model; also called *holdout data*. This book uses the term *holdout set* instead and uses the term *testing* to refer to certain validation checks (e.g., in the *Split-Validation* and *Cross-Validation* nested operators in RapidMiner) during the model-tuning phase.

Training data   (or **training set**) The portion of the data used to fit a model.

Unsupervised learning   An analysis in which one attempts to learn patterns in the data other than predicting an output value of interest.

Validation data   (or **validation set**) The portion of the data used to assess how well the model fits, to adjust models, and to select the best model from among those that have been tried.

Variable   See **Attribute**. In RapidMiner, the term *attribute* is used.

1.8   ROAD MAPS TO THIS BOOK

The book covers many of the widely used predictive and classification methods as well as other machine learning tools. Figure 1.2 outlines machine learning from a process perspective and where the topics in this book fit in. Chapter numbers are indicated beside the topic. Table 1.1 provides a different perspective: it organizes supervised and unsupervised machine learning procedures according to the type and structure of the data.

Order of Topics

The book is divided into nine parts: Part I (Chapters 1–2) gives a general overview of machine learning and its components. Part II (Chapters 3–4) focuses on the early stages of data exploration and dimension reduction.

Part III (Chapter 5) discusses performance evaluation. Although it contains only one chapter, we discuss a variety of topics, from predictive performance metrics to misclassification costs. The principles covered in this part are crucial for the proper evaluation and comparison of supervised learning methods.

Part IV includes eight chapters (Chapters 6–13), covering a variety of popular supervised learning methods (for classification and/or prediction). Within this part, the topics are generally organized according to the level of sophistication of the algorithms, their popularity, and ease of understanding. The final chapter introduces ensembles and combinations of methods.

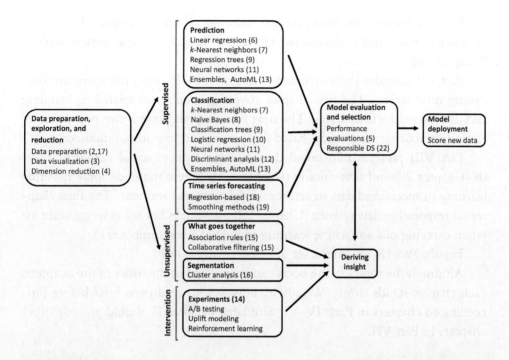

FIGURE 1.2   MACHINE LEARNING FROM A PROCESS PERSPECTIVE. NUMBERS IN PARENTHESES INDICATE CHAPTER NUMBERS

TABLE 1.1   ORGANIZATION OF MACHINE LEARNING METHODS IN THIS BOOK, ACCORDING TO THE NATURE OF THE DATA[a]

| | Supervised | | Unsupervised |
	Continuous response	Categorical response	No response
Continuous predictors	Linear regression (6)	Logistic regression (10)	Principal components (4)
	Neural nets (11)	Neural nets (11)	Cluster analysis (16)
	k-Nearest neighbors (7)	Discriminant analysis (12)	Collaborative filtering (15)
	Ensembles (13)	k-Nearest neighbors (7)	
		Ensembles (13)	
Categorical predictors	Linear regression (6)	Neural nets (11)	Association rules (15)
	Neural nets (11)	Classification trees (9)	Collaborative filtering (15)
	Regression trees (9)	Logistic regression (10)	
	Ensembles (13)	Naïve Bayes (8)	
		Ensembles (13)	

[a]Numbers in parentheses indicate the chapter number.

Part V (Chapter 14) introduces the notions of experiments, intervention, and user feedback. This single chapter starts with A/B testing and then its use in uplift modeling and finally expands into reinforcement learning, explaining the basic ideas and formulations that utilize user feedback for learning best treatment assignments.

Part VI focuses on unsupervised learning of relationships. It presents association rules and collaborative filtering (Chapter 15) and cluster analysis (Chapter 16).

Part VII includes three chapters (Chapters 17–19), with the focus on forecasting time series. The first chapter covers general issues related to handling and understanding time series. The next two chapters present two popular forecasting approaches: regression-based forecasting and smoothing methods.

Part VIII presents two broad data analytics topics: social network analysis (Chapter 20) and text mining (Chapter 21). These methods apply machine learning to specialized data structures: social networks and text. The final chapter on responsible data science (Chapter 22) introduces key issues to consider for when carrying out a machine learning project in a responsible way.

Finally, Part IX includes a set of cases.

Although the topics in the book can be covered in the order of the chapters, each chapter stands alone. We advise, however, to read parts I–III before proceeding to chapters in Parts IV–VI. Similarly, Chapter 17 should precede other chapters in Part VII.

1.9 Using RapidMiner Studio

To facilitate hands-on machine learning experience, this book uses *RapidMiner Studio* (commonly referred in this book as RapidMiner), a commercial machine learning software, available for free (limited to data with 10,000 records), particularly for educational purposes (no data limitations). It provides an interactive environment with a drag-and-drop interface in which you can easily perform machine learning tasks by creating and executing processes based on relevant operators.

RapidMiner helps you get started quickly on machine learning and offers a variety of operators for analyzing data. The illustrations, exercises, and cases in this book are written in relation to this software. RapidMiner has extensive coverage of machine learning techniques for classification, prediction, mining associations and text, forecasting, and data exploration and reduction. It offers a variety of operators supporting supervised learning algorithms: neural nets, classification and regression trees, k-nearest-neighbor classification, naive Bayes, logistic regression, linear regression, and discriminant analysis, all for predictive modeling. It provides for automatic partitioning of data into training, validation, and holdout samples and for the deployment of the model to new data. It also offers unsupervised algorithms: association rules, principal components analysis, k-means clustering, and hierarchical clustering, as well as visualization tools and data-handling utilities. With its short learning curve, free educational license program, it is an ideal companion to a book on machine learning for the business student.

To download RapidMiner Studio, visit www.rapidminer.com and create an account. Follow the instructions there to download and install the latest version of RapidMiner Studio for your operating system. For information on RapidMiner's Educational License Program, visit https://rapidminer.com/educational-program/.

Once RapidMiner Studio is downloaded and installed with a license, upon launching, the primary interface looks similar to that shown in Figure 1.3. The RapidMiner interface provides five different views, highlighted in blue. Clicking on these views allows one to toggle between them. The Design and Process views are the most frequently used. We will also introduce Turbo Prep and Auto Model views later in the book. The Deployments view is needed only when putting chosen models into production use.

The Design view is where a data scientist can create machine learning processes by combining and configuring various operators. One such process is shown in the figure (the process is elaborated later in Section 2.6). In RapidMiner, an *operator* is a container (internally containing code) performing a specific machine learning task (e.g., selecting attributes), each with its own parameters. The Design view includes multiple display units called panels, which can be moved and resized. The default panels include Repository, Operators, Process, Parameters, and Help. Additional panels can be activated from the View menu. The *View > Restore Default View* option from the main menu is often useful for restoring the default location and size of these panels.

To keep different artifacts organized, RapidMiner uses the notion of *repository*, which is a folder-like structure for organizing data, processes, and models (for deployment). After creating a repository, it is best practice to create subfolders *data* and *processes*. The Repository panel is useful for managing the repositories and related artifacts. Upon designing a process in the Process panel, it can be stored in the *processes* subfolder by right-clicking and selecting the *Store Process Here* option. For example, the process *02-02-West Roxbury Preprocessing* is stored in the processes subfolder in the MLBA repository. To execute a process, the blue "play" button is used, shown among the icons above the Repository view. If the process executes properly and the output ports are connected to some modeling artifacts (e.g., performance metrics), the view switches automatically to the Results view for the user to analyze the results. The Operators panel is useful for quickly searching or navigating through a plethora of operators available for different tasks. The Parameters panel is used for configuring operators, and the Help panel is self-explanatory.

For more details on the RapidMiner interface, see https://academy. rapidminer.com/courses/rapidminer-studio-gui-intro.

FIGURE 1.3   PANELS IN THE DESIGN VIEW OF RAPIDMINER STUDIO

Importing and Loading Data in RapidMiner

RapidMiner allows importing data directly into a process through a variety of *Read…* operators (such as *Read CSV*, *Read Excel*, and more). With this approach, a local link to the source data is created, and any updates to the source data are immediately reflected upon rerunning the process. Another approach that is designed to be portable across computers but lacks data updates is to import the data into RapidMiner by selecting the data subfolder and then using the *Import Data* wizard to store the data there in native RapidMiner format called *ExampleSet*. This ExampleSet (data) can then be used in any process with the *Retrieve* operator. We use the latter approach in this book.

For more details on importing and loading data in RapidMiner, see https://academy.rapidminer.com/learning-paths/get-started-with-rapidminer-and-machine-learning.

RapidMiner Extensions

RapidMiner offers a variety of special-purpose extensions (e.g., Deep Learning) that provide additional operators for performing specific machine learning tasks.

These extensions can be searched, installed, and updated from the *Marketplace (Updates and Extensions)* option in RapidMiner Extensions menu. We will use some such extensions in the book, and we will mention them at appropriate places.

One such extension worth mentioning here is the *Python Scripting* extension. It includes operators such as *Python Transformer*, *Python Learner*, *Execute Python*, and *Python Forecaster* that allow Python packages to be used from within Rapid-Miner. To use the Python extension, you will need an installation of Python and supporting packages. The easiest way to do that is by installing *anaconda*, which is a packaged distribution of Python and most commonly used data science packages. To install anaconda and integrate it with RapidMiner, first close Rapid-Miner Studio, and visit https://www.anaconda.com. We recommend installing anaconda's *Individual Edition*. Once anaconda is installed and RapidMiner is launched, RapidMiner automatically detects the path for Python, and all installed packages are available to be used from Python operators in RapidMiner.

We will demonstrate the use of Python extensions in Chapters 12 and 20. Further, Python's *pandas* and *statsmodels* packages are particularly powerful for handling time series data and time series forecasting. While outside the scope of this book, we encourage interested readers to explore techniques described in Chapters 17–19 using these packages.

CHAPTER 2

Overview of the Machine Learning Process

In this chapter, we give an overview of the steps involved in machine learning (ML), starting from a clear goal definition and ending with model deployment. The general steps are shown schematically in Figure 2.1. We also discuss issues related to data collection, cleaning, and preprocessing. We introduce the notion of *data partitioning*, where methods are trained on a set of training data and then their performance is evaluated on a separate set of holdout data, as well as explain how this practice helps avoid overfitting. Finally, we illustrate the steps of model building by applying them to data.

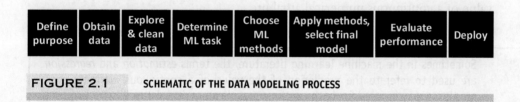

| Define purpose | Obtain data | Explore & clean data | Determine ML task | Choose ML methods | Apply methods, select final model | Evaluate performance | Deploy |

FIGURE 2.1   SCHEMATIC OF THE DATA MODELING PROCESS

2.1 INTRODUCTION

In Chapter 1, we saw some very general definitions of business analytics and machine learning. In this chapter, we introduce a variety of machine learning methods. The core of this book focuses on what has come to be called *predictive analytics*, the tasks of classification and prediction as well as pattern discovery, which have become key elements of a "business analytics" function in most large firms. These terms are described next.

Machine Learning for Business Analytics: Concepts, Techniques and Applications in RapidMiner, First Edition.
Galit Shmueli, Peter C. Bruce, Amit V. Deokar, and Nitin R. Patel

2.2 CORE IDEAS IN MACHINE LEARNING

Classification

Classification is perhaps the most basic form of predictive analytics. The recipient of an offer can respond or not respond. An applicant for a loan can repay on time, repay late, or declare bankruptcy. A credit card transaction can be normal or fraudulent. A packet of data traveling on a network can be benign or threatening. A bus in a fleet can be available for service or unavailable. The victim of an illness can be recovered, still be ill, or be deceased.

A common task in machine learning is to examine data where the classification is unknown or will occur in the future, with the goal of predicting what that classification is or will be. Similar data where the classification is known are used to develop rules, which are then applied to the data with the unknown classification.

Prediction

Prediction is similar to classification, except that we are trying to predict the value of a numerical attribute (e.g., amount of purchase) rather than a class (e.g., purchaser or nonpurchaser). Of course, in classification we are trying to predict a class, but the term *prediction* in this book refers to the prediction of the value of a continuous numerical attribute.

> Sometimes in the machine learning literature, the terms *estimation* and *regression* are used to refer to the prediction of the value of a continuous attribute, and *prediction* may be used for both continuous and categorical data.

Association Rules and Recommendation Systems

Large databases of customer transactions lend themselves naturally to the analysis of associations among items purchased, or "what goes with what." *Association rules*, or *affinity analysis*, is designed to find such general associations patterns between items in large databases. The rules can then be used in a variety of ways. For example, grocery stores can use such information for product placement. They can use the rules for weekly promotional offers or for bundling products. Association rules derived from a hospital database on patients' symptoms during consecutive hospitalizations can help find "which symptom is followed by what other symptom" to help predict future symptoms for returning patients.

Online recommendation systems, such as those used on Amazon and Netflix, use *collaborative filtering*, a method that uses individual users' preferences and tastes given their historic purchase, rating, browsing, or any other measurable behavior indicative of preference, as well as other users' history. In contrast to *association rules* that generate rules general to an entire population, collaborative filtering generates "what goes with what" at the individual user level. Hence, collaborative filtering is used in many recommendation systems that aim to deliver personalized recommendations to users with a wide range of preferences.

Predictive Analytics

Classification, prediction, and, to some extent, association rules and collaborative filtering constitute the analytical methods employed in *predictive analytics*. The term predictive analytics is sometimes used to also include data pattern identification methods such as clustering.

Data Reduction and Dimension Reduction

The performance of some machine learning algorithms is often improved when the number of attributes is limited, and when large numbers of records can be grouped into homogeneous groups. For example, rather than dealing with thousands of product types, an analyst might wish to group them into a smaller number of groups and build separate models for each group. Or a marketer might want to classify customers into different "personas" and must therefore group customers into homogeneous groups to define the personas. This process of consolidating a large number of records (or cases) into a smaller set is termed *data reduction*. Methods for reducing the number of cases are often called *clustering*.

Reducing the number of attributes is typically called *dimension reduction*. Dimension reduction is a common initial step before deploying supervised learning methods, intended to improve predictive power, manageability, and interpretability.

Data Exploration and Visualization

One of the earliest stages of engaging with data is exploring it. Exploration is aimed at understanding the global landscape of the data and detecting unusual values. Exploration is used for data cleaning and manipulation as well as for visual discovery and "hypothesis generation."

Methods for exploring data include looking at various data aggregations and summaries, both numerically and graphically. This includes looking at each attribute separately as well as looking at relationships between attributes. The purpose is to discover patterns and exceptions. Exploration by creating charts and dashboards is called *data visualization* or *visual analytics*. For numerical attributes, we use histograms and boxplots to learn about the distribution of their values, to detect outliers (extreme observations), and to find other information that is relevant to the analysis task. Similarly, for categorical attributes, we use bar charts. We can also look at scatter plots of pairs of numerical attributes to learn about possible relationships, the type of relationship, and, again, to detect outliers. Visualization can be greatly enhanced by adding features such as color and interactive navigation.

Supervised and Unsupervised Learning

A fundamental distinction among machine learning techniques is between supervised and unsupervised methods. *Supervised learning algorithms* are those used in classification and prediction. We must have data available in which the value of the outcome of interest (e.g., purchase or no purchase) is known. Such data are also called "labeled data," since they contain the label (outcome value) for each record. The use of the term "label" reflects the fact that the outcome of interest for a record may often be a characterization applied by a human: a document may be labeled as relevant, or an object in an X-ray may be labeled as malignant. These *training data* are the data from which the classification or prediction algorithm "learns," or is "trained," about the relationship between predictor attributes and the target attribute. Once the algorithm has learned from the training data, it is then applied to another sample of data (the *validation data*) where the outcome is known, to see how well it does in comparison to other models (either a different algorithm or different parameter values of the same algorithm). If many different models are being tried out, it is prudent to save a third sample, which also includes known outcomes (the *holdout data*) to use with the model finally selected to predict how well it will do. The model can then be used to classify or predict the outcome of interest in new cases where the outcome is unknown.

Simple linear regression is an example of a supervised learning algorithm (although rarely called that in the introductory statistics course where you probably first encountered it). The Y variable is the (known) target attribute, and the X variable is a predictor attribute. A regression line is drawn to minimize the sum of squared deviations between the actual Y values and the values predicted by this line. The regression line can now be used to predict Y values for new values of X for which we do not know the Y value.

Unsupervised learning algorithms are those used where there is no target attribute to predict or classify. Hence, there is no "learning" from cases where such a target attribute is known. Association rules, dimension reduction methods, and clustering techniques are all unsupervised learning methods.

Supervised and unsupervised methods are sometimes used in conjunction. For example, unsupervised clustering methods are used to separate loan applicants into several risk-level groups. Then, supervised algorithms are applied separately to each risk-level group for predicting propensity of loan default.

SUPERVISED LEARNING REQUIRES GOOD SUPERVISION

In some cases, the value of the target attribute (the "label") is known because it is an inherent component of the data. Web logs will show whether a person clicked on a link or didn't click. Bank records will show whether a loan was paid on time or not. In other cases, the value of the known target must be supplied by a human labeling process to accumulate enough data to train a model. E-mail must be labeled as spam or legitimate, documents in legal discovery must be labeled as relevant or irrelevant. In either case, the machine learning algorithm can be led astray if the quality of the supervision is poor.

Gene Weingarten reported in the January 5, 2014, *Washington Post* magazine how the strange phrase "defiantly recommend" is making its way into English via autocorrection. "Defiantly" is closer to the common misspelling *definatly* than *definitely*, so Google, in the early days, offered it as a correction when users typed the misspelled word "definatly" on google.com. In the ideal supervised learning model, humans guide the autocorrection process by rejecting *defiantly* and substituting *definitely*. Google's algorithm would then learn that this is the best first-choice correction of "definatly." The problem was that too many people were lazy, just accepting the first correction that Google presented. All these acceptances then cemented "defiantly" as the proper correction.

2.3 THE STEPS IN A MACHINE LEARNING PROJECT

This book focuses on understanding and using machine learning algorithms (steps 4 to 7 below). However, some of the most serious errors in analytics projects result from a poor understanding of the problem—an understanding that must be developed before we get into the details of algorithms to be used. Here is a list of steps to be taken in a typical machine learning effort:

1. *Develop an understanding of the purpose of the machine learning project*: How will the stakeholder use the results? Who will be affected by the results? Will the analysis be a one-shot effort or an ongoing procedure?

2. *Obtain the data to be used in the analysis*: This often involves random sampling from a large database to capture records to be used in an analysis. How well this sample reflects the records of interest affects the ability of the machine learning results to generalize to records outside of this sample. It may also involve pulling together data from different databases or sources. The databases could be internal (e.g., past purchases made by customers) or external (credit ratings). While machine learning deals with very large databases, usually the analysis to be done requires only thousands or tens of thousands of records.

3. *Explore, clean, and preprocess the data*: This step involves verifying that the data are in reasonable condition. How should missing data be handled?

Are the values in a reasonable range, given what you would expect for each attribute? Are there obvious outliers? The data are reviewed graphically: for example, a matrix of scatterplots showing the relationship of each attribute with every other attribute. We also need to ensure consistency in the definitions of fields, units of measurement, time periods, and so on. In this step, new attributes are also typically created from existing ones. For example, "duration" can be computed from start and end dates.

4. *Reduce the data dimension, if necessary*: Dimension reduction can involve operations such as eliminating unneeded attributes, transforming attributes (e.g., turning "money spent" into "spent >$100" vs. "spent ≤$100"), and creating new attributes (e.g., an attribute that records whether at least one of several products was purchased). Make sure that you know what each attribute means and whether it is sensible to include it in the model.

5. *Determine the machine learning task* (classification, prediction, clustering, etc.): This involves translating the general question or problem of step 1 into a more specific machine learning question.

6. *Partition the data (for supervised tasks)*: If the task is supervised (classification or prediction), randomly partition the dataset into three parts: training, validation, and holdout datasets.

7. *Choose the machine learning techniques to be used* (regression, neural nets, hierarchical clustering, etc.).

8. *Use algorithms to perform the task*: This is typically an iterative process— trying multiple variants and often using multiple variants of the same algorithm (choosing different attributes or parameter settings within the algorithm). Where appropriate, feedback from the algorithm's performance on validation data is used to refine the parameter settings.

9. *Interpret the results of the algorithms*: This involves making a choice as to the best algorithm to deploy and, where possible, testing the final choice on the holdout data to get an idea as to how well it will perform. (Recall that each algorithm may also be tested on the validation data for tuning purposes; in this way, the validation data become a part of the fitting process and are likely to underestimate the error in the deployment of the model that is finally chosen.)

10. *Deploy the model*: This step involves integrating the model into operational systems and running it on real records to produce decisions or actions. For example, the model might be applied to a purchased list of possible customers, and the action might be "include in the mailing if the predicted amount of purchase is >$10." A key step here is "scoring" the new records, or using the chosen model to predict the target value for each new record.

The foregoing steps encompass the steps in SEMMA, a methodology developed by the software company SAS:

Sample Take a sample from the dataset; partition into training, validation, and holdout datasets.

Explore Examine the dataset statistically and graphically.

Modify Transform the attributes and impute missing values.

Model Fit predictive models (e.g., regression tree, neural network).

Assess Compare models using a validation dataset.

IBM SPSS Modeler (previously SPSS-Clementine) has a similar methodology, termed CRISP-DM (CRoss-Industry Standard Process for Data Mining). All these frameworks include the same main steps involved in predictive modeling.

2.4 PRELIMINARY STEPS

Organization of Data

Datasets are nearly always constructed and displayed so that attributes are in columns and records are in rows. In the example (data: *WestRoxbury.csv*) shown in Section 2.6 (home values in West Roxbury, Boston, in 2014), 14 attributes are recorded for over 5000 homes. The spreadsheet is organized so that each row represents a home—the first home's assessed value was \$344,200, its tax was \$4430, its size was 9965 ft^2, it was built in 1880, and so on. In supervised learning situations, one of these attributes will be the target attribute, typically listed in the first or last column (in this case, it is TOTAL VALUE, in the first column).

Sampling from a Database

Quite often, we want to perform our modeling on less than the total number of records that are available. Machine learning algorithms will have varying limitations on what they can handle in terms of the numbers of records and attributes, limitations that may be specific to computing power and capacity as well as software limitations. Even within those limits, many algorithms will execute faster with smaller samples.

Accurate models can often be built with as few as several hundred or thousand records. Hence, we will want to sample a subset of records for model building. In RapidMiner, the *Sample* operator can be used for this purpose.

Oversampling Rare Events in Classification Tasks

If the event we are interested in classifying is rare, such as customers purchasing a product in response to a mailing, or fraudulent credit card transactions, sampling a random subset of records may yield so few events (e.g., purchases) that we have little information on them. We would end up with lots of data on nonpurchasers and nonfraudulent transactions but little on which to base a model that distinguishes purchasers from nonpurchasers or fraudulent from nonfraudulent. In such cases, we would want our sampling procedure to overweight the rare class (purchasers or frauds) relative to the majority class (nonpurchasers, non-frauds) so that our sample would end up with a healthy complement of purchasers or frauds.

Assuring an adequate number of responder or "success" cases to train the model is just part of the picture. A more important factor is the costs of misclassification. Whenever the response rate is extremely low, we are likely to attach more importance to identifying a responder than to identifying a nonresponder. In direct-response advertising (whether by traditional mail, email, web, or mobile advertising), we may encounter only one or two responders for every hundred records—the value of finding such a customer far outweighs the costs of reaching him or her. In trying to identify fraudulent transactions, or customers unlikely to repay debt, the costs of failing to find the fraud or the nonpaying customer are likely to exceed the cost of more detailed review of a legitimate transaction or customer.

If the costs of failing to locate responders are comparable to the costs of misidentifying responders as nonresponders, our models would usually achieve highest overall accuracy if they identified everyone as a nonresponder (or almost everyone, if it is easy to identify a few responders without catching many nonresponders). In such a case, the misclassification rate is very low—equal to the rate of responders—but the model is of no value.

More generally, we want to train our model with the asymmetric costs in mind so that the algorithm will catch the more valuable responders, probably at the cost of "catching" and misclassifying more nonresponders as responders than would be the case if we assume equal costs. This subject is discussed in detail in Chapter 5.

Preprocessing and Cleaning the Data

Types of Attributes   There are several ways of classifying attributes. Attributes can be numerical or text (character/string). They can be continuous (able to assume any real numerical value, usually in a given range), integer (taking only integer values), categorical (assuming one of a limited number of values), or date–time (able to assume date and time values). Categorical attributes can be either coded as numerical $(1, 2, 3)$ or text (payments current, payments not current, bankrupt). Categorical attributes can also be unordered (called *nominal attributes*) with categories such as North America, Europe, and Asia; or they can be ordered (called *ordinal attributes*) with categories such as high value, low value, and nil value. Date–time attributes can have values denoting either date or time, or both.

In RapidMiner, continuous attributes are generally referred to as having *numeric* type, but are more specifically assigned either *integer* or *real* value type.[1] Categorical attributes are assigned to have *nominal* type by default, but can be specifically designated as either *binominal* (having only two categories) or *polynominal* (having more than two categories). RapidMiner does not distinguish between nominal and ordinal attributes.[2] Date–time attributes are assigned to have *date-time* type by default but can be specifically designated as either *date* or *time* type. Lastly, RapidMiner also has a *text* attribute type for free text without structure.

Continuous attributes can be handled by most machine learning routines. Machine learning grew out of problems with categorical outcomes; the roots of statistics lie in the analysis of continuous attributes. Sometimes, it is desirable to convert continuous attributes to categorical attributes. This is done most typically in the case of target attributes, where the numerical attribute is mapped to a decision (e.g., credit scores above a certain level mean "grant credit," a medical test result above a certain level means "start treatment"). RapidMiner has operators for this type of conversion available under *Blending > Attributes > Types* in the Operators panel.

Handling Categorical Attributes Categorical attributes can also be handled by most machine learning routines, but often require special handling. If the categorical attribute is ordered (age group, degree of creditworthiness, etc.), we can sometimes code the categories numerically (1, 2, 3,...) and treat the attribute as if it were a continuous attribute. The smaller the number of categories, and the less they represent equal increments of value, the more problematic this approach becomes, but it often works well enough.

Nominal categorical attributes, however, often cannot be used as is. In many cases, they must be decomposed into a series of binary attributes with 1/0 values, called *dummy variables*. For example, a single categorical attribute that can have possible values of "student," "unemployed," "employed," or "retired" would be split into four separate dummy variables where 1 denotes "yes" and 0 denotes "no":

Student—1/0   *Employed*—1/0
Unemployed—1/0   *Retired*—1/0

---

[1]In this book, we will use the terms continuous and numeric interchangeably.
[2]In this book, we will use the terms categorical and nominal interchangeably.

In some algorithms (e.g., regression models), only three of the dummy variables should be used; if the values of three are known, the fourth is also known. For example, given that these four values are the only possible ones, we can know that if a person is neither student, unemployed, nor employed, he or she must be retired. In fact, due to this redundant information, linear regression and logistic regression algorithms will produce incorrect results or fail if you use all four variables. Yet, in other algorithms (e.g., k-nearest neighbors), we must include all four dummy variables. This is called *one-hot encoding*.

In RapidMiner, the *Nominal to Numerical* operator can convert categorical attributes to numerical attributes with *coding type* specified as *dummy coding*, thus creating binary dummies. Optionally, a comparison group can also be specified for each categorical attribute to remove the corresponding redundant category.

Attribute Selection   More is not necessarily better when it comes to selecting attributes for a model. Other things being equal, parsimony, or compactness, is a desirable feature in a model. For one thing, the more attributes we include, the greater the number of records we will need to assess relationships among the attributes. Fifteen records may suffice to give us a rough idea of the relationship between Y and a single predictor attribute X. If we now want information about the relationship between Y and 15 predictor attributes $X_1, \ldots, X_{15}$, 15 records will not be enough (each estimated relationship would have an average of only one record's worth of information, making the estimate very unreliable). In addition, models based on many attributes are often less robust, as they require the collection of more data in the future, are subject to more data quality and availability issues, and require more data cleaning and preprocessing. The process of attribute selection is also called *feature selection*.

How Many Attributes and How Much Data?   Statisticians give us procedures to learn with some precision how many records we would need to achieve a given degree of reliability with a given dataset and a given model. These are called "power calculations" and are intended to assure that an average population effect will be estimated with sufficient precision from a sample. Predictive analytics needs are usually different because the focus is not on identifying an average effect but rather on predicting individual records. This purpose typically requires larger samples than those used for statistical inference. A good rule of thumb is to have 10 records for every predictor attribute. Another, used by Delmaster and Hancock (2001, p. 68) for classification procedures, is to have at least $6 \times m \times p$ records, where m is the number of target attribute classes and p is the number of attributes.

In general, compactness or parsimony is a desirable feature in a machine learning model. Even when we start with a small number of attributes, we often end up with many more after creating new attributes (e.g., converting a categorical attribute into a set of dummy variables). Data visualization and dimension reduction methods help reduce the number of attributes so that redundancies are avoided.

Even when we have an ample supply of data, there are good reasons to pay close attention to the attributes that are included in a model. Someone with domain knowledge (i.e., knowledge of the business process and the data) should be consulted, as knowledge of what the attributes represent is typically critical for building a good model and avoiding errors and legal violations.

For example, suppose we're trying to predict the total purchase amount spent by customers, and we have a few predictor columns that are coded $X_1, X_2, X_3, \ldots$, where we don't know what those codes mean. We might find that X_1 is an excellent predictor of the total amount spent. However, if we discover that X_1 is the amount spent on shipping, calculated as a percentage of the purchase amount, then obviously a model that uses shipping amount cannot be used to predict purchase amount, since the shipping amount is not known until the transaction is completed. This is known as *target leakage*. Another example is if we are trying to predict loan default at the time a customer applies for a loan. If our dataset includes only information on approved loan applications, we will not have information about what distinguishes defaulters from nondefaulters among denied applicants. A model based on approved loans alone can therefore not be used to predict defaulting behavior at the time of loan application but rather only once a loan is approved. Finally, in certain applications (e.g., credit scoring), attributes such as gender and race are legally prohibited.

Outliers   The more data we are dealing with, the greater the chance of encountering erroneous values resulting from measurement error, data-entry error, or the like. If the erroneous value is in the same range as the rest of the data, it may be harmless. If it is well outside the range of the rest of the data (e.g., a misplaced decimal), it may have a substantial effect on some of the machine learning procedures we plan to use.

Values that lie far away from the bulk of the data are called *outliers*. The term *far away* is deliberately left vague because what is or is not called an outlier is basically an arbitrary decision. Analysts use rules of thumb such as "anything over three standard deviations away from the mean is an outlier," but no statistical rule can tell us whether such an outlier is the result of an error. In this statistical sense, an outlier is not necessarily an invalid data point; it is just a distant one.

The purpose of identifying outliers is usually to call attention to values that need further review. We might come up with an explanation looking at the data—in the case of a misplaced decimal, this is likely. We might have no explanation but know that the value is wrong—a temperature of 178 °F for a sick person. We might conclude that the value is within the realm of possibility and leave it alone. Or, it might be that the outliers are what we are looking for—unusual financial transactions or travel patterns. All these are judgments best made by someone with *domain knowledge*, knowledge of the particular application being considered: direct mail, mortgage finance, and so on, as opposed to technical knowledge of statistical or machine learning procedures. Statistical procedures can do little beyond identifying the record as something that needs review.

If manual review is feasible, some outliers may be identified and corrected. In any case, if the number of records with outliers is very small, they might be treated as missing data. How do we inspect for outliers? One technique is to sort the records by the first attribute, then review the data for very large or very small values for that attribute. Then repeat for each successive attribute. Another option is to examine the minimum and maximum values of each attribute using RapidMiner's *Statistics* tab from the *Results* view for the dataset. For a more automated approach that considers each record as a unit, clustering techniques (see Chapter 16) could be used to identify clusters of one or a few records that are distant from others. Those records could then be examined.

Missing Values   Typically, some records will contain missing values. If the number of records with missing values is small, those records might be omitted. However, if we have a large number of attributes, even a small proportion of missing values can affect a lot of records. Even with only 30 attributes, if only 5% of the values are missing (spread randomly and independently among records and attributes), almost 80% of the records would have to be omitted from the analysis. (The chance that a given record would escape having a missing value is $0.95^{30} = 0.215$.)

An alternative to omitting records with missing values is to replace the missing value with an imputed value, based on the other values for that attribute across all records. For example, among 30 attributes, if household income is missing for a particular record, we might substitute the average household income across all records. Doing so does not, of course, add any information about how household income affects the target attribute. It merely allows us to proceed with the analysis and not lose the information contained in this record for the other 29 attributes. Note that using such a technique will understate the variability in a dataset. However, we can assess variability and the performance of our machine learning technique using the holdout data, and therefore this need not present a major problem. RapidMiner offers the ability to replace missing values using fairly simple substitutes (e.g., average, minimum, maximum) using the *Replace Missing Values* operator. More sophisticated procedures do exist—for example, using linear regression, based on other attributes, to fill in the missing values—employing RapidMiner's *Impute Missing Values* operator. These methods have been elaborated mainly for analysis of medical and scientific studies, where each patient or subject record comes at great expense.

In machine learning, where data are typically plentiful, simpler methods usually suffice.

Some datasets contain attributes that have a very large number of missing values. In other words, a measurement is missing for a large number of records. In that case, dropping records with missing values will lead to a large loss of data. Imputing the missing values might also be useless, as the imputations are based on a small number of existing records. An alternative is to examine the importance of the predictor. If it is not very crucial, it can be dropped. If it is important, perhaps a proxy attribute with fewer missing values can be used instead. When such a predictor is deemed central, the best solution is to invest in obtaining the missing data.

Significant time may be required to deal with missing data, as not all situations are susceptible to automated solutions. In a messy dataset, for example, a "0" might mean two things: (1) the value is missing, or (2) the value is actually zero. In the credit industry, a "0" in the "past due" attribute might mean a customer who is fully paid up or a customer with no credit history at all—two very different situations. Human judgment may be required for individual cases or to determine a special rule to deal with the situation.

Normalizing (Standardizing) and Rescaling Data   Some algorithms require that the data be normalized before the algorithm can be implemented effectively. To normalize an attribute, we subtract the mean from each value and then divide by the standard deviation. This operation is also sometimes called *standardizing* or *z-transformation*. In effect, we are expressing each value as the "number of standard deviations away from the mean," also called a *z-score*.

Normalizing is one way to bring all attributes to the same scale. Another popular approach is rescaling each attribute to a [0,1] scale. This is done by subtracting the minimum value and then dividing by the range. Subtracting the minimum shifts the attribute origin to zero. Dividing by the range shrinks or expands the data to the range [0,1]. This is sometimes called *range transformation*.

To consider why normalizing or scaling to [0,1] might be necessary, consider the case of clustering. Clustering typically involves calculating a distance measure that reflects how far each record is from a cluster center or from other records. With multiple attributes, different units will be used: days, dollars, counts, and so on. If the dollars are in the thousands and everything else is in the tens, the dollar attribute will come to dominate the distance measure. Moreover, changing units from, say, days to hours or months could alter the outcome completely.

Some machine learning software tools provide an option to normalize the data in those algorithms where it may be required. It is an option rather than an automatic feature of such algorithms because there are situations where we want each attribute to contribute to the distance measure in proportion to its original scale. In RapidMiner, the *Normalize* operator is configured and used to perform normalization or range transformation prior to implementing the modeling algorithms.

2.5 PREDICTIVE POWER AND OVERFITTING

In supervised learning, a key question presents itself: How well will our prediction or classification model perform when we apply it to new data? We are particularly interested in comparing the performance of different models so that we can choose the model that we think will do the best when it is implemented in practice. A key concept is to make sure that our chosen model generalizes beyond the dataset that we have at hand. To assure generalization, we use the concept of *data partitioning* and try to avoid *overfitting*. These two important concepts are described next.

Overfitting

The more attributes we include in a model, the greater the risk of overfitting the particular data used for modeling. What is overfitting?

In Table 2.1, we show hypothetical data about advertising expenditures in one time period and sales in a subsequent time period. A scatter plot of the data is shown in Figure 2.2. We could connect up these points with a smooth but complicated function, one that interpolates all these data points perfectly and leaves no error (residuals). This can be seen in Figure 2.3. However, we can see that such a curve is unlikely to be accurate, or even useful, in predicting future sales on the basis of advertising expenditures. For instance, it is hard to believe that increasing expenditures from \$400 to \$500 will actually decrease revenue.

A basic purpose of building a model is to represent relationships among attributes in such a way that this representation will do a good job of predicting future outcome values on the basis of future predictor values. Of course, we want the model to do a good job of describing the data we have, but we are more interested in its performance with future data.

TABLE 2.1	HYPOTHETICAL DATA ON ADVERTISING EXPENDITURES AND SUBSEQUENT SALES
Advertising	**Sales**
239	514
364	789
602	550
644	1386
770	1394
789	1440
911	1354

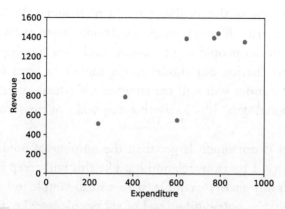

FIGURE 2.2   SCATTER PLOT FOR ADVERTISING AND SALES DATA

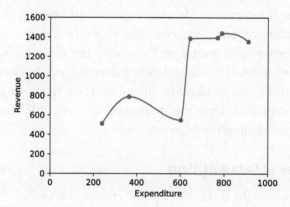

FIGURE 2.3   OVERFITTING: THIS FUNCTION FITS THE DATA WITH NO ERROR

In the hypothetical advertising example, a simple straight line might do a better job than the complex function in terms of predicting future sales on the basis of advertising. Instead, we devised a complex function that fits the data perfectly, and in doing so, we overreached. We ended up modeling some variation in the data that is nothing more than chance variation. We mistreated the noise in the data as if it were a signal.

Similarly, we can add predictors to a model to sharpen its performance with the data at hand. Consider a database of 100 individuals, 50 of whom have contributed to a charitable cause. Information about income, family size, and zip code might do a fair job of predicting whether or not someone is a contributor. If we keep adding additional predictors, we can improve the performance of the model with the data at hand and reduce the misclassification error to a negligible level. However, this low error rate is misleading because it probably includes spurious effects that are specific to the 100 individuals but not beyond that sample.

For example, one of the attributes might be height. We have no basis in theory to suppose that tall people might contribute more or less to charity, but if there are several tall people in our sample and they just happened to contribute heavily to charity, our model might include a term for height—the taller you are, the more you will contribute. Of course, when the model is applied to additional data, it is likely that this will not turn out to be a good predictor.

If the dataset is not much larger than the number of predictor attributes, it is very likely that a spurious relationship like this will creep into the model. Continuing with our charity example, with a small sample just a few of whom are tall, whatever the contribution level of tall people may be, the algorithm is tempted to attribute it to their being tall. If the dataset is very large relative to the number of predictors, this is less likely to occur. In such a case, each predictor must help predict the outcome for a large number of cases, so the job it does is much less dependent on just a few cases that might be flukes.

Somewhat surprisingly, even if we know for a fact that a higher degree curve is the appropriate model, if the model-fitting dataset is not large enough, a lower degree function (i.e., not as likely to fit the noise) is likely to perform better. Overfitting can also result from the application of many different models, from which the best performing model is selected.

Creation and Use of Data Partitions

At first glance, we might think it is best to choose the model that did the best job of classifying or predicting the target attribute of interest with the data at hand. However, when we use the same data both to develop the model and to assess its performance, we introduce an "optimism" bias. This is because when we choose the model that works best with the data, this model's superior performance comes from two sources:

- A superior model
- Chance aspects of the data that happen to match the chosen model better than they match other models.

The latter is a particularly serious problem with techniques (such as trees and neural nets) that do not impose linear or other structure on the data, and thus end up overfitting it.

To address the overfitting problem, we simply divide (partition) our data and develop our model using only one of the partitions. After we have a model, we try it out on another partition and see how it performs, which we can measure in several ways. In a classification model, we can count the proportion of held-back records that were misclassified. In a prediction model, we can measure the residuals (prediction errors) between the predicted values and the actual values.

This evaluation approach in effect mimics the deployment scenario, where our model is applied to data that it hasn't "seen."

We typically deal with two or three partitions: a training set, a validation set, and sometimes an additional holdout set. Partitioning the data into training, validation, and holdout sets is done either randomly according to predetermined proportions or by specifying which records go into which partition according to some relevant variable (e.g., in time series forecasting, the data are partitioned according to their chronological order). In most cases, the partitioning should be done randomly to minimize the chance of getting a biased partition. It is also possible (although cumbersome) to divide the data into more than three partitions by successive partitioning (e.g., divide the initial data into three partitions, then take one of those partitions and partition it further).

Training Partition   The training partition, typically the largest partition, contains the data used to build the various models we are examining. The same training partition is generally used to develop multiple models.

Validation Partition   The validation partition is used to assess the predictive performance of each model so that you can compare models and choose the best one. In some algorithms (e.g., classification and regression trees, k-nearest neighbors), the validation partition may be used in an automated fashion to tune parameters and improve the model.

Holdout Partition   The holdout partition (sometimes called the *test partition* or *evaluation partition*) is used to assess the performance of the chosen model with new data.

Why have both a validation and a holdout partition? When we use the validation data to assess multiple models and then choose the model that performs best with the validation data, we again encounter another (lesser) facet of the overfitting problem—chance aspects of the validation data that happen to match the chosen model better than they match other models. In other words, by using the validation data to choose one of several models, the performance of the chosen model on the validation data will be overly optimistic.

The random features of the validation data that enhance the apparent performance of the chosen model will probably not be present in new data to which the model is applied. Therefore, we may have overestimated the accuracy of our model. The more models we test, the more likely it is that one of them will be particularly effective in modeling the noise in the validation data. Applying the model to the holdout data, which it has not seen before, will provide an unbiased estimate of how well the model will perform with new data. Figure 2.4 shows the three data partitions and their use in the machine learning process. When we

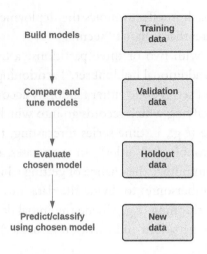

FIGURE 2.4   **THREE DATA PARTITIONS AND THEIR ROLE IN THE MACHINE LEARNING PROCESS**

are concerned mainly with finding the best model and less with exactly how well it will do, we might use only training and validation partitions.

Note that with some algorithms, such as nearest-neighbor algorithms, records in the validation and holdout partitions, and in new data, are compared to records in the training data to find the nearest neighbor(s). As k-nearest neighbors is discussed in this book, the use of two partitions is an essential part of the classification or prediction process, not merely a way to improve or assess it. Nonetheless, we can still interpret the error in the holdout data in the same way that we would interpret error from any other model.

Cross-Validation   When the number of records in our sample is small, data partitioning might not be advisable as each partition will contain too few records for model building and performance evaluation. Furthermore, some machine learning methods are sensitive to small changes in the training data so that a different partitioning can lead to different results. An alternative to data partitioning is cross-validation, which is especially useful with small samples. Cross-validation, or *k-fold cross-validation*, is a procedure that starts with partitioning the data into "folds," or non-overlapping subsamples. Often we choose $k = 5$ folds, meaning that the data are randomly partitioned into five equal parts, where each fold has 20% of the records. A model is then fit k times. Each time, one of the folds is used as the validation set, and the remaining $k-1$ folds serve as the training set. The result is that each fold is used once as the validation set, thereby producing predictions for every record in the dataset. We can then combine the model's predictions on each of the k validation sets in order to evaluate the overall performance of the model. In RapidMiner, cross-validation is achieved using the *Cross Validation* operator by specifying the number of folds in the parameter settings. Sometimes cross-validation is built into a machine learning algorithm, with the results of the cross-validation used for choosing the algorithm's parameters (see, e.g., Chapter 9).

2.6 BUILDING A PREDICTIVE MODEL WITH RAPIDMINER

Let us go through the steps typical to many machine learning tasks using a familiar procedure: multiple linear regression. This will help you understand the overall process before we begin tackling new algorithms. We illustrate the procedure using RapidMiner.

The Internet has revolutionized the real estate industry. Realtors now list houses and their prices on the web, and estimates of house and condominium prices have become widely available, even for units not on the market. In 2014, Zillow (www.zillow.com), a popular online real estate information site in the United States,[3] purchased its major rival, Trulia. By 2015, Zillow had become the dominant platform for checking house prices and, as such, the dominant online advertising venue for realtors. By 2021, another competitor, Redfin, had eclipsed Zillow in market capitalization, largely via its strategy of employing its own agents directly on a salaried basis. What used to be a comfortable 6% commission structure for independent realtors, affording them a handsome surplus (and an oversupply of realtors), was being rapidly eroded by an increasing need to pay for advertising on Zillow and by competition from Redfin. (This, in fact, was the original key to Zillow's business model—redirecting the 6% commission away from realtors and to itself.)

Zillow gets much of the data for its "Zestimates" of home values directly from publicly available city housing data, used to estimate property values for tax assessment. A competitor seeking to get into the market would likely take the same approach. So might realtors seeking to develop an alternative to Zillow.

A simple approach would be a naive, model-less method—just use the assessed values as determined by the city. Those values, however, do not necessarily include all properties, and they might not include changes warranted by remodeling, additions, and so on. Moreover, the assessment methods used by cities may not be transparent or always reflect true market values. However, the city property data can be used as a starting point to build a model, to which additional data (such as that collected by large realtors) can be added later.

Let's look at how Boston property assessment data, available from the city of Boston, might be used to predict home values. The data in *West Roxbury.csv* includes information on single family owner-occupied homes in West Roxbury, a neighborhood in southwest Boston, in 2014. The data include values for

---

[3] "Zestimates may not be as right as you'd like" *Washington Post* Feb. 7, 2015, p. T10, by K. Harney.

various predictor attributes and for a target attribute—assessed home value ("total value"). This dataset has 14 attributes and includes 5802 homes. A sample of the data[4] is shown in Table 2.3, and the "data dictionary" describing each attribute[5] is in Table 2.2.

As we saw earlier, below the header row, each row in the data represents a home. For example, the first home was assessed at a total value of $344.2 thousand (TOTAL VALUE). Its tax bill was $4330. It has a lot size of 9965 square feet (ft^2), was built in 1880, and has two floors, six rooms, and so on.

TABLE 2.2   DESCRIPTION OF VARIABLES IN WEST ROXBURY (BOSTON) HOME VALUE DATASET

TOTAL VALUE	Total assessed value for property, in thousands of USD
TAX	Tax bill amount based on total assessed value multiplied by the tax rate, in USD
LOT SQ FT	Total lot size of parcel (ft^2)
YR BUILT	Year the property was built
GROSS AREA	Gross floor area
LIVING AREA	Total living area for residential properties (ft^2)
FLOORS	Number of floors
ROOMS	Total number of rooms
BEDROOMS	Total number of bedrooms
FULL BATH	Total number of full baths
HALF BATH	Total number of half baths
KITCHEN	Total number of kitchens
FIREPLACE	Total number of fireplaces
REMODEL	When the house was remodeled (recent/old/none)

TABLE 2.3   FIRST 10 RECORDS IN THE WEST ROXBURY HOME VALUES DATASET

TOTAL VALUE	TAX	LOT SQ FT	YR BUILT	GROSS AREA	LIVING AREA	FLOORS	ROOMS	BED ROOMS	FULL BATH	HALF BATH	KIT CHEN	FIRE PLACE	REMODEL
344.2	4330	9965	1880	2436	1352	2	6	3	1	1	1	0	None
412.6	5190	6590	1945	3108	1976	2	10	4	2	1	1	0	Recent
330.1	4152	7500	1890	2294	1371	2	8	4	1	1	1	0	None
498.6	6272	13,773	1957	5032	2608	1	9	5	1	1	1	1	None
331.5	4170	5000	1910	2370	1438	2	7	3	2	0	1	0	None
337.4	4244	5142	1950	2124	1060	1	6	3	1	0	1	1	Old
359.4	4521	5000	1954	3220	1916	2	7	3	1	1	1	0	None
320.4	4030	10,000	1950	2208	1200	1	6	3	1	0	1	0	None
333.5	4195	6835	1958	2582	1092	1	5	3	1	0	1	1	Recent
409.4	5150	5093	1900	4818	2992	2	8	4	2	0	1	0	None

---

[4]The data are a slightly cleaned version of the Property Assessment FY2014 data at https://data.boston.gov/dataset/property-assessment (accessed December 2017).
[5]The full data dictionary provided by the City of Boston is available at https://data.boston.gov/dataset/property-assessment; we have modified a few attribute names.

Predicting Home Values in the West Roxbury Neighborhood
Modeling Process

We now describe in detail the various model stages using the West Roxbury home values example.

1. *Determine the purpose*: Let's assume that the purpose of our machine learning project is to predict the value of homes in West Roxbury.

2. *Obtain the data*: We will use the 2014 West Roxbury housing data. The dataset in question is small enough that we do not need to sample from it—we can use it in its entirety.

3. *Explore, clean, and preprocess the data*: Let's look first at the description of the attributes, also known as the "data dictionary," to be sure that we understand them all. These descriptions are available in Table 2.2. The attribute names and descriptions in this dataset all seem fairly straightforward, but this is not always the case. Often attribute names are cryptic, and their descriptions are unclear or missing.

    It is useful to pause and think about what the attributes mean and whether they should be included in the model. Consider the attribute TAX. At first glance, we consider that the tax on a home is usually a function of its assessed value, so there is some circularity in the model—we want to predict a home's value using TAX as a predictor, yet TAX itself is determined by a home's value. TAX might be a very good predictor of home value in a numerical sense, but would it be useful if we wanted to apply our model to homes whose assessed value might not be known? For this reason, we will exclude TAX from the analysis.

    At this point we would also search for missing data and decide whether to remove rows or columns where data are missing, or impute the missing values.

    It is also useful to check for outliers that might be errors. For example, suppose that the column FLOORS (number of floors) looked like the one in Table 2.4, after sorting the data in descending order based on floors. We can tell right away that the 15 is in error—it is unlikely that a home has 15 floors. All other values are between 1 and 2. Probably, the decimal was misplaced and the value should be 1.5.

TABLE 2.4	OUTLIER IN WEST ROXBURY DATA
Floors	**Rooms**
15	8
2	10
1.5	6
1	6

Last, we create dummy variables for categorical attributes. Here, we have one categorical attribute: REMODEL, which has three categories.

The data preprocessing steps are shown in Figure 2.5. The *Retrieve* operator loads the data already imported in the RapidMiner repository. The *Select Attributes* operator includes all attributes for analysis, except TAX. The *Set Role* operator assigns the *label* role to the target attribute TOTAL VALUE. The *Nominal to Numerical* operator creates dummy variables for the REMODEL attribute.

4. *Reduce the data dimension*: Our dataset has been prepared for presentation with fairly low dimension—it has only 14 attributes, and the single categorical attribute considered has only three categories (and hence adds two or three dummy variables). If we had many more attributes, at this stage, we might want to apply a dimension reduction technique such as condensing multiple categories into a smaller number, or applying principal components analysis to consolidate multiple similar numerical attributes (e.g., LIVING AREA, ROOMS, BEDROOMS, BATH, HALF BATH) into a smaller number of attributes.

5. *Determine the machine learning task*: The specific task is to predict the value of TOTAL VALUE using the predictor attributes. This is a supervised prediction task. For simplicity, we excluded several additional attributes present in the original dataset, which have many categories (BLDG TYPE, ROOF TYPE, and EXT FIN). We therefore use all the numerical attributes (except TAX) and the dummies created for the remaining categorical attributes.

6. *Partition the data (for supervised tasks)*: In this case, we divide the data into two partitions: training and holdout (see Figure 2.6). The training partition is used to build the model, and the holdout partition is used to see how well the model does when applied to new data. We need to specify the proportion of records used in each partition. *Note*: Although not used in our example, a validation partition might also be used when comparing models.

7. *Choose the technique*: In this case, it is multiple linear regression. Having divided the data into training and holdout partitions, we can use Rapid-Miner to build a multiple linear regression model with the training data. We want to predict the value of a house in West Roxbury on the basis of all the other predictors (except TAX).

8. *Use the algorithm to perform the task*: The machine learning process built in RapidMiner is shown in Figure 2.7. The *Data Preprocessing* subprocess contains the same steps mentioned in Figure 2.5, with the addition of the *Split Data* operator used for data partitioning as discussed earlier. We fit a multiple linear regression model between TOTAL VALUE

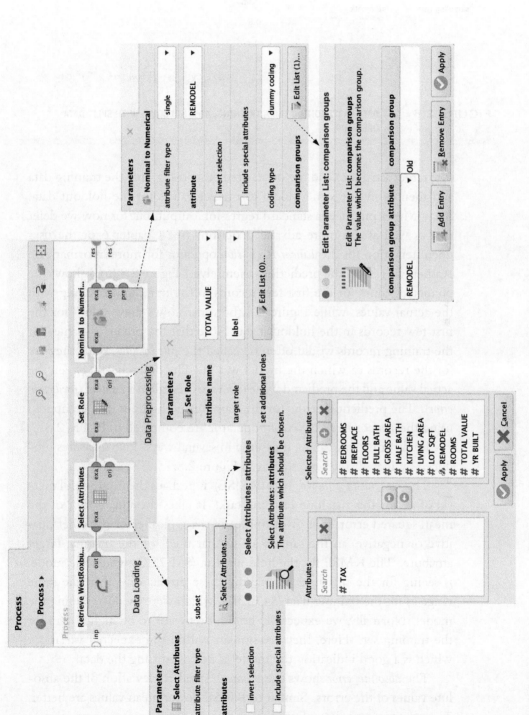

FIGURE 2.5   DATA PREPROCESSING STEPS IN RAPIDMINER FOR WEST ROXBURY DATA

FIGURE 2.6 DATA PARTITIONING (60% TRAINING, 40% HOLDOUT) WITH SPLIT DATA OPERATOR

(the target attribute) and the other predictors using only the training data and then apply the same model to predict values for the holdout data. RapidMiner produces a standard regression output, but for now we defer that as well as the more advanced options (see Chapter 6 or the user documentation for the *Linear Regression* operator for more information). Rather, we review the predictions themselves. Figure 2.8 (top) shows the predicted values for the first few records in the training data along with the actual values, while Figure 2.8 (bottom) shows these values for the first few records in the holdout data. Note that the predicted values for the training records would often be called the *fitted values*, since they are for the records to which the model was fit. The difference between the actual value and the predicted value of a record is called a *residual (prediction error)*. The prediction errors for the training and holdout data computed using the *Performance (Regression)* operator are compared in Figure 2.8.

Prediction error can be measured in several ways. Five measures produced by RapidMiner are shown in Figure 2.8:

The *root_mean_squared_error* (RMSE) is perhaps the most useful metric of all for this machine learning task. It takes the square root of the mean squared error, so it gives an idea of the typical error (whether positive or negative) in the same scale as that used for the original target attribute. The RMSE for the holdout data ($41.71K), which the model is seeing for the first time in making these predictions, is in the same range as for the training data ($43.73K), which were used in training the model. Normally, we expect the holdout set error to be higher than for the training set. Here, they are similar, within the expected variation, which is a good indication the model is not overfitting the data.

The *absolute_error* shows the mean ± standard deviation of the absolute values of the errors. Similar to RMSE, lower mean values are better. The *relative_error*, also referred to as the *absolute percentage error*, gives a

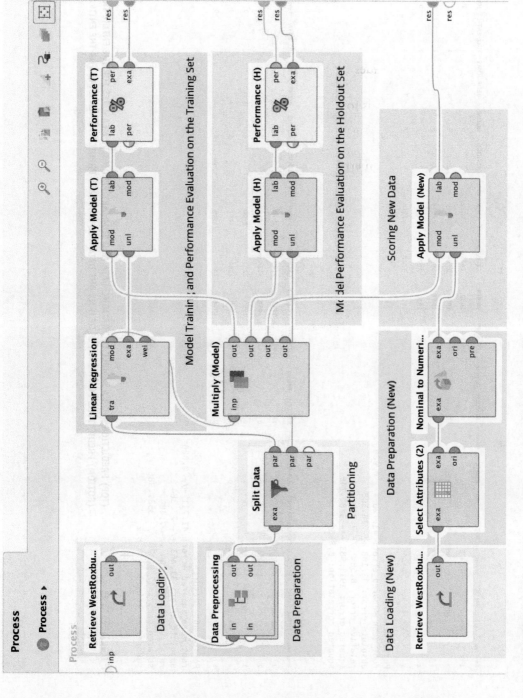

FIGURE 2.7   PREDICTIVE MODELING PROCESS IN RAPIDMINER FOR WEST ROXBURY DATA

Row No.	TOTAL VALUE	prediction(TOTAL VALUE)	REMODEL_None	REMODEL_Recent	LOT SQFT	YR BUILT	GROSS AREA	LIVING AREA	FLOORS	ROOMS	BEDROOMS	FULL BATH	HALF BATH	KITCHEN	FIREPLACE
1	344.200	379.478	1	0	9965	1880	2436	1352	2	6	3	1	1	1	0
2	330.100	355.590	1	0	7500	1890	2294	1371	2	8	4	1	1	1	0
3	498.600	544.043	1	0	13773	1957	5032	2608	1	9	5	1	1	1	1
4	331.500	348.389	1	0	5000	1910	2370	1438	2	7	3	2	0	1	0
5	359.400	404.995	1	0	5000	1954	3220	1916	2	7	3	1	1	1	0

```
PerformanceVector:
root_mean_squared_error: 43.726 +/- 0.000
absolute_error: 33.108 +/- 28.563
relative_error: 8.58% +/- 7.34%
squared_error: 1911.983 +/- 3780.748
squared_correlation: 0.806
```

Row No.	TOTAL VALUE	prediction(TOTAL VALUE)	REMODEL_None	REMODEL_Recent	LOT SQFT	YR BUILT	GROSS AREA	LIVING AREA	FLOORS	ROOMS	BEDROOMS	FULL BATH	HALF BATH	KITCHEN	FIREPLACE
1	412.600	458.019	0	1	6590	1945	3108	1976	2	10	4	2	1	1	0
2	337.400	288.903	0	0	5142	1950	2124	1060	1	6	3	1	0	1	1
3	320.400	312.429	1	0	10000	1950	2208	1200	1	6	3	1	0	1	0
4	333.500	338.221	0	1	6835	1958	2582	1092	1	5	3	1	0	1	1
5	344.500	382.341	1	0	6768	1958	2844	1460	1.500	6	3	2	0	1	1

```
PerformanceVector:
root_mean_squared_error: 41.711 +/- 0.000
absolute_error: 31.463 +/- 27.384
relative_error: 8.30% +/- 7.40%
squared_error: 1739.820 +/- 3531.386
squared_correlation: 0.822
```

FIGURE 2.8   (TOP) PREDICTIONS FOR A SAMPLE OF TRAINING DATA AND SUMMARY PREDICTIVE MEASURES FOR THE ENTIRE TRAINING DATA;
(BOTTOM) PREDICTIONS FOR A SAMPLE OF HOLDOUT DATA AND SUMMARY PREDICTIVE MEASURES FOR THE ENTIRE HOLDOUT DATA

percentage score of how predictions deviate from the actual values. The lower the relative error, the better. The *squared_error* shows the mean of the squared errors (MSE). The *squared_correlation* (R^2) measures the strength of fit in a regression model, based on the training data. It is not useful for evaluating predictive performance.

9. *Interpret the results*: At this stage, we would typically try other prediction algorithms (e.g., regression trees) and see how they do error-wise. We might also try different "settings" on the various models (e.g., we could use the *best subsets* option in multiple linear regression to choose a reduced set of attributes that might perform better with the validation data). For this purpose of model comparison and model tuning, we should utilize a validation dataset instead of the holdout data. After choosing the best model—typically, the model with the lowest error on the validation data while also recognizing that "simpler is better"—we use that model to predict the target attribute in fresh holdout data. These steps are covered in more detail in the analysis of cases.

10. *Deploy the model*: After the best model is chosen, it is applied to new data to predict TOTAL VALUE for homes where this value is unknown. This was, of course, the original purpose. Predicting the output value for new records is called *scoring*. For predictive tasks, scoring produces predicted numerical values. For classification tasks, scoring produces classes and/or propensities. In RapidMiner, we can score new records using one of the models we developed. To do that, we must first create a similar data file with the records to be predicted. For these records, we must include all the predictor values and the target attribute is absent. Then, we must import and load this "new" data in RapidMiner and apply the same data preprocessing steps as the training data, prior to applying the model. Figure 2.9 (top) shows an ExampleSet (imported using data file *WestRoxbury-NewData.csv*) with three homes to be scored using our linear regression model. Note that all the required predictor columns are present, and the output column is absent. The result is shown in Figure 2.9 (bottom), where the predictions are in the second column.

2.7 USING RAPIDMINER FOR MACHINE LEARNING

An important aspect of this modeling process is that the heavy-duty analysis does not necessarily require a huge number of records. The dataset to be analyzed might have millions of records, or be part of a regular ongoing flow, but in applying multiple linear regression or applying a classification tree, the use of a sample of 20,000 is likely to yield as accurate an answer as that obtained when using the entire dataset. The principle involved is the same as the principle

Row No.	TAX	LOT SQFT	YR BUILT	GROSS AREA	LIVING AREA	FLOORS	ROOMS	BEDROOMS	FULL BATH	HALF BATH	KITCHEN	FIREPLACE	REMODEL
1	3850	6877	1963	2240	1808	1	6	3	1	1	1	0	None
2	5386	5965	1963	2998	1637	1.500	8	3	3	0	1	1	Old
3	4608	5662	1961	2805	1750	2	7	4	2	0	1	1	Recent

Row No.	prediction(TOTAL VALUE)	REMODEL_None	REMODEL_Recent	LOT SQFT	YR BUILT	GROSS AREA	LIVING AREA	FLOORS	ROOMS	BEDROOMS	FULL BATH	HALF BATH	KITCHEN	FIREPLACE
1	339.113	1	0	6877	1963	2240	1808	1	6	3	1	1	1	0
2	417.247	0	0	5965	1963	2998	1637	1.500	8	3	3	0	1	1
3	431.719	0	1	5662	1961	2805	1750	2	7	4	2	0	1	1

FIGURE 2.9   (TOP) THREE RECORDS TO BE SCORED AS LOADED IN RAPIDMINER

(BOTTOM) THREE RECORDS SCORED USING LINEAR REGRESSION MODEL

behind polling: if sampled judiciously, 2000 voters can give an estimate of the entire population's opinion within one or two percentage points. (See "How Many Attributes and How Much Data" in Section 2.4 for further discussion.)

Therefore, in most cases, the number of records required in each partition (training, validation, and holdout) can be accommodated within the memory limit allowed of your local machine, as supported by RapidMiner Studio. Of course, we need to get those records into RapidMiner Studio, and for this purpose, RapidMiner provides the *Read Database* operator for accessing and querying data from databases (e.g., MySQL, Oracle) and similar operators (see *Data Access > Cloud Storage* in the Operators panel) for accessing data from cloud storage locations (e.g., Amazon S3, Azure Data Lake, Dropbox). When the number of records is extremely large and records are stored in a large database, RapidMiner Studio supports in-database processing with the *In-Database Processing* extension by conducting data preparation inside the database clusters (e.g., MySQL, PostgreSQL, and Google BigQuery) using their computing power and then sampling the data for modeling.

Similarly, we may need to apply the results of our analysis to a large database, and for this purpose, RapidMiner provides the *Write Database* operator to write the scored data to an external database. RapidMiner models can be stored using the *Store* operator, and RapidMiner's AI Hub (formerly RapidMiner Server) product allows deploying models to production for real-time scoring.

2.8 AUTOMATING MACHINE LEARNING SOLUTIONS[6]

Automating machine learning solutions is often termed "machine learning operations" ("MLOps"), or "AI engineering." In most supervised machine learning applications, the goal is not a static, one-time analysis of a particular dataset. Rather, we want to develop a model that can be used on an ongoing basis to predict or classify new records. Our initial analysis will be in prototype mode, while we explore and define the problem and test different models. We will follow all the steps outlined earlier in this chapter.

At the end of that process, we will typically want our chosen model to be deployed in an automated fashion. For example, the US Internal Revenue Service (IRS) receives several hundred million tax returns per year—it does not want to have to pull each tax return out into an Excel sheet or other environment separate from its main database to determine the predicted probability that the return is fraudulent. Rather, it would prefer that determination be made as part of the normal tax filing environment and process. Music streaming services, such as Pandora or Spotify, need to determine "recommendations" for

---

[6]This section copyright 2021 Peter Bruce, Galit Shmueli and Victor Diloreto; used by permission.

next songs quickly for each of millions of users; there is no time to extract the data for manual analysis.

In practice, this is done by building the chosen algorithm into the computational setting in which the rest of the process lies. A tax return is entered directly into the IRS system by a tax preparer, a predictive algorithm is immediately applied to the new data in the IRS system, and a predicted classification is decided by the algorithm. Business rules would then determine what happens with that classification. In the IRS case, the rule might be "if no predicted fraud, continue routine processing; if fraud is predicted, alert an examiner for possible audit."

This flow of the tax return from data entry, into the IRS system, through a predictive algorithm, then back out to a human user is an example of a "data pipeline." The RapidMiner flow diagrams presented in this text are examples of simple pipelines. In real-world model deployments, the different components of the system communicate with one another via application programming interfaces (APIs) that establish locally valid rules for transmitting data and associated communications. An API for a machine learning algorithm would establish the required elements for a predictive algorithm to work—the exact predictor attributes, their order, data formats, and so on. It would also establish the requirements for communicating the results of the algorithm. Algorithms to be used in an automated data pipeline will need to be compliant with the rules of the APIs where they operate.

Finally, once the computational environment is set and functioning, the machine learning work is not done. The environment in which a model operates is typically dynamic, and predictive models often have a short shelf life—one leading consultant finds they rarely continue to function effectively for more than a year. So, even in a fully deployed state, models must be periodically checked and reevaluated. Once performance flags, it is time to return to prototype mode and see if a new model can be developed.

As you can imagine, these computational environments are complex, and, as of 2022, large companies are only beginning to construct them. They are often driven to do so by the force of circumstance. In the following, we describe two examples of such environments.

Predicting Power Generator Failure[7]

Sira-Kvina, a major hydro-electric power company that supplies 7% of Norway's power, found that generator failures were taking a long time to diagnose, leading to lengthy off-line periods and loss of revenue and customer dissatisfaction.

---

[7]Thanks to Victor Diloreto, Chief Technical Officer of Elder Research, Inc., who wrote portions of this segment.

The company was using an engineering checklist approach: imagine a more complex version of the troubleshooting guide that comes with a fancy appliance, or the advice you encounter when trying to fix a software problem. Such an approach, however, could not begin to make use of all the data that comes in from hundreds of sensors producing tens of thousands of readings per day. A team from Elder Research investigated one particularly lengthy and costly outage and, after much data wrangling, visualization, and analysis, identified a set of separate events which, when they happened together, caused the failure. Moreover, generator failures were often preceded by a set of defined temperature spikes in one specific sensor (you can read a summary of the analysis at www.statistics.com/sira-kvina-hydro-power-the-case-of-the-faulty-generator). But an after-the-fact detective hunt is inherently unsatisfactory, since the generator down-time has already occurred. What is really needed is *proactive preventive maintenance*, triggered by advance warnings that are predictive of failure. Elder built such a system for Sira-Kvina. Machine learning models that predict generator failure are the key analytical component, but they are embedded in a system that must also handle, in addition to training and fitting a model, the following tasks:

- collecting and ingesting data from sensors
- transforming data (especially aggregating and disaggregating granular time series data)
- passing alerts from models to humans and other elements of the system
- providing visualization tools for analysts
- applying case management of anomalies
- adding manual labels applied by analysts, to facilitate further training.

Dozens of tools are involved in this structure. Figure 2.10 illustrates how different layers of tools contribute to this process.

The "Infrastructure" base layer provides base computing capability, memory, and networking, either on-premises or in the cloud. The next layer up supports

FIGURE 2.10   LAYERS OF TOOLS SUPPORTING MACHINE LEARNING AUTOMATION

basic services for the layers above it. "Security" provides user admin capabilities, permission levels, and networking and access rules. "Monitoring" ingests logs, implements needed thresholds and issues alerts. "Automation" has a more limited meaning than the overall topic of this section: it refers to bringing up, configuring, and tearing down tools and infrastructure as needed. "Resource management" provides the oversight of the various resources used throughout the stack. This area is closely coupled to monitoring: understanding what resources could be coming close to exhaustion is important for maintenance purposes.

"Testing/debugging" is self-explanatory, while the "data collection" layer refers primarily to the data store (data warehouse, data lake, or data lakehouse). In the Sira-Kvina case, there is a raw immutable data store (IDS) where all source data is collected, plus an analytic base table (ABT) that holds derivatives of the main data store needed for analysis. The "data ETL" (Extract, Transform, Load) layer provides the tools to create these derivatives. The verification step within this layer checks that the transformations, aggregations, or any formula used to take a raw piece of data and convert it to something else is doing the job we think it's supposed to do. This verification function is wired into the monitoring capability of the system, which flags any issue with an alert to maintainers of the system. The modeling layer contains the model(s) that make predictions (i.e., the primary focus of this book) and is accompanied by the model-monitoring section, which checks that the model is performing to expectations. Tools in the latter are tied into the lower-level infrastructure monitoring to generate alerts when a model is missing on expectations. Finally, the "delivery" layer is the user window into the system, and can represent simple things like a spreadsheet or a text file, or be as elaborate as an enterprise-wide tool like Tableau or Power BI.

From the above, you can see that Sira-Kvina's predictive models occupy only a small part of the data pipeline through which sensor data could flow and, when needed, trigger alerts to operators about system components that need attention. For a more far-reaching structure, consider Uber.

Uber's Michelangelo

Uber, which provides ride-sharing, meal delivery services, and more, uses real-time predictive models for several purposes including:

- matching the optimal driver for a customer ride request
- predicting customer pickup time
- predicting ride duration
- estimating pricing (including which peak pricing tier applies)
- predicting Uber Eats delivery time.

To integrate model-building with deployment, Uber built its own machine learning (ML) structure (MLOps) called Michelangelo. Prior to Michelangelo, in Uber's words, "the impact of ML at Uber was limited to what a few data scientists and engineers could build in a short time frame with mostly open source tools. Specifically, there were no systems in place to build reliable, uniform, and reproducible pipelines for creating and managing training and prediction data at scale."

Uber is a company essentially built on data science; at more traditional companies, the model deployment challenge is exacerbated by the fact that data science and data engineering are often considered separate jobs and disciplines. One major retailer described the problem as follows: "Our highly trained data scientists would build great models, give them to the engineers, who would say 'thank you very much, now we will need to build it again from scratch'."

Uber's Michelangelo is a development and deployment environment that Uber's data scientists use for a variety of models. It provides integration with the company's data stores and standard tools to build pipelines to ingest data. It has tools to split data into training and validation partitions, and to ensure that new data to be predicted follows the same format.

Some of Uber's goals (e.g., predicting the restaurant prep time component of Uber Eats delivery time) are not extremely time-sensitive, and batch processing can be used. Others (e.g., finding a driver) require nearly instantaneous action ("low-latency" response). Michelangelo supports both batch processing and real-time low-latency processing (Uber calls it "online"). Uber is constantly adding huge amounts of granular customer and driver data to its data store, so Michelangelo must have sufficient compute, data storage, and data flow capacity to scale efficiently. It also provides a facility to standardize feature definition and storage, so that data can be shared easily across users. It provides visualization and exploration tools for the prototyping and prep phases. Finally, it collects and makes available (via APIs and via a web user interface) standard information about each model[8]:

- Who trained the model
- Start and end times of the training job
- Full model configuration (features used, hyper parameter values, etc.)
- Reference to training and test datasets
- Distribution and relative importance of each feature
- Model accuracy metrics
- Standard charts and graphs for each model type (e.g., ROC curve, PR curve, and confusion matrix for a binary classifier)

---

[8]This list is from the Uber Engineering blog at https://eng.uber.com/michelangelo-machine-learning-platform; see also the discussion of "Model Cards" in Chapter 22.

- Full learned parameters of the model

- Summary statistics for model visualization.

Finally, to ensure that model performance does not degrade over time, Michelangelo has facilities for periodically storing a sample of predictions, comparing predictions to outcomes, and sending signals to operators when the margin exceeds a certain standard.

A variety of tools, both proprietary and open source, can be used to build the MLOps pipeline. In the Sira-Kvina case, the infrastructure layer was built in the cloud using Amazon Web Services Cloud Development Kit (AWS CDK). AWS's Simple Notification Service (SNS) was used to transmit verification and monitoring messages between layers. Uber built Michelangelo with open source tools such as the Cassandra distributed database system and Kafka brokers to stream verification and monitoring messages.

In this book, our focus will be on the prototyping phase—all the steps that go into properly defining the model and developing and selecting a model. You should be aware, though, that most of the actual work of implementing a machine learning solution lies in the automated deployment phase. Much of this work is not in the analytic domain; rather, it lies in the domains of databases and computer engineering, to assure that detailed nuts and bolts of an automated dataflow all work properly. Nonetheless, some familiarity with the requirements and components of automated pipelines will benefit the data scientist, as it will facilitate communication with the engineers who must ultimately deploy their work.

2.9 ETHICAL PRACTICE IN MACHINE LEARNING

Prior to the advent of Internet-connected devices, the biggest source of big data was public interaction on the Internet. Social media users, as well as shoppers and searchers on the internet, have made an implicit deal with the big companies that provide these services: users can take advantage of powerful search, shopping, and social interaction tools for free, and, in return, the companies get access to user data. Since the first edition of this book was published in 2007, ethical issues in machine learning and data science have received increasing attention, and new rules and laws have emerged. As a business analytics professional or data scientist, you must be aware of the rules and follow them, but you must also think about the implications and use of your work once it goes beyond the prototyping phase. It is now common for businesses, governments, and other organizations to require the explicit incorporation of ethical principles and audits into machine learning and AI applications. Chapter 22, Responsible Data Science, covers this topic in more detail.

MACHINE LEARNING SOFTWARE TOOLS:
THE STATE OF THE MARKET

by Herb Edelstein

Over time, three things are steadily increasing: the amount of data available for analysis, the power of the computing environment, and the number of organizations taking advantage of the first two changes for a widening variety of analytical and predictive goals. Software products for machine learning must deliver more comprehensive coverage than ever before. The term "data science" has become ubiquitous and covers the spectrum of tasks required for business analytics, starting with data engineering (including data gathering, building databases, and making the data suitable for analytics) and machine learning. Machine learning starts with describing and understanding the data, often utilizing advanced visualization techniques followed by sophisticated model building. After the models are constructed, they must be efficiently deployed, so an organization can meet its goals. At the same time, the amount of data collected today presents a great opportunity to tease out subtle relationships that allow precise predictions while unfortunately making it easy to find spurious relationships or statistically significant results that have no practical value. The range of users that must be supported has also increased. Software must support people with diverse backgrounds, ranging from extensive education in machine learning, statistics, and programming to professionals performing such tasks as sales and marketing, risk analysis, fraud detection, reliability prediction, and engineering and scientific analysis. One of the biggest contributors to the hardware environment for machine learning is the spread of high-powered graphic processing units (GPUs). While originally intended for accelerating 3D graphics, meeting the computational requirements for fast 3D graphics also significantly accelerates machine learning. The algorithms used by the major cloud vendors all take advantage of GPUs. However, not all GPUs have the same interface and therefore not all stand-alone software will necessarily take advantage of the GPUs on your computer. Machine learning has also improved model building. As you read this book, you will see that the various algorithms have a plethora of tuning options to help you build the best model. While many experienced model builders can do a good job of manual tuning, it is impossible to try all the combinations of parameters that control the learning process (called hyperparameters) by hand, so an increasing number of products offer the ability to automatically tune the hyperparameters. The more hyperparameters, the larger the number of combinations to be searched. Autotuning can be particularly useful in building the neural networks used for deep learning.

R and Python

One of the most common open source statistical analysis and machine learning software languages is R. It is the successor to a Bell Labs program called S, which was commercialized as S+. Widely used in the academic community, R has become one of the most popular machine learning tools. New algorithms are frequently available first in R. It includes an enormous collection of machine learning algorithms contained in what are known as "packages," along with an abundance of statistical algorithms, data management tools, and visualization tools. Over 10,000 packages are in the CRAN (Comprehensive R Archive Network) library, and there are numerous packages outside of CRAN. This large number provides a great deal of choice. There are multiple packages that will perform essentially the same task, allowing the user to choose the one they think is most appropriate. However, there is a downside to all these options in that there is no uniformity in the R community. For example, in addition to the base R graphing tools, there are the packages Lattice, ggplot2, Plotly, and others. Because it is essentially a special-purpose programming language, R has enormous flexibility but a steeper learning curve than many of the Graphical User Interface (GUI)-based tools. The most common tool used with R is RStudio, an interactive development environment that facilitates the use of R. RStudio has also created a collection of packages called the "tidyverse" which are designed to enhance the ability of R to manipulate and graph data. These have become widely used in the R community. In particular, R has excelled in creating publication quality visualizations using the ggplot2 package (part of the tidyverse) which is based on Leland Wilkinson's groundbreaking book *The Grammar of Graphics*. Some GUIs for R try to improve its usability. R Commander is the oldest of these and like R is extensible with add-on packages. Its creator views it as a gateway to writing R code for more complex analyses. BlueSky is a more recent interface that not only is more comprehensive than R Commander but also allows the user to create their own dialogs to add R functionality.

Python is a widely used general programming language (developed in the 1980s by Guido van Rossum and named after the British comedy group Monty Python) that has overtaken R as the most popular machine learning package. This is due in part to its speed advantage over R, its data-wrangling capabilities, and its better functionality as a programming language. Furthermore, there is an interface to R that allows you to access R functionality should you need to. Pandas is an open source Python library that provides extensive data-wrangling capabilities. Scikit-Learn is another open source Python library that provides a very comprehensive suite of tools for machine learning that is widely used in the Python community. Python is more often used for deep neural networks than R. While R is still dominating in academia, Python appears to be dominating in commercial applications.

Stand-Alone Machine Learning Software

Many stand-alone software packages have appeared that are intended to simplify the process of creating machine learning models. The number of machine learning packages has grown considerably in response to the increasing demand. IBM offers two machine learning platforms: Watson and SPSS Modeler. Watson is cloud based and offers the same ability to utilize GPUs as the other major cloud providers. SPSS Modeler is aimed at local implementation. However, Watson Studio includes Modeler which can run under Studio. In addition to running on IBM's cloud servers, Watson is also available to run on local computers. SAS is the largest company specializing in statistical software. Recognizing the growing importance of machine learning, SAS added Enterprise Miner, a workflow drag-and-drop software, in 1999 to address this need. More recently, SAS created Viya Machine Learning. SAS Enterprise Miner has multiple client interfaces, whereas Viya's interface is a unified HTML5 interface. While both Enterprise Miner and Viya can operate in the cloud, Viya has a wider range of interfaces to the major cloud providers. It is aimed more directly at the data science and machine learning communities. SAS's JMP Pro has a comprehensive set of machine learning tools. It is widely used in the science and engineering world, but also competes in commercial and government settings. It has a unique GUI that is centered on what you are trying to accomplish. For example, to analyze data, you go to the Analyze menu, choose Predictive Modeling, and then select a modeling method (which JMP calls a platform). JMP has its own scripting language, JSL, for tasks that are more complicated than can be accomplished through the GUI, but it also interfaces with R and Python.

Analytic Solver Data Mining (ASDM) is an add-in for Microsoft Excel that provides access to a suite of machine learning tools as well as data engineering capabilities without the need for programming. It is widely used in MBA programs because of its accessibility to students, but it is also used in industry, especially with its cloud interface to Microsoft's Azure. The original version (XLMiner) was developed by one of the authors of this book (Patel). It provides not only traditional machine learning tools such as tree-based learning and neural nets, but also a variety of ensemble methods which have become central to accurate prediction. Additionally, ASDM provides text mining capabilities.

Drag-and-Drop Workflow Interfaces

Since machine learning solutions are typically deployed in workflow pipelines (data ingestion > model fitting > model assessment > data scoring), some software use a drag-and-drop icon and arrows interface, where icons represent different stages of the process, and arrows connect different stages. While there are a variety of such software, we'll mention a few: IBM Modeler is based on the SPSS Clementine program, which had one of the first workflow-based interfaces. This style of interface links the data engineering, exploration, machine learning, model evaluation, and deployment steps together. Modeler has a wide range of statistical and machine learning algorithms, and provides interfaces to Watson, Python, and R for additional functionality. Orange is a visual interface for Python and Scikit-Learn using wrappers designed to make analysis easier. Developed at the University of Ljubljana in Slovenia, Orange is open source software that uses a workflow interface to provide a greatly improved way to use Python for analysis.

RapidMiner Studio was originally developed in Germany in 2001 (the original name was YALE) and has grown into a widely used platform for machine learning. It has a workflow drag-and-drop interface that supports data import, data cleansing, graphics, a large variety of machine learning tools, and model evaluation. One of the most difficult problems in building good models is feature selection. RapidMiner provides a number of tools including genetic algorithms for feature selection. Its Turbo Prep and Auto Model interfaces offer support for data preparation tasks and auto-tuning hyperparameters for standard machine learning algorithms, respectively. RapidMiner also has integration with R and Python to extend its capabilities.

Cloud Computing

Cloud computing vendors are actively promoting their services for machine learning. These products are oriented more toward application developers than machine learning prototypers and business analysts. A big part of the attraction of machine learning in the cloud is the ability to store and manage enormous amounts of data without requiring the expense and complexity of building an in-house capability. This can also enable a more rapid implementation of large distributed multi-user applications. Many of the non-cloud-based machine learning vendors provide interfaces to cloud storage to enable their tools to work with mammoth amounts of data. For example, RapidMiner offers a product Rapid-Miner AI Hub (formerly RapidMiner Server) that leverages the standard cloud computing platforms (Amazon AWS, Google Cloud, MS Azure) for automation and deployment of machine learning models. Amazon has several machine learning services. SageMaker is a machine learning platform that provides developers with functionality including acquiring and wrangling data, building models based on its large collection of algorithms, and deploying the resulting models. Models can be used with data stored in Amazon Web Services (AWS or exported for use in local environments. There is also an automatic machine learning process that will choose the appropriate algorithm and create the model. AWS also has what it calls Deep Learning AMI's (Amazon Machine Images) that are preconfigured virtual machines with deep learning frameworks such as TensorFlow.

Google is very active in cloud analytics with its Vertex AI. The user can either custom train models or use Vertex AI's AutoML which will automatically build models based on your selected targets. Unfortunately, this is not a transparent process, and there is a limitation in the size of the data—100 GB or 100 million rows of tabular data. Models such as TensorFlow deep learning models can be exported for use in local environments. Microsoft is an active player in cloud analytics with its Azure Machine Learning. Azure ML also supports a workflow interface making it more accessible to the nonprogrammer data scientist. Along with Amazon and Google, Azure Machine Learning also supports an automated machine learning mode. ASDM's cloud version is based on Microsoft Azure. Machine learning plays a central role in enabling many organizations to optimize everything from manufacturing and production to marketing and sales. New storage options and analytical tools promise even greater capabilities. The key is to select technology that's appropriate for an organization's unique goals and constraints. As always, human judgment is the most important component of a machine learning solution. The focus of *Machine Learning for Business Analytics* is on a comprehensive understanding of the different techniques and algorithms used in machine learning, and less on the data management requirements of real-time deployment of machine learning models.

***

Herb Edelstein is president of Two Crows Consulting (www.twocrows.com), a leading data mining consulting firm near Washington, DC. He is an internationally recognized expert in data mining and data warehousing, a widely published author on these topics, and a popular speaker.
© 2022 Herb Edelstein.

PROBLEMS

2.1 Assuming that machine learning techniques are to be used in the following cases, identify whether the task required is supervised or unsupervised learning.

   a. Deciding whether to issue a loan to an applicant based on demographic and financial data (with reference to a database of similar data on prior customers).

   b. In an online bookstore, making recommendations to customers concerning additional items to buy based on the buying patterns in prior transactions.

   c. Identifying a network data packet as dangerous (virus, hacker attack) based on comparison to other packets whose threat status is known.

   d. Identifying segments of similar customers.

   e. Predicting whether a company will go bankrupt based on comparing its financial data to those of similar bankrupt and nonbankrupt firms.

   f. Estimating the repair time required for an aircraft based on a trouble ticket.

   g. Automated sorting of mail by zip code scanning.

   h. Printing of custom discount coupons at the conclusion of a grocery store checkout based on what you just bought and what others have bought previously.

2.2 Describe the difference in roles assumed by the validation partition and the holdout partition.

2.3 Consider the sample from a database of credit applicants in Table 2.5. Comment on the likelihood that it was sampled randomly and whether it is likely to be a useful sample.

TABLE 2.5   SAMPLE FROM A DATABASE OF CREDIT APPLICATIONS

OBS	CHECK ACCT	DURATION	HISTORY	NEW CAR	USED CAR	FURNITURE	RADIO TV	EDUC	RETRAIN	AMOUNT	SAVE ACCT	RESPONSE
1	0	6	4	0	0	0	1	0	0	1169	4	1
8	1	36	2	0	1	0	0	0	0	6948	0	1
16	0	24	2	0	0	0	1	0	0	1282	1	0
24	1	12	4	0	1	0	0	0	0	1804	1	1
32	0	24	2	0	0	1	0	0	0	4020	0	1
40	1	9	2	0	0	0	1	0	0	458	0	1
48	0	6	2	0	1	0	0	0	0	1352	2	1
56	3	6	1	1	0	0	0	0	0	783	4	1
64	1	48	0	0	0	0	0	0	1	14,421	0	0
72	3	7	4	0	0	0	1	0	0	730	4	1
80	1	30	2	0	0	1	0	0	0	3832	0	1
88	1	36	2	0	0	0	0	1	0	12,612	1	0
96	1	54	0	0	0	0	0	0	1	15,945	0	0
104	1	9	4	0	0	1	0	0	0	1919	0	1
112	2	15	2	0	0	0	0	1	0	392	0	1

2.4 Consider the sample from a bank database shown in Table 2.6; it was selected randomly from a larger database to be the training set. *Personal Loan* indicates whether a solicitation for a personal loan was accepted and is the target attribute. A campaign is planned for a similar solicitation in the future, and the bank is looking for a model that will identify likely responders. Examine the data carefully and indicate what your next step would be.

TABLE 2.6   SAMPLE FROM A BANK DATABASE

OBS	AGE	EXPERIENCE	INCOME	ZIP CODE	FAMILY	CC AVG	EDUC	MORTGAGE	PERSONAL LOAN	SECURITIES ACCT
1	25	1	49	91107	4	1.6	1	0	0	1
4	35	9	100	94112	1	2.7	2	0	0	0
5	35	8	45	91330	4	1	2	0	0	0
9	35	10	81	90089	3	0.6	2	104	0	0
10	34	9	180	93023	1	8.9	3	0	1	0
12	29	5	45	90277	3	0.1	2	0	0	0
17	38	14	130	95010	4	4.7	3	134	1	0
18	42	18	81	94305	4	2.4	1	0	0	0
21	56	31	25	94015	4	0.9	2	111	0	0
26	43	19	29	94305	3	0.5	1	97	0	0
29	56	30	48	94539	1	2.2	3	0	0	0
30	38	13	119	94104	1	3.3	2	0	1	0
35	31	5	50	94035	4	1.8	3	0	0	0
36	48	24	81	92647	3	0.7	1	0	0	0
37	59	35	121	94720	1	2.9	1	0	0	0
38	51	25	71	95814	1	1.4	3	198	0	0
39	42	18	141	94114	3	5	3	0	1	1
41	57	32	84	92672	3	1.6	3	0	0	1

2.5   Using the concept of overfitting, explain why when a model is fit to training data, zero error with those data is not necessarily good.

2.6   In fitting a model to classify prospects as purchasers or nonpurchasers, a certain company drew the training data from internal data that include demographic and purchase information. Future data to be classified will be lists purchased from other sources, with demographic (but not purchase) data included. It was found that "refund issued" was a useful predictor in the training data. Why is this not an appropriate attribute to include in the model?

2.7   A dataset has 1000 records and 50 attributes with 5% of the values missing, spread randomly throughout the records and attributes. An analyst decides to remove records with missing values. About how many records would you expect to be removed?

2.8   Normalize the data in Table 2.7, showing calculations.

TABLE 2.7

Age	Income ($)
25	49,000
56	156,000
65	99,000
32	192,000
41	39,000
49	57,000

2.9   The distance between two records can be measured in several ways. Consider Euclidean distance, measured as the square root of the sum of the squared differences. For the first two records in Table 2.7, it is

$$\sqrt{(25-56)^2 + (49,000-156,000)^2}.$$

Can normalizing the data change which two records are farthest from each other in terms of Euclidean distance?

2.10 Two models are applied to a dataset that has been partitioned. Model A is considerably more accurate than model B on the training data, but slightly less accurate than model B on the validation data. Which model are you more likely to consider for final deployment?

2.11 The dataset *ToyotaCorolla.csv* contains data on used cars on sale during the late summer of 2004 in the Netherlands. It has 1436 records containing details on 38 attributes, including *Price*, *Age*, *Kilometers*, *HP*, and other specifications. We plan to analyze the data using various machine learning techniques described in future chapters.

a. The dataset has two categorical attributes, *Fuel_Type* and *Color*. Describe how you would convert these to binary attributes. Confirm this using RapidMiner's operators to transform categorical data into dummies. What would you do with the attribute *Model*?

b. Prepare the dataset (as factored into dummies) for machine learning techniques of supervised learning by creating partitions using RapidMiner's *Split Data* operator. Select attributes, and use default values for the random seed and partitioning percentages for training (50%), validation (30%), and holdout (20%) sets. Describe the roles that these partitions will play in modeling.

2.12 [For class or group discussion:] Sort the West Roxbury data by YR BUILT and report any anomalies. Discuss the implications for the analysis done in this chapter, and possible steps to take.

PART II

Data Exploration and Dimension Reduction

CHAPTER 3

Data Visualization

In this chapter, we describe a set of plots that can be used to explore the multi-dimensional nature of a dataset. We present basic plots (bar charts, line charts, and scatter plots), distribution plots (boxplots and histograms), and different enhancements that expand the capabilities of these plots to visualize more information. We focus on how the different visualizations and operations can support machine learning tasks, from supervised tasks (prediction, classification, and time series forecasting) to unsupervised tasks, and provide a few guidelines on specific visualizations to use with each machine learning task. We also describe the advantages of interactive visualization over static plots. This chapter concludes with a presentation of specialized plots suitable for data with special structure (hierarchical, network, and geographical).

3.1 INTRODUCTION[1]

The popular saying "a picture is worth a thousand words" refers to the ability to condense diffused verbal information into a compact and quickly understood graphical image. In the case of numbers, data visualization and numerical summarization provide us with both a powerful tool to explore data and an effective way to present results (Few, 2012).

Where do visualization techniques fit into the machine learning process, as described so far? They are primarily used in the preprocessing portion of the machine learning process. Visualization supports data cleaning by finding incorrect values (e.g., patients whose age is 999 or −1), missing values, duplicate rows, columns with all the same value, and the like. Visualization techniques are

---

[1] This and subsequent sections in this chapter copyright ©2019 Datastats, LLC and Galit Shmueli. Used by permission.

Machine Learning for Business Analytics: Concepts, Techniques and Applications in RapidMiner, First Edition.
Galit Shmueli, Peter C. Bruce, Amit V. Deokar, and Nitin R. Patel
© 2023 John Wiley & Sons, Inc. Published 2023 by John Wiley & Sons, Inc.

also useful for attribute derivation and selection: they can help determine which attributes to include in the analysis and which might be redundant. They can also help with determining appropriate bin sizes, should binning of numerical attributes be needed, [e.g., a numerical target attribute might need to be converted to a binary (binominal type) attribute if a yes/no decision is required]. They can also play a role in combining categories as part of the data reduction process. Finally, if the data have yet to be collected and collection is expensive (as with the Pandora project at its outset; see Chapter 7), visualization methods can help determine, using a sample, which attributes and metrics are useful.

In this chapter, we focus on the use of graphical presentations for the purpose of *data exploration*, particularly with relation to predictive analytics. Although our focus is not on visualization for the purpose of data reporting, this chapter offers ideas as to the effectiveness of various graphical displays for the purpose of data presentation. These offer a wealth of useful presentations beyond tabular summaries and basic bar charts, which are currently the most popular form of data presentation in the business environment. For an excellent discussion of using charts to report business data, see Few (2012). In terms of reporting machine learning results graphically, we describe common graphical displays elsewhere in the book, some of which are technique-specific [e.g., dendrograms for hierarchical clustering (Chapter 16), network charts for social network analysis (Chapter 20), and tree charts for classification and regression trees (Chapter 9)] while others are more general [e.g., receiver operating characteristic (ROC) curves and lift charts for classification (Chapter 5) and profile plots and heatmaps for clustering (Chapter 16)].

Note: The term "graph" has two meanings in statistics. It can refer, particularly in popular usage, to any of a number of figures to represent data (e.g., line chart, bar plot, histogram, etc.). In a more technical use, it refers to the data structure and visualization in networks (see Chapter 20). Using the terms "chart" or "plot" for the visualizations we explore in this chapter avoids this confusion.

Data exploration is a mandatory initial step whether or not more formal analysis follows. Graphical exploration can support free-form exploration for the purpose of understanding the data structure, cleaning the data (e.g., identifying unexpected gaps or "illegal" values), identifying outliers, discovering initial patterns (e.g., correlations among attributes and surprising clusters), and generating interesting questions. Graphical exploration can also be more focused, geared toward specific questions of interest. In the machine learning context, a combination is needed: free-form exploration performed with the purpose of supporting a specific goal.

Graphical exploration can range from generating very basic plots to using operations such as filtering and zooming interactively to explore a set of interconnected visualizations that include advanced features such as color and multiple panels. This chapter is not meant to be an exhaustive guidebook on visualization techniques, but instead discusses main principles and features that support data exploration in a machine learning context. We start by describing varying levels of sophistication in terms of visualization and show the advantages of different features and operations. Our discussion is from the perspective of how visualization supports the subsequent machine learning goal. In particular, we distinguish between supervised and unsupervised learning; within supervised learning, we also further distinguish between classification (categorical target attribute) and prediction (numerical target attribute).

3.2 DATA EXAMPLES

To illustrate data visualization, we use two datasets used in additional chapters in the book.

Example 1: Boston Housing Data

The Boston Housing data contain information on census tracts in Boston[2] for which several measurements are taken (e.g., crime rate, pupil/teacher ratio). It has 14 attributes. A description of each attribute is given in Table 3.1, and a sample of the first nine records is shown in Figure 3.1. The *Filter Example Range*[3] operator is used to select the first nine records by setting *first example* = 1 and *last example* = 9. In addition to the original 13 attributes, the dataset contains the attribute CAT.MEDV, which was created by categorizing median value (MEDV) into two categories: high and low.

We consider three possible tasks:

1. A supervised predictive task, where the target attribute of interest is the median value of a home in the tract (MEDV).

2. A supervised classification task, where the target attribute of interest (class label) is the binary attribute CAT.MEDV that indicates whether the home value is above or below $30,000.

3. An unsupervised task, where the goal is to cluster census tracts.

(MEDV and CAT.MEDV are not used together in any of the three cases).

---

[2]The Boston Housing dataset was originally published by Harrison and Rubinfeld in "Hedonic prices and the demand for clean air," *Journal of Environmental Economics & Management*, vol. 5, pp. 81–102, 1978. A census tract includes 1200–8000 homes.

[3]RapidMiner also has a related operator called *Filter Examples*, located under *Blending* > *Examples* > *Filter* in the Operators panel, which allows selecting a subset of records by specifying different attribute-based filtering conditions. In all these cases, *examples* means records.

TABLE 3.1   DESCRIPTION OF ATTRIBUTES IN BOSTON HOUSING DATASET

CRIM	Crime rate
ZN	Percentage of residential land zoned for lots over 25,000 ft^2
INDUS	Percentage of land occupied by nonretail business
CHAS	Does tract bound Charles River (= 1 if tract bounds river, = 0 otherwise)
NOX	Nitric oxide concentration (parts per 10 million)
RM	Average number of rooms per dwelling
AGE	Percentage of owner-occupied units built prior to 1940
DIS	Weighted distances to five Boston employment centers
RAD	Index of accessibility to radial highways
TAX	Full-value property tax rate per $10,000
PTRATIO	Pupil-to-teacher ratio by town
LSTAT	Percentage of lower status of the population
MEDV	Median value of owner-occupied homes in $1000s
CAT.MEDV	Is median value of owner-occupied homes in tract above $30,000 (CAT.MEDV = 1) or not (CAT.MEDV = 0)

Row No.	CRIM	ZN	INDUS	CHAS	NOX	RM	AGE	DIS	RAD	TAX	PTRATIO	LSTAT	MEDV	CAT. MEDV
1	0.006	18	2.310	0	0.538	6.575	65.200	4.090	1	296	15.300	4.980	24	0
2	0.027	0	7.070	0	0.469	6.421	78.900	4.967	2	242	17.800	9.140	21.600	0
3	0.027	0	7.070	0	0.469	7.185	61.100	4.967	2	242	17.800	4.030	34.700	1
4	0.032	0	2.180	0	0.458	6.998	45.800	6.062	3	222	18.700	2.940	33.400	1
5	0.069	0	2.180	0	0.458	7.147	54.200	6.062	3	222	18.700	5.330	36.200	1
6	0.030	0	2.180	0	0.458	6.430	58.700	6.062	3	222	18.700	5.210	28.700	0
7	0.088	12.500	7.870	0	0.524	6.012	66.600	5.561	5	311	15.200	12.430	22.900	0
8	0.145	12.500	7.870	0	0.524	6.172	96.100	5.950	5	311	15.200	19.150	27.100	0
9	0.211	12.500	7.870	0	0.524	5.631	100	6.082	5	311	15.200	29.930	16.500	0

FIGURE 3.1   FIRST NINE RECORDS IN THE BOSTON HOUSING DATA

Example 2: Ridership on Amtrak Trains

Amtrak, a US railway company, routinely collects data on ridership. Here, we focus on forecasting future ridership using the series of monthly ridership between January 1991 and March 2004. The data and their source are described in Chapter 17. Hence, our task here is (numerical) time series forecasting.

3.3 BASIC CHARTS: BAR CHARTS, LINE CHARTS, AND SCATTER PLOTS

The three most effective basic charts are bar charts, line charts, and scatter plots. These charts are easy to create in RapidMiner and are the most commonly used in the current business world, in both data exploration and presentation (unfortunately, pie charts are also popular, although they are usually ineffective visualizations). Basic charts support data exploration by displaying one or two columns of data (attributes) at a time. This is useful in the early stages of getting familiar with the data structure, the amount and types of attributes, the volume and type of missing values, etc.

The nature of the machine learning task and domain knowledge about the data will affect the use of basic charts in terms of the amount of time and effort allocated to different attributes. In supervised learning, there will be more focus on the target attribute. In scatter plots, the target attribute is typically associated with the y-axis. In unsupervised learning (for the purpose of data reduction or clustering), basic charts that convey relationships (such as scatter plots) are preferred.

In RapidMiner, charts are generally constructed through the Visualizations tab in the Results view. Alternatively, RapidMiner's *Turbo Prep* view is an interface that can be invoked from the Results view for any data. While the Turbo Prep view is particularly geared toward conducting data preparation tasks such as data transformation, generating attributes, etc., it can also be used to invoke the Charts panel (same as the Visualizations tab in the Results view). Further, the Turbo Prep view also provides a quick way to build an aggregation like a pivot table (equivalent to using the *Pivot* operator in a RapidMiner process), then visualizing it as a table or a bar chart.[4]

Figure 3.2 (top left) displays a line chart for the time series of monthly railway passengers on Amtrak. Line charts are used primarily for showing time series. The choice of time frame to plot, as well as the temporal scale, should depend on the horizon of the forecasting task and on the nature of the data.

Bar charts are useful for comparing a single statistic (e.g., average, count, percentage) across groups. The height of the bar (or length in a horizontal display) represents the value of the statistic, and different bars correspond to different groups. Two examples using Turbo Prep view are shown in the bottom panels in Figure 3.2. The left panel shows a bar chart for a numerical attribute (MEDV), and the right panel shows a bar chart for a categorical attribute (CAT.MEDV). In each, separate bars are used to denote tracts in Boston that are near the Charles River vs. those that are not (thereby comparing the two categories of CHAS). The chart with the numerical target MEDV (bottom left) uses the average MEDV on the y-axis. This supports the predictive task: the numerical target is on the y-axis, and the x-axis is used for a potential categorical predictor.[5] (Note that the x-axis on a bar chart must be used only for categorical attributes, because

---

[4]In constructing a pivot table, an appropriate aggregation function (e.g., *sum*, *average*) should be applied to the aggregation attribute.

[5]We refer here to a bar chart with vertical bars. The same principles apply if using a bar chart with horizontal lines, except that the x-axis is now associated with the numerical attribute and the y-axis with the categorical attribute.

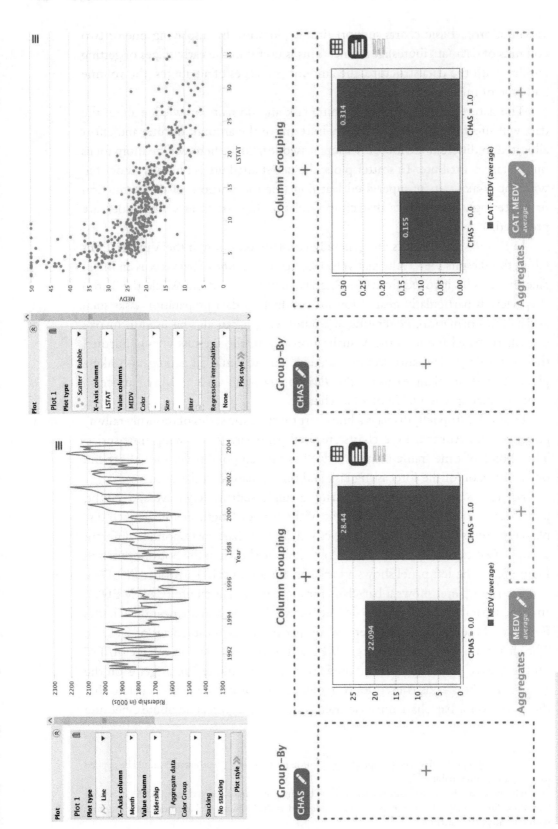

FIGURE 3.2

BASIC CHARTS: (TOP LEFT) LINE CHART, (TOP RIGHT) SCATTER PLOT, (BOTTOM LEFT) BAR CHART FOR NUMERICAL ATTRIBUTE, AND (BOTTOM RIGHT) BAR CHART FOR CATEGORICAL ATTRIBUTE the order of bars in a bar chart should be interchangeable.) For the classification task (bottom right), the y-axis indicates the percent of tracts with MEDV above $30K, and the x-axis is a binary attribute[6] indicating proximity to the Charles river. This plot shows us that the tracts bordering the Charles are much more likely to have median values above $30K.

The top-right panel in Figure 3.2 displays a scatter plot of MEDV vs. LSTAT. This is an important plot in the prediction task. Note that the target MEDV is again on the y-axis (and LSTAT on the x-axis is a potential predictor). Because both attributes in a basic scatter plot must be numerical, it cannot be used to display the relation between CAT.MEDV and potential predictors for the classification task (but we can enhance it to do so—see Section 3.4). For unsupervised learning, this particular scatter plot helps study the association between two numerical attributes in terms of information overlap, as well as identifying clusters of observations.

All three basic charts highlight global information such as the overall level of ridership or MEDV, as well as changes over time (line chart), differences between subgroups (bar chart), and relationships between numerical attributes (scatter plot).

Distribution Plots: Boxplots and Histograms

Before moving on to more sophisticated visualizations that enable multidimensional investigation, we note two important charts that are usually not considered "basic charts" but are very useful in statistical and machine learning contexts. The *boxplot* and the *histogram* are two charts that display the entire distribution of a numerical attribute. Although averages are very popular and useful summary statistics, there is usually much to be gained by looking at additional statistics such as the median and standard deviation of an attribute and even more so by examining the entire distribution. Whereas bar charts can only use a single aggregation, boxplots and histograms display the entire distribution of a numerical attribute. Boxplots are also effective for comparing subgroups by generating side-by-side boxplots or for looking at distributions over time by creating a series of boxplots.

Distribution plots are useful in supervised learning for determining potential machine learning methods and attribute transformations. For example, skewed numerical attributes might warrant transformation (e.g., moving to a logarithmic scale) if used in methods that assume normality (e.g., linear regression, discriminant analysis).

---

[6]Even though CAT.MEDV is a binary attribute, for this data visualization, we consider it as numerical type and do not convert it to binominal type since the aggregation function *average* cannot be applied to a binominal attribute in a pivot table.

A histogram represents the frequencies of all x values with a series of vertical connected bars. For example, in Figure 3.3 (top), there are over 150 tracts where the MEDV is between $20K and $25K.

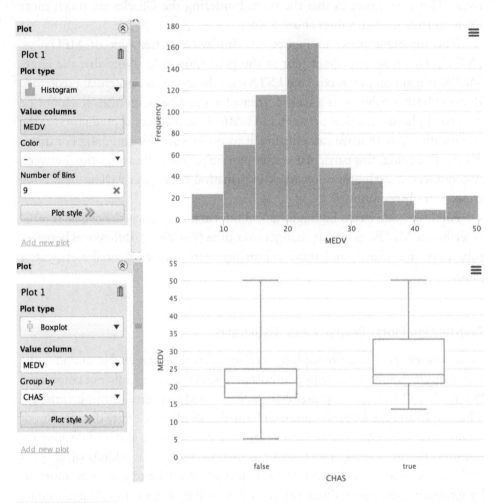

FIGURE 3.3   DISTRIBUTION CHARTS FOR NUMERICAL ATTRIBUTE MEDV. (TOP) HISTOGRAM AND (BOTTOM) BOXPLOT

A boxplot represents the attribute being plotted on the y-axis (although the plot can potentially be turned in a 90° angle, so that the boxes are parallel to the x-axis). Figure 3.3 (bottom) shows two boxplots (called a side-by-side boxplot). The box encloses 50% of the data—for example, in the right-hand box, half of the tracts have MEDV between $20,000 and $33,000. The horizontal line inside the box represents the median (50th percentile). The top and bottom of the box represent the 75th and 25th percentiles, respectively. Lines extending above and below the box cover the rest of the data range; outliers may be depicted as points or circles. Sometimes, the average is marked by a + (or similar) sign. Comparing the average and the median helps in assessing how skewed the data are. Boxplots are often arranged in a series with a different plot for each of the various values of a second attribute,[7] shown on the x-axis.

Because histograms and boxplots are geared toward numerical attributes, their basic form is useful for *prediction* tasks. Boxplots can also support *unsupervised learning* by displaying relationships between a numerical attribute (y-axis) and a categorical attribute (x-axis). For example, the histogram of MEDV in the top panel in Figure 3.3 reveals a skewed distribution. Transforming the target attribute to log(MEDV) might improve results of a linear regression predictor. Compare the side-by-side boxplot in Figure 3.3 to the bottom-left bar chart in Figure 3.2 that only displays the average values. We see that not only is the average MEDV for river-bounding tracts (CHAS=1) higher than the non-river-bounding tracts (CHAS=0) but also the entire distribution is higher (median, quartiles, and min). We can also see that all river-bounding tracts have MEDV above $10K, unlike non-river-bounding tracts. This information is useful for identifying the potential importance of this predictor (CHAS) and for choosing machine learning methods that can capture the non-overlapping area between the two distributions (e.g., trees).

Boxplots and histograms applied to numerical attributes can also provide directions for deriving new attributes; for example, they can indicate how to bin a numerical attribute (e.g., binning a numerical target in order to use a naive Bayes classifier, or in the Boston Housing example, choosing the threshold to convert MEDV to CAT.MEDV).

Finally, side-by-side boxplots are useful in classification tasks for evaluating the potential of numerical predictors. This is done by using the x-axis for the categorical target attribute and the y-axis for a numerical predictor. An example is shown in Figure 3.4, where we can see the effects of four numerical predictors on CAT.MEDV (first transformed to binominal type). The pairs that are most separated (e.g., PTRATIO and INDUS) indicate potentially useful predictors.

The main weakness of basic charts and distribution plots, in their basic form (that is, using position in relation to the axes to encode values), is that they can only display two attributes and therefore cannot reveal high-dimensional information. Each of the basic charts has two dimensions, where each dimension is dedicated to a single attribute. In machine learning, the data are usually multivariate by nature, and the analytics are designed to capture and measure multivariate information. Visual exploration should therefore also incorporate this important aspect. In the next section, we describe how to extend basic charts (and distribution plots) to multidimensional data visualization by adding

---

[7]The "group by" attribute has to be of binominal or polynominal type. Here, CHAS is first transformed to binominal type using the *Numerical to Binominal* operator.

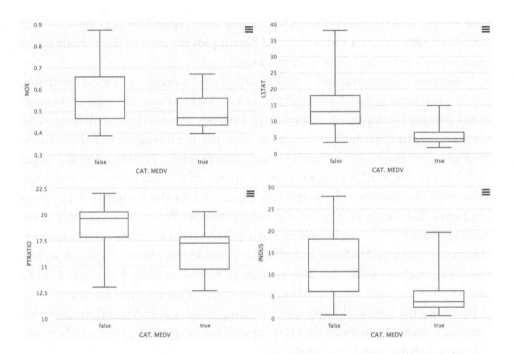

FIGURE 3.4   SIDE-BY-SIDE BOXPLOTS FOR EXPLORING THE CAT.MEDV TARGET ATTRIBUTE BY
DIFFERENT NUMERICAL PREDICTORS. IN A SIDE-BY-SIDE BOXPLOT, ONE AXIS IS
USED FOR A CATEGORICAL ATTRIBUTE, AND THE OTHER FOR A NUMERICAL
ATTRIBUTE. PLOTTING A CATEGORICAL TARGET AND A NUMERICAL PREDICTOR
COMPARES THE PREDICTOR'S DISTRIBUTION ACROSS THE TARGET CATEGORIES.
PLOTTING A NUMERICAL TARGET AND A CATEGORICAL PREDICTOR DISPLAYS THE
DISTRIBUTION OF THE TARGET ATTRIBUTE ACROSS DIFFERENT LEVELS OF THE
PREDICTOR

features, employing manipulations, and incorporating interactivity. We then
present several specialized charts geared toward displaying special data structures
(Section 3.5).

Heatmaps: Visualizing Correlations and Missing Values

A *heatmap* is a graphical display of numerical data where color is used to denote
values. In a machine learning context, heatmaps are especially useful for two
purposes: for visualizing correlation tables and for visualizing missing values in
the data. In both cases, the information is conveyed in a two-dimensional table.
A correlation table for p attributes has p rows and p columns. A data table
contains p columns (attributes) and n rows (observations). If the number of
rows is huge, then a subset can be used. In both cases, it is much easier and
faster to scan the color-coding rather than the values. Note that heatmaps are
useful when examining a large number of values, but they are not a replacement
for more precise graphical displays, such as bar charts, because color differences
cannot be perceived accurately.

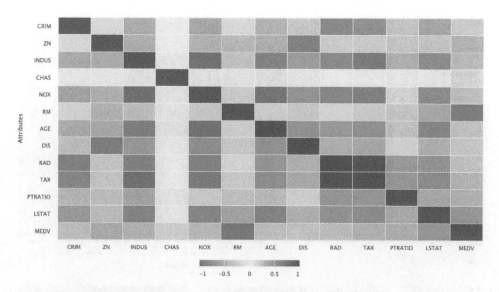

FIGURE 3.5   HEATMAP OF A CORRELATION TABLE. DARKER VALUES DENOTE STRONGER CORRELATION. RED/BLUE REPRESENTS POSITIVE/NEGATIVE VALUES, RESPECTIVELY

An example of a correlation table heatmap is shown in Figure 3.5, displaying all the pairwise correlations between 13 attributes (MEDV and 12 predictors). Darker shades correspond to stronger (positive or negative) correlation, making it easy to quickly spot the high and low correlations. Adding color—here red and blue—can be used to distinguish positive and negative values. This heatmap was produced in RapidMiner using the *Correlation Matrix* operator.

In a missing value heatmap, rows correspond to records and columns to attributes. Figure 3.6 (top) shows an example of a missing value heatmap for a dataset (*NYPD_Motor_Vehicle_Collisions_1000.csv*) on motor vehicle collisions.[8] Note that RapidMiner generates a heatmap visualization with only numerical attributes. In the missing value heatmap in Figure 3.6 (top), missing value cells are denoted with white color while the rest are shown in blue.[9] The missing data heatmap helps visualize the level and amount of "missingness" in the dataset. Some patterns of "missingness" easily emerge: attributes that are missing for nearly all observations and clusters of rows that are missing many values. Attributes with little missingness are also visible. This information can then be used for determining how to handle the missingness (e.g., dropping some attributes, dropping some records, imputing, or via other techniques).

---

[8]The data were obtained from https://data.cityofnewyork.us/Public-Safety/NYPD-Motor-Vehicle-Collisions/h9gi-nx95

[9]The exception is *Unique Key*, which is shown in color based on its values, but is irrelevant for understanding missing values.

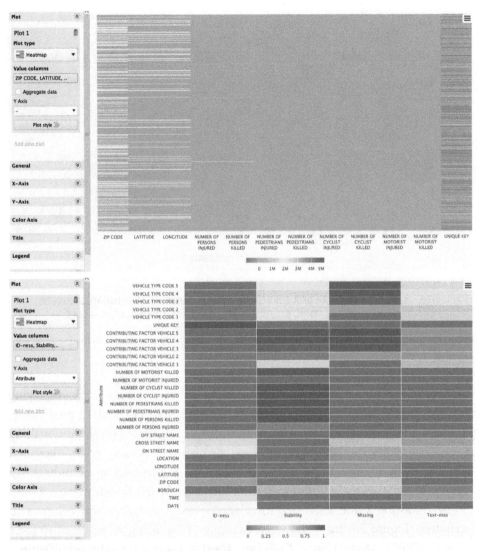

FIGURE 3.6   HEATMAPS FOR A DATASET ON MOTOR VEHICLE COLLISIONS. (TOP) MISSING VALUES HEATMAP. WHITE DENOTES MISSING VALUE. (BOTTOM) QUALITY MEASURES FOR THE ATTRIBUTE, WHERE RED/BLUE REPRESENTS HIGH/LOW VALUES, RESPECTIVELY

RapidMiner's *Quality Measures* operator computes useful quality character-istics for every attribute in the data on a 0–1 scale: *ID-ness*, *Stability*, *Missing*, and *Text-ness*, which can then be plotted as a heatmap for insights. Figure 3.6 (bottom) shows an example of such a heatmap for the collisions dataset. *ID-ness* of an attribute is the ratio of the number of different values for that attribute to the number of total records. It measures whether an attribute has nearly all different values. *Stability* is the ratio of the number of records with the most fre-quent non-missing value to the total number of records with non-missing values.

It measures how constant the values for a certain attribute are. *Missing* is the ratio of the number of missing values to the total number of records and is a measure of "missingness." *Text-ness* measures the degree to which an attribute contains free text information.

3.4 MULTIDIMENSIONAL VISUALIZATION

Basic charts can convey richer information with features such as color, size, and multiple panels, and by enabling operations such as rescaling, aggregation, and interactivity. These additions allow looking at more than one or two attributes at a time. The beauty of these additions is their effectiveness in displaying complex information in an easily understandable way. Effective features are based on understanding how visual perception works (see Few, 2021 for a discussion). The purpose is to make the information more understandable, not just to represent the data in higher dimensions (such as three-dimensional plots that are usually ineffective visualizations).

Adding Attributes: Color, Size, Shape, Multiple Panels, and Animation

In order to include more attributes in a plot, we must consider the type of attribute to include. To represent additional categorical information, the best way is to use hue, shape, or multiple panels. For additional numerical information, we can use color intensity or size. Temporal information can be added via animation.

Incorporating additional categorical and/or numerical attributes into the basic (and distribution) charts means that we can now use all of them for both prediction and classification tasks. For example, we mentioned earlier that a basic scatter plot cannot be used for studying the relationship between a categorical target and predictors (in the context of classification). However, a very effective chart for classification is a scatter plot of two numerical predictors color-coded by the categorical target attribute. An example is shown in Figure 3.7 (top), with color denoting CAT.MEDV.

In the context of prediction, color-coding supports the exploration of the conditional relationship between the numerical target attribute (on the y-axis) and a numerical predictor. Color-coded scatter plots then help assess the need for creating interaction terms (e.g., is the relationship between MEDV and LSTAT different for tracts near vs. away from the river?).

Color can also be used to include further categorical attributes into a bar chart, as long as the number of categories is small. When the number of categories is large, a better alternative is to use multiple panels. Creating multiple panels (also called "trellising") is done by splitting the observations according to a categorical attribute and creating a separate chart (of the same type) for

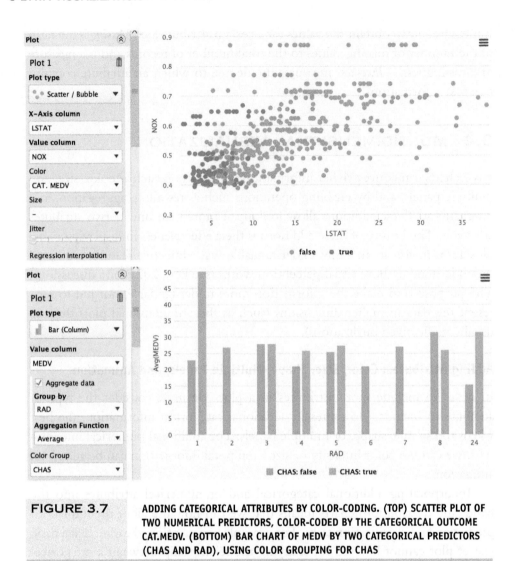

FIGURE 3.7   ADDING CATEGORICAL ATTRIBUTES BY COLOR-CODING. (TOP) SCATTER PLOT OF TWO NUMERICAL PREDICTORS, COLOR-CODED BY THE CATEGORICAL OUTCOME CAT.MEDV. (BOTTOM) BAR CHART OF MEDV BY TWO CATEGORICAL PREDICTORS (CHAS AND RAD), USING COLOR GROUPING FOR CHAS

each category. RapidMiner supports color grouping by an attribute but not creating multiple panels. An example is shown in Figure 3.7 (bottom), where a bar chart of average MEDV by RAD is broken down into CHAS categories with color grouping. We see that the average MEDV for different highway accessibility levels (RAD) behaves differently for tracts near the river (green bars) compared with tracts away from the river (blue bars). This is especially salient for RAD = 1. We also see that there are no near-river tracts in RAD levels 2, 6, and 7. Such information might lead us to create an interaction term between RAD and CHAS and to consider condensing some of the bins in RAD. All these explorations are useful for prediction and classification.

A special chart that uses scatter plots with multiple panels is the *scatter plot matrix*. In it, all pairwise scatter plots are shown in a single display. The panels in a matrix scatter plot are organized in a special way, such that each column and each row correspond to an attribute; thus, the intersections create all the possible pairwise scatter plots. The scatter plot matrix is useful in unsupervised learning for studying the associations between numerical attributes, detecting outliers, and identifying clusters. For supervised learning, it can be used for examining pairwise relationships (and their nature) between predictors to support attribute transformations and attribute selection (see Correlation Analysis in Chapter 4). For prediction, it can also be used to depict the relationship of the outcome with the numerical predictors.

An example of a scatter plot matrix is shown in Figure 3.8, with MEDV and three predictors. Below and above the diagonal are the scatter plots. Attribute names indicate the x-axis and y-axis attributes. For example, the plots in the bottom row all have MEDV on the y-axis (which allows studying the individual target–predictor relations). We can see different types of relationships from the different shapes (e.g., an exponential relationship between MEDV and LSTAT and a highly skewed relationship between CRIM and INDUS), which can indicate needed transformations. Along the diagonal, where just a single attribute is involved, the frequency distribution for that attribute is displayed. Note that the plots above and to the right of the diagonal are mirror images of those below and to the left, but with the two axes flipped.

Once hue is used, further categorical attributes can be added via shape and multiple panels. However, one must proceed cautiously in adding multiple

FIGURE 3.8   SCATTER PLOT MATRIX FOR MEDV AND THREE NUMERICAL PREDICTORS

attributes, as the display can become over-cluttered and then visual perception is lost.

Adding a numerical attribute via size is useful especially in scatter plots (thereby creating "bubble plots"), because in a scatter plot points represent individual observations. In plots that aggregate across observations (e.g., boxplots, histograms, bar charts), size and hue are not normally incorporated.

Finally, adding a temporal dimension to a chart to show how the information changes over time can be achieved via animation. A famous example is Rosling's animated scatter plots showing how world demographics changed over the years (www.gapminder.org). However, while animations of this type work for "statistical storytelling," they are not very effective for data exploration.

Manipulations: Rescaling, Aggregation and Hierarchies, Zooming, and Filtering

Most of the time spent in machine learning projects is spent in data preprocessing. Typically, considerable effort is expended getting all the data in a format that can actually be used in the machine learning software. Additional time is spent processing the data in ways that improve the performance of the machine learning procedures. This preprocessing step includes attribute transformation and derivation of new attributes to help models perform more effectively. Transformations include changing the numeric scale of an attribute, binning numerical attributes, and condensing categories in categorical attributes. The following manipulations support the preprocessing step and the choice of adequate machine learning methods. They do so by revealing patterns and their nature.

Rescaling   Changing the scale in a display can enhance the chart and illuminate relationships. For example, in Figure 3.9, we see the effect of changing both axes of the scatter plot (top) and the y-axis of a boxplot (bottom) to logarithmic (log) scale. In RapidMiner, this is done by selecting the *Logarithmic* option for each axis in the plot settings. Whereas the original charts (left) are hard to understand, the patterns become visible in log scale (right). In the scatter plots, the nature of the relationship between MEDV and CRIM is hard to determine in the original scale, because too many of the points are "crowded" near the y-axis. The rescaling removes this crowding and allows a better view of the linear relationship between the two log-scaled attributes (indicating a log–log relationship). In the boxplot, displaying the crowding toward the x-axis in the original units does not allow us to compare the two box sizes, their locations, lower outliers, and most of the distribution information. Rescaling removes the "crowding to the x-axis" effect, thereby allowing a comparison of the two boxplots.

Aggregation and Hierarchies   Another useful manipulation of scaling is changing the level of aggregation. For a temporal scale, we can aggregate by

FIGURE 3.9   RESCALING CAN ENHANCE PLOTS AND REVEAL PATTERNS. (LEFT) ORIGINAL SCALE AND (RIGHT) LOGARITHMIC SCALE

different granularity (e.g., monthly, daily, hourly) or even by a "seasonal" factor of interest such as month of year or day of week. A popular aggregation for time series is a moving average, where the average of neighboring values within a given window size is plotted. Moving average plots enhance visualizing a global trend (see Chapter 17).

Non-temporal attributes can be aggregated if some meaningful hierarchy exists: geographical (tracts within a zip code in the Boston Housing example), organizational (people within departments within business units), etc. Figure 3.10 illustrates two types of aggregation for the railway ridership time series. The original monthly series is shown in the top-left panel. Seasonal aggregation (by month-of-year) is shown in the top-right panel, where it is easy to see the peak in ridership in July–August and the dip in January–February. The bottom-right panel shows temporal aggregation, where the series is now displayed in yearly aggregates. This plot reveals the global long-term trend in ridership and the generally increasing trend from 1996 on.

Examining different scales, aggregations, or hierarchies supports both supervised and unsupervised tasks in that it can reveal patterns and relationships at various levels and can suggest new sets of attributes with which to work.

Zooming and Panning   The ability to zoom in and out of certain areas of the data on a plot is important for revealing patterns and outliers. We are often interested in more detail on areas of dense information or of special interest. Panning refers to the operation of moving the zoom window to other areas (popular in mapping applications such as Google Maps). An example of zooming is shown in the bottom-left panel of Figure 3.10, where the ridership series is zoomed in to the first two years of the series.

FIGURE 3.10   TIME SERIES LINE CHARTS USING DIFFERENT AGGREGATIONS (RIGHT PANELS), ADDING CURVES (TOP-LEFT PANEL), AND ZOOM IN (BOTTOM-LEFT PANEL)

Zooming and panning support supervised and unsupervised methods by detecting areas of different behavior, which may lead to creating new interaction terms, new attributes, or even separate models for data subsets. In addition, zooming and panning can help choose between methods that assume global behavior (e.g., regression models) and data-driven methods (e.g., exponential smoothing forecasters and k-nearest neighbors classifiers) and indicate the level of global/local behavior (as manifested by parameters such as k in k-nearest neighbors, the size of a tree, or the smoothing parameters in exponential smoothing).

Filtering   Filtering means removing some of the observations from the visualization. The purpose of filtering is to focus the attention on certain data while eliminating "noise" created by other data. Filtering supports supervised and unsupervised learning in a similar way to zooming and panning: it assists in identifying different or unusual local behavior.

Reference: Trend Lines and Labels

Trend lines and in-plot labels also help detect patterns and outliers. Trend lines serve as a reference and allow us to more easily assess the shape of a pattern. Although linearity is easy to visually perceive, more elaborate relationships such as exponential and polynomial trends are harder to assess by eye. Trend lines are useful in line charts and in scatter plots. An example is shown in the top-left panel of Figure 3.10, where a polynomial curve is overlaid on the original line chart (see also Chapter 17).

The RapidMiner process for generating the charts in Figure 3.10 is shown in Figure 3.11. The *Extract Coefficients (Polynomial Fit)* operator is used to fit a quadratic curve to the time series by specifying *degree* = 2. For the other charts, month and year are extracted from the original data using the *Date to Nominal* and *Date to Numerical* operators sequentially. Along the way, the original attribute Month is renamed to Date, and the newly generated attributes are named Month and Year using the *Rename* operator.

FIGURE 3.11   PROCESS FOR CREATING THE TIME SERIES LINE CHARTS IN FIGURE 3.10

In displays that are not overcrowded, the use of in-plot labels can be useful for better exploration of outliers and clusters. RapidMiner scatter plots can be enabled to show x and y values as labels, and data points can be color-coded by an attribute. An example (data: *Utilities.csv*) is shown in Figure 3.12 (a reproduction of Figure 16.1 with the addition of tooltips). The figure shows different utilities on a scatter plot that compares fuel cost with total sales. Although the color-coding of data points may not be of visual aid here due to similar color shades, the interactive tooltip feature allows the user to view the Company label by hovering over any data point. We might be interested in clustering the data and using clustering algorithms to identify clusters of utilities that differ markedly with respect to fuel cost and sales. Figure 3.12, with the interactive tooltips, helps visualize these clusters and their members (e.g., Nevada and Puget are part of a clear cluster with low fuel costs and high sales). For more on clustering and on this example, see Chapter 16.

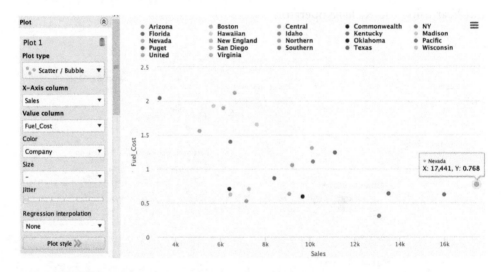

FIGURE 3.12   **SCATTER PLOT WITH INTERACTIVE TOOLTIPS**

Scaling Up to Large Datasets

When the number of observations (rows) is large, charts that display each individual observation (e.g., scatter plots) can become ineffective. Aside from using aggregated charts such as boxplots, some alternatives are:

1. Sampling—drawing a random sample and using it for plotting

2. Reducing marker size

3. Using more transparent marker colors and removing fill[10]

---

[10]RapidMiner does not support the feature of transparent marker coloring.

4. Breaking down the data into subsets (e.g., by creating multiple panels)

5. Using aggregation (e.g., bubble plots where size corresponds to number of observations in a certain range)

6. Using jittering (slightly moving each marker by adding a small amount of noise).

An example of the advantage of plotting a sample over the large dataset is shown in Figure 12.2 in Chapter 12, where a scatter plot of 5000 records is plotted alongside a scatter plot of a sample. Figure 3.13 illustrates an improved plot of the full dataset by using smaller markers and using jittering to uncover overlaid points. We can see that larger areas of the plot are dominated by the blue class, the red class is mainly on the right, while there is a lot of overlap in the high-income area.

FIGURE 3.13   SCATTER PLOT OF LARGE DATASET WITH REDUCED MARKER SIZE AND JITTERING

Multivariate Plot: Parallel Coordinates Plot

Another approach toward presenting multidimensional information in a two-dimensional plot is via specialized charts such as the *parallel coordinates plot*. In this plot, a vertical axis is drawn for each attribute. Then each observation is represented by drawing a line that connects its values on the different axes, thereby creating a "multivariate profile." An example is shown in Figure 3.14 for the Boston Housing data. In this display, the data is colored by the two categories of CAT.MEDV, in order to compare the profiles of tracts in the two classes (for a classification task). We see that the more expensive tracts (orange lines) consistently have low CRIM, low LSAT, and high RM compared with cheaper

FIGURE 3.14   PARALLEL COORDINATES PLOT FOR BOSTON HOUSING DATA. EACH OF THE ATTRIBUTES (SHOWN ON THE HORIZONTAL AXIS) IS SCALED TO 0-1. COLORS ARE USED TO DISTINGUISH CAT.MEDV (ORANGE: HOMES BELOW $30,000)

tracts (green lines), which are more mixed on CRIM, and LSAT, and have a medium level of RM. This observation gives indication of useful predictors and suggests possible binning for some numerical predictors.

Parallel coordinates plots are also useful in unsupervised tasks. They can reveal clusters, outliers, and information overlap across attributes. A useful manipulation is to reorder the columns to better reveal observation clusterings.

Interactive Visualization

Similar to the interactive nature of the machine learning process, interactivity is key to enhancing our ability to gain information from graphical visualization. In the words of Few (2021), an expert in data visualization:

> We can only learn so much when staring at a static visualization such as a printed graph …If we can't interact with the data …we hit the wall.

By interactive visualization, we mean an interface that supports the following principles:

1. Making changes to a chart is *easy, rapid, and reversible*.

2. Multiple concurrent charts and tables can be easily combined and displayed on a single screen.

3. A set of visualizations can be linked so that operations in one display are reflected in the other displays.

Let us consider a few examples where we contrast a static plot generator (e.g., Excel or RapidMiner) with an interactive visualization interface.

Histogram Rebinning   Consider the need to bin a numerical attribute and using a histogram for that purpose. A static histogram would require replotting for each new binning choice. If the user generates multiple plots, then the screen becomes cluttered. If the same plot is recreated, then it is hard to compare different binning choices. In contrast, an interactive visualization would provide an easy way to change bin width interactively (see, e.g., the slider below the histogram in Figure 3.15), and then the histogram would automatically and rapidly replot as the user changes the bin width.

Aggregation and Zooming   Consider a time series forecasting task, given a long series of data. Temporal aggregation at multiple levels is needed for determining short- and long-term patterns. Zooming and panning are used to identify unusual periods. A static plotting software requires the user to compute new attributes for each temporal aggregation (e.g., aggregate daily data to obtain weekly aggregates). Zooming and panning requires manually changing the min and max values on the axis scale of interest (thereby losing the ability to quickly move between different areas without creating multiple charts). An interactive visualization tool would provide immediate temporal hierarchies which the user can easily switch between. Zooming would be enabled as a slider near the axis (see, e.g., the sliders on the top-left panel in Figure 3.15), thereby allowing direct manipulation and rapid reaction.

Combining Multiple Linked Plots That Fit in a Single Screen   To support a classification task, multiple plots are created of the target attribute vs. potential categorical and numerical predictors. These can include side-by-side boxplots, color-coded scatter plots, and multipanel bar charts. The user wants to detect possible multidimensional relationships (and identify possible outliers) by selecting a certain subset of the data (e.g., a single category of some attribute) and locating the observations on the other plots. In a static interface, the user would have to manually organize the plots of interest and resize them to fit within a single screen. A static interface would usually not support inter-plot linkage, and even if it did, the entire set of plots would have to be regenerated each time a selection is made. In contrast, an interactive visualization would provide an easy way to automatically organize and resize the set of plots to fit within a screen. Linking the set of plots would be easy, and in response to the users selection on one plot, the appropriate selection would be automatically highlighted in the other plots (see example in Figure 3.15).

Interactive Visualization Software   In earlier sections, we used plots to illustrate the advantages of visualizations, because "a picture is worth a thousand words." The advantages of an interactive visualization are even harder to

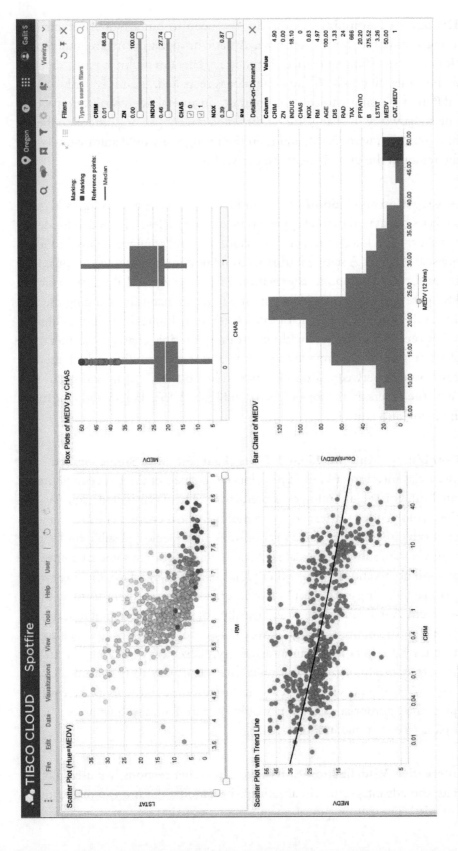

FIGURE 3.15 MULTIPLE INTER-LINKED PLOTS IN A SINGLE VIEW. NOTE THE MARKED OBSERVATION IN THE TOP-LEFT PANEL, WHICH IS ALSO HIGHLIGHTED IN ALL OTHER PLOTS. PRODUCED IN SPOTFIRE

convey in words. As Ben Shneiderman, a well-known researcher in information visualization and interfaces puts it:

> A picture is worth a thousand words. An interface is worth a thousand pictures.

The ability to interact with charts and link them together turns plotting into an analytical tool that supports continuous exploration of the data. Several commercial visualization tools provide powerful capabilities along these lines; two very popular ones are Spotfire (http://spotfire.tibco.com) and Tableau (www.tableausoftware.com). Figure 3.15 was generated using Spotfire.

Tableau and Spotfire have spent hundreds of millions of dollars on software R&D and review of interactions with customers to hone interfaces that allow analysts to interact with data via plots smoothly and efficiently. JMP by SAS (www.jmp.com) is a "statistical discovery" software that also has strong interactive visualization capabilities. All three offer free trial versions. Machine learning platforms like RapidMiner and programming environments like R and Python, which have become popular for statistical analysis, machine learning, and presentation graphics, can produce excellent static plots but are less suitable for interactive visualization, where a sophisticated and highly engineered user interface is required.

3.5 SPECIALIZED VISUALIZATIONS

In this section, we mention a few specialized visualizations that are able to capture data structures beyond the standard time series and cross-sectional structures— special types of relationships that are usually hard to capture with ordinary plots. In particular, we address hierarchical data, network data, and geographical data— three types of data that are becoming increasingly available.

Visualizing Networked Data

Network analysis techniques were spawned by the explosion of social and product network data. Examples of social networks are networks of sellers and buyers on eBay and networks of Facebook users. An example of a product network is the network of products on Amazon (linked through the recommendation system). Network data visualization is available in various network-specialized software and also in general-purpose software.

A network diagram consists of actors and relations between them. "Nodes" are the actors (e.g., users in a social network or products in a product network) and represented by circles. "Edges" are the relations between nodes and are represented by lines connecting nodes. For example, in a social network such as Facebook, we can construct a list of users (nodes) and all the pairwise relations (edges) between users who are "Friends." Alternatively, we can define edges as a posting that one user posts on another user's Facebook page. In this setup, we might have more than a single edge between two nodes. Networks can also have nodes of multiple types. A common structure is networks with two types of nodes. An example of a two-type node network is shown in Figure 3.16, where we see a set of transactions between a network of sellers and buyers on the online auction site www.eBay.com [the data (*ebayNetwork.csv*) are for auctions selling Swarovski beads and took place during a period of several months; from Jank and Yahav (2010)]. The circles with numerical labels represent sellers, and the unlabeled circles represent buyers. Each panel shows a single seller (the label is the seller's ID), with one or more buyers. We can see that this marketplace is dominated by three or four high-volume sellers. We can also see that many buyers interact with a single seller. The market structures for many individual products can be reviewed quickly in this way. Network providers can use the information, for example, to identify possible partnerships to explore with sellers.

Figure 3.16 was produced using NodeXL (www.smrfoundation.org/nodexl), which is an Excel-based tool. The plot's appearance can be customized, and various interactive features are available such as zooming, scaling, and panning the plot, dynamically filtering nodes and edges, altering the plot's layout, finding clusters of related nodes, and calculating network metrics (see Chapter 20 for details and examples).

Network plots can be potentially useful in the context of association rules (see Chapter 15). For example, consider a case of mining a dataset of consumers'

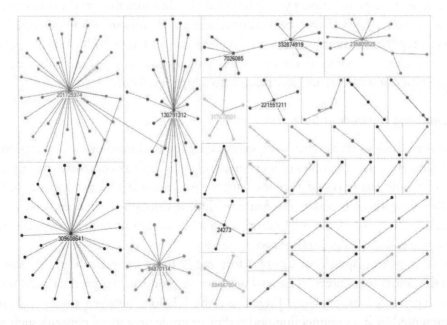

FIGURE 3.16   NETWORK GRAPH OF TRANSACTIONS BETWEEN EBAY SELLERS AND BUYERS OF SWAROVSKI BEADS. EACH PANEL SHOWS A SINGLE SELLER (THE LABEL IS THE SELLER'S ID), WITH ONE OR MORE BUYERS. PRODUCED USING NODEXL

grocery purchases to learn which items are purchased together ("what goes with what"). A network can be constructed with items as nodes and edges connecting items that were purchased together. After a set of rules is generated by the machine learning algorithm (which often contains an excessive number of rules, many of which are unimportant), the network plot can help visualize different rules for the purpose of choosing the interesting ones. For example, a popular "beer and diapers" combination would appear in the network plot as a pair of nodes with very high connectivity. An item which is almost always purchased regardless of other items (e.g., milk) would appear as a very large node with high connectivity to all other nodes.

Visualizing Hierarchical Data: Treemaps

We discussed hierarchical data and the exploration of data at different hierarchy levels in the context of plot manipulations. *Treemaps* are useful visualizations specialized for exploring large datasets that are hierarchically structured (tree-structured). They allow exploration of various dimensions of the data while maintaining the hierarchical nature of the data. An example is shown in Figure 3.17, which displays a large set of auctions from eBay.com (data: *EbayTreemap.csv*),[11] hierarchically ordered by item brand, category, and sub category. The levels in the hierarchy of the treemap are visualized as rectangles

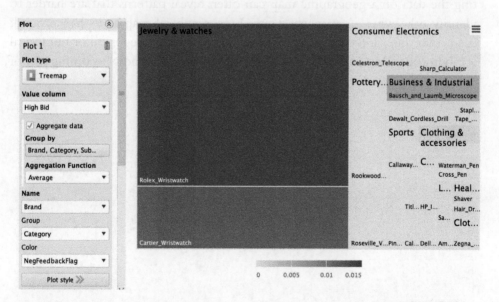

FIGURE 3.17   TREEMAP SHOWING NEARLY 11,000 EBAY AUCTIONS, ORGANIZED BY ITEM CATEGORY, SUBCATEGORY, AND BRAND. RECTANGLE SIZE REPRESENTS AVERAGE CLOSING PRICE (REFLECTING ITEM VALUE). SHADE REPRESENTS % OF SELLERS WITH NEGATIVE FEEDBACK (DARKER = HIGHER %)

---

[11]We thank Sharad Borle for sharing this dataset.

containing sub-rectangles. Categorical attributes can be included in the display by using hue. Numerical attributes can be included via rectangle size and color intensity (ordering of the rectangles is sometimes used to reinforce size). In Figure 3.17, size is used to represent the average closing price (which reflects item value), and color intensity represents the percent of sellers with negative feedback (a negative seller feedback indicates buyer dissatisfaction in past transactions and is often indicative of fraudulent seller behavior). Consider the task of classifying ongoing auctions in terms of a fraudulent outcome. From the treemap, we see that the highest proportion of sellers with negative ratings (black) is concentrated in expensive item auctions (Rolex and Cartier wristwatches).

Ideally, treemaps should be explored interactively, zooming to different levels of the hierarchy. One example of an interactive online application of treemaps is currently available at www.drasticdata.nl. One of their treemap examples displays player-level data from the 2014 World Cup, aggregated to team level. The user can choose to explore players and team data.

Visualizing Geographical Data: Map Charts

Many datasets used for machine learning now include geographical information. Zip codes are one example of a categorical attribute with many categories, where it is not straightforward to create meaningful attributes for analysis. Plotting the data on a geographic map can often reveal patterns that are harder to identify otherwise. A map chart uses a geographical map as its background; then color, hue, and other features are used to include categorical or numerical attributes. Besides specialized mapping software, maps are now becoming part of

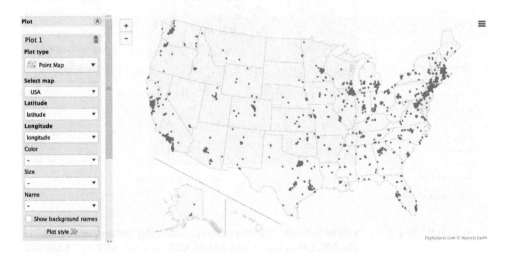

FIGURE 3.18   MAP CHART OF STATISTICS.COM STUDENTS' AND INSTRUCTORS' LOCATIONS ON A US MAP

general-purpose software, and Google Maps provides application programming interfaces (APIs) that allow organizations to overlay their data on a Google map. Similarly, Highcharts.com provides Javascript APIs for creating map charts that are integrated in RapidMiner. Figure 3.18 shows a map chart created in Rapid-Miner showing locations of students and instructors for Statistics.com (data: *SC-US-students-GPS-data-2016.csv*).

Figure 3.19 shows two world map charts comparing countries' "well-being" (according to a 2006 Gallup survey)[12] in the top map, to gross domestic product (GDP) in the bottom map (data: *countries.csv*, *Veerhoven.csv*, and *gdp.csv*). Darker shade means higher value.

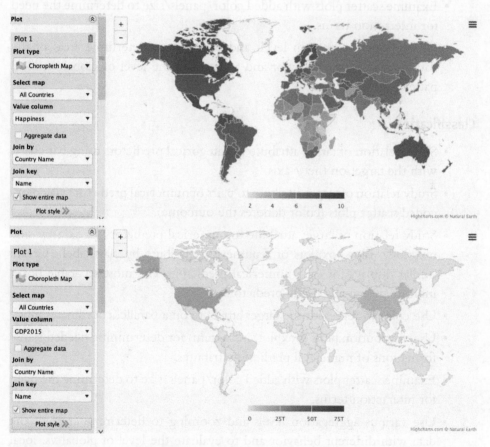

FIGURE 3.19 WORLD MAPS COMPARING "WELL-BEING" (TOP) TO GDP (BOTTOM). SHADING BY AVERAGE "GLOBAL WELL-BEING" SCORE (TOP) OR GDP (BOTTOM) OF COUNTRY. DARKER CORRESPONDS TO HIGHER SCORE OR LEVEL

---

[12]Data from Veerhoven, R., World Database of Happiness, Erasmus University Rotterdam. Available at http://worlddatabaseofhappiness.eur.nl

3.6 SUMMARY: MAJOR VISUALIZATIONS AND OPERATIONS, BY MACHINE LEARNING GOAL

Prediction

- Plot target attribute on the y-axis of boxplots, bar charts, and scatter plots.
- Study relation of target attribute to categorical predictors via side-by-side boxplots, bar charts, and multiple panels.
- Study relation of target attribute to numerical predictors via scatter plots.
- Use distribution plots (boxplot, histogram) for determining needed transformations of the target attribute (and/or numerical predictors).
- Examine scatter plots with added color/panels/size to determine the need for interaction terms.
- Use various aggregation levels and zooming to determine areas of the data with different behavior and to evaluate the level of global vs. local patterns.

Classification

- Study relation of target attribute to categorical predictors using bar charts with the target on the y-axis.
- Study relation of target attribute to pairs of numerical predictors via color-coded scatter plots (color denotes the outcome).
- Study relation of target attribute to numerical predictors via side-by-side boxplots. Plot boxplots of a numerical attribute by class label. Create similar displays for each numerical predictor. The most separable boxes indicate potentially useful predictors.
- Use color to represent the target attribute on a parallel coordinates plot.
- Use distribution plots (boxplot, histogram) for determining needed transformations of numerical predictor attributes.
- Examine scatter plots with added color/panels/size to determine the need for interaction terms.
- Use various aggregation levels and zooming to determine areas of the data with different behavior and to evaluate the level of global vs. local patterns.

Time Series Forecasting

- Create line charts at different temporal aggregations to determine types of patterns.
- Use zooming and panning to examine various shorter periods of the series to determine areas of the data with different behavior.

- Use various aggregation levels to identify global and local patterns.
- Identify missing values in the series (that will require handling).
- Overlay trend lines of different types to determine adequate modeling choices.

Unsupervised Learning

- Create scatter plot matrices to identify pairwise relationships and clustering of observations.
- Use heatmaps to examine the correlation table.
- Use various aggregation levels and zooming to determine areas of the data with different behavior.
- Generate a parallel coordinates plot to identify clusters of observations.

PROBLEMS

3.1   **Shipments of Household Appliances: Line Charts.** The file *ApplianceShipments.csv* contains the series of quarterly shipments (in millions of dollars) of US household appliances between 1985 and 1989.

   a. Create a well-formatted time plot of the data using RapidMiner.

   b. Does there appear to be a quarterly pattern? For a closer view of the patterns, zoom in to the range of 3500–5000 on the y-axis.

   c. Using RapidMiner, create one chart with four separate lines, one line for each of Q1, Q2, Q3, and Q4. In RapidMiner, this can be achieved by adding attributes for quarter and year using the *Generate Attributes* operator. [*Hint*: The function expressions *prefix(Quarter, 2)* and *suffix(Quarter, 4)* can be used to create separate attributes for quarter and year, respectively.] Then, in your visualization, using Shipments as the value column, create a line chart aggregating the data with the *average* aggregation function, grouping it by year and then color-grouping it by quarter. This will plot shipment vs. year for each quarter as a separate series on a line chart. Zoom in to the range of 3500–5000 on the y-axis. Does there appear to be a difference between quarters?

   d. Using RapidMiner, create a line chart of the series at a yearly aggregated level (i.e., the total shipments in each year).

3.2   **Sales of Riding Mowers: Scatter Plots.** A company that manufactures riding mowers wants to identify the best sales prospects for an intensive sales campaign. In particular, the manufacturer is interested in classifying households as prospective owners or nonowners on the basis of Income (in \$1000s) and Lot Size (in 1000 ft^2). The marketing expert looked at a random sample of 24 households, given in the file *RidingMowers.csv*.

   Using RapidMiner, create a scatter plot of Lot Size vs. Income, color-coded by the target attribute owner/nonowner.

3.3   **Laptop Sales at a London Computer Chain: Bar Charts and Boxplots.** The file *LaptopSalesJanuary2008.csv* contains data for all sales of laptops at a computer chain in London in January 2008. This is a subset of the full dataset that includes data for the entire year.

   a. Create a bar chart, showing the average retail price by store. Which store has the highest average? Which has the lowest?

   b. To better compare retail prices across stores, create side-by-side boxplots of retail price by store. Now compare the prices in the two stores from (a). Does there seem to be a difference between their price distributions?

3.4   **Laptop Sales at a London Computer Chain: Interactive Visualization.** The next exercises are designed for using an interactive visualization tool. The file *LaptopSales.csv* is a comma-separated file with nearly 300,000 rows. ENBIS (the European Network for Business and Industrial Statistics) provided these data as part of a contest organized in the fall of 2009.

   Scenario: Imagine that you are a new analyst for a company called Acell (a company selling laptops). You have been provided with data about products and sales. You need to help the company with their business goal of planning a product strategy and pricing policies that will maximize Acell's projected revenues in 2009. Using an interactive visualization tool, answer the following questions.

a. Price Questions:

    i. At what price are the laptops actually selling?

    ii. Does price change with time? (*Hint*: Make sure that the date column is recognized as such. The software should then enable different temporal aggregation choices, e.g., plotting the data by weekly or monthly aggregates or even by day of week.)

    iii. Are prices consistent across retail outlets?

    iv. How does price change with configuration?

b. Location Questions:

    i. Where are the stores and customers located?

    ii. Which stores are selling the most?

    iii. How far would customers travel to buy a laptop?

       ○ *Hint 1*: You should be able to aggregate the data, for example, plot the sum or average of the prices.

       ○ *Hint 2*: Use the coordinated highlighting between multiple visualizations in the same page, for example, select a store in one view to see the matching customers in another visualization.

       ○ *Hint 3*: Explore the use of filters to see differences. Make sure to filter in the zoomed out view. For example, try to use a "store location" slider as an alternative way to dynamically compare store locations. This might be more useful to spot outlier patterns if there were 50 store locations to compare.

    iv. Try an alternative way of looking at how far customers traveled. Do this by creating a new data column that computes the distance between customer and store.

c. Revenue Questions:

    i. How do the sales volume in each store relate to Acell's revenues?

    ii. How does this relationship depend on the configuration?

d. Configuration Questions:

    i. What are the details of each configuration? How does this relate to price?

    ii. Do all stores sell all configurations?

CHAPTER 4

Dimension Reduction

In this chapter, we describe the important step of dimension reduction. The dimension of a dataset, which is the number of attributes, must be reduced for the machine learning algorithms to operate efficiently. This process is part of the pilot/prototype phase of supervised learning and is done before deploying a model. We present and discuss several dimension reduction approaches: (1) incorporating domain knowledge to remove or combine categories, (2) using data summaries to detect information overlap between attributes (and remove or combine redundant attributes or categories), (3) using data conversion techniques such as converting categorical attributes into numerical attributes, and (4) employing automated reduction techniques, such as principal component analysis (PCA), where a new set of attributes (which are weighted averages of the original attributes) is created. These new attributes are uncorrelated, and a small subset of them usually contains most of their combined information. Hence, we can reduce dimension by using only a subset of the new attributes. Finally, we mention supervised learning methods such as regression models and classification and regression trees, which can be used for removing redundant attributes and for combining "similar" categories of categorical attributes.

4.1 INTRODUCTION

In machine learning, one often encounters situations where there is a large number of attributes in the database. Even when the initial number of attributes is small, this set quickly expands in the data preparation step, where new derived attributes are created (e.g., dummies for categorical attributes and new forms of existing attributes). In such situations, it is likely that subsets of attributes are highly correlated with each other. Including highly correlated attributes in

Machine Learning for Business Analytics: Concepts, Techniques and Applications in RapidMiner, First Edition.
Galit Shmueli, Peter C. Bruce, Amit V. Deokar, and Nitin R. Patel
© 2023 John Wiley & Sons, Inc. Published 2023 by John Wiley & Sons, Inc.

a classification or prediction model or including attributes that are unrelated to the target attribute can lead to overfitting, and prediction accuracy and reliability can suffer. A large number of attributes also poses computational problems for some supervised and unsupervised algorithms (aside from questions of correlation). In model deployment, superfluous attributes can increase costs due to the collection and processing of these attributes.

4.2   CURSE OF DIMENSIONALITY

The *dimensionality* of a model is the number of predictors or input attributes used by the model. The *curse of dimensionality* is the affliction caused by adding attributes to multivariate data models. As attributes are added, the data space becomes increasingly sparse, and classification and prediction models fail because the available data are insufficient to provide a useful model across so many attributes. An important consideration is the fact that the difficulties posed by adding an attribute increase exponentially with the addition of each attribute. One way to think of this intuitively is to consider the location of an object on a chessboard. It has two dimensions and 64 squares or choices. If you expand the chessboard to a cube, you increase the dimensions by 50%—from two dimensions to three dimensions. However, the location options increase by 800%, to 512 ($8 \times 8 \times 8$). In statistical distance terms, the proliferation of variables means that nothing is close to anything else anymore—too much noise has been added, and patterns and structure are no longer discernible. The problem is particularly acute in big data applications, including genomics, where, for example, an analysis might have to deal with values for thousands of different genes. One of the key steps in machine learning, therefore, is finding ways to reduce dimensionality with minimal sacrifice of accuracy. In the artificial intelligence literature, dimension reduction is often referred to as *factor selection*, *feature selection*, or *feature extraction*.

4.3   PRACTICAL CONSIDERATIONS

Although machine learning prefers automated methods over domain knowledge, it is important at the first step of data exploration to make sure that the attributes measured are reasonable for the task at hand. The integration of expert knowledge through a discussion with the data provider (or user) will probably lead to better results. Practical considerations include: Which attributes are most important for the task at hand, and which are most likely to be useless? Which attributes are likely to contain much error? Which attributes will be available for measurement (and what will it cost to measure them) in the future if the analysis is repeated? Which attributes can actually be measured before the outcome (target) occurs? For example, if we want to predict the closing price of an ongoing online auction, we cannot use the number of bids as a predictor because this will not be known until the auction closes.

Example 1: House Prices in Boston

We return to the Boston Housing example introduced in Chapter 3. For each neighborhood, a number of attributes are given, such as the crime rate, the student/teacher ratio, and the median value of a housing unit in the neighborhood. A description of all 14 attributes is given in Table 4.1. The first nine records of the data are shown in Table 4.2. The first row represents the first neighborhood, which had an average per capita crime rate of 0.006, 18% of the residential land zoned for lots over 25,000 ft^2, 2.31% of the land devoted to nonretail business, no border on the Charles River, and so on.

TABLE 4.1   DESCRIPTION OF ATTRIBUTES IN THE BOSTON HOUSING DATASET

CRIM	Crime rate
ZN	Percentage of residential land zoned for lots over 25,000 ft^2
INDUS	Percentage of land occupied by nonretail business
CHAS	Does tract bound Charles River? (= 1 if tract bounds river, = 0 otherwise)
NOX	Nitric oxide concentration (parts per 10 million)
RM	Average number of rooms per dwelling
AGE	Percentage of owner-occupied units built prior to 1940
DIS	Weighted distances to five Boston employment centers
RAD	Index of accessibility to radial highways
TAX	Full-value property tax rate per $10,000
PTRATIO	Pupil-to-teacher ratio by town
LSTAT	Percentage of lower status of the population
MEDV	Median value of owner-occupied homes in $1000s
CAT.MEDV	Is median value of owner-occupied homes in tract above $30,000 (CAT.MEDV = 1) or not (CAT.MEDV = 0)?

TABLE 4.2   FIRST NINE RECORDS IN THE BOSTON HOUSING DATA

CRIM	ZN	INDUS	CHAS	NOX	RM	AGE	DIS	RAD	TAX	PTRATIO	LSTAT	MEDV	CAT.MEDV
0.00632	18.0	2.31	0	0.538	6.575	65.2	4.09	1	296	15.3	4.98	24.0	0
0.02731	0.0	7.07	0	0.469	6.421	78.9	4.9671	2	242	17.8	9.14	21.6	0
0.02729	0.0	7.07	0	0.469	7.185	61.1	4.9671	2	242	17.8	4.03	34.7	1
0.03237	0.0	2.18	0	0.458	6.998	45.8	6.0622	3	222	18.7	2.94	33.4	1
0.06905	0.0	2.18	0	0.458	7.147	54.2	6.0622	3	222	18.7	5.33	36.2	1
0.02985	0.0	2.18	0	0.458	6.43	58.7	6.0622	3	222	18.7	5.21	28.7	0
0.08829	12.5	7.87	0	0.524	6.012	66.6	5.5605	5	311	15.2	12.43	22.9	0
0.14455	12.5	7.87	0	0.524	6.172	96.1	5.9505	5	311	15.2	19.15	27.1	0
0.21124	12.5	7.87	0	0.524	5.631	100.0	6.0821	5	311	15.2	29.93	16.5	0

4.4 DATA SUMMARIES

As we have seen in the chapter on data visualization, an important initial step of data exploration is getting familiar with the data and their characteristics through summaries and graphs. The importance of this step cannot be overstated. The better you understand the data, the better the results from the modeling or mining process.

Numerical summaries and graphs of the data are very helpful for data reduction. The information that they convey can assist in combining categories of a categorical attribute, in choosing attributes to remove, in assessing the level of information overlap between attributes, and more. Before discussing such strategies for reducing the dimension of a dataset, let us consider useful summaries and tools.

Summary Statistics

RapidMiner offers several features that assist in summarizing data. The *Statistics* tab of the *Results* view gives an overview of the entire set of attributes in the data through key statistics: *min, max, average, standard deviation,* and *missing*. Additionally, the *Aggregation* operator can be used to compute other statistics such as median for any variable in the data. These summary statistics are also very helpful for learning about the characteristics of each attribute. First, they give us information about the scale and type of values that the attribute takes. The min and max statistics can be used to detect extreme values that might be errors. The mean and median give a sense of the central values of that variable, and a large deviation between the two also indicates skew. The standard deviation gives a sense of how dispersed the data are (relative to the mean). The *missing* count gives us the number of empty cells and can alert us about missing values.

Figure 4.1 shows the summary statistics for the Boston Housing example. We immediately see that the different attributes have very different ranges of values. We will soon see how variation in scale across attributes can distort analyses if not treated properly. Another observation that can be made based on the attribute distributions is that the mean of the first attribute, CRIM (as well as several others), is much larger than the median, indicating right skew. None of the attributes have missing values. There also do not appear to be indications of extreme values that might result from typing errors.

Next, we summarize relationships between two or more attributes. For numerical attributes, we can compute a complete matrix of correlations between each pair of attributes, using the *Correlation Matrix* operator. Figure 4.2 shows the correlation matrix for the Boston Housing attributes. We see that most

Name	⊢ ⊣ Type	Missing	Statistics		Filter (14 / 14 attributes): Search for Attribute		
∧ CRIM	Real	0		Min 0.006	Max 88.976	Average 3.614	Deviation 8.602
∧ ZN	Real	0		Min 0	Max 100	Average 11.364	Deviation 23.322
∧ INDUS	Real	0		Min 0.460	Max 27.740	Average 11.137	Deviation 6.860
∧ CHAS	Integer	0		Min 0	Max 1	Average 0.069	Deviation 0.254
∧ NOX	Real	0		Min 0.385	Max 0.871	Average 0.555	Deviation 0.116
∧ RM	Real	0		Min 3.561	Max 8.780	Average 6.285	Deviation 0.703
∧ AGE	Real	0		Min 2.900	Max 100	Average 68.575	Deviation 28.149
∧ DIS	Real	0		Min 1.130	Max 12.127	Average 3.795	Deviation 2.106
∧ RAD	Integer	0		Min 1	Max 24	Average 9.549	Deviation 8.707
∧ TAX	Integer	0		Min 187	Max 711	Average 408.237	Deviation 168.537
∧ PTRATIO	Real	0		Min 12.600	Max 22	Average 18.456	Deviation 2.165
∧ LSTAT	Real	0		Min 1.730	Max 37.970	Average 12.653	Deviation 7.141
∧ MEDV	Real	0		Min 5	Max 50	Average 22.533	Deviation 9.197
∧ CAT. MEDV	Integer	0		Min 0	Max 1	Average 0.166	Deviation 0.372

Showing attributes 1 – 14   Examples: 506   Special Attributes: 0   Regular Attributes: 14

FIGURE 4.1   SUMMARY STATISTICS FOR THE BOSTON HOUSING DATA

Attributes	CRIM	ZN	INDUS	CHAS	NOX	RM	AGE	DIS	RAD	TAX	PTRATIO	LSTAT	MEDV	CAT. MEDV
CRIM	1	-0.200	0.407	-0.056	0.421	-0.219	0.353	-0.380	0.626	0.583	0.290	0.456	-0.388	-0.152
ZN	-0.200	1	-0.534	-0.043	-0.517	0.312	-0.570	0.664	-0.312	-0.315	-0.392	-0.413	0.360	0.365
INDUS	0.407	-0.534	1	0.063	0.764	-0.392	0.645	-0.708	0.595	0.721	0.383	0.604	-0.484	-0.366
CHAS	-0.056	-0.043	0.063	1	0.091	0.091	0.087	-0.099	-0.007	-0.036	-0.122	-0.054	0.175	0.109
NOX	0.421	-0.517	0.764	0.091	1	-0.302	0.731	-0.769	0.611	0.668	0.189	0.591	-0.427	-0.233
RM	-0.219	0.312	-0.392	0.091	-0.302	1	-0.240	0.205	-0.210	-0.292	-0.356	-0.614	0.695	0.641
AGE	0.353	-0.570	0.645	0.087	0.731	-0.240	1	-0.748	0.456	0.506	0.262	0.602	-0.377	-0.191
DIS	-0.380	0.664	-0.708	-0.099	-0.769	0.205	-0.748	1	-0.495	-0.534	-0.232	-0.497	0.250	0.119
RAD	0.626	-0.312	0.595	-0.007	0.611	-0.210	0.456	-0.495	1	0.910	0.465	0.489	-0.382	-0.198
TAX	0.583	-0.315	0.721	-0.036	0.668	-0.292	0.506	-0.534	0.910	1	0.461	0.544	-0.469	-0.274
PTRATIO	0.290	-0.392	0.383	-0.122	0.189	-0.356	0.262	-0.232	0.465	0.461	1	0.374	-0.508	-0.443
LSTAT	0.456	-0.413	0.604	-0.054	0.591	-0.614	0.602	-0.497	0.489	0.544	0.374	1	-0.738	-0.470
MEDV	-0.388	0.360	-0.484	0.175	-0.427	0.695	-0.377	0.250	-0.382	-0.469	-0.508	-0.738	1	0.790
CAT. MEDV	-0.152	0.365	-0.366	0.109	-0.233	0.641	-0.191	0.119	-0.198	-0.274	-0.443	-0.470	0.790	1

FIGURE 4.2   **CORRELATION TABLE FOR BOSTON HOUSING DATA**

correlations are low and that many are negative.[1] We will return to the importance of the correlation matrix soon, in the context of correlation analysis.

Aggregation and Pivot Tables

Another very useful approach for exploring the data is aggregation by one or more attributes. RapidMiner's *Turbo Prep* view provides an alternative interface for quickly conducting data preparation tasks, including such aggregations. For example, Figure 4.3 illustrates an example of aggregation by a single attribute.[2] The pivot table shows the number of neighborhoods that bound the Charles River vs. those that do not (the attribute CHAS is chosen as the grouping attribute). It appears that the majority of neighborhoods (471 of 506) do not bound the river.

RapidMiner supports various aggregation functions to apply to the aggregate attribute such as *sum*, *average*, *median*, and *sum (count)*, among others. For categorical attributes, we obtain a breakdown of the records by the combination of categories. For instance, we compute the average MEDV by CHAS and RM as follows. The numerical attribute RM (the average number of rooms per dwelling in the neighborhood) is first grouped into bins of size 1 with the *Discretize by User Specification* operator[3] from RapidMiner's Design view as shown in the top of Figure 4.4. Then, Turbo Prep is invoked from the Results view to

---

[1] The *Matrix Visualization* tab from the Results view for the *Correlation Matrix* operator can help distinguish positive and negative values, similar to the heatmap shown in Chapter 3.

[2] The *Aggregate* operator can be used for aggregating by a single attribute from the usual Design view.

[3] There are other binning operators as well for different use cases, namely, *Discretize by Size* (user-specified bin size), *Discretize by Binning* (user-specified number of bins of equal range), *Discretize by*

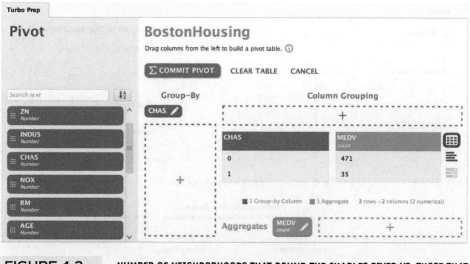

FIGURE 4.3   NUMBER OF NEIGHBORHOODS THAT BOUND THE CHARLES RIVER VS. THOSE THAT DO NOT

create a pivot table[4] as shown in the bottom of Figure 4.4. Note the ? values, denoting that there are no neighborhoods in the dataset with those combinations (e.g., bounding the river and having on average three rooms).

In classification tasks, where the goal is to find predictors that distinguish between two classes, a good exploratory step is to produce summaries for each class. This can assist in detecting useful predictors that display some separation between the two classes. Data summaries are useful for almost any machine learning task and are therefore an important preliminary step for cleaning and understanding the data before carrying out further analyses.

4.5 CORRELATION ANALYSIS

In datasets with a large number of attributes (which are likely to serve as predictors), there is usually much overlap in the information covered by the set of attributes. One simple way to find redundancies is to look at a correlation matrix. This shows all the pairwise correlations between attributes. Pairs that have a very strong (positive or negative) correlation contain a lot of overlap in information and are good candidates for data reduction by removing one of the attributes. Removing attributes that are strongly correlated to others is useful for avoiding multicollinearity problems that can arise in various models. (*Multicollinearity* is

---

Frequency (user-specified number of bins of equal frequency), and *Discretize by Entropy* (a nominal attribute is created from the numeric attribute so as to minimize the entropy—requires class label).

[4]The *Pivot* operator can be used for aggregating by one or more attributes from the usual Design view. The *Pivot* operator can be thought of as a generalization of the *Aggregate* Operator by additionally specifying the column grouping attribute.

FIGURE 4.4   AVERAGE MEDV BY CHAS AND RM: (TOP) CONVERTING RM TO A CATEGORICAL
ATTRIBUTE (BINNING) (BOTTOM) USING TURBO PREP TO CREATE PIVOT TABLE

the presence of two or more predictors sharing the same linear relationship with the target attribute.)

Correlation analysis is also a good method for detecting duplications of attributes in the data. Sometimes, the same attribute appears accidentally more than once in the dataset (under a different name) because the dataset was merged from multiple sources, the same phenomenon is measured in different units, and so on. Using correlation table heatmaps, as shown in Figure 4.2 and Chapter 3, can make the task of identifying strong correlations easier.

4.6 REDUCING THE NUMBER OF CATEGORIES IN CATEGORICAL ATTRIBUTES

When a categorical attribute (i.e., having a nominal type) has many categories, and this attribute is destined to be a predictor, many machine learning methods will require converting it into many dummy attributes. In particular, an attribute with m categories will be transformed into either m or $m - 1$ dummy attributes (depending on the method). This means that even if we have very few original categorical attributes, they can greatly inflate the dimension of the dataset. One way to handle this is to reduce the number of categories by combining close or similar categories. Combining categories requires incorporating expert knowledge and common sense. Pivot tables are useful for this task: we can examine the sizes of the various categories and how the target attribute behaves in each category. Generally, categories that contain very few observations are good candidates for combining with other categories. Use only the categories that are most relevant to the analysis, and label the rest as "other." In classification tasks (with a target attribute of nominal type, i.e., class label), a pivot table broken down by the label classes can help identify categories that do not separate the classes. Those categories too are candidates for inclusion in the "other" category. An example is shown in Figure 4.5, where the distribution of class label CAT.MEDV is broken down by ZN (treated here as a categorical attribute).[5] We can see that the distribution of CAT.MEDV is identical for ZN = 17.5, 90, 95, and 100 (where all neighborhoods have CAT.MEDV = 1). These four categories can then be combined into a single category. Similarly, categories ZN where all neighborhoods have CAT.MEDV = 0 can be combined. Further combination is also possible based on similar bars.

In a time series context where we might have a categorical variable denoting season (such as month, or hour of day) that will serve as a predictor, reducing categories can be done by examining the time series plot and identifying similar

---

[5]To arrange ZN values from low to high values in the chart, we first perform a *Transform* action in Turbo Prep to sort ZN in ascending order.

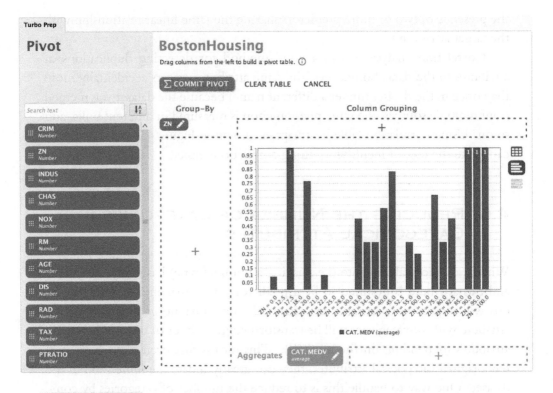

FIGURE 4.5   DISTRIBUTION OF CAT.MEDV (GREEN DENOTES CAT.MEDV = 0) BY ZN. SIMILAR BARS INDICATE LOW SEPARATION BETWEEN CLASSES AND CAN BE COMBINED

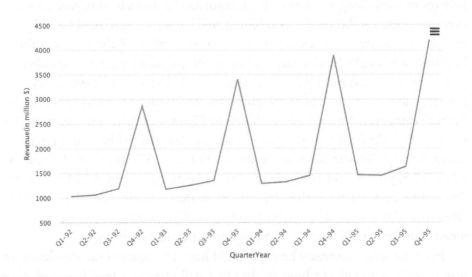

FIGURE 4.6   QUARTERLY REVENUES OF TOYS "R" US, 1992–1995

periods. For example, the time plot in Figure 4.6 shows the quarterly revenues of Toys "R" Us between 1992 and 1995. Only quarter four periods appear different, and therefore, we can combine quarters one to three into a single category.

4.7 CONVERTING A CATEGORICAL ATTRIBUTE TO A NUMERICAL ATTRIBUTE

Sometimes the categories in a categorical attribute represent intervals. Common examples are age group or income bracket. If the interval values are known (e.g., category 2 is the age interval 20–30), we can replace the categorical value ("2" in the example) with the mid-interval value (here "25"). The result will be a numerical attribute which no longer requires multiple dummy attributes.

4.8 PRINCIPAL COMPONENT ANALYSIS

Principal component analysis (PCA) is a useful method for dimension reduction, especially when the number of attributes is large. PCA is especially valuable when we have subsets of measurements that are measured on the same scale and are highly correlated. In that case, it provides a few attributes (often as few as three) that are weighted linear combinations of the original attributes and that retain the majority of the information of the full original set. PCA is intended for use with numerical attributes. For categorical attributes, other methods such as correspondence analysis are more suitable.

Example 2: Breakfast Cereals

Data were collected on the nutritional information and consumer rating of 77 breakfast cereals.[6] The consumer rating is a rating of cereal "healthiness" for consumer information (not a rating by consumers). For each cereal, the data include 13 numerical attributes, and we are interested in reducing this dimension. For each cereal, the information is based on a bowl of cereal rather than a serving size, because most people simply fill a cereal bowl (resulting in constant volume, but not weight). A snapshot of these data is given in Table 4.3, and the description of the different attributes is given in Table 4.4.

We focus first on two attributes: *calories* and *consumer rating*. These are given in Table 4.5. The average calories across the 77 cereals is 106.88 with standard deviation of 19.48. The average consumer rating is 42.67 with standard deviation 14.05. This is shown in Figure 4.7 (middle). The two attributes are strongly

---

[6]The data are available at https://dasl.datadescription.com/datafile/cereals/

TABLE 4.3   SAMPLE FROM THE 77 BREAKFAST CEREALS DATASET

Cereal name	mfr	Type	Calories	Protein	Fat	Sodium	Fiber	Carbo	Sugars	Potass	Vitamins
100% Bran	N	C	70	4	1	130	10	5	6	280	25
100% Natural Bran	Q	C	120	3	5	15	2	8	8	135	0
All-Bran	K	C	70	4	1	260	9	7	5	320	25
All-Bran with Extra Fiber	K	C	50	4	0	140	14	8	0	330	25
Almond Delight	R	C	110	2	2	200	1	14	8		25
Apple Cinnamon Cheerios	G	C	110	2	2	180	1.5	10.5	10	70	25
Apple Jacks	K	C	110	2	0	125	1	11	14	30	25
Basic 4	G	C	130	3	2	210	2	18	8	100	25
Bran Chex	R	C	90	2	1	200	4	15	6	125	25
Bran Flakes	P	C	90	3	0	210	5	13	5	190	25
Cap'n'Crunch	Q	C	120	1	2	220	0	12	12	35	25
Cheerios	G	C	110	6	2	290	2	17	1	105	25
Cinnamon Toast Crunch	G	C	120	1	3	210	0	13	9	45	25
Clusters	G	C	110	3	2	140	2	13	7	105	25
Cocoa Puffs	G	C	110	1	1	180	0	12	13	55	25
Corn Chex	R	C	110	2	0	280	0	22	3	25	25
Corn Flakes	K	C	100	2	0	290	1	21	2	35	25
Corn Pops	K	C	110	1	0	90	1	13	12	20	25
Count Chocula	G	C	110	1	1	180	0	12	13	65	25
Cracklin' Oat Bran	K	C	110	3	3	140	4	10	7	160	25

TABLE 4.4   DESCRIPTION OF THE ATTRIBUTES IN THE BREAKFAST CEREAL DATASET

Variable	Description
mfr	Manufacturer of cereal (American Home Food Products, General Mills, Kellogg, etc.)
type	Cold or hot
calories	Calories per serving
protein	Grams of protein
fat	Grams of fat
sodium	Milligrams of sodium
fiber	Grams of dietary fiber
carbo	Grams of complex carbohydrates
sugars	Grams of sugars
potass	Milligrams of potassium
vitamins	Vitamins and minerals: 0, 25, or 100, indicating the typical percentage of FDA recommended
shelf	Display shelf (1, 2, or 3, counting from the floor)
weight	Weight in ounces of one serving
cups	Number of cups in one serving
rating	Rating of the cereal calculated by consumer reports

correlated with a negative correlation of -0.69. In RapidMiner, the *Correlation Matrix* operator can be used to compute correlation as shown in Figure 4.7 (top and bottom). Roughly speaking, 69% of the total variation in both attributes is actually "co-variation," or variation in one attribute that is duplicated by similar variation in the other attribute. Can we use this fact to reduce the number of attributes while making maximum use of their unique contributions to the overall variation? Since there is redundancy in the information that the two

TABLE 4.5   CEREAL CALORIES AND RATINGS

Cereal	Calories	Rating	Cereal	Calories	Rating
100% Bran	70	68.40297	Just Right Fruit & Nut	140	36.471512
100% Natural Bran	120	33.98368	Kix	110	39.241114
All-Bran	70	59.42551	Life	100	45.328074
All-Bran with Extra Fiber	50	93.70491	Lucky Charms	110	26.734515
Almond Delight	110	34.38484	Maypo	100	54.850917
Apple Cinnamon Cheerios	110	29.50954	Muesli Raisins, Dates & Almonds	150	37.136863
Apple Jacks	110	33.17409	Muesli Raisins, Peaches & Pecans	150	34.139765
Basic 4	130	37.03856	Mueslix Crispy Blend	160	30.313351
Bran Chex	90	49.12025	Multi-Grain Cheerios	100	40.105965
Bran Flakes	90	53.31381	Nut&Honey Crunch	120	29.924285
Cap'n'Crunch	120	18.04285	Nutri-Grain Almond-Raisin	140	40.69232
Cheerios	110	50.765	Nutri-grain Wheat	90	59.642837
Cinnamon Toast Crunch	120	19.82357	Oatmeal Raisin Crisp	130	30.450843
Clusters	110	40.40021	Post Nat. Raisin Bran	120	37.840594
Cocoa Puffs	110	22.73645	Product 19	100	41.50354
Corn Chex	110	41.44502	Puffed Rice	50	60.756112
Corn Flakes	100	45.86332	Puffed Wheat	50	63.005645
Corn Pops	110	35.78279	Quaker Oat Squares	100	49.511874
Count Chocula	110	22.39651	Quaker Oatmeal	100	50.828392
Cracklin' Oat Bran	110	40.44877	Raisin Bran	120	39.259197
Cream of Wheat (Quick)	100	64.53382	Raisin Nut Bran	100	39.7034
Crispix	110	46.89564	Raisin Squares	90	55.333142
Crispy Wheat & Raisins	100	36.1762	Rice Chex	110	41.998933
Double Chex	100	44.33086	Rice Krispies	110	40.560159
Froot Loops	110	32.20758	Shredded Wheat	80	68.235885
Frosted Flakes	110	31.43597	Shredded Wheat 'n'Bran	90	74.472949
Frosted Mini-Wheats	100	58.34514	Shredded Wheat spoon size	90	72.801787
Fruit & Fibre Dates, Walnuts & Oats	120	40.91705	Smacks	110	31.230054
Fruitful Bran	120	41.01549	Special K	110	53.131324
Fruity Pebbles	110	28.02577	Strawberry Fruit Wheats	90	59.363993
Golden Crisp	100	35.25244	Total Corn Flakes	110	38.839746
Golden Grahams	110	23.80404	Total Raisin Bran	140	28.592785
Grape Nuts Flakes	100	52.0769	Total Whole Grain	100	46.658844
Grape-Nuts	110	53.37101	Triples	110	39.106174
Great Grains Pecan	120	45.81172	Trix	110	27.753301
Honey Graham Ohs	120	21.87129	Wheat Chex	100	49.787445
Honey Nut Cheerios	110	31.07222	Wheaties	100	51.592193
Honey-comb	110	28.74241	Wheaties Honey Gold	110	36.187559
Just Right Crunchy Nuggets	110	36.52368			

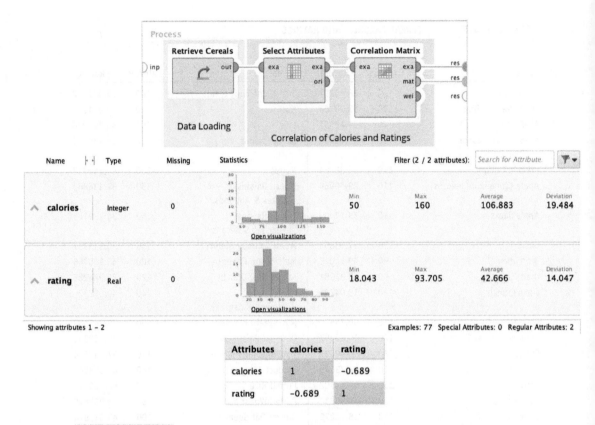

FIGURE 4.7 (TOP) PROCESS FOR CORRELATION ANALYSIS OF *CALORIES* AND *RATING*, (MIDDLE) DESCRIPTIVE STATISTICS, AND (BOTTOM) CORRELATION MATRIX

attributes contain, it might be possible to reduce the two attributes to a single attribute without losing too much information. The idea in PCA is to find a linear combination of the two attributes that contains most, even if not all, of the information so that this new attribute can replace the two original attributes. Information here is in the sense of variability: What can explain the most variability *among* the 77 cereals? The total variability here is the sum of the variances[7] of the two attributes, which in this case is $19.48^2 + 14.05^2 = 576.87$. This means that *calories* accounts for $66\% = 19.48^2/567.87$ of the total variability and *rating* for the remaining 34%. If we drop one of the attributes for the sake of dimension reduction, we lose at least 34% of the total variability. Can we redistribute the total variability between two new attributes in a more polarized way? If so, it might be possible to keep only the one new attribute that (hopefully) accounts for a large portion of the total variation.

Figure 4.8 shows a scatter plot of *rating* vs. *calories*. The line z_1 is the direction in which the variability of the points is largest. It is the line that captures the

---

[7]The variance is the squared standard deviation.

FIGURE 4.8   SCATTER PLOT OF *RATING* VS. *CALORIES* FOR 77 BREAKFAST CEREALS, WITH THE TWO PRINCIPAL COMPONENT DIRECTIONS

most variation in the data if we decide to reduce the dimensionality of the data from two to one. Among all possible lines, it is the line for which, if we project the points in the dataset orthogonally to get a set of 77 (one-dimensional) values, the variance of the z_1 values will be maximum. This is called the *first principal component* (PC). It is also the line that minimizes the sum-of-squared perpendicular distances from the line. The z_2-axis is chosen to be perpendicular to the z_1-axis. In the case of two attributes, there is only one line that is perpendicular to z_1, and it has the second largest variability, but its information is uncorrelated with z_1. This called the *second principal component*. In general, when we have more than two attributes, once we find the direction z_1 with the largest variability, we search among all the orthogonal directions to z_1 for the one with the next-highest variability. That is z_2. The idea is then to find the coordinates of these lines and to see how they redistribute the variability.

Running PCA in RapidMiner is done with the *Principal Component Analysis* operator. Figure 4.9 shows the process, and Figure 4.10 shows the output from running PCA on the two attributes *calories* and *rating*. The *Eigenvectors* table gives the weights that are used to project the original points onto the two new directions. The weights for z_1 are given by $(0.847, -0.532)$, and for z_2 they are given by $(-0.532, -0.847)$. The *Eigenvalues* table gives the reallocated variance: z_1 accounts for 86% of the total variability, and z_2 for the remaining 14%. Therefore, if we drop z_2, we still maintain 86% of the total variability.

The weights are used to compute principal component scores, which are the projected values of *calories* and *rating* onto the new axes (after subtracting the means). The *transform* method of the PCA object can be used to determine the score from the original data. The first column is the projection onto z_1 using

FIGURE 4.9   PROCESS FOR PRINCIPAL COMPONENT ANALYSIS OF *CALORIES* AND *RATING*

FIGURE 4.10   PRINCIPAL COMPONENT ANALYSIS OF *CALORIES* AND *RATING*:
(TOP) EIGENVECTORS TABLE AND (BOTTOM) EIGENVALUES TABLE

the weights $(0.847, -0.532)$. The second column is the projection onto z_2 using the weights $(-0.532, -0.847)$. For example, the first score for the 100% Bran cereal (with 70 calories and a rating of 68.4) is $(0.847)(70 - 106.88) - (0.532)(68.4 - 42.67) = -44.922$.

Note that the means of the new attributes z_1 and z_2 are zero, because we have subtracted the mean of each attribute. The sum of the variances $\text{var}(z_1) + \text{var}(z_2)$ is equal to the sum of the variances of the original attributes, $\text{var}(calories) + \text{var}(rating)$. Furthermore, the variances of z_1 and z_2 are 498 and 79, respectively, so the first principal component, z_1, accounts for 86% of the total variance.

Since it captures most of the variability in the data, it seems reasonable to use one attribute, the first principal score, to represent the two attributes in the original data. Next, we generalize these ideas to more than two attributes.

Principal Components

Let us formalize the procedure described above so that it can easily be generalized to $p > 2$ attributes. Denote the original p attributes by $X_1, X_2, \ldots, X_p$. In PCA, we are looking for a set of new attributes $Z_1, Z_2, \ldots, Z_p$ that are weighted averages of the original attributes (after subtracting their mean):

$$Z_i = a_{i,1}(X_1 - \bar{X}_1) + a_{i,2}(X_2 - \bar{X}_2) + \cdots + a_{i,p}(X_p - \bar{X}_p), \quad i = 1, \ldots, p$$

(4.1)

where each pair of Z's has correlation $= 0$. We then order the resulting Z's by their variance, with Z_1 having the largest variance and Z_p having the smallest variance. The software computes the weights $a_{i,j}$, which are then used in computing the principal component scores.

A further advantage of the principal components compared with the original data is that they are uncorrelated (correlation coefficient $= 0$). If we construct regression models using these principal components as predictors, we will not encounter problems of multicollinearity.

Let us return to the breakfast cereal dataset with all 15 attributes and apply PCA to the 13 numerical attributes. Figure 4.11 shows the process (top left)[8] and the resulting output (top right and bottom). Note that the first three components account for more than 96% of the total variation associated with all 13 of the original attributes. This suggests that we can capture most of the variability in the data with less than 25% of the original dimensions in the data. In fact, the first two principal components alone capture 92.6% of the total variation. However, these results are influenced by the scales of the attributes, as we describe next.

Normalizing the Data

A further use of PCA is to understand the structure of the data. This is done by examining the weights to see how the original attributes contribute to the different principal components. In our example, it is clear that the first principal component is dominated by the sodium content of the cereal: it has the highest (in this case, positive) weight. This means that the first principal component is in fact measuring how much sodium is in the cereal. Similarly, the second principal

---

[8]The operator *Filter Examples* with the parameter *condition class = no_missing_attributes* is used to consider only those records that don't have any missing values. The *Set Role* operator is used to assign the *id* role to the *name* attribute.

Component	Standard Deviation	Proportion of Variance	Cumulative Variance
PC 1	83.764	0.540	0.540
PC 2	70.914	0.387	0.926
PC 3	22.644	0.039	0.966
PC 4	19.181	0.028	0.994
PC 5	8.423	0.005	0.999
PC 6	2.092	0.000	1.000
PC 7	1.699	0.000	1.000
PC 8	0.780	0.000	1.000
PC 9	0.658	0.000	1.000
PC 10	0.370	0.000	1.000
PC 11	0.186	0.000	1.000
PC 12	0.063	0.000	1.000
PC 13	0.000	0.000	1.000

Attribute	PC 1	PC 2	PC 3	PC 4	PC 5	PC 6	PC 7	PC 8	PC 9	PC 10	PC 11	PC 12	PC 13
calories	-0.078	0.009	0.629	0.601	0.455	0.119	0.094	0.026	0.009	0.065	0.009	0.004	0.042
protein	0.001	-0.009	0.001	-0.003	0.056	0.113	0.258	-0.655	-0.202	-0.256	-0.045	-0.005	-0.616
fat	0.000	-0.003	0.016	0.025	-0.016	-0.132	0.373	0.118	0.124	-0.841	-0.062	-0.009	0.318
sodium	-0.980	-0.141	-0.136	0.001	0.014	0.023	0.005	-0.001	-0.004	-0.001	0.000	0.000	0.010
fiber	0.005	-0.031	-0.018	-0.020	0.014	0.263	0.043	0.659	0.227	-0.144	0.021	0.001	-0.648
carbo	-0.017	0.017	0.017	-0.026	0.349	-0.538	-0.672	-0.006	-0.025	-0.300	-0.042	0.014	-0.206
sugars	-0.003	0.000	0.098	0.115	-0.299	0.648	-0.567	-0.103	-0.117	-0.320	-0.028	0.019	0.136
potass	0.135	-0.987	0.037	0.042	-0.047	-0.050	-0.018	-0.015	0.001	0.006	0.000	0.001	0.006
vitamins	-0.094	-0.017	0.692	-0.714	-0.037	0.016	0.012	-0.004	0.012	0.001	-0.002	0.001	0.010
shelf	0.002	-0.004	0.012	-0.006	-0.008	-0.060	0.092	0.328	-0.935	-0.046	0.068	-0.010	0.000
weight	-0.001	-0.001	0.004	0.003	0.003	0.009	-0.024	0.003	0.002	0.006	-0.093	-0.995	0.000
cups	-0.001	0.002	0.001	-0.001	0.002	-0.010	-0.020	-0.062	0.054	-0.080	0.989	-0.092	-0.000
rating	0.075	-0.072	-0.308	-0.335	0.758	0.413	0.018	-0.012	-0.036	-0.023	0.003	0.003	0.188

FIGURE 4.11   (TOP LEFT) PROCESS FOR PCA USING ALL 13 NUMERICAL ATTRIBUTES IN THE BREAKFAST CEREALS DATASET, (TOP RIGHT) REALLOCATED VARIANCE, AND (BOTTOM) ALL 13 PRINCIPAL COMPONENTS

component seems to be measuring the amount of potassium. Since both these attributes are measured in milligrams, whereas the other nutrients are measured in grams, the scale is obviously leading to this result. The variances of potassium and sodium are much larger than the variances of the other attributes, and thus the total variance is dominated by these two variances. A solution is to normalize the data before performing the PCA. Normalization (or standardization) means replacing each original attribute by a standardized version of the variable that has unit variance. This is easily accomplished by dividing each attribute by its standard deviation. The effect of this normalization is to give all attributes equal importance in terms of variability.

When should we normalize the data like this? It depends on the nature of the data. When the units of measurement are common for the attributes (e.g., dollars), and when their scale reflects their importance (sales of jet fuel, sales of heating oil), it is probably best not to normalize (i.e., not to rescale the data so that they have unit variance). If the attributes are measured in different units so that it is unclear how to compare the variability of different variables (e.g., dollars for some, parts per million for others) or if for attributes measured in the same units, scale does not reflect importance (earnings per share, gross revenues), it is generally advisable to normalize. In this way, the differences in units of measurement do not affect the principal components' weights. In the rare situations where we can give relative weights to attributes, we multiply the normalized attributes by these weights before doing the PCA.

Returning to the breakfast cereal data, we normalize the 13 attributes due to the different scales of the attributes, using the *Normalize* operator, and then perform PCA. The output is given in Figure 4.12.

Now we find that we need seven principal components to account for more than 90% of the total variability. The first two principal components account for only 52% of the total variability, and thus reducing the number of attributes to two would mean losing a lot of information. Examining the weights, we see that the first principal component measures the balance between two quantities: (1) calories and cups (large negative weights) vs. (2) protein, fiber, potassium, and consumer rating (large positive weights). High scores on principal component 1 mean that the cereal is low in calories and the amount per bowl while it is high in protein and potassium. Unsurprisingly, this type of cereal is associated with a high consumer rating. The second principal component is most affected by the weight of a serving, and the third principal component by the carbohydrate content. We can continue labeling the next principal components in a similar fashion to learn about the structure of the data.

When the data can be reduced to two dimensions, a useful plot is a scatter plot of the first vs. second principal scores with labels for the observations

Process

Retrieve Cereals — Normalize — Principal Compone...

Data Loadin...

Normalization prior to PCA

Preprocessing

Set Role — Select Attributes

Filter Examples

Component	Standard Deviation	Proportion of Variance	Cumulative Variance
PC 1	1.906	0.280	0.280
PC 2	1.774	0.242	0.522
PC 3	1.382	0.147	0.669
PC 4	1.010	0.078	0.747
PC 5	0.995	0.076	0.823
PC 6	0.850	0.056	0.879
PC 7	0.819	0.052	0.930
PC 8	0.645	0.032	0.962
PC 9	0.562	0.024	0.987
PC 10	0.303	0.007	0.994
PC 11	0.252	0.005	0.999
PC 12	0.139	0.001	1.000
PC 13	?	-0.000	1.000

Attribute	PC 1	PC 2	PC 3	PC 4	PC 5	PC 6	PC 7	PC 8	PC 9	PC 10	PC 11	PC 12	PC 13
calories	-0.300	0.393	0.115	0.204	-0.204	-0.256	0.026	-0.002	-0.030	0.500	-0.214	-0.492	0.234
protein	0.307	0.165	0.277	0.301	-0.320	0.121	-0.283	-0.427	-0.535	-0.022	0.032	0.100	-0.186
fat	-0.040	0.346	-0.205	0.187	-0.587	0.348	0.051	0.063	0.460	-0.145	-0.067	0.291	0.090
sodium	-0.183	0.137	0.389	0.120	0.338	0.664	0.284	0.177	-0.215	-0.001	-0.087	0.054	0.239
fiber	0.453	0.180	0.070	0.039	0.255	0.064	-0.112	0.216	0.244	0.295	-0.531	0.059	-0.442
carbo	-0.192	-0.149	0.562	0.088	-0.183	-0.326	0.260	0.167	0.117	0.241	0.179	0.476	-0.225
sugars	-0.228	0.351	-0.355	-0.023	0.315	-0.152	-0.228	-0.063	-0.225	0.252	-0.003	0.614	0.167
potass	0.402	0.301	0.068	0.091	0.148	0.025	-0.149	0.262	0.167	0.177	0.729	-0.121	0.128
vitamins	-0.116	0.173	0.388	-0.604	0.049	0.129	-0.294	-0.457	0.346	0.052	0.019	-0.000	0.060
shelf	0.171	0.265	-0.002	-0.639	-0.329	-0.052	0.175	0.414	-0.416	-0.046	-0.059	0.017	0.000
weight	-0.050	0.450	0.247	0.153	0.221	-0.399	-0.014	0.075	0.065	-0.692	-0.113	-0.031	0.000
cups	-0.295	-0.212	0.140	0.047	-0.121	0.099	-0.749	0.499	-0.050	-0.077	-0.055	-0.032	-0.000
rating	0.438	-0.252	0.182	0.038	-0.058	-0.186	-0.063	0.015	0.063	0.012	-0.276	0.189	0.743

FIGURE 4.12 (TOP LEFT) PROCESS FOR PCA USING ALL *NORMALIZED* 13 NUMERICAL ATTRIBUTES IN THE BREAKFAST CEREALS DATASET, (TOP RIGHT) REALLOCATED VARIANCE, AND (BOTTOM) ALL 13 PRINCIPAL COMPONENTS

(if the dataset is not too large). To illustrate this, Figure 4.13 displays the first two principal component scores for the breakfast cereals.[9]

We can see that as we move from right (bran cereals) to left, the cereals are less "healthy" in the sense of high calories, low protein and fiber, and so on. Also, moving from bottom to top, we get heavier cereals (moving from puffed rice to raisin bran). These plots are especially useful if interesting clusters of observations can be found. For instance, we see here that children's cereals are close together on the middle-left part of the plot.

Using Principal Components for Classification and Prediction

When the goal of the data reduction is to have a smaller set of attributes that will serve as predictors, we can proceed as follows: apply PCA to the predictors using the training data. Use the output to determine the number of principal components to be retained. The predictors in the model now use the (reduced number of) principal scores columns. For the holdout set, we can use the weights computed from the training data to obtain a set of principal scores by applying the weights to the attributes in the holdout set. These new attributes are then treated as the predictors.

One disadvantage of using a subset of principal components as predictors in a supervised task is that we might lose predictive information that is nonlinear (e.g., a quadratic effect of a predictor on the target attribute or an interaction between predictors). This is because PCA produces linear transformations, thereby capturing linear relationships between the original attributes.

4.9 DIMENSION REDUCTION USING REGRESSION MODELS

In this chapter, we discussed methods for reducing the number of columns using summary statistics, plots, and PCA. All these are considered exploratory methods. Some of them completely ignore the target attribute (e.g., PCA), whereas in other methods we informally try to incorporate the relationship between the predictors and the target attribute (e.g., combining similar categories, in terms of their target attribute behavior). Another approach to reducing the number of predictors, which directly considers the predictive or classification task, is by fitting a regression model. For prediction, a linear regression model is used (see Chapter 6), and for classification, a logistic regression model is used (see Chapter 10). In both cases, we can employ subset selection procedures

---

[9]In RapidMiner, the scatter plot is interactive, i.e., hovering over each data point in the scatter plot shows the cereal name and the first and second principal scores for that data point as a tooltip.

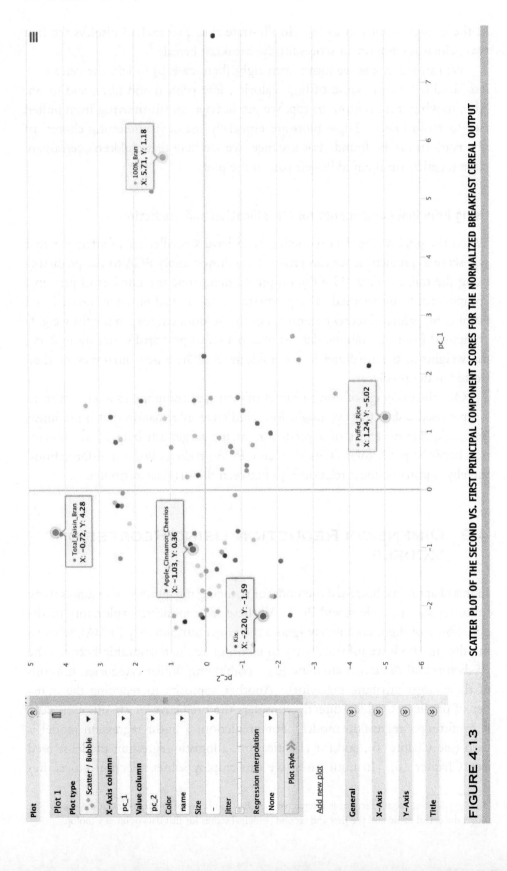

FIGURE 4.13   SCATTER PLOT OF THE SECOND VS. FIRST PRINCIPAL COMPONENT SCORES FOR THE NORMALIZED BREAKFAST CEREAL OUTPUT

that algorithmically choose a subset of predictor attributes among the larger set (see details in the relevant chapters).

Fitted regression models can also be used to further combine similar categories: categories that have coefficients that are not statistically significant (i.e., have a high p-value) can be combined with the reference category, because their distinction from the reference category appears to have no significant effect on the target attribute. Moreover, categories that have similar coefficient values (and the same sign) can often be combined, because their effect on the target attribute is similar. See the example in Chapter 10 on predicting delayed flights for an illustration of how regression models can be used for dimension reduction.

4.10 DIMENSION REDUCTION USING CLASSIFICATION AND REGRESSION TREES

Another method for reducing the number of columns and for combining categories of a categorical attribute is by applying classification and regression trees (see Chapter 9). Classification trees are used for classification tasks and regression trees for prediction tasks. In both cases, the algorithm creates binary splits on the predictors that best classify/predict the class label (e.g., above/below age 30). Although we defer the detailed discussion to Chapter 9, we note here that the resulting tree diagram can be used for determining the important predictors. Predictors (numerical or categorical) that do not appear in the tree can be removed. Similarly, categories that do not appear in the tree can be combined.

PROBLEMS

4.1   **Breakfast Cereals.** Use the data for the breakfast cereals example in Section 4.8 to explore and summarize the data as follows:

    a. Which attributes are quantitative/numerical? Which are nominal?

    b. Compute the mean, median, min, max, and standard deviation for each of the quantitative attributes. This can be done using RapidMiner as shown in Figure 4.1. The median for each attribute can be computed using the *Aggregate* operator.

    c. Plot a histogram for each of the quantitative attributes. Based on the histograms and summary statistics, answer the following questions:

        i. Which attributes have the largest variability?

        ii. Which attributes seem skewed?

        iii. Are there any values that seem extreme?

    d. Plot a side-by-side boxplot comparing the calories in hot vs. cold cereals. What does this plot show us?

    e. Plot a side-by-side boxplot of consumer rating as a function of the shelf height. If we were to predict consumer rating from shelf height, does it appear that we need to keep all three categories of shelf height? (*Hint*: Transform shelf height to a nominal attribute to be able to use it for grouping in a side-by-side boxplot.)

    f. Compute the correlation table along with a heatmap for the quantitative attributes (*Correlation Matrix* operator).

        i. Which pair of attributes is most strongly correlated?

        ii. How can we reduce the number of attributes based on these correlations?

        iii. How would the correlations change if we normalized the data first?

    g. Consider the first principal component (PC) of the analysis of the 13 numerical attributes in Figure 4.11 (bottom). Describe briefly what this PC represents.

4.2   **University Rankings.** The dataset on American college and university rankings (available from www.dataminingbook.com) contains information on 1302 American colleges and universities offering an undergraduate program. For each university, there are 17 measurements that include continuous measurements (such as tuition and graduation rate) and categorical measurements (such as location by state and whether it is a private or a public school).

    a. Remove all categorical attributes (*Hint*: Do not only consider the attributes parsed as Nominal type). Then remove all records with missing numerical measurements from the dataset.

    b. Conduct a principal component analysis on the cleaned data and comment on the results. Should the data be normalized? Discuss what characterizes the components you consider key.

4.3   **Chemical Features of Wine.** Figure 4.14 shows the PCA output on data (non-normalized) in which the attributes represent chemical characteristics of wine, and each case is a different wine.

    a. The data are in the file *Wine.csv*. Observe the Eigenvalues table, and explain why the value for PC1 is so much greater than that of any other column.

    b. Comment on the use of normalization (standardization) in part (a).

Attribute	PC 1	PC 2	PC 3	PC 4	PC 5	PC 6	PC 7
Alcohol	0.002	−0.001	0.017	−0.141	−0.020	−0.194	0.923
Malic_Acid	−0.001	−0.002	0.122	−0.160	0.613	−0.742	−0.150
Ash	0.000	−0.005	0.052	0.010	−0.020	−0.042	0.045
Ash_Alcalinity	−0.005	−0.026	0.939	0.331	−0.064	0.024	0.032
Magnesium	0.018	−0.999	−0.030	0.005	0.006	0.002	0.002
Total_Phenols	0.001	−0.001	−0.040	0.075	−0.315	−0.279	−0.020
Flavanoids	0.002	0.000	−0.085	0.169	−0.525	−0.434	−0.039
Nonflavanoid_Phenols	−0.000	0.001	0.014	−0.011	0.030	0.022	−0.005
Proanthocyanins	0.001	−0.005	−0.025	0.050	−0.251	−0.242	−0.310
Color_Intensity	0.002	−0.015	0.291	−0.879	−0.332	−0.003	−0.113
Hue	0.000	0.001	−0.026	0.060	−0.052	0.024	0.031
OD280_OD315	0.001	0.003	−0.070	0.178	−0.261	−0.289	0.102
Proline	1.000	0.018	0.005	0.003	0.002	0.001	−0.001

Component	Standard Deviation	Proportion of Varian...	Cumulative Variance
PC 1	314.963	0.998	0.998
PC 2	13.135	0.002	1.000
PC 3	3.072	0.000	1.000
PC 4	2.234	0.000	1.000
PC 5	1.109	0.000	1.000
PC 6	0.917	0.000	1.000
PC 7	0.528	0.000	1.000
PC 8	0.389	0.000	1.000
PC 9	0.335	0.000	1.000
PC 10	0.268	0.000	1.000
PC 11	0.194	0.000	1.000
PC 12	0.145	0.000	1.000
PC 13	0.091	0.000	1.000

FIGURE 4.14   PRINCIPAL COMPONENT ANALYSIS OF NONNORMALIZED WINE DATA: (TOP) EIGENVECTORS TABLE (PARTIAL) AND (BOTTOM) EIGENVALUES TABLE

4.4   **Sales of Toyota Corolla Cars.** The file *ToyotaCorolla.csv* contains data on used cars (Toyota Corollas) on sale during late summer of 2004 in the Netherlands. It has 1436 records containing details on 38 attributes, including Price, Age, Kilometers, Horsepower (HP), and other specifications. The goal will be to predict the price of a used Toyota Corolla based on its specifications.

   a. Identify an outlier observation, possibly caused due to a data entry error. This can be done by analyzing the data summary as shown in Figure 4.1. Filter out this observation for the subsequent analysis.

   b. Identify the categorical attributes. (*Hint*: Do not consider just those attributes parsed as Nominal type).

   c. Explain the relationship between a categorical attribute and the series of numeric attributes with dummy coding derived from it.

   d. How many numeric attributes with dummy coding are required to capture the information in a categorical attribute with N categories?

   e. Use RapidMiner to convert the categorical attributes in this dataset into numeric attributes with dummy coding, and explain in words, for one record, the values in the derived numeric dummy attributes.

   f. Use RapidMiner to produce a correlation matrix along with a heatmap. Comment on the relationships among attributes.

PART III

Performance Evaluation

CHAPTER 5

Evaluating Predictive Performance

In this chapter, we discuss how the predictive performance of machine learning methods can be assessed. We point out the danger of overfitting to the training data and the need to test model performance on data that were not used in the training step. We discuss popular performance metrics. For prediction, metrics include average error, mean absolute percentage error (MAPE), and root mean squared error (RMSE) (based on the holdout data). For classification tasks, metrics based on the confusion matrix include overall accuracy, specificity and sensitivity, and metrics that account for misclassification costs. We also show the relation between the choice of threshold value and classification performance and present the receiver operating characteristic (ROC) curve, which is a popular chart for assessing method performance at different threshold values. When the goal is to accurately classify the most interesting or important records, called *ranking*, rather than accurately classify the entire sample (e.g., the 10% of customers most likely to respond to an offer or the 5% of claims most likely to be fraudulent), lift charts are used to assess performance. We also discuss the need for oversampling rare classes and how to adjust performance metrics for the oversampling. Finally, we mention the usefulness of comparing metrics based on the holdout data with those based on the training data for the purpose of detecting overfitting. While some differences are expected, extreme differences can be indicative of overfitting.

5.1 INTRODUCTION

In supervised learning, we are interested in predicting the target attribute (considered a special attribute with the role *label* in RapidMiner) for new records. The target attribute acts as a "supervisor" guiding the machine learning process.

Machine Learning for Business Analytics: Concepts, Techniques and Applications in RapidMiner, First Edition.
Galit Shmueli, Peter C. Bruce, Amit V. Deokar, and Nitin R. Patel

Three main types of outcomes of interest are:

Predicted numerical value: when the target attribute is numerical (e.g., house price)

Predicted class membership: when the target attribute is categorical (e.g., buyer/nonbuyer)

Propensity: the probability of class membership, when the target attribute is categorical (e.g., the propensity to default).

Prediction methods are used for generating numerical predictions, while classification methods ("classifiers") are used for generating propensities and, using a threshold value on the propensities, we can generate predicted class memberships.

A subtle distinction to keep in mind is the two distinct predictive uses of classifiers: one use, *classification*, is aimed at predicting class membership for new records. The other, *ranking*, is detecting among a set of new records the ones most likely to belong to a class of interest.

Let's now examine the approach for judging the usefulness of a prediction method used for generating numerical predictions (Section 5.2), a classifier used for classification (Section 5.3), and a classifier used for ranking (Section 5.4). In Section 5.5, we'll look at evaluating performance under the scenario of oversampling.

5.2 EVALUATING PREDICTIVE PERFORMANCE

First, let us emphasize that predictive accuracy is not the same as goodness of fit. Classical statistical measures of performance are aimed at finding a model that fits well to the data on which the model was trained. In machine learning, we are interested in models that have high predictive accuracy when applied to *new* records. Measures such as R^2 and standard error of estimate are common metrics in classical regression modeling, and residual analysis is used to gauge goodness of fit in that situation. However, these measures do not tell us much about the ability of the model to predict new records.

For assessing prediction performance, several measures are used. In all cases, the measures are based on the holdout set, which serves as a more objective ground than the training set to assess predictive accuracy. This is because records in the holdout set are more similar to the future records to be predicted, in the sense that they are not used to select predictors or to estimate the model parameters. In machine learning, model parameters are learned through the process of model training. Models are trained on the training set and applied to the holdout set, and measures of accuracy then use the prediction errors on that holdout set.

RapidMiner's *Performance (Regression)* operator calculates prediction measures on a labeled dataset that is typically output by the *Apply Model* operator. The computation results are available in the Results view as a Performance Vector (list of performance measures) by connecting the performance output port of the operator to the process output port. For most measures, the mean and the standard deviation values are displayed.

Naive Benchmark: The Average

The benchmark criterion in prediction is using the average target attribute value (thereby ignoring all predictor information). In other words, the prediction for a new record is simply the average across the target attribute values of the records in the training set ($\bar{y}$). This is sometimes called a naive benchmark. Depending on the business context, occasionally it might make sense to use an alternative benchmark value (e.g., when predicting this week's sales, we may use last week's sales as a benchmark). A good predictive model should outperform the benchmark criterion in terms of predictive accuracy.

Prediction Accuracy Measures

The prediction error for record i is defined as the difference between its actual outcome value and its predicted outcome value: $e_i = y_i - \hat{y}_i$. A few popular numerical measures of predictive accuracy are as follows:

MAE (mean absolute error/deviation) = $\frac{1}{n} \sum_{i=1}^{n} |e_i|$. This gives the magnitude of the average absolute error.

Mean error = $\frac{1}{n} \sum_{i=1}^{n} e_i$. This measure is similar to MAE except that it retains the sign of the errors so that negative errors cancel out positive errors of the same magnitude. It therefore gives an indication of whether the predictions are on average over- or underpredicting the target attribute.

MPE (mean percentage error) = $100 \times \frac{1}{n} \sum_{i=1}^{n} e_i/y_i$. This gives the percentage score of how predictions deviate from the actual values (on average), taking into account the direction of the error.

MAPE (mean absolute percentage error) = $100 \times \frac{1}{n} \sum_{i=1}^{n} |e_i/y_i|$. This measure gives a percentage score of how predictions deviate (on average) from the actual values.

RMSE (root mean squared error) = $\sqrt{\frac{1}{n} \sum_{i=1}^{n} e_i^2}$. This is similar to the standard error of estimate in linear regression, except that it is computed on the holdout data rather than on the training data. It has the same units as the target attribute.

In RapidMiner, the *Performance (Regression)* operator computes *absolute error*, and its mean value corresponds to MAE. Similarly, the *relative error* is computed, and its mean value corresponds to MAPE. RMSE is also available as *root mean squared error* in this operator. Error and percentage error can be computed with the *Generate Attributes* operator, and their average values correspond to mean error and MPE, respectively.

Such measures can be used to compare models and to assess their degree of prediction accuracy. Note that all these measures are influenced by outliers. To check outlier influence, we can compute median-based measures (and compare to the above mean-based measures) or simply plot a histogram or boxplot of the errors. Plotting the prediction errors' distribution is in fact very useful and can highlight more information than the metrics alone.

To illustrate the use of predictive accuracy measures and charts of prediction error distribution, consider the charts and error metrics shown in Figures 5.1 and 5.2. These are the result of fitting a certain predictive model to prices of used Toyota Corolla cars.[1] The training set includes 600 cars and the holdout set includes 400 cars. Results are displayed separately for the training and holdout sets. We can see from the histogram and boxplot corresponding to the holdout set that most errors are in the [−2000, 2000] range.

FIGURE 5.1   HISTOGRAMS AND BOXPLOTS OF TOYOTA PRICE PREDICTION ERRORS, FOR TRAINING (LEFT) AND HOLDOUT (RIGHT) SETS

---

[1] The data preprocessing subprocess and other operators in Figure 5.2 (top) are explained in Chapter 6.

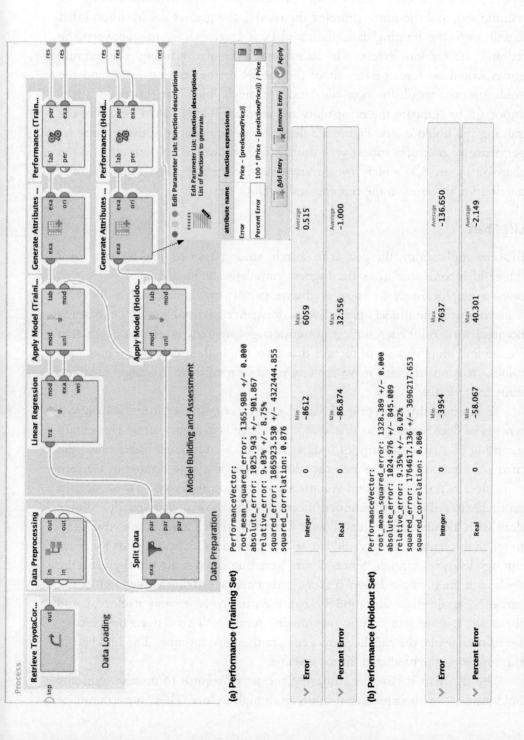

(a) Performance (Training Set)

```
PerformanceVector:
root_mean_squared_error: 1365.988 +/- 0.000
absolute_error: 1025.943 +/- 901.867
relative_error: 9.03% +/- 8.75%
squared_error: 1865923.530 +/- 4322444.855
squared_correlation: 0.876
```

	Min	Max	Average
> Error	Integer	0	-8612	6059	0.515
> Percent Error	Real	0	-86.874	32.556	-1.000

(b) Performance (Holdout Set)

```
PerformanceVector:
root_mean_squared_error: 1328.389 +/- 0.000
absolute_error: 1024.976 +/- 845.009
relative_error: 9.35% +/- 8.02%
squared_error: 1764617.136 +/- 3696217.653
squared_correlation: 0.860
```

	Min	Max	Average
> Error	Integer	0	-3954	7637	-136.650
> Percent Error	Real	0	-58.067	40.301	-2.149

FIGURE 5.2   (TOP) PROCESS FOR TRAINING AND EVALUATING A PREDICTIVE MODEL FOR TOYOTA CAR PRICES AND (BOTTOM) PREDICTION ERROR METRICS FOR TRAINING AND HOLDOUT SETS

Comparing Training and Holdout Performance

Errors that are based on the training set tell us about model fit, whereas those that are based on the holdout set (called "prediction errors") measure the model's ability to predict new data (predictive performance). We expect training errors to be smaller than the holdout errors (because the model was fitted using the training set), and the more complex the model, the greater the likelihood that it will *overfit* the training data (indicated by a greater difference between the training and holdout errors). In an extreme case of overfitting, the training errors would be zero (perfect fit of the model to the training data), and the holdout errors would be non-zero and non-negligible. For this reason, it is important to compare the error plots and metrics (RMSE, MAE, etc.) of the training and holdout sets. Figure 5.2 illustrates this comparison: the training set performance measures appear very similar to those for the holdout set, and the charts in Figure 5.1, which reveal more than the metrics alone, show a similar distribution of errors in the training and holdout sets.

Lift Chart

In some applications, the goal is to search, among a set of new records, for a subset of records that gives the highest cumulative predicted values. In such cases, a graphical way to assess predictive performance is through a *lift chart*. This compares the model's predictive performance to a baseline model that has no predictors. A lift chart for a continuous target attribute is relevant only when we are searching for a set of records that gives the highest cumulative predicted values. It is not relevant if we are interested in predicting the target attribute value for *each* new record.

To illustrate this type of goal, called *ranking*, consider a car rental firm that renews its fleet regularly so that customers drive late-model cars. This entails disposing of a large quantity of used vehicles on a continuing basis. Since the firm is not primarily in the used car sales business, it tries to dispose of as much of its fleet as possible through volume sales to used car dealers. However, it is profitable to sell a limited number of cars through its own channels. Its volume deals with the used car dealers allow it flexibility to pick and choose which cars to sell in this fashion, so it would like to have a model for selecting cars for resale through its own channels. Since all cars were purchased some time ago and the deals with the used car dealers are for fixed prices (specifying a given number of cars of a certain make and model class), the cars' costs are now irrelevant, and the dealer is interested only in maximizing revenue. This is done by selecting for its own resale, the cars likely to generate the most revenue. The lift chart in this case gives the predicted lift for revenue.

The lift chart is based on ordering the set of records of interest (typically holdout data) by their predicted value, from high to low. Then, we accumulate the actual values and plot their cumulative value on the y-axis as a function of the number of records accumulated (the x-axis value). This curve is compared with assigning a naive prediction ($\bar{y}$) to each record and accumulating these average values, which results in a diagonal line. The further away the lift curve is from the diagonal benchmark line, the better the model is doing in separating records with high-value outcomes from those with low-value outcomes. The same information can be presented in a decile lift chart, where the ordered records are grouped into 10 deciles, and for each decile, the chart presents the ratio of model lift to naive benchmark lift.

Figure 5.3 shows a lift chart and decile lift chart based on fitting a linear regression model to the Toyota data.[2,3] The charts are based on the holdout data of 400 cars. It can be seen that the model's predictive performance in terms of lift is better than the baseline model, since its lift curve is higher than that of the baseline model. The lift and decile charts in Figure 5.3 would be useful in the following scenario: choosing the top 10% of the cars that gave the highest predicted sales, for example, we would gain 1.62 times the amount of revenue, compared with choosing 10% of the cars at random. This lift number can also be computed from the lift chart by comparing the sales for 40 random cars (the value of the baseline curve at $x = 40$), which is \$467,195 (= the sum of the actual sales for the 400 holdout set cars divided by 10), with the actual sales of the 40 cars that have the highest predicted values (the value of the lift curve at $x = 40$), which is \$754,717. The ratio between these numbers is 1.62.

5.3 JUDGING CLASSIFIER PERFORMANCE

The need for performance measures arises from the wide choice of classifiers and predictive methods. Not only do we have several different methods, but also even within a single method there are usually many options that can lead to completely different results. A simple example is the choice of predictors used within a particular predictive algorithm. Before we study these various algorithms in detail and face decisions on how to set these options, we need to know how we will measure success.

A natural criterion for judging the performance of a classifier is the probability of making a *misclassification error*. Misclassification means that the record

---

[2] RapidMiner provides the *Lift Chart (Simple)* and *Create Lift Chart* operators for creating lift charts that work with classification problems with categorical target attributes (explained later in this chapter), but not for prediction problems with continuous target attributes. We created a subprocess called *Lift Chart Process*, available through the textbook companion website, that can be used with prediction problems with minor reconfiguration. Note that it requires RapidMiner's *Series* extension. Figure 5.3 is generated using this process.

[3] Figure 5.3 (top) is actually a *cumulative gains chart*, but since RapidMiner refers to such a chart as *lift chart*, we will use the term "lift chart" in this book.

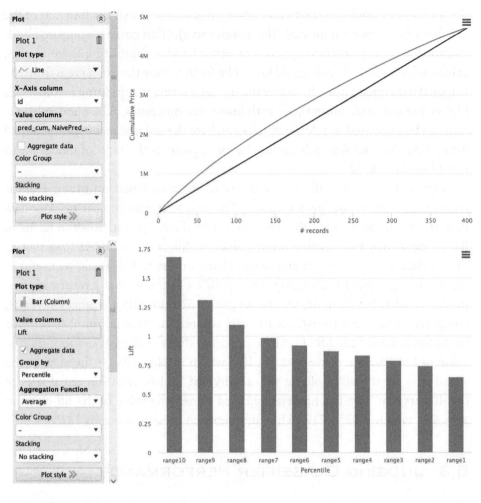

FIGURE 5.3   LIFT CHART (TOP) AND DECILE LIFT CHART (BOTTOM) FOR CONTINUOUS TARGET ATTRIBUTE (SALES OF TOYOTA CARS)

belongs to one class but the model classifies it as a member of a different class. A classifier that makes no errors would be perfect, but we do not expect to be able to construct such classifiers in the real world due to "noise" and not having all the information needed to classify records precisely. Is there a minimal probability of misclassification that we should require of a classifier?

Benchmark: The Naive Rule

A very simple rule for classifying a record into one of m classes, ignoring all predictor information $(x_1, x_2, \ldots, x_p)$ that we may have, is to classify the record as a member of the majority class. In other words, "classify as belonging to the most prevalent class." The *naive rule* is used mainly as a baseline or benchmark for evaluating the performance of more complicated classifiers. Clearly, a classifier that uses external predictor information (on top of the class membership allocation) should outperform the naive rule. There are various performance measures based on the naive rule that measure how much better than the naive rule a certain classifier performs. Similar to using the sample mean ($\bar{y}$) as the naive benchmark in the numerical target attribute case, the naive rule for classification relies solely on the y information and excludes any additional predictor information.

Class Separation

If the classes are well separated by the predictor information, even a small dataset will suffice in finding a good classifier, whereas if the classes are not separated at all by the predictors, even a very large dataset will not help. Figure 5.4 illustrates this for a two-class case. Panel (a) includes a small dataset ($n = 24$ records) where two predictors (income and lot size) are used for separating owners from nonowners (we thank Dean Wichern for this example, described in Johnson and Wichern, 2002). Here, the predictor information seems useful in that it separates the two classes (owners/nonowners). Panel (b) shows a much larger dataset ($n = 5000$ records) where the two predictors (income and monthly average credit card spending) do not separate the two classes well in most of the higher ranges (loan acceptors/nonacceptors).

The Confusion (Classification) Matrix

In practice, most accuracy measures are derived from the *confusion matrix*, also called *classification matrix*. This matrix summarizes the correct and incorrect classifications that a classifier produced for a certain dataset. Rows and columns of the confusion matrix correspond to the predicted and true (actual) classes, respectively. Table 5.1 shows an example of a classification (confusion) matrix for a two-class (0/1) problem resulting from applying a certain classifier to 3000 records. The two diagonal cells (upper left, lower right) give the number of correct classifications, where the predicted class coincides with the actual class of the record. The off-diagonal cells give counts of misclassification. The upper right cell gives the number of class 1 members that were misclassified as 0's (in this example, there were 85 such misclassifications). Similarly, the lower left cell gives the number of class 0 members that were misclassified as 1's (25 such records). In RapidMiner, we can obtain a confusion matrix using the *Performance (Binominal Classification)* operator when the label is of binominal (two-class) type. We will see an example later in this chapter.

The confusion matrix gives estimates of the true classification and misclassification rates. Of course, these are estimates and they can be incorrect, but if we have a large enough dataset and neither class is very rare, our estimates will be

FIGURE 5.4   HIGH (a) AND LOW (b) LEVELS OF SEPARATION BETWEEN TWO CLASSES, USING TWO PREDICTORS

reliable. Sometimes, we may be able to use public data such as US Census data to estimate these proportions. However, in most business settings, we will not know them.

Using the Holdout Data

To obtain an honest estimate of future classification error, we use the confusion matrix that is computed from the *holdout data*. In other words, we first partition the data into training and holdout sets by random selection of records. We then

TABLE 5.1	CONFUSION MATRIX BASED ON 3000 RECORDS AND TWO CLASSES	
	Actual class 0	Actual class 1
Predict 0	2689	85
Predict 1	25	201

construct a classifier using the training data and then apply it to the holdout data. This will yield the predicted classifications for records in the holdout set (see Figure 2.4 in Chapter 2). We then summarize these classifications in a confusion matrix. Although we can summarize our results in a confusion matrix for training data as well, the resulting confusion matrix is not useful for getting an honest estimate of the misclassification rate for new data due to the danger of overfitting.

In addition to examining the holdout data confusion matrix to assess the classification performance on new data, we compare the training data confusion matrix with the holdout data confusion matrix, in order to detect overfitting: although we expect somewhat inferior results on the holdout data, a large discrepancy in training and holdout performance might be indicative of overfitting.

Accuracy Measures

Different accuracy measures can be derived from the classification matrix. Consider a two-class case with classes C_0 and C_1 (e.g., non-buyer/buyer). The schematic confusion matrix in Table 5.2 uses the notation $n_{i,j}$ to denote the number of records that are class C_i members and were classified as C_j members. Of course, if $i \neq j$, these are counts of misclassifications. The total number of records is $n = n_{0,0} + n_{0,1} + n_{1,0} + n_{1,1}$.

TABLE 5.2	CONFUSION MATRIX: MEANING OF EACH CELL	
	Actual class	
	C_0	C_1
Predicted class C_0	$n_{0,0}$ = number of C_0 records classified correctly	$n_{1,0}$ = number of C_1 records classified incorrectly as C_0
C_1	$n_{0,1}$ = number of C_0 records classified incorrectly as C_1	$n_{1,1}$ = number of C_1 records classified correctly

A main accuracy measure is the *estimated misclassification rate*, also called the *overall error rate*. It is given by

$$\text{err} = \frac{n_{1,0} + n_{0,1}}{n},$$

where n is the total number of records in the validation dataset. In the example in Table 5.1, we get err $= (85 + 25)/3000 = 3.67\%$.

We can measure accuracy by looking at the correct classifications—the full half of the cup—instead of the misclassifications. The *overall accuracy* of a classifier is estimated by

$$\text{accuracy} = 1 - \text{err} = \frac{n_{1,1} + n_{0,0}}{n}.$$

In the example, we have $(201 + 2689)/3000 = 96.33\%$.

Propensities and Threshold for Classification

The first step in most classification algorithms is to estimate the probability that a record belongs to each of the classes. These probabilities are also called *propensities* (also called *confidences* in RapidMiner). Propensities are typically used either as an interim step for generating predicted class membership (classification) or for rank-ordering the records by their probability of belonging to a class of interest. Let us consider their first use in this section. The second use is discussed in Section 5.4.

THRESHOLD VALUES FOR TRIAGE

In some cases, it is useful to have two thresholds and allow a "cannot say" option for the classifier. In a two-class situation, this means that for a record, we can make one of three predictions: the record belongs to C_1, or the record belongs to C_0, or we cannot make a prediction because there is not enough information to pick C_1 or C_0 confidently. Records that the classifier cannot classify are subjected to closer scrutiny either by using expert judgment or by enriching the set of predictor variables by gathering additional information that is perhaps more difficult or expensive to obtain. An example is classification of documents found during legal discovery (reciprocal forced document disclosure in a legal proceeding). Under traditional human-review systems, qualified legal personnel are needed to review what might be tens of thousands of documents to determine their relevance to a case. Using a classifier and a triage outcome, documents could be sorted into clearly relevant, clearly not relevant, and the gray area documents requiring human review. This substantially reduces the costs of discovery.

If overall classification accuracy (involving all the classes) is of interest, the record can be assigned to the class with the highest probability. In many contexts, a single class is of special interest, which is also called the *positive class*. So, we will focus on the positive class and compare the propensity of belonging to that class to a *threshold value* (or *cutoff value*) set by the analyst. This approach can be used with two classes or more than two classes, though it may make sense in such cases to consolidate classes so that you end up with two: the class of interest and

TABLE 5.3	24 RECORDS WITH THEIR ACTUAL CLASS AND THE PROBABILITY (PROPENSITY) OF THEM BEING CLASS "OWNER" MEMBERS, AS ESTIMATED BY A CLASSIFIER		

Actual class	Probability of class "owner"	Actual class	Probability of class "owner"
Owner	0.9959	Owner	0.5706
Owner	0.9889	Nonowner	0.4738
Owner	0.9840	Nonowner	0.3382
Owner	0.9770	Nonowner	0.3218
Owner	0.9658	Owner	0.2462
Owner	0.8539	Nonowner	0.1770
Owner	0.7574	Nonowner	0.1270
Nonowner	0.7078	Nonowner	0.0962
Nonowner	0.6515	Nonowner	0.0613
Owner	0.6367	Nonowner	0.0428
Owner	0.6184	Nonowner	0.0354
Owner	0.6071	Nonowner	0.0098

all other classes. If the probability of belonging to the class of interest is above the threshold, the record is assigned to that class.

The default threshold value in two–class classifiers is 0.5. Thus, if the probability of a record being a class C_1 member is greater than 0.5, that record is classified as a C_1. Any record with an estimated probability of less than 0.5 would be classified as a C_0. It is possible, however, to use a threshold that is either higher or lower than 0.5. A threshold greater than 0.5 will end up classifying fewer records as C_1's, whereas a threshold less than 0.5 will end up classifying more records as C_1. Typically, the misclassification rate will rise in either case.

Consider the data in Table 5.3, showing the actual class for 24 records, sorted by the probability that the record is an "owner" (as estimated by a machine learning algorithm). If we adopt the standard 0.5 as the threshold, our misclassification rate is 3/24, whereas if we instead adopt a threshold of 0.25, we classify more records as owners, and the misclassification rate goes up (comprising more nonowners misclassified as owners) to 6/24. Conversely, if we adopt a threshold of 0.75, we classify fewer records as owners. The misclassification rate goes up (comprising more owners misclassified as nonowners) to 5/24. All this can be seen in the classification tables in Figure 5.5 (bottom). Figure 5.5 (top) shows a RapidMiner process for specifying any desired threshold value using the *Create Threshold* and *Apply Threshold* operators.[4]

To see the entire range of threshold values and how the accuracy or misclassification rates change as a function of the threshold, we can plot the performance measure of interest vs. the threshold. The results for the riding-mowers example are shown in Figure 5.6. We can see that the accuracy level is pretty stable around 0.8 for threshold values between 0.2 and 0.8.

---

[4]If the record's propensity of the positive class is greater than the threshold value specified in the *Create Threshold* operator, the prediction is set to the value of the *second class*; otherwise, it is set to the value of the *first class*.

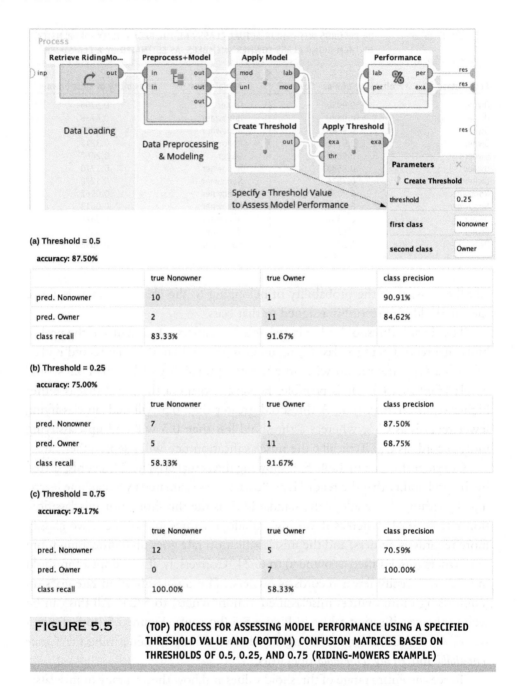

(a) Threshold = 0.5

accuracy: 87.50%

	true Nonowner	true Owner	class precision
pred. Nonowner	10	1	90.91%
pred. Owner	2	11	84.62%
class recall	83.33%	91.67%	

(b) Threshold = 0.25

accuracy: 75.00%

	true Nonowner	true Owner	class precision
pred. Nonowner	7	1	87.50%
pred. Owner	5	11	68.75%
class recall	58.33%	91.67%	

(c) Threshold = 0.75

accuracy: 79.17%

	true Nonowner	true Owner	class precision
pred. Nonowner	12	5	70.59%
pred. Owner	0	7	100.00%
class recall	100.00%	58.33%	

FIGURE 5.5   (TOP) PROCESS FOR ASSESSING MODEL PERFORMANCE USING A SPECIFIED THRESHOLD VALUE AND (BOTTOM) CONFUSION MATRICES BASED ON THRESHOLDS OF 0.5, 0.25, AND 0.75 (RIDING-MOWERS EXAMPLE)

Why would we want to use threshold values different from 0.5 if they increase the misclassification rate? The answer is that it might be more important to classify owners properly than nonowners, and we would tolerate a greater misclassification of the latter.[5] Or the reverse might be true; in other words, the

---

[5] The process shown in Figure 5.5 (top) can be modified to find the "best" threshold value by nesting the operators shown in the pink panel inside the *Optimize Parameters (Grid)* operator and then specifying the performance metric to be optimized in the *Performance (Binominal Classification)* operator. The threshold values to be iterated over are specified in the parameter settings.

FIGURE 5.6   **PLOTTING ACCURACY AND OVERALL ERROR (CLASSIFICATION ERROR) AS A FUNCTION OF THE THRESHOLD VALUE (RIDING-MOWERS EXAMPLE)**

costs of misclassification might be asymmetric. We can adjust the threshold value in such a case to classify more records as the high-value class, that is, accept more misclassifications where the misclassification cost is low. Keep in mind that we are doing so after the machine learning model has already been selected—we are not changing that model. It is also possible to incorporate costs into the picture before deriving the model. These subjects are discussed in greater detail below.

Performance in Case of Unequal Importance of Classes

Suppose that it is more important to predict membership correctly in class C_1 than in class C_0. An example is predicting the financial status (bankrupt/solvent) of firms. It may be more important to predict correctly a firm that is going bankrupt than to predict correctly a firm that is going to remain solvent. The classifier is essentially used as a system for detecting or signaling bankruptcy. In such a case, the overall accuracy is not a good measure for evaluating the classifier. Suppose that the important (positive) class is C_1. The following pair of accuracy measures are the most popular:

> The **sensitivity** (also termed **recall**) of a classifier is its ability to correctly detect all the important class members. This is measured by $n_{1,1}/(n_{1,1} + n_{1,0})$, the percentage of C_1 (positive) members that are correctly classified. Sensitivity is also called the *True Positive Rate (TPR)*.

> The **specificity** of a classifier is its ability to rule out C_0 (negative class) members correctly. This is measured by $n_{0,0}/(n_{0,1} + n_{0,0})$, the percentage of C_1 (negative) members that are correctly classified. Specificity is also called the *True Negative Rate (TNR)*.

It can be useful to plot these measures against the threshold value in order to find a threshold value that balances these measures.

ROC Curve A more popular method for plotting the two measures is through *ROC* (receiver operating characteristic) *curves*. Starting from the lower left, the ROC curve plots the pairs {sensitivity, specificity} as the threshold value descends from 1 to 0. (A typical alternative presentation is to plot 1-specificity on the x-axis, which allows 0 to be placed on the left end of the axis and 1 on the right.) Better performance is reflected by curves that are closer to the top-left corner. The comparison curve is the diagonal, which reflects the average performance of a guessing classifier that has no information about the predictors or target attribute. This guessing classifier guesses that a proportion α of the records is 1's and therefore assigns each record an equal probability $P(Y = 1) = \alpha$. In this case, on average, a proportion α of the 1's will be correctly classified (Sensitivity = α), and a proportion α of the 0s will be correctly classified ($1 - $ Specificity = α). As we increase the threshold value $1 - \alpha$ from 0 to 1, we get the diagonal line Sensitivity = $1 -$ Specificity. Note that the naive rule is one point on this diagonal line, where α = proportion of actual 1's.

A common metric to summarize an ROC curve is "area under the curve (AUC)," which ranges from 1 (perfect discrimination between classes) to 0.5 (no better than random guessing). AUC is commonly used to compare models, especially when there are many models and algorithms under consideration. It has the advantage of simplicity and can be compared across datasets with different positive class rates. However, the AUC has several critical deficiencies. For example, some areas of the ROC curve are irrelevant (e.g., if extremely low sensitivity is unacceptable). Second, when ROC curves of different models cross, AUC comparisons can be misleading: a larger AUC value might correspond to poorer performance over almost the entire range of threshold values (Hand, 2009). For further issues, see Lobo et al. (2008). We therefore advocate not using AUC as a single performance metric for selecting a model.

The ROC curve for the owner/nonowner example and its corresponding AUC, generated using RapidMiner's *Performance (Binominal Classification)* operator, are shown in Figure 5.7. The red curve shows the ROC curve, while the blue curve shows the corresponding threshold values.[6]

Precision and Recall In addition to sensitivity and specificity, there is another performance measure called *precision* that is often considered in tandem with recall (sensitivity):

The **precision** of a classifier is its ability to correctly detect only the important (positive) class members. This is measured by $n_{1,1}/(n_{1,1} + n_{0,1})$, the

---

[6]For any point on the ROC curve (red), to find the corresponding threshold value, drop a vertical line from that point on to the blue curve. Then, read the threshold value off of the y-axis.

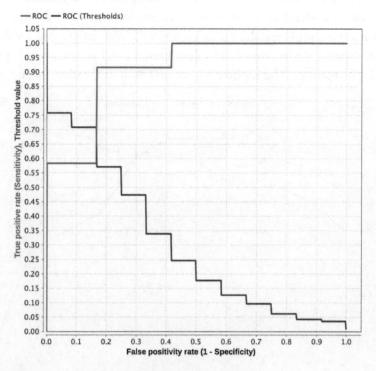

AUC: 0.910 (positive class: Owner)

FIGURE 5.7   **ROC CURVE FOR RIDING-MOWERS EXAMPLE**

percentage of correctly classified positive (C_1) members among all those classified as positive.

For a two-class classifier, there tends to be a tradeoff between precision and recall. While precision is a measure of *exactness* (what percentage of members classified as C_1 actually belong to C_1), recall is a measure of *completeness* (what percentage of C_1 members are classified as such). Depending on the business context, precision may be more important than recall, and vice versa. For example, for credit card fraud detection (positive class = fraudulent), we would want recall close to 1 since we want to find *all* transactions that are truly fraudulent, and we can accept low precision (mistakenly classifying non-fraudulent transactions as fraudulent) if the cost of such misclassification is not too high. The threshold value can be selected based on whether precision or recall is a more important consideration.

A metric called *F1-score* (referred to as *f-measure* in RapidMiner) is used to combine precision and recall values into a single measure, giving them equal weights. F1-score is given by

$$\frac{2 \times \text{precision} \times \text{recall}}{(\text{precision} + \text{recall})}.$$

We can plot precision, recall, and F1–score against the threshold to see the precision–recall tradeoff as a function of threshold values. The results for the riding-mowers example are shown in Figure 5.8. We can see that recall is relatively stable around 0.9 for threshold values between 0.2 and 0.6, while precision is generally increasing. The highest F1–score 0.88 is at threshold value of 0.5.

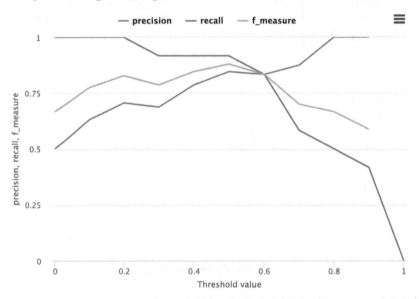

FIGURE 5.8   **PRECISION, RECALL, AND F1-SCORE AS A FUNCTION OF THE THRESHOLD VALUE**

COMPUTING RATES: FROM WHOSE POINT OF VIEW?

Sensitivity and specificity measure the performance of a classifier from the point of view of the "classifying agency" (e.g., a company classifying customers or a hospital classifying patients). They answer the question: "how well does the classifier segregate the important class members?" It is also possible to measure accuracy from the perspective of the entity being classified (e.g., the customer or the patient), who asks "given my predicted class, what is my chance of actually belonging to that class?" The terms "false discovery rate" and "false omission rate" are measures of performance from the perspective of the individual entity. If C_1 is the important (positive) class, then they are defined as follows:

The false discovery rate (FDR) or *fallout* is the proportion of C_1 predictions that are wrong, equal to $n_{0,1}/(n_{1,1} + n_{0,1})$. Note that this is a ratio within the row of C_1 predictions (i.e., it uses only records that were classified as C_1).

The false omission rate (FOR) is the proportion of C_0 predictions that are wrong, equal to $n_{1,0}/(n_{1,0} + n_{0,0})$. Note that this is a ratio within the row of C_0 predictions (that is, it uses only records that were classified as C_0).

Asymmetric Misclassification Costs

Implicit in our discussion of the lift curve, which measures how effective we are in identifying the members of one particular class, is the assumption that the error of misclassifying a record belonging to one class is more serious than for the other class. For example, misclassifying a household as unlikely to respond to a sales offer when it belongs to the class that would respond incurs a greater cost (the opportunity cost of the foregone sale) than the converse error. In the former case, you are missing out on a sale worth perhaps tens or hundreds of dollars. In the latter, you are incurring the costs of contacting someone who will not purchase. In such a scenario, using the misclassification rate as a criterion can be misleading.

Note that we are assuming that the cost (or benefit) of making correct classifications is zero. At first glance, this may seem incomplete. After all, the benefit (negative cost) of classifying a buyer correctly as a buyer would seem substantial. Also, in other circumstances (e.g., using our classification algorithm to score fresh data to implement our decisions), it will be appropriate to consider the actual net dollar impact of each possible classification (or misclassification). Here, however, we are attempting to assess the value of a classifier in terms of classification error, so it greatly simplifies matters if we can capture all cost/benefit information in the misclassification cells. So, instead of recording the benefit of classifying a respondent household correctly, we record the cost of failing to classify it as a respondent household. It amounts to the same thing, and our goal becomes the minimization of costs, whether the costs are actual costs or missed benefits (opportunity costs).

Consider the situation where the sales offer is mailed to a random sample of people for the purpose of constructing a good classifier. Suppose that the offer is accepted by 1% of those households. For these data, if a classifier simply classifies every household as a non-responder, it will have an error rate of only 1% but it will be useless in practice. A classifier that misclassifies 2% of buying households as nonbuyers and 20% of the nonbuyers as buyers would have a higher error rate but would be better if the profit from a sale is substantially higher than the cost of sending out an offer. In these situations, if we have estimates of the cost of both types of misclassification, we can use the confusion matrix to compute the expected cost of misclassification for each record in the holdout data. This enables us to compare different classifiers using overall expected costs (or profits) as the criterion.

Suppose that we are considering sending an offer to 1000 more people, where on average 1% of whom respond (1). Naively classifying everyone as a 0 has an error rate of only 1%. Using a machine learning process, suppose that we can produce these classifications:

	Actual class 0	Actual class 1
Predict 0	970	2
Predict 1	20	8

These classifications have an error rate of $100 \times (20 + 2)/1000 = 2.2\%$—higher than the naive rate.

Now suppose that the profit from a responder is $10 and the cost of sending the offer is $1. Classifying everyone as a 0 still has a misclassification rate of only 1%, but yields a profit of $0. Using the machine learning process, despite the higher misclassification rate, yields a profit of $60.

The matrix of profit is as follows (nothing is sent to the predicted 0's so there are no costs or sales in that row):

Profit	Actual class 0	Actual class 1
Predict 0	0	0
Predict 1	– $20	$80

Looked at purely in terms of costs, when everyone is classified as a 0, there are no costs of sending the offer; the only costs are the opportunity costs of failing to make sales to the ten 1's = $100. The cost (actual costs of sending the offer, plus the opportunity costs of missed sales) of using the machine learning process to select people to send the offer to is only $48:

Costs	Actual class 0	Actual class 1
Predict 0	0	$20
Predict 1	$20	$8

However, this does not improve the actual classifications themselves. A better method is to change the classification rules (and hence the misclassification rates) as discussed in the preceding section, to reflect the asymmetric costs.

A popular performance measure that includes costs is the *average misclassification cost*, which measures the average cost of misclassification per classified record.[7] Denote by q_1 the cost of misclassifying a class C_1 record (as belonging

---

[7]RapidMiner's *Performance (Costs)* operator can be used to compute misclassification costs for a specified cost matrix.

to class C_0) and by q_0 the cost of misclassifying a class C_0 record (as belonging to class C_1). The average misclassification cost is

$$\frac{q_1 n_{1,0} + q_0 n_{0,1}}{n}.$$

Thus, we are looking for a classifier that minimizes this quantity. This can be computed, for instance, for different threshold values.

It turns out that the optimal parameters are affected by the misclassification costs only through the ratio of these costs. This can be seen if we write the foregoing measure slightly differently:

$$\frac{q_1 n_{1,0} + q_0 n_{0,1}}{n} = \frac{n_{1,0}}{n_{1,1} + n_{1,0}} \frac{n_{1,1} + n_{1,0}}{n} q_1 + \frac{n_{0,1}}{n_{0,1} + n_{0,0}} \frac{n_{0,1} + n_{0,0}}{n} q_0.$$

Minimizing this expression is equivalent to minimizing the same expression divided by a constant. If we divide by q_1, it can be seen clearly that the minimization depends only on q_0/q_1 and not on their individual values. This is very practical, because in many cases it is difficult to assess the costs associated with misclassifying a C_1 member and a C_0 member, but estimating the ratio is easier.

This expression is a reasonable estimate of future misclassification cost if the proportions of classes C_1 and C_0 in the sample data are similar to the proportions of classes C_1 and C_0 that are expected in the future. If, instead of a random sample, we draw a sample such that one class is oversampled (as described in the next section), then the sample proportions of C_1's and C_0's will be distorted compared with the future or population. We can then correct the average misclassification cost measure for the distorted sample proportions by incorporating estimates of the true proportions (from external data or domain knowledge), denoted by $p(C_1)$ and $p(C_0)$, into the formula

$$\frac{n_{1,0}}{n_{1,1} + n_{1,0}} p(C_1) q_1 + \frac{n_{0,1}}{n_{0,1} + n_{0,0}} p(C_0) q_0.$$

Using the same logic as above, it can be shown that optimizing this quantity depends on the costs only through their ratio (q_0/q_1) and on the prior probabilities only through their ratio $[p(C_0)/p(C_1)]$. This is why software packages that incorporate costs and prior probabilities might prompt the user for ratios rather than actual costs and probabilities.

Generalization to More Than Two Classes

All the comments made above about two-class classifiers extend readily to classification into more than two classes. Let us suppose that we have m classes $C_1, C_2, \ldots, C_m$. The confusion matrix has m rows and m columns. The misclassification cost associated with the diagonal cells is, of course, always zero. Incorporating prior probabilities of the various classes (where now we have m such numbers) is still done in the same manner. However, evaluating misclassification costs becomes much more complicated: for an m-class case, we have $m(m-1)$ types of misclassifications. Constructing a matrix of misclassification costs thus becomes prohibitively complicated.

5.4 JUDGING RANKING PERFORMANCE

We now turn to the predictive goal of detecting, among a set of new records, the ones most likely to belong to a class of interest. Recall that this differs from the goal of predicting class membership for each new record.

Lift Charts for Binary Data

We already introduced lift charts in the context of a numerical outcome (Section 5.2). We now describe lift charts, also called *lift curves, gains curves,* or *gains charts,* for a binary outcome. This is a more common usage than for predicted continuous outcomes. The lift chart helps us determine how effectively we can "skim the cream" by selecting a relatively small number of records and getting a relatively large portion of the responders. The input required to construct a lift chart is a holdout dataset that has been "scored" by appending to each record the propensity (confidence) that it will belong to a given class.

Let's continue with the case in which a particular class is relatively rare and of much more interest than the other class: tax cheats, debt defaulters, or responders to a mailing. We would like our classification model to sift through the records and sort them according to which ones are most likely to be tax cheats, responders to the mailing, and so on. We can then make more informed decisions. For example, we can decide how many and which tax returns to examine if looking for tax cheats. The model will give us an estimate of the extent to which we will encounter more and more non-cheaters as we proceed through the sorted data starting with the records most likely to be tax cheats. Or we can use the sorted data to decide to which potential customers a limited-budget mailing should be targeted. In other words, we are describing the case when our goal is to obtain a rank ordering among the records according to their class membership propensities.

TABLE 5.4	RECORDS SORTED (HIGH TO LOW) BY PROPENSITY OF OWNERSHIP FOR THE MOWER EXAMPLE (PROPENSITIES = "CONFIDENCE VALUES")		
Obs	Propensity of 1	Actual class	Cumulative actual class
1	0.995878736	1	1
2	0.988923857	1	2
3	0.983964725	1	3
4	0.977001941	1	4
5	0.965836468	1	5
6	0.853925069	1	6
7	0.757405588	1	7
8	0.707844886	0	7
9	0.651520021	0	7
10	0.636720244	1	8
11	0.618440668	1	9
12	0.607053621	1	10
13	0.570624041	1	11
14	0.473775468	0	11
15	0.338220430	0	11
16	0.321829297	0	11
17	0.246205114	1	12
18	0.176997864	0	12
19	0.127035768	0	12
20	0.096216296	0	12
21	0.061262671	0	12
22	0.042799852	0	12
23	0.035405521	0	12
24	0.009795937	0	12

Sorting by Propensity (Confidence)   To construct a lift chart, we sort the set of records by propensity, in descending order. This is the propensity to belong to the important *positive* class, say, C_1. Then, in each row, we compute the cumulative number of C_1 members (Actual Class = C_1). For example, Table 5.4 shows the 24 records ordered in descending class "1" propensity. The right-most column accumulates the number of actual 1's.[8] The lift chart then plots this cumulative column against the number of records, as shown in the lift chart in Figure 5.9.

Interpreting the Lift Chart   What is considered good or bad performance? The ideal ranking performance would place all the 1's at the beginning (the actual 1's would have the highest propensities and be at the top of the table)

---

[8]In RapidMiner, cumulative sum of a numeric attribute can be computed using the *Integrate* operator available in the *Series* extension.

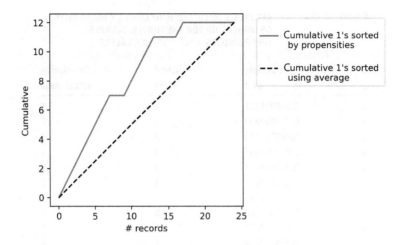

FIGURE 5.9   LIFT CHART FOR THE MOWER EXAMPLE

and all the 0's at the end. A lift chart corresponding to this ideal case would be a diagonal line with slope 1 which turns into a horizontal line (once all the 1's were accumulated). In the example, the lift curve for the best possible classifier—a classifier that makes no errors—would overlap the existing curve at the start, continue with a slope of 1 until it reached all the twelve 1's, and then continue horizontally to the right.

In contrast, a useless model would be one that randomly assigns propensities (shuffling the 1's and 0's randomly in the Actual Class column). Such behavior would increase the cumulative number of 1's, on average, by $\frac{\#1's}{n}$ in each row. In fact, this is the diagonal dotted line joining the points $(0,0)$ to $(24,12)$ seen in Figure 5.9. This serves as a reference line. For any given number of records (the x-axis value), it represents the expected number of 1 classifications (=gains) if we did not have a model but simply selected records at random. It provides a benchmark against which we can evaluate the ranking performance of the model. In this example, although our model is not perfect, it seems to perform much better than the random benchmark.

How do we read a lift chart? For a given number of records (x-axis), the lift curve value on the y-axis tells us how much better we are doing compared with random assignment. For example, looking at Figure 5.9, if we use our model to choose the top 10 records, the lift curve tells us that we would be right for about eight of them. If we simply select 10 records at random, we expect to be right for $10 \times 12/24 = 5$ records. In terms of lift, the model gives us a "lift" in detecting class 1 members of $8/5 = 1.6$. The lift will vary with the number of records we choose to act on. A good classifier will give us a high lift when we act on only a few records. As we include more records, the lift will typically decrease.

FIGURE 5.10   DECILE LIFT CHART FOR THE MOWERS EXAMPLE

Decile Lift Charts

The information from the lift chart can be portrayed as a *decile lift chart*, as shown in Figure 5.10, which is widely used in direct marketing predictive modeling. The decile lift chart aggregates all the lift information into 10 buckets. The bars show the percentage of records that are ranked by the model as "the most probable 1's" in each decile. The orange curve superimposed on the bars shows the cumulative percentage of actual 1's predicted as such by the model (called *cumulative gains*). Based on this curve, we can determine the factor (lift) by which our model outperforms a random assignment of 0's and 1's, taking one decile at a time. We see that taking 10% of the records that are ranked by the model as "the most probable 1's" (having the highest propensities) yields 25%/10% = 2.5 times as many 1's as would a random selection of 10% of the records. In this example, the decile lift chart indicates that we can even use the model to select the top 40% records with the highest propensities and still perform almost twice as well as random.

In RapidMiner, the decile lift chart can be generated with the *Lift Chart (Simple)* operator.[9] The operator requires the model and the data as inputs, in addition to specifying the *target class* as its parameter. While lift charts can be constructed for both training and holdout data, the lift chart based on the holdout data is a better estimator of performance for new records.

---

[9]RapidMiner also has the *Create Lift Chart* operator that automatically bins the propensities on the x-axis and shows counts and percentages as two y-axes.

Beyond Two Classes

A lift chart cannot be used with a multiclass classifier unless a single "important class" is defined and the classifications are reduced to "important" and "unimportant" classes (or, equivalently, *positive* and *negative* classes).

Lift Charts Incorporating Costs and Benefits

When the benefits and costs of correct and incorrect classifications are known or can be estimated, the lift chart is still a useful presentation and decision tool. As before, we need a classifier that assigns to each record a propensity that it belongs to a particular class. The procedure is then as follows:

1. Sort the records in descending order of predicted probability of success (where *success* = belonging to the class of interest).
2. For each record, record the cost (benefit) associated with the actual outcome.
3. For the highest propensity (i.e., first) record, its x-axis value is 1, and its y-axis value is its cost or benefit (computed in Step 2) on the lift curve.
4. For the next record, again calculate the cost (benefit) associated with the actual outcome. Add this to the cost (benefit) for the previous record. This sum is the y-axis coordinate of the second point on the lift curve. Its x-axis value is 2.
5. Repeat Step 4 until all records have been examined. Connect all the points, and this is the lift curve.
6. The reference line is a straight line from the origin to the point y = total net benefit and $x = n$ (n = number of records).

Note: It is entirely possible for a reference line that incorporates costs and benefits to have a negative slope if the net value for the entire dataset is negative. For example, if the cost of mailing to a person is \$0.65, the value of a responder is \$25, and the overall response rate is 2%, the expected net value of mailing to a list of 10,000 is $(0.02 \times \$25 \times 10,000) - (\$0.65 \times 10,000) = \$5000 - \$6500 = -\$1500$. Hence, the y-value at the far right of the lift curve ($x = 10,000$) is -1500, and the slope of the reference line from the origin will be negative. The optimal point will be where the lift curve is at a maximum (i.e., mailing to about 3000 people) in Figure 5.11.

Lift as a Function of Threshold

We could also plot the lift as a function of the threshold value. The only difference is the scale on the x-axis. When the goal is to select the top records based on a certain budget, the lift vs. number of records is preferable. In contrast, when

Reference line has negative slope

$1500

3000

10,000

$ −1500

FIGURE 5.11   **LIFT CURVE INCORPORATING COSTS**

the goal is to find a threshold that distinguishes well between the two classes, the lift vs. threshold value is more useful.

5.5 OVERSAMPLING

As we saw briefly in Chapter 2, when classes are present in very unequal proportions, simple random sampling may produce too few of the rare class to yield useful information about what distinguishes them from the dominant class. In such cases, stratified sampling is often used to oversample the records from the rarer class and improve the performance of classifiers. It is often the case that the rarer events are the more interesting or important ones: responders to a mailing, those who commit fraud, defaulters on debt, and the like. This same stratified sampling procedure is sometimes called *weighted sampling* or *undersampling* , the latter referring to the fact that the more plentiful class is undersampled, relative to the rare class. We shall stick to the term *oversampling*.

> In all discussions of *oversampling*, we assume the common situation in which there are two classes, one of much greater interest than the other. Data with more than two classes do not lend themselves to this procedure.

Consider the data in Figure 5.12, where × represents non–responders and ○, responders. The two axes correspond to two predictors. The dashed vertical line does the best job of classification under the assumption of equal costs: it results in just one misclassification (one ○ is misclassified as an ×). If we incorporate more realistic misclassification costs—let's say that failing to catch a o is five times as costly as failing to catch an ×—the costs of misclassification jump to 5. In such a case, a horizontal line as shown in Figure 5.13 does a better job: it results in misclassification costs of just 2.

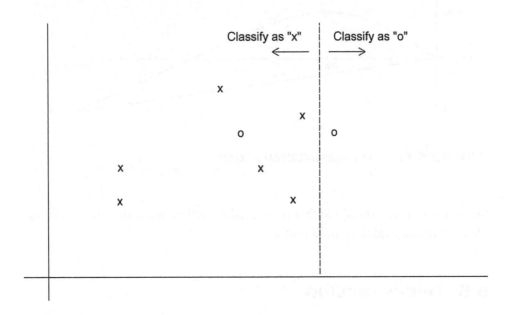

FIGURE 5.12   CLASSIFICATION ASSUMING EQUAL COSTS OF MISCLASSIFICATION

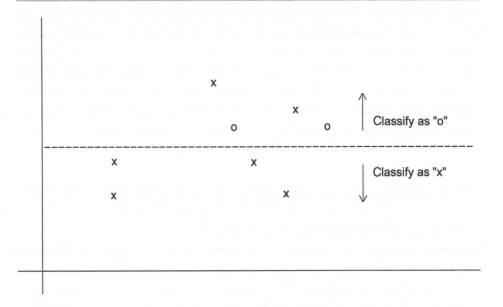

FIGURE 5.13   CLASSIFICATION ASSUMING UNEQUAL COSTS OF MISCLASSIFICATION

Oversampling is one way of incorporating these costs into the training process. In Figure 5.14, we can see that classification algorithms would automatically determine the appropriate classification line if four additional o's were present at each existing o. We can achieve appropriate results either by taking five times as many o's as we would get from simple random sampling (by sampling with replacement if necessary) or by replicating the existing o's fourfold.

Oversampling without replacement in accord with the ratio of costs (the first option above) is the optimal solution, but may not always be practical. There may not be an adequate number of responders to assure that there will be enough of them to fit a model if they constitute only a small proportion of the total. Also, it is often the case that our interest in discovering responders is known to be much greater than our interest in discovering non-responders, but the exact ratio of costs is difficult to determine. When faced with very low response rates in a classification problem, practitioners often sample equal numbers of responders and non-responders as a relatively effective and convenient approach.

In RapidMiner, the *Sample* operator can be used to specify different sampling rates for each class with its *balance data* parameter, thus allowing the majority class to be undersampled appropriately. Alternatively, the *Sample (Balance)* operator in the Mannheim RapidMiner Toolbox extension can also be used for balancing the data by oversampling the rare class records (by replication) or downsampling from the majority class.

Sometimes, an algorithmic approach may be considered for oversampling the rare class to match the number of majority class records. For example,

FIGURE 5.14   CLASSIFICATION USING OVERSAMPLING TO ACCOUNT FOR UNEQUAL COSTS

the *SMOTE Upsampling* operator from RapidMiner's *Operator Toolbox* extension implements the SMOTE (Synthetic Minority Over-sampling Technique) proposed by Chawla et al. (2002). This technique involves synthetically generating records for the minority class. First, a record from the rare class is randomly selected, and k samples similar to it are found using the k-nearest-neighbors algorithm (see Chapter 7). One of these neighbors is selected, and then synthetic records are generated through a combination of these two records.

Finally, RapidMiner also provides the *Generate Weight (Stratification)* operator that assigns weights to each record based on the class proportions. These weights may be then used along with the data in some machine learning models.

Whatever approach is used, when it comes time to assess and predict model performance, we will need to adjust for the oversampling in one of two ways:

1. Score the model to a holdout set that has been selected without oversampling (i.e., via simple random sampling), or

2. Score the model to an oversampled holdout set, and reweight the results to remove the effects of oversampling.

The first method is more straightforward and easier to implement. We describe how to oversample and how to evaluate performance for each of the two methods.

> When classifying data with very low response rates, practitioners typically:
> - train models on data that are 50% responder and 50% non-responder
> - validate the models with an unweighted (simple random) sample from the original data.

Creating an Over-sampled Training Set

How is weighted sampling done? When responders are sufficiently scarce that you will want to use all of them, one common procedure is as follows:

1. The response and non-response data are separated into two distinct sets, or *strata*.

2. Records are then randomly selected for the training set from each stratum. Typically, one might select half the (scarce) responders for the training set and then an equal number of non-responders.

3. The remaining responders are put in the validation set.

4. Non-responders are randomly selected for the validation set in sufficient numbers to maintain the original ratio of responders to non-responders.

5. If a holdout set is required, it can be taken randomly from the validation set.

Evaluating Model Performance Using a Non-oversampled Holdout Set

Although the oversampled data can be used to train models, they are often not suitable for evaluating model performance, because the number of responders will (of course) be exaggerated. The most straightforward way of gaining an unbiased estimate of model performance is to apply the model to regular data (i.e., data not oversampled). In short, train the model on oversampled data, but validate it with regular data.

Evaluating Model Performance if Only Oversampled Holdout Set Exists

In some cases, very low response rates may make it more practical to use over-sampled data not only for the training data but also for the holdout data. This might happen, for example, if an analyst is given a dataset for exploration and prototyping that is already oversampled to boost the proportion with the rare response of interest (perhaps because it is more convenient to transfer and work with a smaller dataset). In such cases, it is still possible to assess how well the model will do with real data, but this requires the oversampled holdout set to be reweighted, in order to restore the class of records that were underrepresented in the sampling process. This adjustment should be made to the confusion matrix and to the lift chart in order to derive good accuracy measures. These adjustments are described next.

I. Adjusting the Confusion Matrix for Oversampling   Suppose that the response rate in the data as a whole is 2% and that the data were oversampled, yielding a sample in which the response rate is 25 times higher (50% responders). The relationship is as follows:

Responders: 2% of the whole data; 50% of the sample

Non-responders: 98% of the whole data, 50% of the sample

Each responder in the whole data is worth 25 responders in the sample (50/2). Each non-responder in the whole data is worth 0.5102 non-responders in the sample (50/98). We call these values *oversampling weights*.

Assume that the holdout confusion matrix looks like this.

CONFUSION MATRIX, OVERSAMPLED DATA (HOLDOUT)

	Actual 0	Actual 1	Total
Predicted 0	390	80	470
Predicted 1	110	420	530
Total	500	500	1000

At this point, the misclassification rate appears to be $(80 + 110)/1000 = 19\%$, and the model ends up classifying 53% of the records as 1's. However, this reflects the performance on a sample where 50% are responders.

To estimate predictive performance when this model is used to score the original population (with 2% responders), we need to undo the effects of the oversampling. The actual number of responders must be divided by 25, and the actual number of non-responders divided by 0.5102:

The revised confusion matrix is as follows:

CONFUSION MATRIX, REWEIGHTED

	Actual 0	Actual 1	Total
Predicted 0	$390/0.5102 = 764.4$	$80/25 = 3.2$	
Predicted 1	$110/0.5102 = 215.6$	$420/25 = 16.8$	
Total	980	20	1000

The adjusted misclassification rate is $(3.2 + 215.6)/1000 = 21.9\%$. The model ends up classifying $(215.6 + 16.8)/1000 = 23.24\%$ of the records as 1's, when we assume 2% responders.

II. Adjusting the Lift Chart for Oversampling   The lift chart is likely to be more useful measures in low-response situations, where our interest lies not so much in classifying all the records correctly as in finding a model that guides us toward those records most likely to contain the response of interest (under the assumption that scarce resources preclude examining or contacting all the records). Typically, our interest in such a case is in maximizing value or minimizing cost, so we will show the adjustment process incorporating the benefit/cost element. The following procedure can be used:

1. Sort the holdout records in order of the predicted probability of success (where success = belonging to the class of interest).

2. For each record, record the cost (benefit) associated with the actual outcome.

3. Divide that value by the oversampling rate. For example, if responders are overweighted by a factor of 25, divide by 25.

4. For the highest probability (i.e., first) record, the value above is the y-coordinate of the first point on the lift curve. The x-coordinate is index number 1.

5. For the next record, again calculate the adjusted value associated with the actual outcome. Add this to the adjusted cost (benefit) for the previous

record. This sum is the y-coordinate of the second point on the lift curve. The x-coordinate is index number 2.

6. Repeat Step 5 until all records have been examined. Connect all the points, and this is the lift curve.

7. The reference line is a straight line from the origin to the point $y = $ total net benefit and $x = n$ ($n = $ number of records).

PROBLEMS

5.1 A machine learning process has been applied to a transaction dataset and has classified 88 records as fraudulent (30 correctly so) and 952 as non-fraudulent (920 correctly so). Construct the confusion matrix and calculate the classification error (overall error) rate.

5.2 Suppose that this process has an adjustable threshold (cutoff) mechanism by which you can alter the proportion of records classified as fraudulent. Describe how moving the threshold up or down would affect the following:

a. The classification error rate for records that are truly fraudulent.

b. The classification error rate for records that are truly non-fraudulent.

5.3 Consider Figure 5.15, the decile lift chart for the transaction data model, applied to new data.

FIGURE 5.15   DECILE LIFT CHART FOR TRANSACTION DATA

a. Interpret the meaning of the first and second bars from the left.

b. Explain how you might use this information in practice.

c. Another analyst comments that you could improve the accuracy of the model by classifying everything as non-fraudulent. If you do that, what is the error rate?

d. Comment on the usefulness, in this situation, of these two metrics of model performance (error rate and lift).

5.4 FiscalNote is a startup founded by a Washington, DC entrepreneur and funded by a Singapore sovereign wealth fund, the Winklevoss twins of Facebook fame, and others. It uses machine learning techniques to predict for its clients whether legislation in the US Congress and in US state legislatures will pass or not. The company reports 94% accuracy (*Washington Post*, November 21, 2014, "Capital Business").

Considering just bills introduced in the US Congress, do a bit of internet research to learn about numbers of bills introduced and passage rates. Identify the possible types of misclassifications, and comment on the use of overall accuracy as a metric. Include a discussion of other possible metrics and the potential role of propensities.

5.5   A large number of insurance records are to be examined to develop a model for predicting fraudulent claims. Of the claims in the historical database, 1% were judged to be fraudulent. A sample is taken to develop a model, and oversampling is used to provide a balanced sample in light of the very low response rate. When applied to this sample ($n = 800$), the model ends up correctly classifying 310 frauds and 270 non-frauds. It missed 90 frauds and classified 130 records incorrectly as frauds when they were not.

    a. Produce the confusion matrix for the sample as it stands.

    b. Find the adjusted misclassification rate (adjusting for the oversampling).

    c. What percentage of new records would you expect to be classified as fraudulent?

5.6   A firm that sells software services has been piloting a new product and has records of 500 customers who have either bought the services or decided not to. The target value is the estimated profit from each sale (excluding sales costs). The global mean is about $2128. However, the cost of the sales effort is not cheap—the company figures it comes to $2500 for each of the 500 customers (whether they buy or not). The firm developed a predictive model in hopes of being able to identify the top spenders in the future. The decile lift chart for the holdout set is shown in Figure 5.16.

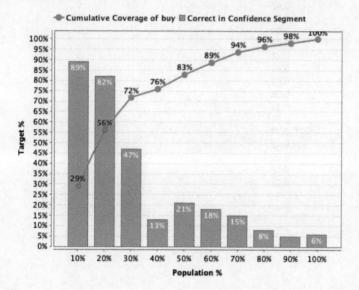

FIGURE 5.16   DECILE LIFT CHART FOR SOFTWARE SERVICES PRODUCT SALES (HOLDOUT SET)

    a. If the company begins working with a new set of 1000 leads to sell the same services, similar to the 500 in the pilot study, without any use of predictive modeling to target sales efforts, what is the estimated profit?

    b. If the firm wants the average profit on each sale to roughly double the sales effort cost and applies an appropriate threshold with this predictive model to a new set of 1000 leads, how far down the new list of 1000 should it proceed (how many deciles)?

    c. Still considering the new list of 1000 leads, if the company applies this predictive model with a lower threshold of $2500, how far should it proceed down the ranked leads, in terms of deciles?

d. Why use this two-stage process for predicting sales—why not simply develop a model for predicting profit for the 1000 new leads?

5.7 Table 5.5 shows a small set of predictive model holdout partition results for a classification model, with both actual values and propensities.

a. Calculate error rates, sensitivity, and specificity using threshold values of 0.25, 0.5, and 0.75.

b. Create a lift chart using Excel, similar to Figure 5.9.

TABLE 5.5	PROPENSITIES AND ACTUAL CLASS MEMBERSHIP FOR HOLDOUT DATA
Propensity of 1	Actual
0.03	0
0.52	0
0.38	0
0.82	1
0.33	0
0.42	0
0.55	1
0.59	0
0.09	0
0.21	0
0.43	0
0.04	0
0.08	0
0.13	0
0.01	0
0.79	1
0.42	0
0.29	0
0.08	0
0.02	0

Prediction and Classification Methods

CHAPTER 6

Multiple Linear Regression

In this chapter, we introduce linear regression models for the purpose of prediction. We discuss the differences between fitting and using regression models for the purpose of inference (as in classical statistics) and for prediction. A predictive goal calls for evaluating model performance on a holdout set and for using predictive metrics. We then raise the challenges of using many predictors and describe variable selection algorithms that are often implemented in linear regression procedures. Finally, we introduce regularized regression techniques, which are particularly useful for datasets with a large number of highly-correlated predictors.

6.1 INTRODUCTION

The most popular model for making predictions is the *multiple linear regression model* encountered in most introductory statistics courses and textbooks. This model is used to fit a relationship between a numerical *target attribute* Y and a set of *predictors* $X_1, X_2, \ldots, X_p$. Attributes are also called *variables* (particularly in statistics), and other terms for the target attribute include *outcome*, *response*, or *dependent variable*. The value of a target attribute is often called a *label*, and in RapidMiner you can assign an attribute a "label" role, meaning it is the target. Predictors also have alternative terms: *independent variables*, *inputs*, *regressors*, or *covariates*. The assumption is that the following function approximates the relationship between the predictors and target attribute:

$$Y = \beta_0 + \beta_1 x_1 + \beta_2 x_2 + \cdots + \beta_p x_p + \epsilon, \tag{6.1}$$

where $\beta_0, \ldots, \beta_p$ are *coefficients* and ϵ is the *noise* or *unexplained* part. Data are then used to estimate the coefficients and to quantify the

Machine Learning for Business Analytics: Concepts, Techniques and Applications in RapidMiner, First Edition.
Galit Shmueli, Peter C. Bruce, Amit V. Deokar, and Nitin R. Patel.

noise. In predictive modeling, the data are also used to evaluate model performance.

Regression modeling means not only estimating the coefficients but also choosing which predictors to include and in what form. For example, a numerical predictor can be included as is, or in logarithmic form $[\log(X)]$, or in a binned form (e.g., age group). Choosing the right form depends on domain knowledge, data availability, and needed predictive power.

Multiple linear regression is applicable to numerous predictive modeling situations. Examples are predicting customer activity on credit cards from their demographics and historical activity patterns, predicting expenditures on vacation travel based on historical frequent flyer data, predicting staffing requirements at help desks based on historical data and product and sales information, predicting sales from cross-selling of products from historical information, and predicting the impact of discounts on sales in retail outlets.

6.2 EXPLANATORY VS. PREDICTIVE MODELING

Before introducing the use of linear regression for prediction, we must clarify an important distinction that often escapes those with earlier familiarity with linear regression from courses in statistics. In particular, the two popular but different objectives behind fitting a regression model are as follows:

1. Explaining or quantifying the average effect of inputs on an outcome (explanatory or descriptive task, respectively).

2. Predicting the outcome value for new records, given their input values (predictive task).

The classical statistical approach is focused on the first objective. In that scenario, the data are treated as a random sample from a larger population of interest. The regression model estimated from this sample is an attempt to capture the *average* relationship in the larger population. This model is then used in decision-making to generate statements such as "a unit increase in service speed (X_1) is associated with an average increase of 5 points in customer satisfaction (Y), all other factors $(X_2, X_3, \ldots, X_p)$ being equal." If X_1 is known to *cause* Y, then such a statement indicates actionable policy changes—this is called explanatory modeling. When the causal structure is unknown, then this model quantifies the degree of *association* between the inputs and outcome variable, and the approach is called descriptive modeling.

In predictive analytics, however, the focus is typically on the second goal: predicting new individual records. Here, we are not interested in the coefficients themselves, nor in the "average record," but rather in the predictions that this model can generate for new records. In this scenario, the model is used for micro-decision-making at the record level. In our previous example, we would use the regression model to predict customer satisfaction for each new customer of interest.

Both explanatory and predictive modeling involve using a dataset to fit a model (i.e., to estimate coefficients), checking model validity, assessing its performance, and comparing with other models. However, the modeling steps and performance assessment differ in the two cases, usually leading to different final models. Therefore, the choice of model is closely tied to whether the goal is explanatory or predictive.

In explanatory and descriptive modeling, where the focus is on modeling the average record, we try to fit the best model to the data in an attempt to learn about the underlying relationship in the population. In contrast, in predictive modeling, the goal is to find a regression model that best predicts new individual records. A regression model that fits the existing data too well is not likely to perform well with new data. Hence, we look for a model that has the highest predictive power by evaluating it on a holdout set and using predictive metrics (see Chapter 5).

Let us summarize the main differences in using a linear regression in the two scenarios:

1. A good explanatory model is one that fits the data closely, whereas a good predictive model is one that predicts new records accurately. Choices of input variables and their form can therefore differ.

2. In explanatory models, the entire dataset is used for estimating the best-fit model, to maximize the amount of information that we have about the hypothesized relationship in the population. When the goal is to predict outcomes of new individual records, the data are typically split into a training set and a holdout set. The training set is used to estimate the model, and the holdout set[1] is used to assess this model's predictive performance on new, unobserved data.

3. Performance measures for explanatory models measure how close the data fit the model (how well the model approximates the data) and how strong the average relationship is, whereas in predictive models performance is measured by predictive accuracy (how well the model predicts new individual records).

4. In explanatory models, the focus is on the coefficients (β), whereas in predictive models the focus is on the predictions ($\hat{y}$).

---

[1] When we are comparing different model options (e.g., different predictors) or multiple models, the data should be partitioned into three sets: training, validation, and holdout. The validation set is used for selecting the model with the best performance, while the holdout set is used to assess the performance of the "best model" on new, unobserved data before model deployment.

For these reasons, it is extremely important to know the goal of the analysis before beginning the modeling process. A good predictive model can have a looser fit to the data on which it is based, and a good explanatory model can have low prediction accuracy. In the remainder of this chapter, we focus on predictive models because these are more popular in machine learning and because most statistics textbooks focus on explanatory modeling.

6.3 ESTIMATING THE REGRESSION EQUATION AND PREDICTION

Once we determine the predictors to include and their form, we estimate the coefficients of the regression formula from the data using a method called *ordinary least squares* (OLS). This method finds values $\hat{\beta}_0, \hat{\beta}_1, \hat{\beta}_2, \ldots, \hat{\beta}_p$ that minimize the sum of squared deviations between the actual target values (Y) and their predicted values based on that model ($\hat{Y}$).

To predict the value of the target for a record with predictor values $x_1, x_2, \ldots, x_p$, we use the equation

$$\hat{Y} = \hat{\beta}_0 + \hat{\beta}_1 x_1 + \hat{\beta}_2 x_2 + \cdots + \hat{\beta}_p x_p. \tag{6.2}$$

Predictions based on this equation are the best predictions possible in the sense that they will be unbiased (equal to the true values on average) and will have the smallest mean squared error compared with any unbiased estimates *if* we make the following assumptions:

1. The noise ϵ (or equivalently, Y) follows a normal distribution.
2. The choice of predictors and their form is correct (*linearity*).
3. The records are independent of each other.
4. The variability in the target values for a given set of predictors is the same regardless of the values of the predictors (*homoskedasticity*).

An important and interesting fact for the predictive goal is that *even if we drop the first assumption and allow the noise to follow an arbitrary distribution, these estimates are very good for prediction,* in the sense that among all linear models, as defined by Eq. (6.1), the model using the least squares estimates, $\hat{\beta}_0, \hat{\beta}_1, \hat{\beta}_2, \ldots, \hat{\beta}_p$, will have the smallest mean squared errors. The assumption of a normal distribution is required in explanatory modeling, where it is used for constructing confidence intervals and statistical tests for the model parameters.

Even if the other assumptions are violated, it is still possible that the resulting predictions are sufficiently accurate and precise for the purpose they are intended for. The key is to evaluate predictive performance of the model, which is the main priority. Satisfying assumptions is of secondary interest, and residual analysis can give clues to potential improved models to examine.

Example: Predicting the Price of Used Toyota Corolla Cars

A large Toyota car dealership offers purchasers of new Toyota cars the option to buy their used car as part of a trade-in. In particular, a new promotion promises to pay high prices for used Toyota Corolla cars for purchasers of a new car. The dealer then sells the used cars for a small profit. To ensure a reasonable profit, the dealer needs to be able to predict the price that the dealership will get for the used cars. For that reason, data were collected on all previous sales of used Toyota Corollas at the dealership. The data include the sales price and other information on the car, such as its age, mileage, fuel type, and engine size. A description of each of the attributes used in the analysis is given in Table 6.1.

TABLE 6.1	ATTRIBUTES IN THE TOYOTA COROLLA EXAMPLE
Attribute	**Description**
Price	Offer price in Euros
Age_08_04	Age in months as of August 2004
KM	Accumulated kilometers on odometer
Fuel_Type	Fuel type (*Petrol, Diesel, CNG*)
HP	Horsepower
Met_Color	Metallic color? (Yes = 1, No = 0)
Automatic	Automatic (Yes = 1, No = 0)
CC	Cylinder volume in cubic centimeters
Doors	Number of doors
Quarterly_Tax	Quarterly road tax in Euros
Weight	Weight in kilograms

A sample of this dataset is shown in Table 6.2. The total number of records in the dataset is 1436 cars (we use the first 1000 cars from the dataset *Toyoto-Corolla.csv* for analysis). Figure 6.1 shows the RapidMiner data preprocessing steps for linear regression starting with the *Select Attributes* operator, which selects the target attribute Price and the 10 predictors listed in Table 6.2 as well as the Id attribute. The *Set Role* assigns the *label* role to the target attribute Price and *id* role to the Id attribute. Notice that the Fuel_Type predictor has three categories (Petrol, Diesel, and CNG). We would therefore require two dummy variables in the model: Fuel_Type_Petrol (0/1) and Fuel_Type_Diesel (0/1); the third, for CNG (0/1), is redundant given the information on the first two dummies. Including the redundant dummy would cause the regression to fail, since the redundant dummy will be a perfect linear combination of the other two. Thus, we use the *Nominal to Numerical* operator on the Fuel_Type predictor to apply dummy coding (*coding type = dummy coding*) using CNG as the

TABLE 6.2			PRICES AND ATTRIBUTES FOR USED TOYOTA COROLLA CARS (SELECTED ROWS AND COLUMNS ONLY)							

Price	Age_08_04	KM	Fuel_Type	HP	Met_Color	Auto-matic	CC	Doors	Quarterly_tax	Weight
13,500	23	46,986	Diesel	90	1	0	2000	3	210	1165
13,750	23	72,937	Diesel	90	1	0	2000	3	210	1165
13,950	24	41,711	Diesel	90	1	0	2000	3	210	1165
14,950	26	48,000	Diesel	90	0	0	2000	3	210	1165
13,750	30	38,500	Diesel	90	0	0	2000	3	210	1170
12,950	32	61,000	Diesel	90	0	0	2000	3	210	1170
16,900	27	94,612	Diesel	90	1	0	2000	3	210	1245
18,600	30	75,889	Diesel	90	1	0	2000	3	210	1245
21,500	27	19,700	Petrol	192	0	0	1800	3	100	1185
12,950	23	71,138	Diesel	69	0	0	1900	3	185	1105
20,950	25	31,461	Petrol	192	0	0	1800	3	100	1185
19,950	22	43,610	Petrol	192	0	0	1800	3	100	1185
19,600	25	32,189	Petrol	192	0	0	1800	3	100	1185
21,500	31	23,000	Petrol	192	1	0	1800	3	100	1185
22,500	32	34,131	Petrol	192	1	0	1800	3	100	1185
22,000	28	18,739	Petrol	192	0	0	1800	3	100	1185
22,750	30	34,000	Petrol	192	1	0	1800	3	100	1185
17,950	24	21,716	Petrol	110	1	0	1600	3	85	1105
16,750	24	25,563	Petrol	110	0	0	1600	3	19	1065
16,950	30	64,359	Petrol	110	1	0	1600	3	85	1105
15,950	30	67,660	Petrol	110	1	0	1600	3	85	1105
16,950	29	43,905	Petrol	110	0	1	1600	3	100	1170
15,950	28	56,349	Petrol	110	1	0	1600	3	85	1120
16,950	28	32,220	Petrol	110	1	0	1600	3	85	1120
16,250	29	25,813	Petrol	110	1	0	1600	3	85	1120
15,950	25	28,450	Petrol	110	1	0	1600	3	85	1120
17,495	27	34,545	Petrol	110	1	0	1600	3	85	1120
15,750	29	41,415	Petrol	110	1	0	1600	3	85	1120
11,950	39	98,823	CNG	110	1	0	1600	5	197	1119

comparison group.[2] The processed data will have 11 predictors. Based on initial data exploration, we observe an outlier value of 16,000 for the CC variable for one observation, which we correct to 1600 using the *Map* operator. Finally, we select the first 1000 cars for analysis using the *Filter Example Range* operator.

Figure 6.2 (top) presents the RapidMiner process for estimating the linear regression model with the training set and measuring performance with this set

---

[2]If a comparison group is specified when using dummy coding, RapidMiner automatically creates only k-1 dummy variables if there are k categories for a predictor. In contrast, if no comparison group is specified when using dummy coding, RapidMiner creates k dummy variables corresponding to each of the k categories of a predictor.

FIGURE 6.1   DATA PREPROCESSING FOR TOYOTA COROLLA DATA

as well. The *Data Preprocessing* subprocess contains the same steps mentioned in Figure 6.1. Using the *Split Data* operator, the data is first partitioned randomly into training (60%) and holdout (40%) sets. We fit a multiple linear regression model between price (the label) and the other predictors using only the training set. The *Multiply* operator simply sends one copy of the training set for model building and another copy of the same data for applying the model with the *Apply Model* operator. The *Linear Regression* operator is used for model building, which can be found in the Operators panel under *Modeling > Predictive > Functions > Linear Regression*. In the *Linear Regression* operator, make sure to set the parameter *feature selection = None* for the current analysis since we want to use all the predictors to build our model (variable selection is discussed in Section 6.4). The *Generate Attributes* operator is used to compute the residuals for later analysis. That is, we create a new attribute Residual which is the difference between the target attribute Price and the model's newly created prediction(Price) attribute, as shown in the parameter list box in Figure 6.2. The performance metrics of interest are selected in the *Performance (Regression)* operator. Figure 6.2 (bottom) shows the performance metrics for the training set. With this being a prediction task rather than an explanatory task, these performance metrics on the training data are of lesser concern. We will be more interested in the performance on the holdout data. The estimated model coefficients are shown in Figure 6.3.

The regression coefficients are then used to predict prices of individual used Toyota Corolla cars based on their age, mileage, and so on. The process is shown

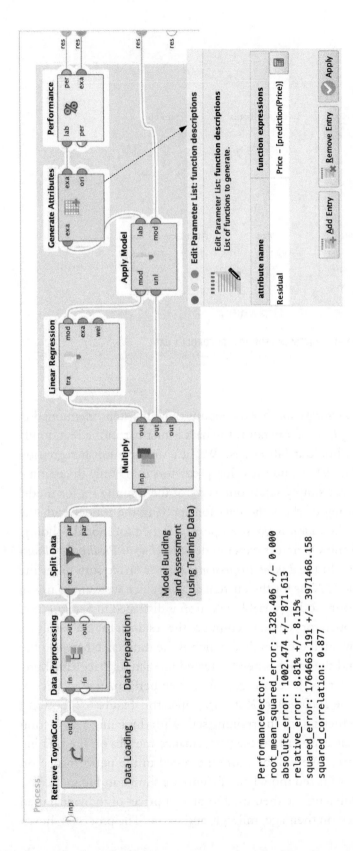

PerformanceVector:
root_mean_squared_error: 1328.406 +/- 0.000
absolute_error: 1002.474 +/- 871.613
relative_error: 8.81% +/- 8.15%
squared_error: 1764663.191 +/- 3971468.158
squared_correlation: 0.877

FIGURE 6.2   (TOP) LINEAR REGRESSION PROCESS FOR MODELING PRICE VS. CAR ATTRIBUTES;
(BOTTOM) MODEL PERFORMANCE FOR THE TRAINING SET

Attribute	Coefficient	Std. Error	Std. Coefficient	Tolerance	t–Stat	p–Value	Code
CC	–2.826	0.803	–0.139	0.956	–3.519	0.000	****
Fuel_Type_Diesel	3778.479	812.362	0.330	0.999	4.651	0.000	****
Fuel_Type_Petrol	3586.422	656.342	0.322	0.998	5.464	0.000	****
Age_08_04	–135.700	4.733	–0.604	0.509	–28.673	0	****
KM	–0.019	0.002	–0.175	0.696	–8.120	0.000	****
HP	60.422	7.196	0.259	0.882	8.397	0.000	****
Met_Color	105.637	120.097	0.013	0.985	0.880	0.379	
Automatic	450.350	260.488	0.026	0.999	1.729	0.084	*
Doors	34.421	61.727	0.009	0.947	0.558	0.577	
Quarterly_Tax	20.094	2.638	0.234	0.968	7.618	0.000	****
Weight	11.883	1.486	0.194	0.698	7.998	0.000	****
(Intercept)	–663.783	1772.583	?	?	–0.374	0.708	

FIGURE 6.3   LINEAR REGRESSION MODEL OF PRICE VS. CAR ATTRIBUTES

in Figure 6.4. Here, the holdout set (second output port of the *Split Data* operator) is wired to the unlabeled data input port of the *Apply Model* operator. The results show a sample of predicted prices for six cars in the holdout set, using the estimated model. It gives the predictions and their errors (relative to the actual prices) for these six cars. Below the predictions, we have overall measures of predictive accuracy. Note that for this holdout data, RMSE = \$1394, the mean absolute error (MAE) is \$1059, and the mean relative error (also known as the mean absolute percentage error, or MAPE) is 9.44%. A histogram of the residuals (Figure 6.5) shows that most of the errors are between ±\$2000. This error magnitude might be small relative to the car price but should be taken into account when considering the profit. Another observation of interest is the large positive residuals (under-predictions), which may or may not be a concern, depending on the application. Measures such as RMSE, MAE, and MAPE are used to assess the predictive performance of a model and to compare models.

6.4 VARIABLE SELECTION IN LINEAR REGRESSION

Reducing the Number of Predictors

A frequent problem in machine learning is that of using a regression equation to predict the value of the target (i.e., the label) when we have many attributes available to choose as predictors in our model. Given the high speed of modern algorithms for multiple linear regression calculations, it is tempting in such a

Row No.	Id	Price	prediction(Price)	Residual	CC	Fuel_Type_Diesel	Fuel_Type_Petrol	Age_08_04	KM	HP	Met_Color	Automatic	Doors	Quarterly_Tax	Weight
1	4	14950	16637.430	-1687	2000	1	0	26	48000	90	0	0	3	210	1165
2	5	13750	16332.318	-2582	2000	1	0	30	38500	90	0	0	3	210	1170
3	6	12950	15638.685	-2688	2000	1	0	32	61000	90	0	0	3	210	1170
4	9	21500	21596.308	-96	1800	0	1	27	19700	192	0	0	3	100	1185
5	10	12950	14408.781	-1458	1900	1	0	23	71138	69	0	0	3	185	1105
6	15	22500	20752.632	1748	1800	0	1	32	34131	192	1	0	3	100	1185

PerformanceVector:
root_mean_squared_error: 1394.251 +/- 0.000
absolute_error: 1058.568 +/- 907.396
relative_error: 9.44% +/- 8.30%
squared_error: 1943934.645 +/- 4077633.176
squared_correlation: 0.859

FIGURE 6.4   LINEAR REGRESSION PROCESS MEASURING HOLDOUT SET PERFORMANCE. RESULTS SHOW PREDICTED PRICES (AND ERRORS) FOR 6 CARS IN HOLDOUT SET AND SUMMARY PREDICTIVE MEASURES FOR ENTIRE HOLDOUT SET

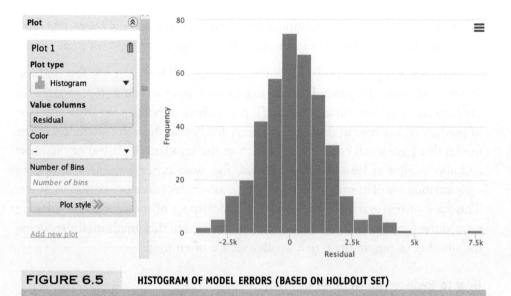

FIGURE 6.5   HISTOGRAM OF MODEL ERRORS (BASED ON HOLDOUT SET)

situation to take a kitchen-sink approach: Why bother to select a subset? Just use all the attributes in the model.

Another consideration favoring the inclusion of numerous attributes is the hope that a previously hidden relationship will emerge. For example, a company found that customers who had purchased anti-scuff protectors for chair and table legs had lower credit risks. However, there are several reasons for exercising caution before throwing all possible predictors into a model:

- It may be expensive or not feasible to collect a full complement of predictors for future predictions.

- We may be able to measure fewer predictors more accurately (e.g., in surveys).

- The more predictors, the higher the chance of missing values in the data. If we delete or impute records with missing values, multiple predictors will lead to a higher rate of record deletion or imputation.

- *Parsimony* is an important property of good models. We obtain more insight into the influence of predictors in models with few parameters.

- Estimates of regression coefficients are likely to be unstable, due to *multicollinearity* in models with many variables. (Multicollinearity is the presence of two or more predictors sharing the same linear relationship with the outcome variable.) Regression coefficients are more stable for parsimonious models. One very rough rule of thumb is to have a number of records n larger than $5(p + 2)$, where p is the number of predictors.

- It can be shown that using predictors that are uncorrelated with the outcome variable increases the variance of predictions.

- It can be shown that dropping predictors that are actually correlated with the outcome variable can increase the average error (bias) of predictions.

The last two points mean that there is a trade-off between too few and too many predictors. In general, accepting some bias can reduce the variance in predictions. This *bias–variance trade-off* is particularly important for large numbers of predictors, because in that case, it is very likely that there are attributes in the model that have small coefficients relative to the standard deviation of the noise and also exhibit at least moderate correlation with other variables. Dropping such attributes will improve the predictions, as it reduces the prediction variance. This type of bias–variance trade-off is a basic aspect of most machine learning procedures for prediction and classification. In light of this, methods for reducing the number of predictors p to a smaller set are often used.

How to Reduce the Number of Predictors

The first step in trying to reduce the number of predictors should always be to use domain knowledge. It is important to understand what the various predictors are measuring and why they are relevant for predicting the label. With this knowledge, the set of predictors should be reduced to a sensible set that reflects the problem at hand. Some practical reasons for predictor elimination are the expense of collecting this information in the future, inaccuracy, high correlation with another predictor, many missing values, or simply irrelevance. Also helpful in examining potential predictors are summary statistics and graphs, such as frequency and correlation tables, predictor-specific summary statistics and plots, and missing value counts.

The next step makes use of computational power and statistical performance metrics. In general, there are two types of methods for reducing the number of predictors in a model. The first is an *exhaustive search* for the "best" subset of predictors by fitting regression models with all the possible combinations of predictors. The exhaustive search approach is not practical in many applications due to the large number of possible models. The second approach is to search through a partial set of models. We describe these two approaches next. In any case, using computational variable selection methods involves comparing many models and choosing the best one. In such cases, it is advisable to have a *validation set* in addition to the training and holdout sets. The validation set is used to compare the models and select the best one. The holdout set is then used to evaluate the predictive performance of this selected model.

Exhaustive Search   The idea here is to evaluate all subsets of predictors. Since the number of subsets for even moderate values of p is very large, after the algorithm creates the subsets and runs all the models, we need some way to examine the most promising subsets and to select from them. The challenge is to select a model that is not too simplistic in terms of excluding important parameters (the model is *underfit*), nor overly complex thereby modeling random noise (the model is *overfit*). Several criteria for evaluating and comparing models are based on metrics computed from the training data, which give a penalty on the number of predictors. One popular criterion is the *adjusted R^2*, which is defined as

$$R^2_{\text{adj}} = 1 - \frac{n-1}{n-p-1}(1 - R^2)$$

where R^2 is the proportion of explained variability in the model (in a model with a single predictor, this is the squared correlation). Like R^2, higher values of R^2_{adj} indicate better fit. Unlike R^2, which does not account for the number of predictors used, R^2_{adj} uses a penalty on the number of predictors. This avoids the artificial increase in R^2 that can result from simply increasing the number of predictors but not the amount of information.

A second popular set of criteria for balancing underfitting and overfitting, which are also computed from the training set, are the *Akaike Information Criterion (AIC)* and Schwartz's *Bayesian Information Criterion (BIC)*. AIC and BIC measure the goodness of fit of a model but also include a penalty that is a function of the number of parameters in the model. As such, they can be used to compare various models for the same dataset. *AIC* and *BIC* are estimates of prediction error based on information theory. For linear regression, AIC and BIC can be computed from the formulas:

$$\text{AIC} = n\ln(\text{SSE}/n) + n(1 + \ln(2\pi)) + 2(p+1), \qquad (6.3)$$
$$\text{BIC} = n\ln(\text{SSE}/n) + n(1 + \ln(2\pi)) + \ln(n)(p+1), \qquad (6.4)$$

where SSE is the model's sum of squared errors. In general, models with smaller AIC and BIC values are considered better.

Note that for a fixed size of subset, R^2, R^2_{adj}, AIC, and BIC all select the same subset. In fact, there is no difference between them in the order of merit they ascribe to subsets of a fixed size. This is good to know if comparing models with the same number of predictors, but often we want to compare models with different numbers of predictors.

A different approach for evaluating and comparing models uses metrics computed from the validation set. Metrics such as validation RMSE, MAE, or MAPE can be used for this purpose. This is also the approach we demonstrate with RapidMiner, since RapidMiner's *Performance (Regression)* operator does not provide the measures R^2_{adj}, AIC, and BIC.

Figure 6.6 shows the process for conducting exhaustive search on the Toyota Corolla price data (with the 11 predictors). The *Data Preprocessing* subprocess contains the same steps mentioned in Figure 6.1. The *Optimize Selection (Brute Force)* wrapper operator can be used with any modeling algorithm operator such as the *Linear Regression* operator. Within this feature selection subprocess, we use the same steps mentioned in Figure 6.4, from *Split Data* operator onward. For

FIGURE 6.6   EXHAUSTIVE SEARCH FOR REDUCING PREDICTORS IN TOYOTA COROLLA EXAMPLE

each model combination, the model is built using the training set, and the performance on the validation set[3] is recorded. For the *Split Data* operator within the feature selection subprocess, the *local random seed* parameter is set to a specific number (we select the default: 1992) to ensure that the exact same training and validation sets are used for each model combination. The performance metric to be optimized is specified in the *Performance (Regression)* operator inside the feature selection subprocess. In this case, we specified RMSE as the optimization criterion. For the *Optimize Selection (Brute Force)* operator, activating the *user result individual selection* option enables the user to interactively select the desired model out of all model combinations (2047 combinations in this example).

The results of applying an exhaustive search are shown in Figure 6.7 (top 10 models shown). If the *user result individual selection* option is not selected, the model with the "best" performance metric (i.e., lowest validation RMSE in this case) is automatically chosen. In this example, the model with index 1535 containing ten predictors has the lowest validation RMSE. A closer look at all the generated models shows eight models with close performance: a 10-predictor model, three 9-predictor models, three 8-predictor models, and a 7-predictor model. These all have similar values of validation RMSE, MAE, and MAPE. The dominant predictor in all the top 10 models is the age of the car, with horsepower, weight, mileage, and CC playing important roles as well.

Note that selecting a model with the best validation performance runs the risk of overfitting, in the sense that we choose the best model that fits the validation data. Therefore, consider more than just the single top performing model, and among the good performers, favor models that have less predictors.

---

[3] We now treat the previous holdout set as a validation set, because we are using it to compare models and select one.

Index	Features	Names
1535	10	CC, Fuel_Type_Petrol, Age_08_04, KM, HP, Met_Color, Automatic, Doors, Quarterly_Tax, Weight
1519	9	CC, Fuel_Type_Petrol, Age_08_04, KM, HP, Automatic, Doors, Quarterly_Tax, Weight
1527	9	CC, Fuel_Type_Petrol, Age_08_04, KM, HP, Met_Color, Doors, Quarterly_Tax, Weight
1531	9	CC, Fuel_Type_Petrol, Age_08_04, KM, HP, Met_Color, Automatic, Quarterly_Tax, Weight
1515	8	CC, Fuel_Type_Petrol, Age_08_04, KM, HP, Automatic, Quarterly_Tax, Weight
1511	8	CC, Fuel_Type_Petrol, Age_08_04, KM, HP, Doors, Quarterly_Tax, Weight
1523	8	CC, Fuel_Type_Petrol, Age_08_04, KM, HP, Met_Color, Quarterly_Tax, Weight
1507	7	CC, Fuel_Type_Petrol, Age_08_04, KM, HP, Quarterly_Tax, Weight
1257	6	CC, Age_08_04, KM, HP, Automatic, Weight
1769	7	CC, Fuel_Type_Diesel, Age_08_04, KM, HP, Automatic, Weight

Index	root_mean_squared_error ↑	absolute_error	relative_error	squared_error	squared_correlation
1535	1379.528	1063.575	0.095	1903097.876	0.861
1519	1379.913	1064.317	0.095	1904160.166	0.861
1527	1380.063	1066.267	0.095	1904572.758	0.861
1531	1380.124	1063.864	0.095	1904743.051	0.861
1515	1380.367	1064.490	0.095	1905411.893	0.861
1511	1380.376	1066.883	0.095	1905438.694	0.861
1523	1380.780	1066.659	0.095	1906553.052	0.861
1507	1380.945	1067.148	0.095	1907009.770	0.861
1257	1384.337	1053.973	0.095	1916389.760	0.860
1769	1384.443	1047.027	0.094	1916683.345	0.860

FIGURE 6.7   EXHAUSTIVE SEARCH RESULTS (PARTIAL) FOR THE TOYOTA COROLLA EXAMPLE

Finally, remember to evaluate the performance of the selected model on the holdout set.

Popular Subset Selection Algorithms   The second method of finding the best subset of predictors relies on a partial, iterative search through the space of all possible regression models. The end product is one best subset of predictors (although there do exist variations of these methods that identify several close-to-best choices for different sizes of predictor subsets). This approach is computationally cheaper, but it has the potential of missing "good" combinations of predictors. None of the methods guarantee that they yield the best subset for any criterion, such as R^2_{adj}. They are reasonable methods for situations with a large number of predictors, but for a moderate number of predictors, the exhaustive search is preferable.

Three popular iterative search algorithms are *forward selection, backward elimination*, and *stepwise regression*. In *forward selection*, we start with no predictors and then add predictors one by one. Each predictor added is the one (among all predictors) that has the largest contribution to R^2 on top of the predictors that are already in it. The algorithm stops when the contribution of additional predictors is not statistically significant. The main disadvantage of this method is that the algorithm will miss pairs or groups of predictors that perform very well together but perform poorly as single predictors. This is similar to interviewing job candidates for a team project one by one, thereby missing groups of candidates who perform superiorly together ("colleagues"), but poorly on their own or with non-colleagues.

In *backward elimination*, we start with all predictors and then at each step eliminate the least useful predictor (according to statistical significance). The algorithm stops when all the remaining predictors have significant contributions. The weakness of this algorithm is that computing the initial model with all predictors can be time-consuming and unstable. *Stepwise regression* is like forward selection except that at each step, we consider dropping predictors that are not statistically significant, as in backward elimination.

In RapidMiner, forward selection, backward elimination, and stepwise selection can each be performed with the *Iterative T-Test* feature selection option in the *Linear Regression* operator itself. There are two key model parameters, *forward alpha* and *backward alpha*, for this option. The *forward alpha* parameter sets a significance level (default value is 0.05) for deciding when to enter a predictor into the model, and the *backward alpha* sets a significance level (default value is 0.05) for deciding when to remove a predictor from the model. For forward selection, increasing the *forward alpha* level makes it easier to enter predictors into the model, while for backward selection, decreasing the *backward alpha* level makes it easier to remove predictors from the model. For forward selection, the *forward alpha* is set to the desired significance level for adding predictors to the model, and the *backward alpha* is set to 0. In the case of backward selection, the assignment is reversed. For stepwise regression, both alpha values are assigned desired significance levels. Other than this feature selection specification in the *Linear Regression* operator, the process setup is similar to Figure 6.4.

Figure 6.8 shows the results of forward selection for the Toyota Corolla example, which suggest a 7-predictor model. The results of backward selection shown in Figure 6.9 also suggest the same 7-predictor model. This need not be the case with other datasets. Stepwise selection, with both *forward alpha* and *backward alpha* set to 0.05, ends up with an 8-predictor model.

There is a popular (but false) notion that stepwise regression is superior to forward selection and backward elimination because of its ability to add and to drop predictors. The subset selection algorithms yield fairly good solutions, but we need to carefully determine the number of predictors to retain by running a few searches and using the combined results to determine the subsets to choose. Once one or more promising models are selected, we run them to evaluate their validation predictive performance. For example, Figure 6.10 shows the

Parameters ✕		Attribute	Coefficient	Std. Error	Std. Coefficient
⌐ **Linear Regression**		Fuel_Type_Diesel	1997.865	656.780	0.175
feature selection ∨	Iterative T–Test ▼ ①	Fuel_Type_Petrol	3605.533	659.252	0.324
max iterations	10 ①	Age_08_04	−136.256	4.736	−0.607
forward alpha	0.05 ①	KM	−0.020	0.002	−0.185
backward alpha	0.0 ①	HP	40.749	4.632	0.175
☐ *eliminate colinear features* ①		Quarterly_Tax	19.963	2.646	0.232
☑ *use bias* ①		Weight	12.676	1.423	0.206
ridge	1.0E-8 ①	(Intercept)	−3425.002	1598.244	?

```
PerformanceVector:
root_mean_squared_error: 1410.337 +/- 0.000
absolute_error: 1082.654 +/- 903.831
relative_error: 9.70% +/- 8.23%
squared_error: 1989049.219 +/- 3969841.150
squared_correlation: 0.855
```

FIGURE 6.8   FORWARD SELECTION MODEL PARAMETERS AND RESULTS FOR REDUCING PREDICTORS IN TOYOTA COROLLA EXAMPLE

Parameters ✕		Attribute	Coefficient	Std. Error	Std. Coefficient
⌐ **Linear Regression**		Fuel_Type_Diesel	1997.865	656.780	0.175
feature selection ∨	Iterative T–Test ▼ ①	Fuel_Type_Petrol	3605.533	659.252	0.324
max iterations	10 ①	Age_08_04	−136.256	4.736	−0.607
forward alpha	0.0 ①	KM	−0.020	0.002	−0.185
backward alpha	0.05 ①	HP	40.749	4.632	0.175
☐ *eliminate colinear features* ①		Quarterly_Tax	19.963	2.646	0.232
☑ *use bias* ①		Weight	12.676	1.423	0.206
ridge	1.0E-8 ①	(Intercept)	−3425.002	1598.244	?

```
PerformanceVector:
root_mean_squared_error: 1410.337 +/- 0.000
absolute_error: 1082.654 +/- 903.831
relative_error: 9.70% +/- 8.23%
squared_error: 1989049.219 +/- 3969841.150
squared_correlation: 0.855
```

FIGURE 6.9   BACKWARD ELIMINATION MODEL PARAMETERS AND RESULTS FOR REDUCING PREDICTORS IN TOYOTA COROLLA EXAMPLE

validation performance of the 8-predictor model from stepwise, which turns out to be only very slightly better than the 11-predictor model (Figure 6.4) in terms of validation metrics. In other words, with only 8 predictors, we can achieve validation performance similar to a larger 11-predictor model. At the same time, the 8-predictor model is not one of the top 10 models selected by exhaustive search (Figure 6.7), yet its performance is similar.

Parameters	X
Linear Regression	
feature selection	Iterative T-Test
max iterations	10
forward alpha	0.05
backward alpha	0.05
eliminate colinear features	
use bias	✓
ridge	1.0E-8

Attribute	Coefficient	Std. Error	Std. Coefficient
CC	-2.523	0.783	-0.124
Fuel_Type_Diesel	3442.609	791.106	0.301
Fuel_Type_Petrol	3520.104	654.631	0.316
Age_08_04	-135.665	4.702	-0.604
KM	-0.019	0.002	-0.177
HP	57.867	7.026	0.248
Quarterly_Tax	19.993	2.626	0.233
Weight	12.516	1.413	0.204
(Intercept)	-1210.794	1728.348	?

```
PerformanceVector:
root_mean_squared_error: 1391.393 +/- 0.000
absolute_error: 1061.550 +/- 899.492
relative_error: 9.46% +/- 8.17%
squared_error: 1935973.908 +/- 4015491.712
squared_correlation: 0.859
```

FIGURE 6.10   STEPWISE REGRESSION MODEL PARAMETERS AND RESULTS FOR REDUCING PREDICTORS IN TOYOTA COROLLA EXAMPLE

There are a few other feature selection options in the *Linear Regression* operator in RapidMiner. First, the default feature selection option is *M5Prime* that uses a variant of regression trees (Chapter 9) called "model trees" to select a model with fewer features, by comparing AIC values of models. Second, the *greedy* option uses an internal forward selection approach to iteratively select attributes based on AIC values of models. This is similar to the forward selection approach explained earlier. Third, the *T-test* option uses a feature selection approach based on statistical significance and removes all attributes whose coefficient is not significantly different from zero. In contrast to the *Iterative T-test* option which removes predictors one at a time, the *T-test* option at once removes all statistically insignificant attributes (those with p-values above the *alpha* parameter). As with other feature selection techniques, we need to carefully compare the feature selection results of these methods and assess their validation predictive performance, also considering model parsimony.

Regularization (Shrinkage Models)

Selecting a subset of predictors is equivalent to setting some of the model coefficients to zero. This approach creates an interpretable result—we know which predictors were dropped and which are retained. A more flexible alternative, called *regularization* or *shrinkage*, "shrinks" the coefficients toward zero. Recall that adjusted R^2 incorporates a penalty according to the number of predictors p. Shrinkage methods also impose a penalty on the model fit, except that the penalty is not based on the *number* of predictors but rather on some aggregation of the coefficient values (predictors are typically first normalized to have the same scale).

The reasoning behind constraining the magnitude of the $\hat{\beta}$ coefficients is that highly correlated predictors will tend to exhibit coefficients with high standard errors, since small changes in the training data might radically shift which of the correlated predictors gets emphasized. This instability (high standard errors) leads to poor predictive power. By constraining the combined magnitude of the coefficients, this variance is reduced.

The two most popular shrinkage methods are *ridge regression* and *lasso*. They differ in terms of the penalty used: in ridge regression, the penalty is based on the sum of squared coefficients $\sum_{j=1}^{p} \beta_j^2$ (called L2 penalty), whereas lasso uses the sum of absolute values $\sum_{j=1}^{p} |\beta_j|$ (called L1 penalty), for p predictors (excluding an intercept). It turns out that the lasso penalty effectively shrinks some of the coefficients to zero, thereby resulting in a subset of predictors.

Whereas in linear regression coefficients are estimated by minimizing the training data SSE, in ridge regression and lasso the coefficients are estimated by minimizing the training data SSE, subject to the penalty term. In RapidMiner, regularized linear regression can be run using the *Generalized Linear Model* (GLM) operator that is based on the GLM implementation from the H2O.ai company. The *Generalized Linear Model* operator can be found in the Operators panel under *Modeling > Predictive > Functions > Generalized Linear Model*. The operator implements regularization as a combination of L1 and L2 penalties, specified by two parameters, λ and α.

The parameter α controls the penalty distribution between the L1 and L2 penalties and can have a value between 0 and 1. *Ridge regression* model is obtained with $\alpha = 0$ (only L2 penalty), while a *lasso* model is obtained with $\alpha = 1$ (only L1 penalty). Choosing $0 < \alpha < 1$ produces a model that is a combination of L1 and L2 penalties (called "elastic net"). The λ parameter controls the amount or strength of regularization applied to the model and can have values ≥ 0. When $\lambda = 0$, no regularization is applied (the α parameter is ignored), yielding ordinary regression.[4]

The process for building a regularized linear regression model is similar to that shown in Figure 6.4 with the exception of using the *Generalized Linear Model* operator instead of the *Linear Regression* operator. The optimal λ parameter values can be automatically searched by enabling the *lambda search* option. Figures 6.11 and 6.12 show the operator specifications for ridge regression and lasso models, respectively, along with the corresponding results for the Toyota Corolla example. We see that, in this case, the validation performance of the optimized Ridge regression is almost the same as the ordinary regression, while

---

[4]The elastic net regularization penalty is defined as $\lambda(\alpha L1 + \frac{1}{2}(1 - \alpha)L2)$, i.e., the weighted sum of the L1 and L2. This penalty is also equivalent to $aL1 + bL2$, such that $\lambda = a + b$ and $\alpha = a/(a+b)$.

Parameters ✕		
GLM (Generalized Linear Model)		
family	AUTO ▼ ①	
solver	AUTO ▼ ①	
☐ reproducible ✔	①	
✔ use regularization	①	
lambda	①	
✔ lambda search	①	
number of lambdas	0	①
lambda min ratio	0.0	①
☐ early stopping	①	
alpha	0.0	①

Attribute	Coefficient	Std. Coefficient
CC	0.083	15.564
Fuel_Type_Diesel	65.054	21.532
Fuel_Type_Petrol	404.812	137.725
Age_08_04	−100.042	−1687.804
KM	−0.024	−837.899
HP	36.194	587.918
Met_Color	164.026	76.036
Automatic	192.977	42.093
Doors	109.968	105.228
Quarterly_Tax	9.758	429.973
Weight	12.996	802.059
Intercept	−1547.517	11982.168

```
PerformanceVector:
root_mean_squared_error: 1494.473 +/- 0.000
absolute_error: 1142.062 +/- 963.920
relative_error: 9.93% +/- 8.86%
squared_error: 2233448.057 +/- 4487146.191
squared_correlation: 0.856
```

FIGURE 6.11   RIDGE REGRESSION APPLIED TO THE TOYOTA COROLLA DATA

Parameters ✕		
GLM (Generalized Linear Model)		
family	AUTO ▼ ①	
solver	AUTO ▼ ①	
☐ reproducible ✔	①	
✔ use regularization	①	
lambda	①	
✔ lambda search	①	
number of lambdas	100	①
lambda min ratio	0.05	①
☐ early stopping	①	
alpha	1.0	①

Attribute	Coefficient	Std. Coefficient
CC	0	0
Fuel_Type_Diesel	0	0
Fuel_Type_Petrol	0	0
Age_08_04	−137.132	−2313.548
KM	−0.016	−576.323
HP	35.035	569.083
Met_Color	0	0
Automatic	0	0
Doors	0	0
Quarterly_Tax	3.197	140.867
Weight	12.743	786.440
Intercept	1806.708	11982.168

```
PerformanceVector:
root_mean_squared_error: 1429.825 +/- 0.000
absolute_error: 1084.943 +/- 931.289
relative_error: 9.66% +/- 9.67%
squared_error: 2044399.946 +/- 4236385.986
squared_correlation: 0.854
```

FIGURE 6.12   LASSO REGRESSION APPLIED TO THE TOYOTA COROLLA DATA

that of the optimized lasso regression is slightly worse than the ordinary linear regression. Looking at the coefficients, we see that the lasso approach lead to a model with four predictors (Age_08_04, KM, HP, Weight). The real strength of these methods becomes more evident when the dataset contains a large number of predictors with high correlation.

Finally, additional ways to reduce the dimension of the data are by using principal components (Chapter 4) and regression trees (Chapter 9).

PROBLEMS

6.1 **Predicting Boston Housing Prices.** The file *BostonHousing.csv* contains information collected by the US Bureau of the Census concerning housing in the area of Boston, Massachusetts. The dataset includes information on 506 census housing tracts in the Boston area. The goal is to predict the median house price in new tracts based on information such as crime rate, pollution, and number of rooms. The dataset contains 13 predictors, and the target attribute is the median house price (MEDV). Table 6.3 describes each of the predictors and the target attribute.

TABLE 6.3 **DESCRIPTION OF ATTRIBUTES FOR BOSTON HOUSING EXAMPLE**

CRIM	Per capita crime rate by town
ZN	Proportion of residential land zoned for lots over 25,000 ft^2
INDUS	Proportion of nonretail business acres per town
CHAS	Charles River dummy variable (=1 if tract bounds river; =0 otherwise)
NOX	Nitric oxide concentration (parts per 10 million)
RM	Average number of rooms per dwelling
AGE	Proportion of owner-occupied units built prior to 1940
DIS	Weighted distances to five Boston employment centers
RAD	Index of accessibility to radial highways
TAX	Full-value property-tax rate per $10,000
PTRATIO	Pupil/teacher ratio by town
LSTAT	Percentage lower status of the population
MEDV	Median value of owner-occupied homes in $1000s

a. Why should the data be partitioned into training, validation, and holdout sets? What will the training set be used for? What will the validation and holdout sets be used for?

b. Partition the data into training/validation/holdout with proportions 60 : 25 : 15. Fit a multiple linear regression model to the median house price (MEDV) as a function of CRIM, CHAS, and RM. Write the equation for predicting the median house price from the predictors in the model.

c. Using the estimated regression model, what median house price is predicted for a tract in the Boston area that does not bound the Charles River, has a crime rate of 0.1, and where the average number of rooms per house is 6?

d. Reduce the number of predictors:

i. Which predictors are likely to be measuring the same thing among the 13 predictors? Discuss the relationships among INDUS, NOX, and TAX.

ii. Compute the correlation table for the 12 numerical predictors using the *Correlation Matrix* operator in RapidMiner, and search for highly correlated pairs. These have potential redundancy and can cause multicollinearity. Choose which ones to remove based on this table.

iii. Use three subset selection algorithms: *backward, forward*, and *stepwise* to reduce the remaining predictors. Compute the validation performance for each of the three selected models. Compare RMSE, MAPE, and mean error, as well as histograms of the errors. Finally, describe the best model.

iv. Evaluate the performance of the best model on the holdout data. Report its holdout RMSE, MAPE, and mean error.

6.2 **Predicting Software Reselling Profits.** Tayko Software is a software catalog firm that sells games and educational software. It started out as a software manufacturer and then added third-party titles to its offerings. It recently revised its collection of items in a new catalog, which it mailed out to its customers. This mailing yielded 2000 purchases. Based on these data, Tayko wants to devise a model for predicting the spending amount that a purchasing customer will yield. The file *Tayko.csv* contains information on 2000 purchases. Table 6.4 describes the attributes to be used in the problem (the data file contains additional attributes).

TABLE 6.4	DESCRIPTION OF ATTRIBUTES FOR TAYKO SOFTWARE EXAMPLE
FREQ	Number of transactions in the preceding year
LAST_UPDATE	Number of days since last update to customer record
WEB	Whether customer purchased by Web order at least once
GENDER	Male or female
ADDRESS_RES	Whether it is a residential address
ADDRESS_US	Whether it is a US address
SPENDING (target attribute)	Amount spent by customer in test mailing ($)

a. Explore the spending amount by creating a pivot table for the categorical attributes and computing the average and standard deviation of spending in each category. (*Hint:* Consider using the *Turbo Prep* view.)

b. Explore the relationship between spending and each of the two continuous predictors by creating two scatterplots (Spending vs. Freq, and Spending vs. last_update_days_ago). Does there seem to be a linear relationship?

c. To fit a predictive model for Spending:

   i. Partition the 2000 records into training and holdout sets.

   ii. Run a multiple linear regression model for Spending vs. all six predictors. Give the estimated predictive equation.

   iii. Based on this model, what type of purchaser is most likely to spend a large amount of money?

   iv. If we used backward elimination to reduce the number of predictors, which predictor would be dropped first from the model?

   v. Show how the prediction and the prediction error are computed for the first purchase in the holdout set.

   vi. Evaluate the predictive accuracy of the model by examining its performance on the holdout set.

   vii. Create a histogram of the model residuals. Do they appear to follow a normal distribution? How does this affect the predictive performance of the model?

6.3 **Predicting Airfare on New Routes.**
The following problem takes place in the United States in the late 1990s, when many major US cities were facing issues with airport congestion, partly as a result of the 1978 deregulation of airlines. Both fares and routes were freed from regulation, and low-fare carriers such as Southwest (SW) began competing on existing routes and starting non-stop service on routes that previously lacked it. Building completely new airports is generally not feasible, but sometimes decommissioned military bases or smaller municipal airports can be reconfigured as regional or larger commercial airports. There are

numerous players and interests involved in the issue (airlines, city, state and federal authorities, civic groups, the military, airport operators), and an aviation consulting firm is seeking advisory contracts with these players. The firm needs predictive models to support its consulting service. One thing the firm might want to be able to predict is fares, in the event a new airport is brought into service. The firm starts with the file *Airfares.csv*, which contains real data that were collected between Q3—1996 and Q2—1997. The attributes in these data are listed in Table 6.5 and are believed to be important in predicting FARE. Some airport-to-airport data are available, but most data are at the city-to-city level. One question that will be of interest in the analysis is the effect that the presence or absence of Southwest has on FARE.

TABLE 6.5   DESCRIPTION OF ATTRIBUTES FOR AIRFARE EXAMPLE

S_CODE	Starting airport's code
S_CITY	Starting city
E_CODE	Ending airport's code
E_CITY	Ending city
COUPON	Average number of coupons (a one-coupon flight is a nonstop flight, a two-coupon flight is a one-stop flight, etc.) for that route
NEW	Number of new carriers entering that route between Q3—1996 and Q2—1997
VACATION	Whether (Yes) or not (No) a vacation route
SW	Whether (Yes) or not (No) Southwest Airlines serves that route
HI	Herfindahl index: measure of market concentration
S_INCOME	Starting city's average personal income
E_INCOME	Ending city's average personal income
S_POP	Starting city's population
E_POP	Ending city's population
SLOT	Whether or not either endpoint airport is slot-controlled (this is a measure of airport congestion)
GATE	Whether or not either endpoint airport has gate constraints (this is another measure of airport congestion)
DISTANCE	Distance between two endpoint airports in miles
PAX	Number of passengers on that route during period of data collection
FARE	Average fare on that route

a. Explore the numerical predictors and target attribute (FARE) by creating a correlation table and examining some scatterplots between FARE and those predictors. What seems to be the best single predictor of FARE?

b. Explore the categorical predictors (excluding the first four) by computing the percentage of flights in each category. Create a pivot table with the average fare in each category. Which categorical predictor seems best for predicting FARE?

c. Find a model for predicting the average fare on a new route:

   i. Convert categorical attributes into numerical attributes with dummy coding. Then, partition the data into training and validation sets. The model will be fit to the training data and evaluated on the validation set.

   ii. Use stepwise regression to reduce the number of predictors. You can ignore the first four predictors (S_CODE, S_CITY, E_CODE, E_CITY). Report the estimated model selected.

   iii. Repeat (ii) using exhaustive search instead of stepwise regression. Compare the resulting best model to the one you obtained in (ii) in terms of the predictors that are in the model.

iv. Compare the predictive accuracy of both models (ii) and (iii) using measures such as RMSE and average error as well as lift charts.

v. Using model (iii), predict the average fare on a route with the following characteristics: COUPON = 1.202, NEW = 3, VACATION = No, SW = No, HI = 4442.141, S_INCOME = $28,760, E_INCOME = $27,664, S_POP = 4,557,004, E_POP = 3,195,503, SLOT = Free, GATE = Free, PAX = 12,782, DISTANCE = 1976 miles.

vi. Predict the reduction in average fare on the route in (v) if Southwest decides to cover this route [using model (iii)].

vii. In reality, which of the factors will not be available for predicting the average fare from a new airport (i.e., before flights start operating on those routes)? Which ones can be estimated? How?

viii. Select a model that includes only factors that are available before flights begin to operate on the new route. Use an exhaustive search to find such a model.

ix. Use the model in (viii) to predict the average fare on a route with characteristics COUPON = 1.202, NEW = 3, VACATION = No, SW = No, HI = 4442.141, S_INCOME = $28,760, E_INCOME = $27,664, S_ POP = 4,557,004, E_POP = 3,195,503, SLOT = Free, GATE = Free, PAX = 12,782, DISTANCE = 1976 miles.

x. Compare the predictive accuracy of this model with model (iii). Is this model good enough, or is it worthwhile reevaluating the model once flights begin on the new route?

d. In competitive industries, a new entrant with a novel business plan can have a disruptive effect on existing firms. If a new entrant's business model is sustainable, other players are forced to respond by changing their business practices. If the goal of the analysis was to evaluate the effect of Southwest Airlines' presence on the airline industry rather than predicting fares on new routes, how would the analysis be different? Describe technical and conceptual aspects.

6.4 **Predicting Prices of Used Cars.** The file *ToyotaCorolla.csv* contains data on used cars (Toyota Corolla) on sale during late summer of 2004 in the Netherlands. It has 1436 records containing details on 38 attributes, including Price, Age, Kilometers, HP, and other specifications. The goal is to predict the price of a used Toyota Corolla based on its specifications. (The example in Section 6.3 is a subset of this dataset.)

Split the data into training (50%), validation (30%), and holdout (20%) datasets.

Run a multiple linear regression with the target attribute Price and predictors Age_08_04, KM, Fuel_Type, HP, Automatic, Doors, Quarterly_Tax, Mfr_Guarantee, Guarantee_Period, Airco, Automatic_airco, CD_Player, Powered_Windows, Sport_Model, and Tow_Bar.

a. What appear to be the three or four most important car specifications for predicting the car's price?

b. Using metrics you consider useful, assess the performance of the model in predicting prices.

k-Nearest Neighbors (k-NN)

In this chapter, we describe the k-nearest neighbors (k-NN) algorithm that can be used for classification (of a categorical label) or prediction (of a numerical label). To classify or predict a new record, the method relies on finding "similar" records in the training data. These "neighbors" are then used to derive a classification or prediction for the new record by voting (for classification) or averaging (for prediction). We explain how similarity is determined, how the number of neighbors is chosen, and how a classification or prediction is computed. k-NN is a highly automated data-driven method. We discuss the advantages and weaknesses of the k-NN method in terms of performance and practical considerations such as computational time.

7.1 THE k-NN CLASSIFIER (CATEGORICAL LABEL)

The idea in k-NN methods is to identify k records in the training dataset that are similar to a new record that we wish to classify. We then use these similar (neighboring) records to classify the new record into a class, assigning the new record to the predominant class among these neighbors. Denote the values of the predictors for this new record by $x_1, x_2, \ldots, x_p$. We look for records in our training data that are similar or "near" the record to be classified in the predictor space (i.e., records that have values close to $x_1, x_2, \ldots, x_p$). Then, based on the classes to which those proximate records belong, we assign a class to the record that we want to classify.

Determining Neighbors

The k-NN algorithm is a classification method that does not make assumptions about the form of the relationship between the class membership

Machine Learning for Business Analytics: Concepts, Techniques and Applications in RapidMiner, First Edition.
Galit Shmueli, Peter C. Bruce, Amit V. Deokar, and Nitin R. Patel
© 2023 John Wiley & Sons, Inc. Published 2023 by John Wiley & Sons, Inc.

(Y) and the predictors $X_1, X_2, \ldots, X_p$. This is a nonparametric method because it does not involve estimation of parameters in an assumed function form, such as the linear form assumed in linear regression (Chapter 6). Instead, this method draws information from similarities between the predictor values of the records in the dataset.

A central question is how to measure the distance between records based on their predictor values. The most popular measure of distance is the Euclidean distance. The Euclidean distance between two records $(x_1, x_2, \ldots, x_p)$ and $(u_1, u_2, \ldots, u_p)$ is

$$\sqrt{(x_1 - u_1)^2 + (x_2 - u_2)^2 + \cdots + (x_p - u_p)^2}. \tag{7.1}$$

You will find a host of other distance metrics in Chapters 12 and 16 for both numerical and categorical variables. However, the k-NN algorithm relies on many distance computations (between each record to be predicted and every record in the training set), and therefore the Euclidean distance, which is computationally cheap, is the most popular in k-NN.

To equalize the scales that the various predictors may have, note that in most cases, predictors should first be standardized before computing a Euclidean distance.

Classification Rule

After computing the distances between the record to be classified and existing records, we need a rule to assign a class to the record to be classified, based on the classes of its neighbors. The simplest case is $k = 1$, where we look for the record that is closest (the nearest neighbor) and classify the new record as belonging to the same class as its closest neighbor. It is a remarkable fact that this simple, intuitive idea of using a single nearest neighbor to classify records can be very powerful when we have a large number of records in our training set. It turns out that the misclassification error of the 1–nearest neighbor scheme has a misclassification rate that is no more than twice the error when we know exactly the probability density functions for each class.

The idea of the *1-nearest neighbor* can be extended to $k > 1$ neighbors as follows:

1. Find the nearest k neighbors to the record to be classified.
2. Use a majority decision rule to classify the record, where the record is classified as a member of the majority class of the k neighbors.

Example: Riding Mowers

A riding-mower manufacturer would like to find a way of classifying families in a city into those likely to purchase a riding mower and those not likely to buy one. A pilot random sample is undertaken of 12 owners and 12 nonowners in the city. The data are shown in Table 7.1. We first partition the data into training data (14 households) and validation data (10 households). Obviously, this dataset is too small for partitioning, which can result in unstable results, but we will continue with this partitioning for illustration purposes. A scatter plot of the training data is shown in Figure 7.1.

TABLE 7.1	LOT SIZE, INCOME, AND OWNERSHIP OF A RIDING MOWER FOR 24 HOUSEHOLDS		
Household number	Income ($000s)	Lot size (000s ft^2)	Ownership of riding mower
1	60.0	18.4	Owner
2	85.5	16.8	Owner
3	64.8	21.6	Owner
4	61.5	20.8	Owner
5	87.0	23.6	Owner
6	110.1	19.2	Owner
7	108.0	17.6	Owner
8	82.8	22.4	Owner
9	69.0	20.0	Owner
10	93.0	20.8	Owner
11	51.0	22.0	Owner
12	81.0	20.0	Owner
13	75.0	19.6	Nonowner
14	52.8	20.8	Nonowner
15	64.8	17.2	Nonowner
16	43.2	20.4	Nonowner
17	84.0	17.6	Nonowner
18	49.2	17.6	Nonowner
19	59.4	16.0	Nonowner
20	66.0	18.4	Nonowner
21	47.4	16.4	Nonowner
22	33.0	18.8	Nonowner
23	51.0	14.0	Nonowner
24	63.0	14.8	Nonowner
25	60.0	20.0	?

Now consider a new household with $60,000 income and 20,000 ft^2 lot size (also shown in Figure 7.1). Among the households in the training set, the one closest to the new household (in Euclidean distance after normalizing income and lot size) is household 4, with $61,500 income and 20,800 ft^2 lot size. If we use a 1-NN classifier, we would classify the new household as an owner,

FIGURE 7.1 SCATTER PLOT OF *LOT SIZE* VS. *INCOME* FOR THE 14 HOUSEHOLDS IN THE TRAINING SET AND THE NEW HOUSEHOLD TO BE CLASSIFIED

like household 4. If we use $k = 3$, the three nearest households are 4, 9, and 14, as can be seen visually in the scatter plot.[1] Two of these neighbors are owners of riding mowers, and one is a nonowner. The majority vote is therefore **Owner**, and the new household would be classified as an owner.

Figure 7.2 shows the RapidMiner process for training a k-NN model and then evaluating its performance with the validation data. In preparing the data, first, the target attribute **Ownership** is transformed to *Binominal* data type using the *Nominal to Binominal* operator. Next, this attribute is assigned the *label* role with the *Set Role* operator. The numeric attributes to be used as predictors (**Income** and **Lot_Size**) are then normalized using the z-transformation with

---

[1] RapidMiner's **k**-NN procedure automatically computes these distances but does not display them. You can compute distances yourself using the *Cross Distances* operator, as shown in the chapter Appendix.

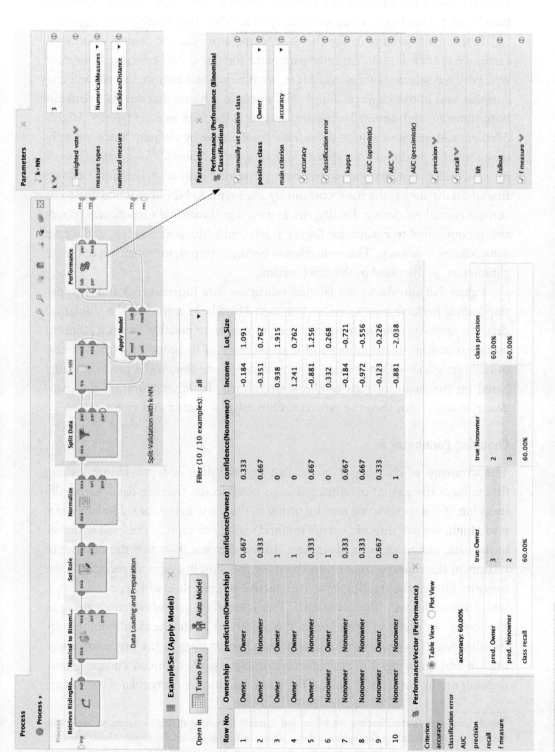

FIGURE 7.2   PROCESS FOR TRAINING AND EVALUATING A *k*-NN CLASSIFIER ON THE RIDING-MOWERS OWNERSHIP DATA

the *Normalize* operator.[2] The *Split Data* operator is configured with 0.58 and 0.42 partition ratios for training and validation data, respectively. The *k-NN* operator used to implement the *k*-NN method can be found in the Operators panel under *Modeling > Predictive > Lazy > k-NN*. The number of neighbors, (k) is the main parameter for the *k-NN* operator, and its default value is 5. Here, we specify $k = 3$. Another parameter for the *k-NN* operator is *weighted vote*, which is selected by default. Here, we unselect this option, but we will discuss this later in this chapter. The *k-NN* operator assumes that our data contains both numeric and nominal attributes and so it specifies *measure types = Mixed-Measures* and *mixed measure = MixedEuclideanDistance* by default. Since we only have numeric predictors, we specify *measure types = NumericalMeasures* and specify a Euclidean distance metric by setting *numerical measure = EuclideanDistance*. Euclidean distance is the most commonly used with *k*-NN in practice due to its computational efficiency. Finally, the *Performance (Binominal Classification)* operator is configured to ensure that `Owner` is selected as the positive class, and we set *main criterion = accuracy*. The *main criterion* becomes important when we optimize parameters, as discussed in the next section.

Figure 7.2 also shows the labeled validation data (normalized) and the corresponding performance metrics. For each household record in the validation data, the *confidence(Owner)* represents the proportion of positive class (i.e., `Owner`) members among its neighbors and is an estimate of its propensity (probability) of belonging to the `Owner` class. The *prediction(Ownership)* is the predicted label based on the majority class of the k neighbors. In other words, if the *confidence(Owner)* > 0.5, then the *prediction(Ownership)* is `Owner` and vice versa.

Choosing Parameter k

The advantage of choosing $k > 1$ is that higher values of k provide smoothing that reduces the risk of overfitting due to noise in the training data. Generally speaking, if k is too low, we may be fitting to the noise in the data. However, if k is too high, we will miss out on the method's ability to capture the local structure in the data, one of its main advantages. In the extreme, $k = n =$ the number of records in the training dataset. In that case, we simply assign all records to the majority class in the training data, irrespective of the values of $(x_1, x_2, \ldots, x_p)$, which coincides with the naive rule! This is clearly a case of oversmoothing in the absence of useful information in the predictors about the class membership. In other words, we want to balance between overfitting to the predictor information and ignoring this information completely. A balanced choice greatly depends on the nature of the data. The more complex and irregular the structure

---

[2]Ideally, during the normalization, the means and standard deviations should be computed only with the *training* data, excluding the *validation* data. This can be done with the *Group Models* operator, as discussed in Chapter 2. In practice, while working with large datasets, this does not make much difference since the distribution of both partitions is quite similar.

of the data, the lower the optimum value of k. Typically, values of k fall in the range of 1–20, and often an odd number is chosen to avoid ties.

So how is k chosen? Answer: We choose the k with the best classification performance. We use the training data to classify the records in the validation data and then compute error rates for various choices of k. For our example, if we choose $k = 1$, we will classify in a way that is very sensitive to the local characteristics of the training data. On the other hand, if we choose a large value of k, such as $k = 14$, we would simply predict the most frequent class in the dataset in all cases. This is a very stable prediction, but it completely ignores the information in the predictors. To find a balance, we examine the accuracy (of predictions in the validation set) that results from different choices of k between 1 and 14. For an even number k, if there is a tie in classifying a household, the tie is broken randomly.[3]

The RapidMiner process for choosing k is shown in Figure 7.3. The *Optimize Parameters (Grid)* operator can be found in the Operators panel under *Modeling > Optimization > Parameters > Optimize Parameters (Grid)*. This operator is a subprocess which contains the same training and validation process shown earlier in Figure 7.2 (with the orange background). Recall that we had configured the *Performance (Binominal Classification)* operator such that the main criterion is *accuracy*. Thus, the "optimal" k is chosen to optimize accuracy on the validation set. The training–validation process is iterated for a range of k values specified in the parameter settings of the *Optimize Parameters (Grid)* operator. (*Note*: The user needs to carefully specify the minimum and maximum parameter values, the scale of the search range, and the number of steps in the parameter search range.) The number of steps option specifies the number of values to be checked in the parameter's min–max search range, and the scale option (e.g., linear, logarithmic, etc.) specifies the pattern of values to be searched; for example, for a large dataset, selecting a small set of k values can speed up computation. The output in Figure 7.4 shows all the chosen performance metrics for each iteration, and the "optimal" k can be selected by sorting.[4] Here, we would choose $k = 5$, which is the lowest k value that maximizes our accuracy in the validation set.[5] Note, however, that now the validation set is used as part of the training process (to set parameter k) and does not reflect a true holdout set as before. Ideally, we would want a third test set to evaluate the performance of the method on data that it did not see.[6]

---

[3]If you are interested in reproducibility of results, check the accuracy only for each odd k.

[4]RapidMiner also provides the *ParameterSet* output panel which directly shows the best parameter value based on the optimized performance criteria.

[5]Partitioning such a small dataset is unwise in practice, as results will heavily rely on the particular partition. For instance, if you use a different partitioning, you might obtain a different "optimal" k. We use this example for illustration only.

[6]A test set can be implemented by adding another *Split Data* operator prior to the *Optimize Parameters (Grid)* operator in the process and then using the *Apply Model* and *Performance (Binominal Classification)* operators to evaluate the performance on the test set.

FIGURE 7.3   PROCESS FOR CHOOSING k BY MEASURING THE ACCURACY OF DIFFERENT k
VALUES ON VALIDATION SET

Once k is chosen, we rerun the algorithm on the combined training and
validation sets to generate classifications of new records. An example process is
shown in Figure 7.5, where the k-NN operator is now configured to use five
nearest neighbors to classify the new household. Note that the *Group Models*
operator is used to sequentially apply the normalization and k-NN to the new
household data.[7]

---

[7]If the k-NN model is directly used, the new household data in the non-normalized form will be
compared with the standardized data (combined training and testing set) to find the nearest neighbors,
which would be incorrect.

Optimize Parameters (Grid)	✕

Optimize Parameters (Grid) (14 rows, 8 columns)

iteration	k–NN.k ↑	accuracy	classification_error	AUC	precision	recall	f_measure
1	1	0.700	0.300	0.500	1	0.400	0.571
2	2	0.800	0.200	0.860	0.800	0.800	0.800
3	3	0.800	0.200	0.880	1	0.600	0.750
4	4	0.600	0.400	0.660	0.571	0.800	0.667
5	5	0.900	0.100	0.860	0.833	1	0.909
6	6	0.500	0.500	0.720	0.500	0.800	0.615
7	7	0.800	0.200	0.840	0.800	0.800	0.800
8	8	0.800	0.200	0.800	0.800	0.800	0.800
9	9	0.700	0.300	0.780	0.667	0.800	0.727
10	10	0.600	0.400	0.740	0.600	0.600	0.600
11	11	0.700	0.300	0.800	1	0.400	0.571
12	12	0.900	0.100	0.980	0.833	1	0.909
13	13	0.700	0.300	0.700	0.750	0.600	0.667
14	14	0.500	0.500	0.500	0.500	1	0.667

FIGURE 7.4   PERFORMANCE METRICS FOR DIFFERENT k VALUES TO FIND OPTIMAL k

Setting the Threshold Value

k-NN uses a majority decision rule to classify a new record, where the record is classified as a member of the majority class of the k neighbors. The definition of "majority" is directly linked to the notion of a threshold value applied to the class membership probabilities. Let us consider a Binominal label case. For a new record, the proportion of positive class members among its neighbors is an estimate of its propensity (probability) of belonging to the positive class. In the riding-mowers example with $k = 5$, it turns out that the five nearest neighbors to the new household (with income = \$60,000 and lot size = 20,000 ft^2) are households 4, 9, 14, 1, and 3. Since four of these are owners and one is a nonowner, we can estimate for the new household a probability of 0.8 of being an owner (and 0.2 for being a nonowner). Using a simple majority rule is equivalent to setting the threshold value to 0.5. In Figure 7.5, we see that the software assigned class **Owner** to this record.

As mentioned in Chapter 5, changing the threshold value affects the confusion matrix (and the error rates). Hence, in some cases, we might want to choose a threshold other than the default 0.5 for the purpose of maximizing accuracy or for incorporating misclassification costs. This is particularly likely to be the

FIGURE 7.5   **CLASSIFYING A NEW HOUSEHOLD USING THE "OPTIMAL" *k* = 5**

case when the class of primary interest (the positive class) is relatively rare, and the threshold for classifying records as positive must be lowered. Recall from Chapter 5 that the operators *Create Threshold* and *Apply Threshold* can used for this purpose.

Weighted *k*-NN

In using a majority vote approach, *k*-NN assigns equal weight to each of the *k* neighbors. For example, with $k = 3$, each neighbor's vote has a weight $= 1/3$. Weighted *k*-NN improves the *k*-NN algorithm by using an incredibly simple yet powerful idea that the closer the neighbor, the heavier its weight in the overall vote. Each neighbor's weight is determined by the inverse of its distance from the record to be predicted (normalized by the sum of inverse distances of all *k* neighbors). Thus, given $d_1, d_2, \ldots, d_k$ distances to each of the *k* neighbors, the weight for neighbor 1 is computed as

$$w_1 = \frac{1/d_1}{\left(1/d_1 + 1/d_2 + \ldots + 1/d_k\right)}. \tag{7.2}$$

Then, to compute the confidence (probability) of belonging to a certain class, we sum up the weights of the neighbors with that class.

For example, returning to our example with $k = 3$, suppose the distances from the new record to its three nearest neighbors (and their labels) were $d_1 = 0.5$ (Nonowner), $d_2 = 0.2$ (Nonowner), and $d_3 = 0.1$ (Owner). Using Eq. (7.2), we get weights $w_1 = 0.12$, $w_2 = 0.29$, and $w_3 = 0.59$. The confidence (probability) of belonging to the Owner class is then 0.59 (and for belonging to Nonowner class is $0.12 + 0.29 = 0.41$). Assuming a 0.5 threshold, the predicted class for the record would be Owner even though the majority vote is Nonowner.

Note: The k-NN operator in RapidMiner uses *weighted vote* by default.

k-NN with More Than Two Classes

The k-NN classifier can easily be applied to a label attribute with m classes, where $m > 2$. The "majority rule" means that a new record is classified as a member of the majority class of its k neighbors. An alternative, when there is a specific class that we are interested in identifying (and are willing to "overidentify" records as belonging to this class), is to calculate the proportion of the k neighbors that belong to this class of interest, use that as an estimate of the probability (propensity) that the new record belongs to that class, and then refer to a user-specified threshold value to decide whether to assign the new record to that class. For more on the use of a threshold value in classification where there is a single class of interest, see Chapter 5.

Working with Categorical Attributes

It usually does not make sense to calculate Euclidean distance between two non-numeric categories (e.g., cookbooks and maps, in a bookstore). Therefore, before k-NN can be applied, nominal (categorical) predictor attributes must be converted to binary dummies. In contrast to the situation with statistical models such as regression, all m binaries should be created and used with k-NN. While mathematically this is redundant, since $m - 1$ dummies contain the same information as m dummies, this redundant information does not create the multicollinearity problems that it does for linear models. Moreover, in k-NN, the use of $m - 1$ dummies can yield different classifications than the use of m dummies and lead to an imbalance in the contribution of the different categories to the model.

RapidMiner does not require converting categorical variables to binary dummies. Instead, for nominal attributes, set *measure types* = *NominalMeasures* in the k-NN operator parameter settings, along with an appropriate distance or similarity metric (in *nominal measure*). When a similarity metric is used, the distance is internally computed as the negative of the similarity value. When the data contains both numeric and nominal attributes, set *measure types = Mixed-Measures* along with *mixed measure = MixedEuclideanDistance*. This setting uses Euclidean distance for numeric attributes and augments it for nominal attributes by using a distance of 0 for identical values and 1 otherwise. For more details on various distance and similarity metrics (measures) for both numerical and categorical variables, see Chapters 12, 16, and 15.

7.2 *k*-NN FOR A NUMERICAL LABEL

The idea of k–NN can readily be extended to predicting a continuous value (as is our aim with multiple linear regression models). The first step of determining neighbors by computing distances remains unchanged. The second step, where a majority vote of the neighbors is used to determine class, is modified such that we take the average label value of the k-nearest neighbors to determine the prediction. Often, this average is a weighted average, with the weight decreasing with increasing distance from the point at which the prediction is required. In RapidMiner, using the weighted vote option in the k-*NN* operator computes the weighted average.

Another modification is in the error metric used for determining the "optimal k." Rather than the overall error rate used in classification, RMSE or another prediction error metric should be used in prediction (see Chapter 5).

PANDORA

Pandora is an Internet music radio service that allows users to build customized "stations" that play music similar to a song or artist that they have specified. When it started, Pandora used a k-NN style clustering/classification process called the Music Genome Project to locate new songs or artists that are close to the user-specified song or artist.

Pandora was the brainchild of Tim Westergren, who worked as a musician and a nanny when he graduated from Stanford in the 1980s. Together with Nolan Gasser, who was studying medieval music, he developed a "matching engine" by entering data about a song's characteristics into a spreadsheet. The first result was surprising—a Beatles song matched to a Bee Gees song, but they built a company around the concept. The early days were hard—Westergren racked up over $300,000 in personal debt, maxed out 11 credit cards, and ended up in the hospital once due to stress-induced heart palpitations. A venture capitalist finally invested funds in 2004 to rescue the firm, and it eventually went public.

In simplified terms, the process works roughly as follows for songs:

1. Pandora established hundreds of variables on which a song can be measured on a scale from 0 to 5. Four such variables from the beginning of the list are

- Acid Rock Qualities
- Accordion Playing

- Acousti-Lectric Sonority
- Acousti-Synthetic Sonority

2. Pandora pays musicians to analyze tens of thousands of songs and rate each song on each of these attributes. Each song will then be represented by a row vector of values between 0 and 5, for example, for Led Zeppelin's Kashmir:

   Kashmir 4 0 3 3 ... (high on acid rock attributes, no accordion, etc.)

   This step represents a significant investment and lies at the heart of Pandora's value because these variables have been tested and selected because they accurately reflect the essence of a song and provide a basis for defining highly individualized preferences.

3. The online user specifies a song that s/he likes (the song must be in Pandora's database).

4. Pandora then calculates the statistical distance[1] between the user's song and the songs in its database. It selects a song that is close to the user-specified song and plays it.

5. The user then has the option of saying "I like this song," "I don't like this song," or saying nothing.

6. If "like" is chosen, the original song and the new song are merged into a 2-song cluster[2] that is represented by a single vector comprising means of the variables in the original two song vectors.

7. If "dislike" is chosen, the vector of the song that is not liked is stored for future reference. (If the user does not express an opinion about the song, in our simplified example here, the new song is not used for further comparisons.)

8. Pandora looks in its database for a new song, one whose statistical distance is close to the "like" song cluster[3] and not too close to the "dislike" song. Depending on the user's reaction, this new song might be added to the "like" cluster or "dislike" cluster.

Over time, Pandora develops the ability to deliver songs that match a particular taste of a particular user. A single user might build up multiple stations around different song clusters. Clearly, this is a less limiting approach than selecting music in terms of which "genre" it belongs to.

While the process described above is a bit more complex than the basic "classification of new data" process described in this chapter, the fundamental process—classifying a record according to its proximity to other records—is the same at its core. Note the role of domain knowledge in this machine learning process—the variables have been tested and selected by the project leaders, and the measurements have been made by human experts. In another sense, this human role represented the Achilles heel of Pandora—it was costly and constituted a bottleneck obstructing the flow of new songs into the system.

Music streaming services later came to omit this step of pre-labeling songs and to rely on machine learning algorithms that get input only from users. Collaborative filtering, for example, recommends songs that are liked by other people who share your tastes (i.e., like the same songs); see Chapter 15 for more on collaborative filtering. Deep learning networks (which were not practically available at Pandora's inception) can take the sound waves in songs and derive features from them, in the same way that these networks derive features from images. These derived features can then be used to predict user choices. See Chapter 11 for more on neural networks.

Pandora was a pioneer in licensed music streaming but was later eclipsed by Spotify and Apple Music, which offered features that Pandora's "customized radio station" model did not, such as the ability to play a specific song on demand and the ability to download music.

Further reading: See www.pandora.com, Wikipedia's article on the Music Genome Project, and Joyce John's article "Pandora and the Music Genome Project," *Scientific Computing*, vol. 23, no. 10: 14, pp. 40–41, Sep. 2006.

---

[1]See Section 12.5 in Chapter 12 for an explanation of statistical distance.

[2]See Chapter 16 for more on clusters.

[3]See Case 23.6 "Segmenting Consumers of Bath Soap" for an exercise involving the identification of clusters, which are then used for classification purposes.

7.3   ADVANTAGES AND SHORTCOMINGS OF *k*-NN ALGORITHMS

The main advantage of *k*-NN methods is their simplicity and lack of parametric assumptions. In the presence of a large enough training set, these methods perform surprisingly well, especially when each class is characterized by multiple combinations of predictor values. For instance, in real estate databases, there are likely to be multiple combinations of {home type, number of rooms, neighborhood, asking price, etc.} that characterize homes that sell quickly vs. those that remain for a long period on the market.

There are three difficulties with the practical exploitation of the power of the *k*-NN approach. First, although no time is required to estimate parameters from the training data (as would be the case for parametric models such as regression), the time to find the nearest neighbors in a large training set can be prohibitive. A number of ideas have been implemented to overcome this difficulty. The main ideas are as follows:

- Reduce the time taken to compute distances by working in a reduced dimension using dimension reduction techniques such as principal components analysis (Chapter 4).

- Use sophisticated data structures such as search trees to speed up identification of the nearest neighbor. This approach often settles for an "almost nearest" neighbor to improve speed. An example is using *bucketing*, where the records are grouped into buckets so that records within each bucket are close to each other. For a to-be-predicted record, buckets are ordered by their distance to the record. Starting from the nearest bucket, the distance to each of the records within the bucket is measured. The algorithm stops when the distance to a bucket is larger than the distance to the closest record thus far.

Second, the number of records required in the training set to qualify as large increases exponentially with the number of predictors p. This is because the expected distance to the nearest neighbor goes up dramatically with p unless the size of the training set increases exponentially with p. This phenomenon is known as the *curse of dimensionality*, a fundamental issue pertinent to all classification, prediction, and clustering techniques. This is why we often seek to reduce the number of predictors through methods such as selecting subsets of the predictors for our model or by combining them using methods such as principal components analysis, singular value decomposition, and factor analysis (see Chapter 4).

Third, k-NN is a "lazy learner": the time-consuming computation is deferred to the time of prediction. For every record to be predicted, we compute its distances from the entire set of training records only at the time of prediction. This behavior prohibits using this algorithm for real-time prediction of a large number of records simultaneously.

APPENDIX: COMPUTING DISTANCES BETWEEN RECORDS IN RAPIDMINER

In RapidMiner's k-*NN* operator, distances between records are computed automatically. If you want to see the distances, the *Cross Distances* operator can be used to compute distances between a *request set* (here, normalized new household data) and a *reference set* (here, normalized training data). Figure 7.6 shows how to compute the Euclidean distance between the new household and each training record.

Row No.	request	document	distance
1	25	4	0.352
2	25	9	0.430
3	25	14	0.487
4	25	1	0.690
5	25	13	0.737
6	25	16	0.821
7	25	18	1.157
8	25	22	1.390
9	25	10	1.614
10	25	21	1.665
11	25	19	1.725
12	25	5	2.019
13	25	24	2.247
14	25	6	2.418

FIGURE 7.6   PROCESS FOR COMPUTING EUCLIDEAN DISTANCES BETWEEN THE NEW HOUSEHOLD AND THE TRAINING DATA

PROBLEMS

7.1 **Calculating Distance with Categorical Predictors.** This exercise with a tiny dataset illustrates the calculation of Euclidean distance and the creation of binary dummies. The online education company Statistics.com segments its customers and prospects into three main categories: IT professionals (IT), statisticians (Stat), and other (Other). It also tracks, for each customer, the number of years since first contact (years). Consider the following customers; information about whether they have taken a course or not (the target attribute to be predicted) is included:

Customer 1: Stat, 1 year, did not take course

Customer 2: Other, 1.1 year, took course

a. Consider now the following new prospect:

Prospect 1: IT, 1 year

Using the above information on the two customers and one prospect, create one dataset for all three with the categorical predictor attribute transformed into two binaries and a similar dataset with the categorical predictor attribute transformed into three binaries. (*Hint:* Use *Create ExampleSet* operator in RapidMiner, and enter the data with dummy coded attributes for course categories; also add an *id* attribute and then set it to *id* role.)

b. For each derived dataset, calculate the Euclidean distance between the prospect and each of the other two customers. (*Note:* While it is typical to normalize data for k-NN, this is not an iron-clad rule, and you may proceed here without normalization.)

c. Using k-NN with $k = 1$, classify the prospect as taking or not taking a course using each of the two derived datasets. Does it make a difference whether you use two or three dummies?

7.2 **Personal Loan Acceptance.** Universal Bank is a relatively young bank growing rapidly in terms of overall customer acquisition. The majority of these customers are liability customers (depositors) with varying sizes of relationship with the bank. The customer base of asset customers (borrowers) is quite small, and the bank is interested in expanding this base rapidly to bring in more loan business. In particular, it wants to explore ways of converting its liability customers to personal loan customers (while retaining them as depositors).

A campaign that the bank ran last year for liability customers showed a healthy conversion rate of over 9% success. This has encouraged the retail marketing department to devise smarter campaigns with better target marketing. The goal is to use k-NN to predict whether a new customer will accept a loan offer. This will serve as the basis for the design of a new campaign.

The file *UniversalBank.csv* contains data on 5000 customers. The data include customer demographic information (age, income, etc.), the customer's relationship with the bank (mortgage, securities account, etc.), and the customer response to the last personal loan campaign (Personal Loan). Among these 5000 customers, only 480 (=9.6%) accepted the personal loan that was offered to them in the earlier campaign.

Data Preprocessing. Transform the target attribute to *Binominal* type, and then specify the *positive* class (loan acceptance) as *acceptor* (replacing *true*) and the other class as *nonacceptor* (replacing *false*) using the *Map* operator in RapidMiner. Ensure that Education, a categorical predictor, is of *Polynominal* type. Also ensure that binary (0/1) predictors, namely, CD Account, CreditCard, Online, and Securities Account, are configured as *Binominal* type attributes. Consider all attributes as predictors except ID and ZIP Code.

Partition the data into training (60%) and holdout (40%) sets.

a. Consider the following customer:
Age = 40, Experience = 10, Income = 84, Family = 2, CCAvg = 2, Education = 2, Mortgage = 0, Securities Account = false, CD Account = false, Online = true, and Credit Card = true. Perform a k-NN classification with the selected predictors using $k = 1$. Use the default threshold value of 0.5. How would this customer be classified?

b. What is a choice of k that balances between overfitting and ignoring the predictor information? Use RapidMiner's *Optimize Parameters (Grid)* operator with nested 10-fold cross-validation on the training set to experiment with different k values, maximizing model accuracy. Report the confusion matrix, accuracy, precision, and recall for the 10-fold cross-validation performance (averaged) for the best k.

c. Show the confusion matrix for the holdout data that results from using the best k. Report and interpret classification performance metrics for the holdout set.

d. Consider the following customer:
Age = 40, Experience = 10, Income = 84, Family = 2, CCAvg = 2, Education = 2, Mortgage = 0, Securities Account = false, CD Account = false, Online = true, and Credit Card = true. Classify the customer using the best k.

e. Would you recommend using accuracy as the metric for finding the best k for this business context? Comment on whether any alternative performance metrics, if any, would be better for optimizing model performance in finding the best k.

7.3   **Predicting Housing Median Prices.** The file *BostonHousing.csv* contains information on over 500 census tracts in Boston, where for each tract multiple attributes are recorded. The last column (CAT.MEDV) was derived from median value (MEDV) such that it obtains the value 1 if MEDV > 30 and 0 otherwise. Consider the goal of predicting the MEDV of a tract, given the information in the first 12 columns.

Partition the data into training (60%) and holdout (40%) sets.

a. Perform a k-NN prediction with all 12 predictors (ignore the CAT.MEDV attribute), trying values of k from 1 to 10 with RapidMiner's *Optimize Parameters (Grid)* operator. Use nested 10-fold cross-validation on the training set within this operator. Make sure to normalize the data with the *Normalize* operator, and use the *Group Models* operator so that the normalization from the training data is used for validation as well. What is the best k? What does it mean?

b. Predict the MEDV for a tract with the following information, using the best k:

CRIM	ZN	INDUS	CHAS	NOX	RM	AGE	DIS	RAD	TAX	PTRATIO	LSTAT
0.2	0	7	0	0.538	6	62	4.7	4	307	21	10

c. If we used the above k-NN algorithm to score the training data, what would be the error of the training set?

d. Report the error rate (averaged) from the 10-fold cross-validation for the best-k. Why is the validation data error overly optimistic compared with the error rate when applying this k-NN predictor to new data?

e. Report the error rate for the holdout set using the optimized k-NN predictor. Compare this with the validation error rate found earlier and comment.

f. If the purpose is to predict MEDV for several thousands of new tracts, what would be the disadvantage of using k-NN prediction? List the operations that the algorithm goes through to produce each prediction.

CHAPTER 8

The Naive Bayes Classifier

In this chapter, we introduce the naive Bayes classifier, which can be applied to data with categorical predictors. We review the concept of conditional probabilities and then present the complete, or exact, Bayesian classifier. We next see how it is impractical in most cases and learn how to modify it and use instead the *naive Bayes* classifier, which is more generally applicable.

8.1 INTRODUCTION

The naive Bayes method (and, indeed, an entire branch of statistics) is named after the Reverend Thomas Bayes (1702–1761). To understand the naive Bayes classifier, we first look at the complete, or exact, Bayesian classifier. The basic principle is simple. For each record to be classified:

1. Find all the other records with the same predictor profile (i.e., where the predictor values are the same).

2. Determine what classes the records belong to and which class is most prevalent.

3. Assign that class to the new record.

Alternatively (or in addition), it may be desirable to tweak the method so that it answers the question: "What is the propensity of belonging to the class of interest?" instead of "Which class is the most probable?" Obtaining class probabilities allows using a sliding threshold to classify a record as belonging to class C_i, even if C_i is not the most probable class for that record. This approach is useful when there is a specific class of interest that we are interested in identifying, and we are willing to "overidentify" records as belonging to this class (see Chapter 5

Machine Learning for Business Analytics: Concepts, Techniques and Applications in RapidMiner, First Edition.
Galit Shmueli, Peter C. Bruce, Amit V. Deokar, and Nitin R. Patel
© 2023 John Wiley & Sons, Inc. Published 2023 by John Wiley & Sons, Inc.

for more details on the use of thresholds for classification and on asymmetric misclassification costs).

Threshold Probability Method

1. Establish a threshold probability for the class of interest above which we consider that a record belongs to that class.
2. Find all the training records with the same predictor profile as the new record (i.e., where the predictor values are the same).
3. Determine the probability that those records belong to the class of interest.
4. If that probability is above the threshold probability, assign the new record to the class of interest.

Conditional Probability

Both procedures incorporate the concept of *conditional probability*, or the probability of event A given that event B has occurred [denoted $P(A|B)$]. In this case, we will be looking at the probability of the record belonging to class C_i given that its predictor values are $x_1, x_2, \ldots, x_p$. In general, for a response with m classes $C_1, C_2, \ldots, C_m$ and the predictor values $x_1, x_2, \ldots, x_p$, we want to compute

$$P(C_i | x_1, \ldots, x_p). \tag{8.1}$$

To classify a record, we compute its probability of belonging to each of the classes in this way and then classify the record to the class that has the highest probability or use the threshold probability to decide whether it should be assigned to the class of interest.

From this definition, we see that the Bayesian classifier works only with categorical predictors. If we use a set of numerical predictors, then it is highly unlikely that multiple records will have identical values on these numerical predictors. In that case, one option is to convert numerical predictors to categorical predictors by binning. Another option is to use a related method called *Gaussian naive Bayes classifier* that can incorporate numerical predictors, and is discussed later in this chapter. For now, we will focus on categorical predictors only.

Example 1: Predicting Fraudulent Financial Reporting

An accounting firm has many large companies as customers. Each customer submits an annual financial report to the firm, which is then audited by the accounting firm. For simplicity, we will designate the outcome of the audit as "fraudulent" or "truthful," referring to the accounting firm's assessment of the customer's financial report. The accounting firm has a strong incentive to be accurate in identifying fraudulent reports—if it passes a fraudulent report as truthful, it would be in legal trouble.

The accounting firm notes that, in addition to all the financial records, it also has information on whether or not the customer has had prior legal trouble (criminal or civil charges of any nature filed against it). This information has not been used in previous audits, but the accounting firm is wondering whether it could be used in the future to identify reports that merit more intensive review. Specifically, it wants to know whether having had prior legal trouble is predictive of fraudulent reporting.

In this case, each customer is a record, and the class label of interest, $Y = \{\text{fraudulent, truthful}\}$, has two classes into which a company can be classified: $C_1 = $ fraudulent and $C_2 = $ truthful. The predictor attribute—"prior legal trouble"—has two values: 0 (no prior legal trouble) and 1 (prior legal trouble).

The accounting firm has data on 1500 companies that it has investigated in the past. For each company, it has information on whether the financial report was judged fraudulent or truthful and whether the company had prior legal trouble. The data were partitioned into a training set (1000 firms) and a holdout set (500 firms). Counts in the training set are shown in Table 8.1.

TABLE 8.1   PIVOT TABLE FOR FINANCIAL REPORTING EXAMPLE

	Prior legal ($X = 1$)	No prior legal ($X = 0$)	Total
Fraudulent (C_1)	50	50	100
Truthful (C_2)	180	720	900
Total	230	770	1000

8.2 APPLYING THE FULL (EXACT) BAYESIAN CLASSIFIER

Now consider the financial report from a new company, which we wish to classify as either fraudulent or truthful by using these data. To do this, we compute the probabilities, as above, of belonging to each of the two classes.

If the new company had prior legal trouble, the probability of belonging to the fraudulent class would be $P(\text{fraudulent} \mid \text{prior legal}) = 50/230$ (of the 230 companies with prior legal trouble in the training set, 50 had fraudulent financial reports). The probability of belonging to the other class, "truthful," is, of course, the remainder $= 180/230$.

Using the "Assign to the Most Probable Class" Method

If a company had prior legal trouble, we assign it to the "truthful" class. Similar calculations for the case of no prior legal trouble are left as an exercise to the reader. In this example, using the rule "assign to the most probable class," all records are assigned to the "truthful" class. This is the same result as the naive rule of "assign all records to the majority class."

Using the Threshold Probability Method

In this example, we are more interested in identifying the fraudulent reports—those are the ones that can land the auditor in jail. We recognize that, to identify the fraudulent reports, some truthful reports will be misidentified as fraudulent, and the overall classification accuracy may decline. Our approach is, therefore, to establish a threshold value for the probability of being fraudulent and classify all records above that value as fraudulent. The Bayesian formula for the calculation of this probability that a record belongs to class C_i is as follows:

$$P(C_i|x_1,\ldots,x_p) = \frac{P(x_1,\ldots,x_p|C_i)P(C_i)}{P(x_1,\ldots,x_p|C_1)P(C_1) + \cdots + P(x_1,\ldots,x_p|C_m)P(C_m)}.$$
$$(8.2)$$

In this example (where frauds are rarer), if the threshold were established at 0.20, we would classify a prior legal trouble record as fraudulent because $P(\text{fraudulent} \mid \text{prior legal}) = 50/230 = 0.22$. The user can treat this threshold as a "slider" to be adjusted to optimize performance, like other parameters in any classification model.

Practical Difficulty with the Complete (Exact) Bayes Procedure

The approach outlined above amounts to finding all the records in the sample that are exactly like the new record to be classified in the sense that all the predictor values are all identical. This was easy in the small example presented above, where there was just one predictor.

When the number of predictors gets larger (even to a modest number like 20), many of the records to be classified will be without exact matches. This can be understood in the context of a model to predict voting on the basis of demographic attributes. Even a sizable sample may not contain even a single match for a new record who is a male Hispanic with high income from the US Midwest who voted in the last election, did not vote in the prior election, has three daughters and one son, and is divorced. And this is just eight variables, a small number for most machine learning exercises. The addition of just a single new attribute with five equally frequent categories reduces the probability of a match by a factor of 5.

8.3 SOLUTION: NAIVE BAYES

In the naive Bayes solution, we no longer restrict the probability calculation to those records that match the record to be classified. Instead we use the entire dataset.

Returning to our original basic classification procedure outlined at the beginning of the chapter, recall that the procedure for classifying a new record was as follows:

1. Find all the other records with the same predictor profile (i.e., where the predictor values are the same).

2. Determine what classes the records belong to and which class is most prevalent.

3. Assign that class to the new record.

The naive Bayes modification (for the basic classification procedure) is as follows:

1. For class C_1, estimate the individual conditional probabilities for each predictor $P(x_j|C_1)$—these are the probabilities that the predictor value in the record to be classified occurs in class C_1. For example, for X_1 this probability is estimated by the proportion of x_1 values among the C_1 records in the training set.

2. Multiply these probabilities by each other and then by the proportion of records belonging to class C_1.

3. Repeat Steps 1 and 2 for all the classes.

4. Estimate a probability for class C_i by taking the value calculated in Step 2 for class C_i and dividing it by the sum of such values for all classes.

5. Assign the record to the class with the highest probability for this set of predictor values.

The above steps lead to the naive Bayes formula for calculating the probability that a record with a given set of predictor values $x_1, \ldots, x_p$ belongs to class C_1 among m classes. The formula can be written as follows:

$$P_{nb}(C_1 \mid x_1, \ldots x_p) =$$

$$\frac{P(C_1)[P(x_1 \mid C_1)P(x_2 \mid C_1) \cdots P(x_p \mid C_1)]}{P(C_1)[P(x_1 \mid C_1)P(x_2 \mid C_1) \cdots P(x_p \mid C_1)] + \cdots + P(C_m)[P(x_1 \mid C_m)P(x_2 \mid C_m) \cdots P(x_p \mid C_m)]}.$$

$$(8.3)$$

This is a somewhat formidable formula; see Example 2 for a simpler numerical version. Note that all the needed quantities can be obtained from pivot tables of Y vs. each of the categorical predictors.

The Naive Bayes Assumption of Conditional Independence

In probability terms, we have made a simplifying assumption that the exact *conditional probability* of seeing a record with predictor profile $x_1, x_2, \ldots, x_p$ within a certain class, $P(x_1, x_2, \ldots, x_p | C_i)$, is well approximated by the product of the individual conditional probabilities $P(x_1 | C_i) \times P(x_2 | C_i) \times \cdots \times P(x_p | C_i)$. These two quantities are identical when the predictors are independent within each class.

For example, suppose that "lost money last year" is an additional attribute in the accounting fraud example. The simplifying assumption we make with naive Bayes is that, within a given class, we no longer need to look for the records characterized both by "prior legal trouble" and "lost money last year." Rather, assuming that the two are independent, we can simply multiply the probability of "prior legal trouble" by the probability of "lost money last year." Of course, complete independence is unlikely in practice, where some correlation between predictors is expected.

In practice, despite the assumption violation, the procedure works quite well—primarily because what is usually needed is not a propensity for each record that is accurate in absolute terms but just a reasonably accurate *rank ordering* of propensities. Even when the assumption is violated, the rank ordering of the records' propensities is typically preserved.

Note that if all we are interested in is a rank ordering, and the denominator remains the same for all classes, it is sufficient to concentrate only on the numerator. The disadvantage of this approach is that the probability values it yields (the propensities), while ordered correctly, are not on the same scale as the exact values that the user would anticipate.

Using the Threshold Probability Method

The above procedure is for the basic case where we seek maximum classification accuracy for all classes. In the case of the *relatively rare class of special interest*, the procedure is as follows:

1. Establish a threshold probability for the class of interest above which we consider that a record belongs to that class.

2. For the class of interest, compute the probability that each individual predictor value in the record to be classified occurs in the training data.

3. Multiply these probabilities times each other and then times the proportion of records belonging to the class of interest.

4. Estimate the probability for the class of interest by taking the value calculated in Step 3 for the class of interest and dividing it by the sum of the similar values for all classes.

5. If this value falls above the threshold, assign the new record to the class of interest; otherwise not.

6. Adjust the threshold value as needed, as a parameter of the model.

Example 2: Predicting Fraudulent Financial Reports, Two Predictors

Let us expand the financial reports example to two predictors and, using a small subset of data, compare the complete (exact) Bayes calculations with the naive Bayes calculations.

Consider the 10 customers of the accounting firm listed in Table 8.2. For each customer, we have information on whether it had prior legal trouble, whether it is a small or large company, and whether the financial report was found to be fraudulent or truthful. Using this information, we will calculate the conditional probability of fraud, given each of the four possible combinations $\{y, small\}$, $\{y, large\}$, $\{n, small\}$, $\{n, large\}$.

TABLE 8.2   INFORMATION ON 10 COMPANIES

Company	Prior legal trouble	Company size	Status
1	Yes	Small	Truthful
2	No	Small	Truthful
3	No	Large	Truthful
4	No	Large	Truthful
5	No	Small	Truthful
6	No	Small	Truthful
7	Yes	Small	Fraudulent
8	Yes	Large	Fraudulent
9	No	Large	Fraudulent
10	Yes	Large	Fraudulent

Complete (Exact) Bayes Calculations: The probabilities are computed as

$P(\text{fraudulent}|\text{PriorLegal} = y, \text{Size} = \text{small}) = 1/2 = 0.5$

$P(\text{fraudulent}|\text{PriorLegal} = y, \text{Size} = \text{large}) = 2/2 = 1$

$P(\text{fraudulent}|\text{PriorLegal} = n, \text{Size} = \text{small}) = 0/3 = 0$

$P(\text{fraudulent}|\text{PriorLegal} = n, \text{Size} = \text{large}) = 1/3 = 0.33$

Naive Bayes Calculations: Now we compute the naive Bayes probabilities. For the conditional probability of fraudulent behaviors given {PriorLegal = y, Size = small}, the numerator is a multiplication of the proportion of {PriorLegal = y} instances among the fraudulent companies, times the proportion of {Size = small} instances among the fraudulent companies, times the proportion of fraudulent companies: $(3/4)(1/4)(4/10) = 0.075$. To get the actual probabilities, we must also compute the numerator for the conditional probability of truthful behaviors given {PriorLegal = y, Size = small}: $(1/6)(4/6)(6/10)$ = 0.067. The denominator is then the sum of these two conditional probabilities $(0.075 + 0.067 = 0.14)$. The conditional probability of fraudulent behaviors given {PriorLegal = y, Size = small} is therefore $0.075/0.14 = 0.53$. In a similar fashion, we compute all four conditional probabilities:

$$P_{\text{nb}}(\text{fraudulent}|\text{PriorLegal} = y, \text{Size} = \text{small}) = \frac{(3/4)(1/4)(4/10)}{(3/4)(1/4)(4/10) + (1/6)(4/6)(6/10)} = 0.53$$

$P_{\text{nb}}(\text{fraudulent}|\text{PriorLegal} = y, \text{Size} = \text{large}) = 0.87$

$P_{\text{nb}}(\text{fraudulent}|\text{PriorLegal} = n, \text{Size} = \text{small}) = 0.07$

$P_{\text{nb}}(\text{fraudulent}|\text{PriorLegal} = n, \text{Size} = \text{large}) = 0.31$

Note how close these naive Bayes probabilities are to the exact Bayes probabilities. Although they are not equal, both would lead to exactly the same classification for a threshold of 0.5 (and many other values). It is often the case that the rank ordering of probabilities is even closer to the exact Bayes method than the probabilities themselves, and for classification purposes it is the rank orderings that matter.

We now consider a larger numerical example, where information on flights is used to predict flight delays.

Example 3: Predicting Delayed Flights

Predicting flight delays can be useful to a variety of organizations: airport authorities, airlines, and aviation authorities. At times, joint task forces have been formed to address the problem. If such an organization were to provide ongoing real-time assistance with flight delays, it would benefit from some advance notice about flights that are likely to be delayed.

TABLE 8.3   **DESCRIPTION OF ATTRIBUTES FOR FLIGHT DELAYS EXAMPLE**

Day of week (DAY_WEEK)	Coded as 1 = Monday, 2 = Tuesday, ..., 7 = Sunday
Sch. dep. time (CRS_DEP_TIME)	Broken down into 18 intervals between 6:00 AM and 10:00 PM
Origin (ORIGIN)	Three airport codes: DCA (Reagan National), IAD (Dulles), and BWI (Baltimore–Washington Int'l)
Destination (DEST)	Three airport codes: JFK (Kennedy), LGA (LaGuardia), and EWR (Newark)
Carrier (CARRIER)	Eight airline codes: CO (Continental), DH (Atlantic Coast), DL (Delta), MQ (American Eagle), OH (Comair), RU (Continental Express), UA (United), and US (USAirways)

In this simplified illustration, we look at five predictors (see Table 8.3). The outcome of interest is whether or not the flight is delayed (*delayed* here means arrived more than 15 minutes late). Our data consist of all flights from the Washington, DC area into the New York City area during January 2004. A record is a particular flight. The percentage of delayed flights among these 2201 flights is 19.5%. The data were obtained from the Bureau of Transportation Statistics (available at www.transtats.bts.gov). The goal is to accurately predict whether or not a new flight (not in this dataset) will be delayed. The class label is whether the flight was delayed or not (1 = delayed and 0 = on time). In addition, information is collected on the predictors listed in Table 8.3.

Figure 8.1 (top) shows the data preprocessing steps involved. The *Select Attributes* operator selects the six attributes for this analysis. The scheduled departure time CRS_DEP_TIME is used rather than the actual departure time DEP_TIME because the actual departure time will not be known in advance for prediction.

We configure the *Discretize* operator to bin the scheduled departure time CRS_DEP_TIME into hourly intervals between 6:00 AM and 10:00 PM. DAY_WEEK, which is a numeric attribute, is transformed to a *Nominal* data type with the *Nominal to Polynominal* operator. Also, Flight Status is transformed to a *Binominal* data type for conducting 2-class classification and then assigned the *label* role with the *Set Role* operator. The data summary after preprocessing is shown in Figure 8.1 (bottom).

FIGURE 8.1   DATA PREPROCESSING FOR FLIGHT DELAYS DATA

Figure 8.2 shows the process for applying a naive Bayes classifier. The *Data Preprocessing* subprocess contains the same steps mentioned in Figure 8.1.

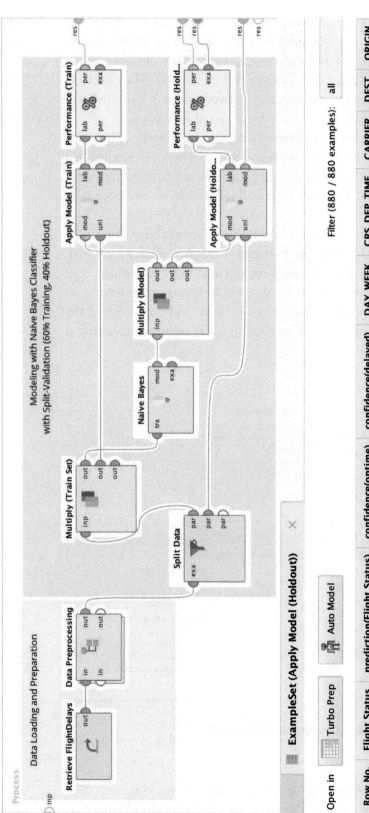

Row No.	Flight Status	prediction(Flight Status)	confidence(ontime)	confidence(delayed)	DAY_WEEK	CRS_DEP_TIME	CARRIER	DEST	ORIGIN
1	ontime	ontime	0.761	0.239	4	1400_1459	OH	JFK	BWI
2	ontime	ontime	0.836	0.164	4	1200_1259	DH	LGA	IAD
3	ontime	ontime	0.712	0.288	4	1700_1759	DH	LGA	IAD
4	ontime	ontime	0.771	0.229	4	1600_1659	DH	JFK	IAD
5	ontime	ontime	0.616	0.384	4	1700_1759	DH	JFK	IAD

FIGURE 8.2   (TOP) PROCESS FOR TRAINING AND EVALUATING A NAIVE BAYES CLASSIFIER ON THE FLIGHT DELAYS DATA AND (BOTTOM) PREDICTIONS FOR FIVE SAMPLE HOLDOUT FLIGHTS

The data were partitioned into training (60%) and holdout (40%) sets using the *Split Data* operator. The *Multiply* operator is used to create two copies of the training set. The naive Bayes method is implemented in RapidMiner using the *Naive Bayes* operator. Unlike most other methods, there are no parameters to be tuned for this model. Laplace correction is enabled by default for the *Naive Bayes* operator and may be optionally disabled. Laplace correction is a *smoothing* technique that handles the problem of zero probability in naive Bayes by adding 1 to each count of attribute categories so that the denominator is never zero while computing conditional probabilities. In practice, this has a negligible effect on the estimated probabilities.

Before using the output, let's see how the algorithm works. Figure 8.3 shows the computed probabilities in the form of a distribution table. The "simple distribution" table in the top left shows the ratios of delayed flights and on time flights in the training set (called prior class probabilities). The remaining tables show the conditional probabilities for each class, as a function of the predictor values. Note that in this example, there are no predictor values that were not represented in the training data. RapidMiner adds a dummy value called "unknown" to each predictor to capture any such missing predictor values.

To classify a new flight, we compute the probability that it will be delayed and the probability that it will be on time. Recall that since both probabilities will have the same denominator, we can just compare the numerators. Each numerator is computed by multiplying all the conditional probabilities of the relevant predictor values and, finally, multiplying by the proportion of that class (in this case $\hat{P}(\text{delayed}) = 0.195$). Let us use an example: to classify a Delta flight from DCA to LGA departing between 10:00 AM and 11:00 AM on a Sunday, we first compute the numerators using the values from the probability distribution table in Figure 8.3:

$\hat{P}(\text{delayed}|\text{Carrier} = \text{DL}, \text{Day\_Week} = 7, \text{Dep\_Time} = 10, \text{Dest} = \text{LGA}, \text{Origin} = \text{DCA})$
$\qquad \propto (0.109)(0.171)(0.023)(0.436)(0.518)(0.195) = 0.0000189,$

$\hat{P}(\text{ontime}|\text{Carrier} = \text{DL}, \text{Day\_Week} = 7, \text{Dep\_Time} = 10, \text{Dest} = \text{LGA}, \text{Origin} = \text{DCA})$
$\qquad \propto (0.199)(0.094)(0.052)(0.550)(0.649)(0.805) = 0.0002795.$

The symbol $\propto$ means "is proportional to," reflecting the fact that this calculation deals only with the numerator in the naive Bayes formula (Equation (8.3)). Comparing the numerators, it is therefore more likely that the flight will be on time. Note that a record with such a combination of predictor values does not exist in the training set, and therefore we use the naive Bayes rather than the exact

SimpleDistribution (Naive Bayes)

SimpleDistribution

Distribution model for label attribute Flight Status

Class ontime (0.805)
5 distributions

Class delayed (0.195)
5 distributions

Attribute ↑	Parameter ↑	ontime	delayed
CRS_DEP_TIME	value=0600_0659	0.066	0.031
CRS_DEP_TIME	value=0700_0759	0.068	0.047
CRS_DEP_TIME	value=0800_0859	0.070	0.062
CRS_DEP_TIME	value=0900_0959	0.051	0.023
CRS_DEP_TIME	value=1000_1059	0.052	0.023
CRS_DEP_TIME	value=1100_1159	0.037	0.016
CRS_DEP_TIME	value=1200_1259	0.069	0.051
CRS_DEP_TIME	value=1300_1359	0.071	0.058
CRS_DEP_TIME	value=1400_1459	0.087	0.152
CRS_DEP_TIME	value=1500_1559	0.059	0.105
CRS_DEP_TIME	value=1600_1659	0.091	0.066
CRS_DEP_TIME	value=1700_1759	0.100	0.152
CRS_DEP_TIME	value=1800_1859	0.037	0.023
CRS_DEP_TIME	value=1900_1959	0.055	0.101
CRS_DEP_TIME	value=2000_2059	0.025	0.012
CRS_DEP_TIME	value=2100_2159	0.062	0.078
CRS_DEP_TIME	value=unknown	0.000	0.000

Attribute ↑	Parameter ↑	ontime	delayed
CARRIER	value=CO	0.043	0.054
CARRIER	value=DH	0.237	0.307
CARRIER	value=DL	0.199	0.109
CARRIER	value=MQ	0.116	0.202
CARRIER	value=OH	0.014	0.008
CARRIER	value=RU	0.170	0.233
CARRIER	value=UA	0.011	0.012
CARRIER	value=US	0.210	0.074
CARRIER	value=unknown	0.000	0.000
DAY_WEEK	value=1	0.124	0.191
DAY_WEEK	value=2	0.139	0.144
DAY_WEEK	value=3	0.147	0.125
DAY_WEEK	value=4	0.189	0.148
DAY_WEEK	value=5	0.185	0.167
DAY_WEEK	value=6	0.122	0.054
DAY_WEEK	value=7	0.094	0.171
DAY_WEEK	value=unknown	0.000	0.000
DEST	value=EWR	0.281	0.358
DEST	value=JFK	0.169	0.206
DEST	value=LGA	0.550	0.436
DEST	value=unknown	0.000	0.000
ORIGIN	value=BWI	0.060	0.086
ORIGIN	value=DCA	0.649	0.518
ORIGIN	value=IAD	0.290	0.397

FIGURE 8.3   PROBABILITY DISTRIBUTION TABLE FOR THE NAIVE BAYES CLASSIFIER TRAINED ON THE FLIGHT DELAYS DATA

Bayes. To compute the actual probability, we divide each of the numerators by their sum:

$$\hat{P}(\text{delayed}|\text{Carrier}=\text{DL, Day\_Week}=7, \text{Dep\_Time}=10, \text{Dest}=\text{LGA, Origin}=\text{DCA})$$
$$= \frac{0.0000189}{0.0000189 + 0.0002795} = 0.063,$$
$$\hat{P}(\text{ontime}|\text{Carrier}=\text{DL, Day\_Week}=7, \text{Dep\_Time}=10, \text{Dest}=\text{LGA, Origin}=\text{DCA})$$
$$= \frac{0.0002795}{0.0000189 + 0.0002795} = 0.937.$$

Of course, we rely on software to compute these probabilities for any records of interest (in the training set, holdout set, or for scoring new data). The bottom part of Figure 8.2 shows five sample records from the holdout data with the predicted probabilities in the *confidence(ontime)* and *confidence(delayed)* columns, as well as the predicted labels in the *prediction(FlightStatus)* column.

Finally, to evaluate the performance of the naive Bayes classifier for our data, we can use the confusion matrix, gains and lift charts, and all the measures that were described in Chapter 5. For our example, the confusion matrices for the training and holdout sets are shown in Figure 8.4. We see that the overall accuracy level is around 80% for both the training and holdout data. In comparison, a naive rule that would classify all 880 flights in the holdout set as "on time" would have missed the 172 delayed flights, also resulting in a 80% accuracy. Thus, by a simple accuracy measure, the naive Bayes model does no better than the naive rule. However, examining the lift chart (Figure 8.5) shows the strength of the naive Bayes in capturing the delayed flights effectively, when the goal is ranking.

(a) Performance on Training Set

accuracy: 80.47%

	true ontime	true delayed	class precision
pred. ontime	1033	227	81.98%
pred. delayed	31	30	49.18%
class recall	97.09%	11.67%	

(b) Performance on Holdout Set

accuracy: 80.23%

	true ontime	true delayed	class precision
pred. ontime	686	151	81.96%
pred. delayed	23	20	46.51%
class recall	96.76%	11.70%	

FIGURE 8.4   CONFUSION MATRICES FOR FLIGHT DELAY USING NAIVE BAYES CLASSIFIER

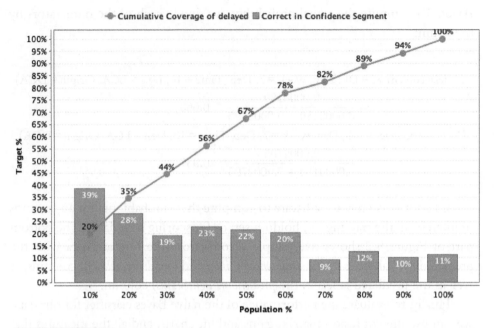

FIGURE 8.5 LIFT CHART FOR NAIVE BAYES CLASSIFIER APPLIED TO FLIGHT DELAY HOLDOUT DATA

Working with Continuous Attributes

Naive Bayes can be extended to numeric (continuous) predictor attributes, most commonly by assuming a Gaussian (normal) distribution for these attributes. This is useful when numeric predictors are present in the data and transforming them to categorical data types can lead to significant information loss. In applying the *Gaussian naive Bayes* method, each numeric attribute is summarized in the form of its mean and standard deviation, for each target class. If we assume a normal (Gaussian) distribution for the numerical attributes, we can use the normal curve to "discretize" the numerical values. This is done by replacing μ and σ with the predictor mean and standard deviation in the Gaussian probability density function $f(x)$:

$$f(x) = \frac{1}{\sigma\sqrt{2\pi}} \exp\left(-\frac{1}{2}\left(\frac{x-\mu}{\sigma}\right)^2\right). \tag{8.4}$$

Using Eq. (8.4), probability density values are computed by the software for each numeric attribute, for each target class. The idea is that the probability of any exact value is zero for a continuous attribute, but by using the probability density function, we are essentially considering a small range around the required exact value. Since this range is the same while computing the density values for each class label, it is possible to use the probability density values in a manner similar to the conditional probability values for categorical predictors in the naive Bayes probability computation. RapidMiner's *Naive Bayes* operator implements the Gaussian naive Bayes method by default when the attributes are numerical. If the attributes' distributions are very far from a normal curve, then RapidMiner offers the *Naive Bayes (Kernel)* operator, which allows more complex distributions using what are known as *kernel* functions.

To illustrate how the naive Bayes computations work for continuous attributes, suppose DISTANCE were to be considered as the predictor for whether the flight was delayed or not. The data from the distribution table shown in Figure 8.6 can be plugged into Eq. (8.4) to compute probability density values[1] for any specific distance value. For example, for Distance = 213, we get $\hat{P}$(Distance = 213 | delayed) = 0.0257737 and $\hat{P}$(Distance = 213 | ontime) = 0.0312124. As before, we compute only the numerator in the naive Bayes formula (Equation (8.3)), indicated with the $\propto$ symbol, as follows:

$$\hat{P}(\text{delayed} \mid \text{Distance} = 213) \propto (0.0257737)(0.195) = 0.005026,$$
$$\hat{P}(\text{ontime} \mid \text{Distance} = 213) \propto (0.0312124)(0.805) = 0.025126.$$

By dividing each of the numerators by their sum, we obtain the actual probability values:

$$\hat{P}(\text{delayed} \mid \text{Distance} = 213) = \frac{0.005026}{0.005026 + 0.025126} = 0.167,$$
$$\hat{P}(\text{ontime} \mid \text{Distance} = 213) = \frac{0.025126}{0.005026 + 0.025126} = 0.833.$$

Attribute	Parameter	ontime	delayed
DISTANCE	mean	212.058	211.658
DISTANCE	standard deviation	12.747	15.420

FIGURE 8.6   **DISTRIBUTION TABLE FOR DISTANCE AS A CONTINUOUS PREDICTOR FOR FLIGHT DELAYS**

---

[1]MS Excel's NORM.DIST function (with cumulative = FALSE parameter) can also be used to compute these probability density values.

8.4   ADVANTAGES AND SHORTCOMINGS OF THE NAIVE BAYES CLASSIFIER

The naive Bayes classifier's beauty is in its simplicity, computational efficiency, good classification performance, and ability to handle categorical attributes directly. In fact, it often outperforms more sophisticated classifiers even when the underlying assumption of independent predictors is far from true. This advantage is especially pronounced when the number of predictors is very large.

Three main issues should be kept in mind, however. First, the naive Bayes classifier requires a very large number of records to obtain good results.

Second, where a predictor category is not present in the training data, naive Bayes assumes that a new record with that category of the predictor has zero probability. This can be a problem if this rare predictor value is important. One example is the binary predictor *Weather* in the flights delay dataset, which we did not use for analysis and which denotes bad weather. When the weather was bad, all flights were delayed. Consider another example, where the class label is *bought high-value life insurance* and a predictor category is *owns yacht*. If the training data have no records with *owns yacht* = 1, for any new records where *owns yacht* = 1, naive Bayes will assign a probability of 0 to the label *bought high-value life insurance*. With no training records with *owns yacht* = 1, of course, no machine learning technique will be able to incorporate this potentially important variable into the classification model—it will be ignored. With naive Bayes, however, the absence of this predictor actively "outvotes" any other information in the record to assign a 0 to the label value (when, in this case, it has a relatively good chance of being a 1). The presence of a large training set (and judicious binning of continuous predictors, if required) helps mitigate this effect. A popular solution in such cases is to use a *smoothing* method such as the Laplace correction implemented in RapidMiner's *Naive Bayes* operator, thus avoiding the issue of zero probability. Also, by automatically adding an "unknown" category to each nominal predictor attribute, RapidMiner accommodates attribute values that may not be present in the training data.

Finally, good performance is obtained when the goal is *classification* or *ranking* of records according to their probability of belonging to a certain class. However, when the goal is to *estimate the probability of class membership (propensity)*, this method provides very biased results. For this reason, the naive Bayes method is rarely used in credit scoring (Larsen, 2005).

SPAM FILTERING

Filtering spam in e-mail has long been a widely familiar application of machine learning. Spam filtering, which is based in large part on natural language vocabulary, is a natural fit for a naive Bayesian classifier, which uses exclusively categorical attributes. Most spam filters are based on this method, which works as follows:

1. Humans review a large number of e-mails, classify them as "spam" or "not spam," and from these select an equal (also large) number of spam e-mails and non-spam e-mails. This is the training data.

2. These e-mails will contain thousands of words; for each word, compute the frequency with which it occurs in the spam dataset and the frequency with which it occurs in the non-spam dataset. Convert these frequencies into estimated probabilities (i.e., if the word "free" occurs in 500 out of 1000 spam e-mails, and only 100 out of 1000 non-spam e-mails, the probability that a spam e-mail will contain the word "free" is 0.5, and the probability that a non-spam e-mail will contain the word "free" is 0.1).

3. If the only word in a new message that needs to be classified as spam or not spam is "free," we would classify the message as spam, since the Bayesian posterior probability is $0.5/(0.5 + 01)$ or 5/6 that, given the appearance of "free," the message is spam.

4. Of course, we will have many more words to consider. For each such word, the probabilities described in Step 2 are calculated and multiplied together, and formula (8.3) is applied to determine the naive Bayes probability of belonging to the classes. In the simple version, class membership (spam or not spam) is determined by the higher probability.

5. In a more flexible interpretation, the ratio between the "spam" and "not spam" probabilities is treated as a score for which the operator can establish (and change) a threshold—anything above that level is classified as spam.

6. Users have the option of building a personalized training database by classifying incoming messages as spam or not spam and adding them to the training database. One person's spam may be another person's substance.

It is clear that, even with the "Naive" simplification, this is an enormous computational burden. Spam filters now typically operate at two levels—at servers (intercepting some spam that never makes it to your computer) and on individual computers (where you have the option of reviewing it). Spammers have also found ways to "poison" the vocabulary-based Bayesian approach, by including sequences of randomly selected irrelevant words. Since these words are randomly selected, they are unlikely to be systematically more prevalent in spam than in non-spam, and they dilute the effect of key spam terms such as "Viagra" and "free." For this reason, sophisticated spam classifiers also include attributes based on elements other than vocabulary, such as the number of links in the message, the vocabulary in the subject line, determination of whether the "From:" e-mail address is the real originator (anti-spoofing), use of HTML and images, and origination at a dynamic or static IP address (the latter are more expensive and cannot be set up quickly).

PROBLEMS

8.1   **Personal Loan Acceptance.** The file *UniversalBank.csv* contains data on 5000 customers of Universal Bank. The data include customer demographic information (age, income, etc.), the customer's relationship with the bank (mortgage, securities account, etc.), and the customer response to the last personal loan campaign (Personal Loan). Among these 5000 customers, only 480 (=9.6%) accepted the personal loan that was offered to them in the earlier campaign. In this exercise, we focus on two predictors: Online (whether or not the customer is an active user of online banking services) and Credit Card (abbreviated CC below) (does the customer hold a credit card issued by the bank) and the class label Personal Loan (abbreviated Loan below).

Partition the data into training (60%) and holdout (40%) sets. (*Hint*: Prior to partitioning the data, review the summary statistics for the data, and perform data preprocessing steps in RapidMiner such as (1) selecting the relevant attributes for the analysis (based on the tasks described below), (2) transforming any 2-class attributes to *Binominal* type and any multi-class categorical attributes to *Polynominal* type and (3) assigning special roles to any attributes as needed for the analysis.)

   a. Create a pivot table for the training data with Online as a column grouping attribute, CC as a row attribute (i.e., group by attribute), and Loan as a secondary row attribute (i.e., group by attribute). The values inside the table should convey the count. Consider using the Turbo Prep view for building the pivot table.

   b. Consider the task of classifying a customer who owns a bank credit card and is actively using online banking services. Looking at the pivot table, what is the probability that this customer will accept the loan offer? [This is the probability of loan acceptance (Loan = true) conditional on having a bank credit card (CC = true) and being an active user of online banking services (Online = true).]

   c. Create two separate pivot tables for the training data. One will have Loan (rows) as a function of Online (columns), and the other will have Loan (rows) as a function of CC.

   d. Compute the following quantities [$P(A \mid B)$ means "the probability of A given B"]:

   i. $P(CC = true \mid Loan = true)$ (the proportion of credit card holders among the loan acceptors)

   ii. $P(Online = true \mid Loan = true)$

   iii. $P(Loan = true)$ (the proportion of loan acceptors)

   iv. $P(CC = true \mid Loan = false)$

   v. $P(Online = true \mid Loan = false)$

   vi. $P(Loan = false)$

   e. Use the quantities computed above to compute the naive Bayes probability $P(Loan = true \mid CC = true, Online = true)$.

   f. Compare this value with the one obtained from the pivot table in (b). Which is a more accurate estimate?

   g. In RapidMiner, run naive Bayes on the data. Examine the model output on the training data, and find an entry that corresponds to $P(Loan = true \mid CC = true, Online = true)$. Compare this with the number you obtained in (e).

8.2   **Automobile Accidents.** The file *accidentsFull.csv* contains information on 42,183 actual automobile accidents in 2001 in the United States that involved one of three levels of injury: NO INJURY, INJURY, or FATALITY. For each accident, additional information is recorded, such as day of week, weather conditions, and road type. A firm might be interested in developing a system for quickly classifying the severity of an accident based on initial reports and associated data in the system (some of which rely on GPS-assisted reporting).

Our goal here is to predict whether an accident just reported will involve an injury (MAX_SEV_IR = 1 or 2) or will not (MAX_SEV_IR = 0). For this purpose, using the *Generate Attributes* operator, create a new attribute called INJURY that takes the value *true* if MAX_SEV_IR = 1 or 2, and otherwise *false*.

a. Using the information in this dataset, if an accident has just been reported and no further information is available, what should the prediction be? (INJURY = true or false?) Why?

b. Select the first 12 records in the dataset, and look only at the response (INJURY) and the two predictors WEATHER_R and TRAF_CON_R. (*Hint*: After selecting only the relevant attributes, review the summary statistics, and consider transforming any 2-class attributes to *Binominal* type and any multi-class categorical attributes to *Polynominal* type. Then, assign special roles to any attributes, as needed. Select the subset of records using the *Filter Example Range* operator.)

   i. Create a pivot table that examines INJURY as a function of the two predictors for these 12 records. Use all three variables in the pivot table as rows/columns.

   ii. Compute the exact Bayes conditional probabilities of an injury (INJURY = true) given the six possible combinations of the predictors.

   iii. Classify the 12 accidents using these probabilities and a threshold of 0.5.

   iv. Compute manually the naive Bayes conditional probability of an injury given WEATHER_R = true and TRAF_CON_R = 1.

   v. Run a naive Bayes classifier on the 12 records and 2 predictors using RapidMiner. Check the model output to obtain probabilities and classifications for all 12 records. Compare this with the exact Bayes classification. Are the resulting classifications equivalent? Is the ranking (=ordering) of observations equivalent?

c. Let us now return to the entire dataset. Partition the data into training (60%) and holdout (40%).

   i. Assuming that no information or initial reports about the accident itself are available at the time of prediction (only location characteristics, weather conditions, etc.), which predictors can we include in the analysis? (Use the data descriptions page from www.dataminingbook.com.)

   ii. Run a naive Bayes classifier on the complete training set with the relevant predictors (and INJURY as the class label). Note that all predictors are categorical. Transform the predictors appropriately to *Binominal* or *Polynominal* type. Show the confusion matrix.

   iii. What is the overall error for the holdout set?

   iv. What is the percent improvement relative to the naive rule (using the holdout set)?

   v. Examine the conditional probabilities in the pivot tables. Why do we get a probability of zero for $P(\text{INJURY} = \text{false} \mid \text{SPD\_LIM} = 5)$?

CHAPTER 9

Classification and Regression Trees

This chapter describes a flexible data-driven method that can be used for both classification (called *classification tree*) and prediction (called *regression tree*). Among the data-driven methods, trees (also known as *decision trees*) are the most transparent and easy to interpret. Trees are based on separating records into subgroups by creating splits on predictors. These splits create logical rules that are transparent and easily understandable, for example, "IF Age < 55 AND Education > 12 THEN class = 1." The resulting subgroups should be more homogeneous in terms of the outcome variable, thereby creating useful prediction or classification rules. We discuss the two key ideas underlying trees: *recursive partitioning* (for constructing the tree) and *pruning* (for cutting the tree back). In the context of tree construction, we also describe a few metrics of homogeneity that are popular in tree algorithms, for determining the homogeneity of the resulting subgroups of records. We explain that limiting tree size is a useful strategy for avoiding overfitting and show how it is done. We also describe alternative strategies for avoiding overfitting. As with other data-driven methods, trees require large amounts of data. However, once constructed, they are computationally cheap to deploy even on large samples. They also have other advantages such as being highly automated, robust to outliers, and able to handle missing values. In addition to prediction and classification, we describe how trees can be used for dimension reduction. Finally, we introduce *random forests* and *boosted trees*, which combine results from multiple trees to improve predictive power.

9.1 INTRODUCTION

If one had to choose a classification technique that performs well across a wide range of situations without requiring much effort from the analyst while being

Machine Learning for Business Analytics: Concepts, Techniques and Applications in RapidMiner, First Edition.
Galit Shmueli, Peter C. Bruce, Amit V. Deokar, and Nitin R. Patel

readily understandable by the consumer of the analysis, a strong contender would be the tree methodology developed by Breiman et al. (1984). Trees, also called decision trees,[1] can be used for both classification and prediction. We discuss the classification procedure first, then in later sections we show how the procedure can be extended to prediction of a numerical outcome. The program that Breiman et al. created to implement these procedures was called CART (Classification And Regression Trees). A related procedure is called C4.5.

What is a classification tree? Figure 9.1 shows a tree for classifying bank customers who receive a loan offer as either acceptors or nonacceptors, based on information such as their income, education level, and average credit card expenditure.

Tree

```
CCAvg > 8.900: acceptor {nonacceptor=0, acceptor=6}
CCAvg ≤ 8.900
|   Mortgage > 529.500
|   |   Mortgage > 626: nonacceptor {nonacceptor=1, acceptor=0}
|   |   Mortgage ≤ 626
|   |   |   Family > 1.500: acceptor {nonacceptor=0, acceptor=8}
|   |   |   Family ≤ 1.500: nonacceptor {nonacceptor=1, acceptor=1}
|   Mortgage ≤ 529.500
|   |   Income > 113.500
|   |   |   Education > 1.500: acceptor {nonacceptor=12, acceptor=184}
|   |   |   Education ≤ 1.500: nonacceptor {nonacceptor=349, acceptor=41}
|   |   Income ≤ 113.500
|   |   |   CCAvg > 2.950: nonacceptor {nonacceptor=128, acceptor=42}
|   |   |   CCAvg ≤ 2.950: nonacceptor {nonacceptor=2221, acceptor=6}
```

FIGURE 9.1   **EXAMPLE OF A TREE FOR CLASSIFYING BANK CUSTOMERS AS LOAN ACCEPTORS OR NONACCEPTORS**

Tree Structure

We have two types of nodes in a tree: decision (= splitting) nodes and leaf nodes. Nodes that have successors are called *decision nodes* because if we were to use a tree to classify a new record for which we knew only the values of the predictor attributes, we would "drop" the record down the tree so that at each

---

[1]While RapidMiner uses the term *decision tree* for its tree operator, we minimize our use of this term to avoid confusion with decision trees used in decision analysis.

decision node, the appropriate branch is taken until we get to a node that has no successors. Such nodes are called the *leaf nodes* (or *terminal nodes* or *leaves* of the tree), and represent the partitioning of the data by predictors.

The type of trees grown by RapidMiner's *Decision Tree* operator are referred to as C4.5-like. For these trees, numerical predictors create binary splits whereas categorical predictors can create as many splits as the predictor has categories. If the tree has only binary-splits at each decision node, then such a tree has the property that the number of leaf nodes is exactly one more than the number of decision nodes.

The *Decision Tree* operator can be located in the Operators panel under *Modeling > Predictive > Trees > Decision Tree*. When using the *Decision Tree* operator, nodes are represented as boxes. For decision nodes, the name of the predictor attribute chosen for splitting appears at the top. Of the two child nodes connected below a decision node, the left box is for records that meet the splitting condition ("> splitting value"), while the right box is for records that meet the complementary condition ("$\leq$ splitting value").

Decision Rules

One of the reasons that tree classifiers are very popular is that they provide easily understandable decision rules (at least if the trees are not too large). Consider the tree in Figure 9.1. The leaf nodes are marked *acceptor* or *nonacceptor* based on the tree's classification for records in that node. The splitting node lists the predictor name and the left and right arrows from the splitting node give the condition for the split (e.g., *CCAvg* ≤ 8.9 from the top node to the right child node.) The colored bar within each leaf node gives a visual indication of the proportion of the two classes in that node. The text description available for each tree (see bottom of Figure 9.1) provides the counts of the two classes in each node.[2] This tree can easily be translated into a set of rules for classifying a bank customer. For example, the bottom-left node under the "Family" decision node in this tree gives us the following rule:

$$\text{IF}(CCAvg \leq 8.9) \text{ AND } (Mortgage > 29.5)$$
$$\text{AND } (Mortgage \leq 626) \text{ AND } (Family > 1.5)$$
$$\text{THEN } Class = \text{acceptor}.$$

Classifying a New Record

To classify a new record, it is "dropped" down the tree. When it has dropped all the way down to a leaf node, we can assign its class simply by taking a "vote" (or average, if the outcome is numerical) of all the training data that belonged

---

[2] In RapidMiner, hovering over leaf nodes interactively shows the record counts and class proportions in each node as well.

to the leaf node when the tree was grown. The class with the highest vote is assigned to the new record. For instance, a new record reaching the rightmost leaf node in Figure 9.1, which has a majority of records that belong to the nonacceptor class, would be classified as "nonacceptor." Alternatively, we can convert the number of nonacceptor class records in the node to a proportion (propensity) and then compare the proportion to a user-specified threshold value. In a binary classification situation (typically, with a success class that is relatively rare and of particular interest), we can also establish a lower threshold to better capture those rare successes (at the cost of lumping in more failures as successes). With a lower threshold, the votes for the *success* class only need attain that lower threshold level for the entire leaf node to be classified as a *success*. The threshold therefore determines the proportion of votes needed for determining the leaf node class. See Chapter 5 for further discussion of the use of a threshold value in classification, for cases where a single class is of interest.

In the following sections, we show how trees are constructed and evaluated.

9.2 CLASSIFICATION TREES

The key idea underlying tree construction is *recursive partitioning* of the space of the predictor attributes. A second important issue is avoiding over-fitting. We start by explaining recursive partitioning (Section 9.2) and then describe approaches for evaluating and fine-tuning trees while avoiding overfitting (Section 9.3).

Recursive Partitioning

Let us denote the target attribute by Y and the predictors by $X_1, X_2, X_3, \ldots, X_p$. In classification, the target will be a categorical attribute (*nominal* type), sometimes called a class label. Specifically, in binary classification, the class label will be of *binominal* type. Recursive partitioning divides up the p-dimensional space of the X predictors into nonoverlapping multidimensional rectangles. The predictor attributes here are considered to be continuous (*numeric* type) or categorical (*nominal* type). This division is accomplished recursively (i.e., operating on the results of prior divisions). First, one of the predictor attributes is selected, say X_i, and a value of X_i, say s_i, is chosen to split the p-dimensional space into two parts: one part that contains all the points with $X_i < s_i$ and the other with all the points with $X_i \geq s_i$. Then, one of these two parts is divided in a similar manner by again choosing a predictor attribute (it could be X_i or another attribute) and a split value for that attribute. This results in three (multidimensional) rectangular regions. This process is continued so that we get smaller and smaller rectangular regions. The idea is to divide the entire X-space up into rectangles such that each rectangle is as homogeneous or "pure" as possible. By *pure*, we mean containing records that belong to just one class. (Of course, this is not always possible, as there may be records that belong to different classes but have exactly the same values for every one of the predictor attributes.)

Let us illustrate recursive partitioning with an example.

Example 1: Riding Mowers

We again use the riding-mower example presented in Chapter 3. A riding-mower manufacturer would like to find a way of classifying families in a city into those likely to purchase a riding mower and those not likely to buy one. A pilot random sample of 12 owners and 12 nonowners in the city is undertaken. The data are shown and plotted in Table 9.1 and Figure 9.2.

TABLE 9.1	LOT SIZE, INCOME, AND OWNERSHIP OF A RIDING MOWER FOR 24 HOUSEHOLDS		
Household number	Income ($000s)	Lot size (000s ft^2)	Ownership of riding mower
1	60.0	18.4	Owner
2	85.5	16.8	Owner
3	64.8	21.6	Owner
4	61.5	20.8	Owner
5	87.0	23.6	Owner
6	110.1	19.2	Owner
7	108.0	17.6	Owner
8	82.8	22.4	Owner
9	69.0	20.0	Owner
10	93.0	20.8	Owner
11	51.0	22.0	Owner
12	81.0	20.0	Owner
13	75.0	19.6	Nonowner
14	52.8	20.8	Nonowner
15	64.8	17.2	Nonowner
16	43.2	20.4	Nonowner
17	84.0	17.6	Nonowner
18	49.2	17.6	Nonowner
19	59.4	16.0	Nonowner
20	66.0	18.4	Nonowner
21	47.4	16.4	Nonowner
22	33.0	18.8	Nonowner
23	51.0	14.0	Nonowner
24	63.0	14.8	Nonowner

If we apply the classification tree procedure to these data, as shown in Figure 9.3, the procedure will choose *Income* for the first split with a splitting value of 84.75. The (X_1, X_2) space is now divided into two rectangles, one with Income $\leq$ 84.75 and the other with Income $>$ 84.75. This is illustrated in Figure 9.4.

Notice how the split has created two rectangles, each of which is much more homogeneous than the rectangle before the split. The left rectangle contains

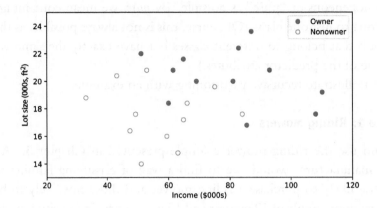

FIGURE 9.2   SCATTER PLOT OF LOT SIZE VS. INCOME FOR 24 OWNERS AND NONOWNERS OF
RIDING MOWERS

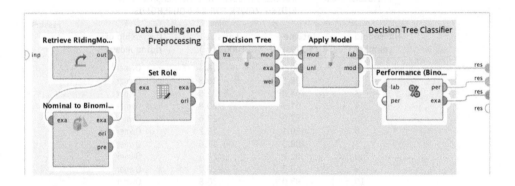

FIGURE 9.3   PROCESS FOR GENERATING CLASSIFICATION TREE FOR OWNERS AND
NONOWNERS OF RIDING MOWERS

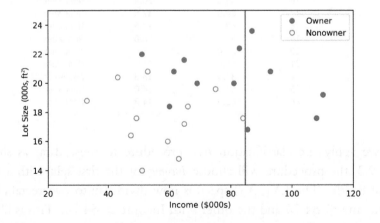

FIGURE 9.4   SPLITTING THE 24 RECORDS BY INCOME VALUE OF 84.75

points that are mostly nonowners (12 nonowners and 7 owners) and the right rectangle contains all owners (5 owners and 0 nonowners).

How was this particular split selected? The algorithm examined each predictor attribute (in this case, Income and Lot Size) and all possible split values for each attribute to find the best split. What are the possible split values for an attribute? They are simply the midpoints between pairs of consecutive values for the predictor. The possible split points for Income are $\{38.1, 45.3, 50.1, \ldots, 109.5\}$ and those for Lot Size are $\{14.4, 15.4, 16.2, \ldots, 23\}$. These split points are ranked according to how much they reduce impurity (heterogeneity) in the resulting rectangle. A pure rectangle is one that is composed of a single class (e.g., owners). The reduction in impurity is defined as overall impurity before the split minus the sum of the impurities for the two rectangles that result from a split.

Categorical Predictors   The previous description used numerical predictors; however, categorical predictors can also be used in the recursive partitioning context. To handle categorical predictors, the split choices for a categorical predictor are all ways in which the set of categories can be divided into two subsets. For example, a categorical predictor with four categories, say $\{a, b, c, d\}$, can be split in seven ways into two subsets: $\{a\}$ and $\{b, c, d\}$; $\{b\}$ and $\{a, c, d\}$; $\{c\}$ and $\{a, b, d\}$; $\{d\}$ and $\{a, b, c\}$; $\{a, b\}$ and $\{c, d\}$; $\{a, c\}$ and $\{b, d\}$; and finally $\{a, d\}$ and $\{b, c\}$. When the number of categories is large, the number of splits becomes very large. As with k-nearest neighbors, a predictor with m categories ($m > 2$) should be factored into m dummies (not $m - 1$). Rapid-Miner's *Decision Tree* operator automatically creates the same number of splits as the number of categories for a categorical predictor. While doing so, it does not require explicitly converting categorical attributes to binary dummies, as long as they are set to be of *Nominal* type or one of its subtypes, i.e., *Polynominal* or *Binominal* type.

Normalization   Whether predictors are numerical or categorical, it does not make any difference if they are standardized (normalized) or not.

Measures of Impurity

There are a number of ways to measure impurity. The two most popular measures are the *Gini index* and an *entropy measure*. We describe both next. Denote the m classes of the target attribute by $k = 1, 2, \ldots, m$.

The *Gini impurity index* for a rectangle A is defined by

$$I(A) = 1 - \sum_{k=1}^{m} p_k^2,$$

where p_k is the proportion of records in rectangle A that belong to class k. This measure takes values between 0 (when all the records belong to the same class) and $(m - 1)/m$ (when all m classes are equally represented). Figure 9.5 shows the values of the Gini index for a two-class case as a function of p_k. It can be seen that the impurity measure is at its peak when $p_k = 0.5$ (that is, when the rectangle contains 50% of each of the two classes).

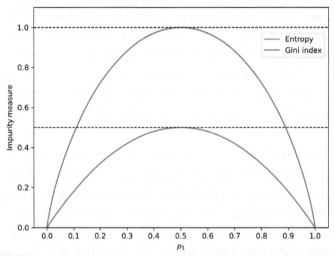

| **FIGURE 9.5** | **VALUES OF GINI INDEX AND ENTROPY MEASURE FOR A TWO-CLASS CASE AS A FUNCTION OF THE PROPORTION OF RECORDS IN CLASS 1 (p_1)** |

A second impurity measure is the *entropy measure*. The entropy for a rectangle A is defined by

$$\text{entropy}(A) = -\sum_{k=1}^{m} p_k \log_2(p_k).$$

This measure ranges between 0 (most pure, all records belong to the same class) and $\log_2(m)$ (when all m classes are represented equally). As shown in Figure 9.5, in the two-class case, the entropy measure is maximized (like the Gini index) at $p_k = 0.5$.

Let us compute the impurity in the riding-mowers example before and after the first split (using Income with the split value of 84.75). The unsplit dataset contains 12 owners and 12 nonowners. This is a two-class case with an equal number of records from each class. Both impurity measures are therefore at their maximum value: Gini = 0.5 and entropy = $\log_2(2) = 1$. After the split, the left rectangle contains 12 nonowners and 7 owners. The impurity measures for this rectangle are:

gini_left = $1 - (12/19)^2 - (7/19)^2 = 0.465$,

entropy_left = $-(12/19) \log_2(12/19) - (7/19) \log_2(7/19) = 0.949$.

The right node contains 5 owners and 0 nonowners and is thus a "pure" node. The impurity measures of the right node are therefore gini_right = 0 and entropy_right = 0.

The combined impurity of the two nodes created by the split is a weighted average of the impurity measures of the two nodes, weighted by the proportion of records in each:

gini = (19/24)(0.465) + (5/24)(0) = 0.368,

entropy = (19/24)(0.949) + (5/24)(0) = 0.752.

Thus, the Gini impurity index decreased from 0.5 before the split to 0.368 after the split. Similarly, the entropy impurity measure decreased from 1 before the split to 0.752 after the split. This decrease in entropy after the split (the difference between entropy before and after the split) is called *information gain*. In the above example, *information gain* = 1 − 0.752 = 0.248. Note that higher values of information gain indicate a better split.

In addition to the Gini index, entropy, and information gain, there is a host of alternative criteria that have been proposed and implemented in different software. Empirical research comparing these different criteria suggests that the choice of splitting criterion will not make much difference on the tree performance, and that each criterion might be superior in some cases but not in others (Rokach and Maimon, 2014).

RapidMiner's *Decision Tree* operator provides the following criteria for generating classification trees: *gini_index, information_gain, gain_ratio* (default), and *accuracy* (maximizes the accuracy for the entire tree).

Gain ratio is a slight modification of *information gain* that takes into account the sizes of the children nodes after a split, trying to avoid splits with variable-size children nodes (that is, a child node with very few records). This can result in simpler trees. In RapidMiner's decision trees that allow more than binary splits (similar to C4.5), gain ratio also penalizes splits with many children. Like information gain, higher values of gain ratio indicate a better split.

Gain ratio adjusts the information gain by taking the *split information* of an attribute split into account. The split information for a rectangle A corresponding to an attribute split is defined by

$$\text{split information}(A) = -\sum_{i=1}^{s} q_i \log_2(q_i)$$

where q_i is the proportion of records in child node i and s is the total number of splits for that attribute. Note that split information captures the distribution of the predictor attribute, without using the label information. In contrast, information gain is computed based on the label information. In the above example,

split information = $-(19/24)\log_2(19/24) - (5/24)\log_2(5/24) = 0.738$,

gain ratio = information gain / split information = 0.248/0.738 = 0.336.

By comparing the reduction in impurity across all possible splits in all possible predictors, the next split is chosen. If we continue splitting the mower data, the next split based on the gain ratio metric is on the Lot Size attribute at the value 21.2. Figure 9.6 shows that once again the tree procedure has astutely chosen to split a rectangle to increase the purity of the resulting rectangles. The upper-left rectangle, which contains records with Income $\leq$ 84.75 and Lot Size $>$ 21.2, has three records that are all owners; whereas the right-side rectangle, which contains records with Income $>$ 84.75 already consists exclusively of five owners. In other words, two rectangles (upper-left and right-side) are now "pure."

We can see how the recursive partitioning is refining the set of constituent rectangles to become purer as the algorithm proceeds. The final stage of the recursive partitioning is shown in Figure 9.7. Notice that each rectangle is now pure: it contains records from just one of the two classes.

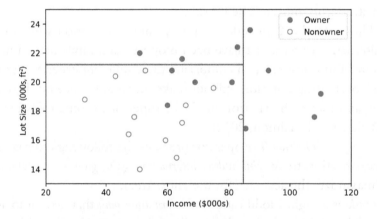

FIGURE 9.6   SPLITTING THE 24 RECORDS FIRST BY INCOME VALUE OF 84.75 AND THEN LOT SIZE VALUE OF 21.2

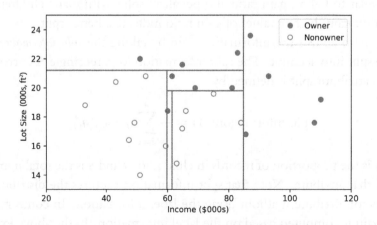

FIGURE 9.7   FINAL STAGE OF RECURSIVE PARTITIONING; EACH RECTANGLE CONSISTING OF A SINGLE CLASS (OWNERS OR NONOWNERS)

The reason the method is called a *classification tree algorithm* is that each split can be depicted as a split of a node into two successor nodes. The first split is shown as a branching of the root node of a tree in Figure 9.8. The tree showing the first three splits is shown in Figure 9.9. The full-grown tree is shown in Figure 9.10.

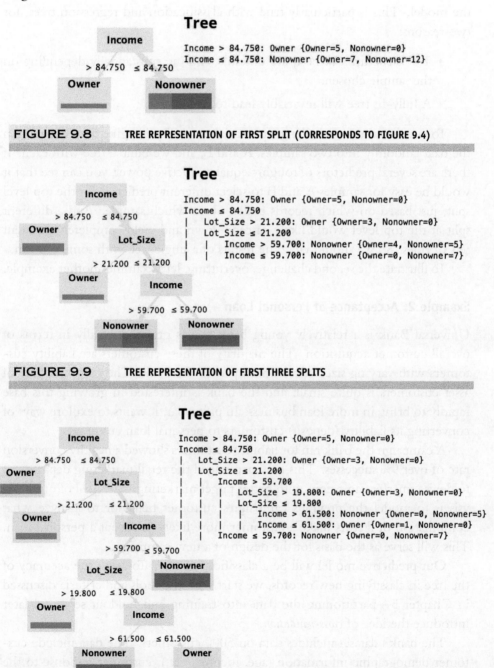

Tree

Income > 84.750: Owner {Owner=5, Nonowner=0}
Income ≤ 84.750: Nonowner {Owner=7, Nonowner=12}

FIGURE 9.8   TREE REPRESENTATION OF FIRST SPLIT (CORRESPONDS TO FIGURE 9.4)

Tree

```
Income > 84.750: Owner {Owner=5, Nonowner=0}
Income ≤ 84.750
|    Lot_Size > 21.200: Owner {Owner=3, Nonowner=0}
|    Lot_Size ≤ 21.200
|    |    Income > 59.700: Nonowner {Owner=4, Nonowner=5}
|    |    Income ≤ 59.700: Nonowner {Owner=0, Nonowner=7}
```

FIGURE 9.9   TREE REPRESENTATION OF FIRST THREE SPLITS

Tree

```
Income > 84.750: Owner {Owner=5, Nonowner=0}
Income ≤ 84.750
|    Lot_Size > 21.200: Owner {Owner=3, Nonowner=0}
|    Lot_Size ≤ 21.200
|    |    Income > 59.700
|    |    |    Lot_Size > 19.800: Owner {Owner=3, Nonowner=0}
|    |    |    Lot_Size ≤ 19.800
|    |    |    |    Income > 61.500: Nonowner {Owner=0, Nonowner=5}
|    |    |    |    Income ≤ 61.500: Owner {Owner=1, Nonowner=0}
|    |    Income ≤ 59.700: Nonowner {Owner=0, Nonowner=7}
```

FIGURE 9.10   TREE REPRESENTATION AFTER ALL SPLITS (CORRESPONDS TO FIGURE 9.7). THIS IS THE FULL GROWN TREE

9.3 EVALUATING THE PERFORMANCE OF A CLASSIFICATION TREE

We have seen with previous methods that the modeling job is not completed by fitting a model to training data; we need out-of-sample data to assess and tune the model. This is particularly true with classification and regression trees, for two reasons:

- Tree structure can be quite unstable, shifting substantially depending on the sample chosen.
- A fully-fit tree will invariably lead to overfitting.

To visualize the first challenge, potential instability, imagine that we partition the data randomly into two samples, A and B, and we build a tree with each. If there are several predictors of roughly equal predictive power, you can see that it would be easy for samples A and B to select different predictors for the top level split, just based on which records ended up in which sample. And a different split at the top level would likely cascade down and yield completely different sets of rules. So we should view the results of a single tree with some caution.

To illustrate the second challenge, overfitting, let's examine another example.

Example 2: Acceptance of Personal Loan

Universal Bank is a relatively young bank that is growing rapidly in terms of overall customer acquisition. The majority of these customers are liability customers with varying sizes of relationship with the bank. The customer base of asset customers is quite small, and the bank is interested in growing this base rapidly to bring in more loan business. In particular, it wants to explore ways of converting its liability (deposit) customers to personal loan customers.

A campaign the bank ran for liability customers showed a healthy conversion rate of over 9% successes. This has encouraged the retail marketing department to devise smarter campaigns with better target marketing. The goal of our analysis is to model the previous campaign's customer behavior to analyze what combination of factors make a customer more likely to accept a personal loan. This will serve as the basis for the design of a new campaign.

Our predictive model will be a classification tree. To assess the accuracy of the tree in classifying new records, we start with the tools and criteria discussed in Chapter 5—partitioning the data into training and holdout sets, and later introduce the idea of *cross-validation*.

The bank's dataset includes data on 5000 customers. The data include customer demographic information (age, income, etc.), customer response to the last personal loan campaign (*Personal Loan*), and the customer's relationship with the bank (mortgage, securities account, etc.). Table 9.2 shows a sample of the bank's customer database for 20 customers, to illustrate the structure of the data. Among these 5000 customers, only 480 (=9.6%) accepted the personal loan that was offered to them in the earlier campaign.

Figure 9.11 shows the data preprocessing steps starting with the *Select Attributes* operator, which selects the 11 predictors listed in Table 9.2 along with *Personal Loan* and *ID* attributes. The *Map* operator is used to replace a few negative values in the data with 0 for the predictor *Experience*.[3] Next, the *Numerical to Binominal* operator transforms the target attribute *Personal Loan* to a 2-class categorical type, with class labels *false* (internally mapped to 0) or *true* (internally mapped to 1). For more meaningful label values during result interpretation, we again use the *Map* operator, this time to specify *acceptor = true* and *nonacceptor = false* for *Personal Loan*. Finally, the *Set Role* operator assigns the *label* role to the target attribute *Personal Loan* and *id* role to the *ID* attribute.

FIGURE 9.11   DATA PREPROCESSING FOR UNIVERSAL BANK LOAN DATA

Figure 9.12 (top) presents the RapidMiner process for building a classification tree on the Universal Bank loan data. The *Data Preprocessing* subprocess contains the same steps mentioned in Figure 9.11. Using the *Split Data* operator, the data is first partitioned randomly into training (3000 records) and holdout

---

[3]The meaning of negative values for the predictor *Experience* is unknown. In practice, domain knowledge should be used to understand more about unusual values prior to their replacement.

TABLE 9.2   SAMPLE OF DATA FOR 20 CUSTOMERS OF UNIVERSAL BANK

ID	Age	Professional experience	Income	Family size	CC avg.	Education	Mortgage	Personal loan	Securities account	CD account	Online banking	Credit card
1	25	1	49	4	1.60	UG	0	No	Yes	No	No	No
2	45	19	34	3	1.50	UG	0	No	Yes	No	No	No
3	39	15	11	1	1.00	UG	0	No	No	No	No	No
4	35	9	100	1	2.70	Grad	0	No	No	No	No	No
5	35	8	45	4	1.00	Grad	0	No	No	No	No	Yes
6	37	13	29	4	0.40	Grad	155	No	No	No	Yes	No
7	53	27	72	2	1.50	Grad	0	No	No	No	Yes	No
8	50	24	22	1	0.30	Prof	0	No	No	No	No	Yes
9	35	10	81	3	0.60	Grad	104	No	No	No	Yes	No
10	34	9	180	1	8.90	Prof	0	Yes	No	No	No	No
11	65	39	105	4	2.40	Prof	0	No	No	No	Yes	No
12	29	5	45	3	0.10	Grad	0	No	No	No	No	No
13	48	23	114	2	3.80	Prof	0	No	Yes	No	Yes	No
14	59	32	40	4	2.50	Grad	0	No	No	No	No	No
15	67	41	112	1	2.00	UG	0	No	Yes	No	Yes	No
16	60	30	22	1	1.50	Prof	0	No	No	No	No	Yes
17	38	14	130	4	4.70	Prof	134	Yes	No	No	No	No
18	42	18	81	4	2.40	UG	0	No	No	No	No	No
19	46	21	193	2	8.10	Prof	0	Yes	Yes	No	No	Yes
20	55	28	21	1	0.50	Grad	0	No	Yes	No	No	Yes

(2000 records) sets. The training set is used to construct the fully-grown tree using the *Decision Tree* operator[4] by setting *maximal depth* = -1.

The result is shown in Figure 9.12 (bottom)—this is the full-grown tree produced by the *Decision Tree* operator. Only the first seven levels are shown for clarity. Although it is difficult to see the exact splits, we note that the top decision node refers to all the records in the training set, of which 2712 customers did not accept the loan and 288 customers accepted the loan. The first split, which is on the CCAvg attribute, generates left and right child nodes. To the left is a leaf node with all acceptors who have monthly average spending on credit cards greater than 8.9. Customers with average credit card spending 8.9 or lower go to the right. The splitting process continues; where it stops depends on the parameter settings of the algorithm. The eventual classification of a customer appears in the leaf nodes. After the first seven levels, the tree has 13 leaf nodes and 4 decision nodes for which the splitting process continues further.

The full-grown tree has no restrictions on the maximum depth of the tree (or the number of leaf nodes), nor on the magnitude of decrease in impurity measure. Of the 62 leaf nodes in the full-grown tree, 36 lead to classification of "nonacceptor" and 26 lead to classification of "acceptor."

Let us assess the performance of this full tree with the holdout data. Each record in the holdout data is "dropped down" the tree and classified according to the leaf node it reaches. These predicted classes can then be compared to the actual outcome via a confusion matrix. When a particular class is of interest, a lift chart is useful for assessing the model's ability to capture those records. The model is applied with the *Apply Model* operator and its performance is assessed using the *Performance (Binominal Classification)* operator. In the *Performance (Binominal Classification)* operator, we recognize the target's positive class label by specifying *positive class = acceptor*. Figure 9.13 shows the confusion matrices for the full-grown tree. We see the training data are perfectly classified (accuracy = 100%), whereas the holdout data have a lower accuracy (98%).

Sensitivity Analysis Using Cross Validation

Due to the issue of tree instability, it is possible that the performance results will differ markedly when using a different partitioning into training and holdout data. It is therefore useful to use cross-validation to evaluate the variability in performance on different data partitioning (see Section 2.5). Figure 9.14 shows the process and the result of using RapidMiner's *Cross-Validation* nested operator

---

[4]The *apply pruning* and *apply prepruning* options are enabled by default. We disable these options to construct the full-grown tree.

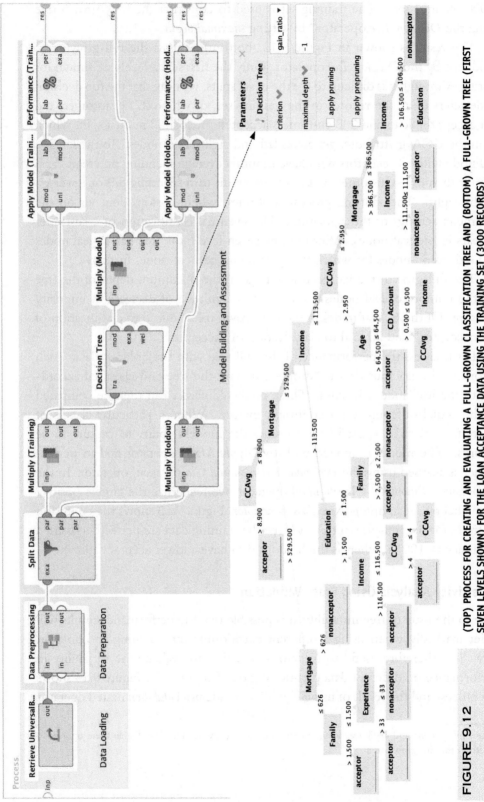

FIGURE 9.12 (TOP) PROCESS FOR CREATING AND EVALUATING A FULL-GROWN CLASSIFICATION TREE AND (BOTTOM) A FULL-GROWN TREE (FIRST SEVEN LEVELS SHOWN) FOR THE LOAN ACCEPTANCE DATA USING THE TRAINING SET (3000 RECORDS)

(a) Performance on Training Set

accuracy: 100.00%

	true nonacceptor	true acceptor	class precision
pred. nonacceptor	2712	0	100.00%
pred. acceptor	0	288	100.00%
class recall	100.00%	100.00%	

(b) Performance on Holdout Set

accuracy: 97.65%

	true nonacceptor	true acceptor	class precision
pred. nonacceptor	1784	23	98.73%
pred. acceptor	24	169	87.56%
class recall	98.67%	88.02%	

FIGURE 9.13 CONFUSION MATRICES AND ACCURACY FOR THE FULL-GROWN CLASSIFICATION TREE, ON THE TRAINING (TOP) AND HOLDOUT (BOTTOM) SETS OF THE PERSONAL LOAN DATA

to perform 5-fold cross-validation on the full-grown tree. The *Log* operator is used to record the performance metrics for each of the five validation folds. We see that the validation accuracy changes significantly across different folds from 0.973 to 0.983.

9.4 AVOIDING OVERFITTING

As the last example illustrated, using a full-grown tree (based on the training data) leads to complete overfitting of the data. As discussed in Chapter 5, overfitting will lead to poor performance on new data. If we look at the overall error at the various levels of the tree, it is expected to decrease as the number of levels grows until the point of overfitting. Of course, for the training data the overall error decreases more and more until it is zero (or close to zero[5]) at the maximum depth of the tree. However, for new data, the overall error is expected to decrease until the point where the tree fully models the relationship between the label and the predictors. After that, the tree starts to model the noise in the training set, and we expect the overall error for the holdout set to start increasing. This is depicted in Figure 9.15. One intuitive reason for the overfitting at the deep levels of

---

[5]Non-zero leaf nodes can result if the training data contains records that have identical values for all predictors, but have different class labels.

accuracy: 97.96% +/– 0.38% (micro average: 97.96%)

	true nonacceptor	true acceptor	class precision
pred. nonacceptor	4469	51	98.87%
pred. acceptor	51	429	89.38%
class recall	98.87%	89.38%	

fold ↑	accuracy	precision	recall	f_measure
1	0.973	0.863	0.854	0.859
2	0.981	0.914	0.885	0.899
3	0.980	0.904	0.885	0.895
4	0.983	0.899	0.927	0.913
5	0.981	0.889	0.917	0.903

FIGURE 9.14   (TOP) PROCESS FOR CREATING AND EVALUATING A FULL-GROWN CLASSIFICATION TREE WITH 5-FOLD CROSS-VALIDATION AND (BOTTOM) HOLDOUT PERFORMANCE METRICS (AVERAGE AND PER FOLD)

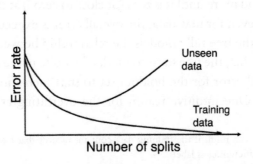

FIGURE 9.15   ERROR RATE AS A FUNCTION OF THE NUMBER OF SPLITS FOR TRAINING VS. HOLDOUT DATA: OVERFITTING

the tree is that these splits are based on very small numbers of observations. In such cases, class difference is likely to be attributed to noise rather than predictor information.

Two ways to try and avoid exceeding this level, thereby limiting overfitting, are by setting rules to stop tree growth (called *prepruning*), or alternatively, by *pruning* the full-grown tree back to a level where it does not overfit. These solutions are discussed next.

Stopping Tree Growth

One can think of different criteria for stopping the tree growth before it starts overfitting the data. Examples are tree depth (i.e., number of splits), minimum number of records in a leaf node, and minimum reduction in impurity. In RapidMiner's *Decision Tree* operator parameter settings, we can control the depth of the tree, the minimum number of records in a node needed to split, the minimum number of records in a leaf node, etc. The problem is that it is not simple to determine what is a good stopping point using such rules.

Let us return to the personal loan example, this time restricting tree depth, the minimum number of records in a leaf node, and the minimum impurity decrease required.[6] The tree parameters and the resulting tree are shown in Figure 9.16 (top). The resulting tree has five terminal nodes, where two are pure but three are not. The smallest terminal node has 40 records.

Figure 9.16 (bottom) displays the confusion matrices for the training and holdout sets of the smaller tree. Compared to the full grown tree, we see that the full tree has higher training accuracy: it is 100% accurate in classifying the training data, which means it has completely pure terminal nodes. The smaller tree achieves the same holdout performance, but importantly, it has a smaller gap in performance between training and holdout, whereas the full tree's training-vs.-holdout performance gap is bigger. The main reason is that the full-grown tree overfits the training data (to perfect accuracy!).

Stopping Tree Growth: Grid Search for Parameter Tuning

As mentioned earlier, the challenge with using tree growth stopping rules such as maximum tree depth is that it is not simple to determine what is a good stopping point using such rules. A solution is to use grid search over combinations of different parameter values. For example, we might want to search for trees with {maximum depths in the range of [5, 30], minimum number of records in leaf nodes between [5, 30], impurity criterion decrease in the range [0.001, 0.01]}.

---

[6]The parameter values chosen are the default values used by RapidMiner's *Decision Tree* operator, except *maximal depth* = 5 and *minimal leaf size* = 40.

Tree

```
Income > 121.500
|   Education > 1.500: acceptor {nonacceptor=0, acceptor=183}
|   Education ≤ 1.500
|   |   Family > 2.500: acceptor {nonacceptor=0, acceptor=40}
|   |   Family ≤ 2.500: nonacceptor {nonacceptor=308, acceptor=0}
Income ≤ 121.500
|   CCAvg > 2.950: nonacceptor {nonacceptor=161, acceptor=53}
|   CCAvg ≤ 2.950: nonacceptor {nonacceptor=2243, acceptor=12}
```

(a) Performance on Training Set
accuracy: 97.83%

	true nonacceptor	true acceptor	class precision
pred. nonacceptor	2712	65	97.66%
pred. acceptor	0	223	100.00%
class recall	100.00%	77.43%	

(b) Performance on Holdout Set
accuracy: 97.35%

	true nonacceptor	true acceptor	class precision
pred. nonacceptor	1808	53	97.15%
pred. acceptor	0	139	100.00%
class recall	100.00%	72.40%	

FIGURE 9.16   (TOP) SMALL CLASSIFICATION TREE AND THE DECISION TREE PARAMETERS USED FOR THE LOAN ACCEPTANCE DATA USING THE TRAINING SET AND (BOTTOM) MODEL PERFORMANCE ON TRAINING AND HOLDOUT SETS

We can use an exhaustive grid search to find the combination that leads to the tree with smallest error (highest accuracy).

If we use the training set to find the tree with the lowest error among all the trees in the searched range, measuring accuracy on that same training data, then we will be overfitting the training data. If we use the holdout set to measure accuracy, then, with the numerous grid search trials, we will be overfitting the holdout data! A solution is therefore to use cross-validation on the training set, and, after settling on the best tree, use that tree with the holdout data to evaluate likely actual performance with new data. This will help detect and avoid possible overfitting.

In RapidMiner, an exhaustive grid search of this type can be achieved using the *Optimize Parameters (Grid)* operator. Figure 9.17 shows the process with this operator containing the *Cross-Validation* subprocess operator [with parameter *number of folds* = 5 and configured similar to Figure 9.14 (top)]. Inside the cross-validation subprocess, the *Decision Tree* operator is used with *prepruning* enabled (default parameter values are used since we specify the search parameters later). If we specify *main criterion* = *accuracy* in the *Performance (Binominal Classification)* operator, accuracy is used as the performance metric for finding the "best" model. Alternatively, we could use another performance metric such as precision, recall or F-measure to find the optimal model based on that metric. We also select the option to manually set the positive class, and use *positive class* = *acceptor* based on our business context. Finally, in the *Optimize Parameters (Grid)* operator parameter settings, we specify the minimum and maximum parameter values to be searched, along with the type (e.g., linear, logarithmic) and the number of steps in the parameter search range, as shown in Figure 9.17.

The final tree is shown in Figure 9.18. Figure 9.19 shows the resulting parameter combination *maximal_depth* 8, *minimal_gain* 0.0082, *minimal_leaf_size* 8. It also shows the model performance on the training set. Figure 9.19 (bottom) shows model performance on the holdout set, which is slightly better than the holdout performance in the full-grown tree.

The exhaustive grid search can quickly become very time consuming. In our example, the grid search assessed $11 \times 6 \times 11 = 726$ combinations. A faster alternative is to increase the step size inside the grid (*steps=*), resulting in fewer intermediate steps. Later, the grid search can be repeated by narrowing the parameter search space and specifying more granular steps.

Stopping Tree Growth: CHAID

CHAID stands for chi-squared automatic interaction detection, a recursive partitioning method that predates classification and regression tree (CART) procedures by several years and is widely used in database marketing applications to this day. It uses a well-known statistical test (the chi-square test for independence) to assess whether splitting a node improves the purity by a statistically significant amount. In particular, at each node, we split on the predictor with the strongest association with the outcome variable. The strength of association is measured by the p-value of a chi-squared test of independence. If for the best predictor the test does not show a significant improvement, the split is not carried out, and the tree is terminated. This method is more suitable for categorical predictors, but it can be adapted to continuous predictors by binning the continuous values

FIGURE 9.17   GRID SEARCH PROCESS FOR TUNING DECISION TREE PARAMETERS

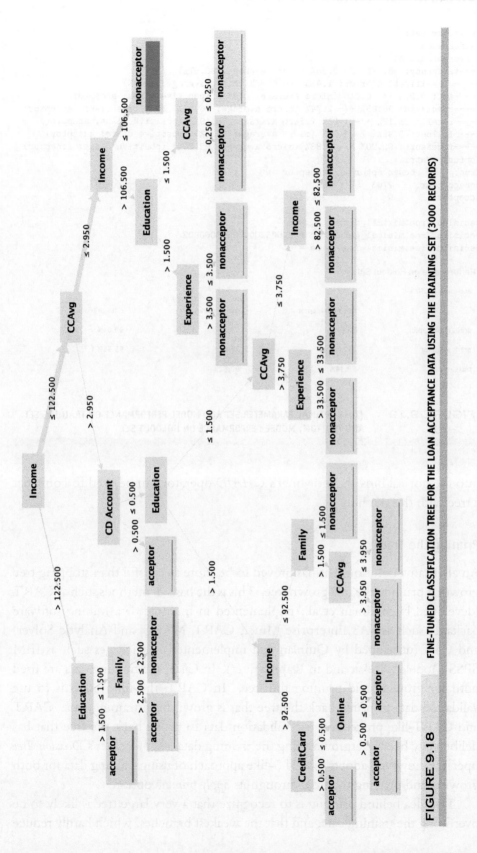

FIGURE 9.18   FINE-TUNED CLASSIFICATION TREE FOR THE LOAN ACCEPTANCE DATA USING THE TRAINING SET (3000 RECORDS)

```
Parameter set:
Performance:
PerformanceVector [
*****accuracy: 98.57% +/- 0.35% (micro average: 98.57%)
-----classification_error: 1.43% +/- 0.35% (micro average: 1.43%)
-----AUC: 0.973 +/- 0.016 (micro average: 0.973) (positive class: acceptor)
-----precision: 96.63% +/- 2.74% (micro average: 96.58%) (positive class: acceptor)
-----recall: 88.19% +/- 1.91% (micro average: 88.19%) (positive class: acceptor)
-----fallout: 0.33% +/- 0.27% (micro average: 0.33%) (positive class: acceptor)
-----f_measure: 92.20% +/- 1.83% (micro average: 92.20%) (positive class: acceptor)
ConfusionMatrix:
True:        nonacceptor     acceptor
nonacceptor:     2703          34
acceptor:          9           254
]
Decision Tree.maximal_depth    = 8
Decision Tree.minimal_gain     = 0.008200000000000002
Decision Tree.minimal_leaf_size = 8
```

Performance on Holdout Set

accuracy: 98.50%

	true nonacceptor	true acceptor	class precision
pred. nonacceptor	1796	18	99.01%
pred. acceptor	12	174	93.55%
class recall	99.34%	90.62%	

FIGURE 9.19   (TOP) OPTIMAL PARAMETER SET AND MODEL PERFORMANCE ON TRAINING SET AND (BOTTOM) MODEL PERFORMANCE ON HOLDOUT SET

into categorical bins. RapidMiner's *CHAID* operator can be used to construct a tree with this method.

Pruning the Tree

An alternative solution that has proved to be more successful than stopping tree growth is pruning the full-grown tree. This is the basis of methods such as CART (developed by Breiman et al., implemented in multiple data mining software packages such as SAS Enterprise Miner, CART, MARS, and Analytic Solver) and C4.5 (developed by Quinlan and implemented in packages such as IBM SPSS Modeler, Weka, and in RapidMiner). In C4.5, the training data are used both for growing and pruning the tree. In CART, the innovation is to use validation data to prune back the tree that is grown from training data. CART and CART-like procedures use validation data to prune back the tree that has deliberately been overgrown using the training data. RapidMiner's *Decision Tree* operator, however, adopts the C4.5-like approach of using training data for both growing and pruning the tree, through its *apply pruning* option.

The idea behind pruning is to recognize that a very large tree is likely to be overfitting the training data, and that the weakest branches, which hardly reduce the error rate, should be removed. Pruning consists of successively selecting a decision node and re-designating it as a leaf node [lopping off the branches extending beyond that decision node (its *subtree*) and thereby reducing the size of the tree]. The pruning process trades off misclassification error in the holdout dataset against the number of decision nodes in the pruned tree to arrive at a tree that captures the patterns—but not the noise—in the training data. Returning to Figure 9.15, we would like to find the point where the curve for the unseen data begins to increase.

CART Approach: To find the degree of pruning that captures the patterns but not the noise, the CART algorithm uses a criterion called the *cost complexity* (CC) of a tree to generate a sequence of trees that are successively smaller to the point of having a tree with just the root node. (What is the classification rule for a tree with just one node?) This means that the first step is to find the best subtree of each size $(1, 2, 3, \ldots)$. Then, we choose among these trees the tree that minimizes the misclassification error rate of the holdout set. This is called the *minimum error tree*. Let us look at this process in a little more detail next.

Constructing the best tree of each size is based on the CC criterion, which is equal to the misclassification error of a tree (based on the training data) plus a penalty factor for the size of the tree. For a tree T that has $L(T)$ leaf nodes, the cost complexity can be written as

$$CC(T) = \text{err}(T) + \alpha L(T),$$

where $\text{err}(T)$ is the fraction of training data observations that are misclassified by tree T and α is a penalty factor for tree size. When $\alpha = 0$, there is no penalty for having too many nodes in a tree, and the best tree using the cost complexity criterion is the full-grown unpruned tree. When we increase α to a very large value the penalty cost component swamps the misclassification error component of the cost complexity criterion function, and the best tree is simply the tree with the fewest leaf nodes: namely the tree with simply one node. The idea is therefore to start with the full-grown tree and then increase the penalty factor α gradually until the cost complexity of the full tree exceeds that of a subtree. Then the same procedure is repeated using the subtree. Continuing in this manner, we generate a succession of trees with a diminishing number of nodes all the way to a trivial tree consisting of just one leaf node.

From this sequence of trees it seems natural to choose the one that gave the lowest misclassification error on the holdout dataset. We call this the *minimum error tree*. To illustrate this, Figure 9.20 shows the error rate for both the training and holdout data as a function of the tree size. It can be seen that the training set error steadily decreases as the tree grows, with a noticeable drop in error rate

# Decision Nodes	% Training Error	% Holdout Error
61	0.00	2.35
60	0.03	2.35
59	0.10	2.40
58	0.10	2.40
57	0.17	2.50
56	0.17	2.50
55	0.30	2.60
54	0.30	2.60
53	0.30	2.60
52	0.40	2.45
51	0.40	2.45
50	0.47	2.45
49	0.47	2.45
48	0.57	2.40
47	0.57	2.40
46	0.60	2.30
45	0.60	2.30
44	0.70	2.25
43	0.73	2.20
42	0.73	2.20
41	0.80	2.35
40	0.80	2.35
39	0.87	2.40
38	0.87	2.40
37	1.00	2.00
36	1.00	2.00
35	1.00	2.00
34	1.07	1.95
33	1.07	1.95
32	1.07	1.95
31	1.07	1.95

# Decision Nodes	% Training Error	% Holdout Error
30	1.27	2.05
29	1.27	2.05
28	1.27	2.05
27	1.27	2.05
26	1.27	2.05
25	1.27	2.05
24	1.33	2.10
23	1.33	2.10
22	1.33	2.10
21	1.33	2.10
20	1.33	2.10
19	1.40	2.05
18	1.40	2.05
17	1.40	2.05
16	1.40	2.05
15	1.73	2.30
14	1.73	2.30
13	1.73	2.30
12	1.73	2.30
11	3.40	3.55
10	3.40	3.55
9	3.40	3.55
8	3.40	3.55
7	3.40	3.55
6	9.13	9.45
5	9.13	9.45
4	9.13	9.45
3	9.17	9.45
2	9.17	9.45
1	9.40	9.60
0	9.60	9.60

Minimum Error Tree

FIGURE 9.20   ERROR RATE AS A FUNCTION OF THE NUMBER OF SPLITS FOR TRAINING VS. HOLDOUT DATA FOR THE LOAN EXAMPLE

between six and seven nodes. The holdout set error rate, however, reaches a minimum at 31 nodes and then starts to increase as the tree grows. At this point the tree is pruned, and we obtain the *minimum error tree*.

RapidMiner's *Pessimistic Pruning* Approach: Unlike the CART-like approach, RapidMiner uses a method called *pessimistic pruning* (Quinlan, 1986), which avoids the need for a separate data partition for pruning. The basic idea in pessimistic pruning is to use only the training set, performing a top–down pass over the tree and determining for each decision node, whether its subtree should be pruned or not. If a decision node is decided to be pruned, its entire subtree is lopped off, resulting in fast pruning on large datasets. Since the error rates using the training data are overly optimistic, a *pessimistic error* estimate is computed for each decision node by assuming that the number of errors follow a binomial distribution. By applying a continuity correction for binomial distribution, the pessimistic error rate for a decision node is

$$e' = e + L(T)/2n,$$

where e is the fraction of misclassified training records in the decision node, n is the number of records in the node, and $L(T)$ is the number of leaf nodes in subtree T. The subtree is pruned unless it improves over the (corrected) error rate of the decision node $(e+1/2)$ by at least[7] $\sqrt{e'(1 - e')/n}$.

Although this method does not have a strong statistical justification, it appears to be a successful heuristic, which compares the number of misclassifications at a node with the number of leaves in the corresponding sub-tree. It is advantageous computationally, as it does not require multiple passes through the tree (like the CART approach). In RapidMiner, pruning is done by selecting the *apply pruning* option in the *Decision Tree* operator.

9.5 CLASSIFICATION RULES FROM TREES

As described in Section 9.1, classification trees provide easily understandable *classification rules* (if the trees are not too large). RapidMiner's *Tree to Rules* operator can be used to display a classification tree in the form of if-then rules. Each leaf node is equivalent to a classification rule. Returning to the example, the left-most leaf node in the fine-tuned tree (Figure 9.18) gives us the rule

IF (*Income* > 122.5) AND (*Education* > 1.5),
THEN *Class* = *acceptor*.

However, in many cases, the number of rules can be reduced by removing redundancies. For example, consider the rule from the right-most leaf node in Figure 9.18:

IF (*Income* ≤ 122.5) AND (*CCAvg* ≤ 2.95) AND (*Income* ≤ 106.5),
THEN *Class* = *nonacceptor*

This rule can be simplified to

IF (*Income* ≤ 106.5) AND (*CCAvg* ≤ 2.95),
THEN *Class* = *nonacceptor*

This transparency in the process and understandability of the algorithm that leads to classifying a record as belonging to a certain class is very advantageous in settings where the final classification is not the only thing of interest. Berry

---

[7]This quantity is equal to one standard error of the pessimistic error rate e'.

and Linoff (2000) give the example of health insurance underwriting, where the insurer is required to show that coverage denial is not based on discrimination. By showing rules that led to denial (e.g., income < \$20K AND low credit history), the company can avoid law suits. Compared to the output of other classifiers, such as discriminant functions, tree-based classification rules are easily explained to managers and operating staff. Their logic is certainly far more transparent than that of weights in neural networks!

9.6 CLASSIFICATION TREES FOR MORE THAN TWO CLASSES

Classification trees can be used with a target attribute that has more than two classes. In terms of measuring impurity, the two measures presented earlier (the Gini impurity index and the entropy measure) and related splitting criteria (information gain and gain ratio) were defined for m classes and hence can be used for any number of classes. The tree itself would have the same structure, except that its leaf nodes would take one of the m-class labels.

9.7 REGRESSION TREES

The tree method can also be used for a numerical target attribute. Regression trees (RT) for prediction operate in much the same fashion as classification trees. The target (Y) is a numerical attribute in this case, but both the principle and the procedure are the same: Many splits are attempted, and for each, we measure "impurity" in each branch of the resulting tree. The tree procedure then selects the split that minimizes the sum of such measures. To illustrate a regression tree, consider the example of predicting prices of Toyota Corolla automobiles (from Chapter 6). The dataset includes information on 1436 sold Toyota Corolla cars. (We use the first 1000 cars from the dataset *ToyotoCorolla.csv*). The goal is to find a predictive model of price as a function of 10 predictors (including mileage, horsepower, number of doors, etc.). A regression tree for these data was built using a training set of 600 records. The process for building this tree is similar to that in Figure 9.17[8] (for data preprocessing steps, see Figure 6.1). The fine-tuned tree, is shown in Figure 9.21 (top). The optimal parameter combination is shown in the bottom left of Figure 9.21.

We see that the top three levels of the regression tree are dominated by age of the car, its weight, and mileage. In the lower levels we can see that individual details of a car, like powered windows, lead to smaller adjustments of the price.

---

[8]The parameter search grid is similar to that in Figure 9.17, except that minimal leaf size is varied from 10 to 50 in 10 linear steps.

(a) Fine-tuned Regression Tree

(b) Optimal Parameters and Performance on Training Set

Parameter set:

Performance:
PerformanceVector [
-----root_mean_squared_error: 1332.535 +/- 114.587 (micro average: 1336.470 +/- 0.000)
-----absolute_error: 970.605 +/- 83.549 (micro average: 970.605 +/- 918.738)
-----relative_error: 8.36% +/- 0.92% (micro average: 8.36% +/- 8.89%)
****squared_error: 1786152.443 +/- 298017.937 (micro average: 1786152.443 +/- 4247589.452)
-----squared_correlation: 0.882 +/- 0.018 (micro average: 0.882)
]
Decision Tree.maximal_depth   = 25
Decision Tree.minimal_gain   = 0.008
Decision Tree.minimal_size_for_split = 31

(c) Performance on Holdout Set

PerformanceVector:
root_mean_squared_error: 1526.495 +/- 0.000
absolute_error: 1038.667 +/- 1118.642
relative_error: 9.43% +/- 11.15%
squared_error: 2330187.994 +/- 6381381.171
squared_correlation: 0.815

FIGURE 9.21   (TOP) FINE-TUNED REGRESSION TREE FOR TOYOTA COROLLA PRICES, (BOTTOM LEFT) OPTIMAL PARAMETER SET AND MODEL PERFORMANCE ON TRAINING SET, AND (BOTTOM RIGHT) MODEL PERFORMANCE ON HOLDOUT SET

Three details differ between regression trees and classification trees: prediction, impurity measures, and evaluating performance. We describe these next.

Prediction

Predicting the target value for a record is performed in a fashion similar to the classification case: We will use the truncated tree from Figure 9.21 to demonstrate how it works. The predictor information is used for "dropping" the record down the tree until reaching a leaf node. For instance, to predict the price of a Toyota Corolla with Age = 60, Mileage (KM) = 160,000, and Horse_Power (HP) = 100, we drop it down the tree and reach the node that has the value $7878.333. This is the price prediction for this car according to the tree. In classification trees, the value of the leaf node (which is one of the categories) is determined by the "voting" of the training records that were in that leaf node. In regression trees, the value of the leaf node is determined by the average outcome value of the training records that were in that leaf node. In the example above, the value $7878.333 is the average price of the 21 cars[9] in the training set that fall in the category of Age > 56.5, KM > 112471.5, and HP $\leq$ 100.

Measuring Impurity

We described two types of impurity measures for nodes in classification trees: the Gini index and the entropy-based measure. In both cases, the index is a function of the *ratio* between the categories of the records in that node. In regression trees, a typical impurity measure is the sum of the squared deviations from the mean of the leaf node. This is equivalent to the sum of the squared errors, because the mean of the leaf node is exactly the prediction. In the example, the impurity of the node with the value $7878.333 is computed by subtracting 7878.333 from the price of each of the 21 cars in the training set that fell in that leaf node, then squaring these deviations, summing them up, and taking the square root of the sum. The lowest impurity possible is zero, when all values in the node are equal.

Evaluating Performance

As stated above, predictions are obtained by averaging the target attribute values in the nodes. We therefore have the usual definition of predictions and errors. The predictive performance of regression trees can be measured in the same way that other predictive methods are evaluated (e.g., linear regression), using summary measures such as RMSE and MAPE.

---

[9]In RapidMiner, hovering over a node in a regression tree shows the number of training records in that node or subtree.

9.8 IMPROVING PREDICTION: RANDOM FORESTS AND BOOSTED TREES

Notwithstanding the transparency advantages of a single tree as described above, in a pure prediction application, where visualizing a set of rules does not matter, better performance is provided by several extensions to trees that combine results from multiple trees. These are examples of *ensembles* (see Chapter 13). One popular multitree approach is *random forests*, introduced by Breiman and Cutler.[10] Random forests are a special case of *bagging*, a method for improving predictive power by combining multiple classifiers or prediction algorithms. See Chapter 13 for further details on bagging.

Random Forests

The basic idea in random forests is to:

1. Draw multiple random samples, with replacement, from the data (this sampling approach is called the *bootstrap*).

2. Using a random subset of predictors at each stage, fit a classification (or regression) tree to each sample (and thus obtain a "forest").

3. Combine the predictions/classifications from the individual trees to obtain improved predictions. Use voting for classification and averaging for prediction.

The process and output in Figure 9.22 illustrates building a random forest in RapidMiner for the personal loan example using the *Random Forest* operator. The holdout accuracy of the random forest in this example (99.00%) is slightly higher than the single fine-tuned tree (98.50%—see Figure 9.19), and slightly higher than the single small tree we fit earlier (97.35%—see Figure 9.16).

Unlike a single tree, results from a random forest cannot be displayed in a tree-like diagram, thereby losing the interpretability that a single tree provides. However, random forests can produce "attribute weights," which measure the relative contribution of the different predictors. The attribute weight for a particular predictor is obtained by computing the decrease in some impurity measure (e.g. Gini or gain ratio) for that predictor in each tree, and then taking an average across the trees. The individual weights are then divided by the sum of all the weights to obtain predictor importance values that sum up to 1. From Figure 9.22 (middle), we see that Income and CCAvg have the highest scores, with Experience and Family being the next two top predictors. Attribute weights for the other predictors are considerably lower.

---

[10]For further details on random forests, see https://www.stat.berkeley.edu/~breiman/ RandomForests/cc_home.htm

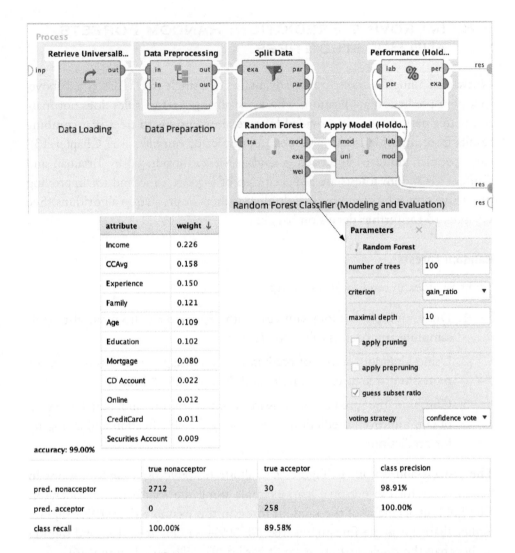

FIGURE 9.22   (TOP) PROCESS FOR RANDOM FOREST CLASSIFIER (PERSONAL LOAN EXAMPLE), (MIDDLE) ATTRIBUTE WEIGHTS, AND (BOTTOM) PERFORMANCE ON HOLDOUT SET

Boosted Trees

The second type of multitree improvement is *boosted trees*, implemented in RapidMiner in the *Gradient Boosted Trees* operator. Here a sequence of trees is fitted, so that each tree concentrates on misclassified records from the previous tree.

1. Fit a single tree.
2. Draw a sample that gives higher selection probabilities to misclassified records.
3. Fit a tree to the new sample.

4. Repeat Steps 2 and 3 multiple times.

5. Use weighted voting to classify records, with heavier weight for later trees.

Figure 9.23 shows the result of running a boosted tree on the loan acceptance example that we saw earlier. We can see that compared to the performance of the single small tree (97.35%—see Figure 9.16), the boosted tree has better performance on the holdout data in terms of overall accuracy (98.73%) and especially in terms of correct classification of 1's—the rare class of special interest. Where does boosting's special talent for finding 1's come from? When one class is dominant (0's constitute over 90% of the data here), basic classifiers are tempted to classify cases as belonging to the dominant class, and the 1's in this case constitute most of the misclassifications with the single tree. The boosting algorithm concentrates on the misclassifications (which are mostly 1's), so it is naturally going to do well in reducing the misclassification of 1's (from 53 in the single small tree to 16 in the boosted tree, in the holdout set).

9.9 ADVANTAGES AND WEAKNESSES OF A TREE

Tree methods are good off-the-shelf classifiers and predictors. They are also useful for attribute selection, with the most important predictors usually showing up at the top of the tree. Trees require relatively little effort from users in the following senses: First, there is no need for transformation of attributes (any monotone transformation of the attributes will give the same trees). Second, feature subset selection is automatic since it is part of the split selection. In the loan example, note that out of the set of 14 predictors available, the small tree automatically selected only four predictors (Income, Education, Family, and CCAvg) and the fine-tuned tree selected eight (Income, Education, Family, CCAvg, CD Account, Experience, CreditCard, and Online).

Trees are also intrinsically robust to outliers, since the choice of a split depends on the *ordering* of values and not on the absolute *magnitudes* of these values. However, they are sensitive to changes in the data, and even a slight change can cause very different splits!

Unlike models that assume a particular relationship between the outcome and predictors (e.g., a linear relationship such as in linear regression and linear discriminant analysis), classification and regression trees are nonlinear and nonparametric. This allows for a wide range of relationships between the predictors and the outcome variable. However, this can also be a weakness: Since the splits are done on one predictor at a time, rather than on combinations of predictors, the tree is likely to miss relationships between predictors, in particular linear structures like those in linear or logistic regression models. Classification trees

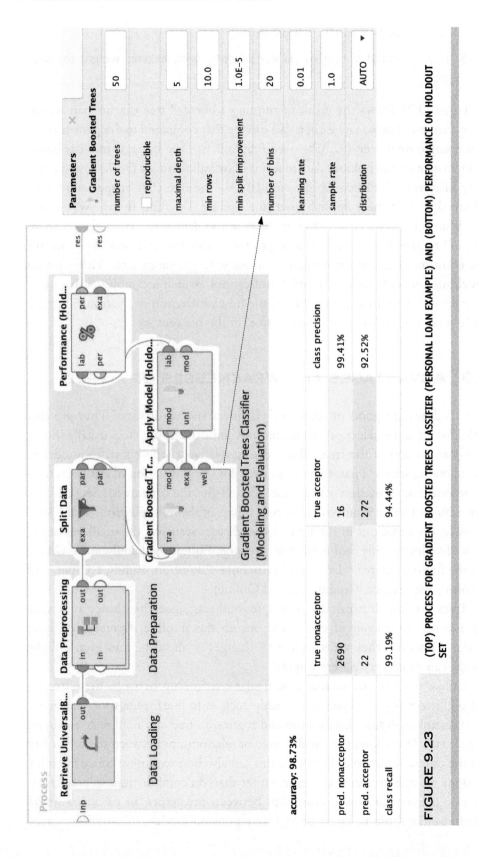

FIGURE 9.23   (TOP) PROCESS FOR GRADIENT BOOSTED TREES CLASSIFIER (PERSONAL LOAN EXAMPLE) AND (BOTTOM) PERFORMANCE ON HOLDOUT SET

FIGURE 9.24   A TWO-PREDICTOR CASE WITH TWO CLASSES. THE BEST SEPARATION IS
ACHIEVED WITH A DIAGONAL LINE, WHICH CLASSIFICATION TREES CANNOT DO

are useful classifiers in cases where horizontal and vertical splitting of the predictor space adequately divides the classes. But consider, for instance, a dataset
with two predictors and two classes, where separation between the two classes
is most obviously achieved by using a diagonal line (as shown in Figure 9.24).
In such cases, a classification tree is expected to have lower performance than
methods such as discriminant analysis. One way to improve performance is
to create new predictors that are derived from existing predictors, which can
capture hypothesized relationships between predictors (similar to interactions in
regression models). Random forests are another solution in such situations.

Another performance issue with classification trees is that they require a large
dataset in order to construct a good classifier. From a computational aspect, trees
can be relatively expensive to grow, because of the multiple sorting involved in
computing all possible splits on every variable. Methods for avoiding overfitting,
such as cross-validation or pruning the data using the validation set, add further
computation time.

Although trees are useful for attribute selection, one challenge is that they
"favor" predictors with many potential split points. This includes categorical
predictors with many categories and numerical predictors with many different
values. Such predictors have a higher chance of appearing in a tree. One simplistic solution is to combine multiple categories into a smaller set and bin numerical
predictors with many values. Alternatively, some special algorithms avoid this
problem by using a two-step process: the first step chooses a predictor (e.g., via
a statistical test) and the second step selects the splitting point on the chosen
predictor. Examples include *conditional inference trees* in the R package `party`

(see Hothorn et al., 2006) and in QUEST classification trees (see Loh and Shih, 1997).

An appealing feature of trees is that they handle missing data without having to impute values or delete records with missing values. Finally, a very important practical advantage of trees is the transparent rules that they generate. Such transparency is often useful in managerial applications, though this advantage is lost in the ensemble versions of trees (random forests, boosted trees).

PROBLEMS

9.1 **Competitive Auctions on eBay.com.** The file *eBayAuctions.csv* contains information on 1972 auctions that transacted on eBay.com during May–June 2004. The goal is to use these data to build a model that will classify auctions as competitive or non-competitive. A *competitive auction* is defined as an auction with at least two bids placed on the item auctioned. The data include attributes that describe the item (auction category), the seller (his/her eBay rating), and the auction terms that the seller selected (auction duration, opening price, currency, day-of-week of auction close). In addition, we have the price at which the auction closed. The task is to predict whether or not the auction will be competitive.

Data Preprocessing. Convert attribute *Duration* into a categorical attribute (nominal type). Convert attribute *Competitive?* to binominal type and assign it the appropriate role in RapidMiner. Consider mapping class labels to meaningful labels using the *Map* operator as well. Split the data into training (60%) and holdout (40%) datasets.

a. Fit a classification tree with the gini index criterion using all predictors. To avoid overfitting, apply pre-pruning (set the minimum number of records in a leaf node to 50 and the maximum tree depth to 7). Write down the results in terms of rules. (*Note*: If you had to slightly reduce the number of predictors due to software limitations, or for clarity of presentation, which would be a good attribute to choose?)

b. Is this model practical for predicting the outcome of a new auction?

c. Describe the interesting and uninteresting information that these rules provide.

d. Fit another classification tree with the gini index criterion, applying pre-pruning (using a tree with a minimum number of records per leaf node = 50 and maximum depth = 7), this time only with predictors that can be used for predicting the outcome of a new auction. Describe the resulting tree in terms of rules. Make sure to report the smallest set of rules required for classification.

e. Plot the resulting tree on a scatter plot: Use the two axes for the two best (quantitative) predictors. Each auction will appear as a point, with coordinates corresponding to its values on those two predictors. Use different colors or symbols to separate competitive and noncompetitive auctions. Draw lines (you can sketch these by hand or use RapidMiner) at the values that create splits. Does this splitting seem reasonable with respect to the meaning of the two predictors? Does it seem to do a good job of separating the two classes?

f. Examine the lift chart and the confusion matrix for the tree. What can you say about the predictive performance of this model?

g. Based on this last tree, what can you conclude from these data about the chances of an auction obtaining at least two bids and its relationship to the auction settings set by the seller (duration, opening price, ending day, currency)? What would you recommend for a seller as the strategy that will most likely lead to a competitive auction?

9.2 **Predicting Delayed Flights.** The file *FlightDelays.csv* contains information on all commercial flights departing the Washington, DC area and arriving at New York during January 2004. For each flight, there is information on the departure and arrival airports, the distance of the route, the scheduled time and date of the flight, and so on. The attribute that we are trying to predict is whether or not a flight is delayed. A delay is defined as an arrival that is at least 15 minutes later than scheduled.

Data Preprocessing. Transform attribute day of week (DAY_WEEK) info a categorical attribute. Bin the scheduled departure time into eight bins. Transform the airline carrier, destination city and origin city to numerical attributes with dummy coding. Use these and all other attributes as predictors (excluding DAY_OF_MONTH, FL_DATE, FL_NUM, and TAIL_NUM). Transform the target attribute to a binominal type and set its appropriate role. By using the *Remap Binominals* operator for the target attribute, specify the positive value = *delayed* and negative value = *ontime*. Partition the data into training (60%) and holdout (40%) sets.

a. Fit a classification tree to the flight delay target attribute using all the relevant predictors. Do not include DEP_TIME (actual departure time) in the model because it is unknown at the time of prediction (unless we are generating our predictions of delays after the plane takes off, which is unlikely). Explain why we excluded DAY_OF_MONTH, FL_DATE, FL_NUM, and TAIL_NUM as predictors in data preprocessing. Use the gain ratio criterion in fitting the tree with maximal depth = 6. Apply pruning and prepruning with default parameters. Express the resulting tree as a set of rules.

b. If you needed to fly between DCA and EWR on a Monday at 7:00 AM, would you be able to use this tree? What other information would you need? Is it available in practice? What information is redundant?

c. Fit the same tree as in (a), this time excluding the Weather predictor. Display this pruned tree. Now, create another tree by increasing the minimal gain required from 0.01 to 0.03. You will find that the tree contains a single leaf node. Display this small tree.

    i. How is the small tree used for classification? (What is the rule for classifying?)

    ii. To what is this rule equivalent?

    iii. Examine the pruned tree. What are the top three predictors according to this tree?

    iv. Why, technically, does the small tree result in a single node?

    v. What is the disadvantage of using the full-grown tree as opposed to an optimally pruned tree?

    vi. Compare this general result from the pruned tree to that from logistic regression in the example in Chapter 10. What are possible reasons for the classification tree's failure to find a good predictive model?

9.3 **Predicting Prices of Used Cars (Regression Trees).** The file *ToyotaCorolla.csv* contains the data on used cars (Toyota Corolla) on sale during late summer of 2004 in the Netherlands. It has 1436 records containing details on 38 attributes, including Price, Age, Kilometers, HP, and other specifications. The goal is to predict the price of a used Toyota Corolla based on its specifications. (The example in Section 9.7 is a subset of this dataset.)

Data Preprocessing. Split the data into training (60%), and holdout (40%) datasets.

a. Run a full-grown regression tree with target attribute Price and predictors Age_08_04, KM, Fuel_Type (first convert to dummies), HP, Automatic, Doors, Quarterly_Tax, Mfr_Guarantee, Guarantee_Period, Airco, Automatic_airco, CD_Player, Powered_Windows, Sport_Model, and Tow_Bar.

    i. Which appear to be the three or four most important car specifications for predicting the car's price?

ii. Compare the prediction errors of the training and holdout sets by examining their RMS error and by plotting the two boxplots. (Note: Use the *Generate Attributes* operator to compute the prediction errors as a new attribute.) How does the predictive performance of the holdout set compare to the training set? Why does this occur?

iii. How might we achieve better holdout predictive performance at the expense of training performance?

iv. Create a smaller tree by using *Optimize Parameters (Grid)* with cv = 5 to find a fine-tuned tree. Compared to the full-grown tree, what is the predictive performance on the holdout set?

b. Let us see the effect of turning the price attribute into a categorical attribute. First, create a new attribute that categorizes price into 20 bins. Now repartition the data keeping Binned_Price instead of Price. Run a classification tree with the same set of predictors as in the RT, and with Binned_Price as the target attribute. As in the less deep regression tree, create a smaller tree by using *Optimize Parameters (Grid)* with cv = 5 to find a fine-tuned tree.

i. Compare the smaller tree generated by the CT with the smaller tree generated by RT. Are they different? (Look at structure, the top predictors, size of tree, etc.) Why?

ii. Predict the price, using the smaller RT and CT, of a used Toyota Corolla with the specifications listed in Table 9.3.

TABLE 9.3   SPECIFICATIONS FOR A PARTICULAR TOYOTA COROLLA

Variable	Value
Age_0804	77
KM	117,000
Fuel_Type	Petrol
HP	110
Automatic	No
Doors	5
Quarterly_Tax	100
Mfg_Guarantee	No
Guarantee_Period	3
Airco	Yes
Automatic_airco	No
CD_Player	No
Powered_Windows	No
Sport_Model	No
Tow_Bar	Yes

iii. Compare the predictions in terms of the predictors that were used, the magnitude of the difference between the two predictions, and the advantages and disadvantages of the two methods.

CHAPTER 10

Logistic Regression

In this chapter, we describe the highly popular and powerful classification method called logistic regression. Like linear regression, it relies on a specific model relating the predictors with the outcome. The user must specify the predictors to include, as well as their form (e.g., including any interaction terms). This means that even small datasets can be used for building logistic regression classifiers and that once the model is estimated, it is computationally fast and cheap to classify even large samples of new records. We describe the logistic regression model formulation and its estimation from data. We also explain the concepts of "logit," "odds," and "probability" of an event that arise in the logistic model context and the relations among the three. We discuss attribute importance and coefficient interpretation, as well as attribute selection for dimension reduction, and extensions to multi-class classification.

10.1 INTRODUCTION

Logistic regression extends the ideas of linear regression to the situation where the target attribute (label) Y is categorical. We can think of a categorical attribute as dividing the records into classes. For example, if Y denotes a recommendation on holding/selling/buying a stock, we have a categorical attribute with three categories. We can think of each of the stocks in the dataset (the records) as belonging to one of three classes: the *hold* class, the *sell* class, and the *buy* class. Logistic regression can be used for classifying a new record, where its class is unknown, into one of the classes, based on the values of its predictor attributes (called *classification*). It can also be used in data where the class is known, to find factors distinguishing between records in different classes in terms of their

Machine Learning for Business Analytics: Concepts, Techniques and Applications in RapidMiner, First Edition.
Galit Shmueli, Peter C. Bruce, Amit V. Deokar, and Nitin R. Patel
© 2023 John Wiley & Sons, Inc. Published 2023 by John Wiley & Sons, Inc.

predictor attributes, or "predictor profile" (called *profiling*). Logistic regression is used in applications such as the following:

1. Classifying customers as returning or nonreturning (classification).

2. Finding factors that differentiate between male and female top executives (profiling).

3. Predicting the approval or disapproval of a loan based on information such as credit scores (classification).

The logistic regression model is used in a variety of fields: whenever a structured model is needed to explain or predict categorical (in particular, binary) outcomes. One such application is in describing choice behavior in econometrics.

In this chapter, we focus on the use of logistic regression for classification. We deal mostly with a binary target attribute (attribute having *Binominal* data type and *label* role in RapidMiner) having two possible classes. In Section 10.4, we show how the results can be extended to the case where Y assumes more than two possible classes. Popular examples of binary targets are success/failure, yes/no, buy/don't buy, default/don't default, and survive/die. For convenience, we often code the values of the binary target attribute Y as 0 and 1.

Note that in some cases we may choose to convert a numeric (continuous) target attribute or a target attribute with multiple classes into a binary target attribute for purposes of simplification, reflecting the fact that decision-making may be binary (approve the loan/don't approve, make an offer/don't make an offer). As with multiple linear regression, the predictor attributes $X_1, X_2, \ldots, X_k$ may be categorical attributes, continuous attributes, or a mixture of these two types. While in multiple linear regression the aim is to predict the value of the continuous Y for a new record, in logistic regression the goal is to predict which class a new record will belong to, or simply to *classify* the record into one of the classes. In the stock example, we would want to classify a new stock into one of the three recommendation classes: sell, hold, or buy. Or, we might want to compute for a new record its *propensity* (=the probability) to belong to each class and then possibly rank a set of new records from highest to lowest propensity in order to act on those with the highest propensity.[1]

In logistic regression, we take two steps: the first step yields estimates of the *propensities* or *probabilities* of belonging to each class. In the binary case, we get an estimate of $p = P(Y = 1)$, the probability of belonging to class 1 (which

---

[1] Potentially, one could use linear regression for classification, by training a linear regression on a 0/1 target attribute (called a *Linear Probability Model*). The model is then used to generate numerical predictions which are converted into binary classifications using a threshold. However, linear probability models, despite their name, do not produce proper predicted probabilities. The numerical predictions they produce are useful for comparison with the classification threshold but are otherwise meaningless.

also tells us the probability of belonging to class 0). In the next step, we use a threshold value on these probabilities in order to classify each case into one of the classes. For example, in a binary case, a threshold of 0.5 means that cases with an estimated probability of $P(Y = 1) \geq 0.5$ are classified as belonging to class 1, whereas cases with $P(Y = 1) < 0.5$ are classified as belonging to class 0. This threshold does not need to be set at 0.5. When the event in question is a low probability but notable or important event (say, 1 = fraudulent transaction), a lower threshold may be used to classify more cases as belonging to class 1.

10.2 THE LOGISTIC REGRESSION MODEL

The idea behind logistic regression is straightforward: instead of using Y directly as the target attribute, we use a function of it, which is called the *logit*. The logit, it turns out, can be modeled as a linear function of the predictors. Once the logit has been predicted, it can be mapped back to a probability.

To understand the logit, we take several intermediate steps: first, we look at $p = P(Y = 1)$, the probability of belonging to class 1 (as opposed to class 0). In contrast to the binary target Y, which only takes the values[2] 0 and 1, p can take any value in the interval $[0, 1]$. However, if we express p as a linear function of the q predictors[3] in the form

$$p = \beta_0 + \beta_1 x_1 + \beta_2 x_2 + \cdots + \beta_q x_q, \tag{10.1}$$

it is not guaranteed that the right-hand side will lead to values within the interval $[0, 1]$. The solution is to use a nonlinear function of the predictors in the form

$$p = \frac{1}{1 + e^{-(\beta_0 + \beta_1 x_1 + \beta_2 x_2 + \cdots + \beta_q x_q)}}. \tag{10.2}$$

This is called the *logistic response function*. For any values $x_1, \ldots, x_q$, the right-hand side will always lead to values in the interval $[0, 1]$. Next, we look at a different measure of belonging to a certain class, known as *odds*. The odds of belonging to class 1 are defined as *the ratio of the probability of belonging to class 1 to the probability of belonging to class 0*:

$$\text{Odds}(Y = 1) = \frac{p}{1 - p}. \tag{10.3}$$

This metric is very popular in horse races, sports, gambling, epidemiology, and other areas. Instead of talking about the *probability* of winning or contacting

---

[2]In RapidMiner, a *Binominal* target attribute takes values *true* or *false* representing 1 or 0, respectively.
[3]Unlike elsewhere in the book, where p denotes the number of predictors, in this chapter, we use q to avoid confusion with the probability p.

a disease, people talk about the *odds* of winning or contacting a disease. How are these two different? If, for example, the probability of winning is 0.5, the odds of winning are $0.5/0.5 = 1$. We can also perform the reverse calculation: given the odds of an event, we can compute its probability by manipulating equation (10.3):

$$p = \frac{\text{odds}}{1 + \text{odds}}. \tag{10.4}$$

Substituting equation (10.2) into equation (10.4), we can write the relationship between the odds and the predictors as

$$\text{Odds}(Y = 1) = e^{\beta_0 + \beta_1 x_1 + \beta_2 x_2 + \cdots + \beta_q x_q}. \tag{10.5}$$

This last equation describes a multiplicative (proportional) relationship between the predictors and the odds. Such a relationship is interpretable in terms of percentages, for example, a unit increase in predictor X_j is associated with an average increase of $e^{\beta_j} \times 100\%$ in the odds (holding all other predictors constant).

Now, if we take a natural logarithm[4] on both sides, we get the standard formulation of a logistic model:

$$\log(\text{odds}) = \beta_0 + \beta_1 x_1 + \beta_2 x_2 + \cdots + \beta_q x_q. \tag{10.6}$$

The $\log(\text{odds})$, called the *logit*, takes values from $-\infty$ (very low odds) to ∞ (very high odds).[5] A logit of 0 corresponds to even odds of 1 (probability = 0.5). Thus, our final formulation of the relation between the target and the predictors uses the logit as the target attribute and models it as a *linear function* of the q predictors.

To see the relationship between the probability, odds, and logit of belonging to class 1, look at Figure 10.1, which shows the odds (a) and logit (b) as a function of p. Notice that the odds can take any non-negative value and that the logit can take any real value.

10.3 EXAMPLE: ACCEPTANCE OF PERSONAL LOAN

Recall the example described in Chapter 9 of acceptance of a personal loan by Universal Bank. The bank's dataset includes data on 5000 customers. The data include the customer's response to the last personal loan campaign (Personal Loan), as well as customer demographic information (Age, Income, etc.) and the customer's relationship with the bank (mortgage, securities account, etc.); see Table 10.1. Among these 5000 customers, only 480 (=9.6%) accepted the personal loan offered to them in a previous campaign. The goal is to build a model that identifies customers who are most likely to accept the loan offer in future mailings.

---

[4]The natural logarithm function is typically denoted ln() or log(). In this book, we use log().

[5]We use the terms *odds* and *odds(Y = 1)* interchangeably.

FIGURE 10.1   (a) ODDS AND (b) LOGIT AS A FUNCTION OF p

TABLE 10.1   DESCRIPTION OF PREDICTORS FOR ACCEPTANCE OF PERSONAL LOAN EXAMPLE

Age	Customer's age in completed years
Experience	Number of years of professional experience
Income	Annual income of the customer ($000s)
Family	Family size of the customer
CCAvg	Average spending on credit cards per month ($000s)
Education	Education level: 1: undergrad; 2: graduate; 3: advanced/professional
Mortgage	Value of house mortgage if any ($000s)
Securities Account	Coded as 1 if customer has securities account with bank
CD Account	Coded as 1 if customer has certificate of deposit (CD) account with bank
Online	Coded as 1 if customer uses Internet banking facilities
CreditCard	Coded as 1 if customer uses credit card issued by Universal Bank

Model with a Single Predictor

Consider first a simple logistic regression model with just one predictor. This is conceptually analogous to the simple linear regression model in which we fit a straight line to relate the target, Y, to a single predictor, X.

Let us construct a simple logistic regression model for classification of customers using the single predictor *Income*. The equation relating the target attribute to the predictor in terms of probabilities is

$$P(\text{Personal Loan} = \textit{Yes} \mid \text{Income} = x) = \frac{1}{1 + e^{-(\beta_0 + \beta_1 x)}},$$

or equivalently, in terms of odds,

$$\text{Odds}(\text{Personal Loan} = \textit{Yes} \mid \text{Income} = x) = e^{\beta_0 + \beta_1 x}. \qquad (10.7)$$

Suppose the estimated coefficients for the model are $\hat{\beta}_0 = -6.04892$ and $\hat{\beta}_1 = 0.036$. So the fitted model is

$$P(\text{Personal Loan} = \textit{Yes} \mid \text{Income} = x) = \frac{1}{1 + e^{6.04892 - 0.036x}}. \qquad (10.8)$$

Although logistic regression can be used for prediction in the sense that we predict the *probability* of a categorical target, it is most often used for classification. To see the difference between the two, consider predicting the probability of a customer accepting the loan offer as opposed to classifying the customer as an acceptor/nonacceptor. From Figure 10.2, it can be seen that the loan acceptance probabilities produced by the logistic regression model (the s-shaped curve in Figure 10.2) can yield values between 0 and 1. To end up with classifications into either 1 or 0 (e.g., a customer either accepts the loan offer or not), we need a threshold, or cutoff value (see section on "Propensities and Threshold for Classification" in Chapter 5). This is true in the case of multiple predictor attributes as well.

In the Universal Bank example, in order to classify a new customer as an acceptor/nonacceptor of the loan offer, we use the information on his/her income by plugging it into the fitted equation in (10.8). This yields an estimated probability of accepting the loan offer. We then compare it with the threshold

FIGURE 10.2   **PLOT OF DATA POINTS (PERSONAL LOAN AS A FUNCTION OF INCOME) AND THE FITTED LOGISTIC CURVE**

value. The customer is classified as an acceptor if the probability of his/her accepting the offer is above the threshold.[6]

Estimating the Logistic Model from Data: Computing Parameter Estimates

In logistic regression, the relation between Y and the β parameters is nonlinear. For this reason, the β parameters are not estimated using the method of least squares (as in multiple linear regression). Instead, a method called *maximum likelihood* is used. The idea, in brief, is to find the estimates that maximize the chance of obtaining the data that we have. This requires iterations using a computer program.[7]

Algorithms to compute the coefficient estimates are less robust than algorithms for linear regression. Computed estimates are generally reliable for well-behaved datasets where the number of records with target attribute values of both 0 and 1 is large; their ratio is "not too close" to either 0 or 1; and when the number of coefficients in the logistic regression model is small relative to the sample size (say, no more than 10%). As with linear regression, collinearity (strong correlation among the predictors) can lead to computational difficulties. Computationally intensive algorithms have been developed recently that circumvent some of these difficulties. For technical details on the maximum likelihood estimation in logistic regression, see Hosmer and Lemeshow (2000).

To illustrate a typical output from such a procedure, we fit a logistic model to the training set of 3000 Universal Bank customers. The target attribute is *Personal Loan*, with 1 defined as the *positive class* representing an acceptor and 0 representing a nonacceptor.

Data Preprocessing   Figure 10.3 shows the data preprocessing steps starting with the *Select Attributes* operator, which selects the 11 predictors listed in Table 10.1 along with *Personal Loan* and *ID* attributes. The *Map* operator is used to replace a few negative values in the data with 0 for the predictor *Experience*.[8] Next, we need to transform the predictor *Education* to be of categorical type using the *Numerical to Polynominal* operator, since RapidMiner parsed it to be

---

[6]Here, we compared the probability with a threshold t. If we prefer to look at *odds* of accepting rather than the probability, an equivalent method is to use the equation in (10.7) and compare the odds with $t/(1-t)$. If the odds are higher than this number, the customer is classified as an acceptor. If it is lower, we classify the customer as a nonacceptor.

[7]The method of maximum likelihood ensures good asymptotic (large sample) properties for the estimates. Under very general conditions, maximum likelihood estimators are: (1) *Consistent* meaning the probability of the estimator differing from the true value approaches zero with increasing sample size, (2) *Asymptotically efficient* meaning the variance is the smallest possible among consistent estimators, and (3) *Asymptotically normally distributed*—This allows us to compute confidence intervals and perform statistical tests in a manner analogous to the analysis of multiple linear regression models, provided that the sample size is *large*.

[8]The meaning of negative values for the predictor *Experience* is unknown. In practice, domain knowledge should be used to understand more about unusual values prior to their replacement.

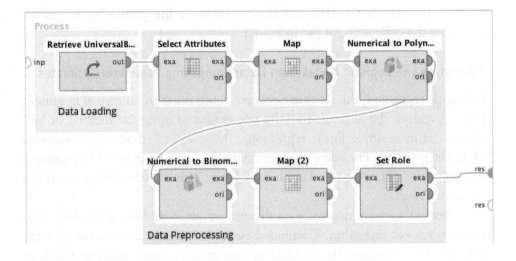

FIGURE 10.3   DATA PREPROCESSING FOR UNIVERSAL BANK LOAN DATA

of numeric type based on its values 1, 2, and 3 in the data. Later, the logistic regression will only use two of the three categories for Education because using all three would create a multicollinearity issue (see Chapter 6). The *comparison group* (reference category) for *Education* is automatically set by RapidMiner based on the first occurring predictor value in the data—in this case, it turns out to be 1 (undergraduate).[9] We also have other predictors, *Securities Account, CD Account, Online,* and *CreditCard*, which are of numeric type with 0/1 values and are treated as dummy variables during logistic regression. In total, the processed data will include 6 = 2 + 1 + 1 + 1 + 1 dummy variables to describe the five categorical predictors from Table 10.1. Together with the six numerical predictors, we have a total of 12 predictors. Following this, the *Numerical to Binominal* operator transforms the target attribute *Personal Loan* to a 2-class categorical type, with class labels *false* (internally mapped to 0) or *true* (internally mapped to 1). For more meaningful label values during result interpretation, we again use the *Map* operator, this time to specify *acceptor = true* and *nonacceptor = false* for *Personal Loan*. Finally, the *Set Role* operator assigns the *label* role to the target attribute *Personal Loan* and *id* role to the *ID* attribute.

Setting Up the Logistic Regression Process   Figure 10.4 (top) presents the RapidMiner process for running a logistic regression on the Universal Bank

---

[9]Due to a software limitation, when using regularization with logistic regression, comparison groups are not automatically set for categorical attributes. In this case, the *Nominal to Numerical* operator can be used to transform each of these attributes to dummy variables by setting *coding type = dummy coding* and by specifying the comparison groups as desired. In the case where the original categorical attributes have numeric values in the data (and RapidMiner parses them as numeric type), prior to the previous step, use the *Numerical to Polynominal* operator to first convert the attributes to categorical type.

FIGURE 10.4   (TOP) PROCESS FOR TRAINING AND EVALUATING A LOGISTIC REGRESSION CLASSIFIER ON THE UNIVERSAL BANK LOAN DATA. (BOTTOM) LOGISTIC REGRESSION MODEL

Attribute	Coefficient	Std. Coefficient	Std. Error	z-Value	p-Value
Education.2	3.972	3.972	0.352	11.277	0
Education.3	4.101	4.101	0.350	11.707	0
Experience	0.048	0.549	0.084	0.572	0.567
Age	−0.038	−0.438	0.084	−0.454	0.650
Income	0.060	2.743	0.004	15.543	0
Family	0.606	0.695	0.099	6.136	0.000
CCAvg	0.186	0.326	0.058	3.214	0.001

Attribute	Coefficient	Std. Coefficient	Std. Error	z-Value	p-Value
Mortgage	0.000	0.025	0.001	0.315	0.753
Securities Account	−1.328	−0.412	0.402	−3.306	0.001
CD Account	3.514	0.841	0.421	8.336	0.000
Online	−0.610	−0.299	0.214	−2.847	0.004
CreditCard	−0.799	−0.366	0.260	−3.076	0.002
Intercept	−12.293	−7.410	2.274	−5.405	0.000

loan data. The *Data Preprocessing* subprocess contains the same steps mentioned in Figure 10.3. Using the *Split Data* operator, the data is first partitioned randomly into training (60%) and holdout (40%) sets. We use the training set to fit a logistic regression model using the *Logistic Regression* operator—located in the Operators panel under *Modeling > Predictive > Logistic Regression*. We then use the holdout set to assess the model's performance using the *Apply Model* and the *Performance (Binominal Classification)* operators. In the *Performance (Binominal Classification)* operator, we recognize the target's positive class label by specifying *positive class = acceptor*. *Multiply* operators are used to copy the model and holdout set and relay them to the *Lift Chart(Simple)* operator to construct a lift chart. In the *Lift Chart(Simple)* operator as well, we specify *target class = acceptor*. We discuss the performance evaluation of the model in Section 10.1.

Estimated Model   The model fit to the training data is shown in Figure 10.4 (bottom) depicting the logistic regression model generated based on the training data. The model based on all 12 predictors has the estimated logistic equation

$$
\begin{aligned}
\text{Logit(Personal Loan = Yes)} \quad = \quad & -12.293 - 0.038\ \text{Age} + 0.048\ \text{Experience} \\
+ \quad & 0.060\ \text{Income} + 0.606\ \text{Family} + 0.186\ \text{CCAvg} \\
+ \quad & 0.000\ \text{Mortgage} - 1.328\ \text{Securities Account} \\
+ \quad & 3.514\ \text{CD Account} - 0.610\ \text{Online} - 0.799\ \text{CreditCard} \\
+ \quad & 3.972\ \text{Education.2} + 4.101\ \text{Education.3.} \qquad (10.9)
\end{aligned}
$$

The positive coefficients for the dummy variables *Education.2, Education.3*, and *CD Account* mean that holding a CD account and having graduate or professional education (all marked by 1 in the dummy variables) are associated with higher probabilities of accepting the loan offer. In contrast, having a securities account, using online banking, and owning a Universal Bank credit card are associated with lower acceptance rates. For the continuous predictors, positive coefficients indicate that a higher value on that predictor is associated with a higher probability of accepting the loan offer (e.g., Income: higher-income customers tend more to accept the offer). Similarly, negative coefficients indicate that a higher value on that predictor is associated with a lower probability of accepting the loan offer (e.g., Age: older customers are less likely to accept the offer).

Interpreting Results in Terms of Odds (for a Profiling Goal)

Logistic models, when they are appropriate for the data, can give useful information about the roles played by different predictor variables. For example, suppose we want to know how increasing family income by one unit will affect the probability of loan acceptance. This can be found straightforwardly if we consider not probabilities, but odds.

Recall that the odds are given by

$$\text{Odds} = e^{\beta_0 + \beta_1 x_1 + \beta_2 x_2 + \cdots + \beta_q x_q}.$$

At first, let us return to the single predictor example, where we model a customer's acceptance of a personal loan offer as a function of his/her income:

$$\text{Odds(Personal Loan} = \textit{Yes} \mid \text{Income}) = e^{\beta_0 + \beta_1 \text{Income}}.$$

We can think of the model as a multiplicative model of odds. The odds that a customer with income zero will accept the loan is estimated by $e^{-6.04892 + (0.036)(0)} = 0.00236$. These are the *base-case odds*. In this example, it is obviously economically meaningless to talk about a zero income; the value zero and the corresponding base-case odds could be meaningful, however, in the context of other predictors. The odds of accepting the loan with an income of \$100K will increase by a multiplicative factor of $e^{(0.036)(100)} = 36.6$ over the base case, so the odds that such a customer will accept the offer are $e^{-6.04892 + (0.036)(100)} = 0.086$.

Suppose that the value of Income, or in general X_1, is increased by one unit from x_1 to $x_1 + 1$, while the other predictors are held at their current value $(x_2, \ldots, x_{12})$. We get the odds ratio

$$\frac{\text{odds}(x_1 + 1, x_2, \ldots, x_{12})}{\text{odds}(x_1, \ldots, x_{12})} = \frac{e^{\beta_0 + \beta_1(x_1+1) + \beta_2 x_2 + \cdots + \beta_{12} x_{12}}}{e^{\beta_0 + \beta_1 x_1 + \beta_2 x_2 + \cdots + \beta_{12} x_{12}}} = e^{\beta_1}.$$

This tells us that a single unit increase in X_1, holding $X_2, \ldots, X_{12}$ constant, is associated with an increase in the odds that a customer accepts the offer by a factor of e^{β_1}. In other words, e^{β_1} is the multiplicative factor by which the odds (of belonging to class 1) increase when the value of X_1 is increased by 1 unit, *holding all other predictors constant*. If $\beta_1 < 0$, an increase in X_1 is associated with a decrease in the odds of belonging to class 1, whereas a positive value of β_1 is associated with an increase in the odds.

When a predictor is a dummy variable, the interpretation is technically the same but has a different practical meaning. For instance, the coefficient for *CD Account* in the 12-predictor model was estimated from the data to be 3.514. Recall that the reference group is customers not holding a CD account. We interpret this coefficient as follows: $e^{3.514} = 33.58$ are the odds that a customer who has a CD account will accept the offer relative to a customer who does not have a CD account, holding all other variables constant. This means that customers who hold CD accounts at Universal Bank are more likely to accept the offer than customers without a CD account (holding all other variables constant).

The advantage of reporting results in odds as opposed to probabilities is that statements such as those above are true for any value of X_1. Unless X_1 is a dummy variable, we cannot apply such statements about the effect of increasing X_1 by a single unit to probabilities. This is because the result depends on the actual value of X_1. So if we increase X_1 from, say, 3 to 4, the effect on p, the probability of belonging to class 1, will be different than if we increase X_1 from 30 to 31. In short, the change in the probability, p, for a unit increase in a particular predictor variable, while holding all other predictors constant, is not a constant—it depends on the specific values of the predictor variables. We therefore talk about probabilities only in the context of specific records.

Evaluating Classification Performance

The general measures of performance that were described in Chapter 5 are used to assess the logistic model performance. Recall that there are several performance measures, the most popular being those based on the confusion matrix (accuracy alone or combined with costs) and the lift charts. As in other classification methods, the goal is to find a model that accurately classifies records to their class, using only the predictor information. A variant of this goal is *ranking* or finding a model that does a superior job of identifying the members of a particular class of interest for a set of new records (which might come at some cost to overall accuracy). Since the training data are used for selecting the model, we expect the model to perform quite well for those data and therefore prefer to test its performance on the holdout set. Recall that the data in the holdout set were not involved in the model building, and thus we can use them to assess the model's ability to classify data that it has not "seen" before.

To obtain the confusion matrix from a logistic regression analysis, we use the estimated equation to predict the probability of class membership (the *propensities*) for each record in the holdout set and use the threshold value to decide on the class assignment of these records. We then compare these classifications with the actual class memberships of these records. In the Universal Bank case, we use the estimated model in equation (10.9) to predict the probability of offer acceptance in a holdout set that contains 2000 customers (these data were not used in the modeling step). Technically, this is done by computing the *logit* using the estimated model in equation (10.9) and then obtaining the probabilities p through the relation $p = e^{\text{logit}} / \left(1 + e^{\text{logit}}\right)$. We then compare these probabilities with our chosen threshold value in order to classify each of the 2000 holdout records as acceptors or nonacceptors.

Figure 10.5 (top) shows propensities for five records in the holdout set. For each customer record in the holdout set, *confidence(acceptor)* is an estimate of its propensity (probability) of belonging to *acceptor* class, and *confidence(nonacceptor)* = 1 - *confidence(acceptor)*. Suppose that we use a threshold of 0.5. We see that

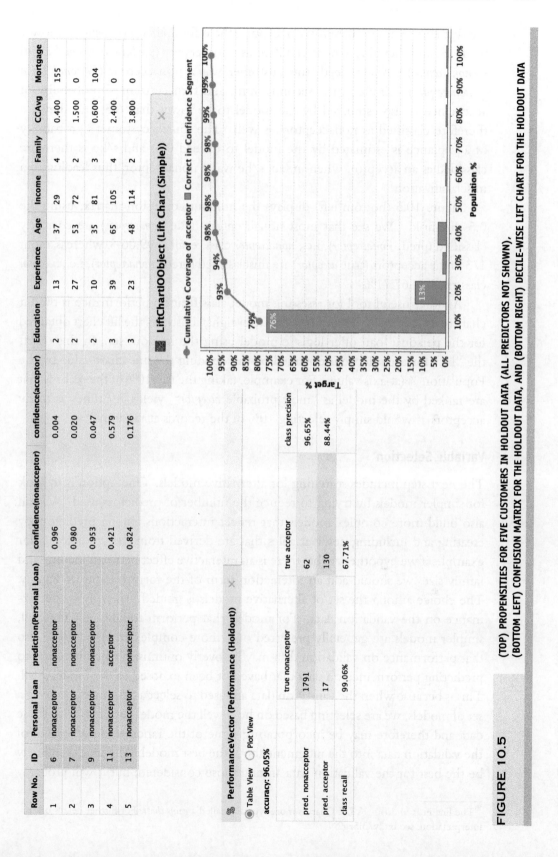

Row No.	ID	Personal Loan	prediction(Personal Loan)	confidence(nonacceptor)	confidence(acceptor)	Education	Experience	Age	Income	Family	CCAvg	Mortgage
1	6	nonacceptor	nonacceptor	0.996	0.004	2	13	37	29	4	0.400	155
2	7	nonacceptor	nonacceptor	0.980	0.020	2	27	53	72	2	1.500	0
3	9	nonacceptor	nonacceptor	0.953	0.047	2	10	35	81	3	0.600	104
4	11	nonacceptor	acceptor	0.421	0.579	3	39	65	105	4	2.400	0
5	13	nonacceptor	nonacceptor	0.824	0.176	3	23	48	114	2	3.800	0

LiftChartIOObject (Lift Chart (Simple))

◆ Cumulative Coverage of acceptor ■ Correct in Confidence Segment

PerformanceVector (Performance (Holdout))

● Table View ○ Plot View

accuracy: 96.05%

	true nonacceptor	true acceptor	class precision
pred. nonacceptor	1791	62	96.65%
pred. acceptor	17	130	88.44%
class recall	99.06%	67.71%	

FIGURE 10.5 (TOP) PROPENSITIES FOR FIVE CUSTOMERS IN HOLDOUT DATA (ALL PREDICTORS NOT SHOWN), (BOTTOM LEFT) CONFUSION MATRIX FOR THE HOLDOUT DATA, AND (BOTTOM RIGHT) DECILE-WISE LIFT CHART FOR THE HOLDOUT DATA

the first customer's probability of accepting the offer (*confidence(acceptor)*) is lower than 0.5, and therefore s/he is classified as nonacceptor (*prediction(Personal Loan) = nonacceptor*). And indeed, this customer was a nonacceptor (*Personal Loan = nonacceptor*). Similarly, the second, third, and fifth customers' probability of acceptance is also estimated by the model to be lower than 0.5, and they are therefore classified as nonacceptors as well. The fourth customer's probability of acceptance is estimated by the model to exceed 0.5, and s/he is therefore classified as an acceptor, when in fact s/he was a nonacceptor, thus leading to a misclassification.

Figure 10.5 (bottom left) displays the holdout confusion matrix, using the 0.5 threshold. We see that most nonacceptors (true *nonacceptor*) are correctly classified (pred. *nonacceptor*), i.e., *nonacceptor* class recall = 99.06%, whereas about 1/3 of the acceptors (true *acceptor*) are misclassified (pred. *nonacceptor*), i.e., *acceptor* class recall = 67.71%.

Another useful tool for assessing model classification performance is the lift chart (see Chapter 5). Figure 10.5 (bottom right) illustrates the lift chart obtained for the personal loan offer logistic model using the holdout set. In this chart, the "lift" for each decile is obtained by the dividing the line chart value by the Population % (x-axis value). For example, taking the top 10% of the records that are ranked by the model as "most probable *acceptors*" yields 7.9 times as many acceptors as would simply selecting 10% of the records at random.[10]

Variable Selection

The next step includes searching for alternative models. One option is to look for simpler models by trying to reduce the number of predictors used. We can also build more complex models that reflect interactions among predictors by creating and including new variables that are derived from the predictors. For example, if we hypothesize that there is an interactive effect between income and family size, we should add an interaction term of the form Income × Family. The choice among the set of alternative models is guided primarily by performance on the validation data. For models that perform roughly equally well, simpler models are generally preferred over more complex models. Note also that performance on validation data may be overly optimistic when it comes to predicting performance on data that have not been exposed to the model at all. This is because when the validation data are used to select a final model among a set of models, we are selecting based on how well the model performs with those data and therefore may be incorporating some of the random idiosyncrasies of the validation data into the judgment about the best model. The model still may be the best for the validation data among those considered, but it will probably

---

[10]The line in RapidMiner's Lift Chart is more typically called a *gains chart*. For further details on its interpretation, see bit.ly/3i5zg2N

not do as well with the unseen data. Therefore, it is useful to evaluate the chosen model on a new holdout set to get a sense of how well it will perform on new data.[11] In addition, one must consider practical issues such as costs of collecting variables, error-proneness, and model complexity in the selection of the final model.

As in linear regression (see Section 6.4 in Chapter 6), in logistic regression, we can use automated variable selection heuristics such as stepwise regression, forward selection, and backward elimination. We can also use regularization using L1 or L2 penalty. In RapidMiner, the *Logistic Regression* operator is designed as a special case of the *Generalized Linear Model* (GLM) operator with *family = binomial* that uses the *logit* link function and is based on the GLM implementation from the H2O.ai company. The *Logistic Regression* operator implements regularization identical to the *Generalized Linear Model* operator as a combination of L1 and L2 penalties, specified by two parameters, λ and α, as discussed in Section 6.4 in Chapter 6. When $\lambda = 0$, no regularization is applied (the α parameter is ignored), yielding ordinary logistic regression. We illustrate the use of regularized logistic regression in Section 10.5.

10.4 LOGISTIC REGRESSION FOR MULTI-CLASS CLASSIFICATION

The logistic model for a binary target attribute can be extended for more than two classes. Suppose that there are m classes. Using a logistic regression model, for each record we would have m probabilities of belonging to each of the m classes. Since the m probabilities must add up to 1, we need to estimate only $m - 1$ probabilities.

When the label classes are distinct from one another and are not related (e.g., by order), we have nominal classes.[12] An example is the choice between several brands of cereal. A simple way to verify that the classes are nominal is when it makes sense to tag them as $A, B, C, \ldots$, and the assignment of letters to classes does not matter. For simplicity, let us assume that there are $m = 3$ brands of cereal that consumers can choose from (assuming that each consumer chooses one). Then, we estimate the probabilities $P(Y = A)$, $P(Y = B)$, and $P(Y = C)$. If we know two of the probabilities, the third probability is determined. We therefore use one of the classes as the reference class. Let us use C as the reference brand.

---

[11] In the prior example, alternative models were not assessed or compared, so we used the *holdout* set for model testing.

[12] In the chapter appendix, we also describe logistic regression for an ordinal label, where the classes have a meaningful order such as *low, medium,* and *high.* RapidMiner supports logistic regression for nominal labels but not for ordinal labels.

The goal is to model the class membership as a function of predictors. So in the cereals example, we might want to predict which cereal will be chosen if we know the cereal's price x.

Next, we form $m - 1$ pseudologit equations that are linear in the predictors. In our example, we would have

$$\text{logit}(A) = \log \frac{P(Y = A)}{P(Y = C)} = \alpha_0 + \alpha_1 x,$$

$$\text{logit}(B) = \log \frac{P(Y = B)}{P(Y = C)} = \beta_0 + \beta_1 x.$$

Once the four coefficients are estimated from the training set, we can estimate the class membership probabilities:

$$P(Y = A) = \frac{e^{a_0 + a_1 x}}{1 + e^{a_0 + a_1 x} + e^{b_0 + b_1 x}},$$

$$P(Y = B) = \frac{e^{b_0 + b_1 x}}{1 + e^{a_0 + a_1 x} + e^{b_0 + b_1 x}},$$

$$P(Y = C) = 1 - P(Y = A) - P(Y = B),$$

where a_0, a_1, b_0, and b_1 are the coefficient estimates obtained from the training set.[13] Finally, a record is assigned to the class that has the highest probability.

Example: Accidents Data

Let's take, for example, data on accidents from the US Bureau of Transportation Statistics. These data can be used to predict whether an accident will result in injuries or fatalities based on predictors such as alcohol involvement, time of day, and road condition. The severity of the accident has three classes: 0 = No Injury, 1 = Nonfatal Injuries, and 2 = Fatalities.

We consider severity as a nominal target variable and fit a simple model with two nominal predictors, alcohol and weather. Alcohol is coded as 1 (involved in the accident) or 2 (not involved in the accident). Weather is coded as 1 (no adverse conditions) or 2 (rain, snow, or other adverse conditions).

Figure 10.6 presents the process for conducting multinomial logistic regression applied to the accidents data. The *Numerical to Polynominal* operator

---

[13]From the two logit equations, we see that $P(Y = A) = P(Y = C) \cdot e^{\alpha_0 + \alpha_1 x}$ and $P(Y = B) = P(Y = C) \cdot e^{\beta_0 + \beta_1 x}$. Since $P(Y = A) + P(Y = B) + P(Y = C) = 1$, we get

$$P(Y = C) = 1 - P(Y = C)e^{\alpha_0 + \alpha_1 x} - P(Y = C)e^{\beta_0 + \beta_1 x} = \frac{1}{e^{\alpha_0 + \alpha_1 x} + e^{\beta_0 + \beta_1 x}}. \quad (10.10)$$

By plugging this form into the two equations above it, we also obtain the membership probabilities in classes A and B.

FIGURE 10.6 NOMINAL (MULTI-CLASS) LOGISTIC REGRESSION IN RAPIDMINER (TOP) RAPIDMINER PROCESS, (MIDDLE) ESTIMATED MODEL, AND (BOTTOM) PREDICTED PROBABILITIES FOR FIVE SAMPLE RECORDS

transforms the target to *Nominal* data type. The *Generalized Linear Model* operator is configured with *family* = *multinomial* parameter. The figure also displays the resulting estimated model and predicted probabilities, i.e., confidence values for a few sample records. The nominal logistic model has estimates for the three intercepts and also has three separate sets of coefficients for the predictors for each level of the target attribute. In practice, it would be useful to evaluate predictive performance on a holdout set.

10.5 EXAMPLE OF COMPLETE ANALYSIS: PREDICTING DELAYED FLIGHTS

Predicting flight delays can be useful to a variety of organizations: airport authorities, airlines, and aviation authorities. At times, joint task forces have been formed to address the problem. Such an organization, if it were to provide ongoing real-time assistance with flight delays, would benefit from some advance notice about flights likely to be delayed.

In this simplified illustration, we look at six predictors (see Table 10.2). The outcome of interest is whether the flight is delayed or not (*delayed* means more than 15 minutes late). Our data consist of all flights from the Washington, DC area into the New York City area during January 2004. The percent of delayed flights among these 2201 flights is 19.5%. The data were obtained from the Bureau of Transportation Statistics website (www.transtats.bts.gov).[14]

TABLE 10.2   **DESCRIPTION OF PREDICTORS FOR FLIGHT DELAYS EXAMPLE**

Day of week (DAY_WEEK)	Coded as 1 = Monday, 2 = Tuesday,...., 7 = Sunday
Departure time (CRS_DEP_TIME)	Broken down into 18 intervals between 6:00 AM and 10:00 PM
Origin (ORIGIN)	Three airport codes: DCA (Reagan National), IAD (Dulles), and BWI (Baltimore–Washington Int'l)
Destination (DEST)	Three airport codes: JFK (Kennedy), LGA (LaGuardia), and EWR (Newark)
Carrier (CARRIER)	Eight airline codes: CO (Continental), DH (Atlantic Coast), DL (Delta), MQ (American Eagle), OH (Comair), RU (Continental Express), UA (United), and US (USAirways)
Weather (Weather)	Coded as 1 if there was a weather-related delay

The goal is to predict accurately whether a new flight, not in this dataset, will be delayed or not. The target attribute, Flight Status, is coded as *delayed* or *ontime*.

Other information available on the website, such as distance and arrival time, is irrelevant because we are looking at a certain route (distance, flight time, etc. should be approximately equal for all flights in the data). A sample of the data for 20 flights is shown in Table 10.3.

Data Visualization

Figure 10.7 shows the process for preparing the data for visualizing the relationships between flight delays and different predictors or combination of predictors. After loading the data, the *Select Attributes* operator is used to select the six

---

[14]In the data, *CRS_DEP_TIME* is the scheduled departure time, and *DEP_TIME* is the actual departure time. Since we are interested in analyzing the effect of departure time, we use *CRS_DEP_TIME* and ignore the actual *DEP_TIME*.

TABLE 10.3   SAMPLE OF 20 FLIGHTS

Flight Status	CARRIER	DAY_WEEK	CRS_DEP_TIME	DEST	ORIGIN	Weather
Ontime	DL	2	728	LGA	DCA	0
Delayed	US	3	1600	LGA	DCA	0
Ontime	DH	5	1242	EWR	IAD	0
Ontime	US	2	2057	LGA	DCA	0
Ontime	DH	3	1603	JFK	IAD	0
Ontime	CO	6	1252	EWR	DCA	0
Ontime	RU	6	1728	EWR	DCA	0
Ontime	DL	5	1031	LGA	DCA	0
Ontime	RU	6	1722	EWR	IAD	0
Delayed	US	1	627	LGA	DCA	0
Delayed	DH	2	1756	JFK	IAD	0
Ontime	MQ	6	1529	JFK	DCA	0
Ontime	US	6	1259	LGA	DCA	0
Ontime	DL	2	1329	LGA	DCA	0
Ontime	RU	2	1453	EWR	BWI	0
Ontime	RU	5	1356	EWR	DCA	0
Delayed	DH	7	2244	LGA	IAD	0
Ontime	US	7	1053	LGA	DCA	0
Ontime	US	2	1057	LGA	DCA	0
Ontime	US	4	632	LGA	DCA	0

FIGURE 10.7   PROCESS FOR VISUALIZING RELATIONSHIPS BETWEEN AVERAGE FLIGHT DELAY AND EACH OF THE SIX PREDICTORS

predictors and the target variable. Then, using the *Nominal to Numerical* operator, *Flight Status* is dummy coded with *ontime* as the comparison group, i.e., level 0, and the transformed variable is named *Flight Status_delayed*. This transformation is done so that aggregation functions such as *count* can be used for grouping during data visualization. The *Discretize by User Specification* operator is then employed to bin and categorize the departure time into hourly intervals between 6:00 AM and 10:00 PM. Similarly, the *Numerical to Polynominal* operator transforms the day of the week into a categorical attribute. Finally, for the purpose of visualization, we sort the data by day of the week and then by the departure time using the *Sort* operator so that the categories appear sorted in the visualizations created.

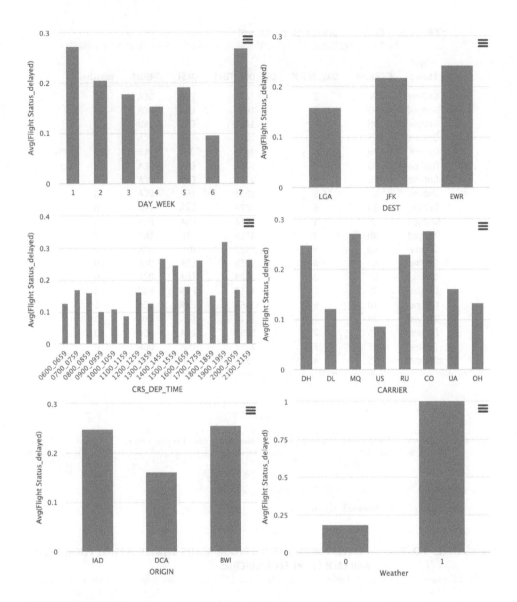

FIGURE 10.8   PROPORTION OF DELAYED FLIGHTS BY EACH OF THE SIX PREDICTORS. TIME OF DAY IS DIVIDED INTO HOURLY BINS

Figure 10.8 shows bar charts depicting the relationships between flight delays and the different predictors. Each bar chart is produced by configuring *Value columns = Flight Status_delayed*, grouping it by the corresponding predictor, and using the *average* aggregation function. From Figure 10.8, we see that Sundays and Mondays saw the largest proportion of delays. Delay rates also seem to differ by carrier, by time of day, as well as by origin and destination airports. For Weather, we see a strong distinction between delays when Weather = 1 (in that case there is always a delay) and Weather = 0.

Figure 10.9 (top) shows the use of the *Pivot* operator to group and aggregate the data. The heatmap in Figure 10.9 (bottom) reveals some specific combinations with high rates of delays, such as Sunday flights by carriers RU or MQ. If you add the information gained from switching the *y*-axis to show origin airport, you can then reach more specific conclusions, such as "Sunday flights by carrier RU departing from BWI or Sunday flights by MQ departing from DCA have a high probability of delay." Similarly, we can also see combinations with very low delay rates.

Our main goal is to find a model that can obtain accurate classifications of new flights based on their predictor information. An alternative goal is finding a certain percentage of flights that are most/least likely to get delayed (*ranking*). And a third different goal is profiling flights: finding out which factors are associated with a delay (not only in this sample but also in the entire population of flights on this route) and for those factors we would like to quantify these effects. A logistic regression model can be used for all these goals, albeit in different ways.

Data Preprocessing

Figure 10.10 shows the process for estimating the logistic regression model after data preprocessing.[15] The *Data Preprocessing* subprocess starts by selecting the predictor and target attributes for analysis with the *Select Attributes* operator. Then, departure time is categorized into hourly intervals using the *Discretize by User Specification* operator, and day of week is transformed into a categorical attribute with the *Numerical to Polynominal* operator. Next, the *Nominal to Binominal* operator is used to transform *Flight Status* to a 2-class attribute. Then, with the *Remap Binominals* operator, we ensure that *delayed* is set as the positive value for the target attribute while model training. Finally, the *Set Role* operator assigns the *label* role to *Flight Status*. We then partition the data with the *Split Data* operator into training set (60%) and holdout set (40%). We use the training set to fit a model and the holdout set to assess the model's performance. The remaining operators are similar to those in Figure 10.4, except that in the *Performance (Binominal Classification)* and *Lift Chart(Simple)* operators, we set the target's positive class label by specifying *positive class = delayed*.

As noted earlier, when using nominal attributes as predictors, the *Logistic Regression* operator automatically sets a *comparison group* (a reference category) for each nominal attribute. This yields a total of 32 dummies (15 scheduled departure time ranges + 7 airline carriers + 6 days of the week + 2 departure

---

[15]For predictive modeling, we need a slightly different preprocessing than that for visualization. For example, in visualization, we converted Flight Status to a 0/1 numerical attribute required for plotting the proportion of delayed flights by each categorical predictor, since the *average* aggregation function used in grouping for histograms supports only numerical attributes. In contrast, for predictive modeling, we require the 2-class target attribute to be of *Binominal* data type.

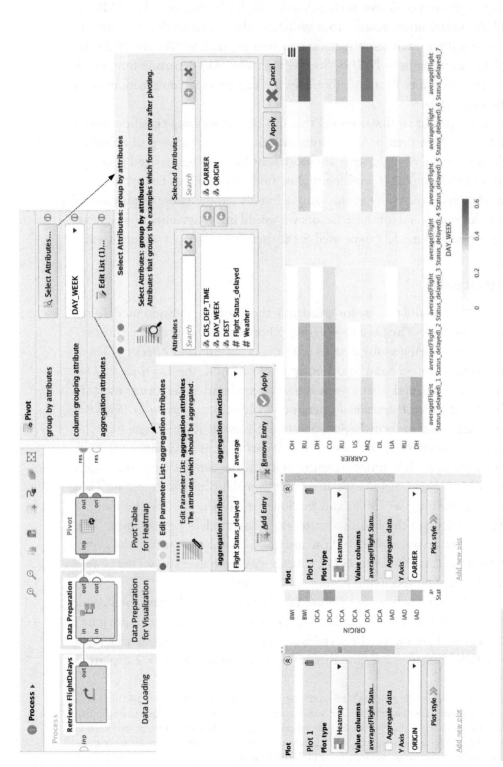

FIGURE 10.9

(TOP) PROCESS FOR PIVOTING THE DATA. (BOTTOM) PERCENT OF DELAYED FLIGHTS (RED = HIGHER %DELAYS) BY DAY OF WEEK, ORIGIN, AND CARRIER. NOTE: Y-AXIS OF THE HEATMAP MAY BE CHANGED TO VIEW THE DATA LABELED BY CARRIER OR ORIGIN

FIGURE 10.10   PROCESS FOR ESTIMATING LOGISTIC REGRESSION MODEL FOR DELAYED FLIGHTS (BASED ON THE TRAINING SET)

airports + 2 arrival airports). In addition, we have a single dummy for Weather. While this is a large number of predictors, we start by using all of them, look at performance, and then explore reducing the dimension.

Model Training

The estimated model with 33 predictors is shown in Figure 10.11. Note that negative coefficients in the logit model translate into odds coefficients $e^{\hat{\beta}}$ lower than 1 and positive logit coefficients translate into odds coefficients larger than 1.

Model Interpretation

The coefficient for arrival airport LGA (DEST.LGA) is estimated as 0.325. Here, the comparison group is JFK. We interpret this coefficient as follows: $e^{0.325} = 1.384$ are the odds of a flight arriving at LGA being delayed relative to a flight to JFK being delayed (the base-case odds), holding all other variables constant. This means that, all else constant, flights to LGA are more likely to be delayed than those to JFK. For departure airports (where BWI is the comparison group), coefficients for both DCA and IAD are negative, indicating that BWI has the highest odds of delay, while DCA has the largest negative coefficient and thereby the lowest odds of delay (holding everything else constant). For carriers (OH is the comparison group), coefficients for all carrier dummies are positive, indicating that OH has the lowest odds of delay, while CO has the largest positive coefficient, indicating the highest odds of delay (holding everything else constant). For day of week, relative to Thursday (DAY_WEEK.4), which is the comparison group, Saturday has the largest negative coefficient and thereby the lowest odds of delay (holding everything else constant). In contrast, Sunday has the largest positive coefficient and thereby the highest odds of delay (holding everything else constant). Also, the odds of delays appear to change over the course of the day, with the most noticeable difference from the comparison group of 6–7 AM being 7–8 PM. Finally, Weather has the largest coefficient, indicating a large gap between flights with Weather = 0 and Weather = 1. Note that we have considered above only coefficient magnitude and not statistical significance. Since our eventual goal is prediction, we will rely instead on predictive performance.

Model Performance

How should we measure the performance of models? One possible measure is "percent of flights correctly classified." Accurate classification can be obtained from the confusion matrix for the holdout data. The confusion matrix gives a sense of the classification accuracy and what type of misclassification is more

Attribute	Coefficient	Std. Coefficient	Std. Error	z–Value	p–Value
CRS_DEP_TIME.0700_0759	0.186	0.186	0.547	0.340	0.734
CRS_DEP_TIME.0800_0859	0.740	0.740	0.520	1.422	0.155
CRS_DEP_TIME.0900_0959	−0.249	−0.249	0.672	−0.370	0.711
CRS_DEP_TIME.1000_1059	−0.127	−0.127	0.648	−0.195	0.845
CRS_DEP_TIME.1100_1159	0.378	0.378	0.685	0.552	0.581
CRS_DEP_TIME.1200_1259	0.604	0.604	0.519	1.163	0.245
CRS_DEP_TIME.1300_1359	0.503	0.503	0.521	0.966	0.334
CRS_DEP_TIME.1400_1459	1.450	1.450	0.468	3.101	0.002
CRS_DEP_TIME.1500_1559	1.238	1.238	0.487	2.541	0.011
CRS_DEP_TIME.1600_1659	0.641	0.641	0.496	1.294	0.196
CRS_DEP_TIME.1700_1759	1.170	1.170	0.456	2.566	0.010
CRS_DEP_TIME.1800_1859	0.585	0.585	0.649	0.902	0.367
CRS_DEP_TIME.1900_1959	1.468	1.468	0.495	2.964	0.003
CRS_DEP_TIME.2000_2059	0.881	0.881	0.755	1.167	0.243
CRS_DEP_TIME.2100_2159	1.015	1.015	0.490	2.073	0.038
CARRIER.DH	1.563	1.563	0.889	1.758	0.079
CARRIER.DL	0.557	0.557	0.930	0.599	0.549
CARRIER.MQ	1.836	1.836	0.917	2.003	0.045
CARRIER.UA	0.052	0.052	1.421	0.037	0.971
CARRIER.US	0.177	0.177	0.944	0.188	0.851
CARRIER.RU	1.936	1.936	0.896	2.162	0.031
CARRIER.CO	1.959	1.959	1.004	1.950	0.051
DAY_WEEK.5	0.197	0.197	0.256	0.769	0.442
DAY_WEEK.6	−0.483	−0.483	0.346	−1.397	0.162
DAY_WEEK.7	0.883	0.883	0.270	3.269	0.001
DAY_WEEK.1	0.637	0.637	0.272	2.344	0.019
DAY_WEEK.2	0.182	0.182	0.279	0.652	0.514
DAY_WEEK.3	0.179	0.179	0.275	0.652	0.515
DEST.LGA	0.325	0.325	0.258	1.259	0.208
DEST.EWR	−0.175	−0.175	0.341	−0.513	0.608
ORIGIN.DCA	−0.390	−0.390	0.431	−0.906	0.365
ORIGIN.IAD	−0.203	−0.203	0.410	−0.494	0.621
Weather	13.222	1.615	71.833	0.184	0.854
Intercept	−3.716	−3.516	0.909	−4.089	0.000

FIGURE 10.11   ESTIMATED LOGISTIC REGRESSION MODEL FOR DELAYED FLIGHTS (BASED ON THE TRAINING SET)

accuracy: 81.59%

	true ontime	true delayed	class precision
pred. ontime	696	149	82.37%
pred. delayed	13	22	62.86%
class recall	98.17%	12.87%	

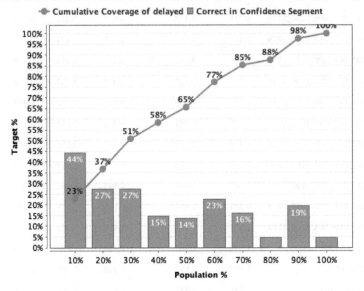

FIGURE 10.12   **CONFUSION MATRIX AND LIFT CHART FOR THE FLIGHT DELAYS HOLDOUT DATA USING ALL PREDICTORS**

frequent. From the confusion matrix and error rates in Figure 10.12, it can be seen that the model more accurately classifies ontime flights and is less accurate in classifying flights that were delayed. (*Note*: The same pattern appears in the confusion matrix for the training data, so it is not surprising to see it emerge for new data.) If there is an asymmetric cost structure so that one type of misclassification is more costly than the other, the threshold value can be selected to minimize the cost. Of course, this tweaking should be carried out on the training data and assessed only using the holdout data.

In most conceivable situations, the purpose of the model would be to identify those flights most likely to be delayed among a set of flights so that resources can be directed toward either reducing the delay or mitigating its effects. Air traffic controllers might work to open up additional air routes or allocate more controllers to a specific area for a short time. Airlines might bring on personnel to rebook passengers and to activate standby flight crews and aircraft. Hotels might allocate space for stranded travelers. In all cases, the resources available are going to be limited and might vary over time and from organization to organization. In this situation, the most useful model would provide an ordering of flights by their probability of delay, letting the model users decide how far down that list to go in taking action. Therefore, model lift is a useful measure of performance—as you move down that list of flights, ordered by their delay probability, how much better does the model do in predicting delay than would a naive model which is simply the average delay rate for all flights? From the lift chart for the holdout data (Figure 10.12), we see that our model is superior to the baseline (simple random selection of flights).

Variable Selection

From the data exploration charts (Figures 10.8 and 10.9) and from the coefficient table for the flights delay model (Figure 10.11), it appears that several of the predictors could be dropped or coded differently. Additionally, we look at the number of flights in different categories to identify categories with very few or no flights—such categories are candidates for removal or merger (see Table 10.4).

TABLE 10.4		NUMBER OF FLIGHTS BY CARRIER AND ORIGIN		
	BWI	DCA	IAD	Total
CO		94		94
DH		27	524	551
DL		388		388
MQ		295		295
OH	30			30
RU	115	162	131	408
UA			31	31
US		404		404
Total	145	1370	686	2201

First, we find that most carriers depart from a single airport (DCA): for those that depart from all three airports, the delay rates are similar regardless of airport. We therefore drop the departure airport distinction by excluding Origin dummies and find that the model performance and fit are not harmed. We also drop the destination airport for a practical reason: not all carriers fly to all airports. Our model would then be invalid for prediction in nonexistent combinations of carrier and destination airport. We also try grouping carriers, day of week, and hour of day into fewer categories that are more distinguishable with respect to delays. For example, Sundays and Mondays seem to have a similar rate of delays, which differs from the lower rate on Tuesday–Saturday. We therefore group the days of week into Sunday + Monday and Other, resulting in a single dummy variable.

Figure 10.13 shows the data preprocessing for generating the new predictors by consolidating categories in existing predictors. The *Generate Attributes* operator is used to specify function expressions as shown in Figure 10.13 (bottom). The new predictors are as follows: *Sun_Mon* (flights on Sunday or

FIGURE 10.13   DATA PREPARATION FOR GENERATING NEW PREDICTORS

Monday), *Carrier_CO_MQ_DH_RU* (flights from select carriers), *2PM_3PM* (flights between 2 PM and 3 PM), and *7PM_8PM* (flights between 7 PM and 8 PM). The original attributes are deselected through the *Select Attributes* operator.

Figure 10.14 displays the estimated smaller model, with its holdout confusion matrix and lift chart. It can be seen that this model competes well with the larger model in terms of classification accuracy and lift while using much less information.

Finally, we try an automated variable selection approach, by using regularization with L1 penalty (lasso). The RapidMiner process is identical to that shown in Figure 10.10, except that we select the *use regularization* option in the *Logistic Regression* operator and then specify the L1 penalty by setting the parameters for *lambda search* option (*number of lambdas* = 100 and *lambda min ratio* = 0.05) and the parameter *alpha* = 1 in the same manner as shown earlier in Chapter 6, Figure 6.12. This results in a regularized model with 20 predictors shown in Figure 10.15 and has the advantage of being more parsimonious than the larger

Attribute	Coefficient	Std. Coefficient	Std. Error	z-Value	p-Value
Weather	13.077	1.597	73.913	0.177	0.860
2PM_3PM	0.825	0.247	0.223	3.705	0.000
7PM_8PM	0.875	0.215	0.264	3.311	0.001
Sun_Mon	0.686	0.295	0.163	4.216	0.000
Carrier_CO_MQ_DH_RU	1.271	0.620	0.180	7.062	0.000
Intercept	−2.739	−1.457	0.178	−15.404	0

accuracy: 82.39%

	true ontime	true delayed	class precision
pred. ontime	699	145	82.82%
pred. delayed	10	26	72.22%
class recall	98.59%	15.20%	

FIGURE 10.14   (TOP) LOGISTIC REGRESSION MODEL WITH FEWER PREDICTORS,
(MIDDLE) CONFUSION MATRIX FOR HOLDOUT DATA, AND
(BOTTOM) LIFT CHART FOR HOLDOUT DATA

model. However, it turns out to be least effective in terms of recall of delayed flights.

We therefore conclude with a 5-predictor model that requires only knowledge of the carrier, the day of week, the hour of the day, and whether it is likely that there will be a delay due to weather. However, this weather variable refers to actual weather at flight time, not a forecast, and is not known in advance! If the aim is to predict in advance whether a particular flight will be delayed, a model without Weather must be used. In contrast, if the goal is profiling (describing) delayed vs. ontime flights, we can keep Weather in the model to allow evaluating the impact of the other factors while holding weather constant [that is,

Attribute	Coefficient	Std. Coefficient	Attribute	Coefficient	Std. Coefficient
DAY_WEEK_5	0	0	CRS_DEP_TIME_1800_1859	0	0
DAY_WEEK_6	–0.501	–0.156	CRS_DEP_TIME_1900_1959	0.833	0.204
DAY_WEEK_7	0.645	0.201	CRS_DEP_TIME_2000_2059	0	0
DAY_WEEK_1	0.363	0.125	CRS_DEP_TIME_2100_2159	0.310	0.077
DAY_WEEK_2	0	0	CARRIER_DH	0.045	0.020
DAY_WEEK_3	0	0	CARRIER_DL	–0.637	–0.246
CRS_DEP_TIME_0700_0759	–0.079	–0.019	CARRIER_MQ	0.314	0.107
CRS_DEP_TIME_0800_0859	0	0	CARRIER_UA	–0.350	–0.037
CRS_DEP_TIME_0900_0959	–0.455	–0.095	CARRIER_US	–0.971	–0.376
CRS_DEP_TIME_1000_1059	–0.252	–0.053	CARRIER_RU	0.143	0.055
CRS_DEP_TIME_1100_1159	0	0	CARRIER_CO	0	0
CRS_DEP_TIME_1200_1259	0	0	DEST_LGA	0	0
CRS_DEP_TIME_1300_1359	0	0	DEST_EWR	0	0
CRS_DEP_TIME_1400_1459	0.681	0.204	ORIGIN_DCA	–0.054	–0.026
CRS_DEP_TIME_1500_1559	0.562	0.142	ORIGIN_IAD	0.043	0.020
CRS_DEP_TIME_1600_1659	0	0	Weather	4.621	0.564
CRS_DEP_TIME_1700_1759	0.579	0.181	Intercept	–1.669	–1.567

accuracy: 81.93%

	true ontime	true delayed	class precision
pred. ontime	709	159	81.68%
pred. delayed	0	12	100.00%
class recall	100.00%	7.02%	

FIGURE 10.15   (TOP) REGULARIZED LOGISTIC REGRESSION MODEL, (MIDDLE) CONFUSION
MATRIX FOR HOLDOUT DATA, AND (BOTTOM) LIFT CHART FOR HOLDOUT DATA

(approximately) comparing days with weather delays to days without weather delays].

To conclude, based on the model built from January 2004 data, the highest chance of an ontime flight from DC to New York is on Tuesday–Saturday in the morning or early evening on Delta, Comair, United, or USAirways. And clearly, good weather is advantageous!

APPENDIX: LOGISTIC REGRESSION FOR ORDINAL CLASSES

Ordinal classes are label classes that have a meaningful order. For example, in stock recommendations, the three classes *buy*, *hold*, and *sell* can be treated as ordered. As a simple rule, if classes can be numbered in a meaningful way, we consider them ordinal. When the number of classes is large (typically, more than 5), we can treat the target attribute as continuous and perform multiple linear regression. When $m = 2$, the logistic model described above is used. We therefore need an extension of the logistic regression for a small number of ordinal classes ($3 \leq m \leq 5$). There are several ways to extend the binary-class case. Here, we describe the *proportional odds* or *cumulative logit method*. For other methods, see Hosmer and Lemeshow (2000).

For simplicity of interpretation and computation, we look at *cumulative* probabilities of class membership. For example, in the stock recommendations, we have $m = 3$ classes. Let us denote them by $1 = buy$, $2 = hold$, and $3 = sell$. The probabilities estimated by the model are $P(Y \leq 1)$ (the probability of a *buy* recommendation) and $P(Y \leq 2)$ (the probability of a *buy* or *hold* recommendation). The three noncumulative probabilities of class membership can easily be recovered from the two cumulative probabilities:

$$
\begin{aligned}
P(Y = 1) &= P(Y \leq 1), \\
P(Y = 2) &= P(Y \leq 2) - P(Y \leq 1), \\
P(Y = 3) &= 1 - P(Y \leq 2).
\end{aligned}
$$

Next, we want to model each logit as a function of the predictors. Corresponding to each of the $m - 1$ cumulative probabilities is a logit. In our example, we would have

$$
\text{logit}(buy) = \log \frac{P(Y \leq 1)}{1 - P(Y \leq 1)},
$$

$$
\text{logit}(buy \text{ or } hold) = \log \frac{P(Y \leq 2)}{1 - P(Y \leq 2)}.
$$

Each of the logits is then modeled as a linear function of the predictors (as in the two-class case). If in the stock recommendations we have a single predictor value x, we compute two logit values using two equations:

$$\text{logit}(buy) = \alpha_0 + \beta_1 x,$$

$$\text{logit}(buy \text{ or } hold) = \beta_0 + \beta_1 x.$$

This means that both lines have the same slope (β_1) but different intercepts. Once the coefficients $\alpha_0, \beta_0, \beta_1$ are estimated, we can compute the class membership probabilities by rewriting the logit equations in terms of probabilities. For the three-class case, for example, we would have

$$P(Y = 1) = P(Y \leq 1) = \frac{1}{1 + e^{-(a_0 + b_1 x)}},$$

$$P(Y = 2) = P(Y \leq 2) - P(Y \leq 1) = \frac{1}{1 + e^{-(b_0 + b_1 x)}} - \frac{1}{1 + e^{-(a_0 + b_1 x)}},$$

$$P(Y = 3) = 1 - P(Y \leq 2) = 1 - \frac{1}{1 + e^{-(b_0 + b_1 x)}},$$

where a_0, b_0, and b_1 are the estimates obtained from the training set.

For each record, we now have the estimated probabilities that it belongs to each of the classes. In our example, each stock would have three probabilities: for a *buy* recommendation, a *hold* recommendation, and a *sell* recommendation. The last step is to classify the record into one of the classes. This is done by assigning it to the class with the highest membership probability. For example, if a stock had estimated probabilities $P(Y = 1) = 0.2$, $P(Y = 2) = 0.3$, and $P(Y = 3) = 0.5$, we would classify it as getting a *sell* recommendation.

This procedure is currently not implemented in RapidMiner, since RapidMiner does not distinguish between ordinal and nominal data types. Programmatic languages like Python and R as well as statistical packages such as Minitab and SAS do have such an implementation.

PROBLEMS

10.1 Financial Condition of Banks. The file *banks.csv* includes data on a sample of 20 banks. The "Financial Condition" column records the judgment of an expert on the financial condition of each bank. This target attribute takes one of two possible values—*weak* or *strong*—according to the financial condition of the bank. The predictors are two ratios used in the financial analysis of banks: TotLns&Lses/Assets is the ratio of total loans and leases to total assets, and TotExp/Assets is the ratio of total expenses to total assets. The goal is to use the two ratios for classifying the financial condition of a new bank.

Run a logistic regression model (on the entire dataset) that models the status of a bank as a function of the two financial measures provided. Transform the target attribute to *Binominal* type, and then specify the *positive* class as *weak* (replacing *true*) for financially weak banks and the other class as *strong* (replacing *false*) using the *Map* operator in RapidMiner. Use the default threshold value of 0.5.

a. Write the estimated equation that associates the financial condition of a bank with its two predictors in three formats:

    i. The logit as a function of the predictors.

    ii. The odds as a function of the predictors.

    iii. The probability as a function of the predictors.

b. Consider a new bank whose total loans and leases/assets ratio = 0.6 and total expenses/assets ratio = 0.11. From your logistic regression model, estimate the following four quantities for this bank (use Excel to do all the intermediate calculations; show your final answers to four decimal places): the logit, the odds, the probability of being financially weak and the classification of the bank (use threshold = 0.5).

c. The threshold value of 0.5 is used in conjunction with the probability of being financially weak. Compute the threshold that should be used if we want to make a classification based on the odds of being financially weak, and the threshold for the corresponding logit.

d. Interpret the estimated coefficient for the total loans & leases-to-total assets ratio (TotLns&Lses/Assets) in terms of the odds of being financially weak.

e. When a bank that is in poor financial condition is misclassified as financially strong, the misclassification cost is much higher than when a financially strong bank is misclassified as weak. To minimize the expected cost of misclassification, should the threshold value for classification (which is currently at 0.5) be increased or decreased?

10.2 Identifying Good System Administrators. A management consultant is studying the roles played by experience and training in a system administrator's ability to complete a set of tasks in a specified amount of time. In particular, she is interested in discriminating between administrators who are able to complete given tasks within a specified time and those who are not. Data are collected on the performance of 75 randomly selected administrators. They are stored in the file *SystemAdministrators.csv*.

The attribute Experience measures months of full-time system administrator experience, while Training measures the number of relevant training credits. The target attribute Completed is either *Yes* or *No*, according to whether or not the administrator completed the tasks.

    a. Create a scatter plot of Experience vs. Training using color to distinguish programmers who completed the task from those who did not complete it. Which predictor(s) appear(s) potentially useful for classifying task completion?

    b. Run a logistic regression model with both predictors using the entire dataset as training data. Among those who completed the task, what is the percentage of programmers incorrectly classified as failing to complete the task?

    c. To decrease the percentage in part (b), should the probability threshold be increased or decreased?

    d. How much experience must be accumulated by a programmer with four years of training before his or her estimated probability of completing the task exceeds 0.5?

10.3 **Sales of Riding Mowers.** A company that manufactures riding mowers wants to identify the best sales prospects for an intensive sales campaign. In particular, the manufacturer is interested in classifying households as prospective owners or nonowners on the basis of Income (in $1000s) and Lot Size (in 1000 ft^2). The marketing expert looked at a random sample of 24 households, given in the file *RidingMowers.csv*. Use all the data to fit a logistic regression of ownership on the two predictors.

    a. What percentage of households in the study were owners of a riding mower?

    b. Create a scatter plot of Income vs. Lot Size using color to distinguish owners from nonowners. From the scatter plot, which class seems to have a higher average income, owners or nonowners?

    c. Among nonowners, what is the percentage of households classified correctly?

    d. To increase the percentage of correctly classified nonowners, should the probability threshold be increased or decreased?

    e. What are the odds that a household with a $60K income and a lot size of 20,000 ft^2 is an owner?

    f. What is the classification of a household with a $60K income and a lot size of 20,000 ft^2? Use threshold = 0.5.

    g. What is the minimum income that a household with 16,000 ft^2 lot size should have before it is classified as an owner?

10.4 **Competitive Auctions on eBay.com.** The file *eBayAuctions.csv* contains information on 1972 auctions transacted on eBay.com during May–June 2004. The goal is to use these data to build a model that will distinguish competitive auctions from noncompetitive ones. A competitive auction is defined as an auction with at least two bids placed on the item being auctioned. The data include variables that describe the item (auction category), the seller (his or her eBay rating), and the auction terms that the seller selected (auction duration, opening price, currency, day of week of auction close). In addition, we have the price at which the auction closed. The goal is to predict whether or not an auction of interest will be competitive.

    Data Preprocessing. Ensure that the categorical predictors are of *Polynominal* type: Category (18 categories), Currency (USD, GBP, Euro), EndDay (Monday–Sunday), and Duration (1, 3, 5, 7, or 10 days). (*Note*: You can choose to leave them as nominal attributes, since the *Logistic Regression* modeling operator in RapidMiner internally converts them into dummies by using the first occurring category in the data for each categorical attribute as its comparison group.)

    a. Create pivot tables for the mean of the binary target attribute (Competitive?) as a function of the various categorical attributes (use the original attributes, not the dummies; also use the target attribute as the original 0/1 numerical attribute). Use the information in the pivot tables to reduce the number of categories that will be used in the model for each categorical attribute. For example, categories that appear most similar with respect to the distribution of competitive auctions could be combined. Remember that new attributes can be created in RapidMiner with the *Generate Attributes* operator.

b. Split the data into training (60%) and holdout (40%) datasets. Run a logistic model with all predictors with a threshold of 0.5.

c. If we want to predict at the start of an auction whether it will be competitive, we cannot use the information on the closing price. Run a logistic model with all predictors as above, excluding closing price. How does this model compare with the full model with respect to predictive accuracy?

d. Interpret the meaning of the coefficient for closing price. Does closing price have a practical significance? Is it statistically significant for predicting competitiveness of auctions? (Use a 10% significance level.)

e. Use regularized logistic regression with L1 penalty on the training data. Compare its selected predictors and classification performance with that of the complete model (excluding closing price).

f. If the major objective is accurate classification, what threshold value should be used?

g. Based on these data, what auction settings set by the seller (duration, opening price, ending day, currency) would you recommend as being most likely to lead to a competitive auction?

CHAPTER 11

Neural Networks

In this chapter, we describe neural networks, a flexible data-driven (albeit black box) method that can be used for classification, prediction, and feature extraction and is the basis for deep learning—a powerful technique that lies behind many artificial intelligence applications like image and voice recognition. We discuss the concepts of "nodes" and "layers" (input layers, output layers, and hidden layers) and how they connect to form the structure of the network. We then explain how a neural network is fitted to data using a numerical example. Because overfitting is a major danger with neural nets, we present a strategy for avoiding it. We describe the different parameters that a user must specify and explain the effect of each on the process. Finally, we move from a detailed description of a basic neural net to a more general discussion of the deeper and more complex neural nets that power deep learning.

RapidMiner

In this chapter, we will use the *Neural Network* modeling operator for building neural networks. RapidMiner supports multiple operators and extensions for working with deep learning models. The *Deep Learning* operator in RapidMiner is based on the deep learning implementation from the H2O.ai company. For more configurable deep learning architectures, the *Deep Learning* RapidMiner extension based on the Deeplearning4j framework[1,2] is available, which we will use later in this chapter. The *Keras* RapidMiner extension is also available for working with deep learning models using the Keras framework.[3] These extensions can be searched and installed through the *Extensions > Marketplace (Updates and Extensions)* menu in RapidMiner.

---

[1] https://deeplearning4j.konduit.ai

[2] The Deep Learning extension requires the *ND4J Back End* extension which is installed automatically during its installation process.

[3] https://keras.io/

Machine Learning for Business Analytics: Concepts, Techniques and Applications in RapidMiner, First Edition.
Galit Shmueli, Peter C. Bruce, Amit V. Deokar, and Nitin R. Patel
© 2023 John Wiley & Sons, Inc. Published 2023 by John Wiley & Sons, Inc.

11.1 INTRODUCTION

Neural networks, also called *artificial neural networks*, are models for classification and prediction. Complex and deep neural networks (deep learning) can also be used for unsupervised tasks such as feature extraction. The neural network is based on a model of biological activity in the brain, where neurons are interconnected and learn from experience. Neural networks mimic the way that human experts learn. The learning and memory properties of neural networks resemble the properties of human learning and memory, and they also have a capacity to generalize from particulars.

Neural nets began to be applied successfully in the late 1990s in areas such as bankruptcy trading and detecting fraud in credit card and monetary transactions. They really took off in the early 2000s with the development of more complex networks and the growing power of computers. Often called "deep learning," these complex networks have been primarily responsible for a powerful revolution in machine learning. Indeed, much of what the public thinks of as "artificial intelligence" has at its heart deep (multilayer) neural networks. Text classification and image recognition are perhaps the most ubiquitous examples, but what has captured the public imagination the most is the promise of self-driving cars. It might surprise many machine learning practitioners today to learn that an application of neural nets from the 1980s was ALVINN, an autonomous vehicle driving application for normal speeds on highways. Using as input a 30×32 grid of pixel intensities from a fixed camera on the vehicle, the classifier provides the direction of steering. The target attribute is a categorical one with 30 classes, such as *sharp left*, *straight ahead*, and *bear right*.

The main strength of neural networks is their high predictive performance. Their structure supports capturing very complex relationships between predictors and a target attribute, which is often not possible with other predictive models.

11.2 CONCEPT AND STRUCTURE OF A NEURAL NETWORK

The idea behind neural networks is to combine the predictor information in a very flexible way that captures complicated relationships among these attributes and between them and the target attribute. For instance, recall that in linear regression models, the form of the relationship between the target and the predictors is specified directly by the user (see Chapter 6). In many cases, the exact form of the relationship is very complicated or is generally unknown. In linear regression modeling, we might try different transformations of the predictors, interactions between predictors, and so on, but the specified form of the

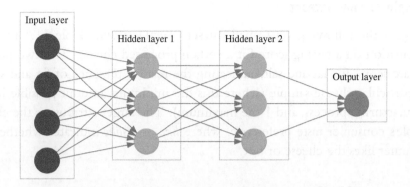

FIGURE 11.1   MULTILAYER FEEDFORWARD NEURAL NETWORK

relationship remains linear. In comparison, in neural networks, the user is not required to specify the correct form. Instead, the network tries to learn about such relationships from the data. In fact, linear regression and logistic regression can be thought of as special cases of very simple neural networks that have only input and output layers and no hidden layers.

Although researchers have studied numerous different neural network architectures, the most successful applications of neural networks in machine learning have been *multilayer feedforward networks*. These are networks in which there is an *input layer* consisting of nodes (sometimes called *neurons*) that simply accept the predictor values and successive layers of nodes that receive input from the previous layers. The outputs of nodes in each layer are inputs to nodes in the next layer. The last layer is called the *output layer*. Layers between the input and output layers are known as *hidden layers*. A feedforward network is a fully connected network with a one-way flow and no cycles. Figure 11.1 shows a diagram for this architecture, with two hidden layers and one node in the output layer representing the target attribute value to be predicted. In a classification problem with m classes, there would be m output nodes (or $m - 1$ output nodes, depending on the software).

11.3 FITTING A NETWORK TO DATA

To illustrate how a neural network is fitted to data, we start with a very small illustrative example. Although the method is by no means operational in such a small example, it is useful for explaining the main steps and operations, for showing how computations are done, and for integrating all the different aspects of neural network data fitting. We will later discuss a more realistic setting.

Example 1: Tiny Dataset

Consider the following very small dataset (*TinyData.csv*). Table 11.1 includes information on a tasting score for a certain processed cheese. The two predictors are scores for fat and salt, indicating the relative presence of fat and salt in the particular cheese sample (where 0 is the minimum amount possible in the manufacturing process, and 1 the maximum). The target attribute is the cheese sample's consumer taste preference, where *like* or *dislike* indicates whether the consumer likes the cheese or not.

TABLE 11.1	TINY EXAMPLE ON TASTING SCORES FOR SIX CONSUMERS WITH TWO PREDICTORS		
Consumer	Fat score	Salt score	Acceptance
1	0.2	0.9	like
2	0.1	0.1	dislike
3	0.2	0.4	dislike
4	0.2	0.5	dislike
5	0.4	0.5	like
6	0.3	0.8	like

Figure 11.2 describes an example of a typical neural net that could be used for predicting cheese preference (*like*/*dislike*) by new consumers, based on these data. We numbered the nodes in the example from N1 to N7. Nodes N1 and N2 belong to the input layer, nodes N3 to N5 belong to the hidden layer, and nodes N6 and N7 belong to the output layer. The values on the connecting arrows are called *weights*, and the weight on the arrow from node i to node j is denoted by $w_{i,j}$. The additional *bias* parameters, denoted by θ_j, serve as an intercept for the output from node j. These are all explained in further detail below.

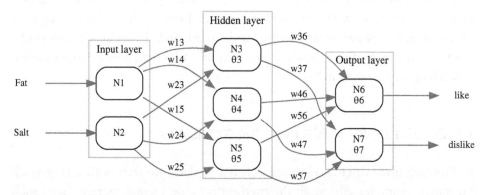

FIGURE 11.2	NEURAL NETWORK FOR THE TINY EXAMPLE. RECTANGLES REPRESENT NODES ("NEURONS"), $w_{i,j}$ ON ARROWS ARE WEIGHTS, AND θ_j INSIDE NODES ARE BIAS VALUES

Computing Output of Nodes

We discuss the input and output of the nodes separately for each of the three types of layers (input, hidden, and output). The main difference is the function used to map from the input to the output of the node.

Input nodes take as input the values of the predictors. Their output is the same as the input. If we have p predictors, the input layer will usually include p nodes. In our example, there are two predictors, and therefore the input layer (shown in Figure 11.2) includes two nodes, each feeding into each node of the hidden layer. Consider the first record: the input into the input layer is Fat = 0.2 and Salt = 0.9, and the output of this layer is also $x_1 = 0.2$ and $x_2 = 0.9$.

Hidden layer nodes take as input the output values from the input layer. The hidden layer in this example consists of three nodes, each receiving input from all the input nodes. To compute the output of a hidden layer node, we compute a weighted sum of the inputs and apply a certain function to it. More formally, for a set of input values $x_1, x_2, \ldots, x_p$, we compute the output of node j by taking the weighted sum[4] $\theta_j + \sum_{i=1}^{p} w_{ij} x_i$, where $\theta_j, w_{1,j}, \ldots, w_{p,j}$ are weights that are initially set randomly and then adjusted as the network "learns." Note that θ_j, also called the *bias* of node j, is a constant that controls the level of contribution of node j.

In the next step, we take a function g of this sum. The function g, also called a *transfer function* or *activation function*, is some monotone function. Examples include the linear function $[g(s) = bs]$, an exponential function $[g(s) = \exp(bs)]$, and a logistic/sigmoidal function $[g(s) = 1/1 + e^{-s}]$. This last function used to be by far the most popular one in neural networks. Its practical value arises from the fact that it has a squashing effect on very small or very large values but is almost linear in the range where the value of the function is between 0.1 and 0.9. Deep learning uses mostly the rectified linear unit (ReLU) activation function or variants of it. This function is identical to the linear function but set to zero for $s < 0$.

If we use a logistic activation function, we can write the output of node j in the hidden layer as

$$\text{Output}_j = g\left(\theta_j + \sum_{i=1}^{p} w_{ij} x_i\right) = \frac{1}{1 + e^{-(\theta_j + \sum_{i=1}^{p} w_{ij} x_i)}}. \qquad (11.1)$$

---

[4]Other options exist for combining inputs, such as taking the maximum or minimum of the weighted inputs rather than their sum, but they are much less popular.

Initializing the Weights and Bias   The values of θ_j and w_{ij} are initialized to small, usually random, numbers around zero. Such values represent a state of no knowledge by the network, similar to a model with no predictors. The initial weights are used in the first round of training.

Returning to our example, suppose that the initial bias and weights for node N3 are $\theta_3 = -0.3$, $w_{1,3} = 0.05$, and $w_{2,3} = 0.01$ (as shown in Figure 11.3). Using the logistic function, we can compute the output of node N3 in the hidden layer (using the first record) as

$$\text{Output}_{N3} = \frac{1}{1 + e^{-[-0.300 + (0.050)(0.20) + (0.010)(0.90)]}} = 0.430.$$

Figure 11.3 shows the initial weights, bias, inputs, and outputs for the first record in our tiny example. If there is more than one hidden layer, the same calculation applies, except that the input values for the second, third, and so on hidden layers would be the output of the preceding hidden layer. This means that the number of input values into a certain node is equal to the number of nodes in the preceding layer. (If there was an additional hidden layer in our example, its nodes would receive input from the three nodes in the first hidden layer.)

Finally, the output layer obtains input values from the (last) hidden layer. It applies the same function as above to create the output. In other words, it takes a weighted sum of its input values and then applies the function g. In our example, output nodes N6 and N7 receive input from the three hidden layer nodes. We can compute the output of these nodes by

$$\text{Output}_{N6} = \frac{1}{1 + e^{-[-0.015 + (0.010)(0.430) + (0.050)(0.511) + (0.015)(0.520)]}}$$
$$= 0.506$$

$$\text{Output}_{N7} = \frac{1}{1 + e^{-[-0.040 + (-0.020)(0.430) + (-0.030)(0.511) + (-0.020)(0.520)]}}$$
$$= 0.481.$$

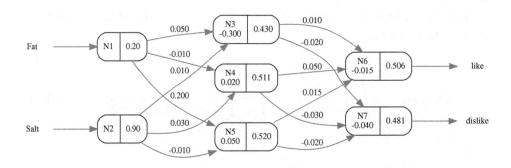

FIGURE 11.3   COMPUTING NODE OUTPUTS (VALUES ARE ON RIGHT SIDE WITHIN EACH NODE) USING THE FIRST RECORD IN THE TINY EXAMPLE AND A LOGISTIC FUNCTION

These two numbers are *almost* the propensities P(Y = *like* | Fat = 0.2, Salt = 0.9) and P(Y = *dislike* | Fat = 0.2, Salt = 0.9). The last step involves normalizing these two values so that they add up to 1. In other words,

$$P(Y = like) = \text{Output}_{N6}/(\text{Output}_{N6} + \text{Output}_{N7}) = 0.506/(0.481 + 0.506) = 0.49$$
$$P(Y = dislike) = 1 - P(Y = like) = 0.481/(0.481 + 0.506) = 0.51.$$

For classification, we use a threshold value (for a binary target attribute) on the propensity. Using a threshold of 0.5, we would classify this record as *like*. For applications with more than two classes, we choose the output node with the largest value.

Relation to Linear and Logistic Regression   Consider a neural network with a single output node and no hidden layers. For a dataset with p predictors, the output node receives $x_1, x_2, \ldots, x_p$, takes a weighted sum of these, and applies the g function. The output of the neural network is therefore $g\left(\theta + \sum_{i=1}^{p} w_i x_i\right)$.

First, consider a numerical target attribute Y. If g is the identity function $[g(s) = s]$, the output is simply

$$\hat{Y} = \theta + \sum_{i=1}^{p} w_i x_i.$$

This is exactly equivalent to the formulation of a multiple linear regression! This means that a neural network with no hidden layers, a single output node, and an identity function g searches only for linear relationships between the target attribute and the predictors.

Now consider a binary target attribute Y. If g is the logistic function, the output is simply

$$\hat{P}(Y = 1) = \frac{1}{1 + e^{-\left(\theta + \sum_{i=1}^{p} w_i x_i\right)}},$$

which is equivalent to the logistic regression formulation!

In both cases, although the formulation is equivalent to the linear and logistic regression models, the resulting estimates for the bias and weights (*coefficients* in linear and logistic regression) can differ, because the estimation method is different. The neural net estimation method is different from *least squares*, the method used to calculate coefficients in linear regression, or the *maximum likelihood* method used in logistic regression. We explain below the method by which the neural network learns.

Preprocessing the Data

When using sigmoidal activation functions such as the logistic function and the hyperbolic tangent function (often called the *tanh* function), neural networks perform best when the predictors are on the same scale, like [0, 1] or [-1, 1]. For this reason, all attributes should be scaled to a [0, 1] or a [-1, 1] interval before training the network. For a numerical attribute X that takes values in the range $[a, b]$ where $a < b$, we rescale the measurements to a [0, 1] scale by subtracting a and dividing by $b - a$. The normalized [0, 1] measurement is then

$$X_{\text{norm}[0,1]} = \frac{X - a}{b - a}.$$

Note that if $[a, b]$ is within the [0, 1] interval, the original scale will be stretched. Similarly, we can rescale the measurements to a [-1, 1] scale by doubling the [0, 1] scaled value and subtracting 1. The normalized [-1, 1] measurement is then

$$X_{\text{norm}[-1,1]} = 2 \times \frac{X - a}{b - a} - 1.$$

If a and b are unknown, we can estimate them from the minimal and maximal values of X in the data. Even if new data exceed this range by a small amount (for example, scaled values are slightly larger than 1), this will not affect the results much.

In RapidMiner, the *Neural Network* operator provides a parameter to automatically normalize the predictors to a [-1, 1] scale prior to network training. Alternatively, the predictors can be scaled to [0, 1] using the *Normalization* operator prior to the *Neural Network* operator.[5] Regardless of the option, all predictors need to be converted to numeric type as follows.

For binary (binominal) attributes, no adjustment is needed other than creating dummy variables. For categorical (nominal) attributes with m categories, if they are ordinal in nature, a choice of m fractions in [0, 1] should reflect their perceived ordering. For example, if four ordinal categories are equally distant from each other, we can map them to [0, 0.25, 0.5, 1]. If the categories are nominal, transforming into $m - 1$ dummies is a good solution. In RapidMiner, the *Nominal to Numerical* operator can be used for dummy coding binary or categorical attributes.

Another operation that improves the performance of the network is to transform highly skewed predictors. In business applications, there tend to be many highly right-skewed attributes (such as income). Taking a log transform of a right-skewed attribute (before rescaling) will usually spread out the values more symmetrically.

---

[5] With this option, the *normalize* parameter in the subsequent *Neural Network* operator should be deselected. Also, the normalization and neural network models must be chained together with the *Group Models* operator so that the normalization from the training set is also applied for the holdout set.

Training the Model

Training the model means estimating θ_j and w_{ij} (bias and weights) that lead to the best predictive results. The process that we described earlier (Section 11.1) for computing the neural network output for a record is repeated for all records in the training set. For each record, the model produces a prediction which is then compared with the actual target attribute value. Their difference is the error for the output node. However, unlike least squares or maximum likelihood, where a global function of the errors (e.g., sum of squared errors) is used for estimating the coefficients, in neural networks, the estimation process uses the errors iteratively to update the estimated parameters (bias and weights).

In particular, the error for the output node is distributed across all the hidden nodes that led to it so that each node is assigned "responsibility" for part of the error. Each of these node-specific errors is then used for updating the weights and bias values.

Back Propagation of Error   The most popular method for using model errors to update weights ("learning") is an algorithm called *back propagation*. As the name implies, errors are computed from the last layer (the output layer) back to the hidden layers.

Let us denote by $\hat{y}_k$ the output from output node k. y_k is 1 or 0 depending on whether the actual class of the observation coincides with node k's label or not (e.g., in Figure 11.3, for a person with output class "like" we have $y_6 = 1$ and $y_7 = 0$). The error associated with output node k is computed by

$$\text{err}_k = \hat{y}_k(1 - \hat{y}_k)(y_k - \hat{y}_k).$$

Notice that this is similar to the ordinary definition of an error $(y_k - \hat{y}_k)$ multiplied by a correction factor. The bias and weights are then updated as follows:

$$\theta_j^{\text{new}} = \theta_j^{\text{old}} + l \times \text{err}_j, \qquad (11.2)$$
$$w_{i,j}^{\text{new}} = w_{i,j}^{\text{old}} + l \times \text{err}_j,$$

where l is a *learning rate* or *weight decay* parameter, a constant ranging typically between 0 and 1, which controls the amount of change in weights from one training cycle to the next.

In our example, the error associated with output node N6 for the first record is $(0.506)(1 - 0.506)(1 - 0.506) = 0.123$. For output node N7, the error is $0.481(1 - 0.481)(0 - 0.481) = -0.120$. These errors are then used to compute the errors associated with the hidden layer nodes, and those bias and weights are updated accordingly using a formula similar to equation (11.2).

Two methods for updating the bias and weights are *case updating* and *batch updating*. In case updating, the parameter values are updated after each record is run through the network (called a *trial*). For example, if we used case updating in the tiny example, the bias and weights would first be updated after running record 1 as follows: using a learning rate of 0.5, $\theta_6, w_{3,6}, w_{4,6}$, and $w_{5,6}$ are updated to

$$\begin{aligned}
\theta_6 &= -0.015 + (0.5)(0.123) = 0.047, \\
w_{3,6} &= 0.010 + (0.5)(0.123) = 0.072, \\
w_{4,6} &= 0.050 + (0.5)(0.123) = 0.112, \\
w_{5,6} &= 0.015 + (0.5)(0.123) = 0.077.
\end{aligned}$$

Similarly, we obtain updated weights $\theta_7 = 0.025$, $w_{3,7} = 0.045$, $w_{4,7} = 0.035$, and $w_{5,7} = 0.045$. These new values are next updated after the second record is run through the network, the third, and so on, until all records are used. This is called one *epoch*, *sweep*, *iteration*, or *training cycle* through the data. Typically, there are many training cycles.

In batch updating, the entire training set is run through the network before each updating of the bias and weights takes place. In that case, the error err_k in the updating equation is the sum of the errors from all records. In practice, case updating tends to yield more accurate results than batch updating but requires a longer run time. This is a serious consideration, since even in batch updating, hundreds or even thousands of sweeps through the training data are executed.

When does the updating stop? The most common conditions are one of the following:

1. When the new values of the bias and weights are only incrementally different from those of the preceding training cycle.

2. When the misclassification rate reaches a required threshold or if there is no improvement in the misclassification rate over the prior training cycle (also called *early stopping* strategy[6]).

3. When the limit on the number of training cycles is reached.

Let us examine the output from running a neural network on the tiny data. Following Figures 11.2 and 11.3, we used a single hidden layer with three nodes. Figure 11.4 (top) shows the RapidMiner process using the *Neural Network* operator for this purpose.

The final bias and weights are shown in Figure 11.4 (bottom). Figure 11.5 shows the final bias and weights in a format similar to that of our previous diagrams.

---

[6]A parameter called *patience* is used in some software (such as in RapidMiner's Deep Learning extension operators) to indicate the number of training cycles to perform after a minimum misclassification rate is reached, to avoid settling at a local minimum. For example, with patience = 5, the updating would continue for five training cycles unless a new minimum misclassification rate is found in which case the process continues again.

FIGURE 11.4   (TOP) RAPIDMINER PROCESS FOR NEURAL NETWORK WITH A SINGLE HIDDEN LAYER (THREE NODES) FOR THE TINY DATA EXAMPLE AND (BOTTOM) FINAL BIAS AND WEIGHTS FOR THE NEURAL NETWORK

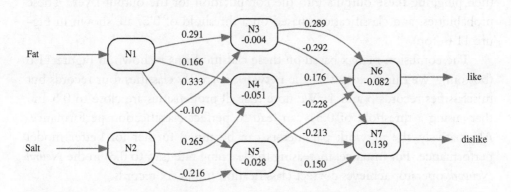

FIGURE 11.5   NEURAL NETWORK FOR THE TINY EXAMPLE WITH FINAL WEIGHTS AND BIAS VALUES (VALUES FROM FIGURE 11.4)

The first part of the output in Figure 11.4 (bottom) shows the estimated parameters that connect the input layer and the hidden layer and then those connecting the hidden layer and output layer. The *bias* values are the *bias nodes* or the *intercepts* and correspond to θ_3, θ_4, and θ_5. The *bias* and *weights* for the predictors are used to compute the output of the hidden layer nodes. They were computed iteratively after choosing a random initial set of values (like the set we chose in Figure 11.3). We use the bias and weights in the way we described earlier to compute the hidden layer's output. With the *normalize* parameter selected in the *Neural Network* operator as shown in Figure 11.4 (top), the predictors are first internally normalized to a [-1, 1] scale, prior to the network training. For instance, for the first record, the normalized values would be computed as Fat = -0.33 and Salt = 1. Then, the output of our previous node N3 is

$$\text{Output}_{N3} = \frac{1}{1 + e^{-[-0.004 + (0.291)(-0.33) + (0.333)(1)]}} = 0.558.$$

Similarly, we can compute the output from the two other hidden nodes for the same record and get $\text{Output}_{N4} = 0.540$ and $\text{Output}_{N5} = 0.448$. The second set of intercepts and weights are for connecting the hidden and output layer nodes. To compute the probability (= propensity) for the *like* output node (N6) for the first record, we use the outputs from the hidden layer that we computed above and get

$$\text{Output}_{N6} = \frac{1}{1 + e^{-[-0.082 + (0.289)(0.558) + (0.176)(0.540) + (-0.228)(0.448)]}} = 0.518.$$

Similarly, we can compute the probability for the *dislike* output node, obtaining the value $\text{Output}_{N7} = 0.482$.

The probabilities for the other five records are computed in the same manner, replacing the input value in the computation of the hidden layer outputs and then plugging these outputs into the computation for the output layer. These probabilities, and classifications based on a threshold of 0.5, are shown in Figure 11.6 (top).

The confusion matrix based on these classifications is shown in Figure 11.6 (bottom). We can observe that the network correctly classifies four records but misclassifies records 3 and 4. We note that all propensities are close to 0.5 and that using a threshold of 0.51 can lead to perfect classification performance. Alternatively, the network parameters can be tuned further for better model performance. For instance, increasing the learning rate (say, to 0.3) in the *Neural Network* operator achieves correct classification for all six records.

Example 2: Classifying Accident Severity

Let's apply the network training process to some real data (*accidentsnn.csv*): US automobile accidents that have been classified by their level of severity as *no*

Row No.	Obs.	Acceptance	prediction(Acceptance)	confidence(like)	confidence(dislike)	Fat	Salt
1	1	like	like	0.518	0.482	0.200	0.900
2	2	dislike	dislike	0.489	0.511	0.100	0.100
3	3	dislike	like	0.503	0.497	0.200	0.400
4	4	dislike	like	0.506	0.494	0.200	0.500
5	5	like	like	0.517	0.483	0.400	0.500
6	6	like	like	0.521	0.479	0.300	0.800

accuracy: 66.67%

	true like	true dislike	class precision
pred. like	3	2	60.00%
pred. dislike	0	1	100.00%
class recall	100.00%	33.33%	

FIGURE 11.6   (TOP) PREDICTIONS AND PROPENSITIES FOR THE TINY DATA EXAMPLE AND (BOTTOM) CONFUSION MATRIX

injury, injury, or *fatality.* A firm might be interested in developing a system for quickly classifying the severity of an accident, based on initial reports and associated data in the system (some of which rely on GPS-assisted reporting). Such a system could be used to assign emergency response team priorities. Table 11.2 shows a small extract (10 records, 4 predictor attributes) from a US government database.

The explanation of the four predictor attributes and target attribute is given in Table 11.3. For the analysis, we convert ALCHL_I to a 0/1 dummy variable (1 = presence of alcohol) and create four dummies for SUR_COND. This gives us a total of seven predictors.

TABLE 11.2   SUBSET FROM THE ACCIDENTS DATA, FOR A HIGH-FATALITY REGION

Consumer	ALCHL_I	PROFIL_I_R	SUR_COND	VEH_INVL	MAX_SEV_IR
1	1	1	1	1	1
2	2	1	1	1	0
3	2	1	1	1	1
4	1	1	1	1	0
5	2	1	1	1	2
6	2	0	1	1	1
7	2	0	1	3	1
8	2	0	1	4	1
9	2	0	1	2	0
10	2	0	1	2	0

TABLE 11.3   DESCRIPTION OF VARIABLES FOR AUTOMOBILE ACCIDENT EXAMPLE

ALCHL_I	Presence (1) or absence (2) of alcohol
PROFIL_I_R	Profile of the roadway: level (1), other (0)
SUR_COND	Surface condition of the road: dry (1), wet (2), snow/slush (3), ice (4), unknown (9)
VEH_INVL	Number of vehicles involved
MAX_SEV_IR	Presence of injuries/fatalities: no injuries (0), injury (1), fatality (2)

With the exception of alcohol involvement and a few other attributes in the larger database, most of the attributes are ones that we might reasonably expect to be available at the time of the initial accident report, before accident details and severity have been determined by first responders. A machine learning model that could predict accident severity on the basis of these initial reports would have value in allocating first responder resources.

To use a neural net architecture for this classification problem, we use seven nodes in the input layer, one for each of the seven predictors, and three nodes (one for each class) in the output layer. We use a single hidden layer and experiment with the number of nodes. If we increase the number of nodes from one to five and examine the resulting confusion matrices, we find that two nodes gives a good balance between improving the predictive performance on the training set without deteriorating the performance on the holdout set. (Networks with more than two nodes in the hidden layer performed as well as the two-node network, but add undesirable complexity.) Figure 11.7 shows the RapidMiner process for the accidents data, and Figure 11.8 (top) shows predictions for five sample records in the holdout set. From the performance shown in Figure 11.8 (bottom), we see that classes 0 and 1 are almost perfectly classified in both the training and holdout data. However, class 2 has a high rate of misclassification.

Our results can depend on how we set the different parameters, and there are a few pitfalls to avoid. We discuss these next.

Avoiding Overfitting

A weakness of the neural network is that it can easily overfit the data, causing the error rate on validation data (and most important, on new data) to be too large. It is therefore important to limit the number of training cycles and not to overtrain on the data (e.g., in RapidMiner's *Neural Network* operator, you can control the number of iterations using the parameter *training cycles*). As in classification and regression trees, overfitting can be detected by examining the performance on the validation set, or better, on a cross-validation set, and seeing when it starts deteriorating, while the training set performance is still improving. This approach is used in some algorithms to limit the number of training cycles. The validation error decreases in the early training cycles of the training process, but after a while, it begins to increase. The point of minimum validation error

FIGURE 11.7   RAPIDMINER PROCESS FOR BUILDING A NEURAL NETWORK WITH TWO NODES IN THE HIDDEN LAYER (ACCIDENTS DATA)

Row No.	MAX_SEV_IR	prediction(MAX_SEV_IR)	confidence(0)	confidence(2)	confidence(1)	VEH_INVL
1	0	0	0.906	0.093	0.000	0
2	2	1	0.010	0.267	0.723	0
3	1	1	0.004	0.102	0.894	0.250
4	1	1	0.005	0.136	0.859	0.250
5	2	1	0.004	0.099	0.897	0

Row No.	ALCHL_I	SUR_COND_2	SUR_COND_4	SUR_COND_3	SUR_COND_9	PROFIL_I_R
1	0	0	0	0	0	0
2	0	0	0	0	0	1
3	0	1	0	0	0	0
4	0	0	0	0	0	1
5	0	1	0	0	0	0

(a) Performance on Training Set

accuracy: 88.15%

	true 0	true 2	true 1	class precision
pred. 0	319	25	0	92.73%
pred. 2	12	37	7	66.07%
pred. 1	0	27	172	86.43%
class recall	96.37%	41.57%	96.09%	

(b) Performance on Holdout Set

accuracy: 86.25%

	true 0	true 2	true 1	class precision
pred. 0	212	12	0	94.64%
pred. 2	8	18	5	58.06%
pred. 1	0	30	115	79.31%
class recall	96.36%	30.00%	95.83%	

FIGURE 11.8   (TOP) PREDICTED PROBABILITIES FOR FIVE SAMPLE HOLDOUT RECORDS AND (BOTTOM) CONFUSION MATRICES FOR TRAINING AND HOLDOUT SET FOR ACCIDENTS DATA

is a good indicator of the best number of training cycles for training, and the weights at that stage are likely to provide the best error rate in new data.

Using the Output for Prediction and Classification

When the neural network is used for predicting a numerical target attribute, the *Neural Network* operator uses a linear activation function. The predictors should be scaled to a [0, 1] or [-1, 1] interval before training the network, as discussed earlier. With the linear activation function, the target prediction is provided in its original units.

For a binary target attribute, although we typically use a threshold of 0.5 with other classifiers, in neural networks there is a tendency for values to cluster around 0.5 (from above and below), as seen in the tiny data example. An alternative is to use the validation set to determine a threshold that produces reasonable predictive performance.

For multi-class classification, where we have a categorical target attribute with m classes, we saw that the *Neural Network* operator produces m output nodes, one for each class. How do we translate these m outputs into a classification rule? Usually, the output node with the largest value (largest probability) determines the net's classification.

11.4 REQUIRED USER INPUT

One of the time-consuming and complex aspects of training a model using back propagation is that we first need to decide on a network architecture. This means specifying the number of hidden layers and the number of nodes in each layer. The usual procedure is to make intelligent guesses using past experience and to do several trial-and-error runs on different architectures. Algorithms exist that grow the number of nodes selectively during training or trim them in a manner analogous to what is done in classification and regression trees (see Chapter 9). Research continues on such methods. As of now, no automatic method seems clearly superior to the trial-and-error approach. A few general guidelines for choosing an architecture follow:

Number of hidden layers: The most popular choice for the number of hidden layers is one. A single hidden layer is usually sufficient to capture even very complex relationships between the predictors.

Size of hidden layer: The number of nodes in the hidden layer also determines the level of complexity of the relationship between the predictors that the network captures. The trade-off is between under- and overfitting. On the one hand, using too few nodes might not be sufficient to capture complex relationships (recall the special cases of a linear relationship such as in linear and logistic regression, in the extreme case of zero nodes or no hidden layer). On the other hand, too many nodes might lead to overfitting. A rule of thumb is to start with p (number of predictors) nodes and gradually decrease or increase while checking for overfitting. The number of hidden layers and the size of each hidden layer can be specified in RapidMiner's *Neural Network* operator with the parameter *hidden layers*. If no hidden layers are specified, the *Neural Network* operator creates a single hidden layer with number of hidden nodes equal to (number of predictors + number of classes) / 2 + 1.

Number of output nodes: For a categorical target attribute with m classes, the number of nodes should equal m (or in some software $m - 1$). For a numerical target attribute, typically a single output node is used unless we are interested in predicting more than one function.

In addition to the choice of architecture, the user should pay attention to the *choice of predictors*. Since neural networks are highly dependent on the quality of their input, the choice of predictors should be done carefully, using domain knowledge, feature selection, and dimension reduction techniques before using the network. We return to this point in the discussion of advantages and weaknesses.

A key parameter that the user can control is the *learning rate* (a.k.a. weight decay), l, which is used primarily to avoid overfitting, by down-weighting new information. This helps to tone down the effect of outliers on the weights and avoids getting stuck in local optima. This parameter typically takes a value in the range $[0, 1]$. Berry and Linoff (2000) suggest starting with a large value (moving away from the random initial weights, thereby "learning quickly" from the data) and then slowly decreasing it as the training cycles progress and as the weights are more reliable. Han and Kamber (2001) suggest the more concrete rule of thumb of setting $l = 1/$(current number of training cycles). This means that at the start, $l = 1$, during the second training cycle it is $l = 0.5$, and then it keeps decaying toward $l = 0$. In RapidMiner, you can set the learning rate in the *Neural Network* operator using the parameter *learning rate*.

11.5 EXPLORING THE RELATIONSHIP BETWEEN PREDICTORS AND TARGET ATTRIBUTE

Neural networks are known to be "black boxes" in the sense that their output does not shed light on the patterns in the data that it models (like our brains). In fact, that is one of the biggest criticisms of the method. However, in some cases, it is possible to learn more about the relationships that the network captures by conducting a sensitivity analysis on the validation set. This is done by setting all predictor values to their mean and obtaining the network's prediction. Then, the process is repeated by setting each predictor sequentially to its minimum, and then maximum, value. By comparing the predictions from different levels of the predictors, we can get a sense of which predictors affect predictions more and in what way.

11.6 DEEP LEARNING[7]

Neural nets had their greatest impact in the period from 2006 onward, with a paper published by AI researcher Geoffrey Hinton, and the rapidly growing popularity of what came to be called *deep learning*. Deep learning involves complex networks with many layers, incorporating processes for dimension reduction and feature discovery.

The data we have dealt with so far in this book are structured data, typically from organizational databases. The predictor attributes, or features, that we think might be meaningful in predicting an outcome of interest already exist in our data. In predicting possible bank failure, for example, we would guess that certain financial ratios (return on assets, return on equity, etc.) might have predictive value. In predicting insurance fraud, we might guess that policy age would be predictive. We are not limited, of course, to attributes that we know are predictive; sometimes a useful predictor emerges in an unexpected way.

With tasks like voice and image recognition, structured high-level predictor information like this is not available. All we have are individual "low-level" sound wave frequency and amplitude or pixel values indicating intensity and color. You'd like to be able to tell the computer "just look for two eyes" and then provide further detail on how an eye appears—a small solid circle (pupil), surrounded by a ring (iris), surrounded by a white area. However, again, all the computer has are columns of (low-level) pixel values—you'd need to do a lot of extra work to define all the different (higher-level) pixel patterns that correspond to eyes. That's where deep learning comes in—it can "learn" how to identify these higher level features by itself.

Deep learning is a rapidly growing and evolving field, with many aspects that distinguish it from simpler predictive models. A full examination of the field of deep learning is beyond the scope of this book, but let us consider one key innovation in the area of algorithmic design that is associated with deep learning and extends the ability of simple neural networks to perform the tasks of supervised and unsupervised learning that we have been discussing. This innovation is "convolution." Convolutional neural networks are used in many different applications and fields and have enabled major advances in voice recognition and the extraction of meaning from text via natural language processing (see Section 21.3 and the discussion of latent semantic indexing in Section 21.4 for a brief discussion of this topic). The basic idea of convolution is illustrated well in the context of image recognition.

---

[7]This section copyright ©2019 Datastats, LLC, Galit Shmueli, and Peter Gedeck. Used by permission.

Convolutional Neural Networks (CNNs)

In a standard neural network, each predictor gets its own weight at each layer of the network. A convolution, by contrast, selects a subset of predictors (pixels) and applies the same operation to the entire subset. It is this grouping that fosters the automated discovery of features. Recall that the data in image recognition tasks consist of a large number of pixel values, which, in a black and white image, range from 0 (black) to 255 (white). Since we are interested in detecting the black lines and shadings, we will reverse this to 255 for black and 0 for white.

Consider the line drawing in Figure 11.9, from a 1893 Funk and Wagnalls publication. Before the computer can begin to identify complex features like eyes, ears, noses, and heads, it needs to master very simple features like lines and borders. For example, the line of the man's chin (Figure 11.10). In a typical convolution, the algorithm considers a small area at a time, say, 3 pixels × 3 pixels. Figure 11.11 illustrates such a case. The line at the chin might look like

FIGURE 11.9   LINE DRAWING, FROM A 1893 FUNK AND WAGNALLS PUBLICATION

FIGURE 11.10   FOCUSING ON THE LINE OF THE MAN'S CHIN

FIGURE 11.11 3×3 PIXEL REPRESENTATION OF LINE ON MAN'S CHIN USING SHADING (a) AND VALUES (b). THE FILTER (c) IDENTIFIES VERTICAL LINES

the Figure 11.11(a); the matrix in Figure 11.11(b) might be our pixel values. In its first convolution operation, the network could apply a filter operation by multiplying the pixel values by a 3×3 matrix of values that happens to be good at identifying vertical lines, such as the matrix in Figure 11.11(c). The sum of the individual cell multiplications is $[0 + 0 + 0 + 200 + 225 + 225 + 0 + 0 + 0] = 650$. This is a relatively high value, compared with what another arrangement of the filter matrix might produce, because both the image section and the filter have high values in the center column and low values elsewhere. (A little experimentation with other 3×3 arrangements of three 1's and six 0's will reveal why this particular matrix is good at identifying vertical lines.) So, for this initial filter action, we can say that the filter has detected a vertical line, and thus we can consolidate the initial nine values of the image section into a single value (say, a value between 0 and 1 to indicate the absence or presence of a vertical line).

Local Feature Map

The "vertical line detector" filter moves across and down the original image matrix, recalculating and producing a single output each time. We end up with a smaller matrix; how much smaller depends on whether the filter moves one pixel at a time, two, or more (called the *stride*). While the original image values were simply individual pixel values, the new, smaller matrix is a map of features, answering the question: "is there a vertical line in this section?"

The fact that the frame for the convolution is relatively small means that the overall operation can identify features that are local in character. We could imagine other local filters to discover horizontal lines, diagonal lines, curves, boundaries, etc. Further layers of different convolutional operations, taking these local feature maps as inputs, can then successively build up higher-level features (corners, rectangles, circles, etc.).

A Hierarchy of Features

The first feature map is of vertical lines; we could repeat the process to identify horizontal lines and diagonal lines. We could also imagine filters to identify

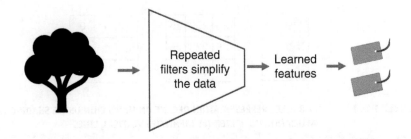

FIGURE 11.12 CONVOLUTION NETWORK PROCESS, SUPERVISED LEARNING: THE REPEATED FILTERING IN THE NETWORK CONVOLUTION PROCESS PRODUCES HIGH-LEVEL FEATURES THAT FACILITATE THE APPLICATION OF CLASS LABELS, WHICH ARE COMPARED WITH ACTUAL CLASSES TO TRAIN THE NETWORK

boundaries between light and dark areas. Then, having produced a set of initial low-level feature maps, the process could repeat, except this time working with these feature maps instead of the original pixel values. This iterative process continues, building up multidimensional matrix maps, or tensors, of higher and higher-level features. As the process proceeds, the matrix representation of higher level features becomes somewhat abstract, so it is not necessarily possible to peer into a deep network and identify, for example, an eye.

In this process, the information is progressively compressed (simplified) as the higher-level features emerge, as illustrated in Figure 11.12.

The Learning Process

How does the net know which convolutional operations to do? To put it simply, it retains the ones that lead to successful classifications. In a basic neural net, the individual weights are what get adjusted in the iterative learning process. In a convolutional network, the net also learns which convolutions to do.

In a supervised learning setting, the network keeps building up features up to the highest level, which might be the goal of the learning task. Consider the task of deciding whether an image contains a face. You have a training set of labeled images with faces and images without faces. The training process yields convolutions that identify hierarchies of features (e.g., edges > circles > eyes) that lead to success in the classification process. Other hierarchies that the net might conceivably encounter (e.g., edges > rectangles > houses) get dropped because they do not contribute to success in the identification of faces. Sometimes it is the case that the output of a single node in the network is an effective classifier, an indication that this node codes for the feature you are focusing on.

Unsupervised Learning

The most magical-seeming accomplishment of deep learning is its ability to identify features and, hence, objects in an unsupervised setting. Famous examples

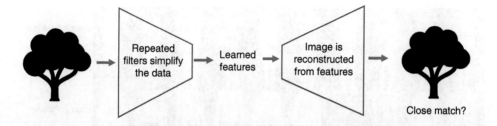

FIGURE 11.13   AUTOENCODER NETWORK PROCESS: THE REPEATED FILTERING IN THE NETWORK CONVOLUTION PROCESS PRODUCES HIGH-LEVEL FEATURES THAT ARE THEN USED TO RECONSTRUCT THE IMAGE. THE RECONSTRUCTED IMAGE IS COMPARED WITH THE ORIGINAL; NETWORK ARCHITECTURES THAT PRODUCE CLOSE MATCHES ARE SAVED AS THE NETWORK IS "TRAINED" WITHOUT BENEFIT OF LABELED DATA

include identifying images with faces and identifying dogs and cats in images (see, e.g., Le et al., 2012). How is this done?

One method is to use a so-called *autoencoder* network. These networks are trained to reproduce the input that is fed into them, by first creating a lower-dimensional representation of the data and then using the created representation to reproduce the original data. The network is trained to retain the features that facilitate accurate reproduction of the input.

Viewed in the context of our image example, autoencoders have the high-level architecture shown in Figure 11.13.

Up to the learned features point (the bottleneck in the image), the network is similar to the supervised network. Once it has developed the learned features, which are a low-dimensional representation of the data, it expands those features into an image by a reverse process. The output image is compared with the input image, and if they are not similar, the network keeps working (using the same backpropagation method we discussed earlier). Once the network reliably produces output images that are similar to the inputs, the process stops.

This internal representation at the bottleneck now has useful information about the general domain (here, images) on which the network was trained. It turns out that the learned features (outputs of nodes at the bottleneck) that emerge in this process are often useful. Since the features can be considered a low-dimensional representation of the original data (similar in spirit to principal components in PCA—see Chapter 4), they can be used, for example, for building a supervised predictive model or for unsupervised clustering.

Example: Classification of Fashion Images

This example demonstrates using a deep learning architecture with CNN for a classification task—to classify fashion images of different types of clothing and footwear. The open source *Fashion MNIST* data made available by Zalando[8]

---

[8]https://github.com/zalandoresearch/fashion-mnist

Class 0: T-shirt/top

Class 1: Trouser

Class 2: Pullover

Class 3: Dress

Class 4: Coat

Class 5: Sandal

Class 6: Shirt

Class 7: Sneaker

Class 8: Bag

Class 9: Ankle boot

FIGURE 11.14   FASHION MNIST DATA: SAMPLE OF 10 IMAGES FROM EACH CLASS

consists of a training set of 60,000 images and a holdout set of 10,000 images. Each image is a 28×28 pixel grayscale image, associated with a label from one of 10 classes. A small sample of 10 images from each class is shown in Figure 11.14.

The dataset is provided in the form of a zipped file *fashion_mnist_png.zip*[9] that contains two folders after unzipping: *train* and *test*. Each folder contains subfolders for each label class (0, 1,...) containing images in *png* file format belonging to that class. In the following, we describe the main steps from preprocessing the data to building a classification model. Figure 11.15 shows the RapidMiner process for image processing and predictive modeling for this example. The RapidMiner extensions *Image Handling* and *Deep Learning* must be installed for these steps. We describe each step separately next.

Data Loading, Partitioning, and Preprocessing   As shown in Figure 11.15, the *Read Image Meta Data* operator is provided with the directory

---

[9]The data in *png* image format is also available at https://github.com/DeepLenin/fashion-mnist_png

FIGURE 11.15   RAPIDMINER PROCESS FOR CLASSIFYING IMAGES FROM FASHION MNIST DATA USING CNN path for the *train* data folder as its parameter and is used to recursively read each image file's metadata which includes its path, filename, width, height, and label. With the *use label* parameter selected, each image is assigned its parent directory name as its label. The same operator is also used to read the holdout set images' metadata from the *test* folder.

Training a deep learning network on the entire training data can be computationally demanding on a local machine. For simplicity, in this example, we sample 4000 images (400 from each class) from the training set with the *Sample (Stratified)* operator.[10] The sample is then partitioned into training (70%) and validation (30%) sets with the *Split Data* operator for tuning the network.

Prior to training and tuning the network, the image pixel values (measuring intensity) must be normalized, aligned with our earlier discussion on preprocessing the data for neural network models. The *Pre-Process Images* nested operator uses the path information from the metadata gathered earlier to read the images individually and scale the image pixels to a [0, 1] scale. The output is a *tensor* object (shown with the *ten* port for *Pre-Process Images* operator), which is a generalized and computationally efficient representation of matrix data in higher dimension.[11] Here, the training tensor object represents 2800 images, each with 28×28 dimension. The validation tensor object represents 1200 images, each with 28×28 dimension.

Training a Deep Learning Network   The normalized training and validation image tensors are input to the *Deep Learning (Tensor)* nested operator, which embeds the deep learning architecture with multiple layers. The *Add Convolutional Layer* operator adds a convolutional layer to create 64 feature maps (activation maps) each with a randomly chosen filter (kernel, k) of size 3 (a 3×3 matrix), a padding[12] (p) of size 1 (a 1×1 matrix), and a stride (s) of 1 (a 1×1 matrix). As discussed earlier, the filter moves across and down each image, recalculating and producing a new feature map. These convolutions are designed to identify basic image features like edges.[13] The ReLU activation function is used to produce the output of each feature map in the layer.

Next, we want to highlight the most dominant feature in an image using the iterative process described earlier in "A Hierarchy of Features." To do this, we

---

[10] To maximize memory usage from your machine for RapidMiner Studio, go to RapidMiner > Preferences > System, leave the parameter "Maximum amount of memory" empty, and restart RapidMiner (if changed). Also, if the machine has less than 16 GB memory, for this example, reduce the sample size (e.g., 650 or 1000) in the *Sample (Stratified)* operator.

[11] You are already familiar with three special types of tensors: a scalar is a rank 0 tensor, a vector is a rank 1 tensor, and a matrix is a rank 2 tensor.

[12] Padding adds empty pixels around the edges of an image. This is done to preserve the original size of an image and to perform full convolutions on the edge pixels, when applying a convolutional filter.

[13] With an image of input dimension $n = n_{width} = n_{height} = 28$, the output dimension for each feature map is given by $(n + 2p - k)/s + 1 = (28 + 2 \times 1 - 3)/1 + 1 = 28$. That is, a 28×28 matrix.

use the convolutional layer output as the input for the max pooling layer with the *Add Pooling Layer* operator, specifying the parameter *Pooling Method = max*. Here, we set kernel size $k = 2$, padding size $p = 0$, and the stride size $s = 2$.[14] Often, we experiment with multiple combinations of convolutional and max pooling layers to determine which configuration is best at identifying different high-level features in the images.

To reduce the chance of overfitting and to make the network more resilient, we randomly drop nodes during training. This is done in RapidMiner with the *Add Dropout Layer* operator, which we use to randomly drop 25% of the nodes from the network. Following this, the *Add Fully-Connected Layer* operator adds a dense layer with the ReLU activation function to learn nonlinear combinations of features learned from the previous convolutional and pooling layers. Finally, the *Add Output Layer* operator uses the Softmax activation function. Like the sigmoid activation function, Softmax results in values in the range [0, 1]. For this multi-class classification task, we have 10 output nodes corresponding to the 10 class labels.

The deep learning network is trained on the train partition, and its performance is measured on the validation partition after each epoch (training cycle). As shown in Figure 11.15, the training is done over 50 epochs allowing early stopping if there is no improvement in the validation set performance (in terms of the multiclass cross entropy metric) for 5 consecutive epochs (patience). After early stopping, the epoch at which the best validation performance was recorded is used. Figure 11.16 (top)[15] shows the learning curve for the deep learning network with early stopping at epoch 35 and the best performance at epoch 30. This shows overfitting starting to occur after epoch 30.

Applying the Predictive Model   The image preprocessing (scaling) on the training set and the learned deep learning network are sequenced together using the *Group Models (Generic)* operator so that these same model settings can be applied for the holdout set. First, the holdout data is sorted with labels in ascending order so that the confusion matrix is ordered properly. Next, the *Apply Model (Generic)* operator applies the sequence of image preprocessing and deep learning model on each image in the holdout set. The output is of the form IOObjectCollection, so the *Append* operator is used to transform it into the familiar ExampleSet format. Finally, the *Performance (Classification)* operator is used to analyze holdout set performance.

Figure 11.16 (middle) shows propensities for a sample of five images from the holdout set. Figure 11.16 (bottom) shows the confusion matrix on the holdout

---

[14]Considering the previous layer's feature maps as input, the output dimension of each feature map is now $(n + 2p - k)/s + 1 = (28 + 2 \times 0 - 2)/2 + 1 = 14$. That is, a 14×14 matrix.

[15]The *Deep Learning* operator uses the term *testing_score* for denoting the *validation_score* here.

Row No.	label	prediction	confidence(0)	confidence(1)	confidence(2)	confidence(3)	confidence(4)
1	0	6	0.427	0.034	0.006	0.052	0.018
2	0	0	0.707	0.000	0.005	0.001	0.000
3	0	0	1.000	0.000	0.000	0.000	0.000
4	0	2	0.339	0.000	0.573	0.000	0.002
5	0	0	0.998	0.000	0.000	0.001	0.000

Row No.	confidence(5)	confidence(6)	confidence(7)	confidence(8)	confidence(9)	Path
1	0.000	0.461	0.000	0.002	0.000	/Users/
2	0.000	0.287	0.000	0.000	0.000	/Users/
3	0.000	0.000	0.000	0.000	0.000	/Users/
4	0.000	0.086	0.000	0.000	0.000	/Users/
5	0.000	0.001	0.000	0.000	0.000	/Users/

accuracy: 84.06%

	true 0	true 1	true 2	true 3	true 4	true 5	true 6	true 7	true 8	true 9	class pr...
pred. 0	723	6	13	21	0	1	127	0	3	0	80.87%
pred. 1	1	946	0	12	2	0	0	0	1	0	98.34%
pred. 2	31	1	728	14	87	0	133	0	4	0	72.95%
pred. 3	62	34	16	880	52	0	43	0	14	0	79.93%
pred. 4	13	6	169	27	785	0	112	0	5	1	70.21%
pred. 5	3	0	0	1	0	966	0	28	7	13	94.89%
pred. 6	152	4	70	40	68	0	568	0	7	2	62.35%
pred. 7	1	0	0	0	0	26	0	935	3	63	90.95%
pred. 8	14	3	4	5	6	0	17	1	956	2	94.84%
pred. 9	0	0	0	0	0	7	0	36	0	919	95.53%
class re...	72.30%	94.60%	72.80%	88.00%	78.50%	96.60%	56.80%	93.50%	95.60%	91.90%	

FIGURE 11.16   (TOP) LEARNING CURVE FOR THE DEEP LEARNING NETWORK, (MIDDLE) PROPENSITIES FOR FIVE RECORDS IN THE HOLDOUT DATA, AND (BOTTOM) CONFUSION MATRIX FOR THE HOLDOUT SET (FASHION MNIST DATA)

set. Remarkably, with only 2800 training images (280 images in each label class) and 1200 validation images, the network was able to achieve an accuracy of 84.06%. From the confusion matrix, we can see that the model does well in identifying classes 1, 5, 7, 8 and 9 but has difficulty with the others. Class 6 (shirts), for example, is often confused with classes 0 (t-shirt/tops), 2 (pullovers), 3 (dresses), and 4 (coats). Using additional training data will likely further improve model performance.[16]

Conclusion

The key to convolutional networks' success is their ability to build, through iteration, multidimensional feature maps of great complexity (requiring substantial computing power and capacity), leading to the development of learned features that form a lower-dimensional representation of the data. You can see that different convolutional architectures (e.g., types of filtering operations) would be suitable for different tasks. The AI community shares pre-trained networks that allow analysts to short-circuit the lengthy and complex training process that is required, as well as datasets that allow training and benchmarking to certain tasks (e.g., datasets of generic images in many different classes, images specifically of faces, satellite imagery, text data, voice data, etc.).

Finally, you may have heard of other types of deep learning. At the time of writing, Recurrent Neural Networks (RNN) are very popular. They are usually implemented with either Long Short-Term Memory (LSTM) or Gated Recurrent Unit (GRU) building blocks. These networks are especially useful for data that are sequential in nature or have temporal behavior, such as time series, music, text and speech (where the order of words in a sentence matters), and user or robot behavior (e.g., clickstream data, where the order of a user's actions can be important). These networks' memory helps them capture such sequences. RapidMiner's Deep Learning extension supports building a variety of sequential deep learning architectures. We illustrated the use of CNN in this chapter. We discuss the use of LSTM for time series forecasting in Chapter 19 and a special application of LSTM for text processing called *word embedding* in Chapter 21. Various sequential deep learning architectures can be composed by using the different types of layers as building blocks with operators such as *Add Recurrent Layer*, *Add LSTM Layer*, and *Add Embedding Layer* and applying the same principles as discussed in this chapter. In deciding whether to use such methods in a given business analytics application, a key consideration is their performance relative to other methods and their required resources (in terms of data and computing).

---

[16]Similar CNN architectures with the complete training data have reported 90%–95% accuracy. See https://github.com/zalandoresearch/fashion-mnist

11.7 ADVANTAGES AND WEAKNESSES OF NEURAL NETWORKS

The most prominent advantage of neural networks is their good predictive performance. They are known to have high tolerance to noisy data and the ability to capture highly complicated relationships between the predictors and an outcome variable. Their weakest point is in providing insight into the structure of the relationship, hence their black box reputation.

Several considerations and dangers should be kept in mind when using neural networks. First, although they are capable of generalizing from a set of examples, extrapolation is still a serious danger. If the network sees only records in a certain range, its predictions outside this range can be completely invalid.

Second, the extreme flexibility of the neural network relies heavily on having sufficient data for training purposes. A related issue is that in classification problems, the network requires sufficient records of the minority class in order to learn it. This is achieved by oversampling, as explained in Chapter 2.

Finally, a practical consideration that can determine the usefulness of a neural network is the computation time. Neural networks are relatively heavy on computation time, requiring a longer runtime than other classifiers. This runtime grows greatly when the number of predictors is increased (as there will be many more weights to compute). In applications where real-time or near-real-time prediction is required, runtime should be measured to make sure that it does not cause unacceptable delay in the decision-making.

PROBLEMS

11.1 Credit Card Use. Consider the hypothetical bank data in Table 11.4 on consumers' use of credit card credit facilities. Create a small worksheet in Excel to illustrate one pass through a simple neural network. (Randomly generate initial weight values.)

TABLE 11.4 DATA FOR CREDIT CARD EXAMPLE AND ATTRIBUTE DESCRIPTIONS

Years	Salary	Used credit
4	43	0
18	65	1
1	53	0
3	95	0
15	88	1
6	112	1

Years: number of years the customer has been with the bank.
Salary: customer's salary (in thousands of dollars).
Used credit: 1 = customer has left an unpaid credit card balance at the end of at least one month in the prior year, 0 = balance was paid off at the end of each month.

11.2 Neural Net Evolution. A neural net typically starts out with random values for bias and weights; hence, it produces essentially random predictions when presented with its first case. What is the key ingredient by which the net evolves to produce a more accurate prediction?

11.3 Car Sales. Consider the data on used cars (*ToyotaCorolla.csv*) with 1436 records and details on 38 attributes, including Price, Age, KM, HP, and other specifications. The goal is to predict the price of a used Toyota Corolla based on its specifications.

- Fit a neural network model to the data. Use a single hidden layer with two nodes.

- Use predictors Age_08_04, KM, Fuel_Type, HP, Automatic, Doors, Quarterly_Tax, Mfr_Guarantee, Guarantee_Period, Airco, Automatic_airco, CD_Player, Powered_Windows, Sport_Model, and Tow_Bar.

- Remember to convert any categorical predictors to dummy variables using the *Nominal to Numerical* operator. Use the *normalize* parameter in the *Neural Network* operator to normalize the data to a [-1, 1] scale prior to model training.

Record the RMS error for the training data and the holdout data. Repeat the process, changing the number of hidden layers and nodes to {single layer with five nodes} and {two layers, five nodes in each layer}.

a. What happens to the RMS error for the training data as the number of layers and nodes increases?

b. What happens to the RMS error for the holdout data?

c. Comment on the appropriate number of layers and nodes for this application.

11.4 Direct Mailing to Airline Customers. East–West Airlines has entered into a partnership with the wireless phone company Telcon to sell the latter's service via direct mail. The file *EastWestAirlinesNN.csv* contains a subset of a data sample of who has already received a test offer. About 13% accepted.

You are asked to develop a model to classify East–West customers as to whether they purchase a wireless phone service contract (target attribute Phone_Sale). This model will be used to classify additional customers.

a. Run a neural net model on these data, using a single hidden layer with five nodes. Remember to first convert categorical attributes into dummies, and use the *normalize* parameter in the *Neural Network* operator to normalize the data to a [-1, 1] scale prior to model training. Create a decile lift chart for the training and holdout sets. Interpret the meaning (in business terms) of the leftmost bar of the holdout decile lift chart.

b. Comment on the difference between the training and holdout lift charts.

c. Run a second neural net model on the data, this time setting the number of hidden nodes to 1. Comment now on the difference between this model and the model you ran earlier and how overfitting might have affected results.

d. What sort of information, if any, is provided about the effects of the various attributes?

CHAPTER 12

Discriminant Analysis

In this chapter, we describe the method of discriminant analysis, which is a model-based approach to classification. We discuss the main principle, where classification is based on the distance of a record from each of the class means. We explain the underlying measure of "statistical distance," which takes into account the correlation between predictors. The output of a discriminant analysis procedure generates estimated "classification functions," which are then used to produce classification scores that can be translated into classifications or propensities (probabilities of class membership). One can also directly integrate misclassification costs into the discriminant analysis setup, and we explain how this is achieved. Finally, we discuss the underlying model assumptions, the practical robustness to some assumption violations, and the advantages of discriminant analysis when the assumptions are reasonably met (e.g., the sufficiency of a small training sample).

12.1 INTRODUCTION

Discriminant analysis is a classification method. Like logistic regression, it is a classical statistical technique that can be used for classification and profiling. It uses sets of measurements on different classes of records to classify new records into one of those classes (*classification*). Common uses of the method have been in classifying organisms into species and subspecies; classifying applications for loans, credit cards, and insurance into low- and high-risk categories; classifying customers of new products into early adopters, early majority, late majority, and laggards; classifying bonds into bond rating categories; classifying skulls of human fossils; as well as in research studies involving disputed authorship, decisions on college admission, medical studies involving alcoholics and nonalcoholics, and

Machine Learning for Business Analytics: Concepts, Techniques and Applications in RapidMiner, First Edition.
Galit Shmueli, Peter C. Bruce, Amit V. Deokar, and Nitin R. Patel

methods to identify human fingerprints. Discriminant analysis can also be used to highlight aspects that distinguish the classes (*profiling*).

We return to two examples that were described in earlier chapters, the Riding-Mowers and Personal Loan Acceptance examples. In each of these, the target attribute has two classes. We close with a third example involving more than two classes.

Example 1: Riding Mowers

We return to the example from Chapter 7, where a riding-mower manufacturer would like to find a way of classifying families in a city into those likely to purchase a riding mower and those not likely to purchase one. A pilot random sample of 12 owners and 12 nonowners in the city is undertaken. The data are given in Table 7.1 in Chapter 7, and a scatter plot is shown in Figure 12.1. We can think of a linear classification rule as a line that separates the two-dimensional region into two parts, with most of the owners in one half-plane and most nonowners in the complementary half-plane. A good classification rule would separate the data so that the fewest points are misclassified: the line shown in Figure 12.1 seems to do a good job in discriminating between the two classes as it makes six misclassifications out of 24 points. Can we do better?

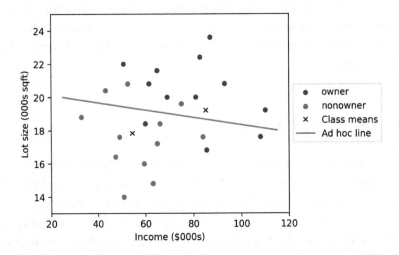

FIGURE 12.1   SCATTER PLOT OF LOT SIZE VS. INCOME FOR 24 OWNERS AND NONOWNERS OF RIDING MOWERS. THE (AD HOC) LINE TRIES TO SEPARATE OWNERS FROM NONOWNERS

Example 2: Personal Loan Acceptance

The riding-mowers example is a classic example and is useful in describing the concept and goal of discriminant analysis. However, in today's business applications, the number of records is much larger, and their separation into classes is much less distinct. To illustrate this, we return to the Universal Bank example described in Chapter 9, where the bank's goal is to identify new customers most likely to accept a personal loan. For simplicity, we will consider only two predictor attributes: the customer's annual income (Income, in $000s) and the average monthly credit card spending (CCAvg, in $000s). The top plot of Figure 12.2 shows the acceptance of a personal loan by a subset of 200 customers from the bank's database as a function of Income and CCAvg. We use a logarithmic scale on both axes to enhance visibility because there are many points condensed in the low-income, low-CC spending area. Even for this small subset, the separation is not clear. The bottom plot shows all 5000 customers and the added complexity of dealing with a large number of records.

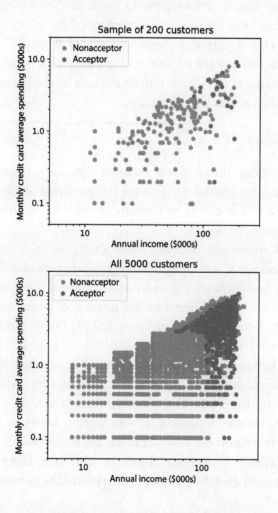

FIGURE 12.2   PERSONAL LOAN ACCEPTANCE AS A FUNCTION OF INCOME AND CREDIT CARD SPENDING FOR 5000 CUSTOMERS OF THE UNIVERSAL BANK (IN LOG SCALE)

12.2 DISTANCE OF A RECORD FROM A CLASS

Finding the best separation between records involves measuring their distance from their class. The general idea is to classify a record to the class to which it is closest. Suppose that we are required to classify a new customer of Universal Bank as being an *acceptor* or a *nonacceptor* of their personal loan offer, based on an income of x. From the bank's database, we find that the mean income for loan acceptors was \$144.75K and for nonacceptors \$66.24K. We can use Income as a predictor of loan acceptance via a simple *Euclidean distance rule*: if x is closer to the mean income of the acceptor class than to the mean income of the nonacceptor class, classify the customer as an *acceptor*; otherwise, classify the customer as a *nonacceptor*. In other words, if $|x - 144.75| < |x - 66.24|$, then classification = *acceptor*; otherwise, *nonacceptor*. Moving from a single predictor attribute (income) to two or more predictor attributes, the equivalent of the mean of a class is the *centroid* of a class. This is simply the vector of means $\bar{\mathbf{x}} = [\bar{x}_1, \ldots, \bar{x}_p]$. The Euclidean distance between a record with p measurements $\mathbf{x} = [x_1, \ldots, x_p]$ and the centroid $\bar{\mathbf{x}}$ is defined as the square root of the sum of the squared differences between the individual values and the means:

$$D_{\text{Euclidean}}(\mathbf{x}, \bar{\mathbf{x}}) = \sqrt{(x_1 - \bar{x}_1)^2 + \cdots + (x_p - \bar{x}_p)^2}. \qquad (12.1)$$

Using the Euclidean distance has three drawbacks. First, the distance depends on the units we choose to measure the predictor attributes. We will get different answers if we decide to measure income in dollars, for instance, rather than in thousands of dollars.

Second, Euclidean distance does not take into account the variability of the attributes. For example, if we compare the variability in income in the two classes, we find that for acceptors, the standard deviation is lower than for nonacceptors (\$31.6K vs. \$40.6K). Therefore, the income of a new customer might be closer to the acceptors' mean income in dollars, but because of the large variability in income for nonacceptors, this customer is just as likely to be a nonacceptor. We therefore want the distance measure to take into account the variance of the different attributes and measure a distance in standard deviations rather than in the original units. This is equivalent to z-scores.

Third, Euclidean distance ignores the correlation between the attributes. This is often a very important consideration, especially when we are using many predictor attributes to separate classes. In this case, there will often be attributes, which by themselves are useful discriminators between classes, but in the presence of other predictor attributes are practically redundant, as they capture the same effects as the other attributes.

A solution to these drawbacks is to use a measure called *statistical distance* (or *Mahalanobis distance*). Let us denote by S the covariance matrix between the p attributes. The definition of a statistical distance is

$$
\begin{aligned}
D_{\text{Statistical}}(\mathbf{x}, \overline{\mathbf{x}}) &= \sqrt{[\mathbf{x} - \overline{\mathbf{x}}]' S^{-1} [\mathbf{x} - \overline{\mathbf{x}}]} \\
&= \sqrt{[(x_1 - \overline{x}_1), (x_2 - \overline{x}_2), \ldots, (x_p - \overline{x}_p)] S^{-1} \begin{bmatrix} x_1 - \overline{x}_1 \\ x_2 - \overline{x}_2 \\ \vdots \\ x_p - \overline{x}_p \end{bmatrix}}
\end{aligned}
$$

$$(12.2)$$

(the notation $'$, which represents *transpose operation*, simply turns the column vector into a row vector). S^{-1} is the inverse matrix of S, which is the p-dimension extension to division. When there is a single predictor ($p = 1$), this formula reduces to a (squared) z-score calculation, since we subtract the mean and divide by the standard deviation. The statistical distance takes into account not only the predictor means, but also the spread of the predictor values and the correlations between the different predictors. To compute a statistical distance between a record and a class, we must compute the predictor means (the centroid) and the covariances between each pair of predictors. These are used to construct the distances. The method of discriminant analysis uses statistical distance as the basis for finding a separating line (or, if there are more than two attributes, a separating hyperplane) that is equally distant from the different class means.[1] It is based on measuring the statistical distances of a record to each of the classes and allocating it to the closest class. This is done through *classification functions*, which are explained next.

12.3 FISHER'S LINEAR CLASSIFICATION FUNCTIONS

Linear classification functions were proposed in 1936 by the noted statistician R. A. Fisher as the basis for improved separation of records into classes. The idea

---

[1] An alternative approach finds a separating line or hyperplane that is "best" at separating the different clouds of points. In the case of two classes, the two methods coincide.

is to find linear functions of the attributes that maximize the ratio of between-class variability to within-class variability. In other words, we would obtain classes that are very homogeneous and differ the most from each other. For each record, these functions are used to compute scores that measure the proximity of that record to each of the classes. A record is classified as belonging to the class for which it has the highest classification score (equivalent to the smallest statistical distance).

The classification functions are estimated using software. In RapidMiner, the *Linear Discriminant Analysis* operator can be found in the Operators panel under *Modeling > Predictive > Linear Discriminant Analysis*. Figure 12.3 shows the RapidMiner process for applying discriminant analysis to the rider-mowers example and the resulting output. Currently, RapidMiner's *Linear Discriminant Analysis* operator only produces the predicted class (predicted labels) for each record as its output (as shown in Figure 12.3). To obtain the estimated classification function (or decision function in case of binary classification), we resort to integrating a Python Scripting extension into our RapidMiner process.

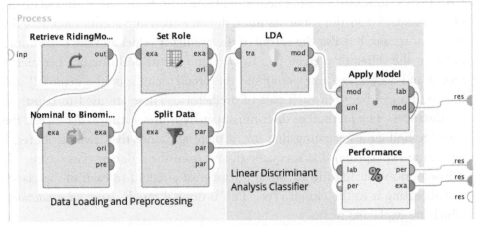

Row No.	Income	Lot_Size	Ownership	prediction(Ownership)
1	64.800	21.600	Owner	Owner
2	61.500	20.800	Owner	Owner
3	87	23.600	Owner	Owner
4	93	20.800	Owner	Owner
5	51	22	Owner	Nonowner

FIGURE 12.3   (TOP) RAPIDMINER PROCESS FOR DISCRIMINANT ANALYSIS OF RIDING-MOWERS DATA AND (BOTTOM) SAMPLE OUTPUT FOR FIVE HOLDOUT SET RECORDS

Using the Python extension shown in Figure 12.4 and explained in the box below, Table 12.1 shows the decision function obtained (displayed in the Log panel in RapidMiner) from running discriminant analysis on the riding mowers data, using two predictors. A negative decision score leads to a "0" (negative class) classification, while a positive score leads to "1" (positive class) classification. (For more than two classes, individual decision functions are returned – see Section 12.7).

DISCRIMINANT ANALYSIS WITH PYTHON SCRIPTING EXTENSION

In RapidMiner's *Linear Discriminant Analysis* operator, only the classifications for each record are displayed. To see the classification function (or decision function in case of binary classification) along with the classification scores and membership probabilities, we can use the *Python Scripting* extension. This extension can be installed from the RapidMiner menu through *Extensions > Marketplace (Updates and Extensions)*.

Figure 12.4 shows how to build a discriminant analysis classifier for the riding-mowers data using the *Python Learner* operator.

When the script is invoked, first the *rm_train* function is called to train a model with the predictors, target attribute, and parameters (optional) as the input. Inside this function, Python's scikit-learn library's *LinearDiscriminantAnalysis()* method is called to create the model instance, which is then fit to the training data. Then, the *rm_apply* function is called to get the classifications, membership probabilities, and classification scores, using the data and the generated model as its inputs. As usual, the *Apply Model* operator simply creates a labeled dataset.

Since the *Python Learner* operator treats any additional attributes derived from the model as probabilities, it automatically renames new attributes in the form *confidence(attribute_name)*. So, to produce meaningful output, the *Rename* operator is used to rename the *confidence(decision_function)* attribute as *decision_function*.

TABLE 12.1   DISCRIMINANT ANALYSIS OUTPUT FOR RIDING-MOWERS DATA, DISPLAYING THE DECISION FUNCTION (USING PYTHON EXTENSION SHOWN IN FIGURE 12.4)

```
Coefficients [[0.12126501 0.61970131]]
Intercept [-19.95494831]
```

USING CLASSIFICATION FUNCTION AND DECISION FUNCTION SCORES TO CLASSIFY RECORDS

For each record, we calculate the value of the classification function (one for each class); whichever class' function has the highest value (= score) is the class assigned to that record. An alternative for a two-class classification case is to use a *decision function*, which is the *difference* between the two individual classification functions. We then use the sign of the decision function to assign the predicted class as positive or negative.

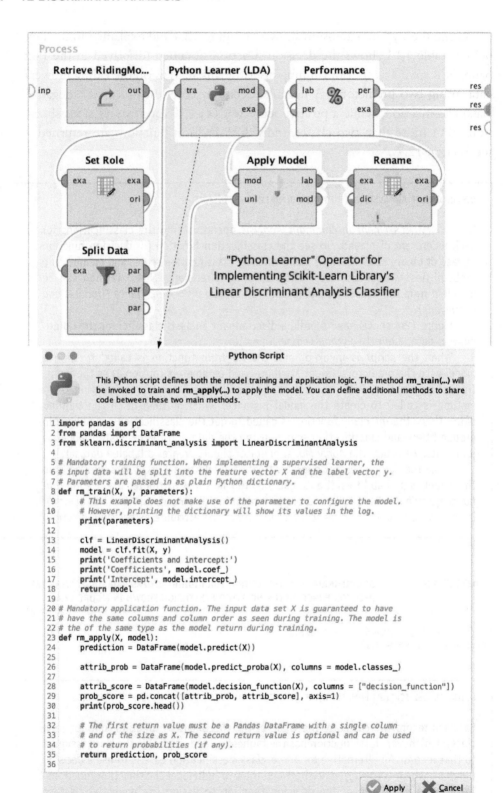

FIGURE 12.4 **PROCESS FOR LINEAR DISCRIMINANT ANALYSIS FOR RIDING-MOWERS DATA USING THE PYTHON SCRIPTING EXTENSION**

To classify a family into the class of *owners* or *nonowners*, we use the classification functions to compute the family's classification scores: A family is classified into the class of *owners* if the owner function score is higher than the nonowner function score and into *nonowners* if the reverse is the case. These functions are specified in a way that can be easily generalized to more than two classes. The values given for the functions are simply the weights to be associated with each attribute in the linear function in a manner analogous to multiple linear regression. For instance, the first household in the holdout set has an income of $64.8K and a lot size of 21.6K ft^2. The decision function is therefore $(0.1213)(64.8) + (0.6197)(21.6) - 19.9549 = 1.29$. Since the value is positive, the household is classified (correctly) by the model as an owner. Such calculations are done by the software and do not need to be done manually. For example, the scores and classifications for the 10 holdout set households—produced by RapidMiner's *Python Scripting* extension shown earlier in Figure 12.4—are given in Figure 12.5.

An alternative way for classifying a record into one of the classes is to compute the probability of belonging to each of the classes and assigning the record to the most likely class. If we have two classes, we need only compute a single probability for each record (of belonging to *owners*, for example). Using a threshold of 0.5 is equivalent to assigning the record to the class with the highest classification score. The advantage of this approach is that we obtain propensities, which can be used for goals such as ranking: we sort the records in order of descending probabilities and generate lift curves.

Let us assume that there are m classes. To compute the probability of belonging to a certain class k, for a certain record i, we need to compute all the classification scores $c_1(i), c_2(i), \ldots, c_m(i)$ and combine them using the following formula:

$$P[\text{record } i (\text{with measurements } x_1, x_2, \ldots, x_p) \text{ belongs to class } k]$$
$$= \frac{e^{c_k(i)}}{e^{c_1(i)} + e^{c_2(i)} + \cdots + e^{c_m(i)}}.$$

Row No.	Income	Lot_Size	Ownership	prediction(Ownership)	confidence(Nonowner)	confidence(Owner)	decision_function
1	64.800	21.600	Owner	Owner	0.216	0.784	1.289
2	61.500	20.800	Owner	Owner	0.403	0.597	0.393
3	87	23.600	Owner	Owner	0.005	0.995	5.220
4	93	20.800	Owner	Owner	0.015	0.985	4.212
5	51	22	Owner	Nonowner	0.534	0.466	−0.137
6	75	19.600	Nonowner	Owner	0.217	0.783	1.286
7	64.800	17.200	Nonowner	Nonowner	0.808	0.192	−1.438
8	49.200	17.600	Nonowner	Nonowner	0.956	0.044	−3.082
9	66	18.400	Nonowner	Nonowner	0.634	0.366	−0.549
10	51	14	Nonowner	Nonowner	0.994	0.006	−5.095

FIGURE 12.5   PREDICTED CLASSES, PROBABILITIES, AND CLASSIFICATION SCORES FOR RIDING-MOWERS HOLDOUT DATA PRODUCED USING THE PYTHON SCRIPTING EXTENSION

These probabilities and their computation for the riding-mowers data in the holdout set are given in Figure 12.5.

Now, when the discriminant model (which was fit to the training partition) is applied to all 24 records, we have four misclassifications, compared with six in in our original (ad hoc) classification. This can be seen in Figure 12.6, which includes the line resulting from the discriminant model.[2]

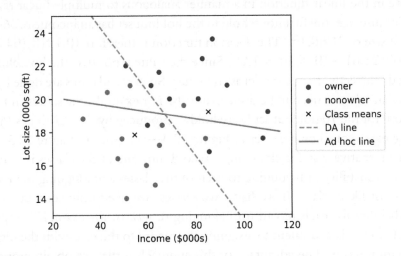

FIGURE 12.6   CLASS SEPARATION OBTAINED FROM THE DISCRIMINANT MODEL (COMPARED TO AD HOC LINE FROM FIGURE 12.1)

12.4 CLASSIFICATION PERFORMANCE OF DISCRIMINANT ANALYSIS

The discriminant analysis method relies on two main assumptions to arrive at classification scores: first, it assumes that the predictor attributes in all classes come from a multivariate normal distribution. When this assumption is reasonably met, discriminant analysis is a more powerful tool than other classification methods, such as logistic regression. In fact, Efron (1975) showed that discriminant analysis is 30% more efficient than logistic regression if the data are multivariate normal, in the sense that we require 30% less records to arrive at the same results. In practice, it has been shown that this method is relatively robust to departures from normality in the sense that predictors can be non-normal

---

[2]The slope of the line is given by $-a_1/a_2$ and the intercept is $-intercept/a_2$, where a_i are the coefficients of the decision function (e.g., here $\frac{21.74}{0.79} + \frac{-0.1}{0.79}$Lot_Size or $27.5 - 0.13$Lot_Size).

and even dummy attributes. This is true as long as the smallest class is sufficiently large (approximately more than 20 records). This method is also known to be sensitive to outliers in both the univariate space of single predictors and in the multivariate space. Exploratory analysis should therefore be used to locate extreme cases and determine whether they can be eliminated.

The second assumption behind discriminant analysis is that the correlation structure between the different predictors within a class is the same across classes. This can be roughly checked by computing the correlation matrix between the predictors separately for each class and comparing matrices. If the correlations differ substantially across classes, the classifier will tend to classify records into the class with the largest variability. When the correlation structure differs significantly and the dataset is very large, an alternative is to use quadratic discriminant analysis (QDA)[3], such as with RapidMiner's *Quadratic Discriminant Analysis* operator.

Notwithstanding the caveats embodied in these statistical assumptions, recall that in a predictive modeling environment, the ultimate test is whether the model works effectively. A reasonable approach is to conduct some exploratory analysis with respect to normality and correlation, train and evaluate a model, and then, depending on classification accuracy and what you learned from the initial exploration, circle back and explore further whether outliers should be examined or choice of predictor attributes revisited.

With respect to the evaluation of classification accuracy, we once again use the general measures of performance that were described in Chapter 5 (judging the performance of a classifier), with the principal ones based on the confusion matrix (accuracy alone or combined with costs) for classification and the lift and gains charts for ranking. The same argument for using the holdout set for evaluating performance still holds. For example, in the riding-mowers example, families shown in holdout set records 5 and 6 are misclassified. This means that the model yields an error rate of 20% for the holdout data.

To obtain the confusion matrix from a discriminant analysis, we either use the classification scores directly or the propensities (probabilities of class membership) that are computed from the classification scores. In both cases, we decide on the class assignment of each record based on the highest score or probability. We then compare these classifications to the actual class memberships of these records. This yields the confusion matrix.

---

[3]In practice, quadratic discriminant analysis has not been found useful except when the difference in the correlation matrices is large and the number of records available for training and testing is large. The reason is that the quadratic model requires estimating many more parameters that are all subject to error [for m classes and p attributes, the total number of parameters to be estimated for all the different correlation matrices is $mp(p + 1)/2$].

12.5 PRIOR PROBABILITIES

So far we have assumed that our objective is to minimize the classification error. The method presented above assumes that the chances of encountering a record from either class are the same. If the probability of encountering a record for classification in the future is not equal for the different classes, we should modify our functions to reduce our expected (long-run average) error rate. The modification is done as follows: let us denote by p_j the prior or future probability of membership in class j (in the two-class case, we have $'p_1$ and $p_2 = 1 - p_1$). We modify the classification function for each class by adding $\log(p_j)$. This effectively increases each of the intercept terms in the classification functions. In a two-class case, this is equivalent to adding to the decision function's intercept the quantity $\log(p_1) - \log(1 - p_1)$. To illustrate this, suppose that the percentage of riding-mower owners in the population is 15%, compared to 50% in the sample. This means that the model should classify fewer households as *owners*. To account for this distortion, we adjust the intercept in the decision function from Table 12.1 and obtain the adjusted intercept $-19.9549 + \log(0.15) - \log(0.85) = -21.5895$. To see how this can affect classifications, consider families corresponding to holdout set records 5 and 6. Family 5 was misclassified as a nonowner, while family 6 was misclassified as an owner in the case involving equal probability of class membership. When we account for the lower probability of owning a mower in the population, family 6 is now classified properly as a nonowner, while family 5 continues to be misclassified as a nonowner.

In addition to shifting the intercept, RapidMiner's *Linear Discriminant Analysis* operator (as well as Python's `scikit-learn` library) uses the priors when averaging the class covariance matrices.

12.6 UNEQUAL MISCLASSIFICATION COSTS

A second practical modification is needed when misclassification costs are not symmetrical. If the cost of misclassifying a class 1 record is very different from the cost of misclassifying a class 2 record, we may want to minimize the expected cost of misclassification rather than the simple error rate (which does not account for unequal misclassification costs). In the two-class case, it is easy to manipulate the classification functions to account for differing misclassification costs (in addition to prior probabilities). We denote by q_1 the cost of misclassifying a class 1 member (into class 2). Similarly, q_2 denotes the cost of misclassifying a class 2 member (into class 1). These costs are integrated into the intercepts of the classification functions by adding $\log(q_1)$ to the intercept for class 1 and

$\log(q_2)$ to the intercept of class 2. This is equivalent to adding the quantity $\log(q_1) - \log(q_2)$ to the intercept of the decision function. To incorporate both prior probabilities and misclassification costs into classification functions, add $\log(p_1 q_1)$ to the intercept of class 1 and $\log(p_2 q_2)$ to that of class 2. To add them into a decision function (for a 2-class problem), add to the intercept the quantity $\log(p_1 q_1) - \log(p_2 q_2)$.

In practice, it is not always simple to come up with misclassification costs q_1 and q_2 for each class. It is usually much easier to estimate the *ratio of costs* q_2/q_1 (e.g., if credit nondefaulter is class 1 and credit defaulter is class 2, the cost of misclassifying a credit defaulter is 10 times more expensive than that of misclassifying a nondefaulter). Luckily, the relationship between the classification functions depends only on this ratio. Therefore, we can set $q_1 = 1$ and $q_2 = ratio$ and simply add $\log(q_2/q_1)$ to the intercept for class 2. For a two-class decision function, we would add to the intercept the quantity: $-\log(q_2/q_1)$.

12.7 CLASSIFYING MORE THAN TWO CLASSES

Example 3: Medical Dispatch to Accident Scenes

Ideally, every automobile accident call to the emergency number 911 results in the immediate dispatch of an ambulance to the accident scene. However, in some cases the dispatch might be delayed (e.g., at peak accident hours or in some resource-strapped towns or shifts). In such cases, the 911 dispatchers must make decisions about which units to send based on sketchy information. It is useful to augment the limited information provided in the initial call with additional information in order to classify the accident as minor injury, serious injury, or death. For this purpose, we can use data (*accidents.csv*) that were collected on automobile accidents in the United States in 2001 that involved some type of injury. For each accident, additional information is recorded, such as day of week, weather conditions, and road type. Table 12.2 shows a small sample of records with 11 measurements of interest.

The goal is to see how well the predictors can be used to classify injury type correctly. To evaluate this, a reduced sample of 1000 records was drawn (with categories combined so that most predictors are binary) and partitioned into training and holdout sets, and a discriminant analysis was performed on the training data containing 600 records. The output structure is very similar to that for the two-class case. The only difference is that each record now has three classification functions (one for each injury type), and the confusion and error matrices are of size 3×3 to account for all the combinations of correct and incorrect classifications (see Figure 12.7).

TABLE 12.2   SAMPLE OF 20 AUTOMOBILE ACCIDENTS FROM THE 2001 DEPARTMENT OF TRANSPORTATION DATABASE

Accident #	RushHour	WRK_ZONE	WKDY	INT_HWY	LGTCON	LEVEL	SPD_LIM	SUR_COND	TRAF_WAY	WEATHER	MAX_SEV
1	1	0	1	1	dark_light	1	70	ice	one_way	adverse	no-injury
2	1	0	1	0	dark_light	0	70	ice	divided	adverse	no-injury
3	1	0	1	0	dark_light	0	65	ice	divided	adverse	non-fatal
4	1	0	1	0	dark_light	0	55	ice	two_way	not_adverse	non-fatal
5	1	0	0	0	dark_light	0	35	snow	one_way	adverse	no-injury
6	1	0	1	0	dark_light	1	35	wet	divided	adverse	no-injury
7	0	0	1	1	dark_light	1	70	wet	divided	adverse	non-fatal
8	0	0	1	0	dark_light	1	35	wet	two_way	adverse	no-injury
9	1	0	1	0	dark_light	0	25	wet	one_way	adverse	non-fatal
10	1	0	1	0	dark_light	0	35	wet	divided	adverse	non-fatal
11	1	0	1	0	dark_light	0	30	wet	divided	adverse	non-fatal
12	1	0	1	0	dark_light	0	60	wet	divided	not_adverse	no-injury
13	1	0	1	0	dark_light	0	40	wet	two_way	not_adverse	no-injury
14	0	0	1	0	day	1	65	dry	two_way	not_adverse	fatal
15	1	0	0	0	day	0	55	dry	two_way	not_adverse	fatal
16	1	0	1	0	day	0	55	dry	two_way	not_adverse	non-fatal
17	1	0	0	0	day	0	55	dry	two_way	not_adverse	non-fatal
18	0	0	1	0	dark	0	55	ice	two_way	not_adverse	no-injury
19	0	0	0	0	dark	0	50	ice	two_way	adverse	no-injury
20	0	0	0	0	dark	1	55	snow	divided	adverse	no-injury

Each accident is classified as one of three injury types (no-injury, non-fatal, or fatal) and has 10 more measurements (extracted from a larger set of measurements)

Row No.	index	fatal	no-injury	non-fatal
1	(Intercept)	−1.973	−0.891	−0.610
2	RushHour	−0.996	0.033	−0.016
3	WRK_ZONE	−0.457	0.220	−0.204
4	WKDY	−1.472	0.166	−0.135
5	INT_HWY	0.755	−0.076	0.061
6	LGTCON_day	0.010	−0.031	0.030
7	LEVEL	0.977	−0.083	0.064
8	SPD_LIM	0.048	0.004	−0.005
9	SUR_COND_dry	−6.000	−0.165	0.258
10	TRAF_two_way	0.753	−0.013	−0.000
11	WEATHER_adverse	−6.597	0.079	0.033

accuracy: 52.83%

	true no-injury	true non-fatal	true fatal	class precision
pred. no-injury	114	95	1	54.29%
pred. non-fatal	172	202	3	53.58%
pred. fatal	6	6	1	7.69%
class recall	39.04%	66.67%	20.00%	

FIGURE 12.7   DISCRIMINANT ANALYSIS FOR THE THREE-CLASS INJURY EXAMPLE: (TOP) CLASSIFICATION FUNCTIONS AND (BOTTOM) CONFUSION MATRIX FOR TRAINING SET. GENERATED USING THE PYTHON SCRIPTING EXTENSION

To obtain the estimated classification functions, predicted scores, and probabilities, we again use the Python Scripting integration, as shown in Figure 12.8. Here, we classify more than two classes using the *Python Learner* operator.[4] The classification functions and the performance output[5] are shown in Figure 12.7, and the predicted classes, probabilities, and classification scores are shown in Figure 12.9.

The rule for classification is still to classify a record to the class that has the highest corresponding classification score. The classification scores are computed, as before, using the classification function coefficients. This can be seen in Figure 12.9. For instance, the *no-injury* classification score for the first accident in the training set is $-0.891 + (0.033)(1) + (0.220)(0) + \cdots + (0.079)(1) = -0.465$. The *non-fatal* score is similarly computed as -0.956, and the *fatal* score as -5.943. Since the *no-injury* score is highest, this accident is (correctly) classified as having no injuries.

We can also compute for each accident, the propensities (estimated probabilities) of belonging to each of the three classes using the same relationship between classification scores and probabilities as in the two-class case. For instance, the probability of the above accident involving nonfatal injuries is estimated by the model as

$$\frac{e^{-0.956}}{e^{-5.943} + e^{-0.465} + e^{-0.956}} = 0.379. \tag{12.3}$$

The probabilities of an accident involving no injuries or fatal injuries are computed in a similar manner. For the first accident in the training set, the highest probability is that of involving no injuries, and therefore it is classified as a *no-injury* accident.

12.8 ADVANTAGES AND WEAKNESSES

Discriminant analysis is typically considered more of a statistical classification method than a data mining method. This is reflected in its absence or short mention in many machine learning resources. However, it is very popular in social sciences and has shown good performance. The use and performance of discriminant analysis are similar to those of multiple linear regression. The two methods therefore share several advantages and weaknesses.

---

[4]The *Rename* operator is used as before (e.g., to rename *confidence(score_fatal)* as *score_fatal*). In this example, since there are three classification functions (one for each injury type), we also use the *Execute Python* operator to display the classification functions as a table in the Results view.

[5]It should be noted that this accuracy is a biased estimate–it is overly optimistic, because we have used the same data for fitting the classification functions and for estimating the accuracy. Therefore, as with all other models, we need to test performance on a holdout set that includes data that was not involved in estimating the classification functions.

FIGURE 12.8   PROCESS FOR LINEAR DISCRIMINANT ANALYSIS FOR THE THREE-CLASS INJURY EXAMPLE USING THE PYTHON SCRIPTING EXTENSION

Row No.	RushHour	WRK_ZONE	WKDY	INT_HWY	LGTCON_day	LEVEL	SPD_LIM	SUR_COND_dry	TRAF_two_way	WEATHER_adverse
1	1	0	1	1	0	1	70	0	0	1
2	1	0	1	0	0	0	55	0	1	0
3	1	0	0	0	0	0	35	0	0	1
4	1	0	1	0	0	1	35	0	0	1
5	1	0	1	0	0	0	25	0	0	1
6	1	0	1	0	0	0	35	0	0	1
7	1	0	1	0	0	0	60	0	0	0
8	1	0	1	1	0	1	45	1	1	0
9	0	0	1	1	0	0	55	1	0	0
10	1	0	1	1	0	0	70	1	0	0

Row No.	MAX_SEV	prediction(MAX_SEV)	confidence(fatal)	confidence(no-injury)	confidence(non-fatal)	score_fatal	score_no-injury	score_non-fatal
1	no-injury	no-injury	0.003	0.619	0.379	-5.943	-0.465	-0.956
2	non-fatal	no-injury	0.263	0.471	0.266	-1.046	-0.464	-1.037
3	no-injury	no-injury	0.000	0.536	0.464	-7.885	-0.625	-0.769
4	no-injury	no-injury	0.000	0.574	0.426	-8.380	-0.542	-0.841
5	non-fatal	no-injury	0.000	0.587	0.413	-9.837	-0.503	-0.854
6	non-fatal	no-injury	0.000	0.609	0.391	-9.356	-0.460	-0.905
7	no-injury	no-injury	0.174	0.539	0.286	-1.559	-0.429	-1.063
8	non-fatal	non-fatal	0.001	0.477	0.522	-6.550	-0.755	-0.666
9	no-injury	non-fatal	0.002	0.493	0.504	-6.047	-0.725	-0.703
10	non-fatal	no-injury	0.002	0.541	0.457	-6.323	-0.626	-0.794

FIGURE 12.9 CLASSIFICATIONS, MEMBERSHIP PROBABILITIES, AND CLASSIFICATION SCORES FOR THE THREE-CLASS INJURY TRAINING DATASET (FIRST 10 RECORDS), USING PYTHON SCRIPTING EXTENSION

Like linear regression, discriminant analysis searches for the optimal weighting of predictors. In linear regression, weighting is with relation to the numerical target attribute, whereas in discriminant analysis, it is with relation to separating the classes of a categorical target attribute. Both use least squares for estimation, and the resulting estimates are robust to local optima.

In both methods, an underlying assumption is normality. In discriminant analysis, we assume that the predictors are approximately from a multivariate normal distribution. Although this assumption is violated in many practical situations (such as with commonly used binary predictors), the method is surprisingly robust. According to Hastie et al. (2001), the reason might be that data can usually support only simple separation boundaries, such as linear boundaries. However, for continuous attributes that are found to be very skewed (as can be seen through a histogram), transformations such as the log transform can improve performance. In addition, the method's sensitivity to outliers commands exploring the data for extreme values and removing those records from the analysis.

An advantage of discriminant analysis as a classifier (like logistic regression in this respect) is that it provides estimates of single-predictor contributions.[6] This is useful for obtaining a ranking of predictor importance and for attribute selection.

Finally, the method is computationally simple, parsimonious, and especially useful for small datasets. With its parametric form, discriminant analysis makes the most out of the data and is therefore especially useful with small samples (as explained in Section 12.4).

---

[6]Comparing predictor contribution requires normalizing all the predictors before running discriminant analysis. Then, compare each coefficient across the two classification functions: coefficients with large differences indicate a predictor with high separation power.

PROBLEMS

12.1 **Personal Loan Acceptance.** Universal Bank is a relatively young bank growing rapidly in terms of overall customer acquisition. The majority of these customers are liability customers with varying sizes of relationship with the bank. The customer base of asset customers is quite small, and the bank is interested in expanding this base rapidly to bring in more loan business. In particular, it wants to explore ways of converting its liability customers to personal loan customers.

A campaign the bank ran for liability customers last year showed a healthy conversion rate of over 9% successes. This has encouraged the retail marketing department to devise smarter campaigns with better target marketing. The goal of our analysis is to model the previous campaign's customer behavior to analyze what combination of factors makes a customer more likely to accept a personal loan. This will serve as the basis for the design of a new campaign.

The file *UniversalBank.csv* contains data on 5000 customers. The data include customer demographic information (e.g., age, income), the customer's relationship with the bank (e.g., mortgage, securities account), and the customer response to the last personal loan campaign (Personal Loan). Among these 5000 customers, only 480 (= 9.6%) accepted the personal loan that was offered to them in the previous campaign.

Partition the data (60% training and 40% holdout), and then perform a discriminant analysis that models Personal Loan as a function of the remaining predictors (excluding zip code). Remember to turn categorical predictors with more than two categories into numerical attributes with dummy coding first. Also, set the target attribute (Personal Loan) to binominal type, and then use the *Map* operator to map *true* and *false* class labels to *acceptor* and *nonacceptor*, respectively, for more meaningful display of results. Specify the positive class as *acceptor* (personal loan acceptance), and use the default cutoff value of 0.5.

a. Compute summary statistics for the predictors separately for loan acceptors and nonacceptors. For continuous predictors, compute the mean and standard deviation. For categorical predictors, compute the percentages. Are there predictors where the two classes differ substantially?

b. Examine the model performance on the holdout set.

   i. What is the accuracy rate?

   ii. Is one type of misclassification more likely than the other?

   iii. Select three customers who were misclassified as *acceptors* and three who were misclassified as *nonacceptors*. The goal is to determine why they are misclassified. First, examine their probability of being classified as acceptors: is it close to the threshold of 0.5? If not, compare their predictor values to the summary statistics of the two classes to determine why they were misclassified. (*Note:* This part requires use of the *Python Learner* operator from the *Python Scripting* extension.)

c. As in many marketing campaigns, it is more important to identify customers who will accept the offer rather than customers who will not accept it. Therefore, a good model should be especially accurate at detecting acceptors. Examine the lift chart for the holdout set, and interpret it in light of this ranking goal.

d. Compare the results from the discriminant analysis with those from a logistic regression (both with cutoff 0.5 and the same predictors). Examine the confusion matrices, the lift charts. Which method performs better on your holdout set in detecting the acceptors?

e. The bank is planning to continue its campaign by sending its offer to 1000 additional customers. Suppose that the cost of sending the offer is $1 and the profit from an accepted offer is $50. What is the expected profitability of this campaign?

f. The cost of misclassifying a loan acceptor customer as a nonacceptor is much higher than the opposite misclassification cost. To minimize the expected cost of misclassification, should the cutoff value for classification (which is currently at 0.5) be increased or decreased?

12.2 Identifying Good System Administrators. A management consultant is studying the roles played by experience and training in a system administrator's ability to complete a set of tasks in a specified amount of time. In particular, she is interested in discriminating between administrators who are able to complete given tasks within a specified time and those who are not. Data are collected on the performance of 75 randomly selected administrators. They are stored in the file *SystemAdministrators.csv*.

Using these data, the consultant performs a discriminant analysis. The variable Experience measures months of full-time system administrator experience, while Training measures number of relevant training credits. The dependent variable Completed is either *Yes* or *No*, according to whether or not the administrator completed the tasks.

a. Create a scatter plot of Experience vs. Training using color or symbol to differentiate administrators who completed the tasks from those who did not complete them. See if you can identify a line that separates the two classes with minimum misclassification.

b. Run a discriminant analysis with both predictors using the entire dataset as training data. Among those who completed the tasks, what is the percentage of administrators who are classified incorrectly as failing to complete the tasks?

c. Given the decision function shown below with the coefficients for Experience and Training, respectively, compute the classification score for an administrator with 4 months of experience and six credits of training. Based on this classification score, how would you classify this administrator?

```
Coefficients [[1.44469947 0.14427824]]
Intercept [-13.60512707]
```

d. How much experience must be accumulated by an administrator with four training credits before his or her estimated probability of completing the tasks exceeds 0.5? (*Hint*: Use the decision function above with different Experience values.)

e. Compare the classification accuracy of this model to that resulting from a logistic regression with cutoff 0.5.

12.3 Detecting Spam E-mail (from the UCI Machine Learning Repository). A team at Hewlett–Packard collected data on a large number of e-mail messages from their postmaster and personal e-mail for the purpose of finding a classifier that can separate e-mail messages that are *spam* vs. *nonspam* (a.k.a. "ham"). The spam concept is diverse: it includes advertisements for products or websites, "make money fast" schemes, chain letters, pornography, and so on. The definition used here is "unsolicited commercial e-mail." The file *Spambase.csv* contains information on 4601 e-mail messages, among which 1813 are tagged "spam." The predictors include 57 attributes; most of them are the average number of times a certain word (e.g., mail, George) or symbol (e.g., #, !) appears in the e-mail. A few predictors are related to the number and length of capitalized words. (*Tip*: While importing the data in RapidMiner, uncheck the box for "Skip Comments," so attributes following any attribute name ending with the # sign will also be imported correctly.)

a. To reduce the number of predictors to a manageable size, examine how each predictor differs between the *spam* and *nonspam* e-mails by comparing the spam-class average and nonspam-class average. Which are the 11 predictors that appear to vary the most between *spam* and *nonspam* e-mails? From these 11, which words or signs occur more often in spam? (*Hint*: Convert the target attribute to binominal type. Then, consider using the *Aggregate* and *Transpose* operators to compute class averages grouped by Spam. For the transposed data, rename the auto-generated attribute names as spam and nonspam to be meaningful, and then filter out the top extra row added by RapidMiner consisting of the class labels. Then, use the *Guess Types* operator to parse the averages as numeric data type. Lastly, use the *Generate Attributes* operator to compute the absolute difference between the class averages.)

b. Partition the data into training and holdout sets and then perform a discriminant analysis on the training data using only the 11 predictors.

c. If we are interested mainly in detecting spam messages, is this model useful? Use the confusion matrix and lift chart for the holdout set for the evaluation.

d. In the sample, almost 40% of the e-mail messages were tagged as spam. However, suppose that the actual proportion of spam messages in these e-mail accounts is 10%. Compute the intercept of the decision function to account for this information, assuming the original decision function intercept to be -2.124.

e. A spam filter that is based on your model is used, so that only messages that are classified as *nonspam* are delivered, while messages that are classified as *spam* are quarantined. In this case, misclassifying a nonspam e-mail (as spam) has much heftier results. Suppose that the cost of quarantining a nonspam e-mail is 20 times that of not detecting a spam message. Compute the intercept of the decision function to account for these costs (assume that the proportion of spam is reflected correctly by the sample proportion and the original decision function has the intercept -2.124).

CHAPTER 13

Generating, Comparing, and Combining Multiple Models

The previous chapters in this part of the book introduced different supervised methods for prediction and classification. Earlier, in Chapter 5, we learned about evaluating predictive performance, which can be used to compare several models and choose the best one. In this chapter, we look at collections of supervised models. First, we introduce the idea of *automated machine learning*, or *AutoML*, which allows us to automatically train many supervised models and see their resulting performance. While in previous chapters we have shown how to manually tune parameters for each supervised method, AutoML automates the full pipeline from data loading to generating a rank-ordered list of candidate models with automatic parameter tuning. We illustrate this process and its results using RapidMiner's *Auto Model* view and highlight some of its key features. We then discuss how model behavior can be understood by analyzing explanations of predictions and simulating different scenarios for attribute values. Finally, we look at an approach for handling multiple models called *ensembles*, which combines multiple supervised models into a "super-model." Instead of choosing a single predictive model, we can combine several models to achieve improved predictive accuracy. We explain the underlying logic of why ensembles can improve predictive accuracy and introduce popular approaches for combining models, including simple averaging, bagging, boosting, and stacking.

13.1 AUTOMATED MACHINE LEARNING (AUTOML)[1]

Machine learning platforms have now started incorporating features for automating the machine learning workflow from data loading to generating a

---

[1] This and subsequent sections in this chapter copyright ©2019 Datastats, LLC, and Galit Shmueli. Used by permission.

Machine Learning for Business Analytics: Concepts, Techniques and Applications in RapidMiner, First Edition.
Galit Shmueli, Peter C. Bruce, Amit V. Deokar, and Nitin R. Patel
© 2023 John Wiley & Sons, Inc. Published 2023 by John Wiley & Sons, Inc.

rank-ordered list of candidate models with automatic parameter tuning. This is called *automated machine learning* or *AutoML*. RapidMiner provides a special view called *Auto Model* that supports the automated machine learning process. The steps in Auto Model follow the general machine learning steps shown earlier in Figure 2.1 and are discussed next in the context of the personal loan example.

AutoML: Explore and Clean Data

Once the data relevant to the business purpose is imported and loaded, machine learning platforms vary in terms of the integration of data preparation steps as part of the AutoML process. Most platforms support some elementary tasks related to data transformation and feature selection; however, since these steps rightly require domain knowledge application, they are handled separately or in a semi-automatic manner.

In RapidMiner, most data preparation is handled by creating a separate process like we have illustrated in examples thus far in the book. Turbo Prep view can be used in conjunction to speed up data extraction, transformation, and loading. The preprocessed data can be stored back into the repository using the *Store* operator, as shown in Figure 13.1 (top). This data can then be loaded from the Auto Model view, as shown in Figure 13.1 (bottom).

AutoML: Determine Machine Learning Task

In this step, we determine the type of task, supervised or unsupervised, and for a supervised task, we determine the target attribute, the important class (if there is one), and potential misclassification costs (if applicable).

RapidMiner's Auto Model supports three machine learning tasks, namely, (1) Predict, (2) Clusters, and (3) Outliers. The *Predict* task encompasses both classification (including binary and multi-class classification) and prediction problems. The *Clusters* task supports non-hierarchical clustering methods like k-means clustering (see Chapter 16 for details), while the *Outliers* task supports distance-based methods [see *Detect Outlier (Distances)* operator for details] to flag certain observations as outliers. We focus on the *Predict* task in this discussion, used for building supervised models.

In the case of the *Predict* task, a target attribute needs to be identified. In the example shown in Figure 13.2 (top), Personal Loan is selected as the target attribute. If the target attribute is numerical, no configuration is needed for the prediction task. However, Auto Model provides an option of transforming the prediction task to a classification task by automatically binning the target into a user-specified number of classes based on equal ranges or equal sizes for the classes. If the target attribute is categorical, a classification task can be configured further, as shown in Figure 13.2 (bottom), by:

1. Defining a cost matrix, if needed, to incorporate asymmetric misclassification costs (see Section 5.3).

FIGURE 13.1   (TOP) STORING PREPARED DATA. (BOTTOM) LOADING DATA WITH AUTO MODEL

2. Specifying the class of highest interest, i.e., positive class.

3. Optionally, mapping the label classes to new values—useful for renaming or reducing the target attribute categories or to transform a multi-class classification task to a binary classification task.

AutoML: Choose Attributes and Machine Learning Methods

At this step, we select the attributes to be used as predictors in the supervised model. As is the case when fitting individual models, the decision should be guided by considerations of data quality and regulatory/ethical requirements (in some applications some attributes are forbidden, such as using gender in loan applications in the United States). We also select the machine learning algorithms we'd like to run. Considerations include potential runtime (for example, some

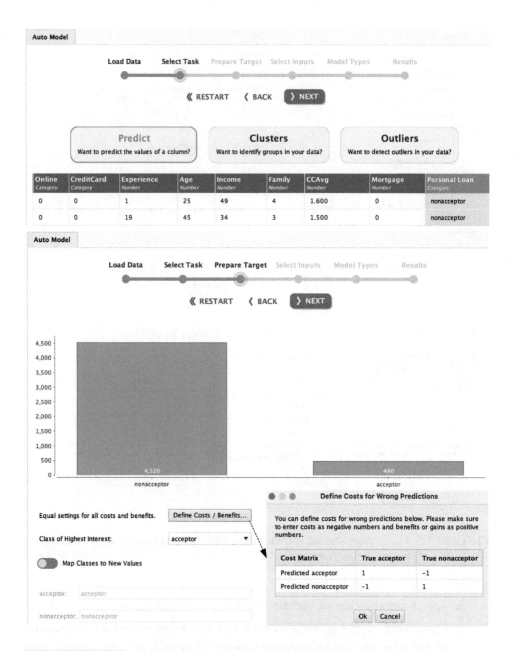

FIGURE 13.2   (TOP) SELECTING "PREDICT" MACHINE LEARNING TASK WITH PERSONAL LOAN AS TARGET. (BOTTOM) PREPARING TARGET WITH AUTO MODEL

algorithms might take much longer to train and/or to score) and the suitability of the algorithm to the type and size of our data and our goal. For example, the k-nearest neighbors algorithm requires a large training sample; simple classification and regression trees are not stable and can result in different trees for slightly different data; linear and logistic regression without regularization have trouble with highly correlated predictors.

In RapidMiner, for any machine learning task, the *Select Input* step in Auto Model uses a traffic-light metaphor[2] to summarize data quality characteristics (*ID-ness*, *Stability*, *Missing*, and *Text-ness*) for each attribute—see Figure 13.3 (top). RapidMiner internally uses the *Quality Measures* operator for this purpose (see Section 3.3 in Chapter 3). Additionally, *Correlation* with the target attribute is indicated for the *Predict* task. Certain attributes may be flagged red because of high stability, high ID-ness, high correlation with the label, etc. (the reason is explained by hovering over the red icon). By default, "red" attributes are deselected but can be overridden by the data scientist. Also, Auto Model uses heuristics to flag any attributes that may potentially cause ethical or legal problems. For example, Age is marked with a warning sign in Figure 13.3 (top) for reconsideration by the data scientist. The data scientist (and domain experts on the team) should consider data quality considerations, target leakage possibilities, and legal/ethical considerations before finalizing feature selection.

Based on the machine learning task and heuristics such as the size of the data, Auto Model's *Model Types* step preselects a set of candidate supervised algorithms, as shown in Figure 13.3 (bottom). For some algorithms, it is useful to select the option for regularization (e.g., for Generalized Linear Model) or optimization (e.g., for Decision Tree) to achieve better model performance at the potential cost of longer runtimes during model training. Based on these options, Auto Model performs model tuning to select optimal model parameters using grid search. The final algorithm choices can be controlled by the data scientist.

AutoML: Evaluate Model Performance

AutoML procedures will typically display the performance of each trained model on the validation set, to allow comparison across algorithms. In RapidMiner, model performance and the model details can be understood from the *Results* step in Auto Model. The Overview dashboard shows a comparative view of models based on their performance on the validation set and on their runtimes. Auto Model splits the data into 60% training and 40% validation sets, and the validation performance is reported. Model performance metrics depend on whether it is a

---

[2]The red/yellow/green bubbles denote the following: **red bubble**: attribute with poor quality—possible reasons may be: (1) high missing: more than 70% of all values are missing, (2) high ID-ness: practically looks like an ID with as many unique values as the records, (3) high stability: more than 90% of the values are constant, and (4) correlation: lower than 0.0001% or higher than 95% correlation with the target attribute, **yellow bubble**: attribute with low quality—possible reasons may be: (1) high ID-ness, combined with high Text-ness: more than 85% of values are distinct text values, (2) correlation: lower than 0.01% or higher than 40% correlation with the target attribute (low correlation may indicate no predictive value, whereas high correlation may indicate a possibility of target leakage), **green bubble**: no data quality issues identified.

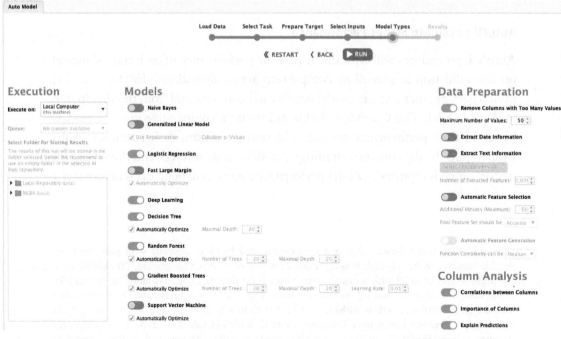

FIGURE 13.3   (TOP) SELECTING PREDICTORS AND
(BOTTOM) SELECTING MODEL TYPES WITH AUTO MODEL

classification or prediction task (see Chapter 5 for details). Figure 13.4 shows the dashboard for the personal loan classification example. We observe that the decision tree has the best accuracy (as well as the best precision, recall, and f-measure), while random forest and gradient boosted trees are close behind but are computationally intensive. Interestingly, the simple decision tree outperforms the more complex tree models. Figure 13.5 shows the validation performance metrics and the confusion matrix for the decision tree model.

AutoML: Model Deployment

Model deployment is increasingly becoming an integrated feature of AutoML. In RapidMiner's Auto Model, for instance, the "best" model selected by the data scientist can be deployed for production through immediate access to the *Deploy* feature. Models may be deployed locally on the machine or remotely on a web server. For local deployment, a local repository folder needs to be specified. For remote deployment, RapidMiner AI Hub has to be pre-configured, and a connection to it has to be set up from within RapidMiner Studio. To enable a monitoring feature to collect model scoring statistics gathered over time requires a setup of a database server. Once a model has been deployed, it can be accessed as a web service and can be integrated with operational systems for real-time scoring and decision making.

Advantages and Weaknesses of Automated Machine Learning

Automated machine learning functionality, such as RapidMiner's Auto Model, can be a valuable tool for beginners and advanced data scientists. For beginners, it can provide a useful starting point for quickly experimenting with a dataset for a business problem by building predictive models that can then be used for further understanding and learning. For advanced users, it can save time in creating common machine learning workflows by relying on automated model selection and tuning for getting quick insights into a business problem before spending extensive efforts on fine-tuning models.

RapidMiner's Auto Model has the additional advantage of providing transparency in modeling. By exporting an auto-generated process from Auto Model, the data scientist can spend more efforts in data understanding, preparation, feature generation, and so on. Also, the data scientist can focus on further fine tuning the models of interest. For example, Auto Model optimizes a decision tree by only changing the *maximal depth* parameter. What would be the effect of changing other parameters such as *minimal leaf size*? While Auto Model speeds up the general model tuning process by considering important model parameters, depending on the problem context or the nature of the data, the data scientist would need to consider further model tuning.

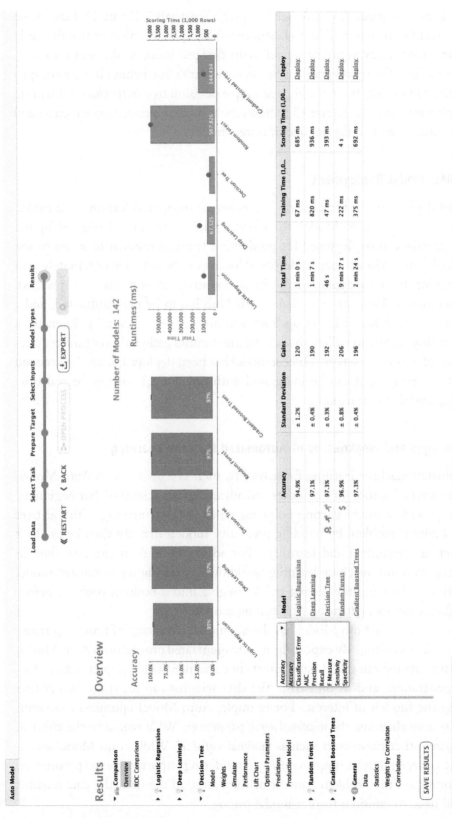

FIGURE 13.4   OVERVIEW OF AUTO MODEL RESULTS: COMPARING ACCURACY AND RUNTIME OF CANDIDATE MODELS (PERSONAL LOAN DATA)

Decision Tree – Performance

Profits

Profits from Model: 1,353   Profits for Best Option (nonacceptor): 1,161   Gain: 192   [Show Costs / Benefits...]

Performances

Criterion	Value	Standard Deviation
Accuracy	97.3%	± 0.3%
Classification Error	2.7%	± 0.3%
AUC	99.0%	± 0.8%
Precision	80.1%	± 5.3%
Recall	94.9%	± 4.8%
F Measure	86.7%	± 2.6%
Sensitivity	94.9%	± 4.8%
Specificity	97.6%	± 0.6%

Confusion Matrix

	true nonacceptor	true acceptor	class precision
pred. nonacceptor	1264	7	99.45%
pred. acceptor	31	127	80.38%
class recall	97.61%	94.78%	

FIGURE 13.5   DECISION TREE MODEL PERFORMANCE: GENERATED WITH AUTO MODEL (PERSONAL LOAN DATA)

The major disadvantage of automated machine learning is its deceptive ability to hide attention to key business-related details and questions. Since the AutoML process lends itself to importing and loading data and generating results fairly quickly, data scientists may not spend adequate time in understanding the nuances of data, exploring and preparing it for the modeling phase, which can lead to garbage-in, garbage-out outcomes, and thoughtless models.

13.2 EXPLAINING MODEL PREDICTIONS

When comparing predictive models, an important aspect is how different predictor attributes affect the predicted values. This is especially important in applications where predicted values must be justified, such as in loan and judicial decisions. Uncovering the effect of predictors on the predicted values is called *explainablility*. "Explaining" predictions provides insight on (1) how the predicted score (e.g., predicted value, class, or probability) is affected by the values of the predictor attributes, and (2) how changes to the values of predictor attributes might change the predicted score. The first is a descriptive question, while the second is a causal question. There are different "explainability" methods, each with its strengths and weaknesses. In the following, we briefly describe two approaches for explaining individual record predictions: LIME and counterfactual explanations. Chapter 22 describes additional approaches, with an emphasis on global explanations that cover the entire dataset.

Explaining Model Predictions: LIME

Given a predicted score for a certain record, the data scientist, decision maker, or even the person being scored might ask "What predictor attributes contributed to this record's predicted score?" The originators of the LIME (Local Interpretable Model-agnostic Explanations) approach described their goal of explaining a prediction as "presenting textual or visual artifacts that provide qualitative understanding of the relationship between the [features ...] and the model's prediction" (Ribeiro et al., 2016). The LIME algorithm generates additional training data around the record to be explained, then generates predicted values for these synthetic data, and subsequently builds a linear regression model on the newly created dataset. Because the linear regression model is trained only on the record and its created "neighbors," it is called a *local* model. We note that even if the overall global relationship between the attributes and the predictions is nonlinear, the *local* linear relationship is useful when the objective is to explain the predictions.

RapidMiner provides an *Explain Predictions* operator that implements the LIME approach.[3] Its explanations are computed as follows:

1. Copy a record, and randomly perturb (slightly change) each attribute value in the copy, thus creating a neighboring record.

2. Use the predictive model to compute a prediction, or a propensity for a class, for the neighboring record.

3. Repeat the above steps to create a set of neighboring records and predictions.

4. Within this set of neighboring records, calculate the correlation between each attribute and the predicted values (or propensities for classification). These are called "local correlations." These local correlations tell you how much individual attributes contribute to the prediction for a given record.

5. Repeat this process for all the records. Note that the local correlations, and thus the information about attribute importance, will differ from record to record.

It may seem counter-intuitive that useful information can be derived from synthetically generated data. Think of the model as a black box, and you are

---

[3]RapidMiner's Explain Predictions algorithm differs from the LIME algorithm in two ways: (1) the Explain Predictions operator algorithm works for both categorical and numerical predictors and target attributes, and (2) the weights are calculated in linear time, making it computationally faster than LIME.

making small changes to the inputs, observing the output, and drawing conclusions about how the inputs are correlated to the output. These local correlation values for each record in the validation set represent local, model-specific attribute weights in its neighborhood, and in RapidMiner they are color-coded green for positive correlation values or red for negative correlation values.

The *Explain Predictions* operator can be used with any supervised model. Auto Model also internally invokes this operator in generating its results. Figure 13.6 (top) shows six sample predictions for the validation set, along with their attributes which are color-coded to provide an "explanation." These explanations are generated with the *Explain Predictions* option chosen in Auto Model's *Model Types* step (see Figure 13.3). Green color marks attributes that support the prediction, and red color marks attributes that contradict the prediction, irrespective of the (mis)classification or accuracy of the prediction. For example, for the validation customer in Row No. 1, who was classified as *nonacceptor*, the value of Education = 1 supports the classification ("similar" customers with Education = 1 are more likely to be nonacceptors), while CD Account = 0 contradicts this classification ("similar" customers with CD Account = 0 are more likely to be acceptors). Such granular prediction explanations can be a valuable tool for conveying model predictions to stakeholders and building their trust in predictive models, particularly in the case of "black box" models like deep learning.

In addition to explanations of record-specific predictions, we can compute "global" model-specific weights by computing the averages of the local attribute weights on the validation set. While these weights give us a good idea of important attributes and can be computed for any modeling algorithm, it is important to recognize their dependency on the validation set in terms of considering their generalizability. Figure 13.6 (bottom) shows these weights for the decision tree model in the loan example. We see that across all the validation records (and their generated "neighbors"), Education has the strongest average correlation with the predicted propensity of loan acceptance.

We note that the record-level interpretability measures are most important for nonlinear and complex relationships, where, say, having a CD account may be very important as a predictor for some customers, but unimportant for others. In contrast, the average weights capture the overall importance of predictors for a specific model when considered in the context of a given validation set.

Counterfactual Explanations of Predictions: What-If Scenarios

Given a record's predicted score and its predictor values, another important question for decision makers and the scored individuals is "What predictor values would have led to a better predicted score?" This causal question asks a counterfactual (what-if) question. Counterfactual explanations of predictions use a "what-if" approach to answer questions such as "What changes to the predictor value(s) would have led to a different classification?" Stated formally,

Decision Tree – Predictions

Row No.	Personal Loan	prediction(Personal Loan)	confidence(nonacceptor)	confidence(acceptor)	cost
1	nonacceptor	nonacceptor	1	0	1
2	nonacceptor	nonacceptor	1	0	1
3	nonacceptor	acceptor	0.204	0.796	0.591
4	nonacceptor	nonacceptor	1	0	1
5	nonacceptor	nonacceptor	1	0	1
6	acceptor	acceptor	0.204	0.796	0.591

Row No.	Education	Securities Account	CD Account	Online	CreditCard	Experience	Age	Income	Family
1	1	0	0	0	0	15	39	11	1
2	2	0	0	1	0	27	53	72	2
3	3	1	0	0	0	23	48	114	2
4	1	1	0	0	0	41	67	112	1
5	3	0	0	1	1	30	60	22	1
6	3	0	0	0	0	14	38	130	4

Decision Tree – Weights

Attribute	Weight
Education	0.185
Age	0.042
Experience	0.041
Income	0.033
Mortgage	0.031
Securities Account	0.026
CD Account	0.025
CreditCard	0.021
Online	0.019
Family	0.015
CCAvg	0.013

FIGURE 13.6   (TOP) SAMPLE PREDICTIONS FOR VALIDATION SET. (BOTTOM) "GLOBAL" MODEL-SPECIFIC WEIGHTS FOR DECISION TREE MODEL: GENERATED WITH AUTO MODEL (PERSONAL LOAN DATA)

"a counterfactual explanation of a prediction describes the smallest change to the feature values that changes the prediction to a predefined output" (Molnar, 2022).[4] Counterfactual explanations are also used in recommender systems to help explain why a user has received a particular recommendation (e.g., "you received this restaurant's ad because you often click on photos of food") and what might have led to a different recommendation (e.g., "had you 'liked' more posts about pets, you would have received an ad for pet accessories").

---

[4]See https://christophm.github.io/interpretable-ml-book/counterfactual.html

RapidMiner provides a *Model Simulator* operator that implements such an approach. This operator is available for every supervised model, as well as in Auto Model, which internally invokes this operator as part of its results. Logically, it functions in a manner similar to the prediction explanations discussed earlier but allows the data scientist to run "what-if" scenarios with various attribute combinations. Here, each scenario is equivalent to a single record.

Figure 13.7 (top), produced by Auto Model for the decision tree model, shows the interface for entering data in the simulator (the default values for numerical attributes are average values, and for nominal attributes they are the most frequent category). The user can change the predictor values and view how such changes affect the predicted score. For classification problems, the model scores the data and computes the propensity for each class and shows the classes bar chart in the right panel. In this example, the propensity that this record belongs to the *acceptor* class is 80%. For prediction problems, the predicted value is shown in the right panel. Like the *Explain Predictions* operator, the simulator displays "important factors," which are the LIME-based local, model-specific attribute weights, with the red/green color-coding.

In addition to manually changing predictor values, the model simulator supports an optimization feature with the "Optimize" button underneath the simulator data entry.[5] This allows the data scientist to ask questions such as "How can I maximize the propensity of loan acceptance given certain constraints?" Constraints can be generic (e.g., staying within two standard deviations around average values of numerical attributes), or can include specific attribute-based constraints (e.g., Age = 45). In the example shown in Figure 13.7, age is held constant at 45, and we see the attribute values that maximize the propensity of *acceptor* given this age. Note that because of the possible inclusion of constraints, and/or the need to fully maximize the target attribute value (in case of prediction) or maximize the propensity of the positive class (in case of classification), these optimal feature values computed by RapidMiner's simulator are not necessarily the smallest feature changes as mentioned earlier in the formal definition of a counterfactual explanation. The resulting attribute values can serve as a guide for business actions, particularly those attributes that can be influenced through business initiatives in a legally compliant and ethically responsible manner. For example, the counterfactual information may indicate that having a credit card account is important for some customers' acceptance of personal loan offers. In such cases, the marketing of the loan might be bundled or associated with credit card upgrades or other offers. Or, if family size seems to be associated with loan acceptance for certain other customers, an offer could be made to them with

---

[5]The Optimize button is based on RapidMiner's *Prescriptive Analytics* operator and is shown in Figure 13.7 (bottom).

Decision Tree – Simulator

FIGURE 13.7   DECISION TREE MODEL SIMULATOR: OPTIMIZED FOR MAXIMIZING PROPENSITY OF ACCEPTOR CLASS FOR AGE = 45 (PERSONAL LOAN DATA) family-centric messaging. On the other hand, some initiatives may run afoul of rules, for example, using gender information to boost response rates.

13.3 ENSEMBLES

AutoML is one way to harness the power of multiple models. Ensembles, in which predictions from multiple models are joined together, are another. Ensembles played a major role in the million-dollar Netflix Prize contest that started in 2006. At the time, Netflix, the largest DVD rental service in the United States, wanted to improve their movie recommendation system (from www.netflixprize.com):

> Netflix is all about connecting people to the movies they love. To help customers find those movies, we've developed our world-class movie recommendation system: Cinematch^{SM}...And while Cinematch is doing pretty well, it can always be made better.

In a bold move, the company decided to share a large amount of data on movie ratings by their users and set up a contest, open to the public, aimed at improving their recommendation system:

> We provide you with a lot of anonymous rating data, and a prediction accuracy bar that is 10% better than what Cinematch can do on the same training data set.

During the contest, an active leader-board showed the results of the competing teams. An interesting behavior started appearing: different teams joined forces to create combined, or *ensemble* predictions, which proved more accurate than the individual predictions. The winning team, called "BellKor's Pragmatic Chaos", combined results from the "BellKor" and "Big Chaos" teams alongside additional members. In a 2010 article in *Chance* magazine, the Netflix Prize winners described the power of their ensemble approach:

> An early lesson of the competition was the value of combining sets of predictions from multiple models or algorithms. If two prediction sets achieved similar RMSEs, it was quicker and more effective to simply average the two sets than to try to develop a new model that incorporated the best of each method. Even if the RMSE for one set was much worse than the other, there was almost certainly a linear combination that improved on the better set.

Why Ensembles Can Improve Predictive Power

The principle of combining methods is popular for reducing risk. For example, in finance, portfolios are created for reducing investment risk. The return from a portfolio is typically less risky, because the variation is smaller than each of the individual components.

In predictive modeling, "risk" is equivalent to variation in prediction error. The more our prediction errors vary, the more volatile our predictive model.

Consider predictions from two different models for a set of n records. $e_{1,i}$ is the prediction error for the ith record by method 1, and $e_{2,i}$ is the prediction error for the same record by method 2.

Suppose that each model produces prediction errors that are, on average, zero (for some records the model over-predicts and for some it under-predicts, but on average the error is zero):

$$E(e_{1,i}) = E(e_{2,i}) = 0.$$

If, for each record, we take an average of the two predictions: $\overline{y}_i = \frac{\hat{y}_{1,i} + \hat{y}_{2,i}}{2}$, then the expected mean error will also be zero:

$$
\begin{aligned}
E\left(y_i - \overline{y}_i\right) &= E\left(y_i - \frac{\hat{y}_{1,i} + \hat{y}_{2,i}}{2}\right) \quad (13.1) \\
&= E\left(\frac{y_i - \hat{y}_{1,i}}{2} + \frac{y_i - \hat{y}_{2,i}}{2}\right) = E\left(\frac{e_{1,i} + e_{2,i}}{2}\right) = 0.
\end{aligned}
$$

This means that the ensemble has the same mean error as the individual models. Now let us examine the variance of the ensemble's prediction errors:

$$\mathrm{Var}\left(\frac{e_{1,i} + e_{2,i}}{2}\right) = \frac{1}{4}\left(\mathrm{Var}(e_{1,i}) + \mathrm{Var}(e_{2,i})\right) + \frac{1}{4} \times 2\mathrm{Cov}\left(e_{1,i}, e_{2,i}\right).$$
(13.2)

This variance can be lower than each of the individual variances $\mathrm{Var}(e_{1,i})$ and $\mathrm{Var}(e_{2,i})$ under some circumstances. A key component is the covariance (or equivalently, correlation) between the two prediction errors. The case of no correlation leaves us with a quantity that can be smaller than each of the individual variances. The variance of the average prediction error will be even smaller when the two prediction errors are negatively correlated.

THE WISDOM OF CROWDS

In his book *The Wisdom of Crowds*, James Surowiecki recounts how Francis Galton, a prominent statistician from the 19th century, watched a contest at a county fair in England. The contest's objective was to guess the weight of an ox. Individual contest entries were highly variable, but the mean of all the estimates was surprisingly accurate—within 1% of the true weight of the ox. On balance, the errors from multiple guesses tended to cancel one another out. You can think of the output of a predictive model as a more informed version of these guesses. Averaging together multiple guesses will yield a more precise answer than the vast majority of the individual guesses. Note that in Galton's story, there were a few (lucky) individuals who scored better than the average. An ensemble estimate will not always be more accurate than all the individual estimates in all cases, but it will be more accurate most of the time.

In summary, using an average of two predictions can potentially lead to smaller error variance and therefore better predictive power. These results generalize to more than two methods; you can combine results from multiple prediction methods or classifiers.

Simple Averaging or Voting

The simplest approach for creating an ensemble is to combine the predictions, classifications, or propensities from multiple models. For example, we might have a linear regression model, a regression tree, and a k-NN algorithm. We use each of the three methods to score, say, a test set. We then combine the three sets of results.

The three models can also be variations that use the same algorithm. For example, we might have three linear regression models, each using a different set of predictors.

Combining Predictions   In prediction tasks, where the target attribute is numerical, we can combine the predictions from the different methods simply by taking an average. In the above example, for each record in the test set, we have three predictions (one from each model). The ensemble prediction is then the average of the three values.

One alternative to a simple average is taking the median prediction, which would be less affected by extreme predictions. Another possibility is computing a weighted average, where weights are proportional to a quantity of interest. For instance, weights can be proportional to the accuracy of the model, or if different data sources are used, the weights can be proportional to the quality of the data.

Ensembles for prediction are useful not only in cross-sectional prediction, but also in time series forecasting (see Chapters 17–19). In forecasting, the same approach of combining future forecasts from multiple methods can lead to more precise predictions. One example is the weather forecasting mobile app Dark Sky (formerly Forecast.io, www.darksky.net/app) which described their algorithm as follows:

> Forecast.io is backed by a wide range of data sources, which are aggregated together statistically to provide the most accurate forecast possible for a given location.

Combining Classifications   In the case of classification, combining the results from multiple classifiers can be done using "voting": for each record, we have multiple classifications. A simple rule would be to choose the most popular class among these classifications. For example, we might use a classification tree, a naive Bayes classifier, and discriminant analysis for classifying a binary target attribute. For each record, we then generate three predicted classes. Simple voting would choose the most common class among the three.

As in prediction, we can assign heavier weights to scores from some models, based on considerations such as model accuracy or data quality. This would be done by setting a "majority rule" that is different from 50%.

RapidMiner provides the *Vote* nested operator in which specific model operators (e.g., *Linear Regression, Decision Tree*) can be embedded. The *Vote* operator can then be used like any other modeling operator. This operator combines predictions by simple averaging and combines classifications by voting.

Combining Propensities   Similar to predictions, propensities can be combined by taking a simple (or weighted) average. Recall that some algorithms, such as naive Bayes (see Chapter 8), produce biased propensities and should therefore not be simply averaged with propensities from other methods.

To illustrate the idea of combining propensities, consider the five models generated with Auto Model earlier (see Figure 13.4): (1) logistic regression, (2) deep learning, (3) decision tree, (4) random forest, and (5) gradient boosted trees. We can export the predictions for the validation set from each of these models from the respective Auto Model "Predictions" result pane. Figure 13.8 (top) shows a process that loads these predictions and combines them in a single data set (within the *Join Data Process* subprocess), keeping only the acceptor class propensities for each model (and, of course, the record ID). Then, using the *Generate Attribute* operator, we compute the average of these propensities for each record, creating the new attribute *pred_prob_avg*. We can either use this new averaged propensity directly (e.g., in ranking tasks or ROC curves), or else we can use it to generate classifications by incorporating a threshold. For example, we can generate another attribute *pred_accept_avg* by applying the condition *pred_prob_avg* $\geq$ 0.5 (that is, using a threshold of 0.5). The ensemble model's classification performance using *pred_accept_avg* is shown in Figure 13.8 (middle) along with sample predictions in Figure 13.8 (bottom). Note that the performance of this ensemble model slightly exceeds the performance of each of the five models shown earlier in Figure 13.4.

Bagging

Another form of ensembles is based on averaging across multiple random data samples. *Bagging*, short for "bootstrap aggregating," comprises two steps:

1. Generating multiple random samples (by sampling with replacement from the original data)—this method is called "bootstrap sampling."

2. Running an algorithm on each sample and producing scores.

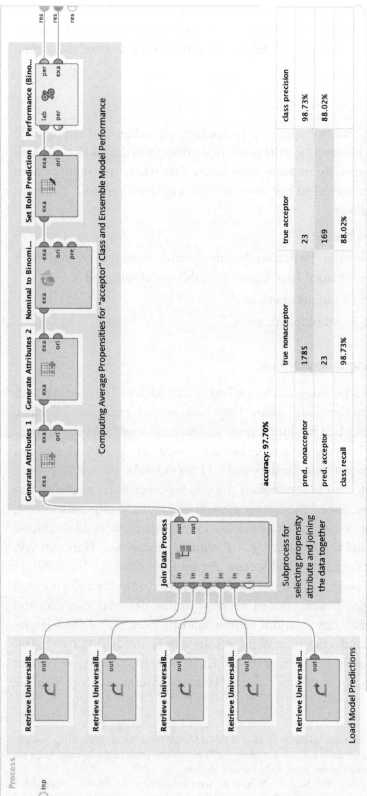

FIGURE 13.8

(TOP) PROCESS FOR COMBINING MODEL PROPENSITIES BY SIMPLE AVERAGING (MIDDLE) ENSEMBLE MODEL PERFORMANCE AND (BOTTOM) SAMPLE PREDICTIONS AND PROPENSITIES FOR VALIDATION DATA (PERSONAL LOAN DATA)

Bagging improves the performance stability of a model and helps avoid over-fitting by separately modeling different data samples and then combining the results. It is therefore especially useful for algorithms such as trees and neural networks.

Boosting

Boosting is a slightly different approach to creating ensembles that sequentially builds better models by leveraging the prediction errors from the previous model. Here, the goal is to directly improve areas in the data where our model makes errors, by forcing the model to pay more attention to those records. The steps in boosting are as follows:

1. Fit a model to the data.
2. Draw a sample from the data so that misclassified records (or records with large prediction errors) have higher probabilities of selection.
3. Fit the model to the new sample.
4. Repeat Steps 2–3 multiple times.

Bagging and Boosting in RapidMiner

Although bagging and boosting can be applied to any machine learning method, most applications are for trees, where they have proved extremely effective. In Chapter 9, we described random forests, an ensemble based on bagged trees, and gradient boosted trees, an ensemble based on boosted trees. We illustrated a random forest implementation for the personal loan example. RapidMiner has a variety of operators to combine classifiers (models for predicting categorical target attributes) and regressors (models for predicting numerical target attributes), including bagging or boosting. The ensemble modeling operators can be found in the Operators panel under *Modeling > Predictive > Ensembles*. Here, we will demonstrate this for decision tree classifiers. Figure 13.9 shows the RapidMiner process to produce a bagged tree using the *Bagging* nested operator and a boosted tree using the *Bayesian Boosting* nested operator for the personal loan data and using them to generate classifications for the validation set.[6] The *Data Preprocessing* subprocess includes the same steps[7] as shown in Figure 10.3 (Chapter 10). The performance output is shown in Figure 13.10. In this example, we see that bagging and boosting both produce slightly better validation accuracy than the single tree.

---

[6] In this chapter, we use the term *validation set* instead of *holdout set* since we are comparing models. Ideally, a separate holdout set should be used to assess the "best" model prior to deployment since we are using that validation set to select, tune, and combine models.

[7] One exception is that we do not include the *Nominal to Numerical* operator for dummy coding, since the *Decision Tree* operator can work well with nominal attributes directly.

FIGURE 13.9   RAPIDMINER PROCESS SHOWING EXAMPLE OF BAGGING AND BOOSTING CLASSIFICATION TREES (PERSONAL LOAN DATA)

(a) Decision Tree Performance on Validation Set

accuracy: 96.65%

	true nonacceptor	true acceptor	class precision
pred. nonacceptor	1788	47	97.44%
pred. acceptor	20	145	87.88%
class recall	98.89%	75.52%	

(b) Bagged Tree Performance on Validation Set

accuracy: 96.95%

	true nonacceptor	true acceptor	class precision
pred. nonacceptor	1791	44	97.60%
pred. acceptor	17	148	89.70%
class recall	99.06%	77.08%	

(c) Boosted Tree Performance on Validation Set

accuracy: 97.70%

	true nonacceptor	true acceptor	class precision
pred. nonacceptor	1772	10	99.44%
pred. acceptor	36	182	83.49%
class recall	98.01%	94.79%	

FIGURE 13.10   PERFORMANCE OF (TOP) SINGLE TREE, (MIDDLE) BAGGED TREES, AND (BOTTOM) BOOSTED TREES (PERSONAL LOAN DATA)

Interestingly, we also observe that the recall of the *acceptor* class has improved quite a bit by using a boosted tree (by trading off some reduction in *acceptor* class precision). This is often observed in boosted ensemble models because of the learning occurring based on prediction errors made in the previous training iteration. As such, this technique is particularly valuable when the data is unbalanced, with a smaller proportion of positive class records (e.g., credit card fraud detection).

Stacking

Yet another form of ensembles is based on the idea of taking heterogeneous "base learners," i.e., different model algorithms, and then using their predictions as predictors for training a meta-learner model. This is called *stacking*, short for "stacked generalization." RapidMiner provides the *Stacking* nested operator for this approach. The steps in stacking are:

1. Fit different models to the data; these are called "base learners."
2. Create a new dataset containing just the predictions from each model and the target attribute (i.e., omitting the original predictors).
3. Fit a new meta-model called a "stacking model learner," to the new dataset.

Advantages and Weaknesses of Ensembles

Combining scores from multiple models is aimed at generating more precise predictions (lowering the prediction error variance). The ensemble approach is most useful when the combined models generate prediction errors that are negatively associated, but it can also be useful when the correlation is low. Ensembles can use simple averaging, weighted averaging, voting, medians, etc. Models can be based on the same algorithm or on different algorithms, using the same sample or different samples. Ensembles have become a major strategy for participants in machine learning contests (e.g., Kaggle), where the goal is to optimize some predictive measure. In that sense, ensembles also provide an operational way to obtain solutions with high predictive power in a fast way, by engaging multiple teams of "data crunchers" working in parallel and combining their results.

Ensembles that are based on different data samples help avoid overfitting. However, remember that you can also overfit the data with an ensemble if you tweak it (e.g., choosing the "best" weights when using a weighted average).

The major disadvantage of an ensemble is the resources that it requires: computationally, as well as in terms of software availability and the analyst's skill and time investment. Ensembles that combine results from different algorithms require developing each of the models and evaluating them. Boosting-type and bagging-type ensembles do not require such effort, but they do have a computational cost (although boosting can be parallelized easily). Ensembles that rely on multiple data sources require collecting and maintaining multiple data sources. And finally, ensembles are "black box" methods, in that the relationship between the predictors and the target attribute usually becomes nontransparent.

13.4 SUMMARY

In practice, the methods discussed earlier in this book are often used not in isolation, but as building blocks in an analytic process whose goal is always to inform and provide insight.

In this chapter, we looked at two ways that multiple models are deployed and at ways in which predicted values can be investigated. Through automated machine learning, the machine learning process of selecting, applying, and tuning different models for better model performance can be made more efficient, while focusing on evaluating the results and comparing the models. In ensembles, multiple models are weighted and combined to produce improved predictions. As models and the modeling process become more complex and less transparent, decision makers and data scientists need tools for understanding individual predicted scores and how they relate to predictor values. We described two popular approaches—LIME and counterfactual explanations—for explaining predicted scores.

PROBLEMS

13.1 **Acceptance of Consumer Loan.** Universal Bank has begun a program to encourage its existing customers to borrow via a consumer loan program. The bank has promoted the loan to 5000 customers, of whom 480 accepted the offer. The data are available in file *UniversalBank.csv*. The bank now wants to develop a model to predict which customers have the greatest probability of accepting the loan, to reduce promotion costs and send the offer only to a subset of its customers.

We will develop several models and then combine them in an ensemble. The models we will use are (1) logistic regression, (2) k-nearest neighbors with $k = 5$, (3) classification trees, and (4) naive Bayes. Use the default values of each model operator in RapidMiner. Preprocess the data using the steps shown in Figure 10.3 (Chapter 10)— one exception is that we do not include the *Nominal to Numerical* operator for dummy coding, since these model operators can work well with nominal attributes directly. Partition the data: 60% training and 40% validation.

a. Fit models to the data using the following modeling operators: (1) *Logistic Regression*, (2) *k-NN* (with $k = 5$), (3) *Decision Tree*, and (4) *Naive Bayes*. Use Personal Loan as the target attribute. Report the validation confusion matrix, accuracy, precision, recall, and AUC for each of the models.

b. Report the first 10 records for the validation data for each model showing the predicted class and propensity (i.e., confidence) values for the positive class. For these records, manually compute and report the confusion matrix and accuracy for each of the models. Taking a majority vote of predicted class by each model, manually compute and report the predicted class for these records. Finally, compute and report the confusion matrix and accuracy based on the majority vote predictions for these records.

c. Use the *Vote* operator to create an ensemble model that is based on the majority vote of predicted target values by the four models. Report the validation confusion matrix, accuracy, precision, recall, and AUC for the ensemble model.

d. Report the first 10 records for the validation data for the ensemble model showing the predicted class and propensity (i.e., confidence) values for the positive class, and manually compute the confusion matrix and accuracy based on these records. Do the ensemble vote model predictions, confusion matrix, and accuracy match with the manually computed predictions earlier?

e. Compare the model performance metrics for the four individual models and the ensemble model.

13.2 **eBay Auctions—Boosting and Bagging.** The file *eBayAuctions.csv* contains information on 1972 auctions that transacted on eBay.com during May–June 2004. The goal is to use these data to build predictive models that will classify auctions as competitive or noncompetitive. A *competitive auction* is defined as an auction with at least two bids placed on the item auctioned. The data include attributes that describe the item (auction category), the seller (his/her eBay rating), and the auction terms that the seller selected (auction duration, opening price, currency, day of week of auction close). In addition, we have the price at which the auction closed. The task is to predict whether or not the auction will be competitive.

Data Preprocessing. Only those attributes that can be used for predicting the outcome of a new auction should be considered. Convert attribute *Duration* into a categorical attribute (nominal type). Convert attribute *Competitive?* to binominal type, and assign it the appropriate role in RapidMiner. Consider mapping class labels to meaningful labels using the *Map* operator as well. Split the data into training (60%) and validation (40%) datasets.

a. Run a classification tree, using the default settings of *Decision Tree* operator. Looking at the validation set, what is the overall accuracy? What is the lift on the first decile? [*Hint*: Use the *Lift Chart (Simple)* operator].

b. Run a boosted tree with the same predictors (use the *Bayesian Boosting* operator with *Decision Tree* operator as the base estimator). For the validation set, what is the overall accuracy? What is the lift on the first decile?

c. Run a bagged tree with the same predictors (use the *Bagging* operator with *Decision Tree* operator as the base estimator). For the validation set, what is the overall accuracy? What is the lift on the first decile?

d. Run a random forest (use the *Random Forest* operator). Compare the bagged tree to the random forest in terms of validation accuracy and lift on first decile. How are the two methods conceptually different?

13.3 **Predicting Delayed Flights (Boosting).** The file *FlightDelays.csv* contains information on all commercial flights departing the Washington, DC area and arriving at New York during January 2004. For each flight, there is information on the departure and arrival airports, the distance of the route, the scheduled time and date of the flight, and so on. The attribute that we are trying to predict is whether or not a flight is delayed. A delay is defined as an arrival that is at least 15 minutes later than scheduled.

Data Preprocessing. Transform attribute day of week (DAY_WEEK) info a categorical attribute.

Bin the scheduled departure time into eight bins. Use these and all other attributes as predictors (excluding DAY_OF_MONTH, FL_DATE, FL_NUM, and TAIL_NUM). Transform the target attribute to a binominal type, and set its appropriate role. By using the *Remap Binominals* operator for the target attribute, specify the positive value = *delayed* and negative value = *ontime*. Partition the data into training (60%) and validation (40%) sets.

a. Fit a classification tree for flight delay using all the relevant predictors—use the *Decision Tree* operator. Do not include DEP_TIME (actual departure time) in the model because it is unknown at the time of prediction (unless we are generating our predictions of delays after the plane takes off, which is unlikely). Explain why we excluded DAY_OF_MONTH, FL_DATE, FL_NUM, and TAIL_NUM as predictors in data preprocessing. Use the gain ratio criterion in fitting the tree with maximal depth = 6. Apply pruning and prepruning with default parameters. Report the confusion matrix, overall accuracy, precision, and recall.

b. Run a boosted classification tree for flight delay using the same predictors as above—use the *Bayesian Boosting* operator with *Decision Tree* operator (same parameters mentioned above) as the base estimator. Report the confusion matrix, overall accuracy, precision, and recall. Compared with the single tree, how does the boosted tree behave in terms of overall accuracy?

c. Compared with the single tree, how does the boosted tree behave in terms of accuracy in identifying delayed flights?

d. Explain why this model might have the best performance over the other models you fit.

PART V

Intervention and User Feedback

CHAPTER 14

Interventions: Experiments, Uplift Models, and Reinforcement Learning

In this chapter, we describe a third paradigm of machine learning, different from supervised and unsupervised learning, that deals with interventions and feedback. Data used in supervised and unsupervised learning are typically *observational data*, being passively collected about the entities of interest (customers, households, transactions, flights, etc.). In contrast, in this chapter, we discuss *experimental data*, resulting from applying interventions to the entities of interest and measuring the outcomes of those interventions. We start with the simplest form of intervention—the A/B test, which is a randomized experiment for testing the causal effect of a treatment or intervention on outcomes of interest. A/B tests are routinely used by internet platforms such as Google, Microsoft, and Uber for testing new features. We then describe *uplift modeling*, a method that combines A/B testing with supervised learning for providing customized targeting. Uplift modeling is commonly used in direct marketing and in political analytics. Finally, we describe *reinforcement learning*, a general machine learning methodology used in personalization, where the algorithm (or *agent*) learns the best treatment assignment policy by interacting with experimental units through dynamic treatment assignment and gathering their feedback.

14.1 A/B TESTING[1]

A/B testing is the marketing industry's term for a standard scientific experiment in which results can be tracked for each individual experimental unit. The idea

---

[1]This and subsequent sections in this chapter copyright © 2019 Datastats, LLC, and Galit Shmueli. Used by permission.

Machine Learning for Business Analytics: Concepts, Techniques and Applications in RapidMiner, First Edition.
Galit Shmueli, Peter C. Bruce, Amit V. Deokar, and Nitin R. Patel.
© 2023 John Wiley & Sons, Inc. Published 2023 by John Wiley & Sons, Inc.

is to test one treatment against another, or a treatment against a control. "Treatment" is simply the term for the intervention you are testing. In a medical trial, it is typically a drug, device, vaccine, or other therapy; in marketing it is typically an offering to a consumer—for example, an e-mail, online ad, push notification, or a webpage shown to a consumer. A display ad in a magazine would not generally qualify, unless it had a specific call to action that allowed the marketer to trace the action (e.g., purchase) to a given ad, plus the ability to split the magazine distribution randomly and provide a different offer to each segment of consumers.

A/B testing has become extremely popular online. Amazon, Microsoft, Facebook, Google, and similar companies conduct thousands to tens of thousands of A/B tests each year, on millions of users, testing user interface changes, enhancements to algorithms (search, ads, personalization, recommendation, etc.), changes to apps, content management system, and more.[2] A/B testing on an Internet or mobile platform involves randomizing user traffic to one of two experiences (current version and new version), computing the difference in relevant outcome metrics between the two groups, and performing statistical tests to rule out differences that are likely due to noise.

In an A/B test, an experimental unit ("subject") can be an individual customer, a user, an online user session, or any unit of interest.

An important element of A/B testing is random allocation—the treatments are assigned or delivered to subjects randomly. That way, any difference between treatment A and treatment B can be attributed to the treatment (unless it is due to chance). For this reason, A/B tests are extremely popular in online advertising, where it is relatively easy to randomly serve different ad designs or content ("treatments") to different users and where user reactions are automatically recorded. A/B tests are also routinely used by Internet platforms and website owners for evaluating new small intended improvements to the user interface design, such as changing the color of a submit button or adding a new navigation link. For example, Optimizely describes a case study showing how Electronic Arts, the maker of the popular SimCity franchise, created and tested several different versions of their pre-order webpage. They hypothesized that placing a call to action higher on the webpage by changing the way the promotional offer was displayed could drive more purchases and increase revenue generated from SimCity.com. Using A/B testing, they found that, contrary to their hypothesis, the version *without* a special promotion offer across the top of the page performed 43% better than the other variation.[3]

In an A/B test, only two measurements are needed for each subject: which treatment it received (A or B) and the outcome. For example, in an online

---

[2]See *Trustworthy online controlled experiments: A practical guide to a/b testing* by Kohavi et al. (2020).
[3]https://www.optimizely.com/insights/blog/ea_simcity_optimizely_casestudy/

TABLE 14.1	EXAMPLE OF RAW DATA RESULTING FROM A/B TEST	
User ID	**Treatment**	**Outcome**
1234	A	Click
1235	A	No click
1236	B	No click
...	...	...

advertising A/B test that compares a new ad design with an existing one, for each user, we would record which ad they were served ($Treat=\{\text{old,new}\}$) and what was the outcome, such as whether they clicked the ad or not ($Y=\{\text{click,no-click}\}$). Table 14.1 shows a schematic sample of such data. In practice, we do not need to keep all individual outcome values for each subject (unless the results will be used beyond the A/B test, such as in uplift modeling). For a binary outcome (e.g., click/no-click), we only need the proportion of clicks in each treatment group. In the ad example, that means the proportion of clicks among users who viewed the old ad ($\hat{p}_A$) and the proportion of clicks among users who viewed the new ad ($\hat{p}_B$). For a numerical outcome (e.g., engagement time), we need only the average and standard deviation of the outcome in each treatment group ($\overline{y}_A, \hat{\sigma}_A$ and $\overline{y}_B, \hat{\sigma}_B$).

Example: Testing a New Feature in a Photo Sharing App

PhoToTo, a fictitious photo sharing app, is interested in testing a new feature that allows users to make uploaded photos disappear after 24 hours. Their goal is to gauge their customers' interest in this feature, with the purpose of increasing user activity and converting users from the free version to the advanced paid version. PhoToTo deploys an A/B test to 2000 of its users who use the free version: 1000 of these users are randomly assigned to an interface with the new feature, while the other 1000 remain with the existing functionality. The experiment is run for a week. For each of the 2000 users, two performance metrics are measured at the end of the experimental week: the total number of uploaded photos and whether the user upgraded to the paid version of PhoToTo. The results of the experiment are shown in Table 14.2. We can see that the average number of photo uploads and the conversion to paid users are both higher in the treatment group where the new feature was introduced. But can we infer the difference between the two groups will generalize when deployed to the larger population of users, or is this a "fluke sample"?

The Statistical Test for Comparing Two Groups (T-Test)

The A/B test is a statistical test comparing the average outcome of a treatment group with that of a control group (or, in general, of two groups A and B).

TABLE 14.2   RESULTS FROM A/B TEST AT PHOTOTO, EVALUATING THE EFFECT OF A NEW FEATURE

Metric	Existing interface (A)	New feature available (B)
Average number of photo uploads	50	60
Standard deviation of photo uploads	50	100
Proportion of conversion to paid users	0.02	0.04

Success is measured by the number of photo uploads and user conversion

Suppose group A receives the existing ad, and group B receives the new design. Suppose the outcome of interest is whether users click on the ad. What if 5% of users shown the new ad clicked and 4% of those shown the existing ad clicked? In many cases, we would now be ready to go with the treatment that did best. This is especially so if we are starting fresh with two new treatments—say, sending our prospects email version A or email version B to promote a new product or testing a new web landing page with a blue banner at the top or an orange banner.

In other cases, there may be a substantial cost difference between the treatments, or we may be testing a new treatment against an existing "standard." In such a case, we may worry about fluke results in an A/B test, particularly if based on a small sample. If random chance produced a result in favor of the costlier or the new treatment, we might not want to switch away from the cheaper or the tried and true standard treatment. Doing so regularly would mean chasing after inconsequential results and losing a firm base of information. In such a case, we can use a statistical test to determine how "unusual" our result is compared with what chance might produce. If our result is very unusual (say, it might not occur more often than 5% of the time in a chance model), we would be prepared to abandon our existing standard in favor of the new treatment. If, on the other hand, our new treatment produced an outcome that occurs 35% of the time by chance anyway, we might stick with the standard treatment. In this way, we minimize our chance of being fooled by chance.

Such a statistical test is termed a *significance test*. The metric "percent of time a chance model produces an outcome at least as unusual as the experiment" is termed a *p-value*. We could calculate p-values by constituting a chance model and simulating results. For example, in a test of engagement times, we could put all the engagement times from both treatments into a hat, shuffle the hat, and then repeatedly draw out pairs of samples like the original samples. Do those pairs rarely yield a difference in mean engagement times across the two re-samples as great as we saw in our actual experiment? If so, we conclude that the difference we saw in the experiment was unlikely to happen by chance: it is "statistically significant." A formula-based equivalent of this procedure is the *t-test for independent samples* (see box) and is included in most statistical software and in some platforms for automating marketing experiments. Conducting independent samples t-test is not possible in RapidMiner, given its focus on machine learning rather than statistical tests. Therefore, we show a simple method to do such a test in Excel instead.

T-TEST FOR COMPARING TWO INDEPENDENT GROUPS

All basic statistics courses and textbooks cover the t-test for testing the difference between two group means (or proportions). Here is a quick reminder of the basics for the case relevant for A/B testing. For testing whether the difference between two group means (or proportions) is significantly in favor of group B (e.g., the new ad design) or not—that is, whether there's evidence the difference between the population means $\mu_B - \mu_A > 0$—we compute the t-statistic:

$$T = \frac{\overline{y}_B - \overline{y}_A}{\text{StandardError}(\overline{y}_B - \overline{y}_A)}.$$

When the outcome metric of interest is binary (e.g., buy/not-buy), a similar formula is used, replacing averages ($\overline{y}$) with proportions ($\hat{p}$).

The denominator of the t-statistic (the standard error of the difference in means or proportions) has the following formulas.[4] For a numerical measure:

$$\text{StandardError}(\overline{y}_B - \overline{y}_A) = \sqrt{s_A^2/n_A + s_B^2/n_B},$$

and for a binary measure:

$$\text{StandardError}(\hat{p}_B - \hat{p}_A) = \sqrt{\frac{\hat{p}_A(1 - \hat{p}_A)}{n_A} + \frac{\hat{p}_B(1 - \hat{p}_B)}{n_B}}.$$

The statistical significance of the t-value (its p-value) is computed by software. Comparing the p-value with a user-determined threshold will then yield a result. For example, if the threshold is 5%, then a p-value below 5% will indicate the click through rate (CTR) on the new design is statistically higher than on the existing design. The results of such tests are subject to two potential errors: false discovery (called Type I error) and missed discovery (Type II error). The choice of threshold value is determined by the false discovery risk level we are prepared to take.

Critically, one must carefully consider the magnitude of the difference and its practical meaning, especially since A/B tests are typically conducted on very large samples of users (tens and even hundreds of thousands of users). Statistical significance is strongly affected by the sample size: the larger the groups, the more likely even a very small difference that is practically meaningless will appear statistically significant. For example, with sufficiently large groups, a CTR of 5.000001% will appear significantly (statistically) higher than 5%.

Returning to our earlier example of the photo sharing app PhoToTo, we can compute the T-statistics for each of the two metrics of interest: the number of uploaded photos and the conversion rate to paid users:

$$T_{\text{photo uploads}} = \frac{60 - 50}{\sqrt{(50^2/1000 + 100^2/1000)}} = 2.828$$

$$T_{\text{paid users}} = \frac{0.04 - 0.02}{\sqrt{(0.04)(0.96)/1000 + (0.02)(0.98)/1000}} = 2.626$$

The corresponding two p-values are as follows: for the increase[5] in average photo uploads, p-value = 0.0024 (in Excel = tdist(2.828,1998,1)); for increase in paid users, p-value = 0.0044 (in Excel = tdist(2.626,1998,1)). Both p-values are very small, thereby indicating that the effect of the new feature on number of uploads and conversion to paid users will generalize to the larger population of users. Note that with much smaller sample sizes, the same outcome values in Table 14.2 could yield statistical insignificance. For example, for $n_A = n_B = 100$, we get p-values of 0.186 and 0.204, respectively.

Multiple Treatment Groups: A/B/n Tests

A/B testing can be extended from two groups (treatment and control, or two groups) to multiple groups. In A/B/n testing, we have n groups. For example, testing three new ad designs against an existing design would use an A/B/4 test. The procedure is very similar to A/B testing, with the difference being the replacement of the t-test with analysis of variance (ANOVA) for a numerical outcome or a chi-square test for comparing proportions. For more on these tests, consult a statistics textbook such as Anderson et al. (2021).

Multiple A/B Tests and the Danger of Multiple Testing

As we mentioned earlier, digital platforms and their business customers (e.g., advertisers and marketers) often perform routine and frequent A/B tests, resulting in thousands of tests. Large companies such as Microsoft have their internal experimentation infrastructure. However, even small companies can perform such testing using services by third parties: Optimizely (https://www.optimizely.com/) is one commercial service that provides online tools for routine A/B testing for online advertisers.

When deploying many A/B tests, there is a high risk of false discoveries: mistakenly concluding that a treatment effect is real, where it is just due to chance. While each statistical t-test carries with it a small probability of false discovery, a combination of many A/B tests dramatically increases the overall false discovery probability. This phenomenon is known as *multiple testing*. Multiple testing

---

[5]We use a *one-sided test*, because we are testing whether the average number of uploads *increases* with the new feature. When the direction of the effect is unknown, we'd use a two-sided test.

can arise from testing multiple metrics (CTR, views, purchases, etc.), running the test for multiple use subgroups (countries, zip codes, device type, etc.), and repeating the same A/B test many times. Kohavi et al. (2020) describe a case of multiple testing that arose in early versions of Optimizely, which allowed those running an A/B test to "peek" at the p-values before the experimental period has been completed. For example, if the A/B test was supposed to run for a week, the tester could peek at test results throughout the week. This peeking was effectively multiple testing, leading to false discoveries of apparent effects. The problem was later detected and eliminated.

Solutions to false discoveries due to multiple testing are based on adjusting the threshold on each p-value, or adjusting the p-values themselves, by considering the total number of tests.[6] However, beyond technical solutions, it is good practice to carefully consider which tests are essential, set the experimental period in advance, disallow "peeking," and select treatments that have reasonable justification (although sometimes new ideas are hard to justify but turn out to be successes).

14.2 UPLIFT (PERSUASION) MODELING

Long before the advent of the Internet, sending messages directly to individuals (i.e., direct mail) held a big share of the advertising market. Direct marketing affords the marketer the ability to invite and monitor direct responses from consumers. This, in turn, allows the marketer to learn whether the messaging is paying off. A message can be tested with a small section of a large list, and, if it pays off, the message can be rolled out to the entire list. With predictive modeling, we have seen that the rollout can be targeted to that portion of the list that is most likely to respond or behave in a certain way. None of this was possible with traditional media advertising (television, radio, newspaper, magazine).

Direct response also made it possible to test one message against another and find out which does better.

An A/B test tells you which treatment does better on average but says nothing about which treatment does better for which individual. A classic example is in political campaigns. Consider the following scenario: the campaign director for Smith, a Democratic Congressional candidate, would like to know which voters should be called to encourage to support Smith. Voters that tend to vote Democratic but are not activists might be more inclined to vote for Smith if they got a call. Active Democrats are probably already supportive of him, and

---

[6]One common method is the "false discovery rate" (FDR), which is the expected number of false discoveries among all discoveries. Using the FDR entails sorting the p-values from low to high and assigning different thresholds.

therefore a call to them would be wasted. Calls to Republicans are not only wasteful, but they could be harmful.

Campaigns now maintain extensive data on voters to help guide decisions about outreach to individual voters. Prior to the 2008 Obama campaign, the practice was to make rule-based decisions based on expert political judgment. Since 2008, it has increasingly been recognized that, rather than relying on judgment or supposition to determine whether an individual should be called, it is best to use the data to develop a model that can predict whether a voter will respond positively to outreach.

Gathering the Data

US states maintain publicly available files of voters, as part of the transparent oversight process for elections. The voter file contains data such as name, address, and date of birth. Political parties have "poll-watchers" at elections to record who votes, so they have additional data on which elections voters voted in. Census data for neighborhoods can be appended, based on voter address. Finally, commercial demographic data can be purchased and matched to the voter data. Table 14.3 shows a small extract of data derived from the voter file for the US state of Delaware.[7] The actual data used in this problem are in the file *Voter-Persuasion.csv* and contain 10,000 records and many additional attributes beyond those shown in Table 14.3.

TABLE 14.3   DATA ON VOTERS (SMALL SUBSET OF ATTRIBUTES AND RECORDS) AND DATA DICTIONARY

Voter	Age	NH_White	Comm_PT	H_F1	Reg_Days	PR_Pelig	E_Elig	Political_C
1	28	70	0	0	3997	0	20	1
2	23	67	3	0	300	0	0	1
3	57	64	4	0	2967	0	0	0
4	70	53	2	1	16,620	100	90	1
5	37	76	2	0	3786	0	20	0

Data dictionary

Age	Voter age in years
NH_White	Neighborhood average of % non-Hispanic white in household
Comm_PT	Neighborhood % of workers who take public transit
H_F1	Single female household (1 = yes)
Reg_Days	Days since voter registered at current address
PR_Pelig	Voted in what % of non-presidential primaries
E_Pelig	Voted in what % of any primaries
Political_C	Is there a political contributor in the home? (1 = yes)

[7]Thanks to Ken Strasma, founder of the microtargeting firm HaystaqDNA and director of targeting for the 2004 Kerry campaign and the 2008 Obama campaign, for these data.

First, the campaign director conducts a survey of 10,000 voters to determine their inclination to vote Democratic. Then, she conducts an experiment, randomly splitting the sample of 10,000 voters in half and mailing a message promoting Smith to half the list (treatment A) and nothing to the other half (treatment B). The control group that gets no message is essential, since other campaigns or news events might cause a shift in opinion. The goal is to measure the change in opinion after the message is sent out, relative to the no-message control group.

The next step is conducting a post-message survey of the same sample of 10,000 voters, to measure whether each voter's opinion of Smith has shifted in a positive direction. A binary attribute, Moved_AD, will be added to the above data, indicating whether opinion has moved in a Democratic direction (1) or not (0).

Table 14.4 summarizes the results of the survey, by comparing the movement in a Democratic direction for each of the treatments. Overall, the message (Message = 1) is modestly effective.

TABLE 14.4 RESULTS OF SENDING A PRO-DEMOCRATIC MESSAGE TO VOTERS

	#Voters	# Moved Dem.	% Moved Dem.
Message = 1 (message sent)	5000	2012	40.2
Message = 0 (no message sent)	5000	1722	34.4

Movement in a Democratic direction among those who got no message is 34.4%. This probably reflects the approach of the election, the heightening campaign activity, and the reduction in the "no opinion" category. It also illustrates the need for a control group. Among those who did get the message, the movement in a Democratic direction is 40.2%. So, overall, the lift from the message is 5.8%.

We can now append two attributes to the voter data shown earlier in Table 14.3: *Message* [whether they received the message (1) or not (0)] and *Moved_AD* [whether they moved in a Democratic direction (1) or not (0)]. The augmented data are shown in Table 14.5.

TABLE 14.5 TARGET ATTRIBUTE (MOVED_AD) AND TREATMENT VARIABLE (MESSAGE) ADDED TO VOTER DATA

Voter	Age	NH_White	Comm_PT	H_F1	Reg_Days	PR_Pelig	E_Elig	Political_C	Message	Moved_AD
1	28	70	0	0	3997	0	20	1	0	1
2	23	67	3	0	300	0	0	1	1	1
3	57	64	4	0	2967	0	0	0	0	0
4	70	53	2	1	16,620	100	90	1	0	0
5	37	76	2	0	3786	0	20	0	1	0

A Simple Model

We can develop a predictive model with Moved_AD as the target attribute and various predictor attributes, *including the treatment Message*. Any classification method can be used; Table 14.6 shows the first few lines from the output of some predictive model used to predict Moved_AD.

TABLE 14.6   CLASSIFICATIONS AND PROPENSITIES FROM PREDICTIVE MODEL (SMALL EXTRACT)

Voter	Message	Actual Moved_AD	Predicted Moved_AD	Predicted Prob.
1	0	1	1	0.5975
2	1	1	1	0.5005
3	0	0	0	0.2235
4	0	0	0	0.3052
5	1	0	0	0.4140

However, our interest is not just how the message did overall, nor is it whether we can predict the probability that a voter's opinion will move in a favorable direction. Rather our goal is to predict how much (positive) impact the message will have on a specific voter. That way the campaign can direct its limited resources toward the voters who are the most persuadable—those for whom sending the message will have the greatest positive effect.

Modeling Individual Uplift

To answer the question about the message's impact on each voter, we need to model the effect of the message at the individual voter level. For each voter, uplift is defined as follows:

Uplift = increase in propensity of favorable opinion after receiving message

To build an uplift model, we follow the following steps to estimate the change in probability of "success" (propensity) that comes from receiving the treatment (the message):

1. Randomly split a data sample into treatment and control groups, conduct an A/B test, and record the target (in our example: Moved_AD).

2. Recombining the data sample, partition it into training and holdout sets; build a predictive model with this target attribute, and include a predictor attribute that denotes treatment status (in our example: Message). If logistic regression is used, additional interaction terms between treatment status and other predictors can be added as predictors to allow the treatment effect to vary across records (in data-driven methods such as trees and KNN this happens automatically).

3. Score this predictive model to a partition of the data; you can use the holdout partition. This will yield, for each holdout record, its propensity of success given its treatment.

4. Reverse the value of the treatment attribute, and re-score the same model to that partition. This will yield for each holdout record its propensity of success had it received the other treatment.

5. Uplift is estimated for each individual by P(Success | Treatment = 1) − P(Success | Treatment = 0).

6. For new data where no experiment has been performed, simply add a synthetic predictor attribute for treatment, and assign first a "1," score the model, then assign a "0," and score the model again. Estimate uplift for the new record(s) as above.

Continuing with the small voter example, the results from Step 3 were shown in Table 14.6—the right column shows the propensities from the model. Next, we retrain the predictive model, but with the values of the treatment attribute Message reversed for each row. Table 14.7 shows the propensities with attribute Message reversed (you can see the reversed values in column Message). Finally, in Step 5, we calculate the uplift for each voter.

TABLE 14.7   **CLASSIFICATIONS AND PROPENSITIES FROM PREDICTIVE MODEL (SMALL EXTRACT) WITH MESSAGE VALUES REVERSED**

Voter	Message	Actual Moved_AD	Predicted Moved_AD	Predicted Prob.
1	1	1	1	0.6908
2	0	1	1	0.3996
3	1	0	0	0.3022
4	1	0	0	0.3980
5	0	0	0	0.3194

Table 14.8 shows the uplift for each voter—the success (Moved_AD = 1) propensity given Message = 1 minus the success propensity given Message = 0.

TABLE 14.8   **UPLIFT: CHANGE IN PROPENSITIES FROM SENDING MESSAGE VS. NOT SENDING MESSAGE**

Voter	Prob. if Message = 1	Prob. if Message = 0	Uplift
1	0.6908	0.5975	0.0933
2	0.5005	0.3996	0.1009
3	0.3022	0.2235	0.0787
4	0.3980	0.3052	0.0928
5	0.4140	0.3194	0.0946

Computing Uplift with RapidMiner

This entire process that we showed manually can be done using RapidMiner as shown in Figure 14.1. The uplift analysis is done in the *Uplift Modeling* subprocess, applied to the 40% holdout set. First, two copies of the logistic regression model and holdout sets are created with the *Multiply* operator. The *Map* operator is used to swap the values of the Message_A (treatment) attribute. The *Apply Model* operator is used to apply the logistic regression model to the treatment and reversed treatment data. The propensities (confidence values) for Moved_AD = 0 or 1 are renamed meaningfully as confidence(Msg) and confidence(NoMsg) for the treatment and reversed treatment data, respectively, using the *Rename* operator. Finally, these two datasets are joined using the *Join* operator, and the uplift is computed as the difference between confidence(Msg) and confidence(NoMsg) using the *Generate Attributes* operator. Figure 14.1 (bottom right) shows the result of implementing the uplift analysis (first five records shown). The output shows the two conditional probabilities, confidence(Msg) = $P(\text{Success}|\text{Treatment} = 1)$ and confidence(NoMsg) = $P(\text{Success}|\text{Treatment} = 0)$, estimated for each record, along with the individual uplift values.

Using the Results of an Uplift Model

Once we have estimated the uplift for each individual, the results can be ordered by uplift. The message could then be sent to all those voters with a positive uplift or, if resources are limited, only to a subset—those with the greatest uplift.

Uplift modeling is used mainly in marketing and, more recently, in political campaigns. It has two main purposes:

- To determine whether to send someone a persuasion message or just leave them alone.

- When a message is definitely going to be sent, to determine which message, among several possibilities, to send.

Technically this amounts to the same thing—"send no message" is simply another category of treatment, and an experiment can be constructed with multiple treatments, for example, no message, message A, and message B. However, practitioners tend to think of the two purposes as distinct and tend to focus on the first. Marketers want to avoid sending discount offers to customers who would make a purchase anyway or renew a subscription anyway. Political campaigns, likewise, want to avoid calling voters who would vote for their candidate in any case. And both parties especially want to avoid sending messages or offers where the effect might be antagonistic—where the uplift is negative.

FIGURE 14.1   (TOP) PROCESS FOR COMPUTING UPLIFT FOR THE VOTERS DATA AND
(BOTTOM RIGHT) INDIVIDUAL UPLIFT FOR FIRST FIVE RECORDS IN HOLDOUT SET

14.3 REINFORCEMENT LEARNING

A/B testing derives causal knowledge about an intervention of interest by actively assigning experimental units (customers, website users, etc.) to treatment/intervention groups, measuring the outcome(s) of interest, and drawing a conclusion about the effectiveness of the intervention. We can think of this process as "learning by interacting" with the experimental units. The notion of *learning by interaction* is what separates supervised and unsupervised learning methods from interventional methods such as A/B testing and reinforcement learning. For example, in recommendation algorithms such as collaborative filtering, we might generate a recommended item (or set of items) for a user. However, unless we actually display the recommendation to the user and measure the outcome, it is impossible to know what the user would have done given the recommendation.

We've seen that interventional methods such as uplift modeling are intended to answer the personalized "what if" question: what would be the user's outcome if s/he were served (or not) a certain recommendation or offer? We now turn to a family of methods called *reinforcement learning*, which are computational algorithms (or *agents*) that "learn by interacting" with experimental units, through dynamic treatment assignment. In both supervised learning and reinforcement learning, the goal is to "learn" a predictive model of the outcome Y as a function of predictors $X_1, X_2, \ldots$. But whereas in supervised learning we train the model on preexisting data, in reinforcement learning we start without data, and the algorithm decides which X (treatment) information to deploy that would generate outcome Y data most useful for learning the optimal treatment-outcome model. In the recommendation example above, a reinforcement learning approach would choose which items to recommend in order to collect user feedback useful for learning the optimal input–output model.

We describe two popular frameworks: multi-armed bandits and Markov decision processes. In both cases the challenge is identifying the best treatment assignment policy in the presence of a plethora of potential interventions (e.g., which news item to display on a user's social media feed, which song to recommend in a music streaming service; which of many coupons to offer a customer on an e-commerce website).

Explore-Exploit: Multi-Armed Bandits

The name *multi-armed bandit* (MAB, or simply "bandit") derives from a gambler playing multiple slot machines, each with a different unknown payoff rate. The gambler's goal is to figure out which machine has the highest payoff rate.

In an A/B test, after learning which treatment did best, you deploy that treatment, and the other treatment(s) get left behind. A MAB uses sequential assignment of experimental units to treatment groups, dynamically updating treatment assignments to new units as the experiment progresses. The idea is to increase the proportion of assignments to the treatment group that shows the best performance (the best slot machine). This is especially useful when there are multiple treatments (e.g., multiple ad designs). For example, if we initially display 10 new ad designs to mobile app users, each with equal probability, and then if initial experimental results indicate the new ad #3 leads to the best outcomes, for the next set of users, we might increase the probability of displaying ad #3 compared with all other designs. However, we do not increase this probability to 100% because there is still uncertainty regarding the superiority of this ad design—perhaps with more data, a different ad design will turn out to be the best one. We therefore still want to continue testing the value of the other nine ad designs. A MAB tries to achieve a dual goal: improving the outcome by increasing the chance of assignment to the "winning" treatment (called *Exploit*) while continuing to evaluate the potential of the "losing" treatment(s) (called *Explore*).

There are different MAB parameters and implementations, which differ in terms of determining how and when to update the treatment assignment probabilities. For example, an *Epsilon First* strategy explores randomly for some period of time and then exploits the treatment with the highest estimated outcome (if one treatment is clearly better than the others, it assigns all new subjects to this treatment). Another approach, the *Epsilon–Greedy* approach, explores ϵ% of the time and exploits $1-\epsilon$% of the time. A variation of the *Epsilon–Greedy* strategy adjusts the ϵ parameter over time, exploring sub-optimal treatments less frequently.

The MAB scenario assumes the intervention effects remain constant from one assignment to the next. However, in some cases the best intervention will depend on a changing context. For example, in music recommendation, it is likely that song preference changes for the same user over different times of the day (waking up, while commuting to work, in the evening, etc.) or across devices (mobile phone, TV, etc.). In such cases, we'd want the algorithm to take into account the context. *Contextual multi-armed bandits*, also known as *contextual bandits*, do exactly this: they search for the best context-specific intervention, thereby combining trial-and-error treatment assignment search with estimating the association between treatment assignment and context variables.

Note: Bandits and contextual bandits are not available in RapidMiner (but can be implemented in R using the package *contextual*).[8]

---

[8] R scripts can be embedded in RapidMiner processes with operators such as the *Execute R* operator from the *R Scripting* extension.

MULTI-ARMED BANDIT: SIMPLE EXAMPLE

Let's consider the scenario of selecting the best online ad to display among 10 different designs, by running a 7-day experiment. Suppose that each day we have a large number of customers accessing the webpage where the ad will be displayed. A 10-armed bandit algorithm that uses an Epsilon-first strategy would take the following steps:

- **Day 1 initialization:** Each ad i has probability $p_i = 0.1$ to be displayed. In other words, each customer is randomly assigned to view one of the 10 ads.
- **Day 1 evaluation and update:** At the end of Day 1, compute the *reward* metric of interest r_i (e.g., CTR, or average ad revenues per ad view), resulting from each of the 10 ads.
- **Day 2 deployment:** All customers assigned to view the best performing Day 1 ad.
- **Day 2 evaluation and update:** At the end of Day 2, compute the average daily *reward* for the displayed ad.
- **Days 3, 5, 7 deployment:** Each customer is randomly assigned to view one of the 10 ads (as in Day 1).
- **Days 3, 5, 7 evaluation and update:** At the end of the day, compute the average daily *reward* for each of the 10 ads (accumulated across the days thus far).
- **Days 4, 6 deployment:** All customers assigned to view the best performing ad thus far.
- **Day 4, 6 evaluation and update:** At the end of the day, compute the average daily *reward* for each of the 10 ads (accumulated across the days thus far).
- **Day 7 experiment conclusion:** The ad with the highest average 7-day reward is selected and will be displayed in the future.

Note that on odd days, where customers are randomized across all 10 ads, the scenario is similar to A/B/10 testing in terms of treatment assignment strategy. The difference is that we do not carry out a statistical test at the end of an odd day to conclude about the best ad. Instead, we accumulate the rewards since Day 1 and reach a conclusion only after the multi-day experiment is complete.

The above example treats each day separately. An alternative is to consider batches of customers visiting the webpage (for example, replacing a day with 10,000 customer visits).

Markov Decision Process (MDP)

In contrast to A/B tests, in bandit algorithms, the allocation of treatments to users is a multi-stage process, in which the allocation at one stage might depend on what happened in the previous stage. Bandit algorithms are actually a special case of a more general staged process, termed a Markov decision process (MDP).

MDPs can allow the algorithm to learn a longer-term relationship between interventions (treatments) and outcomes—for example, a movie recommendation might lead to higher long-term user satisfaction even if the user's immediate reaction is not the most profitable. Hence, MDPs are especially useful in digital environments where long-term goals, such as user satisfaction or brand recognition, are of interest.

A MDP represents the problem of learning the optimal intervention policy through *states* and *rewards*. Consider a music streaming service that provides a recommendation system to its users. Suppose the business goal is to increase overall user engagement with the service (by providing useful recommendations), where engagement is measured by the number of songs played by the user. The algorithm (agent) must discover which song recommendations (interventions) yield the best outcome overall by trying them and recording the user's reactions. To achieve this, we define for the agent an intermediate "reward" such as whether the recommended song was played for at least 30 seconds. The agent's objective is to maximize the total reward over the long run. With such a longer-term optimization, we might recommend an item with a low immediate reward (e.g., low-profit item), but that is likely to lead to profitable rewards in the future. Another advantage of the MDP formulation is that the reward can represent the business value of a particular recommendation so that we might recommend high-profit items even if they have a low probability of purchase.

In addition to the rewards, the MDP records the *state* at each time of treatment assignment. The state includes all the information available to the algorithm about the user, the context, and the items. In the music streaming example, the state might be the user's profile (age, gender, etc.), behavior on the platform (app use frequency, songs played, sharing with friends, etc.), context (time of day, location, device, etc.), and song features (singer, genre, etc.).

The agent's actions (e.g., recommendation or ad displayed) might affect not only the reward but also the next state (e.g., the user's time on app, songs played), thereby affecting future rewards.[9] To capture this, the MDP has a *value function* (specified by the data scientist) that assigns to each state a value corresponding to the expected long-term overall rewards when starting from that state and using a specific treatment assignment policy.

Figure 14.2 shows a schematic of a MDP and how the agent interacts with the user by assigning an intervention (action) and recording the user's reaction (reward) and new state. The terms "agent" and "environment," sometimes called "controller" and "controlled system," reflect the origins of reinforcement learning in engineering applications (such as thermostats for regulating the temperature in a room) and more recently in games such as chess and Go where the algorithm searches for the best next move.

The term "Markov" in MDP implies that we think of rewards, states, and treatment assignments (actions) in discrete time (periods $t = 1, 2, 3, \ldots$) and that the sequence of rewards, states, and actions form a *Markov chain*—this is

---

[9]A MAB is a simplified type of reinforcement learning where the assignment to intervention (action) affects only the immediate reward.

FIGURE 14.2   SCHEMATIC OF REINFORCEMENT LEARNING, WHERE THE SOFTWARE AGENT "LEARNS" THE HUMAN USER BY PROVIDING ACTIONS, RECORDING THE USER'S NEW STATE, AND RECEIVING A REWARD BASED ON THE USER'S REACTION

a sequence of possible events in which the probability of each event depends only on the state attained in the previous event. In other words, to determine its next action (a_{t+1}), the agent only uses information on the most recent state (s_t), reward (r_t), and action (a_t).

For an item recommendation scenario, a generic MDP strategy might look like this:

1. *Initialization:* Using a predictive model, predict what item user u will select next given their user data (state).[10] (This model is based on data without recommendations.)

2. *Action (a_t):* Recommend to user u an item based on the user's data, context, and the item's features (state s_{t_1}). (The item is the result of step 1 for the initial run and then of step 4 thereafter.)

3. *Reward (r_t):* Collect the user's feedback to the recommendation (e.g., purchase, clicks)

4. *Model Update:* Using the pre-recommendation user/context/item data (state s_{t-1}), the recommendation (action a_t), and the user's feedback (reward r_t), the agent updates its predictive model linking the outcome (next step's state and reward) to the input (current step's state and action) $P(s_{t+1}, r_{t+1} | s_t, a_t)$. The agent then computes the value function (the expected long-term overall reward) to choose the next best action.

5. *Repeat* Steps 2–4

There exist a variety of ways to implement MDPs and reinforcement learning algorithms in practice, as well as variations and extensions, some including deep neural networks for the model updating step. The interested reader can learn more in the classic book *Reinforcement Learning* by Sutton and Barto.

---

[10]This means estimating the initial *state transition function* that includes the probabilities of moving from each state to each of the other states.

As a final note about reinforcement learning, it is important to realize that while in this AI technique the data scientist determines the rewards, value function, the set of states, and set of possible actions, this does not guarantee that the agent will arrive at an optimal solution. In his book *Human Compatible*, AI expert Stewart Russell describes how agents designed to achieve a human-designed goal ended up reaching the goal by unacceptable solutions: the ECHO smart home controller was designed to reduce energy consumption by learning from the household behavior. However, inhabitants at Washington State university "often had to sit in the dark if their visitors stayed later than the usual bedtime." The agent has not fully "understood" the human objective, because the goals and rules have not been, and perhaps cannot be, fully specified. By contrast, in games like Go or chess, the ends are easy to define, and the rules can be comprehensively specified. In such games, highly creative solutions may result. The solution path may seem outlandish to a human in its initial stages, but the agent does not care and has been able to determine that it will be ultimately successful.

Reinforcement learning algorithms were designed for tasks that are fully observable, involve short time horizons, and have a small number of states and simple, predictable rules. Stewart Russell (2019) concludes that "Relaxing any of these conditions means that the standard methods will fail."

14.4 SUMMARY

In this chapter, we looked at the use of randomized experiments and user feedback for determining the best intervention. These methods differ from supervised learning and unsupervised learning and involve interaction with the units of interest (customers, website users, etc.). We described A/B testing, uplift modeling, and reinforcement learning.

A/B testing is used to test the effect of an intervention on an outcome of interest. This is done by randomly assigning units to an intervention group or a control (non-intervention) group and comparing the two groups' outcomes. A/B/n testing extends the idea to more than two groups.

In uplift modeling, the results of A/B testing are folded into the predictive modeling process as a predictor variable to guide choices not only about whether to send an offer or persuasion message but also as to who to send it to.

Reinforcement learning uses computational algorithms for identifying best intervention assignments. This is especially useful when there are many possible interventions (such as in recommendation systems) and in environments that allow user–algorithm interaction. The algorithm learns the best intervention policy by trial and error, balancing between exploration (trying different treatment assignments) and exploitation (assigning the best-so-far treatment). Two popular reinforcement learning formulations are MABs and MDPs.

PROBLEMS

14.1 **Marketing Message—A/B Testing.** Which is a more effective marketing message—
a plain text email or an email with images and design elements? Statistics.com conducted an A/B test in June 2012, sending an email to a list of potential customers that
was randomly split into two groups. The measure of success was whether the email
was opened by the receiver or not. For some reason, the email service used by Statis-
tics.com did not produce an even split. The results for each of the 426 sent emails are
in the file *email-A-B-test.csv*.

   a. Before conducting such a test, would you have an opinion as to which would do
better: a message with or without images?

   b. What were the results in terms of open rates? Which message did better? (*Hint:* In
RapidMiner, you can use the *Turbo Prep* view to construct a pivot table to get this
summary.)

   c. We would like to know whether this difference could be due to chance, and so will
conduct a statistical test. Conduct a t-test using Excel to determine whether the
difference is statistically significant and report the p-value.

   d. Summarize your conclusion from the A/B test.

14.2 **Hair Care Product—Uplift Modeling.** This problem uses the dataset in *Hair-Care-
Product.csv*, courtesy of SAS. In this hypothetical case, a promotion for a hair care
product was sent to some members of a buyers club. Purchases were then recorded for
both the members who got the promotion and those who did not.

   a. What is the purchase propensity:

     i. Among those who received the promotion?

     ii. Among those who did not receive the promotion?

   b. Partition the data into training (60%) and validation (40%) and fit:

     i. Uplift using a random forest.

     ii. Uplift using k-NN.

   c. Report the two models' recommendations for the first three members.

PART VI

Mining Relationships Among Records

CHAPTER 15

Association Rules and Collaborative Filtering

In this chapter, we describe the unsupervised learning methods of association rules (also called "affinity analysis" and "market basket analysis") and collaborative filtering. Both methods are popular in marketing for cross-selling products associated with an item that a consumer is considering.

In association rules, the goal is to identify item clusters in transaction-type databases. Association rule discovery in marketing is termed "market basket analysis" and is aimed at discovering which groups of products tend to be purchased together. These items can then be displayed together, offered in post-transaction coupons, or recommended in online shopping. We describe the two-stage process of rule generation and then assessment of rule strength to choose a subset. We look at the popular rule-generating Apriori algorithm and then criteria for judging the strength of rules.

In collaborative filtering, the goal is to provide personalized recommendations that leverage user-level information. User-based collaborative filtering starts with a user and then finds users who have purchased a similar set of items or ranked items in a similar fashion and makes a recommendation to the initial user based on what the similar users purchased or liked. Item-based collaborative filtering starts with an item being considered by a user and then locates other items that tend to be co-purchased with that first item. We explain the technique and the requirements for applying it in practice.

15.1 ASSOCIATION RULES

Put simply, association rules, or *affinity analysis*, constitute a study of "what goes with what." This method is also called *market basket analysis* because it originated with the study of customer transactions databases to determine dependencies

Machine Learning for Business Analytics: Concepts, Techniques and Applications in RapidMiner, First Edition.
Galit Shmueli, Peter C. Bruce, Amit V. Deokar, and Nitin R. Patel

between purchases of different items. Association rules are heavily used in retail for learning about items that are purchased together, but they are also useful in other fields. For example, a medical researcher might want to learn what symptoms appear together. In law, word combinations that appear too often might indicate plagiarism.

Discovering Association Rules in Transaction Databases

The availability of detailed information on customer transactions has led to the development of techniques that automatically look for associations between items that are stored in the database. An example is data collected using barcode scanners in supermarkets. Such *market basket databases* consist of a large number of transaction records. Each record lists all items bought by a customer on a single-purchase transaction. Managers are interested to know if certain groups of items are consistently purchased together. They could use such information for making decisions on store layouts and item placement, for cross-selling, for promotions, for catalog design, and for identifying customer segments based on buying patterns. Association rules provide information of this type in the form of "if–then" statements. These rules are computed from the data; unlike the if–then rules of logic, association rules are probabilistic in nature.

Association rules are commonly encountered in online *recommendation systems* (or *recommender systems*), where customers examining an item or items for possible purchase are shown other items that are often purchased in conjunction with the first item(s). The display from Amazon.com's online shopping system illustrates the application of rules like this under "Frequently bought together." In the example shown in Figure 15.1, a user browsing a Samsung Galaxy S21 cell phone is shown a case and a screen protector that are often purchased along with this phone.

We introduce a simple artificial example and use it throughout the chapter to demonstrate the concepts, computations, and steps of association rules. We end by applying association rules to a more realistic example of book purchases.

Example 1: Synthetic Data on Purchases of Phone Faceplates

A store that sells accessories for cellular phones runs a promotion on faceplates. Customers who purchase multiple faceplates from a choice of six different colors get a discount. The store managers who would like to know what colors of faceplates customers are likely to purchase together collected the transaction database as shown in Table 15.1.

Cell Phones & Accessories › Cell Phones

Samsung Galaxy S21 5G | Factory Unlocked Android Cell Phone | US Version 5G Smartphone | Pro-Grade Camera, 8K Video, 64MP High Res | 128GB, Phantom Violet (SM-G991UZVAXAA)
Visit the SAMSUNG Store
★★★★☆ ˅   351 ratings | 68 answered questions

List Price: $799.99 Details
Price: $749.99 & FREE Returns
You Save: $50.00 (6%)

Pay $41.67/month for 18 months, interest-free upon approval for the Amazon Rewards Visa Card

Model Name	O1
Wireless Carrier	Unlocked
Brand	SAMSUNG
Form Factor	Smartphone
Memory Storage Capacity	128 GB
Operating System	Android

˅ See more

New & Used (9) from $578.24 + $4.79 shipping

Roll over image to zoom in

Frequently bought together

Total price: $772.95
Add all three to Cart

ⓘ These items are shipped from and sold by different sellers. Show details

☑ **This item:** Samsung Galaxy S21 5G | Factory Unlocked Android Cell Phone | US Version 5G Smartphone | Pro-Grade ... $749.99
☑ Ferilinso for Samsung Galaxy S21 Case with 2 Pack Tempered Glass Screen Protector [Hard PC Back+TPU Flexible Fr... $9.97
☑ [4 Pack] Ferilinso 2 Pack Screen Protector for Samsung Galaxy S21 5G with 2 Pack Camera Lens Protector [100% Su... $12.99

Customers who viewed this item also viewed   Page 1 of 5

| SAMSUNG Galaxy S20 FE 5G Factory Unlocked Android Cell Phone 128GB US Version Smartphone Pro-Grade Camera 30X Space... ★★★★☆ 5,605 $597.99 | Samsung Galaxy S21 5G, US Version, 128GB, Phantom Gray - Unlocked (Renewed) ★★★★☆ 117 $590.43 | Samsung Galaxy S21 5G | Factory Unlocked Android Cell Phone | US Version 5G Smartphone | Pro-Grade Camera, 8K Video, 64MP High Res... ★★★★☆ 44 $589.33 | SAMSUNG Galaxy S21 Ultra 5G | Factory Unlocked Android Cell Phone | US Version 5G Smartphone | Pro-Grade Camera, 8K Video,... ★★★★☆ 39 $900.25 | Samsung Galaxy S21+ Plus 5G, US Version, 128GB, Phantom Silver - Unlocked (Renewed) ★★★★☆ 15 $739.98 | {Refurbished} Samsung Galaxy S20 5G, 128GB, Cosmic Gray - Fully Unlocked ★★★★☆ 1,158 5% off $440.00 $464.00 Lowest price in 30 days |

FIGURE 15.1   **RECOMMENDATIONS UNDER "FREQUENTLY BOUGHT TOGETHER" ARE BASED ON ASSOCIATION RULES**

Data Format

Transaction data are usually displayed in one of two formats: a transactions database (with each row representing a list of items purchased in a single transaction) or a binary incidence matrix in which columns are items, rows again represent transactions, and each cell has either a 1 or a 0, indicating the presence or absence of an item in the transaction. For example, Table 15.1 displays the

TABLE 15.1   TRANSACTIONS DATABASE FOR PURCHASES OF DIFFERENT-COLORED CELLULAR PHONE FACEPLATES

Transaction	Faceplate colors purchased			
1	red	white	green	
2	white	orange		
3	white	blue		
4	red	white	orange	
5	red	blue		
6	white	blue		
7	red	blue		
8	red	white	blue	green
9	red	white	blue	
10	yellow			

TABLE 15.2   PHONE FACEPLATE DATA IN BINARY INCIDENCE MATRIX FORMAT

Transaction	Red	White	Blue	Orange	Green	Yellow
1	1	1	0	0	1	0
2	0	1	0	1	0	0
3	0	1	1	0	0	0
4	1	1	0	1	0	0
5	1	0	1	0	0	0
6	0	1	1	0	0	0
7	1	0	1	0	0	0
8	1	1	1	0	1	0
9	1	1	1	0	0	0
10	0	0	0	0	0	1

data (*Faceplate.csv*) for the cellular faceplate purchases in a transactions database. We translate these into binary incidence matrix format in Table 15.2.

Generating Candidate Rules

The idea behind association rules is to examine all possible rules between items in an if–then format and select only those that are most likely to be indicators of true dependence. We use the term *premise* to describe the IF part and *conclusion* to describe the THEN part. Sometimes, premise is also referred to as *antecedent*, and conclusion is also referred to as *consequent*. In association analysis, the premise and conclusion are sets of items (called *itemsets*) that are disjoint (do not have any items in common). Note that itemsets are not records of what people buy; they are simply possible combinations of items, including single items.

Returning to the phone faceplate purchase example, one example of a possible rule is "if red, then white," meaning that if a red faceplate is purchased, a white one is, too. Here, the premise is *red* and the conclusion is *white*. The premise and conclusion each contain a single item in this case. Another possible rule is "if red and white, then green." Here, the premise includes the itemset {*red, white*}, and the conclusion is {*green*}.

The first step in association rules is to generate all the rules that would be candidates for indicating associations between items. Ideally, we might want to look at all possible combinations of items in a database with p distinct items (in the phone faceplate example, $p = 6$). This means finding all combinations of single items, pairs of items, triplets of items, and so on, in the transactions database. However, generating all these combinations requires a long computation time that grows exponentially[1] in p. A practical solution is to consider only combinations that occur with higher frequency in the database. These are called *frequent itemsets*.

Determining what qualifies as a frequent itemset is related to the concept of *support*. The support of a rule is simply the number of transactions that include both the premise and conclusion itemsets. It is called a support because it measures the degree to which the data "support" the validity of the rule. The support is sometimes expressed as a percentage of the total number of records in the database. For example, the support for the itemset {*red, white*} in the phone faceplate example is 4 (or, $100 \times \frac{4}{10} = 40\%$).

What constitutes a frequent itemset is therefore defined as an itemset that has a support that exceeds a selected minimum support, determined by the user.

The Apriori Algorithm

Several algorithms have been proposed for generating frequent itemsets, but the classic algorithm is the *Apriori algorithm* of Agrawal et al. (1993). The key idea of the algorithm is to begin by generating frequent itemsets with just one item (one-itemsets) and to recursively generate frequent itemsets with two items, then with three items, and so on, until we have generated frequent itemsets of all sizes.

It is easy to generate frequent one-itemsets. All we need to do is to count, for each item, how many transactions in the database include the item. These transaction counts are the supports for the one-itemsets. We drop one-itemsets that have support below the desired minimum support to create a list of the frequent one-itemsets.

To generate frequent two-itemsets, we use the frequent one-itemsets. The reasoning is that if a certain one-itemset did not exceed the minimum support, any larger size itemset that includes it will not exceed the minimum support. In general, generating k-itemsets uses the frequent $(k - 1)$-itemsets that were generated in the preceding step. Each step requires a single run through the database, and therefore the Apriori algorithm is very fast even for a large number of unique items in a database.

---

[1]The number of rules that one can generate for p items is $3^p - 2^{p+1} + 1$. Computation time therefore grows by a factor for each additional item. For six items we have 602 rules, while for seven items the number of rules grows to 1932.

FP-Growth Algorithm

Instead of the Apriori algorithm, RapidMiner uses an alternative algorithm called the *FP-Growth algorithm*, proposed by Han et al. (2000) to generate frequent itemsets in a more computationally efficient way. The method is based on the idea of creating a tree structure called *FP-tree* to efficiently represent the transactions occurring in a transaction set. Creating an FP-tree is done in two steps: first, all the items in each transaction are ordered from high to low support. For example, transaction 1 in Table 15.2 would be ordered as *white*, *red*, and *green*; transaction 2 would be ordered as *white*, *orange*, and so on. Then, the FP-tree structure is constructed: the top node is a *null* node. Then, we add a branch (on the left in Figure 15.2) with nodes corresponding to the items in the first transaction. The nodes in Figure 15.2 are labeled with a counter indicating the number of transactions added thus far. After mapping transaction 1, nodes *white*, *red*, and *green* are added, each with a counter = 1. Then, transaction 2 is mapped by navigating down the earlier branch till node *white* (its counter is incremented to 2) and adding a new node *orange* (with its counter = 1). This process continues, and the branches of the tree are created by adding one transaction at a time.

Since different transactions can have common items, they share overlapping paths in the tree. Each branch is thus a sequence of splitting nodes, where a splitting node represents a single item. A branch therefore represents an itemset. The location of the item nodes in the tree is determined by the itemsets in the transactions so that a transaction with a new itemset creates a new branch while transactions sharing the same sequence of items increase the count for each item in the corresponding existing branch. Figure 15.2 shows the FP-tree resulting from the 10 transactions in Table 15.2.

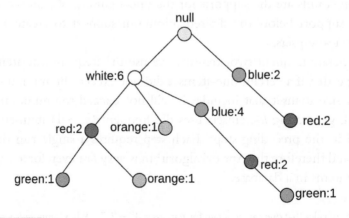

FIGURE 15.2   **FP-TREE FOR PHONE FACEPLATE DATA**

Regardless of whether the Apriori algorithm or FP-Growth algorithm is used, the resulting frequent itemsets are the same. RapidMiner implements the FP-Growth algorithm with the *FP-Growth* operator. The advantage of FP-Growth over Apriori algorithm is that it needs only two passes through the transaction database instead of multiple passes; the first pass records the support count of each item, and the second pass builds the FP-tree. Also, the compact tree structure generated with FP-Growth compresses the transaction data in an efficient format that can be used for computing very large transaction sets in memory.

Selecting Strong Rules

From the abundance of rules generated, the goal is to find only the rules that indicate a strong dependence between premise (antecedent) and conclusion (consequent) itemsets. To measure the strength of association implied by a rule, we use the measures of *confidence*, *lift*, and *conviction* as described below.

Support and Confidence   In addition to support, which we described earlier, there is another measure that expresses the degree of uncertainty about the if–then rule. This is known as the *confidence*[2] of the rule. This measure compares the co-occurrence of the premise and conclusion itemsets in the database with the occurrence of the premise itemsets. Confidence is defined as the ratio of the number of transactions that include all premise and conclusion itemsets (namely, the support) to the number of transactions that include all the premise itemsets:

$$\text{Confidence} = \frac{\text{No. of transactions with both premise and conclusion itemsets}}{\text{No. of transactions with premise itemset}}.$$

For example, suppose that a supermarket database has 100,000 point-of-sale transactions. Of these transactions, 2000 include both orange juice and (over-the-counter) flu medication, and 800 of these include soup purchases. The association rule "IF orange juice and flu medication are purchased THEN soup is purchased on the same trip" has a support of 800 transactions (alternatively, 0.8% = 800/100,000) and a confidence of 40% (=800/2000).

To see the relationship between support and confidence, let us think about what each is measuring (estimating). One way to think of support is that it is the (estimated) probability that a transaction selected randomly from the database will contain all items in the premise and the conclusion:

$$\text{Support} = \hat{P}(\text{premise AND conclusion}).$$

---

[2]The concept of confidence is different from and unrelated to the ideas of confidence intervals and confidence levels used in statistical inference.

In comparison, the confidence is the (estimated) *conditional probability* that a transaction selected randomly will include all the items in the conclusion *given* that the transaction includes all the items in the premise:

$$\text{Confidence} = \frac{\hat{P}(\text{premise AND conclusion})}{\hat{P}(\text{premise})} = \hat{P}(\text{conclusion} \mid \text{premise}).$$

A high value of confidence suggests a strong association rule (in which we are highly confident). However, this can be deceptive because if the premise and/or the conclusion has a high level of support, we can have a high value for confidence even when the premise and conclusion are independent! For example, if nearly all customers buy bananas and nearly all customers buy ice cream, the confidence level of a rule such as "IF bananas THEN ice-cream" will be high regardless of whether there is an association between the items.

Lift A better way to judge the strength of an association rule is to compare the confidence of the rule with a benchmark value, where we assume that the occurrence of the conclusion itemset in a transaction is independent of the occurrence of the premise for each rule. In other words, if the premise and conclusion itemsets are independent, what confidence values would we expect to see? Under independence, the support would be

$$\hat{P}(\text{premise AND conclusion}) = \hat{P}(\text{premise}) \times \hat{P}(\text{conclusion}),$$

and the benchmark confidence would be

$$\frac{\hat{P}(\text{premise}) \times \hat{P}(\text{conclusion})}{\hat{P}(\text{premise})} = \hat{P}(\text{conclusion}).$$

The estimate of this benchmark from the data, called the *benchmark confidence value* for a rule, is computed by

$$\text{Benchmark confidence} = \frac{\text{No. of transactions with conclusion itemset}}{\text{No. of transactions in database}}.$$

We compare the confidence with the benchmark confidence by looking at their ratio: this is called the *lift* of a rule. The lift of the rule is the confidence of the rule divided by the benchmark confidence, assuming independence of conclusion from premise:

$$\text{Lift} = \frac{\text{Confidence}}{\text{Benchmark confidence}}.$$

A lift greater than 1.0 suggests that there is some usefulness to the rule. In other words, the level of association between the premise and conclusion itemsets is higher than would be expected if they were independent. The larger the lift of the rule, the greater the strength of the association.

Conviction   Conviction, proposed by Brin et al. (1997), is a useful metric for measuring the degree of implication (strength of directionality) of a rule and is defined as

$$\text{Conviction} = \frac{\hat{P}(\text{premise}) \times \hat{P}(\text{not conclusion})}{\hat{P}(\text{premise AND not conclusion})}$$

$$= \frac{1 - (\text{support of conclusion})}{1 - \text{confidence of rule}}.$$

The *conviction* of rule {premise, conclusion} considers the directionality of the rule premise $\Rightarrow$ conclusion, rather than simply a co-occurrence (correlation). It measures this directionality by considering an event that *should not happen* if the rule is correct: the event premise-without-conclusion. The probability of this event is the denominator of the conviction metric: $\hat{P}$(premise AND no-conclusion). However, this event (premise-without-conclusion) can also occur when the rule is incorrect, that is, when these two events are unrelated but co-occur purely due to chance. The numerator in conviction computes the probability of such a random co-occurrence: $\hat{P}$(premise) $\times$ $\hat{P}$(no conclusion).

In short, conviction compares the probabilities of the event premise-without-conclusion under an assumption that the rule is correct (denominator) and under an assumption that the rule is incorrect (numerator). When the rule is incorrect, we expect conviction to be close to 1. When the rule is correct, we expect values much larger than 1, indicating how much more unlikely the combination is.

A value of conviction can be interpreted as "the factor by which the event premise-without-conclusion is more unlikely if the rule is correct than by pure chance co-occurrence." For example, consider the rule "if orange juice then flu medication" in our previous example, where we had 100,000 transactions in total. Suppose 10,000 transactions had orange juice (OJ) and no flu medication, 4000 with flu medication and no OJ, 20,000 with both, and 66,000 with neither (see Table 15.3). Then, conviction of "if OJ then flu medication" is calculated as

$$\frac{30,000/100,000 \times 76,000/100,000}{10,000/100,000} = 2.28.$$

This means the 10,000 occurrences of OJ-and-no-flu-medication are more than twice as unlikely if the rule is correct than by pure chance (if the rule is incorrect, we'd expect 22,800 co-occurrences).

In contrast to lift, conviction is a directed metric since it also incorporates the information of the absence of the conclusion. In other words, the conviction of a rule is sensitive to rule direction. Conviction is similar to confidence and ranges from 0 to ∞. It is equal to 0 when the conclusion is always present or the premise is always absent. If the premise and conclusion are independent

TABLE 15.3	EXAMPLE FOR COMPUTING CONVICTION
OJ only (no flu medication)	10,000
Flu medication only (no OJ)	4,000
OJ and flu medication	20,000
No OJ, no flu medication	66,000
Total transactions	100,000

(unrelated), conviction is equal to 1. If the rule always holds (the items always appear together), its value is infinity, corresponding to a confidence value of 1.

To illustrate the computation of support, confidence, lift, and conviction for the cellular phone faceplate example, we use the binary incidence matrix format (Table 15.2) that is better suited to this purpose.

The Process of Rule Selection

Frequent Itemset Selection   The process of selecting strong rules is based on generating all association rules that meet stipulated support and confidence requirements. This is done in two stages. The first stage, described earlier, consists of finding all "frequent" itemsets, those itemsets that have a requisite support.

Now suppose that we want association rules between items for this database that have a support count of at least 2 (equivalent to a percentage support of $2/10 = 20\%$). In other words, these are rules based on items that were purchased together in at least 20% of the transactions. By enumeration, we can see that only the itemsets listed in Table 15.4 have a count of at least 2.

TABLE 15.4	ITEMSETS WITH SUPPORT COUNT OF AT LEAST TWO
Itemset	**Support (count)**
{red}	6
{white}	7
{blue}	6
{orange}	2
{green}	2
{red, white}	4
{red, blue}	4
{red, green}	2
{white, blue}	4
{white, orange}	2
{white, green}	2
{red, white, blue}	2
{red, white, green}	2

The first itemset {*red*} has a support of 6, because six of the transactions included a red faceplate. Similarly, the last itemset {*red, white, green*} has a support of 2, because only two transactions included red, white, and green faceplates.

These frequent itemsets can also be generated by using the FP-Growth algorithm discussed earlier. Using the minimum support threshold, the FP-tree (see Figure 15.2) is "shrunk" into a set of smaller *conditional FP-trees* through a computationally efficient but complex divide-and-conquer method (see Han et al. (2000) for details), resulting in the frequent itemsets.

Association Rules Generation   We generate, from the frequent itemsets, association rules that meet a confidence requirement. The first step is aimed at removing item combinations that are rare in the database. The second stage then filters the remaining rules and selects only those with high confidence. For most association analysis data, the computational challenge is the first stage, as described in the discussion of the Apriori and FP-Growth algorithms.

The computation of confidence in the second stage is simple. Since any subset (e.g., {*red*} in the phone faceplate example) must occur at least as frequently as the set it belongs to (e.g., {*red, white*}), each subset will also be in the list. It is then straightforward to compute the confidence as the ratio of the support for the itemset to the support for each subset of the itemset. We retain the corresponding association rule only if it exceeds the desired cutoff value for confidence. For example, from the itemset {*red, white, green*} in the phone faceplate purchases, we get the following single-conclusion association rules, confidence values, and lift values:

Rule	Confidence		Lift	
{*red, white*} $\Rightarrow$ {*green*}	$\dfrac{\text{Support of \{red, white, green\}}}{\text{Support of \{red, white\}}}$	$= \dfrac{2}{4} = 50\%$	$\dfrac{\text{Confidence of rule}}{\text{Benchmark confidence}}$	$= \dfrac{50\%}{20\%} = 2.5$
{*green*} $\Rightarrow$ {*red*}	$\dfrac{\text{Support of \{green, red\}}}{\text{Support of \{green\}}}$	$= \dfrac{2}{2} = 100\%$	$\dfrac{\text{Confidence of rule}}{\text{Benchmark confidence}}$	$= \dfrac{100\%}{60\%} = 1.67$
{*white, green*} $\Rightarrow$ {*red*}	$\dfrac{\text{Support of \{white, green, red\}}}{\text{Support of \{white, green\}}}$	$= \dfrac{2}{2} = 100\%$	$\dfrac{\text{Confidence of rule}}{\text{Benchmark confidence}}$	$= \dfrac{100\%}{60\%} = 1.67$

If the desired minimum confidence is 70%, we would report only the second and third rules.

After selecting the rules based on the selection criteria, we can compute their conviction values to identify their degree of implication.

Rule	Conviction	
{*red, white*} $\Rightarrow$ {*green*}	$\dfrac{P\{red, white\} \times P\{NOT\ green\}}{P\{red, white, NOT\ green\}}$	$= \dfrac{40\% \times 80\%}{20\%} = 1.6$
{*green*} $\Rightarrow$ {*red*}	$\dfrac{P\{green\} \times P\{NOT\ red\}}{P\{green, NOT\ red\}}$	$= \dfrac{20\% \times 40\%}{0\%} = \infty$
{*white, green*} $\Rightarrow$ {*red*}	$\dfrac{P\{white, green\} \times P\{NOT\ red\}}{P\{white, green, NOT\ red\}}$	$= \dfrac{20\% \times 40\%}{0\%} = \infty$

We can generate association rules in RapidMiner as shown in the process in Figure 15.3 (top). In preparing the data, all attributes, except the Transaction attribute, are transformed to binominal type using the *Numerical to Binominal* operator, and the *Select Attributes* operator is used to select these transformed attributes. With the data prepared, the *FP-Growth* operator is used to find frequent itemsets by specifying the minimum support (20%), and the association rules are selected by specifying minimum confidence level percentage (50%) in the *Create Association Rules* operator.[3,4] *FP-Growth* and *Create Association Rules* operators are both located in RapidMiner's Operators panel under *Modeling > Associations*.

Figure 15.3 (bottom) shows the output with frequent itemsets and the association rules. The output shows information on each rule and its support, confidence, lift, and conviction. (Note that here we consider all possible itemsets, not just {*red, white, green*} as above.) The rules are shown sorted in descending order of conviction and lift values.

Interpreting the Results

We can translate each of the rules from Figure 15.3 (bottom) into an understandable sentence that provides information about performance. For example, we can read rule {*orange*} $\Rightarrow$ {*white*} as follows:

> If *orange* is purchased, then with confidence 100% *white* will also be purchased.
> This rule has a lift of 1.429 and conviction of ∞.

In interpreting results, it is useful to look at the various measures. The support for the rule indicates its impact in terms of overall size: How many transactions are affected? If only a small number of transactions are affected, the rule may be of little use (unless the conclusion is very valuable and/or the rule is very efficient in finding it).

The lift indicates how efficient the rule is in finding conclusion itemsets compared with random selection. A very efficient rule is preferred to an inefficient rule, but we must still consider support: a very efficient rule that has very low support may not be as desirable as a less efficient rule with much greater support.

---

[3]In the *FP-Growth* operator, if the "find min number of itemsets" option is checked, then the operator will find at least as many itemsets as set in the user-specified advanced parameter *min number of itemsets*. It will ignore the "min requirement" (i.e., *min support* or *min frequency*) threshold specified. Thus, if you want to get itemsets that strictly meet only the *min support* or *min frequency* requirement, then uncheck the "find min number of itemsets" checkbox.

[4]The *FP-Growth* operator expects all attributes to be binominal. For a non-binominal attribute in your data, such as an attribute with *id* role, RapidMiner may flag a warning for the *FP-Growth* operator and mark its input port with red color. This warning may be safely ignored, and the operator should run normally using the binominal attributes specified.

FIGURE 15.3 (TOP) PROCESS FOR MINING ASSOCIATION RULES FROM FACEPLATE TRANSACTIONS, (BOTTOM LEFT) FREQUENT ITEMSETS WITH MIN SUPPORT 20%, AND (BOTTOM RIGHT) ASSOCIATION RULES WITH MIN CONFIDENCE 50%

The confidence tells us at what rate conclusions will be found and is useful in determining the business or operational usefulness of a rule: a rule with low confidence may find conclusion itemsets at too low a rate to be worth the cost of (say) promoting the consequent in all the transactions that involve the premise.

The conviction allows us to assess the direction of the rule. For the rule {*red, white*} $\Rightarrow$ {*green*}, the conviction value of 1.6 implies that this rule would be incorrect 60% more often if the relationship between {*red, white*} and {*green*} was purely random. Two rules with their premise and conclusion swapped will have the same lift values but could have different conviction values. From Figure 15.3 (bottom right), we can see that the two rules {*green*} $\Rightarrow$ {*red, white*} and {*red, white*} $\Rightarrow$ {*green*} have the same lift of 2.5 but different conviction values of ∞ and 1.6, respectively. The former with the higher conviction value is preferable because the chance of that relationship being random is lower.

Rules and Chance

What about confidence in the nontechnical sense? How sure can we be that the rules we develop are meaningful? Considering the matter from a statistical perspective, we can ask: Are we finding associations that are really just chance occurrences?

Let us examine the output from an application of this algorithm to a small database of 50 transactions, where each of the nine items is assigned randomly to each transaction. The data are shown in Table 15.5, and the association rules generated are shown in Figure 15.4. Note that we specify the minimum support of 4% for frequent itemset generation and the minimum confidence level of 70% for rule selection. In looking at these tables, remember that "premises" and "conclusion" refer to itemsets, not records.

TABLE 15.5   FIFTY TRANSACTIONS OF RANDOMLY ASSIGNED ITEMS

Transaction	Items					Transaction	Items				Transaction	Items			
1	8					18	8				35	3	4	6	8
2	3	4	8			19					36	1	4	8	
3	8					20	9				37	4	7	8	
4	3	9				21	2	5	6	8	38	8	9		
5	9					22	4	6	9		39	4	5	7	9
6	1	8				23	4	9			40	2	8	9	
7	6	9				24	8	9			41	2	5	9	
8	3	5	7	9		25	6	8			42	1	2	7	9
9	8					26	1	6	8		43	5	8		
10						27	5	8			44	1	7	8	
11	1	7	9			28	4	8	9		45	8			
12	1	4	5	8	9	29	9				46	2	7	9	
13	5	7	9			30	8				47	4	6	9	
14	6	7	8			31	1	5	8		48	9			
15	3	7	9			32	3	6	9		49	9			
16	1	4	9			33	7	9			50	6	7	8	
17	6	7	8			34	7	8	9						

No.	Premises	Conclusion	Support	Confidence	Lift ↓	Conviction ↓
3	8, 3	4	0.040	1	4.545	∞
2	7, 6	8	0.060	1	1.852	∞
4	4, 3	8	0.040	1	1.852	∞
5	1, 5	8	0.040	1	1.852	∞
6	7, 5	9	0.060	1	1.852	∞
7	7, 3	9	0.040	1	1.852	∞
8	7, 2	9	0.040	1	1.852	∞
9	4, 5	9	0.040	1	1.852	∞
1	2	9	0.080	0.800	1.481	2.300

FIGURE 15.4   ASSOCIATION RULES OUTPUT FOR RANDOM DATA

In this example, the lift values highlight Rule [3] as most interesting, as it suggests that purchase of item 4 is almost five times as likely when items 3 and 8 are purchased than if item 4 was not associated with the itemset {3, 8}. We also see that the top 9 rules have conviction of ∞. Yet we know there is no fundamental association underlying these data—they were generated randomly.

Two principles can guide us in assessing rules for possible spuriousness due to chance effects:

1. The more records the rule is based on, the more solid the conclusion.

2. The more distinct rules we consider seriously (perhaps consolidating multiple rules that deal with the same items), the more likely it is that at least some will be based on chance sampling results. For one person to toss a coin 10 times and get 10 heads would be quite surprising. If 1000 people toss a coin 10 times each, it would not be nearly so surprising to have one get 10 heads. Formal adjustment of "statistical significance" when multiple comparisons are made is a complex subject in its own right and beyond the scope of this book. A reasonable approach is to consider rules from the top-down in terms of business or operational applicability and not consider more than what can reasonably be incorporated in a human decision-making process. This will impose a rough constraint on the dangers that arise from an automated review of hundreds or thousands of rules in search of "something interesting."

We now consider a more realistic example, using a larger database and real transactional data.

Example 2: Rules for Similar Book Purchases

The following example (drawn from the Charles Book Club case; see Chapter 23) examines associations among transactions involving various types of books. The database includes 4000 transactions, and there are 11 different types of books. The data, in binary incidence matrix form, are shown in Table 15.6.

TABLE 15.6   SUBSET OF BOOK PURCHASE TRANSACTIONS IN BINARY MATRIX FORMAT

ChildBks	YouthBks	CookBks	DoItYBks	RefBks	ArtBks	GeogBks	ItalCook	ItalAtlas	ItalArt	Florence
0	1	0	1	0	0	1	0	0	0	0
1	0	0	0	0	0	0	0	0	0	0
0	0	0	0	0	0	0	0	0	0	0
1	1	1	0	1	0	1	0	0	0	0
0	0	1	0	0	0	1	0	0	0	0
1	0	0	0	0	1	0	0	0	0	1
0	1	0	0	0	0	0	0	0	0	0
0	1	0	0	1	0	0	0	0	0	0
1	0	0	1	0	0	0	0	0	0	0
1	1	1	0	0	0	1	0	0	0	0
0	0	0	0	0	0	0	0	0	0	0

For instance, the first transaction included *YouthBks* (youth books), *DoItYBks* (do-it-yourself books), and *GeogBks* (geography books). Figure 15.5 shows some of the rules generated for these data, given that we specified a minimal support of 5% (200 transactions out of 4000 transactions) and a minimal confidence of 50%. This resulted in 81 rules (the 25 rules with the highest lift ratio are shown in Figure 15.5).

In reviewing these rules, we see that the information can be compressed. Rules 40, 28, 75, and 80 involve the same four book types, with different premises and conclusions. The same is true of rules 39, 12, and 23, as well as 1 and 15 (the same trio of items). (Item groups like this are easy to track down by looking for rows that share the same support.) This does not mean that the rules are not useful. On the contrary, it can reduce the number of itemsets to be considered for possible action from a business perspective.

15.2 COLLABORATIVE FILTERING[5]

Recommendation systems are a critically important part of websites that offer a large variety of products or services. Examples include the following: Amazon.com offers millions of different products, Netflix has thousands of movies for rental, Google searches over huge numbers of webpages, Internet radio websites such as Spotify and Pandora include a large variety of music albums

---

No.	Premises	Conclusion	Support	Confidence	Lift ↓	Conviction
44	YouthBks, RefBks	CookBks, ChildBks	0.055	0.680	2.810	2.369
40	DoltYBks, RefBks	CookBks, ChildBks	0.061	0.662	2.736	2.244
39	DoltYBks, YouthBks	CookBks, ChildBks	0.067	0.649	2.681	2.159
32	GeogBks, RefBks	CookBks, ChildBks	0.050	0.615	2.540	1.967
30	GeogBks, YouthBks	CookBks, ChildBks	0.063	0.605	2.501	1.920
29	GeogBks, DoltYBks	CookBks, ChildBks	0.060	0.599	2.475	1.890
25	CookBks, ChildBks, GeogBks	YouthBks	0.063	0.578	2.424	1.803
28	CookBks, ChildBks, RefBks	DoltYBks	0.061	0.592	2.323	1.826
18	GeogBks, DoltYBks	YouthBks	0.054	0.540	2.265	1.655
17	CookBks, ChildBks, RefBks	YouthBks	0.055	0.534	2.241	1.634
12	CookBks, ChildBks, DoltYBks	YouthBks	0.067	0.524	2.201	1.602
23	CookBks, ChildBks, YouthBks	DoltYBks	0.067	0.558	2.192	1.687
22	ChildBks, RefBks	DoltYBks	0.071	0.554	2.173	1.669
21	CookBks, ChildBks, GeogBks	DoltYBks	0.060	0.553	2.169	1.665
9	ChildBks, GeogBks	YouthBks	0.075	0.516	2.167	1.575
8	CookBks, GeogBks	YouthBks	0.080	0.514	2.156	1.566
81	ChildBks, YouthBks, RefBks	CookBks	0.055	0.891	2.145	5.369
19	ChildBks, YouthBks	DoltYBks	0.080	0.544	2.136	1.635
16	CookBks, RefBks	DoltYBks	0.074	0.533	2.093	1.596
4	RefBks	CookBks, ChildBks	0.103	0.505	2.089	1.533
75	CookBks, DoltYBks, RefBks	ChildBks	0.061	0.822	2.087	3.407
2	YouthBks	CookBks, ChildBks	0.120	0.504	2.081	1.527
80	ChildBks, DoltYBks, RefBks	CookBks	0.061	0.863	2.076	4.256
1	DoltYBks	CookBks, ChildBks	0.128	0.501	2.072	1.520
15	CookBks, ChildBks	DoltYBks	0.128	0.528	2.072	1.579

FIGURE 15.5   **ASSOCIATION RULES FOR BOOK PURCHASE TRANSACTIONS**

by various artists, travel websites offer many destinations and hotels, and social network websites have many groups. The recommender engine provides personalized recommendations to a user based on the user's information and on similar users' information. Information means behaviors indicative of preference, such as purchase, ratings, and clicking.

The value that recommendation systems provide to users helps online companies convert browsers into buyers, increase cross-selling, and build loyalty.

Collaborative filtering is a popular technique used by such recommendation systems. The term *collaborative filtering* is based on the notions of identifying relevant items for a specific user from the very large set of items ("filtering") by considering preferences of many users ("collaboration").

The Fortune.com article "Amazon's Recommendation Secret" (June 30, 2012) describes the company's use of collaborative filtering not only for providing personalized product recommendations but also for customizing the entire website interface for each user:

> At root, the retail giant's recommendation system is based on a number of simple elements: what a user has bought in the past, which items they have in their virtual shopping cart, items they've rated and liked, and what other customers have viewed and purchased. Amazon calls this homegrown math "item-to-item collaborative filtering," and it's used this algorithm to heavily customize the browsing experience for returning customers.

Data Type and Format

Collaborative filtering requires availability of all item–user information. Specifically, for each item–user combination, we should have some measure of the user's preference for that item. Preference can be a numerical rating or a binary behavior such as a purchase, a "like," or a click.

For n users $(u_1, u_2, \ldots, u_n)$ and p items $(i_1, i_2, \ldots, i_p)$, we can think of the data as an $n \times p$ matrix of n rows (users) by p columns (items). Each cell includes the rating or the binary event corresponding to the user's preference of the item (see schematic in Table 15.7). Typically not every user purchases or rates every item, and therefore a purchase matrix will have many zeros (it is sparse), and a rating matrix will have many missing values. Such missing values sometimes convey "uninterested" (as opposed to non-missing values that convey interest).

TABLE 15.7   SCHEMATIC OF MATRIX FORMAT WITH RATING DATA

User ID	I_1	I_2	$\cdots$	I_p
		Item ID		
U_1	$r_{1,1}$	$r_{1,2}$	$\cdots$	$r_{1,p}$
U_2	$r_{2,1}$	$r_{2,2}$	$\cdots$	$r_{2,p}$
$\vdots$				
U_n	$r_{n,1}$	$r_{n,2}$	$\cdots$	$r_{n,p}$

When both n and p are large, it is not practical to store the preferences data $(r_{u,i})$ in an $n \times p$ table. Instead, the data can be stored in many rows of triplets of the form $(U_u, I_i, r_{u,i})$, where each triplet contains the user ID, the item ID, and the preference information.

Example 3: Netflix Prize Contest

We have been considering both association rules and collaborative filtering as unsupervised techniques, but it is possible to judge how well they do by looking at holdout data to see what users purchase and how they rate items. The famous Netflix contest, mentioned in Chapter 13, did just this and provides a useful example to illustrate collaborative filtering, though the extension into training and validation is beyond the scope of this book.

In 2006, Netflix, the largest movie rental service in North America, announced a US$ 1 million contest (www.netflixprize.com) for the purpose of improving its recommendation system called *Cinematch*. Participants were provided with a number of datasets, one for each movie. Each dataset included all the customer ratings for that movie (and the timestamp). We can think of one large combined dataset of the form [customer ID, movie ID, rating, date] where each record includes the rating given by a certain customer to a certain movie on a certain date. Ratings were on a 1–5 star scale. Contestants were asked to develop a recommendation algorithm that would improve over the existing Netflix system. Table 15.8 shows a small sample from the contest data, organized in matrix format. Rows indicate customers and columns are different movies.

TABLE 15.8   SAMPLE OF RECORDS FROM THE NETFLIX PRIZE CONTEST, FOR A SUBSET OF 10 CUSTOMERS AND 9 MOVIES

Customer ID	Movie ID 1	5	8	17	18	28	30	44	48
30878	4	1			3	3	4	5	
124105	4								
822109	5								
823519	3		1	4			4	5	
885013	4	5							
893988	3						4	4	
1248029	3					2	4		3
1503895	4								
1842128	4						3		
2238063	3								

It is interesting to note that the winning team was able to improve their system by considering not just the ratings for a movie but also *whether* a movie was rated by a particular customer or not. In other words, the information on which movies a customer decided to rate turned out to be critically informative of customers' preferences, more than simply considering the 1–5 rating information[6]:

---

[6]Bell, R. M., Koren, Y., and Volinsky, C., "The BellKor 2008 Solution to the Netflix Prize," https://api.semanticscholar.org/CorpusID:11877045

Collaborative filtering methods address the sparse set of rating values. However, much accuracy is obtained by also looking at other features of the data. First is the information on which movies each user chose to rate, regardless of specific rating value ("the binary view"). This played a decisive role in our 2007 solution, and reflects the fact that the movies to be rated are selected deliberately by the user, and are not a random sample.

This is an example where converting the rating information into a binary matrix of rated/unrated proved to be useful.

User-Based Collaborative Filtering: "People Like You"

One approach to generating personalized recommendations for a user using collaborative filtering is based on finding users with similar preferences and recommending items that they liked but the user hasn't purchased. The algorithm has two steps:

1. Find users who are most similar to the user of interest (neighbors). This is done by comparing the preference of our user with the preferences of other users.

2. Considering only the items that the user has *not* yet purchased, recommend the ones that are most preferred by the user's neighbors.

This is the approach behind Amazon's "Customers Who Viewed This Item Also Viewed..." (see Figure 15.1). It is also used in a Google search for generating the "Similar pages" link shown near each search result.

Step 1 requires choosing a distance (or proximity) metric to measure the distance between our user and the other users. Once the distances are computed, we can use a threshold on the distance or on the number of required neighbors to determine the nearest neighbors to be used in Step 2. This approach is called "user-based top-N recommendation."

A nearest-neighbors approach measures the distance of our user to each of the other users in the database, similar to the k-nearest-neighbors algorithm (see Chapter 7). The Euclidean distance measure we discussed in that chapter does not perform as well for collaborative filtering as some other measures. A popular proximity measure between two users is the Pearson correlation between their ratings. We denote the ratings of items $I_1, \ldots, I_p$ by user U_1 as $r_{1,1}, r_{1,2}, \ldots, r_{1,p}$ and their average by $\bar{r}_1$. Similarly, the ratings by user U_2 are $r_{2,1}, r_{2,2}, \ldots, r_{2,p}$, with average $\bar{r}_2$. The correlation proximity between the two users is defined by

$$\text{Corr}(U_1, U_2) = \frac{\sum (r_{1,i} - \bar{r}_1)(r_{2,i} - \bar{r}_2)}{\sqrt{\sum (r_{1,i} - \bar{r}_1)^2} \sqrt{\sum (r_{2,i} - \bar{r}_2)^2}}, \qquad (15.1)$$

where the summations are only over the items co-rated by both users.

To illustrate this, let us compute the correlation between customer 30878 and customer 823519 in the small Netflix sample in Table 15.8. We'll assume that the data shown in the table is the entire information. First, we compute the average rating by each of these users:

$$\bar{r}_{30878} = (4 + 1 + 3 + 3 + 4 + 5)/6 = 3.333,$$

$$\bar{r}_{823519} = (3 + 1 + 4 + 4 + 5)/5 = 3.4.$$

Note that the average is computed over a different number of movies for each of these customers, because they each rated a different set of movies. The average for a customer is computed over *all* the movies that a customer rated. The calculations for the correlation involve the departures from the average, but *only for the items that they co-rated*. In this case, the co-rated movie IDs are 1, 28, and 30:

$$\text{Corr}(U_{30878}, U_{823519})$$

$$= \frac{(4 - 3.333)(3 - 3.4) + (3 - 3.333)(4 - 3.4) + (4 - 3.333)(5 - 3.4)}{\sqrt{(4 - 3.333)^2 + (3 - 3.333)^2 + (4 - 3.333)^2}\sqrt{(3 - 3.4)^2 + (4 - 3.4)^2 + (5 - 3.4)^2}}$$

$$= 0.6/1.75 = 0.34.$$

The same approach can be used when the data are in the form of a binary matrix (e.g., purchased or didn't purchase.)

Another popular measure is a variant of the Pearson correlation called *cosine similarity*. It differs from the correlation formula by not subtracting the means. Subtracting the mean in the correlation formula adjusts for users' different overall approaches to rating—for example, a customer who always rates highly vs. one who tends to give low ratings.[7]

For example, the cosine similarity between the two Netflix customers is

$$\text{Cos Sim}(U_{30878}, U_{823519}) = \frac{4 \times 3 + 3 \times 4 + 4 \times 5}{\sqrt{4^2 + 3^2 + 4^2}\sqrt{3^2 + 4^2 + 5^2}}$$

$$= 44/45.277 = 0.972$$

Note that when the data are in the form of a binary matrix, say, for purchase or no-purchase, the cosine similarity must be calculated over all items that either user has purchased; it cannot be limited to just the items that were co-purchased.

---

[7]Correlation and cosine similarity are popular in collaborative filtering because they are computationally fast for high-dimensional sparse data, and they account for both the rating values and the number of rated items.

> Collaborative filtering suffers from what is called a *cold start*: it cannot be used as is to create recommendations for new users or new items. For a user who rated a single item, the correlation coefficient between this and other users (in user-generated collaborative filtering) will have a denominator of zero, and the cosine proximity will be 1 regardless of the rating. In a similar vein, users with just one item, and items with just one user, do not qualify as candidates for nearby neighbors.

For a user of interest, we compute his/her similarity to each of the users in our database using a correlation, cosine similarity, or another measure. Then, in Step 2, we look only at the k nearest users, and among all the other items that they rated/purchased, we choose the best one and recommend it to our user. What is the best one? For binary purchase data, it is the item most purchased. For rating data, it could be the highest rated, most rated, or a weighting of the two.

The nearest-neighbors approach can be computationally expensive when we have a large database of users. One solution is to use clustering methods (see Chapter 16) to group users into homogeneous clusters in terms of their preferences and then to measure the distance of our user to each of the clusters. This approach places the computational load on the clustering step that can take place earlier and offline; it is then cheaper (and faster) to compare our user to each of the clusters in real time. The price of clustering is less accurate recommendations, because not all the members of the closest cluster are the most similar to our user.

Item-Based Collaborative Filtering

When the number of users is much larger than the number of items, it is computationally cheaper (and faster) to find similar items rather than similar users. Specifically, when a user expresses interest in a particular item, the item-based collaborative filtering algorithm has two steps:

1. Find the items that were co-rated, or co-purchased, (by any user) with the item of interest.

2. Recommend the most popular or correlated item(s) among the similar items.

Similarity is now computed between items, instead of users. For example, in our small Netflix sample (Table 15.8), the correlation between movie 1 (with average $\bar{r}_1 = 3.7$) and movie 5 (with average $\bar{r}_5 = 3$) is

$$\text{Corr}(I_1, I_5) = \frac{(4 - 3.7)(1 - 3) + (4 - 3.7)(5 - 3)}{\sqrt{(4 - 3.7)^2 + (4 - 3.7)^2}\sqrt{(1 - 3)^2 + (5 - 3)^2}} = 0.$$

The zero correlation is due to the two opposite ratings of movie 5 by the users who also rated 1. One user rated it 5 stars and the other gave it a 1 star.

In a similar fashion, we can compute similarity between all the movies. This can be done offline. In real time, for a user who rates a certain movie highly, we can look up the movie correlation table and recommend the movie with the highest positive correlation to the user's newly rated movie.

According to an industry report[8] by researchers who developed the Amazon item-to-item recommendation system:

> [The item-based] algorithm produces recommendations in real time, scales to massive data sets, and generates high-quality recommendations.

The disadvantage of item-based recommendations is that there is less diversity between items (compared to users' taste), and therefore, the recommendations are often obvious.

Evaluating Performance

Collaborative filtering can be considered an unsupervised learning method, because data are not typically organized for analysis in the form "X was recommended, user did Y." We do, however, have data on what has been purchased or rated by a user without regard to any recommendations. We can "hide" some items in the user–item matrix (this constitutes the holdout set), and use collaborative filtering to make recommendations for the hidden items. This is effectively the same thing as predicting the hidden user rating, or whether the user purchases the item. We can then un-hide the actual user action and see how the recommendations compare to the actual.

Two types of offline learning evaluations are *predictive performance* and *ranking performance*—each measures a different aspect of the recommender system. Predictive performance assesses how close the recommendation is to the actual user's behavior. We have already encountered many such metrics in Chapter 5. In contrast, ranking evaluation considers only performance on the top set of recommended items ("Top-N") produced by the recommender algorithm. This approach is useful in many applications where the a user is shown a set of the "best" recommended items for him/her (such as the results of a Google search). Ranking metrics therefore focus on the accuracy of only the top-ranked items.

Common performance metrics include the following:

Predictive performance for numerical predictions (e.g., ratings):
Metrics such as holdout RMSE and MAE are commonly used. Note that these metrics are strongly influenced by long-tail items: a rare item

---

[8]Linden, G., Smith, B., and York J., "Amazon.com Recommendations: Item-to-Item Collaborative Filtering", *IEEE Internet Computing*, vol. 7, no. 1, p. 76–80, 2003.

that is incorrectly predicted can mask excellent performance on common items. One solution is to weight items within these metrics so that more important/profitable items have higher weights.

Predictive performance for categorical predictions (e.g., click/ no-click)   Metrics based on the holdout confusion matrix such as accuracy, recall and precision, and ROC curves are common.

Ranking performance for numerical predictions (e.g., ratings): A common ranking performance metric is the correlation between the *ordering* of the true ratings and the *ordering* of the predicted ratings. This is known as the Spearman coefficient.

Ranking performance for categorical classifications: Common metrics include Top-N precision and Top-N recall, which are the precision and recall computed only on the top-N recommendation sets and which measure the fraction of relevant items in the recommendation list and the fraction of relevant items that are missed by the list.

There also exist specialized metrics for other important properties of a recommendation algorithm, beyond accuracy, such as novelty, trust, coverage, and serendipity. To learn more about these, see Aggarwal (2016).

Lastly, we note that partitioning the data into training, validation, and holdout sets is done a bit differently than in supervised learning: rather than sampling users, for collaborative filtering evaluation, the sampling is done on *matrix entries* (e.g., $r_{u,i}$ in Table 15.7): these are the user–item combinations in the user–item matrix.

Example 4: Predicting Movie Ratings with MovieLens Data

In this illustration, we analyze movie ratings data from MovieLens,[9] a website that recommends movies for people to watch. The goal is to predict ratings for movies that users have not watched thus far and then use the movies with the highest prediction ratings as top-k recommendations for the user. We use the 100K latest dataset[10] that contains 100,836 ratings provided by 610 users for 9742 movies. The datasets are available through the book website as *ratings.csv* and *movies.csv* files containing ratings data and movies data, respectively. A description of each attribute is given in Table 15.9. Additional movie attributes (e.g., actors) can be retrieved through movie databases such as IMDB.

Figure 15.6 shows the data preprocessing steps, starting with the *Join* operator to merge the ratings and movies data into a single ExampleSet by setting the

---

[9]MovieLens (https://movielens.org) website is managed by the GroupLens research lab at the University of Minnesota.
[10]Source: https://grouplens.org/datasets/movielens/ (Dataset creation date: September 26, 2018); see Harper and Konstan (2015).

| TABLE 15.9 | DESCRIPTION OF ATTRIBUTES IN MOVIELENS DATASET |

Ratings data

userId	Anonymized MovieLens user ID. Each user has rated at least 20 movies.
movieId	Movie ID consistent with that used on the MovieLens website (e.g., information for movie id 1 is available at https://movielens.org/movies/1)
rating	Movie rating provided by user on a 5-star scale, with half-star increments (0.5–5 stars)
timestamp	Timestamp when rating was recorded. Time is in seconds since midnight Coordinated Universal Time (UTC) of January 1, 1970.

Movies data

movieId	Same as ratings data
title	Movie titles, including the year of release in parentheses
genres	Pipe-separated list of genres for corresponding movie title

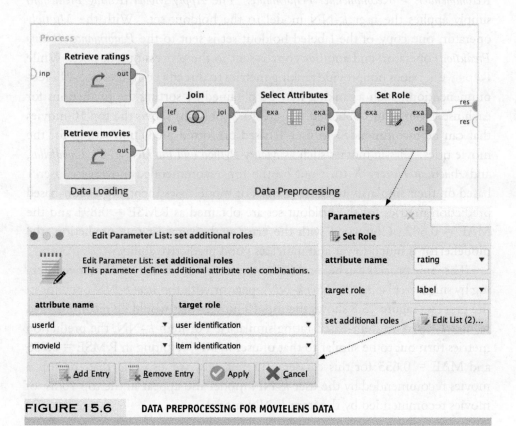

FIGURE 15.6   DATA PREPROCESSING FOR MOVIELENS DATA

parameter *join type* = *inner* and specifying movieId as both the *right_key_attribute* and *left_key_attribute* for joining the data. Next, with the *Select Attributes* operator, all attributes except the rating timestamp are selected for further analysis. Collaborative filtering requires specifying three key roles for certain attributes: *label*, *user identification*, and *item identification*, as shown in Figure 15.6.

Figure 15.7 (top) presents the RapidMiner process for building a user-based collaborative filtering model with the training set and measuring model performance with the holdout set. The *Data Preprocessing* subprocess contains the same steps mentioned in Figure 15.6. Using the *Split Data* operator, the data is partitioned into training (60%) and holdout (40%) sets. *Recommender Extension* has to be installed to implement the collaborative filtering operators. The *User k-NN* operator is used for model building, which can be found in the Operators panel under *Extensions > Recommenders > Item Rating Prediction > Collaborative Filtering Rating Prediction > User k-NN*. In the *User k-NN* operator, we use the default parameters of $k = 80$, *correlation mode* = *cosine*, *Min Rating* = 0, and *Range* = 5 (since the rating is on a 0–5 scale). The model application and performance assessment operators can be found in the Operators panel under *Extensions > Recommenders > Recommender Performance*. The *Apply Model (Rating Prediction)* simply applies the user k-NN model to the holdout set. With the *Multiply* operator, one copy of the labeled holdout set is sent to the *Performance (Rating Prediction)* operator, and another copy is sent to the process output port. While RapidMiner does not provide ranking metrics to directly compute "top-N" recommendations, such a ranking may be obtained by sorting the predictions for each user from results obtained. Figure 15.7 (bottom) shows the top 10 movies that can be recommended to user 1 based on sorted prediction ratings for the movie titles. Classic movies such as *Monty Python and the Holy Grail, Goodfellas,* and *American History X* turn out be the top-recommended movies for user 1 based on their similarity to other users. For model assessment, regression-based prediction metrics for the holdout set are obtained as RMSE = 0.891 and the MAE = 0.682. Compared with the error with average rating prediction, the model error is much lower and indicates good predictive ability.

The same process can be modified to perform item-based collaborative filtering by simply replacing the *User k-NN* operator with the *Item k-NN* operator in the process. Figure 15.8 shows the top-10 movies that would be recommended to user 1 based on item-based rating similarity. For item k-NN, the prediction metrics turn out to be similar to that of user k-NN, resulting in RMSE = 0.855 and MAE = 0.655 for this dataset. Interestingly, we also find that the top 3 movies recommended by the user k-NN model also appear in the top 10 list of movies recommended by the item k-NN model.

Advantages and Weaknesses of Collaborative Filtering

Collaborative filtering relies on the availability of subjective information regarding users' preferences. It provides useful recommendations, even for "long-tail" items, if our database contains sufficient similar users (not necessarily many, but at least a few per user), so that each user can find other users with similar tastes. Similarly, the data should include sufficient per-item ratings or purchases. One

Row No.	rating	userId ↑	movieId	title	genres	prediction →
26	5	1	1136	Monty Python and the Holy Grail (1975)	Adventure|Comedy|Fantasy	5
28	5	1	1213	Goodfellas (1990)	Crime|Drama	5
64	5	1	2329	American History X (1998)	Crime|Drama	5
81	5	1	2959	Fight Club (1999)	Action|Crime|Drama|Thriller	5
7	5	1	260	Star Wars: Episode IV – A New Hope (1977)	Action|Adventure|Sci-Fi	4.995
9	4	1	356	Forrest Gump (1994)	Comedy|Drama|Romance|War	4.973
49	5	1	1927	All Quiet on the Western Front (1930)	Action|Drama|War	4.958
76	5	1	2692	Run Lola Run (Lola rennt) (1998)	Action|Crime	4.933
29	2	1	1219	Psycho (1960)	Crime|Horror	4.932
86	5	1	3147	Green Mile, The (1999)	Crime|Drama	4.928

ExampleSet (40,334 examples, 3 special attributes, 3 regular attributes)

FIGURE 15.7   (TOP) PROCESS FOR USER-BASED COLLABORATIVE FILTERING ON MOVIELENS DATA AND (BOTTOM) 10 HOLDOUT MOVIES FOR USER 1 SORTED BY USER AND RATING PREDICTIONS

Row No.	rating	userId ↑	movieId	title	genres	prediction ↓
28	5	1	1213	Goodfellas (1990)	Crime|Drama	4.911
81	5	1	2959	Fight Club (1999)	Action|Crime|Drama|Thriller	4.890
64	5	1	2329	American History X (1998)	Crime|Drama	4.831
97	5	1	5060	M*A*S*H (a.k.a. MASH) (1970)	Comedy|Drama|War	4.830
26	5	1	1136	Monty Python and the Holy Grail (1975)	Adventure|Comedy|Fantasy	4.823
29	2	1	1219	Psycho (1960)	Crime|Horror	4.775
86	5	1	3147	Green Mile, The (1999)	Crime|Drama	4.764
7	5	1	260	Star Wars: Episode IV – A New Hope (1977)	Action|Adventure|Sci-Fi	4.723
76	5	1	2692	Run Lola Run (Lola rennt) (1998)	Action|Crime	4.711
9	4	1	356	Forrest Gump (1994)	Comedy|Drama|Romance|War	4.711

ExampleSet (40,334 examples, 3 special attributes, 3 regular attributes)

FIGURE 15.8 ITEM-BASED COLLABORATIVE FILTERING ON MOVIELENS DATA: 10 HOLDOUT MOVIES FOR USER 1 SORTED BY USER AND RATING PREDICTIONS

limitation of collaborative filtering is therefore that it cannot generate recommendations for new users, nor for new items. There are various approaches for tackling this challenge.

User-based collaborative filtering looks for similarity in terms of highly rated or preferred items. However, it is blind to data on low-rated or unwanted items. We can therefore not expect to use it as is for detecting unwanted items.

User-based collaborative filtering helps leverage similarities between people's tastes for providing personalized recommendations. However, when the number of users becomes very large, collaborative filtering becomes computationally difficult. Solutions include item-based algorithms, clustering of users, and dimension reduction. The most popular dimension reduction method used in such cases is singular value decomposition (SVD), a computationally superior form of principal components analysis (see Chapter 4).

Although the term "prediction" is often used to describe the output of collaborative filtering, this method is unsupervised by nature. It can be used to generate predicted ratings or purchase indication for a user, but usually we do not have the true outcome value in practice. Evaluating performance is therefore challenging and treats the user's actual behavior as if it were their response to the recommendation. One important way to improve recommendations generated by collaborative filtering is by getting actual user feedback. Once a recommendation is generated, the user can indicate whether the recommendation was adequate or not. For this reason, many recommender systems entice users to provide feedback on their recommendations. When user reactions are measured with respect to the presented recommendations, this is called *online learning*. This is in contrast to *offline learning*, where such "online" feedback information is not used. Lastly, using online learning, many companies now measure the direct impact of a recommender system in terms of a business-relevant metric, such as conversion rate. In Chapter 14, we describe approaches that obtain user feedback that are useful for evaluating recommender systems and other interventions.

Collaborative Filtering vs. Association Rules

While collaborative filtering and association rules are both unsupervised methods used for generating recommendations, they differ in several ways.

Frequent Itemsets vs. Personalized Recommendations Association rules look for frequent item combinations and will provide recommendations only for those items. In contrast, collaborative filtering provides personalized recommendations for every item, thereby catering to users with unusual taste. In this sense, collaborative filtering is useful for capturing the "long tail" of user preferences, while association rules look for the "head." This difference has implications for the data needed: association rules require data on a very large number of "baskets" (transactions) to find a sufficient number of baskets that contain certain combinations of items. In contrast, collaborative filtering does not require many "baskets," but does require data on as many items as possible for many users. Also, association rules operate at the basket level (our database can include multiple transactions for each user), while collaborative filtering operates at the user level.

Because association rules produce generic, impersonal rules (association-based recommendations such as Amazon's "Frequently Bought Together" display the same recommendations to all users searching for a specific item), they can be used for setting common strategies such as product placement in a store or sequencing of diagnostic tests in hospitals. In contrast, collaborative filtering generates user-specific recommendations (e.g., Amazon's "Customers Who Viewed This Item Also Viewed…") and is therefore a tool designed for personalization.

Transactional Data vs. User Data Association rules provide recommendations of items based on their co-purchase with other items in *many transactions/baskets*. In contrast, collaborative filtering provides recommendations of items based on their co-purchase or co-rating by even a small number of other *users*. Considering distinct baskets is useful when the same items are purchased over and over again (e.g., in grocery shopping). Considering distinct users is useful when each item is typically purchased/rated once (e.g., purchases of books, music, and movies).

Binary Data and Ratings Data Association rules treat items as binary data (1 = purchase, 0 = nonpurchase), whereas collaborative filtering can operate on either binary data or on numerical ratings.

Two or More Items In association rules, the premises and conclusion can each include one or more items (e.g., IF milk THEN cookies and cornflakes). Hence, a recommendation might be a bundle of the item of interest with multiple items ("buy milk, cookies, and cornflakes and receive 10% discount"). In contrast, in collaborative filtering, similarity is measured between *pairs* of items or pairs of users. A recommendation will therefore be either for a single item (the most popular item purchased by people like you, which you haven't purchased) or for multiple single items which do not necessarily relate to each other (the top two most popular items purchased by people like you, which you haven't purchased).

These distinctions are sharper for purchases and recommendations of non-popular items, especially when comparing association rules with user-based collaborative filtering. When considering what to recommend to a user who purchased a popular item, then association rules and item-based collaborative filtering might yield the same recommendation for a single item. However, a user-based recommendation will likely differ. Consider a customer who purchases milk every week, as well as gluten-free products (which are rarely purchased by other customers). Suppose that using association rules on the transactions database, we identify the rule "IF milk THEN cookies." Then, the next time our customer purchases milk, s/he will receive a recommendation (e.g., a coupon) to purchase cookies, whether or not s/he purchased cookies and irrespective of his/her gluten-free item purchases. In item-based collaborative filtering, we would look at all items co-purchased with milk across all users and recommend the most popular item among them (which was not purchased by our customer). This might also lead to a recommendation of cookies, because this item was not purchased by our customer.[11] Now consider user-based collaborative filtering. User-based collaborative filtering searches for similar customers—those who purchased the same set of items—and then recommends the item most commonly purchased by these neighbors, which *was not purchased by our customer*. The user-based recommendation is therefore unlikely to recommend cookies and more likely to recommend popular gluten-free items that the customer has not purchased.

15.3 SUMMARY

Association rules (also called market basket analysis) and collaborative filtering are unsupervised methods for deducing associations between purchased items

---

[11] If the rule is "IF milk, THEN cookies and cornflakes," then the association rules would recommend cookies and cornflakes to a milk purchaser, while item-based collaborative filtering would recommend the most popular single item purchased with milk.

from databases of transactions. Association rules search for generic rules about items that are purchased together. The main advantage of this method is that it generates clear, simple rules of the form "IF X is purchased, THEN Y is also likely to be purchased." The method is very transparent and easy to understand.

The process of creating association rules is two-staged. First, a set of candidate rules based on frequent itemsets is generated (the Apriori and FP–Growth algorithms being the most popular rule-generating algorithms). Then from these candidate rules, the rules that indicate the strongest association between items are selected. We use the measures of support and confidence to evaluate the uncertainty in a rule. The user also specifies minimal support and confidence values to be used in the rule generation and selection process. A third measure, the lift, compares the efficiency of the rule to detect a real association with a random combination. Lastly, conviction helps determine the degree of rule implication.

One shortcoming of association rules is the profusion of rules that are generated. There is therefore a need for ways to reduce these to a small set of useful and strong rules. An important nonautomated method to condense the information involves examining the rules for uninformative and trivial rules and for rules that share the same support. Another issue that needs to be kept in mind is that rare combinations tend to be ignored, because they do not meet the minimum support requirement. For this reason, it is better to have items that are approximately equally frequent in the data. This can be achieved by using higher-level hierarchies as the items. An example is to use types of books rather than titles of individual books in deriving association rules from a database of bookstore transactions.

Collaborative filtering is a popular technique used in online recommendation systems. It is based on the relationship between items formed by users who acted similarly on an item, such as purchasing or rating an item highly. User-based collaborative filtering operates on data on item–user combinations, calculates the similarities between users, and provides personalized recommendations to users. An important component for the success of collaborative filtering is that users provide feedback about the recommendations provided and have sufficient information on each item. One disadvantage of collaborative filtering methods is that they cannot generate recommendations for new users or new items. Also, with a huge number of users, user-based collaborative filtering becomes computationally challenging, and alternatives such as item-based methods or dimension reduction are popularly used.

PROBLEMS

15.1 Satellite Radio Customers. An analyst at a subscription-based satellite radio company has been given a sample of data from their customer database, with the goal of finding groups of customers who are associated with one another. The data consist of company data, together with purchased demographic data that are mapped to the company data (see Table 15.10). The analyst decides to apply association rules to learn more about the associations between customers. Comment on this approach.

TABLE 15.10   SAMPLE OF DATA ON SATELLITE RADIO CUSTOMERS

Row ID	zipconvert_2	zipconvert_3	zipconvert_4	zipconvert_5	homeowner dummy	NUMCHLD	INCOME	gender dummy	WEALTH
17	0	1	0	0	1	1	5	1	9
25	1	0	0	0	1	1	1	0	7
29	0	0	0	1	0	2	5	1	8
38	0	0	0	1	1	1	3	0	4
40	0	1	0	0	1	1	4	0	8
53	0	1	0	0	1	1	4	1	8
58	0	0	0	1	1	1	4	1	8
61	1	0	0	0	1	1	1	0	7
71	0	0	1	0	1	1	4	0	5
87	1	0	0	0	1	1	4	1	8
100	0	0	0	1	1	1	4	1	8
104	1	0	0	0	1	1	1	1	5
121	0	0	1	0	1	1	4	1	5
142	1	0	0	0	0	1	5	0	8

15.2 Identifying Course Combinations. The Institute for Statistics Education at Statistics.com offers online courses in statistics and analytics and is seeking information that will help in packaging and sequencing courses. Consider the dataset *CourseTopics.csv*, the first few rows of which are shown in Table 15.11. These data are for purchases of online statistics courses at Statistics.com. Each row represents the courses attended by a single customer. The firm wishes to assess alternative sequencings and bundling of courses. Use association rules to analyze these data, and interpret several of the resulting rules.

TABLE 15.11   DATA ON PURCHASES OF ONLINE STATISTICS COURSES

Intro	DataMining	Survey	CatData	Regression	Forecast	DOE	SW
1	1	0	0	0	0	0	0
0	0	1	0	0	0	0	0
0	1	0	1	1	0	0	1
1	0	0	0	0	0	0	0
1	1	0	0	0	0	0	0
0	1	0	0	0	0	0	0
1	0	0	0	0	0	0	0
0	0	0	1	0	1	1	1
1	0	0	0	0	0	0	0
0	0	0	1	0	0	0	0
1	0	0	0	0	0	0	0

15.3 Cosmetics Purchases. The data shown in Table 15.12 and the output in Figure 15.9 are based on a subset of a dataset on cosmetic purchases (*Cosmetics.csv*) at a large chain drugstore. The store wants to analyze associations among purchases of these items for purposes of point-of-sale display, guidance to sales personnel in promoting cross-sales, and guidance for piloting an eventual time-of-purchase electronic recommender system to boost cross-sales. Consider first only the data shown in Table 15.12, given in binary matrix form.

TABLE 15.12   EXCERPT FROM DATA ON COSMETICS PURCHASES IN BINARY MATRIX FORM

Trans.	Bag	Blush	Nail polish	Brushes	Concealer	Eyebrow pencils	Bronzer
1	0	1	1	1	1	0	1
2	0	0	1	0	1	0	1
3	0	1	0	0	1	1	1
4	0	0	1	1	1	0	1
5	0	1	0	0	1	0	1
6	0	0	0	0	1	0	0
7	0	1	1	1	1	0	1
8	0	0	1	1	0	0	1
9	0	0	0	0	1	0	0
10	1	1	1	1	0	0	0
11	0	0	1	0	0	0	1
12	0	0	1	1	1	0	1

a. Select several values in the matrix and explain their meaning.

b. Consider the results of the association rules analysis shown in Figure 15.9.

    i. For the second row, explain the "confidence" output and how it is calculated.

    ii. For the second row, explain the "support" output and how it is calculated.

    iii. For the second row, explain the "lift" and how it is calculated.

    iv. For the second row, explain the "conviction" and how it is calculated.

    v. For the second row, explain the rule that is represented there in words.

Premises	Conclusion	Support	Confidence	Lift ↓	Conviction ↓
Brushes	Nail Polish	0.149	1	3.571	∞
Concealer, Eye shadow, Blush	Mascara	0.119	0.960	2.688	15.946
Eye shadow, Blush	Mascara	0.169	0.929	2.601	9.002
Blush, Mascara	Eye shadow	0.169	0.918	2.411	7.593
Eyeliner, Lip liner	Concealer	0.120	0.923	2.088	7.254
Eye shadow, Nail Polish	Mascara	0.119	0.908	2.545	7.019
Mascara, Lipstick	Eye shadow	0.110	0.909	2.386	6.809
Concealer, Blush, Mascara	Eye shadow	0.119	0.908	2.384	6.757
Mascara, Bronzer	Eye shadow	0.124	0.905	2.376	6.523
Mascara	Eye shadow	0.321	0.899	2.360	6.138

FIGURE 15.9   ASSOCIATION RULES FOR COSMETICS PURCHASES DATA

   c. Now, use the complete dataset on the cosmetics purchases (in the file *Cosmetics.csv*). Using RapidMiner, apply association rules to these data (for generating frequent itemsets with FP-Growth, use *min_support* = 0.15, and uncheck the option *find min number of itemsets*; for creating association rules, use *min confidence* = 0.5).

      i. How many rules are generated? Sort the rules first by conviction and then by lift, and show the first 10 rules with the premises and conclusion for each rule, as well as their support, confidence, lift and confidence values.

      ii. Interpret the first three rules in the output in words.

      iii. Reviewing the first couple of dozen rules, comment on their redundancy and how you would assess their utility.

15.4 **Course Ratings.** The Institute for Statistics Education at Statistics.com asks students to rate a variety of aspects of a course as soon as the student completes it. The Institute is contemplating instituting a recommendation system that would provide students with recommendations for additional courses as soon as they submit their rating for a completed course. Consider the excerpt from student ratings of online statistics courses (data: *courserating.csv*) shown in Table 15.13 and the problem of what to recommend to student E.N.

   a. First consider *the process of creating* a user-based collaborative filter. This requires computing correlations between all student pairs. For which students, is it possible to compute correlations with E.N.? Compute them.

   b. Based on the single nearest student to E.N., which single course should we recommend to E.N.? Explain why.

   c. Using RapidMiner's *Data to Similarity* operator, compute the cosine similarity between users. (*Note*: Assign the *id* role to the student name attribute.)

   d. Based on the cosine similarities of the nearest students to E.N., which course should be recommended to E.N.?

   e. What is the conceptual difference between using the correlation as opposed to cosine similarities? (*Hint*: How are the missing values in the matrix handled in each case?)

TABLE 15.13   **RATINGS OF ONLINE STATISTICS COURSES: 4 = BEST, 1 = WORST, BLANK = NOT TAKEN**

	SQL	Spatial	PA 1	DM in R	Python	Forecast	R Prog	Hadoop	Regression
L N	4				3	2	4		2
M H	3	4			4				
J H	2	2							
E N	4			4			4		3
D U	4	4							
F L		4							
G L		4							
A H		3							
S A			4						
R W			2					4	
B A			4						
M G			4		4				
A F			4						
K G			3						
D S	4			2			4		

f. With large datasets, it is computationally difficult to compute user-based recommendations in real time, and an item-based approach is used instead. Returning to the rating data (not the binary matrix), let's now take that approach.

    i. If the goal is still to find a recommendation for E.N., for which course pairs is it possible and useful to calculate correlations?

    ii. Just looking at the data, and without yet calculating course pair correlations, which course would you recommend to E.N., relying on item-based filtering? Calculate two course pair correlations involving your guess, and report the results.

15.5 **Movie Ratings.** Consider the MovieLens data (*movies.csv* and *ratings.csv*) discussed in this chapter. After merging the two datasets, split the data into training (60%) and holdout (40%).

a. Perform user-based collaborative filtering with different k values (5, 10, 20, and 40), and apply the model on the holdout data. For each value of k, record the top 5 movies for the first user in the holdout set. Compare the extent of overlap. What role does k play in this model?

b. Perform item-based collaborative filtering with different k values (5, 10, 20, and 40), and conduct the same analysis as in part (a).

c. What is the key difference between user-based collaborative filtering and item-based collaborative filtering? Find and briefly discuss two business applications of each of these recommendation techniques.

d. Based on your experience in solving (a) and (b), identify a practical difficulty a business may face when setting up a recommendation engine using collaborative filtering techniques. What are one or more ways to address this challenge?

CHAPTER 16

Cluster Analysis

This chapter is about the popular unsupervised learning task of clustering, where the goal is to segment the data into a set of homogeneous clusters of records for the purpose of generating insight. Separating a dataset into clusters of homogeneous records is also useful for improving performance of supervised methods, by modeling each cluster separately rather than the entire, heterogeneous dataset. Clustering is used in a vast variety of business applications, from customized marketing to industry analysis. We describe two popular clustering approaches: *hierarchical clustering* and *k-means clustering*. In hierarchical clustering, records are sequentially grouped to create clusters, based on distances between records and distances between clusters. We describe how the algorithm works in terms of the clustering process and mention several common distance metrics used. Hierarchical clustering also produces a useful graphical display of the clustering process and results, called a dendrogram. We present dendrograms and illustrate their usefulness. *k-means clustering* is widely used in large dataset applications. In *k*-means clustering, records are allocated to one of a prespecified set of clusters, according to their distance from each cluster. We describe the *k*-means clustering algorithm and its computational advantages. Finally, we present techniques that assist in generating insight from clustering results.

16.1 INTRODUCTION

Cluster analysis is used to form groups or clusters of similar records based on several measurements made on these records. The key idea is to characterize the clusters in ways that would be useful for the aims of the analysis. This idea has been applied in many areas, including astronomy, archaeology, medicine, chemistry, education, psychology, linguistics, and sociology. Biologists, for example,

Machine Learning for Business Analytics: Concepts, Techniques and Applications in RapidMiner, First Edition.
Galit Shmueli, Peter C. Bruce, Amit V. Deokar, and Nitin R. Patel
© 2023 John Wiley & Sons, Inc. Published 2023 by John Wiley & Sons, Inc.

have made extensive use of classes and subclasses to organize species. A spectac-
ular success of the clustering idea in chemistry was Mendeleev's periodic table
of the elements.

One popular use of cluster analysis in marketing is for *market segmentation:*
customers are segmented based on demographic and transaction history information, and a marketing strategy is tailored for each segment. In countries such
as India, where customer diversity is extremely location-sensitive, chain stores
often perform market segmentation at the store level, rather than chain-wide
(called "micro-segmentation"). Another use is for *market structure analysis:* identifying groups of similar products according to competitive measures of similarity. In marketing and political forecasting, clustering of neighborhoods using US
postal zip codes has been used successfully to group neighborhoods by lifestyles.
Claritas, a company that pioneered this approach, grouped neighborhoods into
40 clusters using various measures of consumer expenditure and demographics.
Examining the clusters enabled Claritas to come up with evocative names, such
as "Bohemian Mix," "Furs and Station Wagons," and "Money and Brains," for
the groups that captured the dominant lifestyles. Knowledge of lifestyles can be
used to estimate the potential demand for products (such as sports utility vehicles)
and services (such as pleasure cruises). Similarly, sales organizations will derive
customer segments and give them names—"personas"—to focus sales efforts.

In finance, cluster analysis can be used for creating *balanced portfolios*: given
data on a variety of investment opportunities (e.g., stocks), one may find clusters based on financial performance variables such as return (daily, weekly, or
monthly), volatility, beta, and other characteristics, such as industry and market
capitalization. Selecting securities from different clusters can help create a balanced portfolio. Another application of cluster analysis in finance is for *industry
analysis*: for a given industry, we are interested in finding groups of similar firms
based on measures such as growth rate, profitability, market size, product range,
and the presence in various international markets. These groups can then be
analyzed to understand industry structure and to determine, for instance, who is
a competitor.

An interesting and unusual application of cluster analysis, described in Berry
and Linoff (1997), is the design of a new set of sizes for army uniforms for
women in the US Army. The study came up with a new clothing size system
with only 20 sizes, where different sizes fit different body types. The 20 sizes are
combinations of five measurements: chest, neck, and shoulder circumference,
sleeve outseam, and neck-to-buttock length (for further details, see McCullugh
et al., 1998). This example is important because it shows how a completely new
insightful view can be gained by examining clusters of records.

Cluster analysis can be applied to huge amounts of data. For instance, Internet search engines use clustering techniques to cluster queries that users submit.

These can then be used for improving search algorithms. The objective of this chapter is to describe the key ideas underlying the most commonly used techniques for cluster analysis and to lay out their strengths and weaknesses.

Typically, the basic data used to form clusters are a table of measurements on several numerical attributes, where each column represents an attribute and a row represents a record. Our goal is to form groups of records so that similar records are in the same group. The number of clusters may be prespecified or determined from the data.

Example: Public Utilities

Table 16.1 gives corporate data on 22 public utilities in the United States (the attribute descriptions are given in the table footnote). We are interested in forming groups of similar utilities. The records to be clustered are the utilities, and the clustering will be based on the eight measurements on each utility. An

TABLE 16.1   DATA ON 22 PUBLIC UTILITIES

Company	Fixed	RoR	Cost	Load	Demand	Sales	Nuclear	Fuel Cost
Arizona Public Service	1.06	9.2	151	54.4	1.6	9077	0.0	0.628
Boston Edison Co.	0.89	10.3	202	57.9	2.2	5088	25.3	1.555
Central Louisiana Co.	1.43	15.4	113	53.0	3.4	9212	0.0	1.058
Commonwealth Edison Co.	1.02	11.2	168	56.0	0.3	6423	34.3	0.700
Consolidated Edison Co. (NY)	1.49	8.8	192	51.2	1.0	3300	15.6	2.044
Florida Power & Light Co.	1.32	13.5	111	60.0	−2.2	11,127	22.5	1.241
Hawaiian Electric Co.	1.22	12.2	175	67.6	2.2	7642	0.0	1.652
daho Power Co.	1.10	9.2	245	57.0	3.3	13,082	0.0	0.309
Kentucky Utilities Co.	1.34	13.0	168	60.4	7.2	8406	0.0	0.862
Madison Gas & Electric Co.	1.12	12.4	197	53.0	2.7	6455	39.2	0.623
Nevada Power Co.	0.75	7.5	173	51.5	6.5	17,441	0.0	0.768
New England Electric Co.	1.13	10.9	178	62.0	3.7	6154	0.0	1.897
Northern States Power Co.	1.15	12.7	199	53.7	6.4	7179	50.2	0.527
Oklahoma Gas & Electric Co.	1.09	12.0	96	49.8	1.4	9673	0.0	0.588
Pacific Gas & Electric Co.	0.96	7.6	164	62.2	−0.1	6468	0.9	1.400
Puget Sound Power & Light Co.	1.16	9.9	252	56.0	9.2	15,991	0.0	0.620
San Diego Gas & Electric Co.	0.76	6.4	136	61.9	9.0	5714	8.3	1.920
The Southern Co.	1.05	12.6	150	56.7	2.7	10,140	0.0	1.108
Texas Utilities Co.	1.16	11.7	104	54.0	−2.1	13,507	0.0	0.636
Wisconsin Electric Power Co.	1.20	11.8	148	59.9	3.5	7287	41.1	0.702
United Illuminating Co.	1.04	8.6	204	61.0	3.5	6650	0.0	2.116
Virginia Electric & Power Co.	1.07	9.3	174	54.3	5.9	10,093	26.6	1.306

Fixed = fixed-charge covering ratio (income/debt); RoR = rate of return on capital
Cost = cost per kilowatt capacity in place; Load = annual load factor
Demand = peak kilowatt-hour demand growth from 1974 to 1975
Sales = sales (kilowatt-hour use per year)
Nuclear = percent nuclear
Fuel Cost = total fuel costs (cents per kilowatthour)

example where clustering would be useful is a study to predict the cost impact of deregulation. To do the requisite analysis, economists would need to build a detailed cost model of the various utilities. It would save a considerable amount of time and effort if we could cluster similar types of utilities and build detailed cost models for just one "typical" utility in each cluster and then scale up from these models to estimate results for all utilities.

For simplicity, let us consider only two of the measurements: Sales and Fuel Cost. Figure 16.1 shows a scatter plot of these two attributes, with labels marking each company. At first glance, there appear to be two or three clusters of utilities: one with utilities that have high fuel costs, a second with utilities that have lower fuel costs and relatively low sales, and a third with utilities with low fuel costs but high sales.

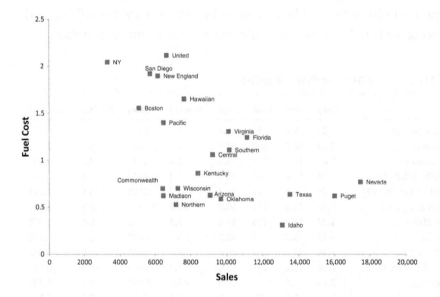

FIGURE 16.1   SCATTER PLOT OF FUEL COST VS. SALES FOR THE 22 UTILITIES

We can therefore think of cluster analysis as a more formal algorithm that measures the distance between records and, according to these distances (here, two-dimensional distances), forms clusters.

Two general types of clustering algorithms for a dataset of n records are hierarchical and non-hierarchical clustering:

Hierarchical methods can be either *agglomerative* or *divisive*. Agglomerative methods begin with n clusters and sequentially merge similar clusters until a single cluster is obtained. Divisive methods work in the opposite direction, starting with one cluster that includes all records. Hierarchical methods are especially useful when the goal is to arrange the clusters into a natural hierarchy.

Non-hierarchical methods such as k-means. Using a prespecified number of clusters, the method assigns records to each cluster. These methods are generally less computationally intensive and are therefore preferred with very large datasets.

We concentrate here on the two most popular methods: hierarchical agglomerative clustering and k-means clustering. In both cases, we need to define two types of distances: distance between two records and distance between two clusters. In both cases, there is a variety of metrics that can be used.

16.2 MEASURING DISTANCE BETWEEN TWO RECORDS

We denote by d_{ij} a *distance metric*, or *dissimilarity measure*, between records i and j. For record i we have the vector of p measurements $(x_{i1}, x_{i2}, \ldots, x_{ip})$, while for record j we have the vector of measurements $(x_{j1}, x_{j2}, \ldots, x_{jp})$. For example, we can write the measurement vector for Arizona Public Service as $[1.06, 9.2, 151, 54.4, 1.6, 9077, 0, 0.628]$.

Distances can be defined in multiple ways, but in general, the following properties are required:

Non-negative: $d_{ij} \geq 0$

Self-proximity: $d_{ii} = 0$ (the distance from a record to itself is zero)

Symmetry: $d_{ij} = d_{ji}$

Triangle inequality: $d_{ij} \leq d_{ik} + d_{kj}$ (the distance between any pair cannot exceed the sum of distances between the other two pairs)

Euclidean Distance

The most popular distance measure is the *Euclidean distance*, d_{ij}, which between two records, i and j, is defined by

$$d_{ij} = \sqrt{(x_{i1} - x_{j1})^2 + (x_{i2} - x_{j2})^2 + \cdots + (x_{ip} - x_{jp})^2}.$$

For instance, the Euclidean distance between Arizona Public Service and Boston Edison Co. can be computed from the raw data by

$$
\begin{aligned}
d_{12} &= \sqrt{(1.06 - 0.89)^2 + (9.2 - 10.3)^2 + (151 - 202)^2 + \cdots + (0.628 - 1.555)^2} \\
&= 3989.408.
\end{aligned}
$$

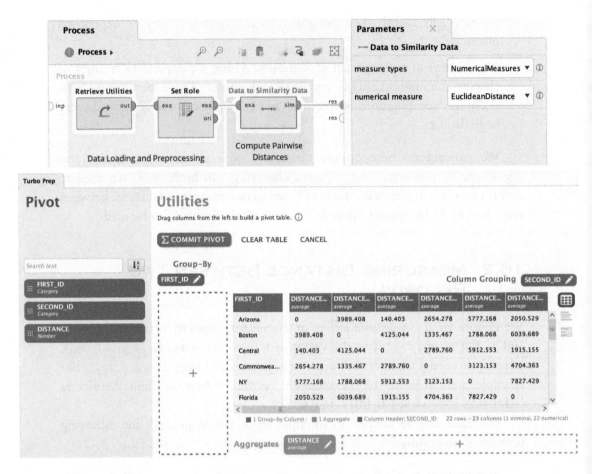

FIGURE 16.2 (TOP) PROCESS FOR COMPUTING EUCLIDEAN DISTANCES BETWEEN THE UTILITIES AND (BOTTOM) PAIRWISE DISTANCES FOR THE FIRST SIX UTILITIES

To compute Euclidean distance in RapidMiner using the *Data to Similarity Data* operator,[1] see Figure 16.2. The pivot table shown can be generated by invoking *Turbo Prep* from the Results view, choosing the *Pivot* option, and then selecting the *Group-By*, *Column Grouping*, and *Aggregates*.

Normalizing Numerical Data

The measure computed above is highly influenced by the scale of each attribute so that attributes with larger scales (e.g., Sales) have a much greater influence over the total distance. It is therefore customary to *normalize* continuous measurements before computing the Euclidean distance. This converts all numeric attributes to the same scale. Normalizing a measurement means subtracting the

---

[1]The *Cross Distances* operator can also be used, particularly for computing distances between records in two different datasets.

| TABLE 16.2 | ORIGINAL AND NORMALIZED MEASUREMENTS FOR SALES AND FUEL COST | | | |

Company	Sales	Fuel Cost	NormSales	NormFuel
Arizona Public Service	9077	0.628	0.0459	−0.8537
Boston Edison Co.	5088	1.555	−1.0778	0.8133
Central Louisiana Co.	9212	1.058	0.0839	−0.0804
Commonwealth Edison Co.	6423	0.7	−0.7017	−0.7242
Consolidated Edison Co. (NY)	3300	2.044	−1.5814	1.6926
Florida Power & Light Co.	11,127	1.241	0.6234	0.2486
Hawaiian Electric Co.	7642	1.652	−0.3583	0.9877
Idaho Power Co.	13,082	0.309	1.1741	−1.4273
Kentucky Utilities Co.	8406	0.862	−0.1431	−0.4329
Madison Gas & Electric Co.	6455	0.623	−0.6927	−0.8627
Nevada Power Co.	17,441	0.768	2.4020	−0.6019
New England Electric Co.	6154	1.897	−0.7775	1.4283
Northern States Power Co.	7179	0.527	−0.4887	−1.0353
Oklahoma Gas & Electric Co.	9673	0.588	0.2138	−0.9256
Pacific Gas & Electric Co.	6468	1.4	−0.6890	0.5346
Puget Sound Power & Light Co.	15,991	0.62	1.9935	−0.8681
San Diego Gas & Electric Co.	5714	1.92	−0.9014	1.4697
The Southern Co.	10,140	1.108	0.3453	0.0095
Texas Utilities Co.	13,507	0.636	1.2938	−0.8393
Wisconsin Electric Power Co.	7287	0.702	−0.4583	−0.7206
United Illuminating Co.	6650	2.116	−0.6378	1.8221
Virginia Electric & Power Co.	10,093	1.306	0.3321	0.3655
Mean	8914.05	1.10	0.00	0.00
Standard deviation	3549.98	0.56	1.00	1.00

average and dividing by the standard deviation (normalized values are also called
z-scores). For instance, the average sales amount across the 22 utilities is 8914.045,
and the standard deviation is 3549.984. The normalized sales for Arizona Public
Service is therefore $(9077 − 8914.045)/3549.984 = 0.046$.

Returning to the simplified utilities data with only two measurements (Sales
and Fuel Cost), we first normalize the measurements (see Table 16.2) and then
compute the Euclidean distance between each pair. Figure 16.3 (bottom) shows
these pairwise distances for the first six utilities.

Other Distance Measures for Numerical Data

It is important to note that the choice of the distance measure plays a major role
in cluster analysis. The main guideline is domain dependent: What exactly is
being measured? How are the different measurements related? What scale should
each measurement be treated as (numerical, or nominal)? Are there outliers?
Finally, depending on the goal of the analysis, should the clusters be distinguished
mostly by a small set of measurements, or should they be separated by multiple
measurements that weight moderately?

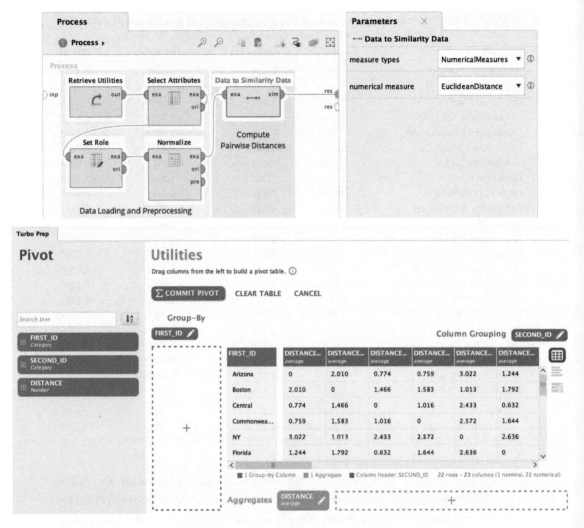

FIGURE 16.3   **(TOP) PROCESS FOR COMPUTING EUCLIDEAN DISTANCES BETWEEN THE UTILITIES BASED ON NORMALIZED SALES AND FUEL COST AND (BOTTOM) PAIRWISE DISTANCES FOR THE FIRST SIX UTILITIES USING NORMALIZED MEASUREMENTS**

Although Euclidean distance is the most widely used distance, it has three main features that need to be kept in mind. First, as mentioned earlier, it is highly scale dependent. Changing the units of one attribute (e.g., from cents to dollars) can have a huge influence on the results. Normalizing is therefore a common solution. However, unequal weighting should be considered if we want the clusters to depend more on certain measurements and less on others. The second feature of Euclidean distance is that it completely ignores the relationship between the measurements. Thus, if the measurements are in fact strongly correlated, a different distance (such as the statistical distance, described later) is likely to be a better choice. The third is that Euclidean distance is sensitive to outliers. If the data are believed to contain outliers and careful removal is not a choice, the use of more robust distances (such as the Manhattan distance, described later) is preferred.

Additional popular distance metrics often used (for reasons such as the ones above) are as follows:

Correlation-based similarity: Sometimes it is more natural or convenient to work with a similarity measure between records rather than distance, which measures dissimilarity. A popular similarity measure is the square of the Pearson correlation coefficient, r_{ij}^2, where the correlation coefficient is defined by

$$r_{ij} = \frac{\sum_{m=1}^{p}(x_{im} - \overline{x}_m)(x_{jm} - \overline{x}_m)}{\sqrt{\sum_{m=1}^{p}(x_{im} - \overline{x}_m)^2 \sum_{m=1}^{p}(x_{jm} - \overline{x}_m)^2}}. \quad (16.1)$$

Such measures can always be converted to distance measures. In the example above, we could define a distance measure $d_{ij} = 1 - r_{ij}^2$.

Statistical distance (also called Mahalanobis distance): This metric has an advantage over the other metrics mentioned in that it takes into account the correlation between measurements. With this metric, measurements that are highly correlated with other measurements do not contribute as much as those that are uncorrelated or mildly correlated. The statistical distance between records i and j is defined as

$$d_{i,j} = \sqrt{(\mathbf{x}_i - \mathbf{x}_j)'S^{-1}(\mathbf{x}_i - \mathbf{x}_j)},$$

where $\mathbf{x}_i$ and $\mathbf{x}_j$ are p-dimensional vectors of the measurements values for records i and j, respectively, and S is the covariance matrix for these vectors ($'$, a transpose operation, simply turns a column vector into a row vector). S^{-1} is the inverse matrix of S, which is the p-dimensional extension to division. For further information on statistical distance, see Chapter 12.

Manhattan distance ("city block"): This distance looks at the absolute differences rather than squared differences and is defined by

$$d_{ij} = \sum_{m=1}^{p} \mid x_{im} - x_{jm} \mid.$$

Maximum coordinate distance: This distance looks only at the measurement on which records i and j deviate most. It is defined by

$$d_{ij} = \max_{m=1,2,\ldots,p} \mid x_{im} - x_{jm} \mid.$$

Distance Measures for Categorical Data

In the case of measurements with binary values, it is more intuitively appealing to use similarity measures than distance measures. Suppose that we have binary values for all the p measurements and, for records i and j, we have the following 2×2 table:

		Record j		
		0	1	
Record i	0	a	b	$a + b$
	1	c	d	$c + d$
		$a + c$	$b + d$	p

where a denotes the number of attributes for which records i and j each have value 0 for that attribute (measurement absent), d is the number of attributes for which the two records each have a value 1 for that attribute (measurement present), and so on. The most useful similarity measures in this situation are as follows:

Matching coefficient: $(a + d)/p$.

Jaccard's coefficient: $d/(b + c + d)$. This coefficient ignores zero matches. This is desirable when we do not want to consider two people to be similar simply because a large number of characteristics are absent in both. For example, if *owns a Corvette* is one of the attributes, a matching "yes" would be evidence of similarity, but a matching "no" tells us little about whether the two people are similar.

Distance Measures for Mixed Data

When the measurements are mixed (some continuous and some binary), a similarity coefficient suggested by Gower is very useful. *Gower's similarity measure* is a weighted average of the distances computed for each attribute, after scaling each attribute to a [0, 1] scale. It is defined as

$$s_{ij} = \frac{\sum_{m=1}^{p} w_{ijm} s_{ijm}}{\sum_{m=1}^{p} w_{ijm}},$$

where s_{ijm} is the similarity between records i and j on measurement m and w_{ijm} is a binary weight given to the corresponding distance.

The similarity measures s_{ijm} and weights w_{ijm} are computed as follows:

1. For continuous measurements, $s_{ijm} = 1 - \frac{|x_{im} - x_{jm}|}{\max(x_m) - \min(x_m)}$ and $w_{ijm} = 1$ unless the value for measurement m is unknown for one or both of the records, in which case $w_{ijm} = 0$.

2. For binary measurements, $s_{ijm} = 1$ if $x_{im} = x_{jm} = 1$ and 0 otherwise. $w_{ijm} = 1$ unless $x_{im} = x_{jm} = 0$.

3. For nonbinary categorical measurements, $s_{ijm} = 1$ if both records are in the same category, and otherwise $s_{ijm} = 0$. As in continuous measurements, $w_{ijm} = 1$ unless the category for measurement m is unknown for one or both of the records, in which case $w_{ijm} = 0$.

16.3 MEASURING DISTANCE BETWEEN TWO CLUSTERS

We define a cluster as a set of one or more records. How do we measure distance between clusters? The idea is to extend measures of *distance between records* into *distances between clusters*. Consider cluster A, which includes the m records $A_1, A_2, \ldots, A_m$, and cluster B, which includes n records $B_1, B_2, \ldots, B_n$. The most widely used measures of distance between clusters are as follows:

Minimum Distance

The distance between the pair of records A_i and B_j that are closest:

$$\min(\text{distance}(A_i, B_j)), \quad i = 1, 2, \ldots, m; \quad j = 1, 2, \ldots, n.$$

Maximum Distance

The distance between the pair of records A_i and B_j that are farthest:

$$\max(\text{distance}(A_i, B_j)), \quad i = 1, 2, \ldots, m; \quad j = 1, 2, \ldots, n.$$

Average Distance

The average distance of all possible distances between records in one cluster and records in the other cluster:

$$\text{Average}(\text{distance}(A_i, B_j)), \quad i = 1, 2, \ldots, m; \quad j = 1, 2, \ldots, n.$$

Centroid Distance

The distance between the two cluster centroids. A *cluster centroid* is the vector of measurement averages across all the records in that cluster. For cluster A, this is the vector $\overline{x}_A = [(1/m \sum_{i=1}^{m} x_{1i}, \ldots, 1/m \sum_{i=1}^{m} x_{pi})]$. The centroid distance between clusters A and B is

$$\text{distance}(\overline{x}_A, \overline{x}_B).$$

Minimum distance, maximum distance, and centroid distance are illustrated visually for two dimensions with a map of Portugal and France in Figure 16.4.

FIGURE 16.4   **TWO-DIMENSIONAL REPRESENTATION OF SEVERAL DIFFERENT DISTANCE MEASURES BETWEEN PORTUGAL AND FRANCE**

For instance, consider the first two utilities (Arizona, Boston) as cluster A and the next three utilities (Central, Commonwealth, Consolidated) as cluster B. Using the normalized scores in Table 16.2 and the distance matrix in Figure 16.3, we can compute each of the distances described above. Using Euclidean distance for each distance calculation, we get the following:

- The closest pair is Arizona and Commonwealth, and therefore the minimum distance between clusters A and B is 0.76.

- The farthest pair is Arizona and Consolidated, and therefore the maximum distance between clusters A and B is 3.02.

- The average distance is $(0.77 + 0.76 + 3.02 + 1.47 + 1.58 + 1.01)/6 = 1.44$.

- The centroid of cluster A is
$$\left[\frac{0.0459 - 1.0778}{2}, \frac{-0.8537 + 0.8133}{2}\right] = [-0.516, \ -0.020]$$
and the centroid of cluster B is
$$\left[\frac{0.0839 - 0.7017 - 1.5814}{3}, \frac{-0.0804 - 0.7242 + 1.6926}{3}\right]$$
$$= [-0.733, 0.296].$$

The distance between the two centroids is then

$$\sqrt{(-0.516 + 0.733)^2 + (-0.020 - 0.296)^2} = 0.38.$$

In deciding among clustering methods, domain knowledge is key. If you have good reason to believe that the clusters might be chain- or sausage-like, minimum distance would be a good choice. This method does not require that cluster members all be close to one another, only that the new members being added be close to one of the existing members. An example of an application where this might be the case would be characteristics of crops planted in long rows or disease outbreaks along navigable waterways that are the main areas of settlement in a region. Another example is laying and finding mines (land or marine). Minimum distance is also fairly robust to small deviations in the distances. However, adding or removing data can influence it greatly.

Maximum and average distance are better choices if you know that the clusters are more likely to be spherical (e.g., customers clustered on the basis of numerous attributes). If you do not know the probable nature of the cluster, these are good default choices, since most clusters tend to be spherical in nature.

We now move to a more detailed description of the two major types of clustering algorithms: hierarchical (agglomerative) and non-hierarchical.

16.4 HIERARCHICAL (AGGLOMERATIVE) CLUSTERING

The idea behind hierarchical agglomerative clustering is to start with each cluster comprising exactly one record and then progressively agglomerating (combining) the two nearest clusters until there is just one cluster left at the end, which consists of all the records.

Returning to the small example of five utilities and two measures (Sales and Fuel Cost) and using the distance matrix (Figure 16.3), the first step in the hierarchical clustering would join Arizona and Commonwealth, which are the closest (using normalized measurements and Euclidean distance). Next, we would recalculate a 4×4 distance matrix that would have the distances between these four clusters: {Arizona, Commonwealth}, {Boston}, {Central}, and {Consolidated}. At this point, we use a measure of distance between clusters such as the ones described in Section 16.3. Each of these distances (minimum, maximum, average, and centroid distance) can be implemented in the hierarchical scheme as described below.

HIERARCHICAL AGGLOMERATIVE CLUSTERING ALGORITHM

1. Start with n clusters (each record = cluster).

2. The two closest records are merged into one cluster.

3. At every step, the two clusters with the smallest distance are merged. This means that either single records are added to existing clusters or two existing clusters are combined.

Single Linkage

In *single linkage clustering* (called *SingleLink* in RapidMiner), the distance measure that we use is the minimum distance (the distance between the nearest pair of records in the two clusters, one record in each cluster). In our utilities example, we would compute the distances between each of {Boston}, {Central}, and {Consolidated} with {Arizona, Commonwealth} to create the 4×4 distance matrix shown in Table 16.3.

TABLE 16.3   DISTANCE MATRIX AFTER ARIZONA AND COMMONWEALTH CONSOLIDATION CLUSTER TOGETHER, USING SINGLE LINKAGE

	Arizona–Commonwealth	Boston	Central	Consolidated
Arizona–Commonwealth	0			
Boston	min(2.01,1.58)	0		
Central	min(0.77,1.02)	1.47	0	
Consolidated	min(3.02,2.57)	1.01	2.43	0

The next step would consolidate {Central} with {Arizona, Commonwealth} because these two clusters are closest. The distance matrix will again be recomputed (this time it will be 3×3), and so on.

This method has a tendency to cluster together at an early stage records that are distant from each other because of a chain of intermediate records in the same cluster. Such clusters have elongated sausage-like shapes when visualized as objects in space.

Complete Linkage

In *complete linkage clustering* (called *CompleteLink* in RapidMiner), the distance between two clusters is the maximum distance (between the farthest pair of records). If we used complete linkage with the five-utilities example, the recomputed distance matrix would be equivalent to Table 16.3, except that the "min" function would be replaced with a "max."

This method tends to produce clusters at the early stages with records that are within a narrow range of distances from each other. If we visualize them as objects in space, the records in such clusters would have roughly spherical shapes.

Average Linkage

Average linkage clustering (called *AverageLink* in RapidMiner) is based on the average distance between clusters (between all possible pairs of records). If we used average linkage with the five-utilities example, the recomputed distance matrix would be equivalent to Table 16.3, except that the "min" function would be replaced with "average." This method is also called *Unweighted Pair-Group Method using Averages* (UPGMA).

Note that unlike average linkage, the results of the single and complete linkage methods depend only on the ordering of the inter-record distances. Linear transformations of the distances (and other transformations that do not change the ordering) do not affect the results.

Centroid Linkage

Centroid linkage clustering is based on centroid distance, where clusters are represented by their mean values for each attribute, which forms a vector of means. The distance between two clusters is the distance between these two vectors. In average linkage, each pairwise distance is calculated, and the average of all such distances is calculated. In contrast, in centroid distance clustering, just one distance is calculated: the distance between group means. This method is also called *Unweighted Pair-Group Method using Centroids* (UPGMC). Centroid Linkage is not available in RapidMiner.

Ward's Method

Ward's method is also agglomerative, in that it joins records and clusters together progressively to produce larger and larger clusters, but operates slightly differently from the general approach described above. Ward's method considers the "loss of information" that occurs when records are clustered together. When each cluster has one record, there is no loss of information, and all individual values remain available. When records are joined together and represented in clusters, information about an individual record is replaced by the information for the cluster to which it belongs. To measure loss of information, Ward's method employs "error sum of squares" (ESS) that measures the difference between individual records and a group mean.

This is easiest to see in univariate data. For example, consider the values (2, 6, 5, 6, 2, 2, 2, 2, 0, 0, 0) with a mean of 2.5. Their ESS is equal to

$$(2 - 2.5)^2 + (6 - 2.5)^2 + (5 - 2.5)^2 + \cdots + (0 - 2.5)^2 = 50.5.$$

The loss of information associated with grouping the values into a single group is therefore 50.5. Now group the records into four groups: (0, 0, 0), (2, 2, 2, 2), (5), (6, 6). The loss of information is the sum of the ESS for each group, which is 0 (each record in each group is equal to the mean for that group, so the ESS for each group is 0). Thus, clustering the 10 records into 4 clusters results in no loss of information, and this would be the first step in Ward's method. In moving to a smaller number of clusters, Ward's method would choose the configuration that results in the smallest incremental loss of information.

Ward's method tends to result in convex clusters that are of roughly equal size, which can be an important consideration in some applications (e.g., in establishing meaningful customer segments). Ward's method is not available in RapidMiner.

Dendrograms: Displaying Clustering Process and Results

A *dendrogram* is a treelike diagram that summarizes the process of clustering. On the x-axis are the records. Similar records are joined by lines whose vertical length reflects the distance between the records. Figure 16.5 (top) shows the process for clustering the 22 utilities using the 8 normalized numeric attributes and generating a dendrogram with RapidMiner's *Clustering (Agglomerative Clustering)* operator.[2] The resultant single linkage dendrogram is shown in Figure 16.5 (bottom).[3]

In most software by choosing a cutoff distance on the y-axis, a set of clusters is created. In RapidMiner, the folder view is used for this purpose. Visually, this means drawing a horizontal line on a dendrogram. Records with connections below the horizontal line (i.e., their distance is smaller than the cutoff distance) belong to the same cluster. For example, for the single linkage dendrogram in Figure 16.5, six clusters can be obtained by choosing a cutoff distance of 2.7 in the folder view. In the folder view, folders have the following naming convention—*cluster number, number of records contained in that cluster* (*distance between the records*). To identify these six clusters, we expand all folders and subfolders with the distance above the desired cutoff value of 2.7. Then, the number of non-expanded folders represents the count of clusters corresponding to that cutoff value, and the records in the non-expanded folders indicate the membership of those clusters. The six clusters are (from right to left on the dendrogram):

{NY} (*folder*: 4:1)
{Nevada} (*folder*: 10:1)
{San Diego} (*folder*: 16:1)
{Idaho, Puget} (*folder*: 32:2)
{Central} (*folder*: 2:1)
{Arizona, Southern, Oklahoma, Texas, Kentucky, Boston, Commonwealth, Madison, Northern, Wisconsin, Hawaiian, New England, United, Pacific, Virginia, Florida} (*folder*: 37:16)

---

[2]This operator supports single linkage, complete linkage, and average linkage clustering.
[3]RapidMiner's dendrogram does not label the individual observations. Instead, the folder view is used in conjunction with the dendrogram to understand the membership details of each subcluster, along with the distance between the records.

FIGURE 16.5

(TOP LEFT) PROCESS FOR SINGLE LINKAGE CLUSTERING OF 22 UTILITIES, USING ALL 8 NUMERIC ATTRIBUTES, (BOTTOM LEFT) DENDROGRAM, AND (BOTTOM RIGHT) CLUSTER MEMBERSHIP AND DISTANCES (6 UNEXPANDED FOLDERS BELOW DISTANCE CUTOFF 2.7 CONTAIN CLUSTER MEMBERS; READ DENDROGRAM FROM RIGHT TO LEFT AND UNEXPANDED FOLDERS FROM BOTTOM TO TOP)

(PARTIAL OUTPUT, MODIFIED FOR CLARITY)

The average linkage dendrogram is shown in Figure 16.6. If we want six clusters using average linkage, we can choose a cutoff distance of 3.5. The resulting six clusters are slightly different. While some records remain in the same cluster in both methods (e.g., Arizona, Florida, Kentucky, Oklahoma, Texas), others change. The six clusters are (from right to left on the dendrogram):

{Idaho, Puget, Nevada} (*folder*: 37:3)
{NY} (*folder*: 4:1)
{San Diego} (*folder*: 16:1)
{Hawaiian, New England, United, Pacific} (folder: 32:4)
{Boston, Virginia, Commonwealth, Wisconsin, Madison, Northern} (*folder*: 33:6)
{Arizona, Southern, Oklahoma, Texas, Florida, Central, Kentucky} (*folder*: 36:7)

Note that if we wanted five clusters, they would be identical to the six above, with the exception that two of the clusters would be merged into a single cluster. For example, in the single linkage case, the two leftmost clusters in the dendrogram would be merged into one cluster. In general, all hierarchical methods have clusters that are nested within each other as we decrease the number of clusters. This is a valuable property for interpreting clusters and is essential in certain applications, such as taxonomy of varieties of living organisms.

Validating Clusters

One important goal of cluster analysis is to come up with *meaningful clusters*. Since there are many variations that can be chosen, it is important to make sure that the resulting clusters are valid, in the sense that they really generate some insight. To see whether the cluster analysis is useful, consider each of the following aspects:

1. *Cluster interpretability*: Is the interpretation of the resulting clusters reasonable? To interpret the clusters, explore the characteristics of each cluster by:

   a. Obtaining summary statistics (e.g., average, min, max) from each cluster on each measurement that was used in the cluster analysis.

   b. Examining the clusters for separation along some common feature (attribute) that was not used in the cluster analysis.

   c. *Labeling the clusters*: Based on the interpretation, trying to assign a name or label to each cluster.

2. *Cluster stability*: Do cluster assignments change significantly if some of the inputs are altered slightly? Another way to check stability is to partition the data and see how well clusters formed based on one part apply to the other part. To do this:

   a. Cluster partition A.

   b. Use the cluster centroids from A to assign each record in partition B (each record is assigned to the cluster with the closest centroid).

FIGURE 16.6

(TOP LEFT) PROCESS FOR AVERAGE LINKAGE CLUSTERING OF 22 UTILITIES, USING ALL 8 NUMERIC ATTRIBUTES, (BOTTOM LEFT) DENDROGRAM, AND (BOTTOM RIGHT) CLUSTER MEMBERSHIP AND DISTANCES (6 UNEXPANDED FOLDERS BELOW DISTANCE CUTOFF 3.5 CONTAIN CLUSTER MEMBERS; READ DENDROGRAM FROM RIGHT TO LEFT AND UNEXPANDED FOLDERS FROM BOTTOM TO TOP)

(PARTIAL OUTPUT, MODIFIED FOR CLARITY)

c. Assess how consistent the cluster assignments are compared with the assignments based on all the data.

3. *Cluster separation*: Examine the ratio of between-cluster variation to within-cluster variation to see whether the separation is reasonable. There exist statistical tests for this task (an F-ratio), but their usefulness is somewhat controversial.

4. *Number of clusters*: The number of resulting clusters must be useful, given the purpose of the analysis. For example, suppose the goal of the clustering is to identify categories of customers and assign labels to them for market segmentation purposes. If the marketing department can only manage to sustain three different marketing presentations, it would probably not make sense to identify more than three clusters.

Returning to the utilities example, we notice that both methods (single and average linkage) identify {NY} and {San Diego} as singleton clusters. Also, both dendrograms imply that a reasonable number of clusters in this dataset is four. One insight that can be derived from the average linkage clustering is that the clusters tend to group geographically. The four non-singleton clusters form (approximately) a southern group, a northern group, an east/west seaboard group, and a west group.

We can further characterize each of the clusters by examining the summary statistics of their measurements or visually looking at a heatmap of their individual measurements. Figure 16.7 shows a heatmap of the four clusters and two singletons, highlighting the different profile that each cluster has in terms of the eight measurements. We see, for instance, that cluster 4 is characterized by utilities with a high percent of nuclear power, cluster 5 is characterized by high fixed charge and RoR, and cluster 2 has high fuel costs.

Limitations of Hierarchical Clustering

Hierarchical clustering is very appealing in that it does not require specification of the number of clusters and in that sense is purely data-driven. The ability to represent the clustering process and results through dendrograms is also an advantage of this method, as it is easier to understand and interpret. There are, however, a few limitations to consider:

1. Hierarchical clustering requires the computation and storage of an $n \times n$ distance matrix. For very large datasets, this can be expensive and slow.

2. The hierarchical algorithm makes only one pass through the data. This means that records that are allocated incorrectly early in the process cannot be reallocated subsequently.

3. Hierarchical clustering also tends to have low stability. Reordering data or dropping a few records can lead to a different solution.

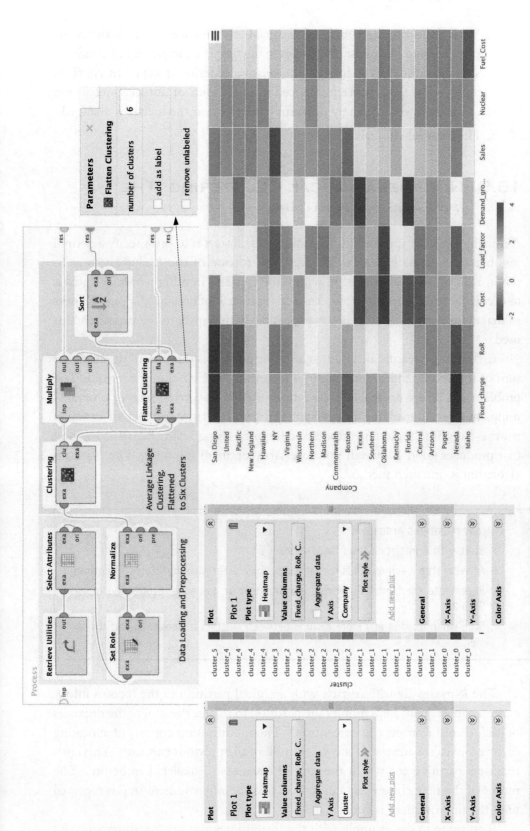

FIGURE 16.7

(TOP) PROCESS FOR FLATTENING AVERAGE LINKAGE CLUSTERED DATA AND (BOTTOM) HEATMAP FOR THE 22 UTILITIES. ROWS ARE SORTED BY THE SIX CLUSTERS. NOTE: Y-AXIS OF THE HEATMAP MAY BE CHANGED TO VIEW THE DATA LABELED BY COMPANY OR CLUSTER

4. With respect to the choice of distance between clusters, single and complete linkage are robust to changes in the distance metric (e.g., Euclidean, statistical distance) as long as the relative ordering is kept. In contrast, average linkage is more influenced by the choice of distance metric and might lead to completely different clusters when the metric is changed.

5. Hierarchical clustering is sensitive to outliers.

16.5 NON-HIERARCHICAL CLUSTERING: THE k-MEANS ALGORITHM

A non-hierarchical approach to forming good clusters is to pre-specify a desired number of clusters, k, and assign each case to one of the k clusters so as to minimize a measure of dispersion within the clusters. In other words, the goal is to divide the sample into a predetermined number k of non-overlapping clusters so that clusters are as homogeneous as possible with respect to the measurements used.

A common measure of within-cluster dispersion is the sum of distances (or sum of squared Euclidean distances) of records from their cluster centroid. The problem can be set up as an optimization problem involving integer programming, but because solving integer programs with a large number of variables is time-consuming, clusters are often computed using a fast, heuristic method that produces good (although not necessarily optimal) solutions. The k-means algorithm is one such method.

---

k-MEANS CLUSTERING ALGORITHM

1. Start with k initial clusters (user chooses k).
2. At every step, each record is reassigned to the cluster with the "closest" centroid.
3. Recompute the centroids of clusters that lost or gained a record, and repeat Step 2.
4. Stop when moving any more records between clusters increases cluster dispersion.

The k-means algorithm starts with an initial partition of the records into k clusters. Subsequent steps modify the partition to reduce the sum of the distances of each record from its cluster centroid. The modification consists of allocating each record to the nearest of the k centroids of the previous partition. This leads to a new partition for which the sum of distances is smaller than before. The means of the new clusters are computed, and the improvement step is repeated until the improvement is very small.

Returning to the example with the five utilities and two measurements, let us assume that $k = 2$ and that the initial clusters are A = {Arizona, Boston} and

B = {Central, Commonwealth, Consolidated}. The cluster centroids were computed in Section 16.3:

$$\bar{x}_A = [-0.516, -0.020] \quad \text{and} \quad \bar{x}_B = [-0.733, 0.296].$$

The distance of each record from each of these two centroids is shown in Table 16.4.

TABLE 16.4	DISTANCE OF EACH RECORD FROM EACH CENTROID	
	Distance from Centroid A	Distance from Centroid B
Arizona	1.0052	1.3887
Boston	1.0052	0.6216
Central	0.6029	0.8995
Commonwealth	0.7281	1.0207
Consolidated	2.0172	1.6341

We see that Boston is closer to cluster B and that Central and Commonwealth are each closer to cluster A. We therefore move each of these records to the other cluster and obtain A = {Arizona, Central, Commonwealth} and B = {Consolidated, Boston}. Recalculating the centroids gives

$$\bar{x}_A = [-0.191, -0.553] \quad \text{and} \quad \bar{x}_B = [-1.33, 1.253].$$

The distance of each record from each of the newly calculated centroids is given in Table 16.5. At this point we stop, because each record is allocated to its closest cluster.

TABLE 16.5	DISTANCE OF EACH RECORD FROM EACH NEWLY CALCULATED CENTROID	
	Distance from Centroid A	Distance from Centroid B
Arizona	0.3827	2.5159
Boston	1.6289	0.5067
Central	0.5463	1.9432
Commonwealth	0.5391	2.0745
Consolidated	2.6412	0.5067

Choosing the Number of Clusters (*k*)

The choice of the number of clusters can either be driven by external considerations (e.g., previous knowledge, practical constraints, etc.), or we can try a few different values for k and compare the resulting clusters. After choosing k, the n records are partitioned into these initial clusters. If there is external reasoning that suggests a certain partitioning, this information should be used. Alternatively, if there exists external information on the centroids of the k clusters, this can be used to initially allocate the records.

In many cases, there is no information to be used for the initial partition. In these cases, the algorithm can be rerun with different randomly generated starting partitions to reduce chances of the heuristic producing a poor solution. The number of clusters in the data is generally not known, so it is a good idea to run the algorithm with different values for k that are near the number of clusters that one expects from the data, to see how the sum of distances reduces with increasing values of k. Note that the clusters obtained using different values of k will not be nested (unlike those obtained by hierarchical methods).

The process for running the k-means algorithm using the *Clustering (k-Means)* operator for all 22 utilities and eight normalized measurements with $k = 6$ is shown in Figure 16.8 (top). The resulting clusters are shown in Figure 16.8 (bottom). As in the results from the hierarchical clustering, we see once

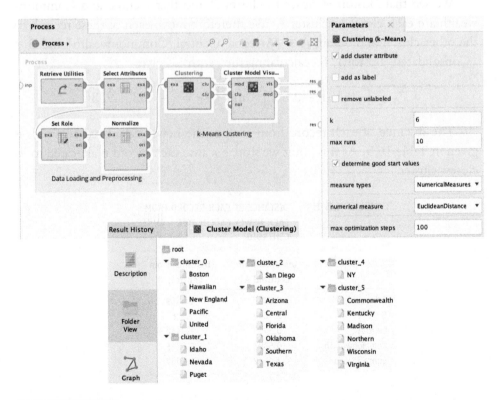

FIGURE 16.8   (TOP) PROCESS FOR k-MEANS CLUSTERING OF 22 UTILITIES INTO $k = 6$ CLUSTERS AND (BOTTOM) RESULTING 6 CLUSTERS (OUTPUT MODIFIED FOR CLARITY)

again that {San Diego} and {NY} are singleton clusters. Similarly, {Idaho, Puget, Nevada} form a cluster as before. The three other clusters (cluster_0: {Boston, Hawaiian, New England, Pacific, and United}, cluster_3: {Arizona, Central, Florida, Oklahoma, Southern, Texas}, and cluster_5: {Commonwealth, Kentucky, Madison, Northern, Wisconsin, Virginia}) are also nearly identical to those that emerged in the hierarchical clustering with average linkage.

To characterize the resulting clusters, we examine the output generated by the *Cluster Model Visualizer* operator. The cluster centroids are shown as a centroid table in Figure 16.9 (top) and as a centroid chart in Figure 16.9 (middle). The overview of clusters shown in Figure 16.9 (bottom) compares the cluster centroids and is useful for cluster interpretation. We see, for instance, that cluster_5 is characterized by highest average Nuclear, relatively low Fuel Cost, and high RoR. We can also see which attributes do the best job of separating the clusters. For example, the spread of clusters for Sales and Fixed–charge is quite high and not so high for the other attributes.

We can also inspect the information on the within-cluster dispersion using the *Performance (Cluster Distance Performance)* operator. From Figure 16.10 (middle), we see that cluster_1, cluster_3, and cluster_5 (with 3, 6, and 6 records, respectively) have the largest within-cluster average squared distances and are thus the most heterogeneous. In contrast, cluster_0, with five records, has a smaller within-cluster average squared distance. This means that cluster cluster_0 is more homogeneous than cluster_1, cluster_3, and cluster_5. Clusters cluster_2 and cluster_4 each have a single record, so within-cluster dispersion is not meaningful.

From the distances between clusters measured by Euclidean distance between the centroids (see Figure 16.10 (bottom)), we can learn about the separation of the different clusters. The *Extract Cluster Prototypes* operator can be used to retrieve the cluster centroids as tabular data, and then the *Data to Similarity Data* operator can be used to find inter-cluster distances. From the pivot table, we can see that cluster_3 (ID: 4) and cluster_5 (ID: 6) are the closest to one another and cluster_2 (ID: 3) and cluster_4 (ID: 5) are the most distant from one another. Also, cluster_2 (ID: 3) and cluster_4 (ID: 5), which are singleton clusters, are most distant from the other clusters, overall, but there is no cluster that is a striking outlier.

When the number of clusters is not predetermined by domain requirements, we can use a graphical approach to evaluate different numbers of clusters. An "elbow chart" is a line chart depicting the decline in cluster heterogeneity as we add more clusters. Figure 16.11 shows the overall average within-cluster squared distance (normalized) for different choices of k. Moving from 1 to 2 tightens clusters considerably (reflected by the large reduction in within-cluster squared distance), and so does moving from 2 to 3 and even to 4. Adding more clusters beyond four brings less improvement to cluster homogeneity.

Cluster	Fixed_charge	RoR	Cost	Load_factor	Demand_growth	Sales	Nuclear	Fuel_Cost
Cluster 0	-0.358	-0.364	0.399	1.157	-0.302	-0.708	-0.403	1.117
Cluster 1	-0.600	-0.833	1.339	-0.481	0.992	1.857	-0.715	-0.966
Cluster 2	-1.919	-1.932	-0.781	1.103	1.847	-0.901	-0.220	1.470
Cluster 3	0.384	0.741	-1.149	-0.522	-0.783	0.434	-0.491	-0.407
Cluster 4	2.037	-0.863	0.578	-1.295	-0.719	-1.581	0.214	1.693
Cluster 5	0.195	0.444	0.182	-0.170	0.350	-0.359	1.185	-0.568

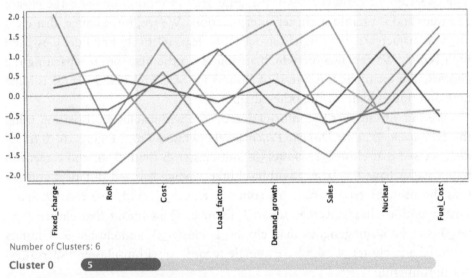

Cluster 0 (5)   Cluster 1 (3)   Cluster 2 (1)   Cluster 3 (6)   Cluster 4 (1)   Cluster 5 (6)

Number of Clusters: 6

Cluster 0   5

Fuel_Cost is on average 78.27% larger, **Load_factor** is on average 71.93% larger, **Nuclear** is on average 56.33% smaller

Cluster 1   3

Sales is on average 117.40% larger, **Nuclear** is on average 100.00% smaller, **Cost** is on average 76.41% larger

Cluster 2   1

Demand_growth is on average 105.85% larger, **Fuel_Cost** is on average 102.97% larger, **RoR** is on average 100.00% smaller

Cluster 3   6

Nuclear is on average 68.75% smaller, **Cost** is on average 65.60% smaller, **Demand_growth** is on average 44.86% smaller

Cluster 4   1

Fuel_Cost is on average 118.59% larger, **Fixed_charge** is on average 103.25% larger, **Sales** is on average 100.00% smaller

Cluster 5   6

Nuclear is on average 165.83% larger, **Fuel_Cost** is on average 39.82% smaller, **RoR** is on average 22.99% larger

FIGURE 16.9   (TOP) CENTROID TABLE k-MEANS CLUSTERING WITH $k = 6$ CLUSTERS, (MIDDLE) CENTROID CHART, AND (BOTTOM) OVERVIEW OF $k = 6$ CLUSTERS (UTILITIES DATA)

PerformanceVector

```
PerformanceVector:
Avg. within centroid distance: 2.690
Avg. within centroid distance_cluster_0: 2.387
Avg. within centroid distance_cluster_1: 3.178
Avg. within centroid distance_cluster_2: 0.000
Avg. within centroid distance_cluster_3: 3.226
Avg. within centroid distance_cluster_4: 0.000
Avg. within centroid distance_cluster_5: 3.059
```

FIGURE 16.10 (TOP) PROCESS FOR COMPUTING k-MEANS CLUSTER DISTANCE PERFORMANCE, (MIDDLE) AVERAGE WITHIN-CLUSTER SQUARED EUCLIDEAN DISTANCES, AND (BOTTOM) EUCLIDEAN DISTANCE BETWEEN CLUSTER CENTROIDS

Yet another domain-independent method to evaluate different number of algorithms is the X-means algorithm introduced by Pelleg and Moore (2000). It is an iterative variant of the k-means algorithm and is implemented in Rapid-Miner with the *X-Means* operator. It uses a heuristic to determine the "correct" number of clusters. It starts with a minimum number of centroids and iteratively

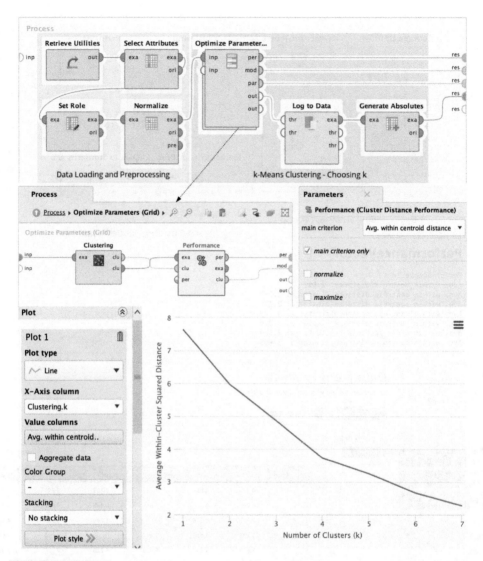

FIGURE 16.11   (TOP) PROCESS FOR COMPARING DIFFERENT CHOICES OF k IN TERMS OF OVERALL AVERAGE WITHIN-CLUSTER SQUARED DISTANCES AND (BOTTOM) ELBOW CHART

proceeds by determining whether splitting a cluster into more clusters based on the Bayesian Information Criteria (BIC) is advantageous.

Finally, we can use the information on the distance between the final clusters to evaluate the cluster validity. The ratio of the sum of within-cluster squared distances to cluster means for a given k to the sum of squared distances to the mean of all the records (in other words, $k = 1$) is a useful measure for the usefulness of the clustering. If the ratio is near 1.0, the clustering has not been very effective, whereas if it is small, we have well-separated groups.

PROBLEMS

16.1 University Rankings. The dataset (*Universities.csv*) on American College and University Rankings (available from www.dataminingbook.com) contains information on 1302 American colleges and universities offering an undergraduate program. For each university, there are 17 measurements, including continuous measurements (such as tuition and graduation rate) and categorical measurements (such as location by state and whether it is a private or public school).

Note that many records are missing some measurements. Our first goal is to estimate these missing values from "similar" records. This will be done by clustering the complete records and then finding the closest cluster for each of the partial records. The missing values will be imputed from the information in that cluster.

   a. Remove all records with missing measurements from the dataset. (*Hint*: Use the *Filter Examples* operator. Remember to set College Name as *id* role.)

   b. For all the continuous measurements, run hierarchical clustering using complete linkage and Euclidean distance. Make sure to normalize the measurements. From the dendrogram: How many clusters seem reasonable for describing these data?

   c. Compare the summary statistics for each cluster, and describe each cluster in this context (e.g., "Universities with high tuition, low acceptance rate..."). (*Hint*: To obtain cluster statistics for hierarchical clustering, first use the *Flatten Clustering* operator to obtain the clustered data as an *ExampleSet*. Then, use the *De-Normalize* and *Apply Model* operators on the flattened clustered data, and then compute cluster characteristics using the *Aggregate* operator.)

   d. Use the categorical measurements that were not used in the analysis (State and Private/Public) to characterize the different clusters. Is there any relationship between the clusters and the categorical information? (*Hint*: Use the *Join* operator (inner) to combine the de-normalized clustered data with the original data containing the State and Private/Public attributes. Then use *Turbo Prep* or the *Pivot* operator.)

   e. What other external information can explain the contents of some or all of these clusters?

   f. Consider Tufts University, which is missing some information. Compute the Euclidean distance of this record from each of the clusters that you found above (using only the measurements that you have). Which cluster is it closest to? Impute the missing values for Tufts by taking the average of the cluster on those measurements. (*Hint*: Use the *Cross Distances* operator to compute distance, and use the *Replace Missing Values* operator for missing value imputation.)

16.2 Pharmaceutical Industry. An equities analyst is studying the pharmaceutical industry and would like your help in exploring and understanding the financial data collected by her firm. Her main objective is to understand the structure of the pharmaceutical industry using some basic financial measures.

Financial data gathered on 21 firms in the pharmaceutical industry are available in the file *Pharmaceuticals.csv*. For each firm, the following attributes are recorded:

   1. Market capitalization (in billions of dollars)

   2. Beta

   3. Price/earnings ratio

4. Return on equity

5. Return on assets

6. Asset turnover

7. Leverage

8. Estimated revenue growth

9. Net profit margin

10. Median recommendation (across major brokerages)

11. Location of firm's headquarters

12. Stock exchange on which the firm is listed

Use cluster analysis to explore and analyze the given dataset as follows:

a. Use only the numerical attributes (1–9) to cluster the 21 firms. Justify the various choices made in conducting the cluster analysis, such as the specific clustering algorithm(s) used, the number of clusters formed, and so on.

b. Interpret the clusters with respect to the numerical attributes used in forming the clusters.

c. Is there a pattern in the clusters with respect to the categorical attributes (10–12) (those not used in forming the clusters)?

d. Provide an appropriate name for each cluster using any or all of the attributes in the dataset.

16.3 **Customer Rating of Breakfast Cereals.** The dataset *Cereals.csv* includes nutritional information, store display, and consumer ratings for 77 breakfast cereals.

Data Preprocessing. Remove all cereals with missing values.

a. Apply hierarchical clustering to the data using Euclidean distance to the normalized measurements. Compare the dendrograms from single linkage and complete linkage, and look at cluster centroids. Comment on the structure of the clusters and on their stability. (*Hint*: To obtain cluster centroids for hierarchical clustering, first use the *Flatten Clustering* operator to obtain the clustered data as an *ExampleSet*. Then, use the *De-Normalize* and *Apply Model* operators on the flattened clustered data to compute cluster centroids using the *Aggregate* operator.)

b. Which method leads to the most insightful or meaningful clusters?

c. Choose one of the methods. How many clusters would you use? What distance is used for this cutoff? (Look at the dendrogram.)

d. The elementary public schools would like to choose a set of cereals to include in their daily cafeterias. Every day a different cereal is offered, but all cereals should support a healthy diet. For this goal, you are requested to find a cluster of "healthy cereals." Should the data be normalized? If not, how should they be used in the cluster analysis?

16.4 **Marketing to Frequent Fliers.** The file *EastWestAirlinesCluster.csv* contains information on 3999 passengers who belong to an airline's frequent flier program. For each passenger, the data include information on their mileage history and on different ways they accrued or spent miles in the last year. The goal is to try to identify clusters of passengers that have similar characteristics for the purpose of targeting different segments for different types of mileage offers.

a. Apply an iterative k-means clustering in RapidMiner using the *X-Means* operator, specifying parameters: k_min = 2, k_max = 10. Make sure to normalize the data first. How many clusters appear?

b. What would happen if the data were not normalized?

c. Compare the cluster centroid to characterize the different clusters, and try to give each cluster a label.

d. To check the stability of the clusters, remove a random 5% of the data (by taking a random sample of 95% of the records), and repeat the analysis. Does the same picture emerge?

e. Which clusters would you target for offers, and what types of offers would you target to customers in that cluster?

Forecasting Time Series

CHAPTER 17

Handling Time Series

In this chapter, we describe the context of business time series forecasting and introduce the main approaches that are detailed in the next chapters and, in particular, regression-based forecasting and smoothing-based methods. Our focus is on forecasting future values of a single time series. These three chapters are meant as an introduction to the general forecasting approach and methods.

In this chapter, we discuss the difference between the predictive nature of time series forecasting vs. the descriptive or explanatory task of time series analysis. A general discussion of combining forecasting methods or results for added precision follows. Next, we present a time series in terms of four components (level, trend, seasonality, and noise) and methods for visualizing the different components and exploring time series data. We close with a discussion of data partitioning (creating training and holdout sets), which is performed differently from cross-sectional data partitioning.

RapidMiner

In this chapter, we will use RapidMiner's time series operators *Lag* and *Extract Coefficients (Polynominal Fit)*. We will also briefly discuss two additional operators for evaluating time series models, namely, *Sliding Window Validation* and *Forecast Validation*. These and other time series modeling operators are located in the *Operators* panel under *Modeling > Time Series*. The *Series Extension* available through RapidMiner's marketplace provides additional operators for processing and analyzing time series data.

Machine Learning for Business Analytics: Concepts, Techniques and Applications in RapidMiner, First Edition.
Galit Shmueli, Peter C. Bruce, Amit V. Deokar, and Nitin R. Patel.
© 2023 John Wiley & Sons, Inc. Published 2023 by John Wiley & Sons, Inc.

17.1 INTRODUCTION[1]

Time series forecasting is performed in nearly every organization that works with quantifiable data. Retail stores use it to forecast sales. Energy companies use it to forecast reserves, production, demand, and prices. Educational institutions use it to forecast enrollment. Governments use it to forecast tax receipts and spending. International financial organizations like the World Bank and International Monetary Fund use it to forecast inflation and economic activity. Transportation companies use time series forecasting to forecast future travel. Banks and lending institutions use it (sometimes badly!) to forecast new home purchases. Also, venture capital firms use it to forecast market potential and to evaluate business plans.

The previous chapters in this book deal with classifying and predicting data where time is not a factor, in the sense that it is not treated differently from other attributes and where the sequence of measurements over time does not matter. These are typically called cross-sectional data. In contrast, this chapter deals with a different type of data: time series.

With today's technology, many time series are recorded on very frequent time scales. Stock data are available at ticker level. Purchases at online and offline stores are recorded in real time. The Internet of Things (IoT) generates huge numbers of time series, produced by sensors and other measurements devices. Although data might be available at a very frequent scale, for the purpose of forecasting, it is not always preferable to use this time scale. In considering the choice of time scale, one must consider the scale of the required forecasts and the level of noise in the data. For example, if the goal is to forecast next-day sales at a grocery store, using minute-by-minute sales data is likely to be less useful for forecasting than using daily aggregates. The minute-by-minute series will contain many sources of noise (e.g., variation by peak and non-peak shopping hours) that degrade its forecasting power, and these noise errors, when the data are aggregated to a cruder level, are likely to average out.

The focus in this part of the book is on forecasting a single time series. In some cases, multiple time series are to be forecasted (e.g., the monthly sales of multiple products). Even when multiple series are being forecasted, the most popular forecasting practice is to forecast each series individually. The advantage of single-series forecasting is its simplicity. The disadvantage is that it does not take into account possible relationships between series. The statistics literature contains models for multivariate time series which directly model the cross-correlations between series. Such methods tend to make restrictive assumptions about the data and the cross-series structure. They also require statistical expertise

---

[1]This and subsequent sections in this chapter, copyright ©2019 Datastats, LLC, and Galit Shmueli. Used by permission.

for estimation and maintenance. Econometric models often include information from one or more series as inputs into another series. However, such models are based on assumptions of causality that are based on theoretical models. An alternative approach is to capture the associations between the series of interest and external information more heuristically. An example is using the sales of lipstick to forecast some measure of the economy, based on the observation by Ronald Lauder, chairman of Estee Lauder, that lipstick sales tend to increase before tough economic times (a phenomenon called the "leading lipstick indicator").

17.2 DESCRIPTIVE VS. PREDICTIVE MODELING

As with cross-sectional data, modeling time series data is done for either descriptive or predictive purposes. In descriptive modeling, or *time series analysis*, a time series is modeled to determine its components in terms of seasonal patterns, trends, relation to external factors, etc. These can then be used for decision-making and policy formulation. In contrast, *time series forecasting* uses the information in a time series (and perhaps other information) to forecast future values of that series. The difference between the goals of time series analysis and time series forecasting leads to differences in the type of methods used and in the modeling process itself. For example, in selecting a method for describing a time series, priority is given to methods that produce understandable results (rather than "black box" methods) and sometimes to models based on causal arguments (explanatory models). Furthermore, describing can be done in retrospect, while forecasting is *prospective* in nature. This means that descriptive models might use "future" information (e.g., averaging the values of yesterday, today, and tomorrow to obtain a smooth representation of today's value), whereas forecasting models cannot.

The focus in this chapter is on time series forecasting, where the goal is to predict future values of a time series. For information on time series analysis, see Chatfield (2003).

17.3 POPULAR FORECASTING METHODS IN BUSINESS

In this part of the book, we focus on two main types of forecasting methods that are popular in business applications. Both are versatile and powerful yet relatively simple to understand and deploy. One type of forecasting tool is linear regression, where the user specifies a certain model and then estimates it from the time series. The other includes more data-driven methods, such as smoothing and deep learning, where the method learns patterns from the data. Each of the two types of tools has advantages and disadvantages, as detailed in Chapters 18 and 19. We also note that machine learning methods such as neural networks and others that are intended for cross-sectional data are also sometimes used for time series forecasting, especially for incorporating external information into the forecasts (see Shmueli and Lichtendahl, 2016).

Combining Methods

Before a discussion of specific forecasting methods in the following two chapters, it should be noted that a popular approach for improving predictive performance is to combine forecasting methods. This is similar to the ensembles approach described in Chapter 13. Combining forecasting methods can be done via two-level (or multi-level) forecasters, where the first method uses the original time series to generate forecasts of future values and the second method uses the residuals from the first model to generate forecasts of future forecast errors, thereby "correcting" the first level forecasts. We describe two-level forecasting in Section 18.4. Another combination approach is via "ensembles," where multiple methods are applied to the time series, and their resulting forecasts are averaged in some way to produce the final forecast. Combining methods can take advantage of the strengths of different forecasting methods to capture different aspects of the time series (also true in cross-sectional data). The averaging across multiple methods can lead to forecasts that are more robust and of higher precision.

17.4 TIME SERIES COMPONENTS

In both types of forecasting methods, regression models and smoothing, and in general, it is customary to dissect a time series into four components: *level, trend, seasonality*, and *noise*. The first three components are assumed to be invisible, as they characterize the underlying series, which we only observe with added noise. Level describes the average value of the series, trend is the change in the series from one period to the next, and seasonality describes a short-term cyclical behavior of the series which can be observed several times within the given series. Finally, noise is the random variation that results from measurement error or other causes not accounted for. It is always present in a time series to some degree.

> Don't get confused by the standard conversational meaning of "season" (winter, spring, etc.). The statistical meaning of "season" refers to any time period that repeats itself in cycles within the larger time series. Also, note that the term "period" in forecasting means simply a span of time, and not the specific meaning that it has in physics, of the distance between two equivalent points in a cycle.

To identify the components of a time series, the first step is to examine a *time plot*. In its simplest form, a time plot is a line chart of the series values over time, with temporal labels (e.g., calendar date) on the horizontal axis. To illustrate this, consider the following example.

Example: Ridership on Amtrak Trains

Amtrak, a US railway company, routinely collects data on ridership. Here we focus on forecasting future ridership using the series of monthly ridership between January 1991 and March 2004.[2]

A time plot for the monthly Amtrak ridership series[3] is shown in Figure 17.1. Note that the values are in thousands of riders.

FIGURE 17.1   **MONTHLY RIDERSHIP ON AMTRAK TRAINS (IN THOUSANDS) FROM JANUARY 1991 TO MARCH 2004**

Looking at the time plot reveals the nature of the series components: the overall level is around 1,800,000 passengers per month. A slight U-shaped trend is discernible during this period, with pronounced annual seasonality, with peak travel during summer (July and August).

A second step in visualizing a time series is to examine it more carefully. A few tools are useful:

---

[2]Data from https://www.bts.gov/archive/publications/multimodal_transportation_indicators/june_ 2010/amtrak_ridership and available on the book companion site www.dataminingbook.com

[3]To import the data in RapidMiner correctly using the *Amtrak.csv* file, change the date format to *dd/MM/yyyy* in the *Format your columns* step of the *Import Data* wizard.

Zoom in: Zooming in to a shorter period within the series can reveal patterns that are hidden when viewing the entire series. This is especially important when the time series is long. Consider a series of the daily number of vehicles passing through the Baregg tunnel in Switzerland (*BareggTunnel.csv*).[4] The series from November 1, 2003 to November 16, 2005 is shown in Figure 17.2 (top). Zooming in to a four-month period (Figure 17.2, bottom) reveals a strong day-of-week pattern that is not visible in the plot of the complete time series.

FIGURE 17.2   (TOP) TIME PLOT OF THE DAILY NUMBER OF VEHICLES PASSING THROUGH THE BAREGG TUNNEL, SWITZERLAND, AND (BOTTOM) ZOOMING IN TO A FOUR-MONTH PERIOD, REVEALING A DAY-OF-WEEK PATTERN

Change scale of series: To better identify the shape of a trend, it is useful to change the scale of the series. One simple option, to check for an exponential trend, is to change the vertical scale to a logarithmic scale

---

[4]Data from http://neural-forecasting-competition.com/downloads/NNGC1/datasets/download. htm

(in RapidMiner, select the *Logarithmic* option for a plot's Y-axis). If the trend on the new scale appears more linear, then the trend in the original series is closer to an exponential trend.

Add trend lines: Another possibility for better discerning the shape of the trend is to add a trend line. By trying different trendlines, one can see what type of trend (e.g., linear, exponential, quadratic) best approximates the data.

Suppress seasonality: It is often easier to see trends in the data when seasonality is suppressed. Suppressing seasonality patterns can be done by plotting the series at a cruder time scale (e.g., aggregating monthly data into years) or creating separate lines or time plots for each season (e.g., separate lines for each day of week). Another popular option is to use moving average charts. We will discuss these in Section 19.2.

Continuing our example of Amtrak ridership, the charts in Figure 17.3 help make the series' components more visible. The RapidMiner process for creating these plots is shown in Figure 17.4.

Some forecasting methods directly model these components by making assumptions about their structure. For example, a popular assumption about trend is that it is linear or exponential over the given time period or part of it. Another common assumption is about the noise structure: many statistical methods assume that the noise follows a normal distribution. The advantage of methods that rely on such assumptions is that when the assumptions are reasonably met, the resulting forecasts will be more robust and the models more understandable. Other forecasting methods, which are data-adaptive, make fewer assumptions about the structure of these components and instead try to estimate them only from the data. Data-adaptive methods are advantageous when such assumptions are likely to be violated or when the structure of the time series changes over time. Another advantage of many data-adaptive methods is their simplicity and computational efficiency.

A key criterion for deciding between model-driven and data-driven forecasting methods is the nature of the series in terms of global vs. local patterns. A global pattern is one that is relatively constant throughout the series. An example is a linear trend throughout the entire series. In contrast, a local pattern is one that occurs only in a short period of the data and then changes, for example, a trend that is approximately linear within four neighboring time points, but the trend size (slope) changes slowly over time.

Model-driven methods are generally preferable for forecasting series with global patterns as they use all the data to estimate the global pattern. For a local pattern, a model-driven model would require specifying how and when the patterns change, which is usually impractical and often unknown. Therefore, data-driven methods are preferable for local patterns. Such methods "learn" patterns from the data, and their memory length can be set to best adapt to

FIGURE 17.3   **PLOTS THAT ENHANCE THE DIFFERENT COMPONENTS OF THE TIME SERIES. (TOP) ZOOM IN TO THREE YEARS OF DATA AND (BOTTOM) ORIGINAL SERIES WITH OVERLAID QUADRATIC TRENDLINE**

the rate of change in the series. Patterns that change quickly warrant a "short memory," whereas patterns that change slowly warrant a "long memory." In conclusion, the time plot should be used to identify not only the time series component but also the global/local nature of the trend and seasonality.

17.5 DATA PARTITIONING AND PERFORMANCE EVALUATION

As in the case of cross-sectional data, to avoid overfitting and to be able to assess the predictive performance of the model on new data, we first partition the

FIGURE 17.4   RAPIDMINER **PROCESS FOR CREATING TIME PLOTS THAT ENHANCE THE DIFFERENT COMPONENTS OF THE TIME SERIES (AMTRAK RIDERSHIP DATA)**

data into a training set and a holdout set (and perhaps an additional validation set for model tuning and comparison). However, there is one important difference between data partitioning in cross-sectional and time series data. In cross-sectional data, the partitioning is usually done randomly, with a random set of records designated as training data and the remainder as holdout data. However, in time series, a random partition would create two time series with "holes." Most standard forecasting methods cannot handle time series with missing values. Therefore, we partition a time series into training and holdout sets differently. The series is trimmed into two periods; the earlier period is set as the training data, and the later period as the holdout data. Methods are then trained on the earlier training period, and their predictive performance is assessed on the later holdout period. This approach also has the advantage of mimicking how the forecasting model will be used in practice: trained on existing data to forecast future values.

Figure 17.5 (top) illustrates data partitioning for the Amtrak ridership data using the *Filter Examples* operator in RapidMiner. The final 36 months are selected as the holdout set and the earlier period is the training set. The filter condition for partitioning uses an *id* attribute (with *id* role) created using the *Generate ID* operator.[5] Figure 17.5 (bottom) shows the partitioned data in a time plot.

DATA PARTITIONING OPERATORS IN RAPIDMINER

In addition to the generic *Filter Examples* operator, RapidMiner also provides other operators for evaluating models on time series data, including *Forecast Validation* and *Sliding Window Validation* operators, both of which are particularly suited for evaluating models over sliding windows. The *Forecast Validation* operator is suitable when evaluating models of type "forecast model" (e.g., time series models created using *ARIMA* or *Holt-Winters* operators). Here, the training set is specified by the *window size* parameter, and the holdout set is specified by the *horizon* parameter. We use this operator in Chapter 19. The *Sliding Window Validation* operator is suitable when using cross-sectional prediction models (such as models created using the *Linear Regression* operator). Here, the training and holdout sets are specified by the *training window size* and *test window size* parameters. Both operators have a *step size* parameter to determine the shift of the window across the entire series.

Evaluation measures typically use the same metrics used in cross-sectional evaluation (see Chapter 5) with *RMSE*, *MAE*, and *MAPE* being the most popular in practice. In evaluating and comparing forecasting methods, another important tool is visualization: examining time plots of the actual and predicted series can shed light on performance and hint toward possible improvements.

Benchmark Performance: Naive Forecasts

While it is tempting to apply "sophisticated" forecasting methods, we must evaluate their value added compared with a very simple approach: the *naive forecast*. A naive forecast is simply the most recent value of the series. In other words, at time t, our forecast for any future period $t+k$ is simply the value of the series at time t. While simple, naive forecasts are sometimes surprisingly difficult to outperform with more sophisticated models. It is therefore important to benchmark against results from a naive-forecasting approach.

When a time series has seasonality, a *seasonal naive forecast* can be generated. It is simply the value on the most recent similar season. For example, to forecast

---

[5]While data can also be partitioned based on the Month attribute, it is easier to work with *id* values in general, so we use this approach in the book.

FIGURE 17.5   (TOP) RAPIDMINER PROCESS FOR DATA PARTITIONING AND (BOTTOM) TRAINING
(123 VALUES) AND HOLDOUT (36 VALUES) SETS FOR AMTRAK RIDERSHIP DATA

April 2001 for the Amtrak ridership, we use the ridership from the most recent April, which is April 2000. Similarly, to forecast April 2002, we also use April 2000 ridership. In Figure 17.6, we show naive (red horizontal line) and seasonal naive forecasts (green line), as well as actual values (orange line), in a three-year holdout set from April 2001 to March 2004. Figure 17.7 shows the RapidMiner process to generate this chart. For naive forecasts, the *Extract Macro* operator captures the final value in the training period and uses it as the naive forecast for the holdout period. Computing seasonal naive forecasts requires using the *Lag* operator set to 12—the number of seasons here. This copies the $(t-12)$th value into a new attribute, Ridership-12. Then, using a subprocess containing *Loop*, *Append*, and *Join* operators, the last 12 values in the training period are repeated for the Ridership-12 attribute in the holdout set. This attribute serves as the seasonal naive forecast for the holdout period.

FIGURE 17.6   NAIVE AND SEASONAL NAIVE FORECASTS IN A THREE-YEAR HOLDOUT SET FOR AMTRAK RIDERSHIP

Performance on the holdout set is more relevant than the performance on the training set because it is more indicative of how the models will perform in the future. Figure 17.8 compares the accuracies of these two naive forecasts for the holdout period. Because Amtrak ridership has strong monthly seasonality, the seasonal naive forecast is the clear winner on all popular measures.

Generating Future Forecasts

Another important difference between cross-sectional and time series partitioning occurs when creating the actual forecasts. Before attempting to forecast future values of the series, the training and holdout sets are recombined into

FIGURE 17.7 RAPIDMINER PROCESS FOR NAÏVE AND SEASONAL NAÏVE FORECASTS IN A THREE-YEAR HOLDOUT SET FOR AMTRAK RIDERSHIP

(a) Performance on Holdout Set (Naive Forecast)

```
PerformanceVector:
root_mean_squared_error: 142.755 +/- 0.000
absolute_error: 115.923 +/- 83.311
relative_error: 6.02% +/- 4.73%
```

(b) Performance on Holdout Set (Seasonal Naive Forecast)

```
PerformanceVector:
root_mean_squared_error: 95.624 +/- 0.000
absolute_error: 84.094 +/- 45.521
relative_error: 4.25% +/- 2.32%
```

FIGURE 17.8 PREDICTIVE ACCURACY OF NAIVE (a) AND SEASONAL NAIVE (b) FORECASTS IN THE HOLDOUT SET FOR AMTRAK RIDERSHIP

one long series, and the chosen method/model is rerun on the complete data. This final model is then used to forecast future values. The three advantages in recombining are the following:

1. The holdout set, which is the most recent period, usually contains the most valuable information in terms of being the closest in time to the forecast period.

2. With more data (the complete time series compared to only the training set), some models can be estimated more accurately.

3. If only the training set is used to generate forecasts, then it will require forecasting farther into the future (e.g., if the holdout set contains four time points, forecasting the next period will require a five-step-ahead forecast from the training set).

PROBLEMS

17.1 Impact of September 11 on Air Travel in the United States. The Research and Innovative Technology Administration's Bureau of Transportation Statistics conducted a study to evaluate the impact of the September 11, 2001 terrorist attack on US transportation. The 2006 study report and the data can be found at https://www.bts.gov/archive/publications/estimated_impacts_of_9_11_on_us_travel/index. The goal of the study was stated as follows:

> The purpose of this study is to provide a greater understanding of the passenger travel behavior patterns of persons making long distance trips before and after 9/11.

The report analyzes monthly passenger movement data between January 1990 and May 2004. Data on three monthly time series are given in file *Sept11Travel.csv* for this period:

(1) Actual airline revenue passenger miles (Air)

(2) Rail passenger miles (Rail)

(3) Vehicle miles traveled (Car)

To assess the impact of September 11, BTS took the following approach: using data before September 11, they forecasted future data (under the assumption of no terrorist attack). Then, they compared the forecasted series with the actual data to assess the impact of the event. Our first step, therefore, is to split each of the time series into two parts: pre- and post-September 11. We now concentrate only on the earlier time series.

a. Is the goal of this study descriptive or predictive?

b. Plot each of the three pre-event time series (Air, Rail, Car).

    i. What time series components appear from the plot?

    ii. What type of trend appears? Change the scale of the series, add trendlines, and suppress seasonality to better visualize the trend pattern.

17.2 Performance on Training and Holdout Data. Two different models were fit to the same time series. The first 100 time periods were used for the training set, and the last 12 periods were treated as a holdout set. Assume that both models make sense practically and fit the data pretty well. Below are the RMSE values for each of the models:

	Training set	Holdout set
Model A	543	690
Model B	669	675

a. Which model appears more useful for explaining the different components of this time series? Why?

b. Which model appears to be more useful for forecasting purposes? Why?

17.3 Forecasting Department Store Sales. The file *DepartmentStoreSales.csv* contains data on the quarterly sales for a department store over a six-year period (data courtesy of Chris Albright).

    a. Create a well-formatted time plot of the data.

    b. Which of the four components (level, trend, seasonality, noise) seem to be present in this series?

17.4 **Shipments of Household Appliances.** The file *ApplianceShipments.csv* contains the series of quarterly shipments (in million dollars) of US household appliances between 1985 and 1989 (data courtesy of Ken Black).

    a. Create a well-formatted time plot of the data.

    b. Which of the four components (level, trend, seasonality, noise) seem to be present in this series?

17.5 **Canadian Manufacturing Workers Workhours.** The time plot in Figure 17.9 describes the average annual number of weekly hours spent by Canadian manufacturing workers (data are available in *CanadianWorkHours.csv*—thanks to Ken Black for the data).

FIGURE 17.9   **AVERAGE ANNUAL WEEKLY HOURS SPENT BY CANADIAN MANUFACTURING WORKERS**

    a. Reproduce the time plot.

    b. Which of the four components (level, trend, seasonality, noise) seem to be present in this series?

17.6 **Souvenir Sales.** The file *SouvenirSales.csv* contains monthly sales for a souvenir shop at a beach resort town in Queensland, Australia, between 1995 and 2001. [Source: Hyndman and Yang (2018).]

    Back in 2001, the store wanted to use the data to forecast sales for the next 12 months (year 2002). They hired an analyst to generate forecasts. The analyst first partitioned the data into training and holdout sets, with the holdout set containing the last 12 months of data (year 2001). She then fit a regression model to sales, using the training set.

    a. Create a well-formatted time plot of the data.

    b. Change the scale on the x-axis or on the y-axis or on both to logarithmic scale to achieve a linear relationship. Select the time plot that seems most linear.

c. Comparing the two time plots, what can be said about the type of trend in the data?

d. Why were the data partitioned? Partition the data into the training and holdout sets as explained above.

17.7 Shampoo Sales. The file *ShampooSales.csv* contains data on the monthly sales of a certain shampoo over a three-year period. [Source: Hyndman and Yang (2018).]

a. Create a well-formatted time plot of the data.

b. Which of the four components (level, trend, seasonality, noise) seem to be present in this series?

c. Do you expect to see seasonality in sales of shampoo? Why?

d. If the goal is forecasting sales in future months, which of the following steps should be taken?

- Partition the data into training and holdout sets.
- Tweak the model parameters to obtain good fit to the validation data.
- Look at MAPE and RMSE values for the training set.
- Look at MAPE and RMSE values for the holdout set.

CHAPTER 18

Regression-Based Forecasting

A popular forecasting tool is based on multiple linear regression models, using suitable predictors to capture trend and/or seasonality. In this chapter, we show how a linear regression model can be set up to capture a time series with a trend and/or seasonality. The model, which is estimated from the data, can then produce future forecasts by inserting the relevant predictor information into the estimated regression equation. We describe different types of common trends (linear, exponential, polynomial) and two types of seasonality (additive and multiplicative). Next, we show how a regression model can be used to quantify the correlation between neighboring values in a time series (called autocorrelation). This type of model, called an autoregressive (AR) model, is useful for improving forecast precision by making use of the information contained in the autocorrelation (beyond trend and seasonality). It is also useful for evaluating the predictability of a series, by evaluating whether the series is a "random walk." The various steps of fitting linear regression and autoregressive models, using them to generate forecasts, and assessing their predictive accuracy, are illustrated using the Amtrak ridership series.

RapidMiner

In this chapter, in addition to *Linear Regression* and related operators used for prediction models, we will use the following time series operators in RapidMiner: *Logarithm*, *Autocorrelation / Autocovariance*, *ARIMA*, *Apply Forecast*, and *Differentiate*. These and other time series modeling operators are located in the *Operators* panel under *Modeling > Time Series*. The *Series Extension* available through RapidMiner's marketplace provides additional operators for processing and analyzing time series data.

Machine Learning for Business Analytics: Concepts, Techniques and Applications in RapidMiner, First Edition.
Galit Shmueli, Peter C. Bruce, Amit V. Deokar, and Nitin R. Patel.
© 2023 John Wiley & Sons, Inc. Published 2023 by John Wiley & Sons, Inc.

18.1   A MODEL WITH TREND[1]

Linear Trend

To create a linear regression model that captures a time series with a global linear trend, the target attribute (Y) is set as the time series values or some function of it, and the predictor attribute (X) is set as a time index. Let us consider a simple example: fitting a linear trend to the Amtrak ridership data described in Chapter 17. This type of trend is shown in Figure 18.1 (bottom).

From the time plot, it is obvious that the global trend is not linear. However, we use this example to illustrate how a linear trend is fitted, and later we consider more appropriate models for this series.

To obtain a linear relationship between Ridership and Time, we set the target attribute Y as the Amtrak ridership and create a new attribute that is a time index $t = 1, 2, 3, \ldots$. This time index is then used as a single predictor in the regression model:

$$Y_t = \beta_0 + \beta_1 t + \epsilon,$$

where Y_t is the ridership at period t and ϵ is the standard noise term in a linear regression. Thus, we are modeling three of the four time series components: level (β_0), trend (β_1), and noise (ϵ). Seasonality is not modeled. A snapshot of the two corresponding columns (Y_t and t) for the first 14 months is shown in Table 18.1.

TABLE 18.1	TARGET ATTRIBUTE (MIDDLE) AND PREDICTOR ATTRIBUTE (RIGHT) USED TO FIT A LINEAR TREND (FIRST 14 MONTHS SHOWN)	
Month	Ridership (Y_t)	t
Jan 91	1709	1
Feb 91	1621	2
Mar 91	1973	3
Apr 91	1812	4
May 91	1975	5
Jun 91	1862	6
Jul 91	1940	7
Aug 91	2013	8
Sep 91	1596	9
Oct 91	1725	10
Nov 91	1676	11
Dec 91	1814	12
Jan 92	1615	13
Feb 92	1557	14

Creating a time index in RapidMiner is done using the *Generate ID* operator, as shown in Figure 18.1. We can then use the resulting *id* as a predictor.

---

[1] This and subsequent sections in this chapter copyright © 2019 Datastats, LLC, and Galit Shmueli. Used by permission.

FIGURE 18.1   (TOP) RAPIDMINER PROCESS FOR FITTING A LINEAR TREND TO AMTRAK
RIDERSHIP AND (BOTTOM) LINEAR TREND FIT

After partitioning the data into training and holdout sets, the next step is to
fit a linear regression model to the training set, with t as the single predictor.
In RapidMiner, we do this by setting the role of *id* as regular attribute—the *use
bias* option in the *Linear Regression* operator also adds an *intercept* to the model.
Applying this to the Amtrak ridership data (with a holdout set consisting of
the last 36 months) results in the estimated model shown in Figure 18.2. The
actual and fitted values and the residuals (or forecast errors) are shown in the

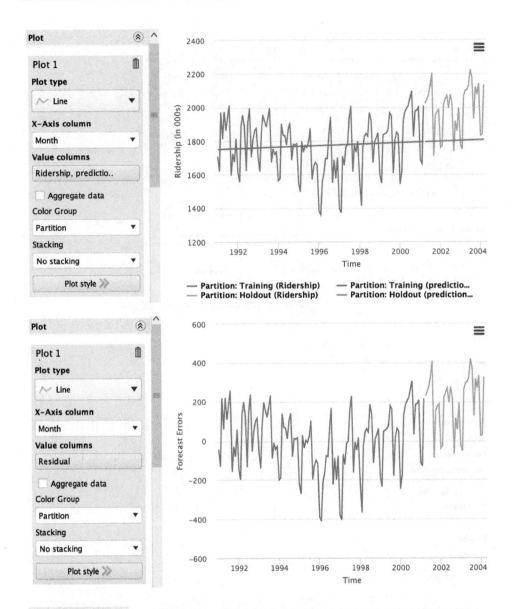

FIGURE 18.2 A LINEAR TREND FIT TO AMTRAK RIDERSHIP IN THE TRAINING PERIOD AND FORECASTED IN THE HOLDOUT PERIOD

two time plots. The RapidMiner process to generate these charts is shown in Figure 18.3.[2]

---

[2]The *Filter Examples* operator with condition *id* <= 123 is used to partition the data. Alternatively, the *Sliding Window Validation* operator with *training window size* = 123, *test window size* = 36, and *step size* = 1 could be used.

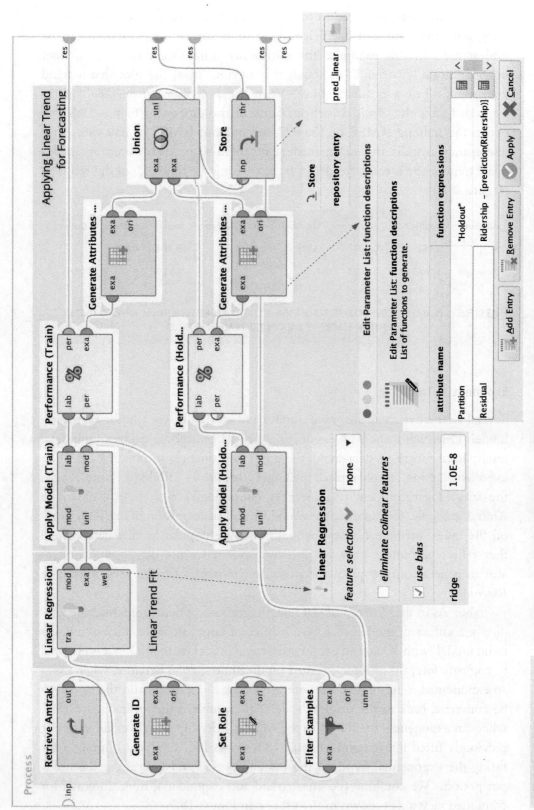

FIGURE 18.3   RAPIDMINER PROCESS FOR FITTING A LINEAR TREND TO AMTRAK RIDERSHIP IN THE TRAINING PERIOD AND FORECASTED IN THE HOLDOUT PERIOD

Figure 18.4 contains a report of the estimated coefficients. Note that examining only the estimated coefficients and their statistical significance can be misleading! In this example, the statistically insignificant trend coefficient might indicate "no trend," although it is obvious from the plot that a trend does exist, albeit a quadratic one. With the *Performance (Regression)* operator added after the *Apply Model* operators in the process in Figure 18.3, we obtain the training RMSE of 158.927 and holdout RMSE of 239.486. This discrepancy is indicative of an inadequate trend shape. However, an inadequate trend shape is easiest to detect by examining the time plot of the residuals (Figure 18.2).

Attribute	Coefficient	Std. Error	Std. Coefficient	Tolerance	t–Stat	p–Value	Code
id	0.351	0.407	0.078	?	0.864	0.390	
(Intercept)	1750.360	29.073	?	?	60.206	0	****

FIGURE 18.4   COEFFICIENTS TABLE FROM A LINEAR REGRESSION MODEL APPLIED TO THE AMTRAK RIDERSHIP DATA IN THE TRAINING PERIOD

Exponential Trend

Several alternative trend shapes are useful and easy to fit via a linear regression model. One such shape is an exponential trend. An exponential trend implies a multiplicative increase/decrease of the series over time ($Y_t = ce^{\beta_1 t + \epsilon}$). To fit an exponential trend, simply replace the target attribute Y with $\log Y$ (where log is the natural logarithm), and fit a linear regression ($\log Y_t = \beta_0 + \beta_1 t + \epsilon$). In the Amtrak example, for instance, we would fit a linear regression of log(Ridership) on the index attribute t. Exponential trends are popular in sales data, where they reflect percentage growth. In RapidMiner, we use the *Logarithm* operator to generate a new predictor attribute *Ridership_log* to be used instead of *Ridership*.

Note: As in the general case of linear regression, when comparing the predictive accuracy of models that have a different target attribute, such as a linear trend model (with Y) and an exponential trend model (with $\log Y$), it is essential to compare forecasts or forecast errors on the same scale. Therefore, when using an exponential trend model, the forecasts of $\log Y$ are made and then need to be converted back to the original scale. An example is shown in Figure 18.5, where an exponential trend is fit to the Amtrak ridership data, overlaid with our previously fitted linear trend. Figure 18.6 shows the RapidMiner process for fitting the exponential trend on the training period and forecasting the holdout period. We combine the linear trend and exponential trend forecasts for combined viewing as shown in the process in Figure 18.7.

FIGURE 18.5 **EXPONENTIAL (RED) AND LINEAR (GREEN) TREND USED TO FORECAST AMTRAK RIDERSHIP**

Polynomial Trend

Another nonlinear trend shape that is easy to fit via linear regression is a polynomial trend and, in particular, a quadratic relationship of the form $Y_t = \beta_0 + \beta_1 t + \beta_2 t^2 + \epsilon$. This is done by creating an additional predictor t^2 (the square of t) and fitting a multiple linear regression with the two predictors t and t^2. In RapidMiner, we create t^2 by generating another predictor attribute *id-sq*, computed as *id* $\times$ *id*. We then include *id* and *id-sq* as predictors. For the Amtrak ridership data, we have already seen a U-shaped trend in the data. We therefore fit a quadratic model using a process similar to Figure 18.3. The fitted and residual charts are shown in Figure 18.8. We conclude from these plots that this shape adequately captures the trend during the training period. The training forecast errors are now devoid of trend and exhibit only seasonality. The forecast now overshoots for the test period, indicating that the quadratic trend that seemed to fit the training data well may not be useful for future data.

In general, any type of trend shape can be fit as long as it has a mathematical representation. However, the underlying assumption is that this shape is applicable throughout the period of data that we have and also during the period that we are going to forecast. Do not choose an overly complex shape. Although it will fit the training data well, it will in fact be overfitting them. To avoid overfitting, always examine the holdout performance, and refrain from choosing overly complex trend patterns.

FIGURE 18.6   RAPIDMINER **PROCESS TO FIT AN EXPONENTIAL TREND FOR FORECASTING AMTRAK RIDERSHIP**

FIGURE 18.7   RAPIDMINER **PROCESS FOR COMBINING THE LINEAR TREND FORECASTED SERIES WITH EXPONENTIAL TREND FORECASTED SERIES**

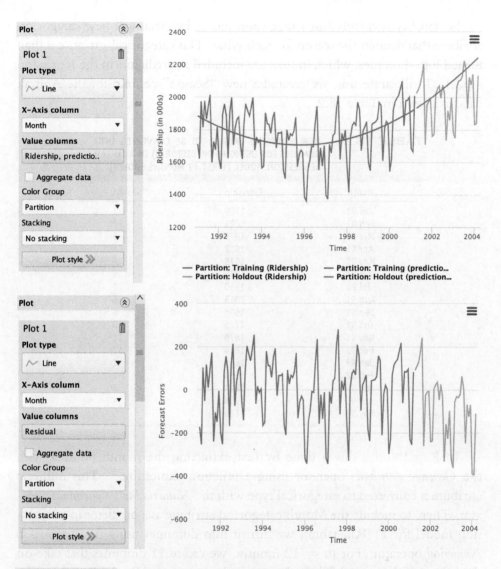

FIGURE 18.8   QUADRATIC TREND MODEL USED TO FORECAST AMTRAK RIDERSHIP. PLOTS OF (TOP) ACTUAL AND FORECASTED VALUES AND (BOTTOM) FORECAST ERRORS

18.2 A MODEL WITH SEASONALITY

A seasonal pattern in a time series means that periods that fall in some seasons have consistently higher or lower values than those that fall in other seasons. Examples are day-of-week patterns, monthly patterns, and quarterly patterns. The Amtrak ridership monthly time series, as can be seen in the time plot, exhibits strong monthly seasonality (with highest traffic during summer months).

Seasonality is captured in a regression model by creating a new categorical attribute that denotes the season for each value. This categorical attribute is then turned into dummies, which in turn are included as predictors in the regression model. To illustrate this, we created a new "Season" column for the Amtrak data, as shown in Table 18.2.

TABLE 18.2	NEW ATTRIBUTE (RIGHT) TO BE CONVERTED INTO DUMMIES FOR USING AS PREDICTOR(S) IN A LINEAR REGRESSION MODEL (FIRST 17 MONTHS SHOWN)	
Month	Ridership	Season
Jan 91	1709	1
Feb 91	1621	2
Mar 91	1973	3
Apr 91	1812	4
May 91	1975	5
Jun 91	1862	6
Jul 91	1940	7
Aug 91	2013	8
Sep 91	1596	9
Oct 91	1725	10
Nov 91	1676	11
Dec 91	1814	12
Jan 92	1615	1
Feb 92	1557	2
Mar 92	1891	3
Apr 92	1956	4
May 92	1885	5

In RapidMiner, this is done by first extracting the month number with the *Generate Attributes* operator using a function expression.[3] This numeric attribute is converted to categorical type with the *Numerical to Polynominal* operator. Then, to include the Month categorical attribute as a predictor in a regression model for Y (Ridership), we turn it into dummies using the *Nominal to Numerical* operator. For $m = 12$ months, we create 11 dummies that take on the value 1 if the period falls in that particular month and 0 otherwise.[4]

Similar to the process shown in Figure 18.3,[5] after partitioning the data into training and holdout sets, we fit the regression model to the training data. The fitted series and the residuals from this model are shown in Figure 18.9. The model appears to capture the seasonality in the data. However, since we have not included a trend component in the model (as shown in Section 18.1), the fitted values do not capture the existing trend. Therefore, the residuals, which are the difference between the actual and the fitted values, clearly display the remaining U-shaped trend.

---

[3] We use the function expression *date_get(Month, DATE_UNIT_MONTH)* + 1. (We add 1 because month numbering in RapidMiner starts with 0.)

[4] Using only $m - 1$ dummies is sufficient. If all $m - 1$ dummies are zero, then the season must be the mth season. Including all m dummies causes multicollinearity.

[5] Here, the generated *id* is not changed to a regular attribute, so it remains with its *id* role and does not serve as a predictor in this model.

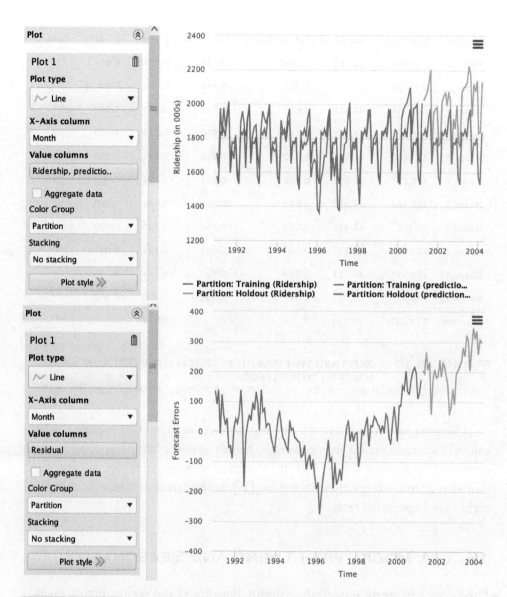

FIGURE 18.9 REGRESSION MODEL WITH SEASONALITY FOR AMTRAK RIDERSHIP. PLOTS OF (TOP) ACTUAL AND FORECASTED VALUES AND (BOTTOM) FORECAST ERRORS

Additive vs. Multiplicative Seasonality

When seasonality is added as described above (create categorical seasonal attribute, then create dummies from it, and then regress on Y), it captures *additive seasonality*. This means that the average value of Y in a certain season is a fixed amount more or less than that in another season. For example, consider the regression coefficients table in Figure 18.10 for the model with additive seasonality that we just fitted. The coefficient for *Season_8* (396.66) indicates that the average number of passengers in August is higher by 396,660 passengers than the average in January (the comparison group).

Attribute	Coefficient	Std. Error	Std. Coefficient	Tolerance	t-Stat	p-Value	Code
Season_2	-42.930	43.243	-0.077	0.705	-0.993	0.323	
Season_3	260.768	43.243	0.467	0.966	6.030	0.000	****
Season_4	245.092	44.311	0.420	0.957	5.531	0.000	****
Season_5	278.222	44.311	0.477	0.970	6.279	0.000	****
Season_6	233.460	44.311	0.400	0.951	5.269	0.000	****
Season_7	345.327	44.311	0.592	0.991	7.793	0.000	****
Season_8	396.660	44.311	0.680	0.999	8.952	0.000	****
Season_9	75.762	44.311	0.130	0.854	1.710	0.090	*
Season_10	200.608	44.311	0.344	0.935	4.527	0.000	****
Season_11	192.355	44.311	0.330	0.931	4.341	0.000	****
Season_12	230.415	44.311	0.395	0.950	5.200	0.000	****
(Intercept)	1573.972	30.578	?	?	51.475	0	****

FIGURE 18.10   COEFFICIENTS TABLE FROM FITTING ADDITIVE SEASONALITY TO THE AMTRAK DATA IN THE TRAINING PERIOD

Using regression models, we can also capture *multiplicative seasonality*, where values in a certain season are, on average, higher or lower by a percentage amount compared to another season. To fit multiplicative seasonality, we use the same model as above, except that we use $\log(Y)$ as the target attribute as described earlier for *Exponential trend*.

18.3 A MODEL WITH TREND AND SEASONALITY

Finally, we can create models that capture both trend and seasonality by including predictors of both types. For example, from our exploration of the Amtrak ridership data, it appears that a quadratic trend and monthly seasonality are both warranted. We therefore fit a model to the training data with 13 predictors: 11 dummies for month and t and t^2 for trend. The coefficients table and fit from this final model are shown in Figures 18.11 and 18.12. If we are satisfied with this model after evaluating its predictive performance on the holdout data and comparing it against alternatives, we would re-fit it to the entire un-partitioned series. This re-fitted model can then be used to generate k-step-ahead forecasts (denoted by F_{t+k}) by plugging in the appropriate month and index terms.

Attribute	Coefficient	Std. Err...	Std. Coefficient	Toleran...	t-Stat	p-Value	Code
Season_2	-43.246	30.241	-0.077	0.773	-1.430	0.156	
Season_3	260.015	30.242	0.465	0.975	8.598	0.000	****
Season_4	260.617	31.021	0.447	0.961	8.401	0.000	****
Season_5	293.797	31.020	0.504	0.972	9.471	0.000	****
Season_6	248.961	31.020	0.427	0.957	8.026	0.000	****
Season_7	360.634	31.020	0.618	0.990	11.626	0	****
Season_8	411.651	31.021	0.706	0.998	13.270	0	****
Season_9	90.316	31.022	0.155	0.876	2.911	0.004	***
Season_10	214.604	31.024	0.368	0.944	6.917	0.000	****
Season_11	205.671	31.026	0.353	0.941	6.629	0.000	****
Season_12	242.929	31.029	0.416	0.957	7.829	0.000	****
id-sq	0.061	0.006	1.732	0.994	10.660	0	****
id	-7.156	0.729	-1.594	0.954	-9.812	0.000	****
(Intercept)	1696.979	27.675	?	?	61.318	0	****

FIGURE 18.11   COEFFICIENTS TABLE FROM FITTING TREND AND SEASONALITY TO AMTRAK DATA IN THE TRAINING PERIOD

However, the predictions on the test data are still missing the mark, indicating that the trend we have identified may not be so global, after all. More on this in the next chapter, where we allow a local trend component.

18.4 AUTOCORRELATION AND ARIMA MODELS

When we use linear regression for time series forecasting, we are able to account for patterns such as trend and seasonality. However, ordinary regression models do not account for dependence between values in different periods, which in cross-sectional data is assumed to be absent. Yet, in the time series context, values in neighboring periods tend to be correlated. Such correlation, called *autocorrelation*, is informative and can help in improving forecasts. If we know that a high value tends to be followed by high values (positive autocorrelation), then we can use that to adjust forecasts. We will now discuss how to compute the autocorrelation of a series and how best to utilize the information for improving forecasts.

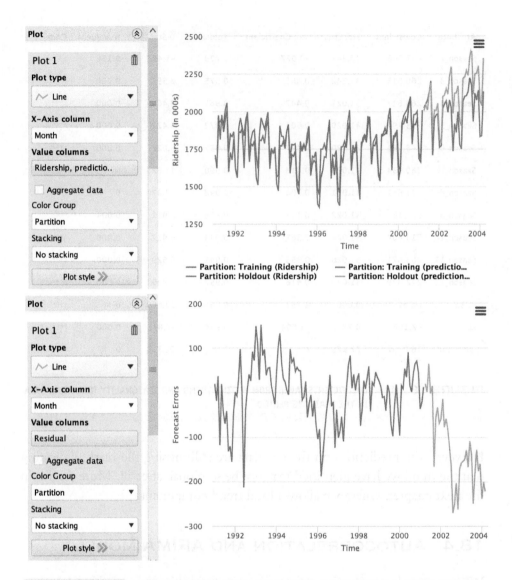

FIGURE 18.12   REGRESSION MODEL WITH TREND AND SEASONALITY FOR AMTRAK RIDERSHIP. PLOTS OF (TOP) ACTUAL AND FORECASTED VALUES AND (BOTTOM) FORECAST ERRORS

Computing Autocorrelation

Correlation between values of a time series in neighboring periods is called *autocorrelation*, because it describes a relationship between the series and itself. To compute autocorrelation, we compute the correlation between the series and a lagged version of the series. A *lagged series* is a "copy" of the original series which is moved forward one or more time periods. A lagged series with lag-1 is the

TABLE 18.3	FIRST 24 MONTHS OF AMTRAK RIDERSHIP SERIES WITH LAG-1 AND LAG-2 SERIES		

Month	Ridership	Lag-1 series	Lag-2 series
Jan 91	1709		
Feb 91	1621	1709	
Mar 91	1973	1621	1709
Apr 91	1812	1973	1621
May 91	1975	1812	1973
Jun 91	1862	1975	1812
Jul 91	1940	1862	1975
Aug 91	2013	1940	1862
Sep 91	1596	2013	1940
Oct 91	1725	1596	2013
Nov 91	1676	1725	1596
Dec 91	1814	1676	1725
Jan 92	1615	1814	1676
Feb 92	1557	1615	1814
Mar 92	1891	1557	1615
Apr 92	1956	1891	1557
May 92	1885	1956	1891
Jun 92	1623	1885	1956
Jul 92	1903	1623	1885
Aug 92	1997	1903	1623
Sep 92	1704	1997	1903
Oct 92	1810	1704	1997
Nov 92	1862	1810	1704
Dec 92	1875	1862	1810

original series moved forward one time period, a lagged series with lag-2 is the original series moved forward two time periods, etc. Table 18.3 shows the first 24 months of the Amtrak ridership series, the lag-1 series, and the lag-2 series.

Next, to compute the lag-1 autocorrelation, which measures the linear relationship between values in consecutive time periods, we compute the correlation between the original series and the lag-1 series e.g., via the operator *Correlation Matrix* to be 0.079. Note that although the original series in Table 18.3 has 24 time periods, the lag-1 autocorrelation will only be based on 23 pairs (because the lag-1 series does not have a value for January 1991). Similarly, the lag-2 autocorrelation, measuring the relationship between values that are two time periods apart, is the correlation between the original series and the lag-2 series (yielding -0.143).

We can use RapidMiner's *Autocorrelation / Autocovariance* operator to compute the autocorrelation function (ACF) of a series and create a plot. For example, the output for the 24-month ridership is shown in Figure 18.13.[6]

---

[6]The *Autocorrelation / Autocovariance* operator requires the *maximum lag* parameter to be set to the number of lags desired + 1, since the autocorrelation with the series itself (lag 0) is counted.

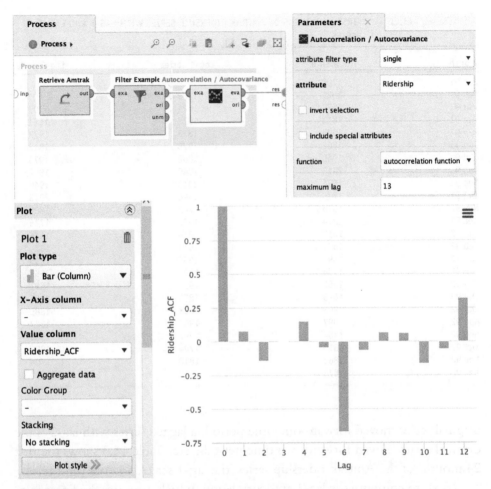

FIGURE 18.13   (TOP) RAPIDMINER PROCESS TO COMPUTE AUTOCORRELATION AND (BOTTOM) AUTOCORRELATION PLOT FOR LAGS 1–12 (FOR FIRST 24 MONTHS OF AMTRAK RIDERSHIP)

A few typical autocorrelation behaviors that are useful to explore are the following:

Strong autocorrelation (positive or negative) at a lag k larger than 1 and its multiples $(2k, 3k, \ldots)$ typically reflects a cyclical pattern. For example, strong positive lag-12 autocorrelation in monthly data will reflect an annual seasonality (where values during a given month each year are positively correlated).

Positive lag-1 autocorrelation (called "stickiness") describes a series where consecutive values move generally in the same direction. In the presence of a strong linear trend, we would expect to see a strong and positive lag-1 autocorrelation.

Negative lag-1 autocorrelation reflects swings in the series, where high values are immediately followed by low values and vice versa.

Examining the autocorrelation of a series can therefore help to detect seasonality patterns. In Figure 18.13, for example, we see that the strongest autocorrelation is at lag 6 and is negative. This indicates a bi-annual pattern in ridership, with six-month switches from high to low ridership. A look at the time plot confirms the high-summer low-winter pattern.

In addition to looking at the autocorrelation of the raw series, it is very useful to look at the autocorrelation of the *residual series* (that is, the forecast errors series). For example, after fitting a regression model (or using any other forecasting method), we can examine the autocorrelation of the series of residuals. If we have adequately modeled the seasonal pattern, then the residual series should show no autocorrelation at the season's lag. Figure 18.14 displays the autocorrelations for the residuals from the regression model with seasonality and quadratic trend shown in Figure 18.12. It is clear that the 6-month (and 12-month) cyclical behavior no longer dominates the series of residuals, indicating

FIGURE 18.14   (TOP) RAPIDMINER PROCESS TO COMPUTE AUTOCORRELATION AND (BOTTOM) AUTOCORRELATION PLOT OF FORECAST ERRORS SERIES FROM FIGURE 18.12

that the regression model captured them adequately. However, we can also see a strong positive autocorrelation from lag 1 on, indicating a positive relationship between neighboring residuals. This is valuable information, which can be used to improve forecasts.

Improving Forecasts by Integrating Autocorrelation Information

In general, there are two approaches to taking advantage of autocorrelation. One is by directly building the autocorrelation into the regression model, and the other is by constructing a second-level forecasting model on the residual series.

Among regression-type models that directly account for autocorrelation are *autoregressive* (AR) models, or the more general class of models called ARIMA (Autoregressive Integrated Moving Average) models. AR models are similar to linear regression models, except that the predictors are the past values of the series. For example, an autoregressive model of order 2, denoted AR(2), can be written as

$$Y_t = \beta_0 + \beta_1 Y_{t-1} + \beta_2 Y_{t-2} + \epsilon. \tag{18.1}$$

Estimating such models is roughly equivalent to fitting a linear regression model with the series as the target attribute and the two lagged series (at lag 1 and 2 in this example) as the predictors. However, it is better to use designated ARIMA estimation methods (e.g., using RapidMiner's *ARIMA* operator) over ordinary linear regression estimation, to produce more accurate results.[7] Although moving from AR to ARIMA models creates a larger set of more flexible forecasting models, it also requires much more statistical expertise. Even with the simpler AR models, fitting them to raw time series that contain patterns such as trends and seasonality requires the user to perform several initial data transformations and to choose the order of the model.[8] These are not straightforward tasks. Because ARIMA modeling is less robust and requires more experience and statistical expertise than other methods, we do not discuss it here and direct the interested reader to classic time series textbooks (e.g., see Chapter 4 in Chatfield, 2003).

However, we do discuss one particular use of AR models that is straightforward to apply in the context of forecasting, which can provide a significant improvement to short-term forecasts. This relates to the second approach for utilizing autocorrelation, which requires constructing a second-level forecasting model for the residuals, as follows:

1. Generate a k-step-ahead forecast of the series (F_{t+k}), using any forecasting method

---

[7] ARIMA model estimation differs from ordinary regression estimation by accounting for the dependence between records.

[8] RapidMiner's *Optimize Parameters Grid* operator can be used to search for "optimal" ARIMA parameter values. However, such an approach is only recommended for a data scientist with advanced statistical expertise.

2. Generate a k-step-ahead forecast of the forecast error (residual) (E_{t+k}), using an AR (or other) model

3. Improve the initial k-step-ahead forecast of the series by adjusting it according to its forecasted error: *Improved* $F^*_{t+k} = F_{t+k} + E_{t+k}$.

In particular, we can fit low-order AR models to series of residuals (or *forecast errors*) which can then be used to forecast future forecast errors. By fitting the series of residuals, rather than the raw series, we avoid the need for initial data transformations (because the residual series is not expected to contain any trends or cyclical behavior besides autocorrelation).

To fit an AR model to the series of residuals, we first examine the autocorrelations of the residual series. We then choose the order of the AR model according to the lags in which autocorrelation appears. Often, when autocorrelation exists at lag-1 and higher, it is sufficient to fit an AR(1) model of the form

$$E_t = \beta_0 + \beta_1 E_{t-1} + \epsilon, \tag{18.2}$$

where E_t denotes the residual (or *forecast error*) at time t. For example, although the autocorrelations in Figure 18.14 appear large from lags 1 to 10 or so, it is likely that an AR(1) would capture all of these relationships. The reason is that if immediate neighboring values are correlated, then the relationship propagates to values that are two periods away, then three periods away, etc.[9]

The result of fitting such an AR(1) model to the Amtrak ridership residual series is shown in Figure 18.15 (bottom). The AR(1) coefficient (0.6042) is the same as the lag-1 autocorrelation (0.604) that we found earlier (Figure 18.14). The forecasted residual for April 2001 is computed by plugging in the most recent mean-centered[10] residual from March 2001 (equal to 12.108 $- (-0.2433)$) into the AR(1) model:

$$-0.2433 + (0.6042)(12.108 - (-0.2433)) = 7.219.$$

You can obtain this number directly by using the *Apply Forecast* operator with the ARIMA model as the input (see output in Figure 18.15 (bottom)). The positive value tells us that the regression model will produce a ridership forecast for April 2001 that is too low and that we should adjust it up by adding 7219 riders. In this particular example, the regression model (with quadratic trend and seasonality) produced a forecast of 2,004,271 riders, and the improved two-stage model [regression + AR(1) correction] corrected it by increasing it to 2,011,490

---

[9] *Partial autocorrelations (function = partial autocorrelation function* parameter in the *Autocorrelation / Autocovariance* operator) measure the contribution of each lag series *over and above* smaller lags. For example, the lag-2 partial autocorrelation is the contribution of lag-2 beyond that of lag-1.

[10] RapidMiner's ARIMA function produces coefficients based on the mean-centered series. Its "constant" is actually the series mean. To generate a forecast, we must first subtract the mean from the plugged in value and then multiply by the AR(1) coefficient.

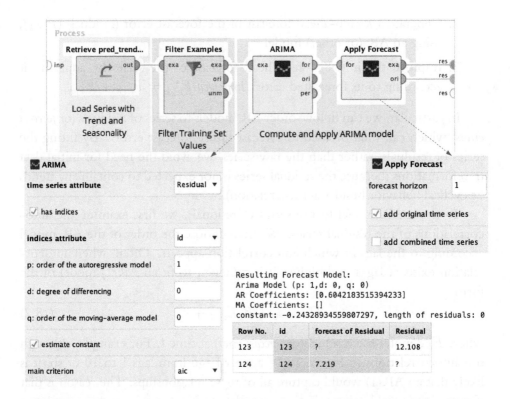

(TOP) RAPIDMINER PROCESS FOR COMPUTING AND APPLYING ARIMA MODEL
AND (BOTTOM) OUTPUT FOR AR(1) MODEL ON RIDERSHIP RESIDUALS

riders. The actual value for April 2001 turned out to be 2,023,792 riders—much closer to the improved forecast.

From the plot of the actual vs. forecasted residual series (Figure 18.16), we can see that the AR(1) model fits the residual series quite well. Note, however, that the plot is based on the training data (until March 2001). To evaluate predictive performance of the two-level model [regression + AR(1)], we would have to examine performance (e.g., via MAPE or RMSE metrics) on the holdout data, in a fashion similar to the calculation that we performed for April 2001. The RapidMiner process for generating the plot in Figure 18.16 and computing the performance on the holdout data is shown in Figure 18.17.

Finally, to examine whether we have indeed accounted for the autocorrelation in the series and that no more information remains in the series, we examine the autocorrelations of the series of residuals-of-residuals (the residuals obtained after the AR(1), which was applied to the regression residuals). This is seen in Figure 18.18 (for RapidMiner process, see Figure 18.17). It is clear that no more autocorrelation remains and that the addition of the AR(1) has adequately captured the autocorrelation information.

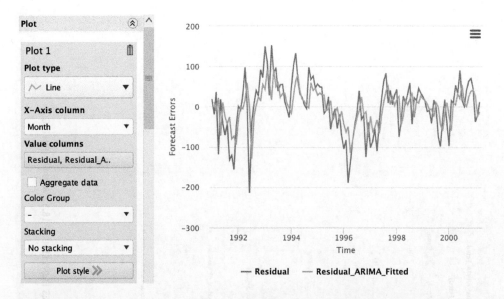

FIGURE 18.16   FITTING AN AR(1) MODEL TO THE RESIDUAL SERIES FROM FIGURE 18.12

We mentioned earlier that improving forecasts via an additional AR layer is useful for short-term forecasting. The reason is that an AR model of order k will usually only provide useful forecasts for the next k periods, and after that forecasts will rely on earlier forecasts rather than on actual data. For example, to forecast the residual of May 2001 when the time of prediction is March 2001, we would need the residual for April 2001. However, because that value is not available, it would be replaced by its forecast. Hence, the forecast for May 2001 would be based on the forecast for April 2001.

Evaluating Predictability

Before attempting to forecast a time series, it is important to determine whether it is predictable, in the sense that its past can be used to predict its future beyond the naive forecast. One useful way to assess predictability is to test whether the series is a *random walk*. A random walk is a series in which changes from one time period to the next are random. According to the efficient market hypothesis in economics, asset prices are random walks, and therefore predicting stock prices is a game of chance.[11]

A random walk is a special case of an AR(1) model, where the slope coefficient is equal to 1:

$$Y_t = \beta_0 + Y_{t-1} + \epsilon_t. \tag{18.3}$$

---

[11]There is some controversy surrounding the efficient market hypothesis, with claims that there is slight autocorrelation in asset prices, which does make them predictable to some extent. However, transaction costs and bid–ask spreads tend to offset any prediction benefits.

FIGURE 18.17   RAPIDMINER PROCESS FOR FITTING AN AR(1) MODEL TO THE RESIDUAL SERIES FROM FIGURE 18.12 AND COMPUTING AUTOCORRELATIONS OF RESIDUALS-OF-RESIDUALS SERIES

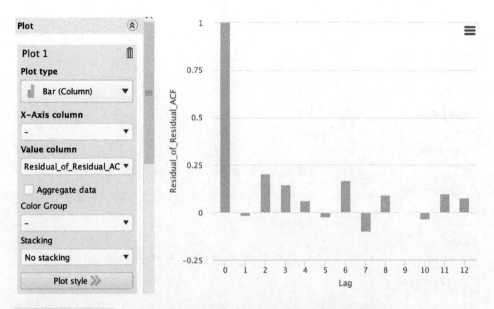

FIGURE 18.18   AUTOCORRELATIONS OF RESIDUALS-OF-RESIDUALS SERIES

We can also write this as

$$Y_t - Y_{t-1} = \beta_0 + \epsilon_t. \tag{18.4}$$

We see from the last equation that the difference between the values at periods $t - 1$ and t is random, hence the term "random walk." Forecasts from such a model are basically equal to the most recent observed value (the naive forecast), reflecting the lack of any other information.

Testing whether a series is a random walk is equivalent to testing whether the lag-1 differenced series $Y_t - Y_{t-1}$ ($t = 2, 3, \ldots$) behaves like a random series. The latter can be done by examining the autocorrelations of the differenced series: if all autocorrelation values are insignificant, then the original series is likely a random walk.

As an example, consider the series of S&P500 monthly closing prices between May 1995 and August 2003 (*SP500.csv*) shown in Figure 18.19. The autocorrelation plot of the lag-1 differenced closing prices series is shown in Figure 18.20. We see that all autocorrelation values are practically zero, indicating that the closing prices series is a random walk. Forecasting this series using any of the methods described earlier (aside from the naive forecast) is therefore futile.

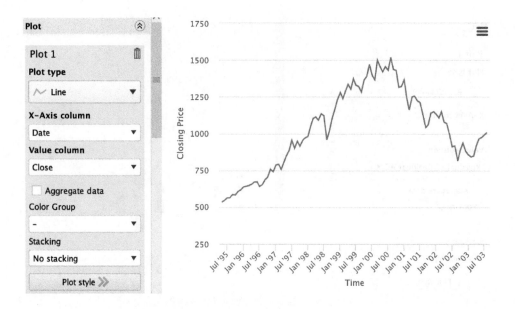

FIGURE 18.19   S&P500 MONTHLY CLOSING PRICES SERIES

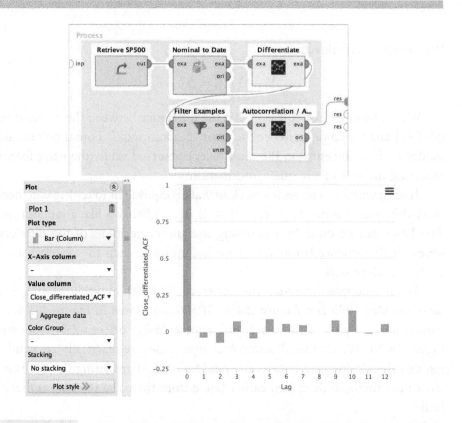

FIGURE 18.20   (TOP) PROCESS FOR COMPUTING AUTOCORRELATIONS OF LAG-1 DIFFERENCED S&P500 MONTHLY CLOSING PRICES. (BOTTOM) AUTOCORRELATION PLOT

PROBLEMS

18.1 Impact of September 11 on Air Travel in the United States. The Research and Innovative Technology Administration's Bureau of Transportation Statistics conducted a study to evaluate the impact of the September 11, 2001 terrorist attack on US transportation. The 2006 study report and the data can be found at https://www.bts.gov/archive/publications/estimated_impacts_of_9_11_on_us_travel/index. The goal of the study was stated as follows:

> The purpose of this study is to provide a greater understanding of the passenger travel behavior patterns of persons making long distance trips before and after 9/11.

The report analyzes monthly passenger movement data between January 1990 and May 2004. Data on three monthly time series are given in file *Sept11Travel.csv* for this period: (1) actual airline revenue passenger miles (Air), (2) rail passenger miles (Rail), and (3) vehicle miles traveled (Car).

To assess the impact of September 11, BTS took the following approach: using data before September 11, they forecasted future data (under the assumption of no terrorist attack). Then, they compared the forecasted series with the actual data to assess the impact of the event. Our first step, therefore, is to split each of the time series into two parts: pre- and post-September 11. We now concentrate only on the earlier time series.

a. Plot the pre-event AIR time series. What time series components appear? (*Hint:* In preparing the data, use *Nominal to Date* and *Parse Numbers* operators to transform the attributes to the correct data type.)

b. Figure 18.21 shows a time plot of the **seasonally adjusted** pre-September-11 AIR series. Which of the following methods would be adequate for forecasting the series shown in the figure?

- Linear regression model seasonality
- Linear regression model with trend
- Linear regression model with trend and seasonality

FIGURE 18.21   SEASONALLY ADJUSTED PRE-SEPTEMBER-11 AIR SERIES

c. Specify a linear regression model for the AIR series that would produce a season-ally adjusted series similar to the one shown in Figure 18.21, with multiplicative seasonality. What is the target attribute? What are the predictors?

d. Run the regression model from (c). Remember to use only pre-event data.

    i. What can we learn from the statistical insignificance of the coefficients for October and September?

    ii. The actual value of AIR (air revenue passenger miles) in January 1990 was 35.153577 billion. What is the residual for this month, using the regression model? Report the residual in terms of air revenue passenger miles.

e. Create an ACF (autocorrelation) plot of the regression residuals.

    i. What does the ACF plot tell us about the regression model's forecasts?

    ii. How can this information be used to improve the model?

f. Fit linear regression models to Air, Rail, and Auto with additive seasonality and an appropriate trend. For Air and Rail, fit a linear trend. For Rail, use a quadratic trend. Remember to use only pre-event data. Once the models are estimated, use them to forecast each of the three post-event series.

    i. For each series (Air, Rail, Auto), plot the complete pre-event and post-event actual series overlayed with the predicted series.

    ii. What can be said about the effect of the September 11 terrorist attack on the three modes of transportation? Discuss the magnitude of the effect, its time span, and any other relevant aspects.

18.2 **Analysis of Canadian Manufacturing Workers' Workhours.** The time plot in Figure 18.22 describes the average annual number of weekly hours spent by Canadian manufacturing workers (*CanadianWorkHours.csv*, data courtesy of Ken Black).

a. Which of the following regression models would fit the series best? (Choose one.)

- Linear trend model
- Linear trend model with seasonality
- Quadratic trend model
- Quadratic trend model with seasonality

FIGURE 18.22 **AVERAGE ANNUAL WEEKLY HOURS SPENT BY CANADIAN MANUFACTURING WORKERS**

b. If we computed the autocorrelation of this series, would the lag-1 autocorrelation exhibit negative, positive, or no autocorrelation? How can you see this from the plot?

c. Compute the autocorrelation of the series and produce an ACF plot. Verify your answer to the previous question.

18.3 **Toys "R" US Revenues.** Figure 18.23 is a time plot of the quarterly revenues of Toys "R" US between 1992 and 1995 (thanks to Chris Albright for suggesting the use of these data, which are available in *ToysRUsRevenues.csv*).[12]

FIGURE 18.23   QUARTERLY REVENUES OF TOYS "R" US, 1992–1995

a. Fit a regression model with a linear trend and additive seasonality. Use the entire series (excluding the last two quarters) as the training set.

b. A partial output of the regression model is shown in Figure 18.24 (where Quarter_2 is the Quarter 2 dummy and Index is the trend). Use this output to answer the following questions:

    i. Which two statistics (and their values) measure how well this model fits the training data?

    ii. Which two statistics (and their values) measure the predictive accuracy of this model?

    iii. After adjusting for trend, what is the average difference between sales in Q3 and sales in Q1?

    iv. After adjusting for seasonality, which quarter (Q1, Q2, Q3, or Q4) has the highest average sales?

---

[12]*Note:* To parse the time attribute in RapidMiner as Date type, first use the *Split* operator to split the QuarterYear attribute values into quarter and year parts, and then use the *Map* operator to replace the quarters with months (e.g., replace Q1 with Mar). Next, use the *Generate Attributes* to combine them again using the *concat* function, and finally parse them as Date type with *Nominal to Date* operator.

Attribute	Coefficient	Std. Error	t-Stat	p-Value	Code
Quarter_Q2	-15.107	119.660	-0.126	0.902	
Quarter_Q3	89.167	128.674	0.693	0.506	
Quarter_Q4	2101.726	129.165	16.272	0.000	****
Index	47.107	11.257	4.185	0.002	***
(Intercept)	906.750	115.346	7.861	0.000	****

(a) Performance on Training Set

```
PerformanceVector:
root_mean_squared_error: 135.080 +/- 0.000
absolute_error: 92.531 +/- 98.410
relative_error: 5.01% +/- 2.84%
squared_correlation: 0.977
```

(b) Performance on Holdout Set

```
PerformanceVector:
root_mean_squared_error: 313.682 +/- 0.000
absolute_error: 254.667 +/- 183.143
relative_error: 7.40% +/- 3.02%
squared_correlation: 1.000
```

FIGURE 18.24   **REGRESSION MODEL FITTED TO TOYS "R" US TIME SERIES AND ITS PREDICTIVE PERFORMANCE IN TRAINING (a) AND HOLDOUT (b) PERIODS**

18.4 Walmart Stock. Figure 18.25 shows the series of Walmart daily closing prices between February 2001 and February 2002 (thanks to Chris Albright for suggesting the use of these data, which are publicly available, for example, at http://finance.yahoo.com and are in the file *WalMartStock.csv*).

FIGURE 18.25   **DAILY CLOSE PRICE OF WALMART STOCK, FEBRUARY 2001–2002**

a. Create a well-formatted time plot of the closing price series.

b. Compute a lag-1 differenced series of the closing prices. Create a time plot of the differenced series. Note your observations by visually inspecting the differenced series.

c. Which of the following is/are relevant for testing whether this stock is a random walk?

- The autocorrelations of the close prices series

- The autocorrelations of the lag-1 differenced close prices series

- The AR(1) constant coefficient

d. Use the relevant information from Figure 18.26 to decide whether this is a random walk. Explain how you reached your conclusion and based on which statistics and/or plots.

FIGURE 18.26   (TOP) AUTOCORRELATIONS OF WALMART STOCK PRICES AND
(BOTTOM) AUTOCORRELATIONS OF LAG-1 DIFFERENCED WALMART STOCK PRICES

e. What are the implications of finding that a time series is a random walk? Choose the correct statement(s) below.

- It is impossible to obtain forecasts that are more accurate than naive forecasts for the series.

- The series is random.

- The changes in the series from one period to the next are random.

18.5 Department Store Sales. The time plot in Figure 18.27 describes actual quarterly sales for a department store over a six-year period (data are available in *DepartmentStore-Sales.csv*, data courtesy of Chris Albright).

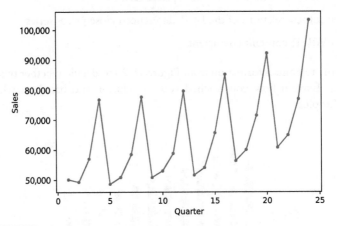

FIGURE 18.27   DEPARTMENT STORE QUARTERLY SALES SERIES

a. The forecaster decided that there is an exponential trend in the series. To fit a regression-based model that accounts for this trend, which of the following operations must be performed?

- Take log of quarter index.
- Take log of sales.
- Take an exponent of sales.
- Take an exponent of quarter index.

b. Fit a regression model with an exponential trend and seasonality, using the first 20 quarters as the training data (remember to first partition the series into training and holdout series).

c. A partial output is shown in Figure 18.28.[13] From the output, after adjusting for trend, are Q2 average sales higher, lower, or approximately equal to the average Q1 sales?

Attribute	Coefficient	Std. Error	t–Stat	p–Value	Code
Quart_2	0.025	0.021	1.202	0.248	
Quart_3	0.165	0.021	7.917	0.000	****
Quart_4	0.434	0.021	20.572	0.000	****
Quarter	0.011	0.001	8.561	0.000	****
(Intercept)	10.749	0.019	574.057	0	****

FIGURE 18.28   OUTPUT FROM REGRESSION MODEL FIT TO DEPARTMENT STORE SALES IN THE TRAINING PERIOD

---

[13]Note that the attribute "Quarter" in the data and the regression model is equivalent to the usual "trend" attribute.

d. Use this model to forecast sales in Q21 and Q22.

e. The plots in Figure 18.29 describe the fit (top) and forecast errors (bottom) from this regression model.

FIGURE 18.29   FIT OF REGRESSION MODEL FOR DEPARTMENT STORE SALES

    i. Recreate these plots.

    ii. Based on these plots, what can you say about your forecasts for Q21 and Q22? Are they likely to over-forecast, under-forecast, or be reasonably close to the real sales values?

f. From the forecast errors plot, which of the following statements appear true?

- Seasonality is not captured well.
- The regression model fits the data well.
- The trend in the data is not captured well by the model.

g. Which of the following solutions is adequate *and* a parsimonious solution for improving model fit?

- Fit a quadratic trend model to the residuals (with Quarter and Quarter^2).[14]
- Fit an AR model to the residuals.
- Fit a quadratic trend model to Sales (with Quarter and Quarter^2).

18.6 Souvenir Sales. The file *SouvenirSales.csv* contains monthly sales for a souvenir shop at a beach resort town in Queensland, Australia, between 1995 and 2001. [Source: Hyndman and Yang (2018).] Figure 18.30 displays the sales time plot. The series is presented twice, in Australian dollars and in log scale. Back in 2001, the store wanted to use the data to forecast sales for the next 12 months (year 2002). They hired an analyst to generate forecasts. The analyst first partitioned the data into training and holdout sets, with the holdout set containing the last 12 months of data (year 2001). She then fit a regression model to sales, using the training set.

FIGURE 18.30   MONTHLY SALES AT AUSTRALIAN SOUVENIR SHOP IN AUSTRALIAN DOLLARS (a) AND IN LOG SCALE (b)

a. Based on the two time plots, which predictors should be included in the regression model? What is the total number of predictors in the model?

b. Run a regression model with Sales (in Australian dollars) as the target attribute and with a linear trend and monthly seasonality. Remember to fit only the training data. Call this model A.

  i. Examine the estimated coefficients: Which month tends to have the highest average sales during the year? Why is this reasonable?

  ii. The estimated trend coefficient in model A is 245.36. What does this mean?

c. Run a regression model with an exponential trend and multiplicative seasonality. Remember to fit only the training data. Call this model B.

  i. Fitting a model to log(Sales) with a linear trend is equivalent to fitting a model to Sales (in dollars) with what type of trend?

  ii. The estimated trend coefficient in model B is 0.02. What does this mean?

  iii. Use this model to forecast the sales in February 2002. (*Hint*: Fit model B to the entire series without partitioning.)

---

[14]Note that the attribute "Quarter" in the dataset is equivalent to the usual "trend" attribute.

d. Compare the two regression models (A and B) in terms of forecast performance. Which model is preferable for forecasting? Mention at least two reasons based on the information in the outputs.

e. Continuing with model B, create an ACF plot until lag-15 for the full series of forecast errors (without partitioning into training/holdout). Now fit an AR model with lag 2 [ARIMA(2,0,0)] to this series of forecast errors. We will use this model to improve the forecast for January 2002.

    i. Examining the ACF plot and the estimated coefficients of the AR(2) model, what can we learn about the forecasts that result from model B?

    ii. Use the autocorrelation information to compute an improved forecast for January 2002, using model B and the AR(2) model above.

f. How would you model these data differently if the goal was to understand the different components of sales in the souvenir shop between 1995–2001? Mention two differences.

18.7 **Shipments of Household Appliances.** The time plot in Figure 18.31 shows the series of quarterly shipments (in million dollars) of US household appliances between 1985 and 1989 (data are available in *ApplianceShipments.csv*, data courtesy of Ken Black). If we compute the autocorrelation of the series, which lag (>0) is most likely to have the largest coefficient (in absolute value)? Create an ACF plot and compare with your answer.

FIGURE 18.31   **QUARTERLY SHIPMENTS OF US HOUSEHOLD APPLIANCES OVER FIVE YEARS**

18.8 **Australian Wine Sales.** Figure 18.32 shows time plots of monthly sales of six types of Australian wines (red, rose, sweet white, dry white, sparkling, and fortified) for 1980–1994. [Data are available in *AustralianWines.csv*, Source: Hyndman and Yang (2018).] The units are thousands of liters. You are hired to obtain short-term forecasts (two to three months ahead) for each of the six series, and this task will be repeated every month.

a. Comment on the suitability of a regression-based forecaster for each wine type.

b. Fortified wine has the largest market share of the above six types of wine. You are asked to focus on fortified wine sales alone and produce as accurate as possible forecasts for the next two months.

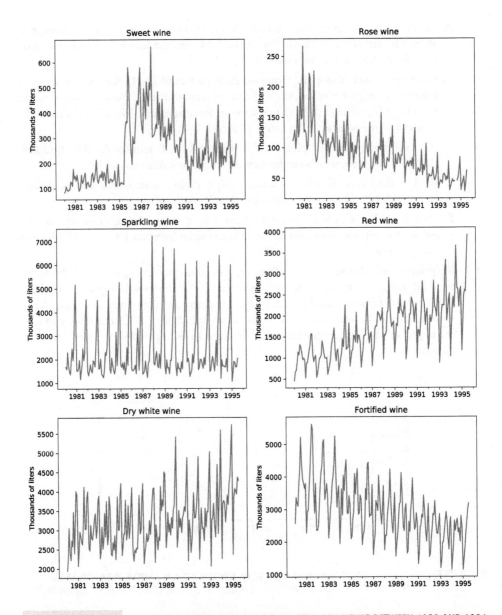

FIGURE 18.32   **MONTHLY SALES OF SIX TYPES OF AUSTRALIAN WINES BETWEEN 1980 AND 1994**

- Start by partitioning the data: use the period until December 1993 as the training set.
- Fit a regression model to sales with a linear trend and additive seasonality.

  i. Create the "actual vs. forecast" plot. What can you say about the model fit?

  ii. Use the regression model to forecast sales in January and February 1994.

c. Create an ACF plot for the training residuals from the above model until lag-12. Examining this plot (only), which of the following statements are reasonable conclusions?

- Decembers (month 12) are not captured well by the model.
- There is a strong correlation between sales on the same calendar month.
- The model does not capture the seasonality well.
- We should try to fit an AR model with lag-12 to the residuals.

CHAPTER 19

Smoothing and Deep Learning Methods for Forecasting

In this chapter, we describe a set of popular and flexible methods for forecasting time series that rely on *smoothing*. Smoothing is based on averaging over multiple periods in order to reduce the noise. We start with two simple smoothers, the *moving average* and *simple exponential smoother*, which are suitable for forecasting series that contain no trend or seasonality. In both cases, forecasts are averages of previous values of the series (the length of the series history considered and the weights used in the averaging differ between the methods). We also show how a moving average can be used, with a slight adaptation, for data visualization. We then proceed to describe smoothing methods suitable for forecasting series with a trend and/or seasonality. Smoothing methods are data-driven and are able to adapt to changes in the series over time. Although highly automated, the user must specify *smoothing constants* that determine how fast the method adapts to new data. We discuss the choice of such constants and their meaning. We then describe basic deep learning methods suitable for forecasting time series: recurrent neural networks (RNN) and Long Short-Term Memory (LSTM) networks. The different methods are illustrated using the Amtrak ridership series.

RapidMiner

In this chapter, we will use the following time series operators in RapidMiner: *Moving Average Filter, Exponential Smoothing, Forecast Validation*, and *Holt-Winters*. These and other time series modeling operators can be located in the *Operators* panel under *Modeling > Time Series*. The *Series Extension* available through RapidMiner's marketplace provides additional operators for processing and analyzing time series data. We also use certain deep learning modeling operators [e.g., *Deep Learning (Tensor), Add LSTM Layer*, etc.] to illustrate the use of deep learning for forecasting.

Machine Learning for Business Analytics: Concepts, Techniques and Applications in RapidMiner, First Edition.
Galit Shmueli, Peter C. Bruce, Amit V. Deokar, and Nitin R. Patel.
© 2023 John Wiley & Sons, Inc. Published 2023 by John Wiley & Sons, Inc.

19.1 SMOOTHING METHODS: INTRODUCTION[1]

A second class of methods for time series forecasting is *smoothing methods*. Unlike regression models, which rely on an underlying theoretical model for the components of a time series (e.g., linear or quadratic trend), smoothing methods are data-driven, in the sense that they estimate time series components directly from the data without assuming a predetermined structure. Data-driven methods are especially useful in series where patterns change over time. Smoothing methods "smooth" out the noise in a series in an attempt to uncover the patterns. Smoothing is done by averaging the series over multiple periods, where different smoothers differ by the number of periods averaged, how the average is computed, how many times averaging is performed, and so on. We now describe two types of smoothing methods that are popular in business applications due to their simplicity and adaptability. These are the moving average method and exponential smoothing.

19.2 MOVING AVERAGE

The moving average is a simple smoother: it consists of averaging values across a window of consecutive periods, thereby generating a series of averages. A moving average with window width w means averaging across each set of w consecutive values, where w is determined by the user.

In general, there are two types of moving averages: a *centered moving average* and a *trailing moving average*. Centered moving averages are powerful for visualizing trends, because the averaging operation can suppress seasonality and noise, thereby making the trend more visible. In contrast, trailing moving averages are useful for forecasting. The difference between the two is in terms of the window's location on the time series.

Centered Moving Average for Visualization

In a centered moving average, the value of the moving average at time t (MA_t) is computed by centering the window around time t and averaging across the w values within the window:

$$MA_t = \left(Y_{t-(w-1)/2} + \cdots + Y_{t-1} + Y_t + Y_{t+1} + \cdots + Y_{t+(w-1)/2}\right)/w.$$

$$(19.1)$$

For example, with a window of width $w = 5$, the moving average at time point $t = 3$ means averaging the values of the series at time points $1, 2, 3, 4, 5$; at

---

[1]This and subsequent sections in this chapter copyright © 2019 Datastats, LLC, and Galit Shmueli. Used by permission.

time point $t = 4$, the moving average is the average of the series at time points $2, 3, 4, 5, 6$, and so on.[2] This is illustrated in Figure 19.1 (a).

(a)

Centered window ($w = 5$)

$t - 2$ $t - 1$ t $t + 1$ $t + 2$

(b)

Trailing window ($w = 5$)

$t - 4$ $t - 3$ $t - 2$ $t - 1$ t

FIGURE 19.1   SCHEMATIC OF CENTERED MOVING AVERAGE (a) AND TRAILING MOVING AVERAGE (b), BOTH WITH WINDOW WIDTH $W = 5$

Choosing the window width in a seasonal series is straightforward: because the goal is to suppress seasonality for better visualizing the trend, the default choice should be the length of a seasonal cycle. Returning to the Amtrak ridership data, the annual seasonality indicates a choice of $w = 12$. Figure 19.2 (red line) shows a centered moving average line overlaid on the original series. We can see a global U shape, but unlike the regression model that fits a strict

FIGURE 19.2   CENTERED MOVING AVERAGE (RED LINE) AND TRAILING MOVING AVERAGE (GREEN LINE) WITH WINDOW $W = 12$, OVERLAID ON AMTRAK RIDERSHIP SERIES

---

[2]For an even window width, such as $w = 4$, we can obtain the moving average at time point $t = 3$ by averaging across two windows: across time points $1, 2, 3, 4$ and across time points $2, 3, 4, 5$. The average of the two averages is the final moving average.

U-shape, the moving average shows some deviation, such as the slight dip during the last year.

Trailing Moving Average for Forecasting

Centered moving averages are computed by averaging across data in the past and the future of a given time point. In that sense, they cannot be used for forecasting because at the time of forecasting, the future is typically unknown. Hence, for purposes of forecasting, we use *trailing moving averages*, where the window of width w is set on the most recent available w values of the series. The k-step-ahead forecast F_{t+k} $(k = 1, 2, 3, \ldots)$ is then the average of these w values (see also bottom plot in Figure 19.1):

$$F_{t+k} = (Y_t + Y_{t-1} + \cdots + Y_{t-w+1})/w.$$

For example, in the Amtrak ridership series, to forecast ridership in February 1992 or later months, given information until January 1992 and using a moving average with window width $w = 12$, we would take the average ridership during the most recent 12 months (February 1991 to January 1992). Figure 19.2 (green line) shows a trailing moving average line overlaid on the original series. The RapidMiner process for generating this chart is shown in Figure 19.3. RapidMiner's window width includes the *filter size left*, *filter size right*, and the point itself. Hence, for a 12-month trailing window, we set *filter size left* = 11 and leave *filter size right* at 0.

Next, we illustrate a 12-month moving average forecaster for the Amtrak ridership. We partition the Amtrak ridership time series, leaving the last 36 months as the holdout period. Applying a moving average forecaster with window $w = 12$, we obtained the output shown in Figure 19.4. The RapidMiner process is shown in Figure 19.5, where the *Extract Macro* operator records the last training MA to be used as a forecast. Note that for the first 12 records of the training period, there is no forecast (because there are less than 12 past values to average). Also, note that the forecasts for all months in the holdout period are identical (1938.481) because the method assumes that information is known only until March 2001.

In this example, it is clear that the moving average forecaster is inadequate for generating monthly forecasts because it does not capture the seasonality in the data. Seasons with high ridership are under-forecasted, and seasons with low ridership are over-forecasted. A similar issue arises when forecasting a series with a trend: the moving average "lags behind," thereby under-forecasting in the presence of an increasing trend and over-forecasting in the presence of a

FIGURE 19.3   RAPIDMINER **PROCESS FOR CREATING CENTERED MOVING AVERAGE AND TRAILING MOVING AVERAGE FOR AMTRAK RIDERSHIP SERIES**

decreasing trend. This "lagging behind" of the trailing moving average can also be seen in Figure 19.2.

In general, the moving average should be used for forecasting *only in series that lack seasonality and trend*. Such a limitation might seem impractical. However, there are a few popular methods for removing trends (de-trending) and removing

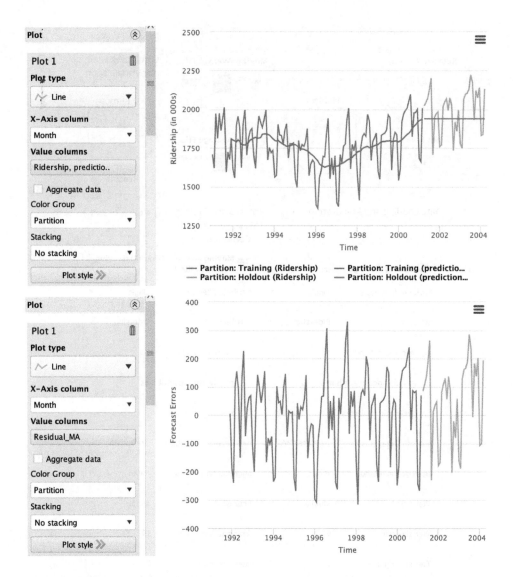

FIGURE 19.4   TRAILING MOVING AVERAGE FORECASTER WITH $W = 12$ APPLIED TO AMTRAK RIDERSHIP SERIES

seasonality (de-seasonalizing) from a series, such as regression models. The moving average can then be used to forecast such de-trended and de-seasonalized series, and then the trend and seasonality can be added back to the forecast. For example, consider the regression model shown in Figure 18.12 in Chapter 18, which yields residuals devoid of seasonality and trend (see bottom chart). We can apply a moving average forecaster to that series of residuals (also called forecast errors), thereby creating a forecast for the next *forecast error*. For example, to forecast ridership in April 2001 (the first period in the holdout set), assuming that we have information until March 2001, we use the regression model

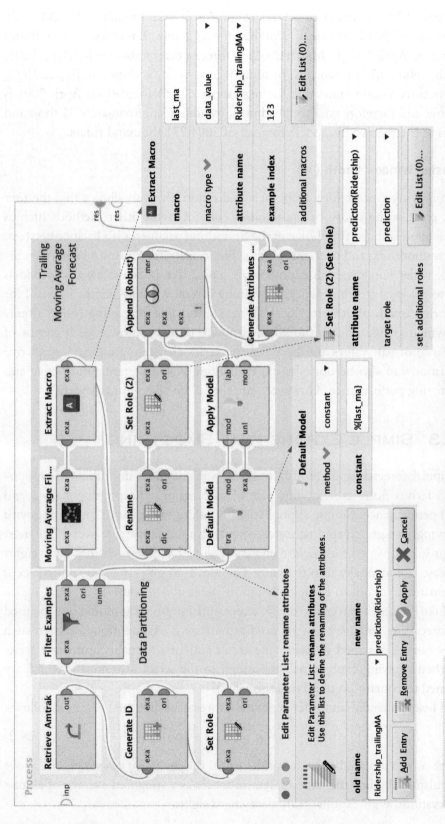

FIGURE 19.5   RAPIDMINER PROCESS FOR CREATING TRAILING MOVING AVERAGE FORECAST WITH $w = 12$ APPLIED TO AMTRAK RIDERSHIP SERIES

in Figure 18.11 to generate a forecast for April 2001 [which yields 2004.271 thousand (=2,004,271) riders]. We then use a 12-month moving average (using the period April 2000 to March 2001) to forecast the *forecast error* for April 2001, which yields 30.781 (manually, or using RapidMiner, as shown in Figure 19.6). The positive value implies that the regression model's forecast for April 2001 is too low, and therefore we should adjust it by adding approximately 31 thousand riders to the regression model's forecast of 2004.271 thousand riders.

Choosing Window Width (w)

With moving average forecasting or visualization, the only choice that the user must make is the width of the window (w). As with other methods such as k-nearest neighbors, the choice of the smoothing parameter is a balance between under-smoothing and over-smoothing. For visualization (using a centered window), wider windows will expose more global trends, while narrow windows will reveal local trends. Hence, examining several window widths is useful for exploring trends of differing local/global nature. For forecasting (using a trailing window), the choice should incorporate domain knowledge in terms of relevance of past values and how fast the series changes. Empirical predictive evaluation can also be done by experimenting with different values of w and comparing performance. However, care should be taken not to overfit!

19.3 SIMPLE EXPONENTIAL SMOOTHING

A popular forecasting method in business is exponential smoothing. Its popularity derives from its flexibility, ease of automation, cheap computation, and good performance. Simple exponential smoothing is similar to forecasting with a moving average, except that instead of taking a simple average over the w most recent values, we take a *weighted average* of *all* past values, such that the weights decrease exponentially into the past. The idea is to give more weight to recent information, yet not to completely ignore older information.

Like the moving average, simple exponential smoothing should only be used for forecasting *series that have no trend or seasonality*. As mentioned earlier, such series can be obtained by removing trend and/or seasonality from raw series and then applying exponential smoothing to the series of residuals (which are assumed to contain no trend or seasonality).

The exponential smoother generates a forecast at time $t+1$ (F_{t+1}) as follows:

$$F_{t+1} = \alpha Y_t + \alpha(1 - \alpha)Y_{t-1} + \alpha(1 - \alpha)^2 Y_{t-2} + \cdots, \tag{19.2}$$

where α is a constant between 0 and 1 called the *smoothing parameter*. The above formulation displays the exponential smoother as a weighted average of all past observations, with exponentially decaying weights.

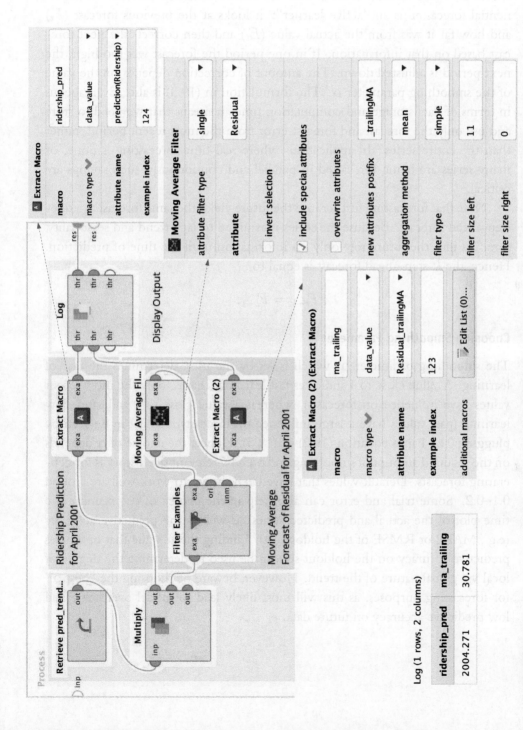

Log (1 rows, 2 columns)

ridership_pred	ma_trailing
2004.271	30.781

FIGURE 19.6   (TOP) RAPIDMINER PROCESS FOR APPLYING MA TO THE RESIDUALS FROM THE REGRESSION MODEL (WHICH LACK TREND AND SEASONALITY), TO FORECAST THE APRIL 2001 RESIDUAL AND (BOTTOM LEFT) PROCESS COMPUTATION OUTPUT

It turns out that we can write the exponential forecaster in another way, which is very useful in practice:

$$F_{t+1} = F_t + \alpha E_t, \tag{19.3}$$

where E_t is the forecast error at time t. This formulation presents the exponential forecaster as an "active learner": it looks at the previous forecast (F_t) and how far it was from the actual value (E_t) and then corrects the next forecast based on that information. If in one period the forecast was too high, the next period is adjusted down. The amount of correction depends on the value of the smoothing parameter α. The formulation in (19.3) is also advantageous in terms of data storage and computation time: it means that we need to store and use only the forecast and forecast error from the most recent period, rather than the entire series. In applications where real-time forecasting is done, or many series are being forecasted in parallel and continuously, such savings are critical.

Note that forecasting further into the future yields the same forecast as a one-step-ahead forecast. Because the series is assumed to lack trend and seasonality, forecasts into the future rely only on information until the time of prediction. Hence, the k-step-ahead forecast is equal to

$$F_{t+k} = F_{t+1}.$$

Choosing Smoothing Parameter α

The smoothing parameter α, which is set by the user, determines the rate of learning. A value close to 1 indicates fast learning (that is, only the most recent values have influence on forecasts), whereas a value close to 0 indicates slow learning (past values have a large influence on forecasts). This can be seen by plugging 0 or 1 into equation (19.2) or (19.3). Hence, the choice of α depends on the required amount of smoothing and on how relevant the history is for generating forecasts. Default values that have been shown to work well are around 0.1–0.2. Some trial and error can also help in the choice of α: examine the time plot of the actual and predicted series, as well as the predictive accuracy (e.g., MAPE or RMSE of the holdout set). Finding the α value that optimizes predictive accuracy on the holdout set can be used to determine the degree of local vs. global nature of the trend. However, beware of choosing the "best α" for forecasting purposes, as this will most likely lead to model overfitting and low predictive accuracy on future data.

To use exponential smoothing in RapidMiner, we use the *Exponential Smoothing* operator. Parameter *alpha* sets the value of α.

To illustrate forecasting with simple exponential smoothing, we return to the residuals from the regression model, which are assumed to contain no trend or seasonality. To forecast the residual on April 2001, we apply exponential smoothing to the entire period until March 2001 and use $\alpha = 0.2$. The model's forecasts are shown in Figure 19.7. The process to generate the forecasts is shown in Figure 19.8. The forecast for the residual (the green line) is 14.143 (in thousands of riders), implying that we should adjust the regression's forecast by adding 14,143 riders to that forecast.

| FIGURE 19.7 | OUTPUT FOR SIMPLE EXPONENTIAL SMOOTHING FORECASTER WITH $\alpha = 0.2$, APPLIED TO THE SERIES OF RESIDUALS FROM THE REGRESSION MODEL (WHICH LACK TREND AND SEASONALITY). THE FORECAST VALUE IS 14.143 |

Relation Between Moving Average and Simple Exponential Smoothing

In both smoothing methods, the user must specify a single parameter: in moving averages, the window width (w) must be set; in exponential smoothing, the smoothing parameter (α) must be set. In both cases, the parameter determines the importance of fresh information over older information. In fact, the two smoothers are approximately equal if the window width of the moving average is equal to $w = 2/\alpha - 1$.

FIGURE 19.8   RAPIDMINER PROCESS FOR APPLYING EXPONENTIAL SMOOTHING WITH α = 0.2 TO THE RESIDUALS FROM THE REGRESSION MODEL (WHICH LACK TREND AND SEASONALITY)

19.4 ADVANCED EXPONENTIAL SMOOTHING

As mentioned earlier, both the moving average and simple exponential smoothing should only be used for forecasting series with no trend or seasonality, series that have only a level and noise. One solution for forecasting series with trend and/or seasonality is first to remove those components (e.g., via regression models). Another solution is to use a more sophisticated version of exponential smoothing, which can capture trend and/or seasonality. In the following, we describe an extension of exponential smoothing that can capture a trend and/or seasonality. These different methods can all be implemented using RapidMiner's *Holt-Winters* operator.

Series with a Trend

For series that contain a trend, we can use "double exponential smoothing." Unlike in regression models, the trend shape is not assumed to be global, but rather, it can change over time. In double exponential smoothing, the local trend is estimated from the data and is updated as more data arrive. Similar to simple exponential smoothing, the level of the series is also estimated from the data and is updated as more data arrive. The k-step-ahead forecast is given by combining the level estimate at time t (L_t) and the trend estimate at time t (T_t):

$$F_{t+k} = L_t + kT_t. \tag{19.4}$$

Note that in the presence of a trend, one-, two-, three-step-ahead (etc.), forecasts are no longer identical. The level and trend are updated through a pair of updating equations:

$$L_t = \alpha Y_t + (1 - \alpha)(L_{t-1} + T_{t-1}), \tag{19.5}$$

$$T_t = \beta (L_t - L_{t-1}) + (1 - \beta)T_{t-1}. \tag{19.6}$$

The first equation means that the level at time t is a weighted average of the actual value at time t and the level in the previous period, adjusted for trend (in the presence of a trend, moving from one period to the next requires factoring in the trend). The second equation means that the trend at time t is a weighted average of the trend in the previous period and the more recent information on the change in level.[3] Here, there are two smoothing parameters, α and β, which determine the rate of learning. As in simple exponential smoothing, they are both constants in the range [0,1], set by the user, with higher values leading to faster learning (more weight to most recent information).

---

[3]There are various ways to estimate the initial values L_1 and T_1, but the differences among these ways usually disappear after a few periods.

Note: RapidMiner does not implement the above method. However, using the *Holt-Winters* operator (described next) can lead to reasonably close results.

Series with a Trend and Seasonality

For series that contain both trend and seasonality, the "Holt-Winters exponential smoothing" method can be used. This is a further extension of double exponential smoothing, where the k-step-ahead forecast also takes into account the seasonality at period $t + k$. Assuming seasonality with M seasons (e.g., for weekly seasonality $M = 7$), the forecast is given by

$$F_{t+k} = (L_t + kT_t)\, S_{t+k-M}. \tag{19.7}$$

(Note that by the time of forecasting t, the series must have included at least one full cycle of seasons in order to produce forecasts using this formula, that is, $t > M$.)

Being an adaptive method, Holt-Winters exponential smoothing allows the level, trend, and seasonality patterns to change over time. These three components are estimated and updated as more information arrives. The three updating equations are given by

$$L_t = \alpha Y_t / S_{t-M} + (1 - \alpha)(L_{t-1} + T_{t-1}), \tag{19.8}$$

$$T_t = \beta\,(L_t - L_{t-1}) + (1 - \beta)T_{t-1}, \tag{19.9}$$

$$S_t = \gamma Y_t / L_t + (1 - \gamma)S_{t-M}. \tag{19.10}$$

The first equation is similar to that in double exponential smoothing, except that it uses the seasonally-adjusted value at time t rather than the raw value. This is done by dividing Y_t by its seasonal index, as estimated in the last cycle. The second equation is identical to double exponential smoothing. The third equation means that the seasonal index is updated by taking a weighted average of the seasonal index from the previous cycle and the current trend-adjusted value. Note that this formulation describes a multiplicative seasonal relationship, where values on different seasons differ by percentage amounts. There is also an additive seasonality version of Holt-Winters exponential smoothing, where seasons differ by a constant amount (for more detail, see Shmueli and Lichtendahl, 2016).

Holt-Winters method is implemented in RapidMiner's *Holt-Winters* operator. The user sets smoothing parameters *alpha*, *beta*, and *gamma*. Parameter *period* is the number of seasons. Parameter *seasonality model* allows specifying additive or multiplicative seasonality.

To illustrate forecasting a series with the Holt-Winters method, consider the raw Amtrak ridership data. As we observed earlier, the data contain both a trend and monthly seasonality. Figure 19.9 depicts the fitted and forecasted values.

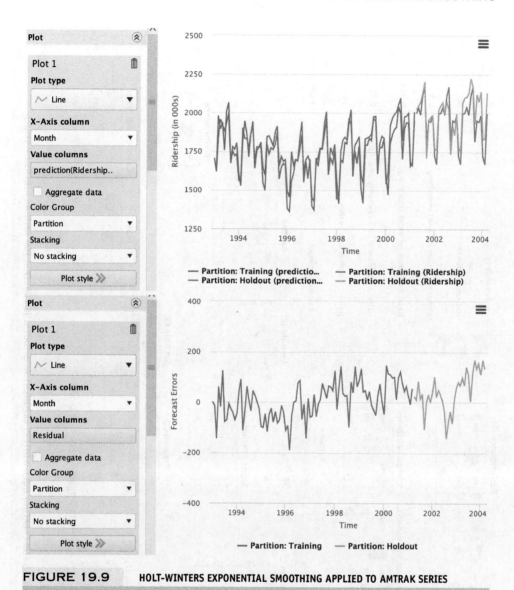

FIGURE 19.9   HOLT-WINTERS EXPONENTIAL SMOOTHING APPLIED TO AMTRAK SERIES

The RapidMiner process is shown in Figure 19.10.[4] The model performs fairly well with an RMSE of 87.75 and MAPE of 3.60% on the holdout set.

Series with Seasonality (No Trend)

Finally, for series that contain seasonality but no trend, we can use a Holt-Winters exponential smoothing formulation that lacks a trend term, by deleting the trend term in the forecasting equation and updating equations. *Note*: RapidMiner does not implement this formulation, but applying the *Holt-Winters*

---

[4]Because *Holt-Winters* is a time series operator in RapidMiner, we use the *Forecast Validation* operators (Training: *window size* = 24, *horizon size* = 1, *step size* = 1; Holdout: *window size* = 123, *horizon size* = 36, *step size* = 1). The *window size* parameter for the training period is set to two seasons (in this case, 24) and for the holdout period to the entire training period (in this case, 123).

FIGURE 19.10 RAPIDMINER PROCESS FOR CREATING HOLT-WINTERS EXPONENTIAL SMOOTHING FORECAST FOR AMTRAK RIDERSHIP SERIES

operator to a series with seasonality and no trend will often lead to reasonable results.

19.5 DEEP LEARNING FOR FORECASTING

While smoothing-based methods have been successfully used for decades, the data-driven toolkit for forecasting time series has recently been supplemented with deep learning methods. Recurrent neural network (RNN) is a type of deep learning method suited for temporal data such as time series or other sequential data such as music, text, and speech. Compared with the multilayer feed-forward network shown in Figure 11.1 in Chapter 11, the RNN has an additional arrow within each hidden layer, as shown in Figure 19.11. This allows the network to "remember" the information it learned in the previous epoch (iteration through the data). In other words, RNNs incorporate a looping mechanism that allows information to flow from one epoch to the next. Here, an epoch means a pass through one subsequence of the series (see below).

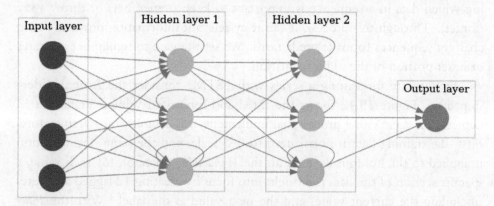

FIGURE 19.11   SCHEMATIC OF RECURRENT NEURAL NETWORK (RNN)

Training an RNN on a time series requires partitioning the training series into a sequence of "rolling windows" (sub-series) of width w. Each sub-series serves as the predictor series and has an associated future period that serves as the label. For example, for one-step-ahead forecasts, we convert the training series $y_1, y_2, \ldots, y_t$ into the set shown in Table 19.1. These sub-series are then fed into the RNN sequentially (into the input layer in Figure 19.11). The arrow from each hidden node to itself then "remembers" the information learned from the previous sub-series.

A simple RNN, however, suffers from "short-term memory" in the sense that it remembers information from very recent periods, but not from longer history. This results from the so-called vanishing gradient problem. Gradients are

TABLE 19.1   CONVERTING A TIME SERIES OF LENGTH
T INTO A SEQUENCE OF SUB-SERIES AND
ASSOCIATED ONE-STEP-AHEAD LABELS

Predictor series	Label
$y_1, y_2, \ldots, y_w$	y_{w+1}
$y_2, y_3, \ldots, y_{w+1}$	y_{w+2}
$\vdots$	$\vdots$
$y_{t-w}, \ldots, y_{t-1}$	y_t

values computed to update the neural network weights during backpropagation. The vanishing gradient problem occurs since the gradient updates become small over time, and the earlier layers that receive a small gradient update stop learning. Because these layers don't learn, a simple RNN can forget what it saw much earlier in the sequence, thus having a short-term memory.

To overcome the short-term memory issue, a variant of RNN called Long Short-Term Memory (LSTM) was developed. LSTM adds to each hidden node special mechanisms called *gates* that can regulate the information flow by learning which data in a sequence is important to keep (remember) or throw away (forget). Through this process, it can relay relevant information down the long chain of sequences to make predictions. We set the gate to remember a greater or lesser portion of the old information.

To illustrate forecasting a series with LSTM, consider the Amtrak ridership data. Figure 19.12 shows the fitted and forecasted values. Figure 19.13 depicts the RapidMiner process that implements this deep learning architecture. First, the training data is normalized to 0–1 scale, and the same normalization is applied to the holdout data. With the *Windowing* operator, for each value, a specific section of the data is brought into focus by creating 12 lagged attributes (including the current value) and the next value as the label. With the *Filter Examples* operator, last 36 values are retained as holdout, and the earlier values are used for training and validation (80% training, 20% validation) during the deep learning process.

The *Deep Learning (Tensor)* nested operator[5] contains the LSTM layer with three *neurons*, a ReLU *activation function*, and the *forget gate bias initialization*

---

[5]The *Deep Learning (Tensor)* requires a *tensor* object as an input and produces a tensor as an output (see Chapter 11). The *Collect* operator is used to convert an *ExampleSet* object to a tensor object, and later, the *Select* operator is used to convert the tensor object back to an *ExampleSet* object. The figure shows some errors (red marks at some ports) because the metadata about the object types is not correctly relayed between the operators due to a technical limitation. These errors can be safely ignored.

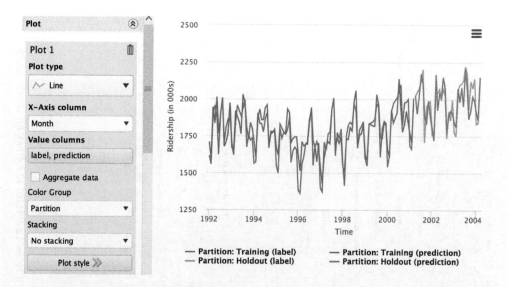

FIGURE 19.12   **ACTUAL AND FORECASTED VALUES USING THE DEEP LEARNING LSTM MODEL FOR AMTRAK RIDERSHIP SERIES**

parameter set to 2. The *forget gate bias initialization* parameter is typically set to values between 1 and 5 and influences the forget gate behavior of keeping or discarding older information. The higher the value, the more older information is remembered and vice versa. Setting it to 0 would be nearly equivalent to an RNN, i.e., no long-term memory at all. This parameter is adjusted by experimentation based on the pattern in the data. The output layer has a single output neuron, an identity *activation function*, and uses mean squared error as the *loss function*. Often, as with other deep learning networks, we experiment with different layer and parameter combinations to determine which combination is best at achieving high predictive performance. Finally, the data is de-normalized for viewing a time plot on the original scale and computing performance metrics.

From the plot of the fitted and forecasted values (Figure 19.12), we can see that the model learns the temporal patterns quite well. The model has RMSE of 90.68 and MAPE of 3.71% on the holdout period (not shown in the process), which is comparable to the Holt-Winters performance. It is also notable that the LSTM's forecasts are consistently too high during the dip periods, especially during the training period. Further parameter tuning might help improve this issue.

FIGURE 19.13   RAPIDMINER PROCESS FOR CREATING TRAILING MOVING AVERAGE FORECAST WITH $w = 12$ APPLIED TO AMTRAK RIDERSHIP SERIES

PROBLEMS

19.1 **Impact of September 11 on Air Travel in the United States.** The Research and Innovative Technology Administration's Bureau of Transportation Statistics conducted a study to evaluate the impact of the September 11, 2001 terrorist attack on US transportation. The 2006 study report and the data can be found at https://www.bts.gov/archive/publications/estimated_impacts_of_9_11_on_us_travel/index. The goal of the study was stated as follows:

> The purpose of this study is to provide a greater understanding of the passenger travel behavior patterns of persons making long distance trips before and after 9/11.

> The report analyzes monthly passenger movement data between January 1990 and May 2004. Data on three monthly time series are given in file *Sept11Travel.csv* for this period: (1) actual airline revenue passenger miles (Air), (2) rail passenger miles (Rail), and (3) vehicle miles traveled (Car).

> To assess the impact of September 11, BTS took the following approach: using data before September 11, they forecasted future data (under the assumption of no terrorist attack). Then, they compared the forecasted series with the actual data to assess the impact of the event. Our first step, therefore, is to split each of the time series into two parts: pre- and post-September 11. We now concentrate only on the earlier time series.

a. Create a time plot for the pre-event AIR time series. What time series components appear from the plot? (*Hint*: In preparing the data, use *Nominal to Date* and *Parse Numbers* operators to transform the attributes to the correct data type.)

b. Figure 19.14 shows a time plot of the **seasonally-adjusted** pre-September-11 AIR series. Which of the following smoothing methods would be adequate for forecasting this seasonally-adjusted series?

- Moving average (with what window width?)
- Simple exponential smoothing
- Double exponential smoothing
- Holt-Winters exponential smoothing

FIGURE 19.14   SEASONALLY-ADJUSTED PRE-SEPTEMBER-11 AIR SERIES

19.2 Relation Between Moving Average and Exponential Smoothing. Assume that we apply a moving average to a series, using a very short window span. If we wanted to achieve an equivalent result using simple exponential smoothing, what value should the smoothing coefficient take?

19.3 Forecasting with a Moving Average. For a given time series of sales, the training set consists of 50 months. The first five months' data are shown below:

Month	Sales
Sept 98	27
Oct 98	31
Nov 98	58
Dec 98	63
Jan 99	59

a. Compute the sales forecast for January 1999 based on a moving average with $w = 4$.

b. Compute the forecast error for the above forecast.

19.4 Optimizing Holt-Winters Exponential Smoothing. The table below shows the optimal smoothing constants from applying exponential smoothing to data, using automated model selection [*Note*: Such automated selection can be performed in RapidMiner with the *Optimize Parameter (Grid)* operator by nesting the *Forecast Validation* operator inside it]:

Level	0.4
Trend	0.0
Seasonality	0.1

a. The value of zero that is obtained for the trend smoothing constant means that (choose one of the following):

- There is no trend.
- The trend is estimated only from the first two periods.
- The trend is updated throughout the data.
- The trend is statistically insignificant.

b. What is the danger of using the optimal smoothing constant values?

19.5 Department Store Sales. The time plot in Figure 19.15 describes actual quarterly sales for a department store over a six-year period (data are available in *DepartmentStoreSales.csv*, data courtesy of Chris Albright).

a. Which of the following methods would **not** be suitable for forecasting this series?

- Moving average of raw series
- Moving average of deseasonalized series
- Simple exponential smoothing of the raw series
- Double exponential smoothing of the raw series
- Holt-Winters exponential smoothing of the raw series

FIGURE 19.15   DEPARTMENT STORE QUARTERLY SALES SERIES

b. The forecaster was tasked to generate forecasts for four quarters ahead. He therefore partitioned the data such that the last four quarters were designated as the holdout period. The forecaster approached the forecasting task by using multiplicative Holt-Winters exponential smoothing. The smoothing parameters used were $\alpha = 0.5, \beta = 0.0001, \gamma = 0.2$ with multiplicative seasonality.

   i. Run this method on the data.

   ii. The forecasts for the holdout set are given in Table 19.2. Compute the MAPE values for the forecasts of Q21 and Q22.

TABLE 19.2   FORECASTS FOR HOLDOUT SERIES USING EXPONENTIAL SMOOTHING

Quarter	Actual	Forecast	Error
21	60,800	59,942.580	857.420
22	64,900	61,399.147	3,500.853
23	76,997	70,742.740	6,254.260
24	103,337	92,704.407	10,632.593

c. The fit and residuals from the exponential smoothing are shown in Figure 19.16. Using all the information thus far, is this model suitable for forecasting Q21 and Q22?

19.6 **Shipments of Household Appliances.** The time plot in Figure 19.17 shows the series of quarterly shipments (in million dollars) of US household appliances between 1985 and 1989 (data are available in *ApplianceShipments.csv*, data courtesy of Ken Black).

a. Which of the following methods would be suitable for forecasting this series if applied to the raw data?

   • Moving average

   • Simple exponential smoothing

   • Double exponential smoothing

   • Holt-Winters exponential smoothing

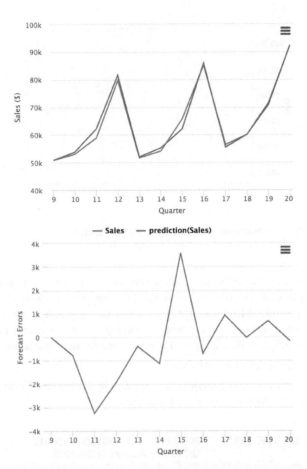

FIGURE 19.16   (TOP) FORECASTS AND ACTUALS AND (BOTTOM) FORECAST ERRORS USING
HOLT-WINTERS EXPONENTIAL SMOOTHING (TRAINING DATA)

FIGURE 19.17   QUARTERLY SHIPMENTS OF US HOUSEHOLD APPLIANCES OVER FIVE YEARS

b. Apply a moving average with window span $w = 4$ to the data. Use all but the last
year as the training set. Create a time plot of the moving average series.

   i. What does the MA(4) chart reveal?

   ii. Use the MA(4) model to forecast appliance sales in Q1-1990.

   iii. Use the MA(4) model to forecast appliance sales in Q1-1991.

    iv. Is the forecast for Q1-1990 most likely to underestimate, overestimate, or accurately estimate the actual sales on Q1-1990? Explain.

    v. Management feels most comfortable with moving averages. The analyst therefore plans to use this method for forecasting future quarters. What else should be considered before using the MA(4) to forecast future quarterly shipments of household appliances?

c. We now focus on forecasting beyond 1989. In the following, continue to use all but the last year as the training set and the last four quarters as the holdout set. First, fit a regression model to sales with a linear trend and quarterly seasonality to the training data. Next, apply Holt-Winters exponential smoothing with smoothing parameters $\alpha = 0.8, \beta = 0.5, \gamma = 1.0$ with multiplicative seasonality to the training data. Choose an adequate "season length."

    i. Compute the MAPE for the holdout period using the regression model.

    ii. Compute the MAPE for the holdout period using Holt-Winters exponential smoothing.

    iii. Which model would you prefer to use for forecasting Q1-1990? Give three reasons.

    iv. If we optimize the smoothing parameters in the Holt-Winters method, are the optimal parameters likely to get values close to zero? Why or why not?

19.7 Shampoo Sales. The time plot in Figure 19.18 describes monthly sales of a certain shampoo over a three-year period. [Data are available in *ShampooSales.csv*, Source: Hyndman and Yang (2018).]

FIGURE 19.18   MONTHLY SALES OF A CERTAIN SHAMPOO

Which of the following methods would be suitable for forecasting this series if applied to the raw data?

- Moving average
- Simple exponential smoothing
- Double exponential smoothing
- Holt-Winters exponential smoothing

19.8 **Natural Gas Sales.** Figure 19.19 is a time plot of quarterly natural gas sales (in billions of BTU) of a certain company, over a period of four years (data is available in *NaturalGasSales.csv*, data courtesy of George McCabe). The company's analyst is asked to use a moving average to forecast sales in Winter 2005.

a. Reproduce the time plot with the overlaying MA(4) line.

b. What can we learn about the series from the MA line?

c. Run a moving average forecaster with adequate season length. Are forecasts generated by this method expected to over-forecast, under-forecast, or accurately forecast actual sales? Why?

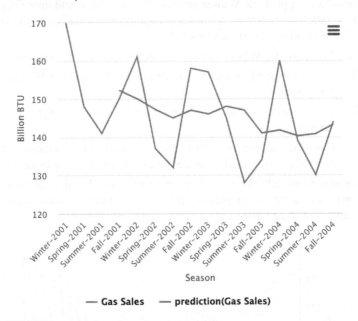

FIGURE 19.19   QUARTERLY SALES OF NATURAL GAS OVER FOUR YEARS

19.9 **Australian Wine Sales.** Figure 19.20 shows time plots of monthly sales of six types of Australian wines (red, rose, sweet white, dry white, sparkling, and fortified) for 1980–1994. [Data are available in *AustralianWines.csv*, Source: Hyndman and Yang (2018).] The units are thousands of liters. You are hired to obtain short-term forecasts (two to three months ahead) for each of the six series, and this task will be repeated every month.

a. Which forecasting method would you choose if you had to choose the same method for all series? Why?

b. Fortified wine has the largest market share of the above six types of wine. You are asked to focus on fortified wine sales alone and produce as accurate as possible forecasts for the next two months.

- Start by partitioning the data using the period until December 1993 as the training set.

- Apply Holt-Winters exponential smoothing to sales with an appropriate season length (use smoothing parameters $\alpha = 0.2, \beta = 0.001, \gamma = 0.001$ with multiplicative seasonality).

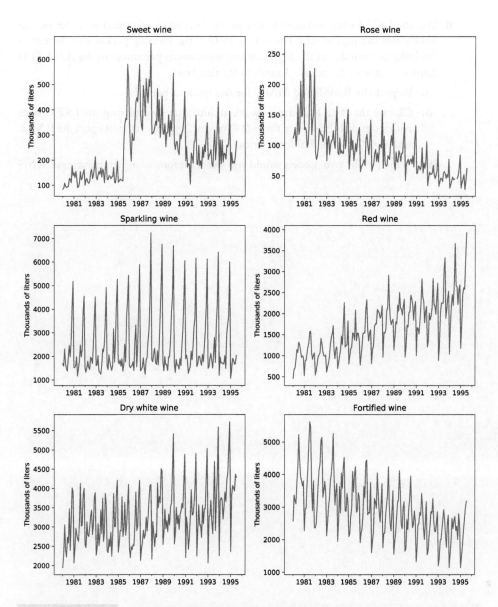

FIGURE 19.20   MONTHLY SALES OF SIX TYPES OF AUSTRALIAN WINES BETWEEN 1980 AND 1994

c. Create an ACF plot for the training residuals from the Holt-Winters exponential smoothing until lag-12.

Examining this plot, which of the following statements are reasonable conclusions?

- Decembers (month 12) are not captured well by the model.

- There is a strong correlation between sales on the same calendar month.

- The model does not capture the seasonality well.

- We should try to fit an autoregressive model with lag-12 to the residuals.

- We should first deseasonalize the data and then apply Holt-Winters exponential smoothing.

d. Use the LSTM deep learning technique to forecast the fortified wine series. As before, use the period until December 1993 as the training period and the rest as the holdout period. Set the *forget gate bias initialization* parameter in the *Add LSTM Layer* operator to 2, and use 3 neurons for that layer.

   i. Report the RMSE and MAPE for the holdout period.

   ii. Change the deep learning network architecture by replacing the LSTM layer with a simple RNN using the *Add Recurrent Layer* operator. Report the RMSE and MAPE for the holdout period.

   iii. Which of the two models would you select for forecasting future values? Why?

Data Analytics

CHAPTER 20

Social Network Analytics[1]

In this chapter, we examine the basic ways to visualize and describe social networks, measure linkages, and analyze the network with both supervised and unsupervised techniques. The methods we use long predate the Internet but gained widespread use with the explosion in social media data. Twitter, for example, makes its feed available for public analysis, and some other social media firms make some of their data available to programmers and developers via an application programming interface (API).

20.1 INTRODUCTION[2]

The use of social media began its rapid growth in the early 2000s with the advent of Friendster and MySpace and, in 2004, Facebook. LinkedIn, catering to professionals, soon followed, as did Twitter, Tumblr, Instagram, Yelp, TripAdvisor, and others. These information-based companies quickly began generating a deluge of data—especially data concerning links among people (friends, followers, connections, etc.).

For some companies, like Facebook, Twitter, and LinkedIn, nearly the entire value of the company lies in the analytic and predictive value of this data from their social networks. As of this writing (March 2022), Facebook was worth more than double General Motors and Ford combined. Other companies, like Amazon and Spotify, use social network data as important components of predictive engines aimed at selling products and services.

---

[1] The organization of ideas in this chapter owes much to Jennifer Golbeck and her book *Analyzing the Social Web* (Golbeck, 2013).

[2] This and the subsequent sections in this chapter copyright © 2019 Datastats, LLC, and Galit Shmueli. Used by permission.

Machine Learning for Business Analytics: Concepts, Techniques and Applications in RapidMiner, First Edition.
Galit Shmueli, Peter C. Bruce, Amit V. Deokar, and Nitin R. Patel
© 2023 John Wiley & Sons, Inc. Published 2023 by John Wiley & Sons, Inc.

Social networks are basically entities (e.g., people) and the connections among them. Let's look at the building blocks for describing, depicting, and analyzing networks. The basic elements of a network are:

- Nodes (also called vertices or vertexes)
- Edges (connections or links between nodes)

A very simple LinkedIn network might be depicted as shown in Figure 20.1 (bottom). This network has six nodes depicting members, with edges connecting some, but not all, of the pairs of nodes. To create this network in RapidMiner, we use the Python scripting extension (see box below). As shown in Figure 20.1 (top), the script parameter in the *Execute Python* operator is customized to construct the network using the *pandas* and *networkx* libraries and then to display the network using the *matplotlib* library in Python.

SOCIAL NETWORK ANALYTICS WITH PYTHON SCRIPTING EXTENSION

We will use RapidMiner's *Python Scripting* extension for performing various social network analytics. This extension can be installed from the RapidMiner menu through *Extensions > Marketplace (Updates and Extensions)*.

In particular, we will use the *Execute Python* operator that executes a Python script specified in the operator's script parameter (or through the script file port). The input ports of the *Execute Python* operator correspond to the arguments of the script. RapidMiner data connected to input ports is automatically converted from RapidMiner's *ExampleSet* format to the *DataFrame* format used in Python's Pandas library. Similarly, the output ports of the *Execute Python* operator correspond to the values returned by the script and are converted back from *DataFrame* format to *ExampleSet* format.

20.2 DIRECTED VS. UNDIRECTED NETWORKS

In the plot shown in Figure 20.1 (bottom), edges are bidirectional or undirected, meaning that if John is connected to Peter, then Peter must also be connected to John, and there is no difference in the nature of these connections. You can see from this plot that there is a group of well-connected members (Peter, John, Dave, and Jenny), plus two less-connected members (Sam and Albert).

Connections might also be directional, or directed. For example, in Twitter, Dave might follow Peter, but Peter might not follow Dave. A simple Twitter network (using the same members and connections) might be depicted using edges with arrows as shown in Figure 20.2.[3]

---

[3]Directed networks can be visualized in RapidMiner using the *Transition Graph* operator.

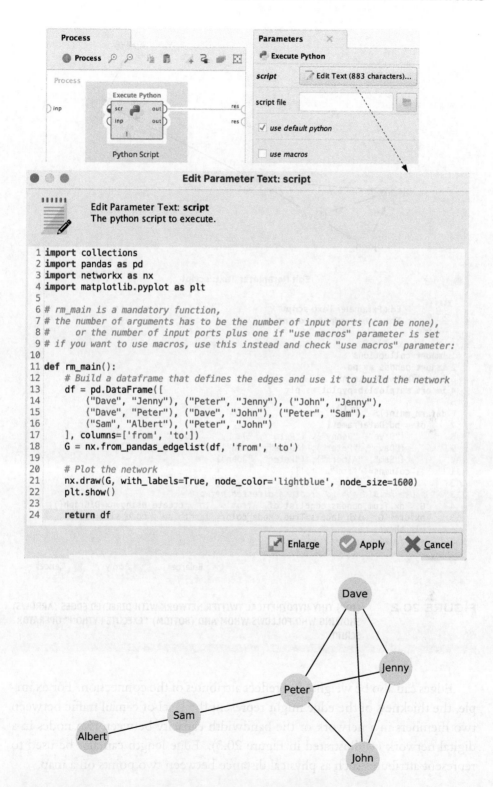

```
1  import collections
2  import pandas as pd
3  import networkx as nx
4  import matplotlib.pyplot as plt
5
6  # rm_main is a mandatory function,
7  # the number of arguments has to be the number of input ports (can be none),
8  #     or the number of input ports plus one if "use macros" parameter is set
9  # if you want to use macros, use this instead and check "use macros" parameter:
10
11 def rm_main():
12     # Build a dataframe that defines the edges and use it to build the network
13     df = pd.DataFrame([
14         ("Dave", "Jenny"), ("Peter", "Jenny"), ("John", "Jenny"),
15         ("Dave", "Peter"), ("Dave", "John"), ("Peter", "Sam"),
16         ("Sam", "Albert"), ("Peter", "John")
17     ], columns=['from', 'to'])
18     G = nx.from_pandas_edgelist(df, 'from', 'to')
19
20     # Plot the network
21     nx.draw(G, with_labels=True, node_color='lightblue', node_size=1600)
22     plt.show()
23
24     return df
```

FIGURE 20.1   (TOP) RAPIDMINER PROCESS AND PYTHON SCRIPT AND
(BOTTOM) OUTPUT DATA AND TINY HYPOTHETICAL LINKEDIN NETWORK.
THE EDGES REPRESENT CONNECTIONS AMONG THE MEMBERS

FIGURE 20.2 (TOP) TINY HYPOTHETICAL TWITTER NETWORK WITH DIRECTED EDGES (ARROWS) SHOWING WHO FOLLOWS WHOM AND (BOTTOM) "EXECUTE PYTHON" OPERATOR SCRIPT

Edges can also be weighted to reflect attributes of the connection. For example, the thickness of the edge might represent the level of e-mail traffic between two members in a network or the bandwidth capacity between two nodes in a digital network (as illustrated in Figure 20.3). Edge length can also be used to represent attributes such as physical distance between two points on a map.

FIGURE 20.3	EDGE WEIGHTS REPRESENTED BY LINE THICKNESS, FOR EXAMPLE, BANDWIDTH CAPACITY BETWEEN NODES IN A DIGITAL NETWORK

20.3 VISUALIZING AND ANALYZING NETWORKS

You have probably seen network plots[4] used as a tool for visualizing and exploring networks; they are used widely in the news media. Jason Buch and Guillermo Contreras, reporters for the *San Antonio Express News*,[5] pored over law enforcement records (data: *drug.csv*) and produced the network diagram shown in Figure 20.4 to understand and illustrate the connections used to launder drug money. You can see that there is a well-connected central node; it is the address of an expensive residence in the gated Dominion community in San Antonio, owned by accused launderers Mauricio and Alejandro Sanchez Garza. There are several entities in the lower left connected only to themselves and one singleton. Nodes are sized according to how central they are to the network (specifically, in proportion to their *eigenvector centrality*, which is discussed in Section 20.4).

Plot Layout

It is important to note that x, y coordinates usually carry no meaning in network plots; the meaning is conveyed in other elements such as node size, edge width, labels, and directional arrows. Consequently, the same network may be depicted

---

[4]In the field of network analysis, the term *graph* refers to the data structure of networks (i.e., lists of edges and nodes). In a more general sense, and in other areas of statistics, the term is used synonymously with "chart" or "plot." Here, to avoid confusion, we will use the term *plot* or *network plot* to refer to the visualization and *network data* to refer to the data itself.

[5]*San Antonio Express News*, May 23, 2012, accessed June 16, 2014.

Edit Parameter Text: script

Edit Parameter Text: **script**
The python script to execute.

```python
1 import collections
2 import pandas as pd
3 import networkx as nx
4 import matplotlib.pyplot as plt
5
6 def rm_main(drug_df):
7     G = nx.from_pandas_edgelist(drug_df, 'Entity', 'Related Entity')
8
9     centrality = nx.eigenvector_centrality(G)
10    node_size=[400*centrality[n] for n in G.nodes()]
11    nx.draw(G, with_labels=False, node_color='skyblue', node_size=node_size)
12    plt.show()
13    return drug_df
```

⬚ Enlarge   ✓ Apply   ✗ Cancel

FIGURE 20.4   (TOP) DRUG-LAUNDERING NETWORK IN SAN ANTONIO, TX, AND
(BOTTOM) "EXECUTE PYTHON" OPERATOR SCRIPT

by two very different looking plots. For example, Figure 20.5 presents two different layouts of the hypothetical LinkedIn network.

As a result, visualization tools face innumerable choices in plot layout. The first step in making a choice is to establish what principles should govern the layout. Dunne and Shneiderman (2009, cited in Golbeck, 2013) list these four plot readability principles:

1. Every node should be visible.

2. For every node, you should be able to count its degree (explained below).

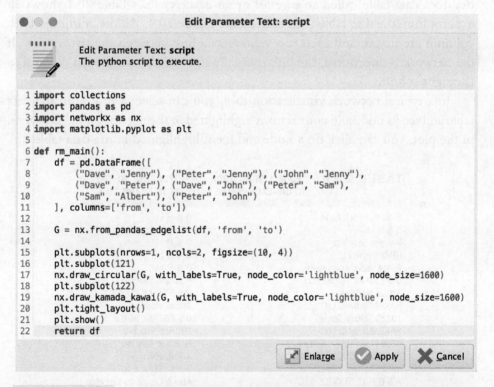

```
1  import collections
2  import pandas as pd
3  import networkx as nx
4  import matplotlib.pyplot as plt
5
6  def rm_main():
7      df = pd.DataFrame([
8          ("Dave", "Jenny"), ("Peter", "Jenny"), ("John", "Jenny"),
9          ("Dave", "Peter"), ("Dave", "John"), ("Peter", "Sam"),
10         ("Sam", "Albert"), ("Peter", "John")
11     ], columns=['from', 'to'])
12
13     G = nx.from_pandas_edgelist(df, 'from', 'to')
14
15     plt.subplots(nrows=1, ncols=2, figsize=(10, 4))
16     plt.subplot(121)
17     nx.draw_circular(G, with_labels=True, node_color='lightblue', node_size=1600)
18     plt.subplot(122)
19     nx.draw_kamada_kawai(G, with_labels=True, node_color='lightblue', node_size=1600)
20     plt.tight_layout()
21     plt.show()
22     return df
```

FIGURE 20.5   (TOP) TWO DIFFERENT LAYOUTS OF THE TINY LINKEDIN NETWORK PRESENTED IN FIGURE 20.1 AND (BOTTOM) "EXECUTE PYTHON" OPERATOR SCRIPT

3. For every link, you should be able to follow it from source to destination.

4. Clusters and outliers should be identifiable.

These general principles are then translated into readability metrics by which plots can be judged. One simple layouts is *circular* (all nodes lie in a circle) and *grid* (all nodes lie at the intersection of grid lines in a rectangular grid).

You can probably think of alternate layouts that more clearly reveal structures such as clusters and singletons, and so can computers using a variety of algorithms. These algorithms typically use a combination of fixed arbitrary starting structures, random tweaking, analogs to physical properties (e.g., springs connecting nodes), and a sequence of iteration and measurement against the readability principles. The Kamada–Kawai force-directed layout available in *networkx* Python library is an example of such an algorithm. A detailed discussion of layout algorithms is beyond the scope of this chapter; see Golbeck (2013, chapter 4) for an introduction to layout issues, including algorithms, the use of size, shape and color, scaling issues, and labeling.

Edge List

A network plot such as the one in Figure 20.4 (drug laundry network) is always tied to a data table called an *edge list* or an *adjacency list*. Table 20.1 shows an excerpt from the data table used to generate Figure 20.4. All the entities in both columns are nodes, and each row represents a link between the two nodes. If the network is directional, the link is usually structured from the left column to the right column.

In a typical network visualization tool, you can select a row from the data table and see its node and connections highlighted in the network plot. Likewise, in the plot, you can click on a node and see it highlighted in the data table.

TABLE 20.1	EDGE LIST EXCERPT CORRESPONDING TO THE DRUG-LAUNDERING NETWORK IN FIGURE 20.4
6451 Babcock Road	Q & M LLC
Q & M LLC	10 Kings Heath
Maurico Sanchez	Q & M LLC
Hilda Riebeling	Q & M LLC
Ponte Vedra Apartments	Q & M LLC
O S F STEAK HOUSE, LLC	Mauricio Sanchez
Arturo Madrigal	O S F STEAK HOUSE
HARBARD BAR, LLC	Arturo Madrigal
10223 Sahara Street	O S F STEAK HOUSE
HARBARD BAR, LLC	Maurico Sanchez
9510 Tioga Drive, Suite 206	Mauricio Sanchez
FDA FIBER, INC	Arturo Madrigal
10223 Sahara Street	O S F STEAK HOUSE
A G Q FULL SERVICE, LLC	Alvaro Garcia de Quevedo
19510 Gran Roble	Arturo Madrigal
Lorenza Madrigal Cristan	19519 Gran Roble
Laredo National Bank	19519 Gran Roble

Adjacency Matrix

The same relationships can be presented in a matrix. The adjacency matrix for the small directed network for Twitter in Figure 20.2 is shown in Table 20.2.

Each cell in the matrix indicates an edge, with the originating node in the left header column and the destination node in the top row of headers. Reading the first row, we see that Dave is following three people—Peter, Jenny, and John.

TABLE 20.2   ADJACENCY MATRIX EXCERPT CORRESPONDING TO THE TWITTER DATA IN FIGURE 20.2

	Dave	Peter	Jenny	Sam	John	Albert
Dave	0	1	1	0	1	0
Peter	0	0	1	1	1	0
Jenny	0	0	0	0	0	0
Sam	0	0	0	0	0	1
John	0	1	1	0	0	0
Albert	0	0	0	0	0	0

Using Network Data in Classification and Prediction

In our discussion of classification and prediction, as well as clustering and data reduction, we were dealing mostly with highly structured data in the form of a data frame—columns were attributes (features), and rows were records. We saw how to use RapidMiner to sample from relational databases to bring data into the tabular format of an ExampleSet.

Highly structured data can be used for network analysis, but network data often start out in a more unstructured or semi-structured format. Twitter provides a public feed of a portion of its voluminous stream of tweets, which has captured researchers' attention and accelerated interest in the application of network analytics to social media data. Network analysis can take this unstructured data and turn it into structured data with usable metrics.

We now turn our attention to those metrics. These metrics can be used not only to describe the attributes of networks but as inputs to more traditional data mining methods.

20.4   SOCIAL DATA METRICS AND TAXONOMY

Several popular network metrics are used in network analysis. Before introducing them, we introduce some basic network terminology used for constructing the metrics:

Edge weight measures the strength of the relationship between the two connected nodes. For example, in an e-mail network, there might be an edge weight that reflects the number of e-mails exchanged between two individuals linked by that edge.

Path and **path length** are important for measuring distance between nodes. A path is the route of nodes needed to go from node A to node B; path length is the number of edges in that route. Typically these terms refer to the shortest route. In a weighted network, the shortest path does not necessarily reflect the path with the fewest edges, but rather the path with the least weight. For example, if the weights reflect a cost factor, the shortest path would reflect the minimal cost.

A connected network is a network where each node in the network has a path, of any length, to all other nodes. A network may be unconnected in its entirety but consist of segments that are connected within themselves. In the money laundering visualization (Figure 20.4), the network as a whole is unconnected—the nodes are not all connected to one another. You can see two independent sub-networks, one large and a small one with four nodes.

A clique is a network in which each node is directly connected by an edge to every other node. The connections must all be single edges—a connection via a multi-node path does not count.

A singleton is an unconnected node. It might arise when an individual signs up for a social network service (e.g., to read reviews) and does not participate in any networking activities.

Node-Level Centrality Metrics

Often we may be interested in the importance or influence of a particular individual or node, which is reflected in how central that node is in the network. The most common way to calculate this is by degree—how many edges are connected to the node. Nodes with many connections are more central. In Figure 20.1, the Albert node is of degree 1, Sam of degree 2, and Jenny of degree 3. In a directed network, we are interested in both indegree and outdegree—the number of incoming and outgoing connections of a node. In Figure 20.2, Peter has indegree of 2 and outdegree of 1.

Another metric for a node's centrality is *closeness*—how close the node is to the other nodes in the network. This is measured by finding the shortest path from that node to all the other nodes and then taking the reciprocal of the average of these path lengths. In Figure 20.1 example, Albert's closeness centrality is $5/(1 + 2 + 3 + 3 + 3) = 0.417$.

Still another metric is *betweenness*—the extent to which a given node lies on the shortest path between pairs of nodes. The calculation starts with the given node, say, node A, and two other nodes, say, B and C, out of perhaps many nodes in a network. The shortest paths between B and C are listed, and the proportion of paths that include A is recorded. The betweenness of a node is the sum of this proportion over all pairs of nodes. In Figure 20.1 example, Peter's node is on all the shortest paths between one of the nodes Dave, Jenny, and John with either Albert or Sam. Because in this example we have only one shortest path between pairs of nodes, this gives an unnormalized betweenness for Peter of 6. To normalize, this number is divided by the number of all possible shortest paths $\binom{n-1}{2} = \frac{(n-1)(n-2)}{2}$. In our example, this is 10, so the normalized betweenness of Peter is 0.6. This proportion is recorded also for all other nodal pairs, and betweenness is the average proportion.

An aphorism relevant for social media networks is "it's not what you know, but who you know." A more accurate rendition would qualify it further—"it's who you know and who they know." A link to a member that has many other connections can be more valuable than a link to a member with few connections. A metric that measures this connectivity aspect is *eigenvector centrality*, which factors in both the number of links from a node and the number of onward connections from those links. The details of the calculation is not discussed here, but the result always lies between 0 (not central) and 1 (maximum centrality). The larger the value for a given node, the more central it is.

Centrality can be depicted on a network plot by the size of a node—the more central the node, the larger it is.

Figure 20.6 shows the script and computed centrality measures for the small undirected LinkedIn data.

Egocentric Network

It is often important to gain information that comes only from the analysis of individuals and their connections. For example, an executive recruiting firm may be interested in individuals with certain job titles and the people those individuals are connected to.

An egocentric network is the network of connections centered around an individual node. A degree 1 egocentric network consists of all the edges connected to the individual node, plus their connections. A degree 2 egocentric network is the network of all those nodes and edges, plus the edges and nodes connected to them. The degree 1 and degree 2 egocentric network for Peter in the LinkedIn network are shown in Figure 20.7. Note that the degree 2 egocentric network for Peter is the entire network shown in Figure 20.1.

Network Metrics

To this point, we have discussed metrics and terms that apply to nodes and edges. We can also measure attributes of the network as a whole. Two main network metrics are *degree distribution* and *density*.

Degree distribution describes the range of *connectedness* of the nodes—how many nodes have, for example, five connections, how many have four connections, how many have three, etc. In the tiny LinkedIn network

● ● ●   **Edit Parameter Text: script**

▦▦▦▦▦   Edit Parameter Text: **script**
░░   The python script to execute.

```
1 import collections
2 import pandas as pd
3 import networkx as nx
4 import matplotlib.pyplot as plt
5
6 def rm_main():
7     df = pd.DataFrame([
8         ("Dave", "Jenny"), ("Peter", "Jenny"), ("John", "Jenny"),
9         ("Dave", "Peter"), ("Dave", "John"), ("Peter", "Sam"),
10        ("Sam", "Albert"), ("Peter", "John")
11    ], columns=['from', 'to'])
12    G = nx.from_pandas_edgelist(df, 'from', 'to')
13
14    # Compute centrality measures for the network
15    df_degree = pd.DataFrame(G.degree(), columns=['node','degree'])
16    df_closeness_cent = pd.DataFrame(list(nx.closeness_centrality(G).items()),
17                        columns=['node','closeness centrality'])
18    df_betweenness_cent = pd.DataFrame(list(nx.betweenness_centrality(G).items()),
19                        columns=['node','betweenness centrality'])
20    df_eigenvector_cent = pd.DataFrame(list(nx.eigenvector_centrality(G, tol=1.e-2).items()),
21                        columns=['node','eigenvector centrality'])
22    return df_degree,df_closeness_cent, df_betweenness_cent,df_eigenvector_cent
```

[☑ Enlarge]   [✓ Apply]   [✗ Cancel]

Row No.	node	degree		Row No.	node	closeness centrality
1	Dave	3		1	Dave	0.625
2	Jenny	3		2	Jenny	0.625
3	Peter	4		3	Peter	0.833
4	John	3		4	John	0.625
5	Sam	2		5	Sam	0.625
6	Albert	1		6	Albert	0.417

Row No.	node	betweenness centrality		Row No.	node	eigenvector centrality
1	Dave	0		1	Dave	0.472
2	Jenny	0		2	Jenny	0.472
3	Peter	0.600		3	Peter	0.529
4	John	0		4	John	0.472
5	Sam	0.400		5	Sam	0.211
6	Albert	0		6	Albert	0.080

FIGURE 20.6   (TOP) "EXECUTE PYTHON" OPERATOR SCRIPT FOR COMPUTING CENTRALITY AND (BOTTOM) CENTRALITY MEASURES FOR THE TINY LINKEDIN NETWORK PRESENTED IN FIGURE 20.1

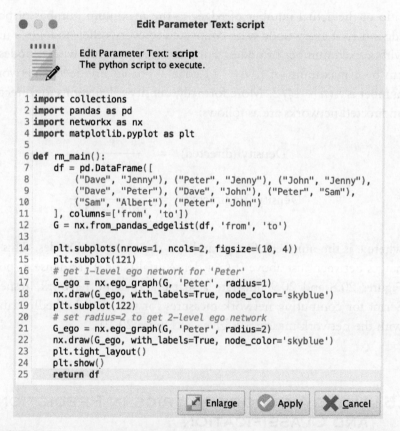

```
1  import collections
2  import pandas as pd
3  import networkx as nx
4  import matplotlib.pyplot as plt
5
6  def rm_main():
7      df = pd.DataFrame([
8          ("Dave", "Jenny"), ("Peter", "Jenny"), ("John", "Jenny"),
9          ("Dave", "Peter"), ("Dave", "John"), ("Peter", "Sam"),
10         ("Sam", "Albert"), ("Peter", "John")
11     ], columns=['from', 'to'])
12     G = nx.from_pandas_edgelist(df, 'from', 'to')
13
14     plt.subplots(nrows=1, ncols=2, figsize=(10, 4))
15     plt.subplot(121)
16     # get 1-level ego network for 'Peter'
17     G_ego = nx.ego_graph(G, 'Peter', radius=1)
18     nx.draw(G_ego, with_labels=True, node_color='skyblue')
19     plt.subplot(122)
20     # set radius=2 to get 2-level ego network
21     G_ego = nx.ego_graph(G, 'Peter', radius=2)
22     nx.draw(G_ego, with_labels=True, node_color='skyblue')
23     plt.tight_layout()
24     plt.show()
25     return df
```

FIGURE 20.7   (TOP) THE DEGREE 1 (a) AND DEGREE 2 (b) EGOCENTRIC NETWORKS FOR PETER, FROM THE LINKEDIN NETWORK IN FIGURE 20.1, AND (BOTTOM) "EXECUTE PYTHON" OPERATOR SCRIPT

(Figure 20.1), we see that Peter, Jenny, and Dave have three connections, John and Sam have two connections, and Albert has one. A table of this degree distribution is shown in Table 20.3.

Density is another way to describe the overall connectedness of network data which focuses on the edges, not the nodes. The metric looks at the

TABLE 20.3	DEGREE DISTRIBUTION OF THE TINY LINKEDIN NETWORK
Degree	Frequency
Degree 0	0
Degree 1	1
Degree 2	1
Degree 3	3
Degree 4	1

ratio of the actual number of edges to the maximum number of potential edges (i.e., if every node were connected to every other node) in a network with a fixed number of nodes. For a directed network with n nodes, there can be a maximum of $n(n-1)$ edges. For an undirected network, the number is $n(n-1)/2$. More formally, density calculations for directed and undirected networks are as follows:

$$\text{Density (directed)} \quad = \quad \frac{e}{n(n-1)}, \tag{20.1}$$

$$\text{Density (undirected)} \quad = \quad \frac{e}{n(n-1)/2}, \tag{20.2}$$

where e is the number of edges and n is the number of nodes. This metric ranges between just above 0 (not dense at all) and 1 (as dense as possible). Figures 20.8 and 20.9 illustrate a sparse and dense network, respectively. Script for computing network measures for the small LinkedIn data along with the network measures is given in Figure 20.10.

20.5 USING NETWORK METRICS IN PREDICTION AND CLASSIFICATION

Network attributes can be used along with other predictors in standard classification and prediction procedures. The most common applications involve the concept of *matching*. Online dating services, for example, will predict for their members which other members might be potentially compatible. Their algorithms typically involve calculation of a distance measure between a member seeking a relationship and candidate matches. It might also go beyond the members' self-reported features and incorporate information about links between the member and candidate matches. A link might represent the action "viewed candidate profile."

FIGURE 20.8   **A RELATIVELY SPARSE NETWORK**

FIGURE 20.9   **A RELATIVELY DENSE NETWORK**

Link Prediction

Social networks such as Facebook and LinkedIn use network information to recommend new connections. The translation of this goal into an analytics problem is:

> "If presented with a network, can you predict the next link to form?"

```
Edit Parameter Text: script

Edit Parameter Text: script
The python script to execute.

1  import collections
2  import pandas as pd
3  import networkx as nx
4
5  def rm_main():
6      df = pd.DataFrame([
7          ("Dave", "Jenny"), ("Peter", "Jenny"), ("John", "Jenny"),
8          ("Dave", "Peter"), ("Dave", "John"), ("Peter", "Sam"),
9          ("Sam", "Albert"), ("Peter", "John")
10     ], columns=['from', 'to'])
11     G = nx.from_pandas_edgelist(df, 'from', 'to')
12
13     degreeCount = collections.Counter(d for node , d in G.degree())
14     degreeDistribution = [0] * (1 + max(degreeCount))
15     for degree, count in degreeCount.items():
16         degreeDistribution[degree] = count
17     degree_list = list(range(0,len(degreeDistribution)))
18     df_degreeDistribution = pd.DataFrame(list(zip(degree_list, degreeDistribution)),
19                                 columns=['degree','degree distribution'])
20     df_density = pd.DataFrame.from_dict({'density': [nx.density(G)]})
21     return df_degreeDistribution, df_density
```

Enlarge   Apply   Cancel

Row No.	degree	degree distribution
1	0	0
2	1	1
3	2	1
4	3	3
5	4	1

Row No.	density
1	0.533

FIGURE 20.10 (TOP) "EXECUTE PYTHON" OPERATOR SCRIPT FOR COMPUTING NETWORK MEASURES AND (BOTTOM) NETWORK MEASURES FOR THE TINY LINKEDIN NETWORK PRESENTED IN FIGURE 20.1

Prediction algorithms list all possible node pairs and then assign a score to each pair that reflects the similarity of the two nodes. The pair that scores as most similar (closest) is the next link predicted to form, if it does not already exist. See Chapter 16 for a discussion of such distance measures. Some attributes used in calculating similarity measures are the same as those based on non-network information (e.g., years of education, age, sex, location). Other metrics used in link prediction apply specifically to network data:

- Shortest path
- Number of common neighbors
- Edge weight

Link prediction is also used in targeting intelligence surveillance. "Collecting everything" may be technically, politically, or legally unfeasible, and an agency must therefore identify a priori a smaller set of individuals requiring surveillance. The agency will often start with known targets and then use link prediction to identify additional targets and prioritize collection efforts.

Entity Resolution

Governments use network analysis to track terrorist networks, and a key part of that effort is identification of individuals. The same individual may appear multiple times from different data sources, and the agencies want to know, for example, whether individual A identified by French surveillance in Tunisia is the same as individual AA identified by Israeli intelligence in Lebanon and individual AAA identified by US intelligence in Pakistan.

One way to evaluate whether an individual appears in multiple databases is to measure distances and use them in a similar fashion to nearest neighbors or clustering. In Chapter 16, we looked in particular at Euclidean distance and discussed this metric not in terms of the network an individual belongs to, but rather in terms of the profile (predictor values) of the individual. When basing entity resolution on these attributes, it is useful to bring domain knowledge into the picture to weight the importance of each attribute. For example, two attributes in an individual's record might be street address and zip code. A match on street address is more definitive than a match on zip code, so we would probably want to give street address more weight in the scoring algorithm. For a more detailed discussion of automated weight calculation and assignment, see p. 137 in Golbeck (2013).

In addition to measuring distance based on individual profiles, we can bring network attributes into the picture. Consider the simple networks for each individual in Figure 20.11, showing connections to known individuals: based on network connections, you would conclude that A and AA are likely the same person while AAA is probably a different person. The metrics that can formalize this search and be used in automated fashion where human–intermediated visualization is not practical are the same ones that are used in link prediction.

Entity resolution is also used extensively in customer record management and search. For example, a customer might contact a company inquiring about a product or service, triggering the creation of a customer record. The same customer might later inquire again or purchase something. The customer database system should flag the second interaction as belonging to the first customer. Ideally, the customer will enter his or her information exactly the same way in each interaction, facilitating the match, but this does not necessarily happen. Failing an exact match, other customers may be proposed as matches based on proximity.

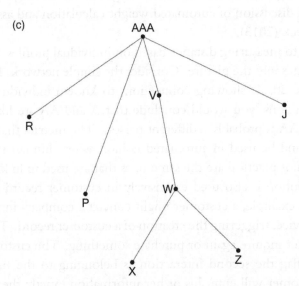

FIGURE 20.11   THE NETWORKS FOR SUSPECT A (a), SUSPECT AA (b), AND SUSPECT AAA (c)

Another area where entity resolution is used is fraud detection. For example, a large telecom used link resolution to detect customers who "disappeared" after accumulating debt but then reappeared by opening a new account. The network of phone calls to and from such people tends to remain stable, assisting the company to identify them.

In traditional business operations, the match may be based on variables such as name, address, and postal code. In social media products, matches may also be calculated on the basis of network similarity.

Collaborative Filtering

We saw in Chapter 15 that collaborative filtering uses similarity metrics to identify similar individuals and thereby develop recommendations for a particular individual. Companies that have a social media component to their business can use information about network connections to augment other data in measuring similarity.

For example, in a company where Internet advertising revenue is important, a key question is what ads to show consumers.

Consider the following small illustration for a company whose business is centered around online users: user A has just logged on and is to be compared with users B–D. Table 20.4 shows some demographic and user data for each of the users.

TABLE 20.4   FOUR MEASUREMENTS FOR USERS A, B, C, AND D

User	Months as customer	Age	Spending	Education
A	7	23	0	3
B	3	45	0	2
C	5	29	100	3
D	11	59	0	3

Our initial step is to compute distances based on these values, to determine which user is closest to user A. First, we convert the raw data to normalized values to place all the measurements on the same scale (for Education, 1 = high school, 2 = college, 3 = post-college degree). Normalizing means subtracting the mean and dividing by the standard deviation. The normalized data are shown in Table 20.5.

Next, we calculate the Euclidean distance between A and each of the other users (see Table 20.6). Based on these calculations, which only take into account the demographic and user data, user C is the closest one to the new user A.

TABLE 20.5   NORMALIZED MEASUREMENTS FOR USERS A, B, C, AND D

User	Months as customer	Age	Spending	Education
A	0.17	−1.14	−0.58	0.58
B	−1.18	0.43	−0.58	−1.73
C	−0.51	−0.71	1.73	0.58
D	1.52	1.42	−0.58	0.58

TABLE 20.6   EUCLIDEAN DISTANCE BETWEEN EACH PAIR OF USERS

Pair	Months as customer	Age	Spending	Education	Euclidean distance
A–B	1.83	2.44	0	5.33	3.1
A–C	0.46	0.18	5.33	0	2.44
A–D	1.83	6.55	0	0	2.89

Let's now bring in network metrics, and suppose that the inter-user distances in terms of shortest path are A–B = 2, A–C = 4, and A–D = 3 (Table 20.7).

TABLE 20.7   NETWORK METRICS

Pair	Shortest path
A–B	2
A–C	4
A–D	3

Finally, we can combine this network metric with the other user measurement distances calculated earlier. There is no need to calculate and normalize differences, as we did with the other user measurements, since the shortest-path metric itself already measures distance between records. We therefore take a weighted average of the network and non-network metrics, using weights that reflect the relative importance we want to attach to each. Using equal weights (Table 20.8), user B is scored as the closest to A and could be recommended as a link for user A (in a social environment) or could be used as a source for product and service recommendations. With different weights, it is possible to obtain different results. Choosing weights is not a scientific process; rather, it depends on the business judgment about the relative importance of the network metrics vs. the non-network user measurements.

TABLE 20.8   COMBINING THE NETWORK AND NON-NETWORK METRICS

Pair	Shortest path	Weight	Non-network	Weight	Mean
A–B	2	0.5	3.1	0.5	2.55
A–C	4	0.5	2.44	0.5	3.22
A–D	3	0.5	2.89	0.5	2.95

In addition to recommending social media connections and providing data for recommendations, network analysis has been used for identifying clusters of similar individuals based on network data (e.g., for marketing purposes), identifying influential individuals (e.g., to target with promotions or outreach), and understanding—in some cases, controlling—the propagation of disease and information.

USING SOCIAL NETWORK DATA

The primary users of social network data are the social networks themselves, those who develop applications (apps) for the networks, and their advertisers. Facebook, Twitter, other networks, and associated app developers use the network data to customize each user's individual experience and increase engagement (that is, encourage more and longer use).

Social network data are also a powerful advertising tool. Facebook generates roughly $50 billion in advertising revenue annually, Twitter $2 billion, and LinkedIn about $5 billion, at this writing. Unlike traditional media, Internet social media platforms offer highly specific microtargeting of ads, the ability to experiment with different ads on a continuous basis to optimize performance, and the ability to measure response and charge advertisers only for the ads that people click on. Facebook gains its advantage from its large user base and the rich information portfolio it has on its regular users (including the identity of a user's connection and information on those connected users).

Perhaps the most well-known example of this advantage was Donald Trump's 2016 campaign for President. Although Trump is most often associated with Twitter, Brad Parscale, Digital Director of the 2016 campaign, gives credit for the victory to Facebook, due to its ability to microtarget ads. He put it this way in a 2018 *60 Minutes* television interview:

> "Facebook now lets you get to places ... that you would never go with
> TV ads. Now, I can find, you know, 15 people in the Florida Panhandle
> that I would never buy a TV commercial for."

Parscale explained that he was able to generate 50,000–60,000 different ads per day, combining both microtargeting and continuous massive experimentation to see what ads worked best with what individuals. Although Trump lost the popular vote by 2.8 million votes overall, he was able to win the Electoral College by a razor thin margin of 77,744 votes in three key states—Pennsylvania, Wisconsin, and Michigan. The ability to surgically target voters where they would be most effective was crucial, and Facebook was instrumental in this effort. Facebook experts were embedded with the Trump campaign to implement the complex job, and Parscale credited the company with a key role in Trump's victory: "Donald Trump won, but I think Facebook was the method."

Facebook and Twitter have in the past made data publicly available via Application Programming Interfaces (APIs). Controversial use of Facebook data via third-party apps has resulted in changes to Facebook procedures and significant limitations. Twitter requires that you register as an app developer to gain access to its API. Twitter data is especially popular with researchers for more than just its network data—it is used for analysis of social trends, political opinions, and consumer sentiment. Social media APIs are updated on a regular basis, as are the limits on

what you can do with the data. See www.dataminingbook.com for updated references on social media API documentation and useful references on using Python
(which can be used within RapidMiner with the *Python Scripting* extension) in conjunction with this data.

As ethical issues in data science have come to the fore, social media has come
in for increased scrutiny. Companies' command of huge amounts of detailed user
data raises privacy concerns, heightened by the use of algorithms to microtarget
advertising. Rapid sharing of user activity and opinion, coupled with powerful
recommender systems, has the effect of magnifying and speeding up malignant
social movements. These topics are covered in greater detail in Chapter 22.

20.6   Collecting Social Network Data with RapidMiner

In this section, we briefly show how to collect data from one of the most used
social networks: Twitter. There are several operators available in RapidMiner
to interface with this social network, as shown in Figure 20.12 (top left). A
connection to Twitter can be configured using an *Access Token* obtained through
a developer account set up with Twitter. The Twitter connection interface is
shown in Figure 20.12 (top right). Figure 20.12 (bottom) shows collected data
for five recent tweets that contain the words "business analytics."

20.7   Advantages and Disadvantages

The key value of social network data to businesses is the information it provides
about individuals and their needs, desires, and tastes. This information can be
used to improve target advertising—and perfectly targeted advertising is the holy
grail of the advertising business. People often disdain or ignore traditional "broad
spectrum" advertising, whereas they pay close attention when presented with
information about something specific that they are interested in. The power of
network data is that they allow capturing information on individual needs and
tastes without measuring or collecting such data directly. Moreover, network
data are often user-provided rather than actively collected.

To see the power of social network data, one need look no further than the
data-based social media giants of the 21st century—Facebook, LinkedIn, Twitter,
Yelp, and others. They have built enormous value based almost exclusively on
the information contained in their social data—they manufacture no products
and sell no services (in the traditional sense) to their users. The main value
they generate is the ability to generate real-time information at the level of the
individual to better target ads.

Row No.	Id	Created-At	From-User	From-User-Id	To-User	To-User-Id	Language	Source
1	14883...	Jan 31, 20...	Zoho Analytics	18212207	?	-1	en	\<a href="h...
2	14882...	Jan 31, 20...	Israel Rivera	581165262	?	-1	en	\<a href="h...
3	14882...	Jan 31, 20...	SelectHub	1446750774	?	-1	en	\<a href="h...
4	14882...	Jan 31, 20...	SonicWall	18147893	?	-1	en	\<a href="h...
5	14881...	Jan 31, 20...	S-Square Sy...	8211206357...	?	-1	en	\<a href="h...

Row No.	Text	Geo-Location-Latitude	Geo-Location-Longitude	Retweet-Count
1	Due to the unprecedented rise in the adoption of b...	?	?	0
2	RT @SonicWall: SonicWall Analytics with Productivity ...	?	?	1
3	Learn about the different applications of business a...	?	?	0
4	SonicWall Analytics with Productivity Reports allows ...	?	?	1
5	#SSquareSolution	?	?	0

FIGURE 20.12 (TOP LEFT) TWITTER OPERATORS IN RAPIDMINER (TOP RIGHT) TWITTER CONNECTION IN RAPIDMINER, AND (BOTTOM) SAMPLE TWEETS

It is important to distinguish between social network *engagement* and the use of social network *analytics*. Many organizations have social media policies and use social media as part of their communications and advertising strategies; however, this does not mean they have access to detailed social network data that they can use for analysis. Abrams Research, an Internet marketing agency, cited the edgy online retailer Zappos in 2009 for the best use of social media, but Zappos' orientation was engagement—use of social media for product support and customer service—rather than analytics.

Reliance on social network analytics comes with hazards and challenges. One major hazard is the dynamic, faddish, and somewhat ephemeral nature of social media use. In part this is because social media involvement is relatively new, and the landscape is changing with the arrival of new players and new technologies. It also stems from the essential nature of social media. People use social media not to provide essential needs like food and shelter, but as a voluntary avocation to provide entertainment and interaction with others. Tastes change, and what's in and out of fashion shifts rapidly in these spheres.

Facebook was a pioneer, and its initial appeal was to the college crowd and later to young adults. Eight years later, nearly half its users were of age 45 years or older, significantly higher than in the rest of the social media industry. These users spend more time per visit and are wealthier than college students, so Facebook may be benefiting from this demographic trend. However, this rapid shift shows how fast the essentials of their business model can shift.

Other challenges lie in the public and personal nature of the data involved. Although individuals nearly always engage with social media voluntarily, this does not mean they do so responsibly or with knowledge of the potential consequences. Information posted on Facebook became evidence in 33% of US divorce cases, and numerous cases have been cited of individuals being fired because of information they posted on Facebook.

One enterprising programmer created the website pleaserobme.com (since removed) that listed the real-time location of people who had "checked in" via FourSquare to a cafe or restaurant, thus letting the world know that they were not at home. FourSquare was not making this information easily available to hackers, but the check-ins were auto-posted to Twitter, where they could be harvested via an API. Thus, information collected for the purpose of enriching the "targetability" of advertising to users ended up creating a liability for both FourSquare and Twitter. Twitter's liability came about indirectly, and it would have been easy for Twitter to overlook this risk in setting up their connection with FourSquare.

In summary, despite the potential for abuse and exposure to risk, the value provided by social network analytics seems large enough to ensure that the analytics methods outlined in this chapter will continue to be in demand.

PROBLEMS

20.1 **Describing a Network.** Consider an undirected network for individuals A, B, C, D, and E. A is connected to B and C. B is connected to A and C. C is connected to A, B, and D. D is connected to C and E. E is connected to D.

   a. Produce a network plot for this network.

   b. What node(s) would need to be removed from the network for the remaining nodes to constitute a clique?

   c. What is the degree for node A?

   d. Which node(s) have the lowest degree?

   e. Tabulate the degree distribution for this network.

   f. Is this network connected?

   g. Calculate the betweenness centrality for nodes A and C.

   h. Calculate the density of the network.

20.2 **Network Density and Size.** Imagine that two new nodes are added to the undirected network in the previous exercise.

   a. By what percent has the number of nodes increased?

   b. By what percent has the number of possible edges increased?

   c. Suppose the new node has a typical (median) number of connections. What will happen to network density?

   d. Comment on comparing densities in networks of different sizes.

   e. Tabulate the degree distribution for this network.

20.3 **Link Prediction.** Consider the network shown in Figure 20.13.

   a. Using the number of common neighbors score, predict the next link to form (that is, suggest which new link has the best chance of success).

   b. Using the shortest path score, identify the link that is least likely to form.

FIGURE 20.13   **NETWORK FOR LINK PREDICTION EXERCISE**

CHAPTER 21

Text Mining

In this chapter, we introduce text as a form of data. First, we discuss a tabular representation of text data in which each column is a word, each row is a document, and each cell is a 0 or 1, indicating whether that column's word is present in that row's document. Then, we consider how to move from unstructured documents to this structured matrix. Finally, we illustrate how to integrate this process into the standard machine learning procedures covered in earlier parts of the book.

RapidMiner

In this chapter, we will use the following RapidMiner extensions that provide some additional operators related to text mining:

- Text Processing
- Operator Toolbox
- Word2Vec

These extensions can be searched and installed through the *Extensions > Marketplace (Updates and Extensions)* menu in RapidMiner.

21.1 INTRODUCTION[1]

Up to this point, and in machine learning in general, we have been primarily dealing with three types of data:

- Numerical

---

[1]This and the subsequent sections in this chapter copyright © 2019 Datastats, LLC, and Galit Shmueli. Used by permission.

Machine Learning for Business Analytics: Concepts, Techniques and Applications in RapidMiner, First Edition.
Galit Shmueli, Peter C. Bruce, Amit V. Deokar, and Nitin R. Patel
© 2023 John Wiley & Sons, Inc. Published 2023 by John Wiley & Sons, Inc.

- Binary (true/false)
- Multicategory

In some common predictive analytics applications, though, data come in text form. An Internet service provider, for example, might want to use an automated algorithm to classify support tickets as urgent or routine so that the urgent ones can receive immediate human review. A law firm facing a massive discovery process (review of large numbers of documents) would benefit from a document review algorithm that could classify documents as relevant or irrelevant. In both of these cases, the predictor attributes (features) are embedded as text in documents.

Text mining methods have gotten a boost from the availability of social media data—the Twitter feed, for example, as well as blogs, online forums, review sites, and news articles. The public availability of web-based text has provided a huge repository of data on which researchers can hone text mining methods. One area of growth has been the application of text mining methods to notes and transcripts from contact centers and service centers.

21.2 THE TABULAR REPRESENTATION OF TEXT: TERM–DOCUMENT MATRIX AND "BAG-OF-WORDS"

Consider the following three sentences:

```
S1. this is the first sentence.
S2. this is a second sentence.
S3. the third sentence is here.
```

We can represent the words (called *terms*) in these three sentences (called *documents*) in a *term–document matrix*, where each column is a word and each row is a sentence. Figure 21.1 (top) shows the matrix for these three sentences.

Note that all the words in all three sentences are represented in the matrix and each word has exactly one row. Order is not important, and the number in the cell indicates the frequency of that term in that sentence. This is the *bag-of-words* approach, where the document is treated simply as a collection of words in which order, grammar, and syntax do not matter.

The three sentences have now been transformed into a tabular data format just like those we have seen to this point. In a simple world, this binary matrix could be used in clustering or, with the appending of a target attribute, for classification or prediction. However, the text mining world is not a simple one. Even confining our analysis to the bag-of-words approach, considerable thinking and preprocessing may be required. Some human review of the documents, beyond simply classifying them for training purposes, may be indispensable.

Row No.	a	first	here	is	second	sentence	the	third	this
1	1	1	0	1	0	1	0	0	1
2	1	0	0	1	1	1	0	0	1
3	0	0	1	1	0	1	1	1	0

FIGURE 21.1   (TOP) TERM–DOCUMENT MATRIX REPRESENTATION OF WORDS IN SENTENCES S1–S3 AND (BOTTOM) PROCESS FOR CREATING THE TERM–DOCUMENT MATRIX

CREATING A TERM–DOCUMENT MATRIX IN RAPIDMINER

Figure 21.1 (bottom) shows a process to create a term–document matrix in RapidMiner. RapidMiner uses a data format called *Document* that serves as a basis for most operators in the Text Processing extension. There are various operators available in this extension to read/process data from files as *Documents* or to transform RapidMiner *ExampleSet* data into *Documents*.

Documents created with the *Create Document* operator are sent to the *Process Document* operator which is a container for any text preprocessing steps to be performed. We discuss this in Section 21.4. For now, it suffices to know that the *Tokenize* operator separates each word using a non-letter character. The parameter *vector creation = Text Occurrences* for the *Process Document* operator creates a vector that stores the count of each word in every document.

21.3 BAG-OF-WORDS VS. MEANING EXTRACTION AT DOCUMENT LEVEL

We can distinguish between two undertakings in text mining:

- Labeling a document as belonging to a class or clustering similar documents
- Extracting more detailed meaning from a document

The first goal requires a sizable collection of documents, or a *corpus*,[2] the ability to extract predictor attributes from documents, and, for the classification task, lots of pre-labeled documents to train a model. The models that are used, though, are the standard statistical and machine learning predictive models that we have already dealt with for numerical and categorical data.

The second goal might involve a single document and is much more ambitious. The computer must learn at least some version of the complex "algorithms" that make up human language comprehension: grammar, syntax, punctuation, etc. In other words, it must undertake the processing of a natural (i.e., noncomputer) language to *understand* documents in that language. Understanding the meaning of one document on its own is a far more formidable task than probabilistically assigning a class to a document based on rules derived from hundreds or thousands of similar documents.

For one thing, text comprehension requires maintenance and consideration of word order. "San Francisco beat Boston in last night's baseball game" is very different from "Boston beat San Francisco in last night's baseball game."

Even identical words in the same order can carry different meanings, depending on the cultural and social context: "Hitchcock shot The Birds in Bodega Bay," to an avid outdoors person indifferent to capitalization and unfamiliar with Alfred Hitchcock's films, might be about bird hunting. Ambiguity resolution is a major challenge in text comprehension—does "bot" mean "bought," or does it refer to robots?

Our focus will remain with the overall focus of the book and the easier goal—probabilistically assigning a class to a document or clustering similar documents. The second goal—deriving understanding from a single document—is the subject of the field of natural language processing (NLP).

---

[2]The term "corpus" is often used to refer to a large, fixed standard set of documents that can be used by text preprocessing algorithms, often to train algorithms for a specific type of text or to compare the results of different algorithms. A specific text mining setting may rely on algorithms trained on a corpus specially suited to that task. One early general-purpose standard corpus was the Brown corpus of 500 English language documents of varying types (named Brown because it was compiled at Brown University in the early 1960s). These days many corpora rely on web-based sources such as Wikipedia and Twitter, which provide huge amounts of documents.

21.4 PREPROCESSING THE TEXT

The simple example we presented had ordinary words separated by spaces and a period to denote the end of the each sentence. A fairly simple algorithm could break the sentences up into the word matrix with a few rules about spaces and periods. It should be evident that the rules required to parse data from real-world sources will need to be more complex. It should also be evident that the preparation of data for text mining is a more involved undertaking than the preparation of numerical or categorical data for predictive models. For example, consider the modified example in Figure 21.2, based on the following sentences:

```
S1.  this is the first    sentence!!
S2.  this is a second Sentence :)
S3.  the third sentence, is here
S4.  forth of all sentences
```

This set of sentences has extra spaces, non–alpha characters, incorrect capitalization, and a misspelling of "fourth."

Tokenization

Our first simple dataset was composed entirely of words found in the dictionary. A real set of documents will have more variety—it will contain numbers, alphanumeric strings like date stamps or part numbers, web and e-mail addresses, abbreviations, slang, proper nouns, misspellings, and more.

Tokenization is the process of taking a text and, in an automated fashion, dividing it into separate "tokens" or terms. A token (term) is the basic unit of analysis. A word separated by spaces is a token. 2+3 would need to be separated into three tokens, while 23 would remain as one token. Punctuation might also stand as its own token (e.g., the @ symbol). These tokens become the row headers in the data matrix. Each text mining software program will have its own list of delimiters (spaces, commas, colons, etc.) that it uses to divide up the text into tokens. By default, the *Tokenize* operator in RapidMiner uses any non-letters as the splitting characters, thus ignoring numbers and punctuation marks as shown in Figure 21.2. It also makes sense to convert all letters to lowercase or uppercase so that words like "sentence" and "Sentence" are treated as the same token. Here, the *Transform Cases* operator converts all characters to lower case. The allowable length of each token may be configured for analysis as well. Here, the *Filter Tokens (by Length)* operator is used to select words that are two or more characters long. In Figure 21.3, we modify the default tokenizer to consider punctuation marks. This captures the emoji and the emphasis of the first sentence.

Row No.	all	first	forth	here	is	of	second	sentence	sentences	the	third	this
1	0	1	0	0	1	0	0	1	0	0	0	1
2	0	0	0	0	1	0	1	1	0	0	0	1
3	0	0	0	1	1	0	0	1	0	1	1	0
4	1	0	1	0	0	1	0	0	1	0	0	0

FIGURE 21.2   (TOP) PROCESS FOR TOKENIZATION OF EXAMPLE 2 SENTENCES S1–S4 AND (BOTTOM) RESULTING TERM–DOCUMENT MATRIX

For a sizeable corpus, tokenization will result in a huge number of attributes—the English language has over a million words, let alone the non-word terms that will be encountered in typical documents. Anything that can be done in the preprocessing stage to reduce the number of terms will aid in the analysis. The initial focus is on eliminating terms that simply add bulk and noise.

Some of the terms that result from the initial parsing of the corpus might not be useful in further analyses and can be eliminated in the preprocessing stage. For example, in a legal discovery case, one corpus of documents might be e-mails, all of which have company information and some boilerplate as part of the signature. These terms might be added to a *stopword list* of terms that are to be automatically eliminated in the preprocessing stage.

Row No.	:)	all	first	forth	here	is	of	second	sentence	sentence!!	sentences	the	third	this
1	0	0	1	0	0	1	0	0	0	1	0	0	0	1
2	1	0	0	0	0	1	0	1	1	0	0	0	0	1
3	0	0	0	0	1	1	0	0	1	0	0	1	1	0
4	0	1	0	1	0	0	1	0	0	0	1	0	0	0

FIGURE 21.3   **(TOP) PROCESS FOR CUSTOMIZED TOKENIZATION OF EXAMPLE 2 SENTENCES S1–S4 AND (BOTTOM) RESULTING TERM–DOCUMENT MATRIX**

Text Reduction

Most text-processing software (RapidMiner included) come with a generic *stopword* list of frequently occurring terms to be removed during preprocessing stages. RapidMiner's *Filter Stopwords (English) operator*[3] contains a large number of terms to be removed (Table 21.1 shows the first 180 stopwords). You can provide your own list of stopwords using a text file parameter to the *Filter Stopwords (Dictionary) operator.*

---

[3]RapidMiner's Text Processing extension uses the stopword list based on the *Word Vector Tool* java library https://sourceforge.net/projects/wvtool/

TABLE 21.1	STOPWORDS USED IN RAPIDMINER'S TEXT PROCESSING EXTENSION

First 180 of 395 stopwords

a	abaft	aboard	about	above	across
afore	aforesaid	after	again	against	agin
ago	aint	albeit	all	almost	alone
along	alongside	already	also	although	always
am	american	amid	amidst	among	amongst
an	and	anent	another	any	anybody
anyone	anything	are	aren	around	as
aslant	astride	at	athwart	away	back
bar	barring	be	because	been	before
behind	being	below	beneath	beside	besides
best	better	between	betwixt	beyond	both
but	by	can	cannot	certain	circa
close	concerning	considering	cos	could	couldn
couldst	dare	dared	daren	dares	daring
despite	did	didn	different	directly	do
does	doesn	doing	done	don	dost
doth	down	during	durst	each	early
either	em	english	enough	ere	even
ever	every	everybody	everyone	everything	except
excepting	failing	far	few	first	five
following	for	four	from	gonna	gotta
had	hadn	hard	has	hasn	hast
hath	have	haven	having.	he	her
here	hers	herself	high	him	himself
his	home	how	howbeit	however	id
if	ill	immediately	important	in	inside
instantly	into	is	isn	it	its
itself	ve	just	large	last	later
least	left	less	lest	let	like
likewise	little	living	long	many	may

Additional techniques to reduce the volume of text ("vocabulary reduction") and to focus on the most meaningful text include the following:

- *Stemming* is a linguistic method that reduces different variants of words to a common core.

- Frequency filters can be used to eliminate either terms that occur in a great majority of documents or very rare terms. Frequency filters can also be used to limit the vocabulary to the *n* most frequent terms.

- Synonyms or synonymous phrases may be consolidated.

- Letter case (uppercase/lowercase) can be ignored.

- A variety of specific terms in a category can be replaced with the category name. This is called *normalization*. For example, different e-mail addresses or different numbers might all be replaced with "emailtoken" or "numbertoken."

Figure 21.4 presents the text reduction step applied to the four sentences example, after tokenization. We can see the number of terms has been reduced to three.

FIGURE 21.4 (TOP) PROCESS FOR TEXT REDUCTION OF EXAMPLE 2 SENTENCES S1–S4 AND (BOTTOM) RESULTING TERM–DOCUMENT MATRIX

Presence/Absence vs. Frequency (Occurrences)

The bag-of-words approach can be implemented in terms of either *frequency* of terms or *presence/absence* of terms. The latter might be appropriate in some circumstances—in a forensic accounting classification model, for example, the presence or absence of a particular vendor name might be a key predictor attribute, without regard to how often it appears in a given document. *Frequency* can be important in other circumstances, however. For example, in processing support tickets, a single mention of "IP address" might be non-meaningful—all support tickets might involve a user's IP address as part of the submission. Repetition of the phrase multiple times, however, might provide useful information that IP address is part of the problem (e.g., DNS resolution).

To implement bag-of-words in RapidMiner, use the *Process Documents* operator. There are three options: for presence/absence, set the parameter *vector creation = Binary Term Occurrences*. The operator will then return a binary matrix (that is, it will convert all non-zero counts to 1's). For term frequency in the sense of occurrences (count), we set *vector creation = Term Occurrences* (as shown in the earlier examples). The third option is using *vector creation = Term Frequency* that produces a normalized matrix of term frequencies, where the count in each document is divided by a normalizing factor. The normalizing factor is document-specific and is computed as the square root of the sum of squares of all the term counts in that document.

Term Frequency–Inverse Document Frequency (TF-IDF)

There are additional popular options that factor in both the frequency of a term in a document and the frequency of documents with that term. One such popular option, which measures the importance of a term to a document, is *Term Frequency–Inverse Document Frequency* (TF-IDF). For a given document d and term t, the term frequency (TF) is the number of times term t appears in document d:

$$\text{TF}(t, d) = \# \text{ times term } t \text{ appears in document } d.$$

To account for terms that appear frequently in the domain of interest, we compute the *Inverse Document Frequency* (IDF) of term t, calculated over the entire corpus and defined as[4]

$$\text{IDF}(t) = \log \left(\frac{\text{total number of documents}}{\# \text{ documents containing term } t} \right).$$

TF-IDF(t, d) for a specific term–document pair is the product of TF(t, d) and IDF(t):

$$\text{TF-IDF}(t, d) = \text{TF}(t, d) \times \text{IDF}(t). \tag{21.1}$$

The TF-IDF matrix contains the value for each term-document combination. The above definition of TF-IDF is a common one; however, there are multiple ways to define and weight both TF and IDF, so there are a variety of possible definitions of TF-IDF.

Often, the TF-IDF(t, d) values are normalized, that is, divided by a normalizing factor of the respective document d. The normalizing factor for a document d is the square root of the sum of squares of all the TF-IDF(t, d) values for that document. For example, Figure 21.5 shows the normalized TF-IDF matrix for the four-sentence example (after tokenization and text reduction done as shown

---

[4]IDF(t) is actually just the fraction, without the logarithm, although using a logarithm is very common.

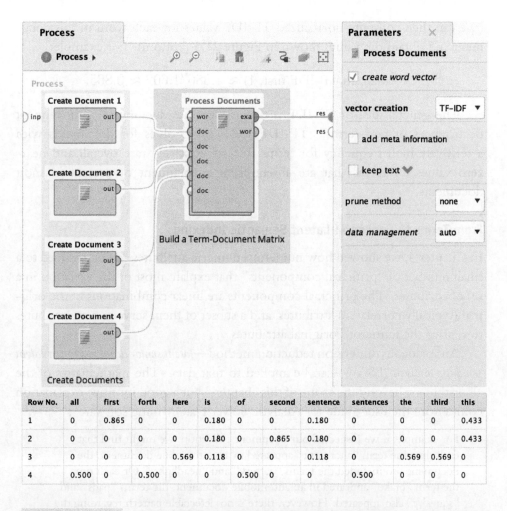

Row No.	all	first	forth	here	is	of	second	sentence	sentences	the	third	this
1	0	0.865	0	0	0.180	0	0	0.180	0	0	0	0.433
2	0	0	0	0	0.180	0	0.865	0.180	0	0	0	0.433
3	0	0	0	0.569	0.118	0	0	0.118	0	0.569	0.569	0
4	0.500	0	0.500	0	0	0.500	0	0	0.500	0	0	0

FIGURE 21.5   (TOP) PROCESS FOR CREATING TF-IDF MATRIX FOR EXAMPLE 2 SENTENCES S1–S4 AND (BOTTOM) RESULTING TF-IDF (NORMALIZED) MATRIX

in Figure 21.2). The *Process Documents* operator uses the natural logarithm for the computation of IDF. For example, the TF–IDF value for the term "first" in document 1 is computed by

$$\text{TF–IDF(first, 1)} = 1 \times \left[\log \left(\frac{4}{1} \right) \right] \approx 1.386.$$

The other TF–IDF values in document 1 are TF–IDF(is, 1) = 0.288, TF–IDF(sentence, 1) = 0.288, TF–IDF(this, 1) = 0.693, and the remaining TF–IDF values for document 1 are 0. The normalization factor for document 1 is therefore computed as

$$\sqrt{1.386^2 + 0.288^2 + 0.288^2 + 0.693^2} \approx 1.602.$$

We can then compute normalized TF-IDF values for each word in this document and obtain the values shown in Figure 21.5 (bottom). For example:

$$\text{Normalized TF-IDF(first, 1)} \approx 1.386/1.602 \approx 0.865.$$

The general idea of TF-IDF is that it identifies documents with frequent occurrences of rare terms. TF-IDF yields high values for documents with a relatively high frequency for terms that are relatively rare overall and near-zero values for terms that are absent from a document or present in most documents.

From Terms to Concepts: Latent Semantic Indexing

In Chapter 4, we showed how numerous numeric attributes can be reduced to a small number of "principal components" that explain most of the variation in a set of attributes. The principal components are linear combinations of the original (typically correlated) attributes, and a subset of them serve as new attributes to replace the numerous original attributes.

An analogous dimension reduction method—*latent semantic indexing* [or *latent semantic analysis* (LSA)]—can be applied to text data. The mathematics of the algorithm are beyond the scope of this chapter,[5] but a good intuitive explanation comes from the user guide for Analytic Solver Data Mining software[6]:

> For example, if we inspected our document collection, we might find that each time the term "alternator" appeared in an automobile document, the document also included the terms "battery" and "headlights." Or each time the term "brake" appeared in an automobile document, the terms "pads" and "squeaky" also appeared. However, there is no detectable pattern regarding the use of the terms "alternator" and "brake" together. Documents including "alternator" might or might not include "brake" and documents including "brake" might or might not include "alternator." Our four terms, battery, headlights, pads, and squeaky describe two different automobile repair issues: failing brakes and a bad alternator.

So, in this case, latent semantic indexing would reduce the four terms to two concepts:

- Brake failure
- Alternator failure

We illustrate latent semantic indexing using RapidMiner in the example in Section 21.6.

---

[5] Generally, in PCA, the dimension is reduced by replacing the covariance matrix by a smaller one; in LSA, dimension is reduced by replacing the term-document matrix by a smaller one.
[6] https://www.solver.com/text-mining-example

Extracting Meaning

In the simple latent semantic indexing example, the concepts to which the terms map (failing brakes, bad alternator) are clear and understandable. In many cases, unfortunately, this will not be true—the concepts to which the terms map will not be obvious. In such cases, latent semantic indexing will greatly enhance the manageability of the text for purposes of building predictive models and sharpen predictive power by reducing noise, but it will turn the model into a black box device for prediction, not so useful for understanding the roles that terms and concepts play. This is OK for our purposes—as noted earlier, we are focusing on text mining to classify or cluster new documents, not to extract meaning.

From Terms to High-Dimensional Word Vectors: Word2Vec

Word embedding is a form of text representation technique in which each word is represented in the form of a multidimensional vector (called *word vector*) so that words that are closer to one another in this vector space would also be similar in meaning. Latent semantic indexing discussed earlier was one such word embedding that considers occurrences of terms at a document level. Yet another form of word embedding approaches is Word2Vec[7] which considers occurrences of terms at a context level and uses prediction-based models to arrive at the word vector representations.

The Word2Vec technique uses a neural network model and trains words against other words in its neighborhood within the corpus. The technique has two variants based on how the model is trained: *continuous bag of words* (CBOW) and *skip-gram*. In both variants, a window of specified length (context) is moved along the text in the training corpus, and in each iteration the network is trained using only the words inside the window. The CBOW model is trained to predict the word in the center of the window (focus word) based on the surrounding words (context words). The skip-gram model is trained to predict the context words based on the focus word. After the training is complete, the hidden layer with its learned weights is used as the word vector representation.

Google has published pretrained Word2Vec word vectors trained with CBOW on a Google News dataset (about 100 billion words) that contain 300-dimensional vectors for three million words and phrases. Interestingly, these high-dimensional word vectors support vector operations that often make semantic sense. For example, the mathematical operation vector(Paris) − vector(France) + vector(Italy) is found to be very similar to vector(Rome), thus implicitly capturing the notion of countries and their capitals.

We illustrate an application of Word2Vec using RapidMiner in Section 21.7.

---

[7]https://code.google.com/archive/p/word2vec/

21.5 IMPLEMENTING MACHINE LEARNING METHODS

After the text has gone through the preprocessing stage, it is then in a numeric matrix format, and you can apply the various data mining methods discussed earlier in this book. Clustering methods can be used to identify clusters of documents—for example, large numbers of medical reports can be mined to identify clusters of symptoms. Prediction methods can be used with tech support tickets to predict how long it will take to resolve an issue. Perhaps the most popular application of text mining is for classification—also termed *labeling*—of documents.

21.6 EXAMPLE: ONLINE DISCUSSIONS ON AUTOS AND ELECTRONICS

This example[8] illustrates a classification task—to classify Internet discussion posts as either auto-related or electronics-related. One post looks like this:

> From: smith@logos.asd.sgi.com (Tom Smith) Subject: Ford Explorer 4WD - do I need performance axle?
> We're considering getting a Ford Explorer XLT with 4WD and we have the following questions (All we would do is go skiing - no off-roading):
> 1. With 4WD, do we need the "performance axle" - (limited slip axle). Its purpose is to allow the tires to act independently when the tires are on different terrain.
> 2. Do we need the all-terrain tires (P235/75X15) or will the all-season (P225/70X15) be good enough for us at Lake Tahoe?
> Thanks,
> Tom
> –
>
> ===
> Tom Smith Silicon Graphics smith@asd.sgi.com 2011 N. Shoreline Rd. MS 8U-815 415-962-0494 (fax) Mountain View, CA 94043
> ===

The posts are taken from Internet groups devoted to autos and electronics, so are pre-labeled. This one, clearly, is auto-related. A related organizational scenario might involve messages received by a medical office that must be classified as medical or non-medical (the messages in such a real scenario would probably have to be labeled by humans as part of the preprocessing).

The posts are in the form a zipped file (*AutoAndElectronics.zip*) that contains two folders after unzipping: *auto posts* and *electronics posts*. Each folder contains a set of 1000 posts organized in small files. In the following, we describe the

---

[8]The dataset is taken from www.cs.cmu.edu/afs/cs/project/theo-20/www/data/news20.html, with minor modifications.

main steps from preprocessing to building a classification model on the data. Figure 21.7 shows the RapidMiner process for text processing and predictive modeling for this example. We describe each step separately next.

Importing the Records

The *Loop Files* operator is used to read the individual files as "documents" from the data folder and convert them to RapidMiner's ExampleSet format. Later, the collection of ExampleSets are appended together and stored as a single data file (ExampleSet) in the repository. This is shown in Figure 21.6.

Row No.	text	metadata_file	file_type	metadata_path		metadata_date	metadata_size
1	Path: cantal...	/103084	autos/103084	/Users/	/AutoAndElectronics/rec.autos/103084	Mar 3, 1997 ...	778
2	Xref: cantal...	/103414	autos/103414	/Users/	/AutoAndElectronics/rec.autos/103414	Mar 3, 1997 ...	2082
3	Path: cantal...	/103070	autos/103070	/Users/	/AutoAndElectronics/rec.autos/103070	Mar 3, 1997 ...	2137
4	Xref: cantal...	/103242	autos/103242	/Users/	/AutoAndElectronics/rec.autos/103242	Mar 3, 1997 ...	2476
5	Newsgroups...	/102955	autos/102955	/Users/	/AutoAndElectronics/rec.autos/102955	Mar 3, 1997 ...	2614

FIGURE 21.6   (TOP) PROCESS FOR LOADING THE TEXT FILES AND STORING THE DATA AS A RAPIDMINER EXAMPLESET (AUTOS AND ELECTRONICS DISCUSSION DATA) AND (BOTTOM) SAMPLE RECORDS FROM THE EXAMPLESET

Data Preparation and Labeling the Records

The data file produced by the process in Figure 21.6 is loaded in a new process. In Figure 21.7, we load the data file with the *Retrieve* operator. Next, the attribute "text" is converted to *Text* format using the *Nominal to Text* operator, and the

FIGURE 21.7   PROCESS FOR LABELING THE RECORDS, PREPROCESSING TEXT, PRODUCING CONCEPT MATRIX, AND FITTING A PREDICTIVE MODEL TO THE AUTOS AND ELECTRONICS DISCUSSION DATA

Generates Attribute operator is used to create a target attribute called "category." A class label is assigned to each record based on the file path—we will use the labels "autos" and "electronics." The text and category attributes are now ready for further processing. This is shown in the Data Preprocessing subprocess in Figure 21.7.

Text Preprocessing in RapidMiner

Prior to text preprocessing, we partition the data (60% training, 40% holdout) so that any text preprocessing and text reduction learned from the training data can be applied to the holdout set during model evaluation. This is done using the *Split Data* operator in Figure 21.7.

The text preprocessing step does *case transformation* of the text to lower case, followed by *tokenization* into words. These tokens are filtered based on length (*min chars* = 4, *max chars* = 25) and then further filtered by removing stopwords. Finally, *stemming* is performed on the selected tokens. The *Process Documents from Data* operator is configured to ignore words that are overall too rare (*prune below percent* = 1) or too common (*prune above percent* = 90). These operations are nested in the *Process Documents from Data* operator as shown in Figure 21.7.

The text preprocessing will produce a "clean" corpus and term–document matrix that can be used to compute the TF-IDF term–document matrix described earlier. The TF-IDF matrix incorporates both the frequency of a term and the frequency with which documents containing that term appear in the overall corpus. Figure 21.7 shows this operation—creating a TF-IDF matrix—the *Process Documents from Data* operator's *vector creation* parameter is set to produce a TF-IDF matrix.

Producing a Concept Matrix

The resulting TF-IDF matrix is probably too large to efficiently analyze in a predictive model (specifically, the number of predictors in the example is 1522), so we use latent semantic indexing to extract a reduced space, termed "concepts." For manageability, we will limit the number of concepts to 20. In RapidMiner, latent semantic indexing can be implemented by the *SVD (Singular Value Decomposition)* operator. Figure 21.7 shows this operation—latent semantic indexing— the *SVD (Singular Value Decomposition)* operator is configured to generate 20 reduced dimensions.

Finally, we can use this reduced set of concepts[9] to facilitate the building of a predictive model. We will not attempt to interpret the concepts for meaning.

---

[9]RapidMiner's Converters extension provides *SVD to ExampleSet* operator that may be used to further analyze the SVD vectors.

Fitting a Predictive Model

At this point, we have transformed the original text data into a familiar form needed for predictive modeling—a single target attribute [class labels: autos (*positive class*) and electronics] and 20 predictors (the concepts).

We can now try applying several classification models to this data. While applying the classification model to the holdout data, we first use the words from the training TF-IDF matrix to compute the TF-IDF matrix for the holdout data. Next, the SVD concepts learned from the training data are applied to the holdout data. Finally, the classification model is applied on this transformed holdout data to evaluate model performance. Figure 21.8 (top) shows the performance of a logistic regression model, with "category" as the target attribute and the 20 concept variables as the predictors.

accuracy: 94.25%

	true autos	true electronics	class precision
pred. autos	378	24	94.03%
pred. electronics	22	376	94.47%
class recall	94.50%	94.00%	

FIGURE 21.8   (TOP) CONFUSION MATRIX FOR THE PREDICTIVE MODEL FIT TO THE AUTOS AND ELECTRONICS DISCUSSION DATA AND (BOTTOM) LIFT CHART

The confusion matrix [Figure 21.8 (top)] shows reasonably high accuracy in separating the two classes of documents—an accuracy of 94.25%. The decile-wise lift chart [Figure 21.8 (bottom)] confirms the high separability of the classes and the usefulness of this model for a ranking goal. For a two-class dataset with a nearly 50/50 split between the classes, the maximum lift per decile is 2, and the lift shown here is just under 2 for the first 50% of the cases and close to 0 for the last 40%.

Next, we'd try other models to see how they compare; this is left as an exercise.

Prediction

The most prevalent application of text mining is classification ("labeling"), but it can also be used for prediction of numerical values. For example, maintenance or support tickets could be used to predict length or cost of repair. The only step that would be different in the above process is the label that is applied after the preprocessing, which would be a numeric value rather than a class.

21.7 EXAMPLE: SENTIMENT ANALYSIS OF MOVIE REVIEWS

This example demonstrates using Word2Vec word embeddings for a classification task—to classify the sentiment of movie reviews as either positive or negative. The file *IMDB-Dataset-10K.xlsx* contains 5000 positive and 5000 negative movie reviews collected from the Internet Movie Database (IMDB) (Maas et al. 2011).[10] In the following, we describe the key steps from preprocessing to building a classification model on the data. Figure 21.9 shows the RapidMiner process for text processing and predictive modeling for this example.

A snippet of a positive review looks like this:

> It is so gratifying to see one great piece of art converted into another without distortion or contrivance. I had no guess as to how such an extraordinary piece of literature could be recreated as a film worth seeing. ...So now my favorite book and movie have the same title.

On the other hand, a snippet of a negative review looks like this:

> I did not expect much from this film, but boy-o-boy, I did not expect the movie to be this bad. ...This is a very bad film! I gave it three out of ten because of few smiles it gave me, but I did never laugh!

Data Loading, Preparation, and Partitioning

Using the *Retrieve* operator, the data is first loaded as an *ExampleSet* in the RapidMiner process. In the *Data Preprocessing* subprocess shown in Figure 21.9,

---

[10]The original large movie dataset is published at https://ai.stanford.edu/~amaas/data/sentiment/ and contains 25K positive and 25K negative movie reviews collected from the Internet Movie Database (IMDB). A stratified sample of 10K records from this dataset is used in this example.

Parameters	
Word2Vec	
Minimal Vocab Frequency	100
Layer Size	200
Window Size	5
Use Negative Samples	5
Iterations	5
Down Sampling Rate	1.0E-4

FIGURE 21.9　RAPIDMINER PROCESS TO PREDICTING REVIEW SENTIMENTS FROM MOVIE REVIEW DATA

the "sentiment" attribute is converted to binominal type using the *Nominal to Binominal* operator, the attribute "review" is converted to *Text* format using the *Nominal to Text* operator, and the *Set Role* operator is used to assign the *label* role to the "sentiment" target attribute. The data is then partitioned (60% training, 40% holdout) with the *Split Data* operator.

Generating and Applying Word2vec Model

The *Word2Vec* operator for training a word2vec model takes as input a collection of documents. The "review" attribute selected with the *Select Attributes* operator is passed to the *Data to Documents* operator which converts the data to a collection of documents (marked with a double-lined connector). The *Loop Collection* nested operator is then used to apply text preprocessing operators to each document. These are the same as shown earlier in Figure 21.7.[11]

Next, the *Word2Vec* operator is used to generate a 200-dimension word embedding model, which is written to a file using the *Write Word2Vec* operator and is also applied to the training document collection using the *Apply Word2Vec (Documents)* operator. This is shown in the left part of the *Word2Vec Features* subprocess in Figure 21.9. A sample of the applied word2vec model for the training data is shown in Figure 21.10 (top). We can see that for each word, 200 attributes (dimensions) are generated. A given word occurring in different documents has the same values for all dimensions. For example, the word "love" has the same dimension values for any movie review it appears in.

At this point, each review consists of 200 values for each of its words. To transform the data into the familiar tabular format with each record corresponding to a movie review, an aggregate value for each of the 200 attributes is required. We can do this in several different ways. Here, we compute the average dimension value for each movie review (that is, the average across all words in the review, which are available in the trained or pretrained word2vec model). This is done by using the *Loop Attributes* operator that iterates over each of the 200 attributes and embeds the *Aggregate* operator to compute the average of all attribute values, grouped by "document id." The output of this process is a collection of 6000 training set documents, each containing two attributes: "document id" and "average(dimension_X)" (for dimension_X). Using the *Merge Attributes* operator, these documents are merged into a single dataset and then joined with the "sentiment" attribute from the original dataset using the *Join* operator. Finally, only the sentiment and the 200 predictors are selected in the data with the *Select Attributes* operator. This is shown in the right part of the *Word2Vec Features* subprocess in Figure 21.9.

---

[11]Stemming is not used with pretrained word2vec word embeddings (e.g., Google's Word2Vec), so following the same approach, we do not use it in this example.

Row No.	word	document id	dimension_0	dimension_1	dimension_2	...	dimension_198	dimension_199
1	mentioned	0	0.067	-0.007	-0.094	...	0.011	-0.035
2	watching	0	0.062	-0.004	-0.086	...	0.004	-0.044
3	episode	0	0.065	-0.012	-0.086	...	-0.004	-0.036
...								
290178	love	5999	0.062	-0.017	-0.093	...	0.016	-0.017
290179	people	5999	0.050	-0.003	-0.077	...	0.003	-0.035
290180	wrong	5999	0.064	-0.009	-0.085	...	0.017	-0.029

id	sentiment	prediction(sentiment)	confidence(positive)	confidence(negative)	average(dimension_0)	average(dimension_1)	average(dimension_2)
1	negative	negative	0.331	0.669	0.054	-0.013	-0.078
2	positive	positive	0.904	0.096	0.053	-0.013	-0.083
3	positive	positive	0.858	0.142	0.048	-0.014	-0.080
4	positive	positive	0.619	0.381	0.060	-0.005	-0.084
5	positive	negative	0.476	0.524	0.050	-0.010	-0.080

FIGURE 21.10   (TOP) APPLICATION OF 200-DIMENSIONAL WORD2VEC MODEL TO TRAINING DATA (SAMPLE OF SIX WORDS WITH FEW DIMENSIONS) AND (BOTTOM) PROPENSITIES FOR FIVE RECORDS IN THE HOLDOUT DATA

FIGURE 21.11   "WORD2VEC FEATURES" SUBPROCESS FOR HOLDOUT DATA

The holdout data is processed similarly and is shown in Figure 21.11. The only difference is that the word2vec model trained earlier and written to a file is now used for the holdout data with the *Read Word2Vec* operator.

Fitting a Predictive Model

The data is now ready for predictive modeling with a single target attribute "sentiment" (class labels: positive and negative) and 200 predictors (the averaged word embedding dimensions). Different classification models may be applied to this data. Figure 21.9 shows the application of logistic regression. Figure 21.12 shows the model performance for the holdout set. Figure 21.10 (bottom) shows sample records from the holdout set with propensities and sentiment predictions.

The confusion matrix [Figure 21.12 (top)] shows a moderately high accuracy in separating reviews with positive and negative sentiments—an accuracy of 82.05%. For a ranking goal, the decile-wise lift chart [Figure 21.12 (bottom)] shows that this model demonstrates high separability of classes with the first 50% of the cases showing an average lift of 1.64.

Using a Pretrained Word2vec Model

A pretrained word2vec model (such as Google's pretrained word2vec word vectors[12]) can be directly used to generate word embedding features rather than

---

[12]Available for download from https://code.google.com/archive/p/word2vec/. *Note*: The file size of *GoogleNews-vectors-negative300.bin.gz* is 3.64GB, and loading will require significant computer memory.

accuracy: 82.05%

	true positive	true negative	class precision
pred. positive	1650	368	81.76%
pred. negative	350	1632	82.34%
class recall	82.50%	81.60%	

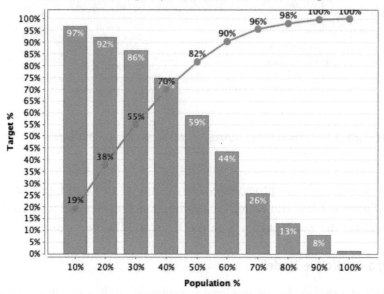

FIGURE 21.12   (TOP) CONFUSION MATRIX FOR THE PREDICTIVE MODEL FIT TO THE WORD2VEC
FEATURES FROM MOVIE REVIEW DATA AND (BOTTOM) LIFT CHART

learning the embedding vectors based on the training data. Figure 21.13 (top) shows the process for using a pretrained word2vec model. This is similar to the process shown in Figure 21.9, except that the word embedding feature generation is done during data preprocessing, given that the word2vec model is already pretrained. The *Word2Vec Features* subprocess is identical to 21.11 except using the pretrained word2vec model in the *Read Word2Vec* operator. Figure 21.13 (middle) shows the confusion matrix for the holdout set, indicating slightly better accuracy than the earlier trained word2vec model. The better model performance is also evident in the lift chart shown in Figure 21.13 (bottom).

accuracy: 83.60%

	true positive	true negative	class precision
pred. positive	1658	314	84.08%
pred. negative	342	1686	83.14%
class recall	82.90%	84.30%	

FIGURE 21.13   (TOP) RAPIDMINER PROCESS FOR SENTIMENT ANALYSIS USING FEATURES BASED
ON GOOGLE'S PRETRAINED WORD2VEC MODEL, (MIDDLE) CONFUSION MATRIX
FOR HOLDOUT SET, AND (BOTTOM) LIFT CHART (MOVIE REVIEW DATA)

21.8 SUMMARY

In this chapter, we drew a distinction between text processing for the purpose of extracting meaning from a single document (natural language processing— NLP) and classifying or labeling numerous documents in probabilistic fashion (text mining). We concentrated on the latter and examined the preprocessing steps that need to occur before text can be mined. Those steps are more varied and involved than those involved in preparing numerical data. The ultimate goal is to produce a matrix in which rows are terms and columns are documents. The nature of language is such that the number of terms is excessive for effective model-building, so the preprocessing steps include vocabulary reduction. A final major reduction takes place if we use, instead of the terms, a limited set of concepts that represents most of the variation in the documents, in the same way that principal components capture most of the variation in numerical data. In word embedding methods that represent words in multidimensional space, aggregation (such as counts or averages) is used for this purpose. Finally, we end up with a quantitative matrix in which the cells represent the frequency or presence of terms and the columns represent documents. To this, we append document labels (classes), and then we are ready to use this matrix for classifying documents using classification methods.

PROBLEMS

21.1 Tokenization. Consider the following text version of a post to an online learning forum in a statistics course:

```
Thanks John!<br /><br /><font size="3">
&quot;Illustrations and demos will be
provided for students to work through on
their own&quot;</font>.
Do we need that to finish project? If yes,
where to find the illustration and demos?
Thanks for your help.\<img title="smile"
alt="smile" src="\url{http://lms.statistics.
com/pix/smartpix.php/statistics_com_1/s/smil
ey.gif}" \><br /> <br />
```

a. Identify 10 non-word tokens in the passage.

b. Suppose this passage constitutes a document to be classified, but you are not certain of the business goal of the classification task. Identify material (at least 20% of the terms) that, in your judgment, could be discarded fairly safely without knowing that goal.

c. Suppose the classification task is to predict whether this post requires the attention of the instructor or whether a teaching assistant might suffice. Identify the 20% of the terms that you think might be most helpful in that task.

d. What aspect of the passage is most problematic from the standpoint of simply using a bag-of-words approach, as opposed to an approach in which meaning is extracted?

21.2 Classifying Internet Discussion Posts. In this problem, you will use the data and scenario described in this chapter's example, in which the task is to develop a model to classify documents as either auto-related or electronics-related.

a. Using the process shown in Figure 21.6, store the data as an *ExampleSet*. Then, load the data in a new process and create a label vector.

b. Following the example in this chapter, preprocess the documents. Explain what would be different if you did not perform the "stemming" step.

c. Use the LSA to create 10 concepts. Explain what is different about the concept matrix, as opposed to the TF-IDF matrix.

d. Using this matrix, fit a predictive model (different from the model presented in the chapter illustration) to classify documents as autos or electronics. Compare its performance with that of the model presented in the chapter illustration.

21.3 Classifying Classified Ads Submitted Online. Consider the case of a website that caters to the needs of a specific farming community and carries classified ads intended for that community. Anyone, including robots, can post an ad via a web interface, and the site owners have problems with ads that are fraudulent, spam, or simply not relevant to the community. They have provided a file with 4143 ads, each ad in a row, and each ad labeled as either -1 (not relevant) or 1 (relevant). The goal is to develop a predictive model that can classify ads automatically.

- Open the file *farm-ads.csv*, and briefly review some of the relevant and non-relevant ads to get a flavor for their contents.

- Following the example in the chapter, preprocess the data in RapidMiner, and create a term–document matrix and a concept matrix. Limit the number of concepts to 20.

  a. Examine the term–document matrix.

    i. Is it sparse or dense?

    ii. Find two non-zero entries and briefly interpret their meaning, in words (you do not need to derive their calculation).

  b. Briefly explain the difference between the term–document matrix and the concept–document matrix. Relate the latter to what you learned in the principal components chapter (Chapter 4).

  c. Using logistic regression, partition the data (60% training, 40% holdout), and develop a model to classify the documents as "relevant" or "non-relevant." Comment on its efficacy.

  d. Why use the concept–document matrix, and not the term-document matrix, to provide the predictor attributes?

21.4 **Clustering Auto Posts.** In this problem, you will use the data and scenario described in this chapter's example. The task is to cluster the auto posts.

  a. Following the example in this chapter, preprocess the documents, except do not create a label vector.

  b. Use the LSA to create 10 concepts.

  c. Before doing the clustering, state how many natural clusters you expect to find.

  d. Perform hierarchical clustering using *complete linkage* criterion, and inspect the dendrogram.

    i. From the dendrogram, how many natural clusters appear?

    ii. Examining the dendrogram as it branches beyond the number of main clusters, select a subcluster and assess its characteristics.

  e. Perform k-means clustering for two clusters, and report how distant and separated they are (using between-cluster distance and within-cluster dispersion).

CHAPTER 22

Responsible Data Science[1]

In this chapter, we go beyond technical considerations of model fitting, selection, and performance and discuss the potentially harmful effects of machine learning. The catalog of harms is now extensive, including a host of cases where AI has deliberately been put to ill purposes in service of big brother surveillance and state suppression of minorities. Our focus, however, is on cases where the intentions of the model developer are good, and the resulting bias or unfairness has been unintentional. We review the principles of responsible data science (RDS) and discuss a concrete framework that can govern data science work to put those principles into practice. We also discuss some key elements of that framework: datasheets, model cards, and model audits.

22.1 INTRODUCTION[2]

Machine learning and AI bring the promise of seemingly unlimited good. After all, the ability to ingest any set of arbitrarily sized, minimally structured data and produce predictions or explanations for these data is applicable to almost every domain. Our societal attention often focuses on the revolutionary future applications of this potential: cars that drive themselves, computers that can hold natural conversations with humans, precision medications tailored to our specific genomes, cameras that can instantly recognize any object, and software that can automatically generate new images or videos. Conversations about these benefits, though, too often ignore the harms that machine learning models can cause.

---

[1] This chapter draws on material from *Responsible Data Science*, Wiley 2021, by Grant Fleming and Peter Bruce, used by permission.

[2] This chapter copyright ©2021 Datastats, LLC. Used by permission

---

Machine Learning for Business Analytics: Concepts, Techniques and Applications in RapidMiner, First Edition.
Galit Shmueli, Peter C. Bruce, Amit V. Deokar, and Nitin R. Patel
© 2023 John Wiley & Sons, Inc. Published 2023 by John Wiley & Sons, Inc.

Example: Predicting Recidivism

Decisions about criminal defendants in the US justice system are based on the weight of probabilistic evidence at multiple stages: whether to arrest, whether to go to trial, arrival at a verdict, and sentencing. At the sentencing phase, judges determine the length and terms of sentences, in part, by assessing the likelihood that a convicted defendant will commit another crime (recidivate). Courts have started relying increasingly on machine learning recidivism algorithms to inform decisions on sentencing. The COMPAS algorithm,[3] sold by Northpointe, Inc., is among the most prominent of these, and critics have charged that it is biased against African–Americans. The algorithm is not public and involves more than 170 predictors. Its advocates retort that COMPAS has good overall predictive performance and that its accuracy, as measured by the area under the ROC curve (Receiver Operating Characteristics curve), is similar for African–American and White defendants. The trouble is that the errors made are quite different:

- African–American defendants are over-predicted to re-offend (leading to tougher sentences).
- White defendants are under-predicted to re-offend (leading to lighter sentences).

The over-prediction errors (penalizing African–Americans) balance out the under-prediction errors (favoring Whites), so the overall error rate is the same for both. A single-minded focus on one overall accuracy metric obscures this bias against African–Americans. We will work through this example in greater detail below.

22.2 UNINTENTIONAL HARM

The COMPAS algorithm did not set out to penalize African–Americans. Its goal was to make sentencing decisions overall more consistent and "scientific." The bias against African–Americans was unintended and unwanted.

Another stark example of unintentional harm was the Optum healthcare algorithm. In 2001, the healthcare company Optum launched Impact-Pro, a predictive modeling tool that purported to predict patients' future need for followup care and assign a risk score, based on a variety of predictor inputs. The result would be better healthcare for patients, as follow-up interventions could be better timed and calibrated. Hospitals could use the tool to better manage resources, and insurers could use it to better set insurance rates. Unfortunately,

---

[3]COMPAS stands for "Correctional Offender Management Profiling for Alternative Sanctions"; a good summary by the public interest group ProPublica can be found here: https://www.propublica.org/article/how-we-analyzed-the-compas-recidivism-algorithm

experience proved that the algorithm was biased against African–Americans: a research team led by Ziad Obermeyer studied these algorithms and found that, for any given risk score, African–American patients consistently experienced more chronic health conditions than did White patients.

It turned out that a key predictor for "future health care need" is "prior healthcare spending." African–American spending on healthcare was, on average, less than that for Whites, but not because of better health. Rather, it was due to lower income levels and less access to health insurance and costly medical facilities. Hence, an African–American individual would be predicted to need less follow-up care than a White individual with similar health.

There are numerous other examples of well-intentioned algorithms going wrong.[4] The algorithms that power social media and Internet ads foster connections among people and with things they are interested in, "bringing the world closer together" in Facebook's words. Those same algorithms can also nurture communities of hate and facilitate the spread of false news and conspiracy theories.

INTENDED HARM

Not all damage from machine learning algorithms is unintentional. In some cases, bad actors "weaponize" algorithms for purposes that are malicious. In other cases, seemingly legitimate law enforcement practices creep into the realm of "big brother":

- Facial recognition and identification technology, combined with the widespread presence of security cameras, enable police departments to track down criminal suspects who would have gone undetected in the pre-technology age. This is a good thing!

- Those same technologies, though, have enabled US immigration authorities to track down and deport undocumented individuals who may have been living and working peacefully for years or decades. This is not so clearly a good thing – the technology empowered bureaucrats (not legislators) to shift the terms of a highly contentious political debate that was broadly agreed on only one thing: authorities should not be sweeping the country to round up and deport long-term residents who are undocumented.

- These technologies have also aided Chinese police authorities in their surveillance and suppression of Uighur and Tibetan communities, a bad thing by the standards of most pluralistic societies that honor the rule of law.

Some might also consider that knowing about damage caused by algorithms and proceeding anyway ("turning a blind eye") constitutes intentional harm. In late 2021, a disaffected employee at Facebook released a trove of internal Facebook

---

[4]The popular author Cathy O'Neil coined the catchphrase "Weapons of Math Destruction" in recounting such examples in her book of the same name (O'Neil, 2016).

research showing that ML-enabled algorithms harmed teenagers (for teen girls with mental health and body-image issues, Instagram exacerbated those issues) and fostered civil discord (2018 algorithm changes for the Facebook newsfeed boosted angry and contentious content). Top executives knew about the internal research but were reluctant to make significant changes in highly profitable platforms.

The framework and process we discuss in this chapter will do little to counter the individual or entity that is determined to develop or repurpose algorithms for harmful purposes. However, the framework outlined below does have an important message for data scientists involved in developing algorithms: anticipate and be mindful of potentially harmful uses to which their work might be put.

22.3 LEGAL CONSIDERATIONS

Many treatments of the ethical aspects of data science focus on legal issues. This is understandable, as avoiding legal jeopardy is a strong motivator. Legal compliance is ultimately a matter for attorneys more than data scientists. The latter may contribute best by pursuing a general framework for responsible data science, so our legal discussion will be brief and focused on two points: the European Union's GDPR and the concept of "protected groups."

The General Data Protection Regulation (GDPR)

The most recognized legal environment for machine learning is the General Data Protection Regulation (GDPR) of the European Union (EU), which went into effect in August 2018. The GDPR provides sweeping protections to those in the EU (whether citizens of EU countries or not) including a "right to be forgotten" (a requirement that technology companies provide mechanisms by which individuals can have their data removed from online platforms), as well as the right to data portability and the right to object to automated decision-making and profiling. The GDPR's focus is strongly on empowering the individual, educated citizen with greater leverage to enforce the privacy of their data. Because the GDPR was the first comprehensive regulatory framework for big data services, it set the pattern for other legal initiatives that followed, including the California Consumer Protection Act (CCPA) and Canada's Personal Information Protection and Electronic Documents Act (PIPEDA). Given the size of the EU market and the global nature of internet activity, the GDPR has become, in effect, a global regulatory regime.

Protected Groups

Regulations and laws that address not simply consumer privacy, but also issues of algorithmic discrimination and bias, are less well developed. However, one guiding principle is that laws that restrict behavior by individuals or corporations do not disappear merely because the decisions are made by algorithms. Decisions or actions that are illegal for a human in a company (discrimination in lending based on gender or age, for example) are also illegal for an algorithm to do in automated fashion. In US law (and in other countries as well), there are various "protected groups" where such restrictions apply. Protected groups may be identified on the basis of race, gender, age, sexual orientation, medical disability, or other factors. Although there may be no AI-specific or big data-specific laws in this area, there is ample and long-standing legal history that must be considered in the deployment of algorithms.

To evaluate fairness and calculate fairness metrics, a "privileged group" is designated. Often this reflects actual societal advantage enjoyed by the group (terminology coinciding with the social justice movement), but it is also a technical requirement. Fairness metrics must be calculated relative to some base group, so the term by itself does not imply privilege in the lay meaning.

22.4 PRINCIPLES OF RESPONSIBLE DATA SCIENCE

Legal statutes and regulations are typically lengthy, detailed, and difficult to understand. Moreover, legal compliance alone is not sufficient to avoid some of the harm caused by machine learning. The potential for reputational harm may be just as great as that for legal jeopardy. In late 2021, Facebook began conducting "reputational reviews" of its services and products. The publicly-stated purpose was to avoid harm to children, but news stories also cited Facebook's desire to anticipate how its algorithms might be criticized. A significant movement has arisen in the data science community to focus greater attention on this potential for harm and how to avoid it. A number of commentators have suggested that data scientists should adhere to a framework for responsible data science: a set of best practices. Common to most suggested frameworks are five principles:

- Non-maleficence (avoiding harm)
- Fairness
- Transparency
- Accountability
- Privacy

Non-maleficence

Non-maleficence covers concepts associated with causing or avoiding harm. At a high level, following this principle requires that data scientists ensure that their models do not cause foreseeable harms or harms of negligence. While unforeseen harms are sometimes unavoidable, they should be accounted for as much as reasonably possible. Harms that ought to be avoided include risks of physical harm, legal risks, reductions in future opportunities, privacy violations, emotional distress, facilitating illegal activities, and other results which could negatively impact individuals.

Non-maleficence is the hardest principle to guarantee in practice, and we recommend thinking of it as more of a goal to strive for than a necessary box to check for every data science project. A model can be fair, transparent, accountable to users, and respecting of privacy yet still make predictions that advantage some people while causing harm for others. Medical triaging algorithms for prioritizing scarce medical resources necessarily place some individuals further back in the queue or out of the queue entirely. Credit scoring algorithms make life difficult for those receiving low credit scores. In such cases, non-maleficence must be considered in the context of other principles.

Fairness

Fairness covers concepts associated with equal representation, anti-discrimination, dignity, and just outcomes. Dimensions of interest for fairness evaluations typically involve human-specific factors like ethnicity, gender, sexual orientation, age, socioeconomic status, education, disability status, presence of preexisting conditions (healthcarc), and history of adverse events. Model fairness is primarily a function of whether the model produces fair outcomes, with input factors (how the model uses certain features, how the features were created, etc.) being less relevant. Like non-maleficence, fairness is a difficult concept to pin down. What is fair for one person or context might be unfair for another. One person might consider it fair for everyone to pay the same absolute amount in taxes. Another person might think everyone should pay the same share of their income in taxes. Another might think the wealthy should pay a higher share of their income in taxes. Yet another might think that the wealthy should pay all the taxes. There is no universally agreed definition, in this case, of what constitutes fairness. Because fairness relies primarily on ensuring fair outcomes, it is easier to translate into practice than the other four principles. However, fairness-improving methods are still very underused. Fairness is almost always talked about exclusively in the context of models that make predictions for individual people, like whether a person should be provided a loan. In actuality, fairness is relevant for any modeling task where the goal is to either minimize differences between groups or maximize predictive performance with respect to specific groups. For example, in a spam email classification task, it might make sense to use fairness interventions to make the spam classification model more balanced in how well it classifies spam across different identified topics. While this is not a use case that deals directly with people, it can still be beneficial to consider fairness.

Transparency

Transparency covers concepts associated with user consent, model interpretability, and explanations for other modeling choices made by the creators of a model. Typically, this communication is conveyed via clear documentation about the data or model.[5] Transparency as a concept is as simple as it appears: where possible, decisions about the modeling process should be recorded and available for inspection. However, transparency quickly becomes complex when trying to move it from principle to practice. For example, the modeling team, regulators, users, and clients all might require mutually exclusive forms of transparency due to their different needs and technical abilities. Documentation about the datasets used, explanations for choices made within the modeling process, and interpretations for individual predictions made for one group might need to be completely revamped for another.

An important related term is the *interpretability* of a model. Some of the greatest advances in machine learning have come with so-called uninterpretable, black box models—models where the learned relationships between predictors and outcomes are so complex that humans cannot discern how one affects the other. Neural nets are one example, and they have become ubiquitous now with the power and popularity of deep learning. Random forests and boosted trees are also examples of black box methods: single trees can easily be translated into decision rules, but when the predictions from many different trees are simply averaged or otherwise aggregated, that interpretability disappears.

Classical statistical models like linear and logistic regression are "intrinsically interpretable." Their coefficients provide clear and direct estimates of the effects of individual predictors.

Without interpretability, we are handicapped in reviewing the ethical impact of our models. If a model is producing biased predictions, how would we know which predictors are instrumental in generating the biased predictions so that we might make corrections? In seeking interpretability, we can follow a two-pronged approach:

- Where possible, include an interpretable model among the final candidates, to serve as a benchmark. If we ultimately choose a better-performing black box model, we'd like to know how much, in terms of performance, we would have to give up if we went with an intrinsically-interpretable model.

---

[5] Under Basel II banking regulations, for example, deployed credit scoring models should be repeatable, transparent and auditable (Saddiqi, 2017).

- Apply interpretability methods, ex post, to a black box model. Some examples of these methods are illustrated in the COMPAS example in Section 22.7.

Accountability

Accountability covers concepts associated with legal compliance, acting with integrity, responding to the concerns of individuals who use or are affected by machine learning algorithms, and allowing for individual recourse for harmful modeling decisions. For example, people who receive a loan denial ideally ought to be entitled to not just an explanation for why that decision was made but also the ability to appeal the decision and an indication of the minimum set of differences that would have resulted in a change in the decision. In practice, accountability typically does not go beyond ensuring that a model achieves legal compliance (which itself has gotten more difficult because of regulation like the GDPR) or, in a few cases, adherence to company or industry standards.

Data Privacy and Security

Privacy covers concepts associated with only gathering necessary information, storing data securely, ensuring that data is de-identified once it is used in a model, and ensuring that other aspects of user data cannot be inferred from the model results. Fortunately, there are already several well-understood approaches for maintaining the privacy of systems (via preventing hacks, unintentional disclosures, physical attacks, etc.). Making data available for analysis in models circumvents some of these protections, and it may be necessary to use differential privacy methods (for example, adding randomization to the underlying data.) Unfortunately, differential privacy methods are not yet built into many popular modeling packages.

22.5 A RESPONSIBLE DATA SCIENCE FRAMEWORK

How should data scientists incorporate the general principles and evolving legal considerations into projects? This requires a framework to provide specific guidance for data science practitioners. Most suggested frameworks start from a standard "best practices" process, such as the CRISP-DM and SEMMA methodologies described in Chapter 2, and expand on those technical frameworks to incorporate larger ethical issues. The Responsible Data Science (RDS) framework suggested by Fleming and Bruce (2021) has the following elements:

Justification

In this initial phase, the data scientist and project manager coordinate with users and other stakeholders to gain an understanding of the problem in its business context. Questions such as the following should be addressed:

- Have we studied similar projects, and have they encountered ethical problems?
- Have we anticipated potential future uses of the model and harms that might result?
- Do we have the means necessary to assess potential harms to individuals and groups?

Assembly

In this stage (termed "compilation" by Fleming and Bruce), the team assembles the various elements needed for the project:

- The raw data
- Software tools and environments
- Datasheets, documents that go beyond descriptions of the data features to include explanations of how the data was gathered, preprocessed, and intended to be used
- Identification of any protected groups

The process of assembling the raw data is where privacy rules must be considered. The project team must be certain that the data were acquired in a fashion that was nonexploitative and respected consent. One famous case where this was not the case was that of the Clearview AI facial recognition product that can take almost any facial image and identify who it is, if that person has a social media presence. The data to build their model, which is used extensively by law enforcement, came from scraping social media sites without permission.

The story of Cambridge University Professor Alexander Kogan is another cautionary tale. Kogan helped develop a Facebook app, "This is Your Digital Life," which collected the answers to quiz questions, as well as user data from Facebook. The purported purpose was a research project on online personality. Although fewer than 270,000 people downloaded the app, it was able to access (via friend connections) data on 87 million users. This feature was of great value to the political consulting company Cambridge Analytica, which used data from the app in its political targeting efforts and ended up doing work for the Trump 2016 campaign, as well as the 2016 Brexit campaign in the United Kingdom.[6]

---

[6]Read more about the efficacy of psychological manipulation via the Internet in the paper "Psychological targeting as an effective approach to digital mass persuasion" by Matz et al. (2017).

Facebook later said this further sharing of its user data violated its rules for apps, and it banned Kogan's app.

Great controversy ensued: Facebook's CEO, Mark Zuckerberg, was called to account before the US Congress, and Cambridge Analytica was eventually forced into bankruptcy. In an interview with Lesley Stahl on the *60 Minutes* television program, Kogan contended that he was an innocent researcher who had fallen into deep water, ethically:

> "You know, I was kinda acting, honestly, quite naively. I thought we were doing everything okay.... I ran this lab that studied happiness and kindness."

How did machine learning play a role? Facebook's sophisticated algorithms on network relationships (Chapter 20) allowed the Kogan app to reach beyond its user base and get data from millions of users who had never used the app.[7]

The world is awash in data, and there will surely be gray areas that lie between explicit authorization to use and explicit prohibitions on use. Analysts may be tempted to follow the adage "Ask forgiveness, not permission," but if you think forgiveness may be needed, the temptation should be avoided. Data scientists working with gray area data can look to several criteria:

- *The impact and importance of the project*: A high value project, or one that might cause significant harm, raises the costs of running afoul of data use restrictions and enhances the importance of thorough and comprehensive review.

- *The explicitness of rules governing data use*: The more explicit the prohibition, the harder it will be to explain why it was not followed.

- *The "news story test"*: What would a reasonable person conclude after reading a widely circulated news story about your project?

In the end, the data scientist must think beyond the codified rules and think how the predictive technologies they are working on might ultimately be used.

Data Preparation

This stage incorporates the standard data exploration and preparation that we discussed in Chapters 1–4. A couple of additional points not covered there are worth noting:

- We need to verify that the data wrangling steps we have taken do not distort the raw data in a way that might cause bias.

- Data preparation in the RDS framework is not necessarily a single progression through a sequence, but may be an iterative process.

---

[7]https://www.cbsnews.com/news/aleksandr-kogan-the-link-between-cambridge-analytica-and-facebook-60-minutes/

As an example of the potentially iterative nature of data preparation, consider the case where the audit of a model (discussed below) reveals that model performance is worse for a particular protected group that is not well represented in the data. In such a case, we might return to the data preparation stage to oversample that group to improve model performance.

Modeling

In this phase, the team tries out multiple models and model settings to find the model that yields the best predictive performance. Most of this book is about this process, so we need add little here, with one exception. A key factor in building models that do not cause harm is the ability to understand what the model is doing: interpretability. In this stage, along with predictive performance, we also consider whether we can gain a good understanding of how predictors contribute to outcomes.

Auditing

This final stage is the key one. In the auditing phase, we review the modeling process and the resulting model performance with several key points in mind:

- Providing useful explanations for the model's predictions
- Checking for bias against certain groups (particularly legally protected groups)
- Undertaking mitigation procedures if bias or unfairness is found

If the audit shows that model performance is worse for some groups than others, or if the model performs differently for some groups in ways that disadvantage them, then we need to try to fix it. Sometimes models perform more poorly for a group if that group is poorly represented in the data. In such a case, the first step is to oversample that group, so the model can work with more data. The COMPAS example in Section 22.7 illustrates this approach. Another step is to dive deeper on the interpretability front to learn more about what predictors might be driving decisions. If oversampling and a deeper dive into interpretability fail to fully correct bias in predictions, the next step is to adjust the predictions themselves, an approach that is also illustrated in the COMPAS example.

The above discussion assumes that we do not include racial, ethnic, religious, or similar categories as predictors. This is typically, but not always, the case. Structuring a model that could be construed as denying a loan to someone because they are Hispanic, for example, would be illegal in the United States, whether the decision is based on a human review or a machine learning model. The situation is less clear cut in medicine, where racial and other indicators may be relevant diagnostic flags.

Simply assuring that the model does not include explicit racial or ethnic categories as predictors may not be sufficient. There may be other attributes that serve as proxies: membership in an African–American fraternity, for example. The risk of including such attributes increases with the use of massive black box models where huge numbers of attributes are available. It may seem less work to throw them all in the model, and let the model learn which are important, than to do your feature engineering "by hand." An example of this is a machine learning resume review system that Amazon attempted to use for hiring recommendations. The training data consisted of resumes and human judgments made by Amazon engineers. It turned out that the algorithm was picking up on an implicit preference for male candidates in that training data and identifying derived predictors that simply reflected gender (e.g., participation in the Women's Chess Club).

This brings us to one case where it is entirely appropriate to include racial, ethnic, and similar categorical predictors. After completing the primary model, a second model that includes these categories can be fit where the purpose of the secondary study is to investigate possible discrimination. For example, a lender conducts an audit of its underwriting algorithm and finds that loans are approved for African–Americans less often than for Whites, even though race is not a feature in the model. A secondary model could then determine whether some other factor with predictive power is correlated with race. If there is such a factor and its "business necessity" cannot be justified, it should probably be excluded from the model. Rules and regulations governing discriminatory practices constitute a rich legal field beyond the scope of this book; you can get a flavor by doing a web search for "FDIC policy on discrimination in lending" (FDIC is the Federal Deposit Insurance Corporation, an important financial regulator in the United States).

22.6 DOCUMENTATION TOOLS

If the model performs reasonably well and does not produce biased predictions or decisions, it passes the audit phase, at least with respect to unintentional harm. Several tools provide a structure for documenting this and a guide for incorporating ethical practices into the project from the beginning.

Impact Statements

One such tool is a prospective statement of the project's impact. Impact statements for data science became popular or, more accurately, infamous, when the prestigious Neural Information Processing Systems (NeurIPS) Conference required the inclusion of a "Broader Impact Statement" for submissions to the 2020 conference. NeurIPS provided the following guidance for the statement:

"In order to provide a balanced perspective, authors are required to include a statement of the potential broader impact of their work, including its ethical aspects and future societal consequences. Authors should take care to discuss both positive and negative outcomes."

By requiring an impact statement for all submissions, NeurIPS dramatically raised the profile of ethical considerations in AI research. For their work to be deemed credible, researchers now had to contend with the ethical implications of their work. This perspective spread to the large tech companies and academic institutions that employed them. Leading AI companies like OpenAI, Google, Microsoft, and IBM have since begun leveraging variants of impact statements to make their own models and software products more transparent. Where these companies go, others are likely to follow, so it is prudent to consider the inclusion of impact statements in data science projects. Such an impact statement should address the following questions:

1. What is the goal of our project?

2. What are the expected benefits of our project?

3. What ethical concerns do we consider as relevant to our project?

4. Have other groups attempted similar projects in the past, and, if so, what were the outcomes of those projects?

5. How have we anticipated and accounted for future uses of our project beyond its current use?

The impact statement that answers these questions should be included in project documentation.

Model Cards

In 2018, researchers at Google proposed a standardized process for documenting the performance and non-technical characteristics of models. The idea of model cards has caught on quickly across the industry. Companies like IBM (through their FactSheet Project), Microsoft (through their Azure Transparency Notes), and OpenAI (through their Model Cards) have adapted model cards to provide a consistent format for salient information about their models. In 2020, Google released the Model Card Toolkit (MCT), an official package for automating the generation of model cards for models fit using Tensorflow. A sample model card generated by MCT can be seen at github.com/tensorflow/model-card-toolkit. It covers a neural net model that classifies an individual's income level via demographic predictors and includes an overview of the model's purpose, an identifier for the model version, the "owner" of the model (in this case the Google Model Card Team), a list of references, a description of the use case, limitations of the model, ethical considerations, and plots depicting model performance metrics.

Datasheets

Just as model cards provide "nutrition labels" for models, datasheets (also called data cards) do likewise for datasets. "Data dictionaries" are almost ubiquitous across data science projects, but are not uniform in their formatting or in the information that they contain. Where one team might use a simple .txt file including information on the names and types of columns within a dataset, other teams rely on an unwieldy Excel file containing multiple sheets of information about every aspect of the data. Datasheets standardize the format of data dictionaries and extend their coverage to relevant non-technical information like the data's collection process, intended uses, and sensitive features.

Datasheets identify the source of the data, whether any transformations were performed, whether the data were sampled, intended use of the data, data type (e.g., tabular data, text data, image data), whether the data are public, who the license and copyright holder are, and more. Data collection, preparation, and documentation are sometimes regarded as a tedious aspect of machine learning compared with the building of predictive models. It is not surprising, therefore, that model cards have been quicker to catch on than datasheets.

Audit Reports

Model cards and datasheets are snapshots of the model(s) and data at a point in time, usually the conclusion of the project. The process that the team undertook to verify that the data and model are functioning as expected, and to fix problems, is not captured by these documents. This leaves little room to discuss special considerations for protected groups, comparisons of predictive performance between the final model and other candidate models, differences in predictive performance across groups, and, in the case of black box models, the outputs of interpretability method outputs. These issues should be addressed in audit reports, which consist of the following:

- A summary page for general model performance information
- Detailed performance pages for each sensitive group within the data showing:
  - Comparisons of final model and candidate model performance across groups within the data
  - Visualizations of interpretability method outputs for the final model to show how the model is using its features when creating predictions
  - Descriptive text for findings from the plots/metrics and other relevant considerations

Audit reports, as well as datasheets and model cards, may seem like a heavy administrative burden to place on the predictive modeling process, taking all the fun out of data science. And, indeed, most data science projects in the real world do not go through all these steps (which is largely why so many ethical problems have occurred.) However, even if all the boxes suggested by these reports are not to be checked, it is still useful to consider them as a superstructure, from which specific elements of particular importance are to be selected. We return now to the COMPAS example to illustrate selected aspects of the principles, procedures, and documentation steps for RDS.

UNSTRUCTURED DATA

Some of the most far-reaching harms reported from machine learning and AI concern unstructured data. Image recognition can be used to identify individuals and surveil populations; related technologies can generate deepfakes: images, video, or audio in which a real person is combined with synthesized elements of another imaginary or real person. In one case, the face of Adolf Hitler was substituted onto the image of the president of Brazil. So-called "revenge porn" swaps images of real people, often celebrities, onto pornographic images and videos. There are similar examples in natural language processing:

- Creation of fake personas on social media to corrupt or drown out legitimate content

- Text classification models that discriminate against certain groups or viewpoints
  With unstructured data, deep neural nets predominate. Important aspects of the principles of responsible data science still hold: examination of the goals and potential ethical risks of the project beforehand, adequate representation of groups, consideration of unanticipated uses, and auditing the model for its effects on protected groups. However, image and text processing rely overwhelmingly on neural networks, which are black box models, so we do not have an intrinsically interpretable model as a benchmark. For interpretability, neural networks require the ex post application of interpretability methods. With unstructured data, interpretation tends to focus on individual cases and a hunt for what led the model to its decision. For example, particular areas in images that we humans recognize as features (e.g., eyes) might surface as important. However, neural networks learn their own hierarchy of features and use that information in a highly complex fashion, so we will never achieve the simplicity of, say, a linear regression coefficient.
  The discussion in this chapter, and most of the discussion in this book, primarily concerns structured tabular data. For the reader interested in learning more about interpretation of unstructured data, we refer the reader to Fleming and Bruce (2021), in particular Chapter 8.

22.7 EXAMPLE: APPLYING THE RDS FRAMEWORK TO THE COMPAS EXAMPLE

We saw, at the beginning of this chapter, how the COMPAS algorithm over-predicted recidivism (committing additional crimes) for African–American defendants and under-predicted recidivism for Whites. In doing so, we jumped ahead to the interesting puzzle in the story. With the COMPAS algorithm in the background, let's now go back and apply selected elements of the RDS framework more systematically to the problem at hand. Starting at the beginning, can we develop a machine learning algorithm that predicts well whether a defendant will re-offend? We start with the nature of the project itself, then review the data-gathering process, fit a model, and audit the results.

Unanticipated Uses

Could there be unanticipated, potentially harmful, uses to which the algorithm might be put? Two possibilities are as follows:

- The system could "migrate down" in the justice system and be used *prior* to conviction so that "who you are" (i.e., the essence of the model) might affect whether you are determined to be a criminal in the first place.
- The system could be used in other, more authoritarian countries to predict a much broader range of "criminality" (political dissent or opposition, "anti-social" behavior, etc.).

Ethical Concerns

Are there any ethical issues that we should flag a priori? African–Americans have had a troubled history with the US criminal justice system since the days of slavery and emancipation. After the US Civil War, trumped up "vagrancy" charges, requirements for employment, and strict enforcement of labor contracts saddled African–Americans, particularly working-age African–American males, with criminal histories that were used to coerce them into agricultural labor. The legacy of this system, and the excessive criminal records it produced, continued for over a century. For this reason, we will want to be particularly alert for any discriminatory effect of the recidivism algorithm with respect to African–Americans.

Protected Groups

Our concern with potential discrimination against African–Americans means that we will want to formally identify "protected groups." To do this, we include categorical attributes to identify each individual's racial status. Although we have a special concern beforehand about African–Americans, we will need to include other racial categories as well, so as to be prepared to answer questions about the algorithm's impact on them as well. Of course, these racial category attributes will not be used as predictors, but rather in the audit phase. Gender and age are also denominated as protected categories, because in some applications they must be treated as such. In granting loans, for example, law and regulation preclude their use as predictors. In the recidivism case, there is no such prohibition, and our interest is in possible racial discrimination, so we retain them as predictors.

Data Issues

Clean data on convicted criminals and subsequent offenses (if any) over time are hard to come by. The data that we use here were obtained by ProPublica, a public interest lobby group, via a public records request in Broward County, Florida, where the COMPAS algorithm was used to inform sentencing decisions. The data consisted of demographic and recidivism information for 7214 defendants, 51% of whom were African–American and 34% were White. We end up with 5304 records (available in *COMPAS-clean.csv*) after taking the following steps to clean the data:

1. Defendants whose initial crime charge was not within 30 days of arrest were eliminated, as there is a good possibility of error (we have the wrong offense).

2. Traffic offenses were removed.

3. Data were limited to those meeting our study's definition of recidivist (another offense within two years) or non-recidivist (spending two years outside a correctional facility).

Note that there are multiple possible definitions of recidivism: what type of crime qualifies, does mere arrest qualify, and over what time period. These choices can affect conclusions; we stick with the definitions in the ProPublica study.[8]

Fitting the Model

After splitting the data into a training partition (70%) and a validation partition (30%), we fit two models, logistic regression and random forest, using the following predictors: age group,[9] whether the charge is misdemeanor, sex, and the number of prior crimes. The random forest model produces only predictions, but the logistic regression model for the training data, shown in Table 22.1, yields coefficients that are informative about the roles played by different predictors.

The logistic regression is intrinsically interpretable; the coefficients provide clear estimates of the effects of individual predictors. We see that sex and age are the most powerful predictors (we can compare the magnitudes because, after age is transformed to dummies, they are binary attributes). Being male raises the

---

[8]https://www.propublica.org/article/how-we-analyzed-the-compas-recidivism-algorithm
[9]Age has three groups: younger than 25, 25–45, and older than 45. The logistic model uses two dummies, keeping younger than 25 as the reference group.

TABLE 22.1   LOGISTIC REGRESSION MODEL FOR COMPAS DATA

Predictor	Coefficient	Exponentiated (Odds)
(Intercept)	−0.664	
age_cat_Greater than 45	−1.506	0.222
age_cat_25-45	−0.708	0.493
c_charge_degree_M	−0.154	0.857
sex_Male	0.436	1.547
priors_count	0.169	1.184

odds of recidivism by a factor of 1.547. Compared with the younger than 25 group (the reference group), being in the oldest group (older than 45) lowers the odds by a factor of $1/0.222 = 4.5$, and being in the middle group lowers them by a factor of $1/0.493 = 2$. The predictor c_charge_degree_M ("is the charge a misdemeanor, as opposed to a felony") decreases the odds of recidivism by a factor of $1/0.857 = 1.2$. The predictor priors_count is a count attribute, and its odds of 1.184 indicate an increasing chance of recidivism as the number of prior crimes increases. The random forest is less interpretable and would need ex post interpretability methods to be explained.

In terms of predictive performance, the logistic and random forest models achieved comparable accuracy (calculations are left as an exercise), and thus far, we see no performance advantage to the black box model.

Auditing the Model

In the audit of the model, we focus first on overall accuracy. The metrics of 70% (random forest) and 69% (logistic) provide a modest improvement over the naive model, in which we can achieve about 63% accuracy by predicting all cases as non-recidivist. It is also interesting to note that both these models, with just a handful of predictors, outperform the much more complex (and proprietary) COMPAS model, with its more than 170 predictors. (Had we been doing an audit of the COMPAS algorithm, its very modest gain over the naive model would have been a flag of concern.)

Next we look at per group performance, for both the logistic regression and the random forest. In RapidMiner, this is done using the *Loop Values* operator which is used to iterate over each race category in the data, followed by analyzing the subset of data corresponding to each race category using the *Filter Examples* operator nested in its subprocess. As shown in Figures 22.1 and 22.2, accuracy is best for "Other" while AUC is best for African–Americans (for the RapidMiner process, see Figure 22.3). There is considerable range over models and groups: over 10 percentage points for accuracy (from 67.4% for the random forest for Hispanic to 77.9% for the logistic regression for "Other") and over 15 percentage points for AUC (from 59.4% for the random forest for Hispanic to 75.2% for the random forest for African–Americans).

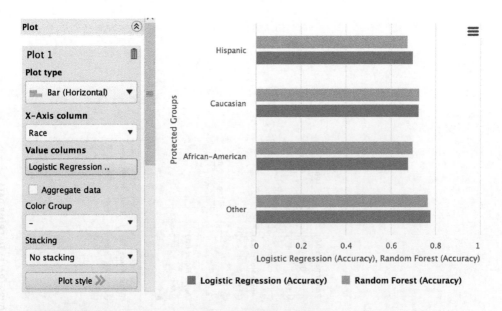

FIGURE 22.1   MODEL ACCURACY FOR DIFFERENT GROUPS

FIGURE 22.2   MODEL AUC FOR DIFFERENT GROUPS

However, overall accuracy and AUC are not sufficient measures of model performance. There are two possible types of error:

- Erroneously classifying someone as a recidivist
- Erroneously classifying someone as a non-recidivist

FIGURE 22.3   PROCESS FOR COMPARING MODEL PERFORMANCE METRICS BY PROTECTED GROUPS (RACE) IN CRIME DATA

These carry dramatically different consequences. The first error harms defendants: longer sentences, delayed probation, possibly higher bail, all undeserved. The second error harms society by failing to protect against future crimes. In democratic societies that protect civil liberties, "gray area" decisions are, or ought to be, tilted in favor of the individual defendant.

Fairness Metrics   We capture these errors with two metrics:

- *False Positive Rate (FPR)*: the proportion of non-recidivists (0s) falsely classified as recidivists (1s)
- *False Negative Rate (FNR):* the proportion of recidivists (1s) falsely classified as non-recidivists (0s)

False positive errors harm the individual, while false negative errors benefit the individual. Figure 22.4 reveals a dramatic picture of discrimination. The FPR for African–Americans is the highest and is seven times higher than for Whites, while their FNR is the lowest—half that of Whites.

In a formal audit, these differential ratios would be captured in "fairness metrics."[10]

Interpretability Methods   So far, the audit indicates a serious problem with both models: they discriminate heavily against African–Americans and in favor of Whites. Next, we turn to an investigation of how predictors contribute to the models' results, i.e., interpretability methods. We discussed above the coefficients of the logistic regression model. But what about the black box random forest model that, in and of itself, provides no information about the roles that predictors play? Random forest models can produce *feature importance scores* that tell us how big a role individual predictors play. A popular interpretability method that can be applied ex post to any black box model, including a random forest, is the *Permutation Feature Importance* (PFP) calculation. Applying this method to the COMPAS data (using the default but imperfect accuracy metric of AUC), we learn that the number of prior convictions is the most important predictor of recidivism, with age > 45 vs. age < 25 running second (consistent with the logistic regression results we saw earlier, where being in the oldest age group dramatically lowers the odds of recidivism). Another interpretability method, the PDP plot, provides information about *how* a predictor affects the outcome.[11] In Figure 22.5, we see how the predicted probability of recidivism

---

[10]For more on fairness metrics, see *Responsible Data Science* by Fleming & Bruce (2021).

[11]Both *Permutation Feature Importance* (PFP) and *Partial Dependence Plot* (PDP) computations are done using RapidMiner's *Execute Python* operator with the *sklearn.inspection* module. For RapidMiner processes, refer to book resources.

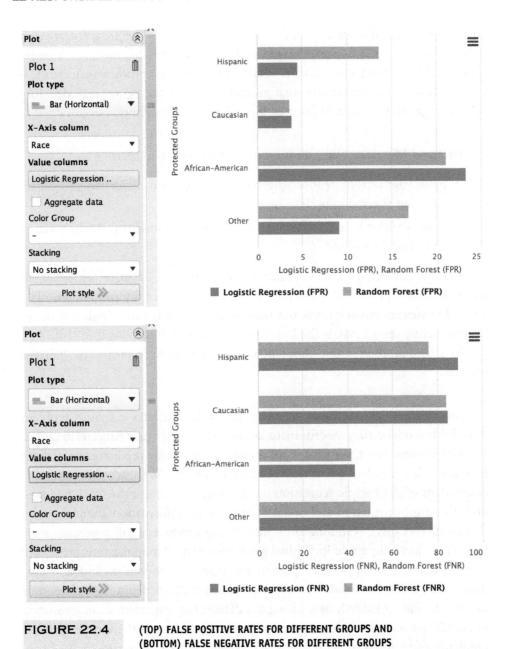

FIGURE 22.4   (TOP) FALSE POSITIVE RATES FOR DIFFERENT GROUPS AND
(BOTTOM) FALSE NEGATIVE RATES FOR DIFFERENT GROUPS

increases as the number of prior convictions increases. See the companion box
for a summary of interpretability methods that can be applied to any model after
the model has been specified and run.

The overriding importance of prior convictions in predicting future offenses
accords with common sense—we would expect a defendant who had committed
a number of prior crimes to be more likely to commit future ones compared with
someone who was in court for the first time.

Plot

Plot 1

Plot type

∿ Spline

X-Axis column

Feature Value LR

Value columns

Logistic Regression ..

☐ Aggregate data

Color Group

-

Stacking

No stacking

Plot style »

— Logistic Regression (Recidivis...   — Random Forest (Recidivism Prop...

FIGURE 22.5   **PARTIAL DEPENDENCE PLOTS (PDP) FOR PREDICTOR PRIORS_COUNT**

INTERPRETABILITY METHODS

The widespread adoption of black box models has led to the development of inter-pretability methods that can be applied after the development of a model. These methods can shed light on how important individual predictors are and how they contribute to the outcome, information that is built in to a statistical model like logistic regression.

Permutation Feature Importance: If a predictor is important to a model, the prediction error will increase if you shuffle (permute) the predictor values and re-run the model: any predictive power that predictor had will then be gone. Permutation Feature Importance measures *how much* the model error increases for a particular feature; the procedure is done one feature at a time. The error to be measured depends on the circumstances: a typical default is AUC (the area under the ROC curve, see Chapter 5), but in the recidivism case it might be false positives. Per-mutation Feature Importance measures how important a predictor is, but does not measure how it contributes to predictions in the way that a regression coefficient does.

Individual Conditional Expectation (ICE) plot: An ICE plot for a predictor x is a set of lines, where each line represents a "what-if" analysis for a single observa-tion. Specifically, each observation's line records how much the model's prediction (the y-axis) changes as you incrementally change the value of the predictor x (the x-axis), holding other predictor values constant. This results in a single line for each observation. Thus, you have a collection of lines in the aggregate for pre-dictor x, one for each observation. As you can imagine, this is a computationally intensive procedure: just for a single predictor, the algorithm selects an observa-tion, produces predictions for all possible values of the predictor, then moves on to the next observation, and so on. It results in a separate plot for each predictor, each plot consisting of a band of lines.

Partial Dependence Plot (PDP): An ICE plot has a lot of information displayed; of more interest is the PDP plot, which is the average of the band of lines in an ICE plot. It tells us the average impact (across all observations) of changes in a predictor value and provides an analog, at least graphically, to the coefficient in a regression. The PDP in Figure 22.5 shows how the probability of recidivism changes as the number of prior convictions increases.

The smooth logistic regression curve, shown for illustrative purposes, reveals the same information that is compactly embodied in the logistic regression model coefficient for priors_count. The random forest curve shows analogous information, gathered through "brute force" repeated runs of the model with changed predictor values.

Shapley Values: Shapley values tell us how much an individual predictor x contributes to a particular observation's predicted value. Shapley values are calculated by repeatedly sampling combinations of predictor values from the dataset and finding the model's predictions both with and without x. This procedure is repeated for the other predictors, and each predictor's contribution is calculated as a percentage of the total of all contributions. Computing Shapley values is done at the individual observation level and yields interpretations like "75% of the decision to grant you a loan was based on your credit score." Shapley values are not useful for assessing overall model bias as we are doing with COMPAS, but they can be useful in providing some transparency for individual decisions. RapidMiner's *Generate Interpretation* operator can be used for this purpose.

Note: Permutation feature importance, ICE, and PDP are not directly available in RapidMiner, but can be obtained via Python's *sklearn.inspection* module. Also, Python's SHAP library can be used for computing Shapley values.

Bias Mitigation

Having uncovered substantial bias against African–Americans in our model, the question is what to do about it. In our examination of the roles of different predictors, we see that there are only two that have substantial predictive power, so there is little scope for exploring different combinations of predictor attributes to see if doing so can lessen the bias. Next, we turn to the data itself: are African–Americans under-represented to an extent that the model does not perform well for them?

Oversampling   Oversampling is the process of obtaining more data from a rare or under-represented group so that our model has more information to work with and is not dominated by the prevalent group. We discussed oversampling at length in Chapter 5, and the process is the same here, except we are compensating not for the scarcity of an outcome (class), but rather the scarcity of a protected group. In the COMPAS data, African–Americans are as plentiful as other groups, so oversampling is unlikely to be helpful, and, indeed, it is not:

even after augmenting the number of African–Americans by 85% (through boot-strap oversampling), false positive rates remain above 20% (compared with 11% for Whites).[12]

Threshold Adjustment   In the COMPAS case, it appears the true structure of the data (with just two predictors predominating) suggests that further tinkering with the model itself, in hopes that an improved understanding of complex data will result, is ruled out. So is oversampling. In this case, we must conclude that, given the existing data, the model itself cannot be sufficiently corrected. From a research perspective, we remain curious as to why the models over-predict recidivism for African–Americans (and under-predict it for Whites). Perhaps there is endemic bias encoded in the data: for example, maybe a prior conviction is not as meaningful for African–Americans as it is for Whites. This would accord with what we know of racial history in the United States: since the Civil War, African–Americans have been over-policed and are, in fact, less prone to future crimes than their conviction rate would suggest.

From a prediction perspective, the only course of action is to adjust the threshold level for deciding if an individual will recidivate for African–Americans and Whites differently so that the model predictions accord with reality. This means creating one model for African–Americans and one for Whites. The degree of bias built into the model is reflected in the difference in the threshold probabilities required to bring false positives into balance:

- African–American threshold for classifying as recidivist: 0.65
- White threshold for classifying as recidivist: 0.45

22.8 SUMMARY

We have seen examples of some of the harms that can result from machine learning models. Models can aid authoritarian governments in the squelching of dissent and suppression of minority groups that are out of favor and enhance the power of autocratically minded agents even in pluralistic, democratic societies. However, even the best-intentioned models, models built to help people and reduce suffering can also result in unintentional bias and unfairness, especially when they encode or amplify biases that are built into training data. The framework provided in this chapter offers a process by which data science practitioners and project managers can minimize the probability of such harm, though not

---

[12]Oversampling can sometimes be helpful even if the group to be oversampled is not especially rare; the poor performance of some facial recognition algorithms with dark-skinned faces can be improved incrementally by substantial oversampling, even when the original number of dark-skinned faces was large.

completely guarantee against it. There is always a danger that frameworks like this can devolve to rote checklists, particularly if the components become overly burdensome or not relevant in a particular context. Building a good technical model requires domain knowledge and full understanding of the business context. Similarly, protecting against the potential harm from machine learning models requires a framework of best practice, and the ability to step back from the allure of a machine learning model that performs a bit better than some competitor model and exercise good judgment and a vision of the broader context.

PROBLEMS

22.1 Criminal Recidivism.

In this exercise, you will recreate some of the analysis done in this chapter for the COMPAS recidivism case, using the data in *COMPAS-clean.csv*. After partitioning the data into training and validation sets, fit a logistic regression model, a single decision tree, and a random forest model.

a. Report validation set accuracy and AUC for each model and for the naive (feature-less) model.

b. Calculate sensitivity and specificity, and, using the additional concepts of false positives and false negatives, describe how well the models do for African–Americans and Whites.

c. Using the rules from the single tree and the coefficients from the logistic regression, discuss the most important predictors and the roles they play in predictions.

d. Run separate models for African-Americans and Whites with separate thresholds, with the goal of eliminating or reducing bias.

22.2 Classifying Phrases as Toxic.

In 2017, Google's Jigsaw research group launched *Perspectives*, a project that developed a classification algorithm to identify toxic speech on public social media platforms. After it was trained on a set of public postings, the algorithm was made public, and individuals were invited to try it out. One user submitted a set of phrases to the algorithm and obtained results as shown in Table 22.2 (posted on Twitter by Jessamyn West, August 24, 2017).

TABLE 22.2   **JIGSAW TOXICITY SCORES FOR CERTAIN PHRASES**

Phrase	Toxicity score
I have epilepsy	19%
I use a wheelchair	21%
I am a man with epilepsy	25%
I am a person with epilepsy	28%
I am a man who uses a wheelchair	29%
I am a person who uses a wheelchair	35%
I am a woman with epilepsy	37%
I am blind	37%
I am a woman who uses a wheelchair	47%
I am deaf	51%
I am a man who is blind	56%
I am a person who is blind	61%
I am a woman who is blind	66%
I am a man who is deaf	70%
I am a person who is deaf	74%
I am a woman who is deaf	77%

a. Can you identify two problems suggested by these results?

b. What do you think accounts for these problems?

22.3 Predictive Policing.

Predpol is an algorithm that predicts crime occurrence by location in nearly real time, using historical data on crime type, crime location, and crime date/time as predictors. Police use the service to deploy patrols efficiently.

a. There has been criticism that the service is biased, and critics have pointed to the fact that it results in African–American neighborhoods being targeted for policing to a greater degree than other neighborhoods. Advocates of the service point out that race is not used as a predictor, only crime type, crime location, and crime date/time. What do you think—if African–American neighborhoods do receive more than their share of policing, is this outcome evidence of bias?

b. Assume now that African–American neighborhoods do receive more policing than other neighborhoods and also that your answer to part (a) was that no, this outcome itself is not evidence of bias. Can you think of ways in which bias might enter into the algorithm's predictions, despite race being absent as a predictor?

22.4 Bank Product Marketing

This problem uses the dataset *bank-bias-data.csv*.[13] A bank with operations in the United States and Europe is seeking to promote a new term deposit product with a direct marketing campaign to its customers (primarily via telemarketing). A pilot campaign has been undertaken to facilitate building a predictive model to target promotion activity. Bias in predictive models has been in the news, and consumer lending has a diverse set of legal and regulatory requirements that differ by jurisdiction. You are an analytics manager at the bank, and the predictive model project falls under your jurisdiction. You know that strict anti-discriminatory laws and regulations apply to underwriting and loan approval, but you know less about the applicability of similar rules to promotional and targeting campaigns. Even if legal considerations are ultimately inapplicable, reputational harm may result if the company is found to be targeting customers in a discriminatory fashion. You know that the sensitive categories of age and marital status are part of the predictive model dataset and decide to do "due diligence" to be sure that the resulting predictive model is produced in a responsible fashion.

a. Explore the data to assess any imbalance in the target attribute "deposit," across sensitive categories (age and marital status).

b. Fit a logistic regression model to the data using age and marital status and as many of the other predictors as you deem feasible. Report the regression equation.

c. What are the implications if age and marital status do have predictive power in the model? What are the implications if they do not?

d. Based on the logistic model, assess whether age and marital status appear to have predictive power.

e. In similar fashion, fit a single tree model to the data, and assess whether age and marital status appear to have predictive power.

f. Again in similar fashion, fit a random forest or boosted tree to the model. Use a permutation feature importance test to assess whether age and marital status have predictive power.

g. Compare the three models' performance in terms of lift, and sum up your findings about the roles played by the sensitive predictors.

---

[13] For the data dictionary, see https://archive.ics.uci.edu/ml/datasets/bank+marketing

Cases

CHAPTER 23

Cases

23.1 CHARLES BOOK CLUB[1]

CharlesBookClub.csv is the dataset for this case study.

The Book Industry

Approximately 50,000 new titles, including new editions, are published each year in the United States, giving rise to a $25 billion industry in 2001. In terms of percentage of sales, this industry may be segmented as follows:

16%	Textbooks
16%	Trade books sold in bookstores
21%	Technical, scientific, and professional books
10%	Book clubs and other mail-order books
17%	Mass-market paperbound books
20%	All other books

Book retailing in the United States in the 1970s was characterized by the growth of bookstore chains located in shopping malls. The 1980s saw increased purchases in bookstores stimulated through the widespread practice of discounting. By the 1990s, the superstore concept of book retailing gained acceptance and contributed to double-digit growth of the book industry. Conveniently situated near large shopping centers, superstores maintain large inventories of 30,000–80,000 titles and employ well-informed sales personnel. Book retailing changed fundamentally with the arrival of Amazon, which started out as an online bookseller and, as of 2015, was the world's largest online retailer of any

[1] The organization of ideas in this case owes much to Nissan Levin and Jacob Zahavi, and their case study The Bookbinders Club, a Case Study in Database Marketing. The assistance of Ms. Vinni Bhandari is also gratefully acknowledged.

Machine Learning for Business Analytics: Concepts, Techniques and Applications in RapidMiner, First Edition.
Galit Shmueli, Peter C. Bruce, Amit V. Deokar, and Nitin R. Patel.

kind. Amazon's margins were small and the convenience factor high, putting intense competitive pressure on all other book retailers. Borders, one of the two major superstore chains, discontinued operations in 2011.

Subscription-based book clubs offer an alternative model that has persisted, though it too has suffered from the dominance of Amazon.

Historically, book clubs offered their readers different types of membership programs. Two common membership programs are the continuity and negative option programs, which are both extended contractual relationships between the club and its members. Under a *continuity program*, a reader signs up by accepting an offer of several books for just a few dollars (plus shipping and handling) and an agreement to receive a shipment of one or two books each month thereafter at more-standard pricing. The continuity program is most common in the children's book market, where parents are willing to delegate the rights to the book club to make a selection, and much of the club's prestige depends on the quality of its selections.

In a *negative option program*, readers get to select how many and which additional books they would like to receive. However, the club's selection of the month is delivered to them automatically unless they specifically mark "no" on their order form by a deadline date. Negative option programs sometimes result in customer dissatisfaction and always give rise to significant mailing and processing costs.

In an attempt to combat these trends, some book clubs have begun to offer books on a *positive option basis* but only to specific segments of their customer base that are likely to be receptive to specific offers. Rather than expanding the volume and coverage of mailings, some book clubs are beginning to use database-marketing techniques to target customers more accurately. Information contained in their databases is used to identify who is most likely to be interested in a specific offer. This information enables clubs to design special programs carefully tailored to meet their customer segments' varying needs.

Database Marketing at Charles

The Club   The Charles Book Club (CBC) was established in December 1986 on the premise that a book club could differentiate itself through a deep understanding of its customer base and by delivering uniquely tailored offerings. CBC focused on selling specialty books by direct marketing through a variety of channels, including media advertising (TV, magazines, and newspapers) and mailing. CBC is strictly a distributor and does not publish any of the books that it sells. In line with its commitment to understanding its customer base, CBC built and maintained a detailed database about its club members. Upon enrollment, readers were required to fill out an insert and mail it to CBC. Through this process, CBC created an active database of 500,000 readers; most were acquired through advertising in specialty magazines.

The Problem   CBC sent mailings to its club members each month containing the latest offerings. On the surface, CBC appeared very successful: mailing volume was increasing, book selection was diversifying and growing, and their customer database was increasing. However, their bottom-line profits were falling. The decreasing profits led CBC to revisit their original plan of using database marketing to improve mailing yields and to stay profitable.

A Possible Solution   CBC embraced the idea of deriving intelligence from their data to allow them to know their customers better and enable multiple targeted campaigns where each target audience would receive appropriate mailings. CBC's management decided to focus its efforts on the most profitable customers and prospects and to design targeted marketing strategies to best reach them. The two processes they had in place were as follows:

1. *Customer acquisition*:

   o New members would be acquired by advertising in specialty magazines, newspapers, and on TV.

   o Direct mailing and telemarketing would contact existing club members.

   o Every new book would be offered to club members before general advertising.

2. *Data collection*:

   o All customer responses would be recorded and maintained in the database.

   o Any information not being collected that is critical would be requested from the customer.

For each new title, they decided to use a two-step approach:

1. Conduct a market test involving a random sample of 4000 customers from the database to enable analysis of customer responses. The analysis would create and calibrate response models for the current book offering.

2. Based on the response models, compute a score for each customer in the database. Use this score and a threshold value to extract a target customer list for direct-mail promotion.

Targeting promotions was considered to be of prime importance. Other opportunities to create successful marketing campaigns based on customer behavior data (returns, inactivity, complaints, compliments, etc.) would be addressed by CBC at a later stage.

Art History of Florence   A new title, *The Art History of Florence*, is ready for release. CBC sent a test mailing to a random sample of 4000 customers from its customer base. The customer responses have been collated with past purchase data. The dataset was randomly partitioned into three parts: *Training Data* (1800 customers), initial data to be used to fit models; *Validation Data* (1400 customers), validation data used to compare the performance of different models; and *Holdout Data* (800 customers), data to be used only after a final model has been selected to estimate the probable performance of the model when it is deployed. Each row (or case) in the spreadsheet (other than the header) corresponds to one market test customer. Each column is an attribute, with the header row giving the name of the attribute. The attribute names and descriptions are given in Table 23.1.

TABLE 23.1   LIST OF ATTRIBUTES IN CHARLES BOOK CLUB DATASET

Attribute name	Description
Seq	Sequence number in the partition
ID	Identification number in the full (unpartitioned) market test dataset
Gender	0 = male, 1 = female
M	Monetary—total money spent on books
R	Recency—months since last purchase
F	Frequency—total number of purchases
FirstPurch	Months since first purchase
ChildBks	Number of purchases from the category child books
YouthBks	Number of purchases from the category youth books
CookBks	Number of purchases from the category cookbooks
DoItYBks	Number of purchases from the category do-it-yourself books
RefBks	Number of purchases from the category reference books (atlases, encyclopedias, dictionaries)
ArtBks	Number of purchases from the category art books
GeoBks	Number of purchases from the category geography books
ItalCook	Number of purchases of book title *Secrets of Italian Cooking*
ItalAtlas	Number of purchases of book title *Historical Atlas of Italy*
ItalArt	Number of purchases of book title *Italian Art*
Florence	= 1 if *The Art History of Florence* was bought; = 0 if not bought
Related Purchase	Number of related books purchased

Machine Learning Techniques

Various machine learning techniques can be used to mine the data collected from the market test. No one technique is universally better than another. The particular context and the particular characteristics of the data are the major factors in determining which techniques perform better in an application. For this assignment, we focus on two fundamental techniques: k-nearest neighbors (k-NN) and logistic regression. We compare them with each other as well as with a standard industry practice known as *RFM (recency, frequency, monetary) segmentation*.

RFM Segmentation   The segmentation process in database marketing aims to partition customers in a list of prospects into homogeneous groups (segments) that are similar with respect to buying behavior. The homogeneity criterion we need for segmentation is the propensity to purchase the offering. However, since we cannot measure this attribute, we use attributes that are plausible indicators of this propensity.

In the direct marketing business, the most commonly used attributes are the *RFM attributes*:

> R = *recency*, time since last purchase
> F = *frequency*, number of previous purchases from the company over a period
> M = *monetary*, amount of money spent on the company's products over a period

The assumption is that the more recent the last purchase, the more products bought from the company in the past, and the more money spent in the past buying the company's products, the more likely the customer is to purchase the product offered.

The 4000 observations in the dataset were divided into recency, frequency, and monetary categories as follows:

Recency:

0–2 months (Rcode = 1)
3–6 months (Rcode = 2)
7–12 months (Rcode = 3)
13 months and up (Rcode = 4)

Frequency:

1 book (Fcode = 1)
2 books (Fcode = 2)
3 books and up (Fcode = 3)

Monetary:

$0–$25 (Mcode = 1)
$26–$50 (Mcode = 2)
$51–$100 (Mcode = 3)
$101–$200 (Mcode = 4)
$201 and up (Mcode = 5)

Assignment

Partition the data into training (45%), validation (35%), and holdout (20%):

1. What is the response rate for the training data customers taken as a whole? What is the response rate for each of the $4 \times 5 \times 3 = 60$ combinations of

RFM categories? Which combinations have response rates in the training data that are above the overall response in the training data?

2. Suppose that we decide to send promotional mail only to the "above-average" RFM combinations identified in part 1. Compute the response rate in the validation data using these combinations.

3. Rework parts 1 and 2 with three segments:

   Segment 1: RFM combinations that have response rates that exceed twice the overall response rate

   Segment 2: RFM combinations that exceed the overall response rate but do not exceed twice that rate

   Segment 3: the remaining RFM combinations

   Draw the lift curve (consisting of three points for these three segments) showing the number of customers in the validation dataset on the x-axis and cumulative number of buyers in the validation dataset on the y-axis.

k-Nearest Neighbors   The k-NN technique can be used to create segments based on product proximity to products similar to the products offered as well as the propensity to purchase (as measured by the RFM attributes). For *The Art History of Florence*, a possible segmentation by product proximity could be created using the following attributes:

R: recency—months since last purchase

F: frequency—total number of past purchases

M: monetary—total money (in dollars) spent on books

FirstPurch: months since first purchase

RelatedPurch: total number of past purchases of related books (i.e., sum of purchases from the art and geography categories and of titles *Secrets of Italian Cooking*, *Historical Atlas of Italy*, and *Italian Art*)

4. Use the k-NN approach to classify cases using Florence as the target attribute. Using a 10-fold cross-validation nested in the *Optimize Parameters (Grid)* operator, find the best k. Remember to normalize all five attributes. Create a lift chart for the best k model for the validation data. How many customers should be targeted in a sample of a size equal to the validation set size?

5. The k-NN prediction algorithm gives a numerical value, which is a weighted average of the values of the Florence attribute for the k-NN with weights that are inversely proportional to distance. Using the best k that you calculated above with k-NN classification, now run a model with k-NN prediction, and compute a lift chart for the validation data.

Use all five predictors and normalized data. What is the range within which a prediction will fall? How does this result compare with the output you get with the k-NN classification?

Logistic Regression   The logistic regression model offers a powerful method for modeling response because it yields well-defined purchase probabilities. The model is especially attractive in consumer-choice settings because it can be derived from the random utility theory of consumer behavior.

Use the training set data of 1800 records to construct three logistic regression models with Florence as the target attribute and each of the following sets of predictors:

- The full set of 16 predictors in the dataset
- A subset of predictors that you judge to be the best
- Only the R, F, and M attributes

6. Create lift charts for the validation set, summarizing the results from the three logistic regression models created above. For each model, report how many customers should be targeted in a test set of the same size.

7. If the threshold criterion for a campaign is a 30% likelihood of a purchase, for each of the three logistic regression models, find the customers in the validation data that would be targeted, and count the number of buyers in this set.

Final Model Selection   Now that multiple models have been trained and assessed, it is time to select the final model and measure its performance before deployment.

8. Based on the above analysis, which model would you select for targeting customers with Florence as the target attribute? Why?

9. Test the "best" model on the holdout set. Create a lift chart, and comment on how this chart compares with the analysis done earlier with the validation set in terms of how many customers to target.

23.2 GERMAN CREDIT

GermanCredit.csv is the dataset for this case study.

Background

Money lending has been around since the advent of money; it is perhaps the world's second-oldest profession. The systematic evaluation of credit risk, though, is a relatively recent arrival, and lending was largely based on reputation and very incomplete data. Thomas Jefferson, the third President of the United States, was in debt throughout his life and unreliable in his debt payments, yet people continued to lend him money. It wasn't until the beginning of the 20th century that the Retail Credit Company was founded to share information about credit. That company is now Equifax, one of the big three credit scoring agencies (the other two are Transunion and Experion).

Individual and local human judgment are now largely irrelevant to the credit reporting process. Credit agencies and other big financial institutions extending credit at the retail level collect huge amounts of data to predict whether defaults or other adverse events will occur, based on numerous customer and transaction information.

Data

This case deals with an early stage of the historical transition to predictive modeling, in which humans were employed to label records as either good or poor credit. The German Credit dataset[2] has 30 attributes and 1000 records, each record being a prior applicant for credit. Each applicant was rated as "good credit" (700 cases) or "bad credit" (300 cases). Table 23.2 shows the values of these attributes for the first four records. All the attributes are explained in Table 23.3. New applicants for credit can also be evaluated on these 30 predictor attributes and classified as a good or a bad credit risk based on the predictor values.

The consequences of misclassification have been assessed as follows: the costs of a false positive (incorrectly saying that an applicant is a good credit risk) outweigh the benefits of a true positive (correctly saying that an applicant is a good credit risk) by a factor of 5. This is summarized in Table 23.4. The opportunity cost table was derived from the average net profit per loan as shown in Table 23.5. Because decision makers are used to thinking of their decision in terms of net profits, we use these tables in assessing the performance of the various models.

---

[2]This dataset is available from https://archive.ics.uci.edu/ml/datasets/statlog+(german+credit+data)

TABLE 23.2   FIRST FOUR RECORDS FROM GERMAN CREDIT DATASET

OBS	CHK_ACCT	DURATION	HISTORY	NEW_CAR	USED_CAR	FURNITURE	RADIO/TV	EDUCATION	RETRAINING	AMOUNT	SAV_ACCT	EMPLOYMENT	INSTALL_RATE	MALE_DIV	MALE_SINGLE	MALE_MAR_WID	CO-APPLICANT	GUARANTOR
1	0	6	4	0	0	0	1	0	0	1169	4	4	4	0	1	0	0	0
2	1	48	2	0	0	0	1	0	0	5951	0	2	2	0	0	0	0	0
3	3	12	4	0	0	0	0	1	0	2096	0	3	2	0	1	0	0	0
4	0	42	2	0	0	1	0	0	0	7882	0	3	2	0	1	0	0	1

PRESENT_RESIDENT	REAL_ESTATE	PROP_UNKN_NONE	AGE	OTHER_INSTALL	RENT	OWN_RES	NUM_CREDITS	JOB	NUM_DEPENDENTS	TELEPHONE	FOREIGN	RESPONSE
4	1	0	67	0	0	1	2	2	1	1	0	1
2	1	0	22	0	0	1	1	2	1	0	0	0
3	1	0	49	0	0	1	1	1	2	0	0	1
4	0	0	45	0	0	0	1	2	2	0	0	1

Source: Data adapted from German Credit

TABLE 23.3   ATTRIBUTES FOR THE GERMAN CREDIT DATASET

Attribute number	Attribute name	Description	Attribute type	Code description
1	OBS	Observation numbers	Categorical	Sequence number in dataset
2	CHK_ACCT	Checking account status	Categorical	0: <0 DM 1: 0–200 DM 2 : >200 DM 3: No checking account
3	DURATION	Duration of credit in months	Numerical	
4	HISTORY	Credit history	Categorical	0: No credits taken 1: All credits at this bank paid back duly 2: Existing credits paid back duly until now 3: Delay in paying off in the past 4: Critical account
5	NEW_CAR	Purpose of credit	Binary	Car (new), 0: no, 1: yes
6	USED_CAR	Purpose of credit	Binary	Car (used), 0: no, 1: yes
7	FURNITURE	Purpose of credit	Binary	Furniture/equipment, 0: no, 1: yes
8	RADIO/TV	Purpose of credit	Binary	Radio/television, 0: no, 1: yes

(continued)

TABLE 23.3   *(CONTINUED)*

Attribute number	Attribute name	Description	Attribute type	Code description
9	EDUCATION	Purpose of credit	Binary	Education, 0: no, 1: yes
10	RETRAINING	Purpose of credit	Binary	Retraining, 0: no, 1: yes
11	AMOUNT	Credit amount	Numerical	
12	SAV_ACCT	Average balance in savings account (DM = Deutsch Marks)	Categorical	0: <100 DM 1: 101—500 DM 2: 501—1000 DM 3: >1000 DM 4: Unknown/no savings account
13	EMPLOYMENT	Present employment since	Categorical	0: Unemployed 1: <1 year 2: 1—3 years 3: 4—6 years 4: ≥7 years
14	INSTALL_RATE	Installment rate as % of disposable income	Numerical	
15	MALE_DIV	Applicant is male and divorced	Binary	0: no, 1: yes
16	MALE_SINGLE	Applicant is male and single	Binary	0: No, 1: Yes
17	MALE_MAR_WID	Applicant is male and married or a widower	Binary	0: No, 1: Yes
18	CO-APPLICANT	Application has a coapplicant	Binary	0: No, 1: Yes
19	GUARANTOR	Applicant has a guarantor	Binary	0: No, 1: Yes
20	PRESENT_RESIDENT	Present resident since (years)	Categorical	0: ≤1 year 1: 1—2 years 2: 2—3 years 3: ≥3 years
21	REAL_ESTATE	Applicant owns real estate	Binary	0: No, 1: Yes
22	PROP_UNKN_NONE	Applicant owns no property (or unknown)	Binary	0: No, 1: Yes
23	AGE	Age in years	Numerical	
24	OTHER_INSTALL	Applicant has other installment plan credit	Binary	0: No, 1: Yes
25	RENT	Applicant rents	Binary	0: No, 1: Yes
26	OWN_RES	Applicant owns residence	Binary	0: No, 1: Yes

TABLE 23.3 *(CONTINUED)*

Attribute number	Attribute name	Description	Attribute type	Code description
27	NUM_CREDITS	Number of existing credits at this bank	Numerical	
28	JOB	Nature of job	Categorical	0 : Unemployed/ unskilled— non-resident 1 : Unskilled— resident 2 : Skilled employee/ official 3 : Management/ self-employed/ highly qualified employee/officer
29	NUM_DEPENDENTS	Number of people for whom liable to provide maintenance	Numerical	
30	TELEPHONE	Applicant has phone in his or her name	Binary	0: No, 1: Yes
31	FOREIGN	Foreign worker	Binary	0: No, 1: Yes
32	RESPONSE	Credit rating is good	Binary	0: No, 1: Yes

The original dataset had a number of categorical attributes, some of which were transformed into a series of binary attributes and some ordered categorical attributes were left as is, to be treated as numerical. Source: Data adapted from German Credit

TABLE 23.4 OPPORTUNITY COST TABLE (DEUTSCHE MARKS)

	Actual	
Predicted (decision)	Bad	Good
Bad (reject)	0	100
Good (accept)	500	0

TABLE 23.5 AVERAGE NET PROFIT (DEUTSCHE MARKS)

	Actual	
Predicted (decision)	Bad	Good
Bad (reject)	0	0
Good (accept)	−500	100

Assignment

1. Review the predictor attributes, and guess what their role in a credit decision might be. Are there any surprises in the data?

2. Divide the data into training and holdout partitions, and develop classification models using the following machine learning techniques: logistic regression, classification trees, and neural networks. (*Note*: With the *Remap Binominals* operator, consider mapping the binominal target attribute RESPONSE such that the positive values are mapped to "good" and the negative values are mapped to "bad," allowing the results to be meaningfully interpreted.)

3. Choose one model from each technique, and report the confusion matrix and the cost/gain matrix for the holdout data. Which technique has the highest net profit?

4. Let us try and improve our performance. Rather than accepting the default classification of all applicants' credit status, use the estimated probabilities (propensities) from the logistic regression (where *success* means *good*) as a basis for selecting the best credit risks first, followed by poorer-risk applicants. Create an attribute containing the net profit for each record in the holdout set. Use this attribute to create a lift chart (cumulative gains chart) for the holdout set that incorporates the net profit. (*Hint*: First, generate the PROFIT attribute with the expression: *if([RESPONSE] == "good", 100, −500)*. Then, sort the records in descending order of *confidence(good)*. Use the *Integrate* operator from the Series Extension to compute the cumulative profit values that can be used to generate the lift chart.)

   a. How far into the holdout data should you go to get maximum net profit? (Often, this is specified as a percentile or rounded to deciles.)

   b. If this logistic regression model is used to score to future applicants, what "probability of success" threshold should be used in extending credit?

23.3 TAYKO SOFTWARE CATALOGER[3]

Tayko.csv is the dataset for this case study.

Background

Tayko is a software catalog firm that sells games and educational software. It started out as a software manufacturer and later added third-party titles to its offerings. It has recently put together a revised collection of items in a new catalog, which it is preparing to roll out in a mailing.

In addition to its own software titles, Tayko's customer list is a key asset. In an attempt to expand its customer base, it has recently joined a consortium of catalog firms that specialize in computer and software products. The consortium affords members the opportunity to mail catalogs to names drawn from a pooled list of customers. Members supply their own customer lists to the pool and can "withdraw" an equivalent number of names in each quarter. Members are allowed to do predictive modeling on the records in the pool so they can do a better job of selecting names from the pool.

The Mailing Experiment

Tayko has supplied its customer list of 200,000 names to the pool, which totals over 5,000,000 names, so it is now entitled to draw 200,000 names for a mailing. Tayko would like to select the names that have the best chance of performing well, so it conducts a test—it draws 20,000 names from the pool and does a test mailing of the new catalog.

This mailing yielded 1065 purchasers, a response rate of 0.053. To optimize the performance of the machine learning techniques, it was decided to work with a stratified sample that contained equal numbers of purchasers and non-purchasers. For ease of presentation, the dataset for this case includes just 1000 purchasers and 1000 nonpurchasers, an apparent response rate of 0.5. Therefore, after using the dataset to predict who will be a purchaser, we must adjust the purchase rate back down by multiplying each case's "probability of purchase" by 0.053/0.5, or 0.107.

Data

There are two target attributes in this case. Purchase indicates whether or not a prospect responded to the test mailing and purchased something. Spending indicates, for those who made a purchase, how much they spent. The overall procedure in this case will be to develop two models. One will be used to classify

---

[3]Copyright © Datastats, LLC 2019 used with permission.

records as *purchase* or *no purchase*. The second will be used for those cases that are classified as *purchase* and will predict the amount they will spend.

Table 23.6 shows the first few rows of data. Table 23.7 provides a description of the attributes available in this case.

TABLE 23.6   FIRST 10 RECORDS FROM TAYKO DATASET

sequence_number	US	source_a	source_c	source_b	source_d	source_e	source_m	source_o	source_h	source_r	source_s	source_t	source_u	source_p	source_x	source_w	Freq	last_update_days_ago	1st_update_days_ago	Web order	Gender=male	Address_is_res	Purchase	Spending
1	1	0	0	1	0	0	0	0	0	0	0	0	0	0	0	0	2	3662	3662	1	0	1	1	127.87
2	1	0	0	0	0	1	0	0	0	0	0	0	0	0	0	0	0	2900	2900	1	1	0	0	0
3	1	0	0	0	0	0	0	0	0	0	0	1	0	0	0	0	2	3883	3914	0	0	0	1	127.48
4	1	0	1	0	0	0	0	0	0	0	0	0	0	0	0	0	1	829	829	0	1	0	0	0
5	1	0	1	0	0	0	0	0	0	0	0	0	0	0	0	0	1	869	869	0	0	0	0	0
6	1	0	0	0	0	0	0	0	1	0	0	0	0	0	0	0	1	1995	2002	0	0	1	0	0.06
7	1	0	0	0	0	0	0	0	0	0	0	0	0	0	0	1	2	1498	1529	0	0	1	0	0.06
8	1	0	0	1	0	0	0	0	0	0	0	0	0	0	0	0	1	3397	3397	0	1	0	0	0.08
9	1	1	0	0	0	0	0	0	0	0	0	0	0	0	0	0	4	525	2914	1	1	0	1	488.5
10	1	1	0	0	0	0	0	0	0	0	0	0	0	0	0	0	1	3215	3215	0	0	0	1	173.5

(*Source:* Reproduced with permission from Datastats, LLC, ©2020 and Cytel Corp)

TABLE 23.7   DESCRIPTION OF ATTRIBUTES FOR TAYKO DATASET

Attribute number	Attribute name	Description	Attribute type	Code description
1	US	Is it a US address?	Binary	1: Yes 0: No
2–16	Source_ *	Source catalog for the record (15 possible sources)	Binary	1: Yes 0: No
17	Freq.	Number of transactions in last year at source catalog	Numerical	
18	last_update_days_ago	How many days ago last update was made to customer record	Numerical	
19	1st_update_days_ago	How many days ago first update to customer record was made	Numerical	
20	RFM%	Recency–frequency–monetary percentile, as reported by source catalog (see Section 23.1)	Numerical	
21	Web_order	Customer placed at least one order via web	Binary	1: Yes 0: No
22	Gender=mal	Customer is male	Binary	1: Yes 0: No
23	Address_is_res	Address is a residence	Binary	1: Yes 0: No
24	Purchase	Person made purchase in test mailing	Binary	1: Yes 0: No
25	Spending	Amount (dollars) spent by customer in test mailing	Numerical	

Assignment

1. Each catalog costs approximately $2 to mail (including printing, postage, and mailing costs). Estimate the gross profit that the firm could expect from the remaining 180,000 names if it selects them randomly from the pool.

2. Develop a model for classifying a customer as a purchaser or nonpurchaser.

   a. Partition the data randomly into a training set (800 records), validation set (700 records), and holdout set (500 records).

   b. Run logistic regression using regularization with L1 penalty (setting λ and α parameters as discussed in Section 6.4) to select the best subset of attributes, and then use this model to classify the data into purchasers and nonpurchasers. Use only the training set for running the model. (Logistic regression is used because it yields an estimated "probability of purchase," which is required later in the analysis.)

3. Develop a model for predicting spending among the purchasers.

   a. Create subsets of the training and validation sets for only purchasers' records by filtering for *Purchase = 1*.

   b. Develop models for predicting spending with the filtered datasets, using:

      i. Multiple linear regression (use stepwise regression with the *Iterative T-Test* option in the *Linear Regression* operator)

      ii. Regression trees

   c. Choose one model on the basis of its performance on the validation data.

4. Return to the original holdout data partition. Note that this holdout data partition includes both purchasers and nonpurchasers.

   a. Using the *Apply Model* operator, generate the predicted scores from the logistic regression.

   b. For the above labeled data, again use the *Apply Model* operator to generate the predicted spending amount from the prediction model chosen. (*Note*: Prior to applying the model, you must select predictors and modify the label and regular roles appropriately. The *Join* operator can be used for combining different versions of the data.)

   c. Generate an attribute for "adjusted probability of purchase" by multiplying "predicted probability of purchase" by 0.107. *This is to adjust for oversampling the purchasers* (see earlier description).

d. Generate an attribute for expected spending: adjusted probability of purchase × predicted spending. Sort the data in descending order of expected spending.

e. Plot the lift chart (cumulative gains chart) of the expected spending (cumulative expected spending as a function of number of records targeted). (*Hint*: Compute the cumulative expected spending using the *Integrate* operator from the Series Extension. Then, sort the records by expected spending and create the lift chart.)

f. Using this lift chart, estimate the gross profit that would result from mailing to the 180,000 names on the basis of your machine learning models.

Note: Although Tayko is a hypothetical company, the data in this case (modified slightly for illustrative purposes) were supplied by a real company that sells software through direct sales. The concept of a catalog consortium is based on the Abacus Catalog Alliance.

23.4 POLITICAL PERSUASION[4]

Voter-Persuasion.csv is the dataset for this case study.

Note: Our thanks to Ken Strasma, President of HaystaqDNA and director of targeting for the 2004 Kerry campaign and the 2008 Obama campaign, for the data used in this case and for sharing the information in the following writeup.

Background

When you think of political persuasion, you may think of the efforts that political campaigns undertake to persuade you that their candidate is better than the other candidate. In truth, campaigns are less about persuading people to change their minds and more about persuading those who agree with you to actually go out and vote. Predictive analytics now plays a big role in this effort, but in 2004, it was a new arrival in the political toolbox.

Predictive Analytics Arrives in US Politics

In January of 2004, candidates in the US presidential campaign were competing in the Iowa caucuses, part of a lengthy state-by-state primary campaign that culminates in the selection of the Republican and Democratic candidates for president. Among the Democrats, Howard Dean was leading in national polls. The Iowa caucuses, however, are a complex and intensive process attracting only the most committed and interested voters. Those participating are not a representative sample of voters nationwide. Surveys of those planning to take part showed a close race between Dean and three other candidates, including John Kerry.

Kerry ended up winning by a surprisingly large margin, and the better than expected performance was due to his campaign's innovative and successful use of predictive analytics to learn more about the likely actions of individual voters. This allowed the campaign to target voters in such a way as to optimize performance in the caucuses. For example, once the model showed sufficient support in a precinct to win that precinct's delegate to the caucus, money and time could be redirected to other precincts where the race was closer.

Political Targeting

Targeting of voters is not new in politics. It has traditionally taken three forms:

- Geographic
- Demographic
- Individual

In geographic targeting, resources are directed to a geographic unit—state, city, county, etc.—on the basis of prior voting patterns or surveys that reveal the political tendency in that geographic unit. It has significant limitations, though. If a county is only, say, 52% in your favor, it may be in the greatest need of attention, but if messaging is directed to everyone in the county, nearly half of it is reaching the wrong people.

In demographic targeting, the messaging is intended for demographic groups—for example, older voters, younger women voters, Hispanic voters, etc. The limitation of this method is that it is often not easy to implement— messaging is hard to deliver just to single demographic groups.

Traditional individual targeting, the most effective form of targeting, was done on the basis of surveys asking voters how they plan to vote. The big limitation of this method is, of course, the cost. The expense of reaching all voters in a phone or door-to-door survey can be prohibitive.

The use of predictive analytics adds power to the individual targeting method and reduces cost. A model allows prediction to be rolled out to the entire voter base, not just those surveyed, and brings to bear a wealth of information. Geographic and demographic data remain part of the picture, but they are used at an individual level.

Uplift

In a classical predictive modeling application for marketing, a sample of data is selected and an offer is made (e.g., on the web) or a message is sent (e.g., by mail), and a predictive model is developed to classify individuals as responding or not-responding. The model is then applied to new data, propensities to respond are calculated, individuals are ranked by their propensity to respond, and the marketer can then select those most likely to respond to mailings or offers.

Some key information is missing from this classical approach: How would the individual respond in the absence of the offer or mailing? Might a high-propensity customer be inclined to purchase irrespective of the offer? Might a person's propensity to buy actually be diminished by the offer? Uplift modeling (see Chapter 14) allows us to estimate the effect of "offer vs. no offer" or "mailing vs. no mailing" at the individual level.

In this case, we will apply uplift modeling to actual voter data that were augmented with the results of a hypothetical experiment. The experiment consisted of the following steps:

1. Conduct a pre-survey of the voters to determine their inclination to vote Democratic.

2. Randomly split the voters into two samples—control and treatment.

3. Send a flyer promoting the Democratic candidate to the treatment group.

4. Conduct another survey of the voters to determine their inclination to vote Democratic.

Data

The data in this case are in the file *Voter-Persuasion.csv*. The target attribute is MOVED_AD, where a 1 = "opinion moved in favor of the Democratic candidate" and 0 = "opinion did not move in favor of the Democratic candidate." This attribute encapsulates the information from the pre- and post-surveys. The important predictor attribute is *Flyer*, a binary attribute that indicates whether or not a voter received the flyer. In addition, there are numerous other predictor attributes from these sources:

1. Government voter files
2. Political party data
3. Commercial consumer and demographic data
4. Census neighborhood data

Government voter files are maintained, and made public, to assure the integrity of the voting process. They contain essential data for identification purposes such as name, address, and date of birth. The file used in this case also contains party identification (needed if a state limits participation in party primaries to voters in that party). Parties also staff elections with their own poll watchers, who record whether an individual votes in an election. These data (termed "derived" in the case data) are maintained and curated by each party and can be readily matched to the voter data by name. Demographic data at the neighborhood level are available from the census and can be appended to the voter data by address matching. Consumer and additional demographic data (buying habits, education) can be purchased from marketing firms and appended to the voter data (matching by name and address).

Assignment

The task in this case is to develop an uplift model that predicts the uplift for each voter. Uplift is defined as the increase in propensity to move one's opinion in a Democratic direction. First, review the attributes in *Voter-Persuasion.csv*, and understand which data source they are probably coming from. Then, answer the following questions and perform the tasks indicated:

1. Overall, how well did the flyer do in moving voters in a Democratic direction? (Look at the target attribute among those who got the flyer, compared with those who did not.)

2. Explore the data to learn more about the relationships between the predictor attributes and MOVED_AD (visualization can be helpful). Which of the predictors seem to have good predictive potential? Show supporting charts and/or tables.

3. Partition the data using the partition attribute that is in the dataset, make decisions about predictor inclusion, and fit three predictive models accordingly. For each model, give sufficient detail about the method used, its parameters, and the predictors used, so that your results can be replicated.

4. Among your three models, choose the best one in terms of predictive power. Which one is it? Why did you choose it?

5. Using your chosen model, report the propensities for the first three records in the validation set.

6. Create a derived attribute that is the opposite of *Flyer*, say, *Flyer-reversed*. Using your chosen model, re-score the holdout data using the *Flyer-reversed* attribute as a predictor, instead of *Flyer*. Report the propensities for the first three records in the validation set.

7. For each record, uplift is computed based on the following difference:

$$P(\text{success} \mid \text{Flyer} = 1) - P(\text{success} \mid \text{Flyer} = 0)$$

Compute the uplift for each of the voters in the validation set, and report the uplift for the first three records.

8. If a campaign has the resources to mail the flyer only to 10% of the voters, what uplift threshold should be used?

23.5 TAXI CANCELLATIONS[5]

Taxi-cancellation-case.csv is the dataset for this case study.[6]

Business Situation

In late 2013, the taxi company Yourcabs.com in Bangalore, India, was facing a problem with the drivers using their platform—not all drivers were showing up for their scheduled calls. Drivers would cancel their acceptance of a call, and, if the cancellation did not occur with adequate notice, the customer would be delayed or even left high and dry.

Bangalore is a key tech center in India, and technology was transforming the taxi industry. Yourcabs.com featured an online booking system (though customers could phone in as well) and presented itself as a taxi booking portal. The Uber ride sharing service started its Bangalore operations in mid-2014.

Yourcabs.com had collected data on its bookings from 2011 to 2013 and posted a contest on Kaggle, in coordination with the Indian School of Business, to see what it could learn about the problem of cab cancellations.

The data presented for this case are a randomly selected subset of the original data, with 10,000 rows, one row for each booking. There are 17 input attributes, including user (customer) ID, vehicle model, whether the booking was made online or via a mobile app, type of travel, type of booking package, geographic information, and the date and time of the scheduled trip. The target attribute of interest is the binary indicator of whether a ride was canceled. The overall cancellation rate is between 7% and 8%.

Assignment

1. How can a predictive model based on these data be used by Yourcabs.com?

2. How can a profiling model (identifying predictors that distinguish canceled/uncanceled trips) be used by Yourcabs.com?

3. Explore, prepare, and transform the data to facilitate predictive modeling. Here are some hints:

   • In exploratory modeling, it is useful to move fairly soon to at least an initial model without solving *all* data preparation issues. One example is the GPS information—other geographic information is available,

---

[5]Copyright © Datastats, LLC and Galit Shmueli 2019; used with permission.

[6]When importing this data in RapidMiner, make sure to change the date format to *dd/MM/yy HH:mm* in the data import wizard so that the *from_date* and *booking_created* attributes import correctly. The *to_date* attribute will import as a categorical type, which can then be converted to a *Date-Time* type with the *Nominal to Date* operator.

so you could defer the challenge of how to interpret/use the GPS information.

- How will you deal with missing data, such as cases where ? is indicated?

- Think about what useful information might be held within the date and time fields (the booking timestamp and the trip timestamp).

- Think also about the categorical attributes and how to deal with them. Should we turn them all into dummies? Use only some?

4. Fit several predictive models of your choice. Do they provide information on how the predictor attributes relate to cancellations?

5. Report the predictive performance of your model in terms of error rates (the confusion matrix). How well does the model perform? Can the model be used in practice?

6. Examine the predictive performance of your model in terms of ranking (lift). How well does the model perform? Can the model be used in practice?

23.6 SEGMENTING CONSUMERS OF BATH SOAP[7]

BathSoapHousehold.csv is the dataset for this case study.

Business Situation

CRISA is an Asian market research agency that specializes in tracking consumer purchase behavior in consumer goods (both durable and nondurable). In one major research project, CRISA tracks numerous consumer product categories (e.g., "detergents") and, within each category, perhaps dozens of brands. To track purchase behavior, CRISA constituted household panels in over 100 cities and towns in India, covering most of the Indian urban market. The households were carefully selected using stratified sampling to ensure a representative sample; a subset of 600 records is analyzed here. The strata were defined on the basis of socioeconomic status and the market (a collection of cities).

CRISA has both transaction data (each row is a transaction) and household data (each row is a household), and for the household data, it maintains the following information:

- Demographics of the households (updated annually)
- Possession of durable goods (car, washing machine, etc., updated annually; an "affluence index" is computed from this information)
- Purchase data of product categories and brands (updated monthly)

CRISA has two categories of clients: (1) advertising agencies that subscribe to the database services, obtain updated data every month, and use the data to advise their clients on advertising and promotion strategies and (2) consumer goods manufacturers, which monitor their market share using the CRISA database.

Key Problems

CRISA has traditionally segmented markets on the basis of purchaser demographics. They would now like to segment the market based on two key sets of attributes more directly related to the purchase process and to brand loyalty:

1. Purchase behavior (volume, frequency, susceptibility to discounts, and brand loyalty)
2. Basis of purchase (promotion, price)

Doing so would allow CRISA to gain information about what demographic attributes are associated with different purchase behaviors and degrees of brand loyalty and thus deploy promotion budgets more effectively. More effective market segmentation would enable CRISA's clients (in this case, a firm called IMRB) to design more cost-effective promotions targeted at appropriate segments. Thus, multiple promotions could be launched, each targeted at different market segments at different times of the year. This would result in a more cost-effective allocation of the promotion budget to different market segments. It would also enable IMRB to design more effective customer reward systems and thereby increase brand loyalty.

Data

The data in Table 23.8 profile each household, each row containing the data for one household.

Measuring Brand Loyalty

Several attributes in this case measure aspects of brand loyalty. The number of different brands purchased by the customer is one measure of loyalty. However, a consumer who purchases one or two brands in quick succession and then settles on a third for a long streak is different from a consumer who constantly switches back and forth among three brands. Therefore, how often customers switch from one brand to another is another measure of loyalty. Yet a third perspective on the same issue is the proportion of purchases that go to different brands—a consumer who spends 90% of his or her purchase money on one brand is more loyal than a consumer who spends more equally among several brands.

All three of these components can be measured with the data in the purchase summary worksheet.

Assignment

1. Use k-means clustering to identify clusters of households based on:
   a. The attributes that describe purchase behavior (including brand loyalty)
   b. The attributes that describe the basis for purchase
   c. The attributes that describe both purchase behavior and basis of purchase

   Note 1: How should k be chosen? Think about how the clusters would be used. It is likely that the marketing efforts would support two to five different promotional approaches.

   Note 2: How should the percentages of total purchases accounted for by various brands be treated? Isn't a customer who buys all brand A just as loyal as a customer who buys all brand B? What will be the effect on any

TABLE 23.8   DESCRIPTION OF ATTRIBUTES FOR EACH HOUSEHOLD

Attribute type	Attribute name	Description
Member ID	Member id	Unique identifier for each household
Demographics	SEC	Socioeconomic class (1 = high, 5 = low)
	FEH	Eating habits(1 = vegetarian, 2 = vegetarian but eat eggs, 3 = nonvegetarian, 0 = not specified)
	MT	Native language (see table in worksheet)
	SEX	Gender of homemaker (1 = male, 2 = female)
	AGE	Age of homemaker
	EDU	Education of homemaker (1 = minimum, 9 = maximum)
	HS	Number of members in household
	CHILD	Presence of children in household (4 categories)
	CS	Television availability (1 = available, 2 = unavailable)
	Affluence Index	Weighted value of durables possessed
Purchase summary over the period	No. of Brands	Number of brands purchased
	Brand Runs	Number of instances of consecutive purchase of brands
	Total Volume	Sum of volume
	No. of Trans	Number of purchase transactions (multiple brands purchased in a month are counted as separate transactions)
	Value	Sum of value
	Trans/Brand Runs	Average transactions per brand run
	Vol/Trans	Average volume per transaction
	Avg. Price	Average price of purchase
Purchase within promotion	Pur Vol	Percent of volume purchased
	No Promo - %	Percent of volume purchased under no promotion
	Pur Vol Promo 6%	Percent of volume purchased under promotion code 6
	Pur Vol Other Promo %	Percent of volume purchased under other promotions
Brandwise purchase	Br. Cd. (57, 144), 55, 272, 286, 24, 481, 352, 5, and 999 (others)	Percent of volume purchased of the brand
Price categorywise purchase	Price Cat 1 to 4	Percent of volume purchased under the price category
Selling propositionwise purchase	Proposition Cat 5 to 15	Percent of volume purchased under the product proposition category

(*Source*: © Cytel, Inc. and Datastats, LLC 2019)

distance measure of using the brand share attributes as is? Consider using a single derived attribute.

2. Select what you think is the best segmentation, and comment on the characteristics (demographic, brand loyalty, and basis for purchase) of these clusters. (This information would be used to guide the development of advertising and promotional campaigns.)

3. Develop a model that classifies the data into these segments. Since this information would most likely be used in targeting direct-mail promotions, it would be useful to select a market segment that would be defined as a *success* in the classification model.

23.7 DIRECT-MAIL FUNDRAISING

Fundraising.csv and *FutureFundraising.csv* are the datasets used for this case study.

Background

Note: Be sure to read the information about oversampling and adjustment in Chapter 5 before starting to work on this case.

A national veterans' organization wishes to develop a predictive model to improve the cost-effectiveness of their direct marketing campaign. The organization, with its in-house database of over 13 million donors, is one of the largest direct-mail fundraisers in the United States. According to their recent mailing records, the overall response rate is 5.1%. Out of those who responded (donated), the average donation is $13.00. Each mailing, which includes a gift of personalized address labels and assortments of cards and envelopes, costs $0.68 to produce and send. Using these facts, we take a sample of this dataset to develop a classification model that can effectively capture donors so that the expected net profit is maximized. Weighted sampling is used, underrepresenting the non-responders so that the sample has equal numbers of donors and non-donors.

Data

The file *Fundraising.csv* contains 3120 records with 50% donors (TARGET_B = 1) and 50% non-donors (TARGET_B = 0). The amount of donation (TARGET_D) is also included but is not used in this case. The descriptions for the 22 attributes (including two target attributes) are listed in Table 23.9.

Assignment

Step 1—Partitioning: Partition the dataset into 60% training and 40% holdout (set the seed to 12345).

Step 2—Model Building: Follow the following steps to build, evaluate, and choose a model.

1. *Select classification tool and parameters*: Run at least two classification models of your choosing. Be sure NOT to use TARGET_D in your analysis. Describe the two models that you chose, with sufficient detail (method, parameters, attributes, etc.) so that it can be replicated.

2. *Classification under asymmetric response and cost*: What is the reasoning behind using weighted sampling to produce a training set with equal numbers of donors and non-donors? Why not use a simple random sample from the original dataset?

3. *Calculate net profit*: For each method, calculate the cumulative gains of net profit for both the training and holdout sets based on the actual

TABLE 23.9	DESCRIPTION OF ATTRIBUTES FOR THE FUNDRAISING DATASET

Attribute	Description
ZIP	Zip code group (zip codes were grouped into five groups; 1 = the potential donor belongs to this zip group.) 00000–19999 $\Rightarrow$ zipconvert_1 20000–39999 $\Rightarrow$ zipconvert_2 40000–59999 $\Rightarrow$ zipconvert_3 60000–79999 $\Rightarrow$ zipconvert_4 80000–99999 $\Rightarrow$ zipconvert_5
HOMEOWNER	1 = homeowner, 0 = not a homeowner
NUMCHLD	Number of children
INCOME	Household income
GENDER	0 = male, 1 = female
WEALTH	Wealth rating uses median family income and population statistics from each area to index relative wealth within each state The segments are denoted 0 to 9, with 9 being the highest-wealth group and zero the lowest. Each rating has a different meaning within each state.
HV	Average home value in potential donor's neighborhood in hundreds of dollars
ICmed	Median family income in potential donor's neighborhood in hundreds of dollars
ICavg	Average family income in potential donor's neighborhood in hundreds
IC15	Percent earning less than $15K in potential donor's neighborhood
NUMPROM	Lifetime number of promotions received to date
RAMNTALL	Dollar amount of lifetime gifts to date
MAXRAMNT	Dollar amount of largest gift to date
LASTGIFT	Dollar amount of most recent gift
TOTALMONTHS	Number of months from last donation to July 1998 (the last time the case was updated)
TIMELAG	Number of months between first and second gift
AVGGIFT	Average dollar amount of gifts to date
TARGET_B	Target attribute: binary indicator for response 1 = donor, 0 = non-donor
TARGET_D	Target attribute: donation amount (in dollars). We will NOT be using this attribute for this case

response rate (5.1%.) Again, the expected donation, given that they are donors, is $13.00, and the total cost of each mailing is $0.68. (*Hint*: To calculate estimated net profit, we will need to undo the effects of the weighted sampling and calculate the net profit that would reflect the actual response distribution of 5.1% donors and 94.9% non-donors. To do this, divide each row's net profit by the oversampling weights applicable to the actual status of that row. The oversampling weight for actual donors is 50%/5.1% = 9.8. The oversampling weight for actual non-donors is 50%/94.9% = 0.53.)

4. *Draw lift charts (cumulative gains curves)*: Draw the different models' net profit cumulative gains curves for the holdout set in a single plot (net profit on the y-axis, proportion of list or number mailed on the x-axis). Is there a model that dominates?

5. *Select best model*: From your answer in (4), what do you think is the "best" model?

Step 3—Testing: The file *FutureFundraising.csv* contains the attributes for future mailing candidates.

6. Using your "best" model from Step 2 (number 5), which of these candidates do you predict as donors and non-donors? List them in descending order of the probability of being a donor. Starting at the top of this sorted list, roughly how far down would you go in a mailing campaign?

23.8 CATALOG CROSS-SELLING[8]

CatalogCrossSell.csv is the dataset for this case study.

Background

Exeter, Inc., is a catalog firm that sells products in a number of different catalogs that it owns. The catalogs number in the dozens but fall into nine basic categories:

1. Clothing
2. Housewares
3. Health
4. Automotive
5. Personal electronics
6. Computers
7. Garden
8. Novelty gift
9. Jewelry

The costs of printing and distributing catalogs are high. By far, the biggest cost of operation is the cost of promoting products to people who buy nothing. Having invested so much in the production of artwork and printing of catalogs, Exeter wants to take every opportunity to use them effectively. One such opportunity is in cross-selling—once a customer has "taken the bait" and purchases one product, try to sell them another while you have their attention.

Such cross-promotion might take the form of enclosing a catalog in the shipment of a purchased product, together with a discount coupon to induce a purchase from that catalog. Or, it might take the form of a similar coupon sent by e-mail, with a link to the web version of that catalog.

But which catalog should be enclosed in the box or included as a link in the e-mail with the discount coupon? Exeter would like it to be an informed choice—a catalog that has a higher probability of inducing a purchase than simply choosing a catalog at random.

Assignment

Using the dataset *CatalogCrossSell.csv*, perform an association rules analysis, and comment on the results. Your discussion should provide interpretations in English of the meanings of the various output statistics (lift ratio, conviction,

---

[8]Copyright © Datastats, LLC 2019; used with permission.

confidence, support) and include a very rough estimate (precise calculations are not necessary) of the extent to which this will help Exeter make an informed choice about which catalog to cross-promote to a purchaser.

Acknowledgment   The data for this case have been adapted from the data in a set of cases provided for educational purposes by the Direct Marketing Education Foundation ("DMEF Academic Data Set Two, Multi Division Catalog Company, Code: 02DMEF"), used with permission.

23.9 TIME SERIES CASE: FORECASTING PUBLIC TRANSPORTATION DEMAND

bicup2006.csv is the dataset for this case study.

Background

Forecasting transportation demand is important for multiple purposes such as staffing, planning, and inventory control. The public transportation system in Santiago de Chile has gone through a major effort of reconstruction. In this context, a business intelligence competition took place in October 2006, which focused on forecasting demand for public transportation. This case is based on the competition, with some modifications.

Problem Description

A public transportation company is expecting an increase in demand for its services and is planning to acquire new buses and to extend its terminals. These investments require a reliable forecast of future demand. To create such forecasts, one can use data on historic demand. The company's data warehouse has data for each 15-minute interval between 6:30 and 22:00, on the number of passengers arriving at the terminal. As a forecasting consultant, you have been asked to create a forecasting method that can generate forecasts for the number of passengers arriving at the terminal.

Available Data

Part of the historic information is available in the file *bicup2006.csv*. The file contains the historic information with known demand for a 3-week period, separated into 15-minute intervals, and dates and times for a future 3-day period (DEMAND = ?), for which forecasts should be generated (as part of the 2006 competition).

Assignment Goal

Your goal is to create a model/method that produces accurate forecasts. To evaluate your accuracy, partition the given historic data into two periods: a training period (the first two weeks) and a holdout period (the last week). Models should be fitted only to the training data and evaluated on the holdout data.

Although the competition winning criterion was the lowest mean absolute error (MAE) on the future 3-day data, this is *not* the goal for this assignment. Instead, if we consider a more realistic business context, our goal is to create a model that generates reasonably good forecasts on any time/day of the week. Consider not only predictive metrics such as MAE, mean absolute percentage error (MAPE), and root mean squared error (RMSE), but also look at actual and forecasted values, overlaid on a time plot, as well as a time plot of the forecast errors.

Assignment

For your final model, present the following summary:

1. Name of the method/combination of methods.

2. A brief description of the method/combination.

3. All estimated equations associated with constructing forecasts from this method.

4. The MAPE and MAE for the training period and the holdout period.

5. Forecasts for the future period (March 22–24), in 15-minute bins.

6. A single chart showing the fit of the final version of the model to the entire period (including training, holdout, and future). Note that this model should be fitted using the combined training plus holdout data.

Tips and Suggested Steps

1. Use exploratory analysis to identify the components of this time series. Is there a trend? Is there seasonality? If so, how many "seasons" are there? Are there any other visible patterns? Are the patterns global (the same throughout the series) or local?

2. Consider the frequency of the data from a practical and technical point of view. What are some options?

3. Compare the weekdays and weekends. How do they differ? Consider how these differences can be captured by different methods.

4. Examine the series for missing values or unusual values. Think of solutions.

5. Based on the patterns that you found in the data, which models or methods should be considered?

6. Consider how to handle actual counts of zero within the computation of MAPE.

23.10 LOAN APPROVAL[9]

UniversalBank-Case.xlsx is the dataset for this case study.

Background

You are a data scientist recently hired by Universal Bank, a mid-sized bank in the southern United States. Most of your work to this point has involved pulling reports from databases, but now you have been given a more interesting task. The bank is facing competition from online lenders that can offer rapid automated loan approvals, and it wants to develop its own predictive model so that it can do likewise. Before building the web infrastructure, which could be costly, the bank wants to pilot a prototype loan approval model, developed by you.

The bank wants to launch its model with the approval process for personal loans extended to existing customers. The bank has only been offering these loans for a relatively short time, so has little data on default rates. It does have data on prior loan applications and whether they were approved or disapproved. You have done some preliminary data prep and feature selection work, resulting in the dataset of 5000 records for this project. Each record is for a customer and consists of feature values for that customer along with a record of the human decision on their loan application. Your end goal is to develop a model to predict that human decision and an accompanying report to the bank's chief lending officer.

Regulatory Requirements

You are somewhat familiar with regulatory requirements with respect to discrimination (do a web search for the US Department of Justice Equal Credit Opportunity Act or ECOA). Bank attorneys have told you that the ECOA requirements pertain to the basis for credit decisions and do not mean that the proportion of approved loans must be the same for all groups.

Getting Started

You have the RDS framework in hand (see Chapter 22). You recognize that some aspects of the framework may take more time (e.g., consulting with other stakeholders and learning more about how the data were produced), but you want to get started with at least a draft so that you can discuss next steps with your superiors.

---

[9]Copyright © 2022 Datastats, LLC, and Galit Shmueli, used with permission.

Assignment

1. Identify any features that might need to be excluded from the modeling task, per the ECOA.

2. Should you simply eliminate these features from the data?

3. Explore the data, with a focus on loan approval rates for different groups.

4. Split the data into training and validation data, and fit several models of your choice to predict whether a personal loan should be approved, using only permitted features. There are a number of possible performance measures; evaluate the model performance by the metric(s) you consider useful.

5. Assess the usefulness of the model from a pure model performance standpoint.

6. Considering the "protected" categories per the ECOA, evaluate whether the model is fair.

7. Describe steps that might be taken to improve the model fairness. Implement any measures that can be taken without going beyond the dataset at hand. (*Hint*: If you did not calculate a correlation matrix earlier, you should do one now.)

8. Write a very short report summarizing your findings.

References

Aggarwal, C. C. (2016). *Recommender Systems* (Vol. 1). Springer Cham.

Agrawal, R., Imielinski, T., and Swami, A. (1993). Mining associations between sets of items in massive databases. In: *Proceedings of the 1993 ACM-SIGMOD International Conference on Management of Data*, pp. 207–216. New York: ACM Press.

Anderson, D. R., Sweeney, D. J., Williams, T. A., Cam, J. D., Cochran, J. J., Fry, M. J., and Ohlmann, J. W. (2021). *Modern Business Statistics with Microsoft Excel*, 7th ed. Boston: Cengage Learning.

Berry, M. J. A., and Linoff, G. S. (1997). *Data Mining Techniques*. New York: Wiley.

Berry, M. J. A., and Linoff, G. S. (2000). *Mastering Data Mining*. New York: Wiley.

Breiman, L., Friedman, J., Olshen, R., and Stone, C. (1984). *Classification and Regression Trees*. Boca Raton, FL: Chapman Hall/CRC (orig. published by Wadsworth).

Brin, S., Motwani, R., Ullman, J. D., and Tsur, S. (1997). Dynamic itemset counting and implication rules for market basket data. In: *Proceedings of the 1997 ACM-SIGMOD International Conference on Management of Data*, pp. 255–264. New York: ACM Press.

Chawla, N. V., Bowyer, K. W., Lawrence, O. H., and Kegelmeyer, W. P. (2002). SMOTE: synthetic minority over-sampling technique. *Journal of Artificial Intelligence Research*, vol. 16, number 1, pp. 321–357.

Chatfield, C. (2003). *The Analysis of Time Series: An Introduction*, 6th ed. Boca Raton, FL: Chapman Hall/CRC.

Delmaster, R., and Hancock, M. (2001). *Data Mining Explained*. Boston, MA: Digital Press.

Efron, B. (1975). The efficiency of logistic regression compared to normal discriminant analysis. *Journal of the American Statistical Association*, vol. 70, number 352, pp. 892–898.

Few, S. (2021). *Now You See It*, 2nd ed. Oakland, CA: Analytics Press.

Few, S. (2012). *Show Me the Numbers*, 2nd ed. Oakland, CA: Analytics Press.

Fleming, G., and Bruce, P. C. (2021). *Responsible Data Science*. Hoboken, NJ: Wiley.

Golbeck, J. (2013). *Analyzing the Social Web*. Waltham, MA: Morgan Kaufmann.

Han, J., and Kamber, M. (2001). *Data Mining: Concepts and Techniques*. San Diego, CA: Academic Press.

Han, J., Pei, J., and Yin, Y. (2000). Mining frequent patterns without candidate generation. In: *Proceedings of the 2000 ACM-SIGMOD International Conference on Management of Data*, pp. 1–12. New York: ACM Press.

Hand, D. J. (2009). Measuring classifier performance: a coherent alternative to the area under the ROC curve. *Machine Learning*, vol. 77, number 1, pp. 103–123.

Machine Learning for Business Analytics: Concepts, Techniques and Applications in RapidMiner, First Edition.
Galit Shmueli, Peter C. Bruce, Amit V. Deokar, and Nitin R. Patel
© 2023 John Wiley & Sons, Inc. Published 2023 by John Wiley & Sons, Inc.

Harper, F. M., and Konstan, J. A. (2015). The MovieLens Datasets: history and context. *ACM Transactions on Interactive Intelligent Systems (TiiS)*, vol. 5, number 4, pp. 19:1–19:19. DOI: 10.1145/2827872.

Harris, H., Murphy, S., and Vaisman, M. (2013). *Analyzing the Analyzers: An Introspective Survey of Data Scientists and Their Work*. Cambridge, MA: O'Reilly Media.

Hastie, T., Tibshirani, R., and Friedman, J. (2001). *The Elements of Statistical Learning*. New York: Springer.

Hosmer, D. W., and Lemeshow, S. (2000). *Applied Logistic Regression*, 2nd ed. New York: Wiley-Interscience.

Hothorn, T., Hornik K., and Zeileis, A. (2006). Unbiased recursive partitioning: a conditional inference framework. *Journal of Computational and Graphical Statistics*, vol. 15, number 3, pp. 651–674.

Hyndman, R., and Yang, Y. Z. (2018). tsdl: Time Series Data Library. v0.1.0. https://pkg.yangzhuoranyang.com/tsdl/.

Jank, W., and Yahav, I. (2010). E-Loyalty networks in online auctions. *The Annals of Applied Statistics*, vol. 4, number 1, pp. 151–178.

Johnson, W., and Wichern, D. (2002). *Applied Multivariate Statistics*. Upper Saddle River, NJ: Prentice Hall.

Kohavi, R., Tang, D., and Xu, Y. (2020). *Trustworthy Online Controlled Experiments: A Practical Guide to A/B Testing*. Cambridge, United Kingdom; New York, NY: Cambridge University Press.

Larsen, K. (2005). Generalized naive Bayes classifiers. *SIGKDD Explorations*, vol. 7, number 1, pp. 76–81.

Le, Q. V., Ranzato, M. A., Monga, R., Devin, M., Chen, K., Corrado, G. S., Dean, J., and Ng, A.Y. (2012). Building high-level features using large scale unsupervised learning. In: *Proceedings of the Twenty-Ninth International Conference on Machine Learning*. Editors: J. Langford and J. Pineau. Edinburgh: Omnipress.

Lobo, J. M., Jiménez-Valverde, A., and Real, R. (2008). AUC: a misleading measure of the performance of predictive distribution models. *Global Ecology and Biogeography*, vol. 17, number 2, pp. 145-151.

Loh, W.-Y., and Shih, Y.-S. (1997). Split selection methods for classification trees. *Statistica Sinica*, vol. 7, pp. 815–840.

Maas, A. L., Daly, R. E., Pham, P. T., Huang, D., Ng, A. Y., and Potts, C. (2011). Learning word vectors for sentiment analysis. In: *Proceedings of the 49th Annual Meeting of the Association for Computational Linguistics: Human Language Technologies - vol. 1*, pp. 142–150. DOI: 10.5555/2002472.2002491.

Molnar, C. (2022). *Interpretable Machine Learning: A Guide for Making Black Box Models Explainable*, 2nd ed. https://christophm.github.io/interpretable-ml-book/.

McCullugh, C. E., Paal, B., and Ashdown, S. P. (1998). An optimisation approach to apparel sizing. *Journal of the Operational Research Society*, vol. 49, number 5, pp. 492–499.

Matz, S. C., Kosinski, S. C., Nave, G., and Stillwell, D. J. (2017). Psychological targeting in digital mass persuasion. In: *Proceedings of the National Academy of Sciences*, vol. 114, number 48, pp. 12714–12719. DOI: 10.1073/pnas.1710966114.

O'Neil, C. (2016). Weapons of Math Destruction. New York: Crown Publishers.

Pelleg, D., and Moore, A. W. (2000). X-means: Extending K-means with efficient estimation of the number of clusters. In: *Proceedings of the Seventeenth International Conference on Machine Learning*, pp. 727–734. DOI: 10.5555/645529.657808.

Pregibon, D. (1999). 2001: a statistical odyssey. Invited talk at *The Fifth ACM SIGKDD International Conference on Knowledge Discovery and Data Mining*. New York: ACM Press, p. 4.

Quinlan, J. R. (1986). Induction of decision trees. *Machine learning*, vol. 1, number 1, pp. 81–106.

Ribeiro, M. T., Singh, S., and Guestrin, C. (2016). Why should I trust you?: explaining the predictions of any classifier. In: *Proceedings of the 22nd ACM SIGKDD International Conference on Knowledge Discovery and Data Mining*. San Francisco, CA: ACM, pp. 1135–1144. DOI: 10.1145/2939672.2939778.

Rokach, L., and Maimon, O. Z. (2014). *Data Mining with Decision Trees: Theory and Applications*, 2nd ed. Singapore: World Scientific.

Russell, S. (2019). *Human Compatible: Artificial Intelligence and the Problem of Control*. New York: Penguin Books.

Saddiqi, N. (2017). *Intelligent Credit Scoring: Building and Implementing Better Credit Risk Scorecards*, 2nd ed. Hoboken, NJ: Wiley.

Shmueli, G., and Lichtendahl, K. C. (2016). *Practical Time Series Forecasting with R: A Hands-On Guide*, 2nd ed.: Axelrod-Schnall Publishers.

Siegel, E. (2013). *Predictive Analytics*. New York: Wiley.

Sutton, R. S., and Barto, A. G. (2018). *Reinforcement Learning: An Introduction*, 2nd ed. Bradford Books.

Data Files Used in the Book

1. accidents.csv
2. accidentsFull.csv
3. accidentsnn.csv
4. Airfares.csv
5. Amtrak.csv
6. ApplianceShipments.csv
7. AustralianWines.csv
8. AutoAndElectronics.zip
9. Bank-bias-data.csv
10. banks.csv
11. BareggTunnel.csv
12. BathSoapHousehold.csv
13. bicup2006.csv
14. BostonHousing.csv
15. CanadianWorkHours.csv
16. CatalogCrossSell.csv
17. Cereals.csv
18. CharlesBookClub.csv
19. COMPAS-clean.csv
20. Cosmetics.csv
21. countries.csv
22. courserating.csv
23. CourseTopics.csv
24. DepartmentStoreSales.csv
25. drug.csv
26. EastWestAirlinesCluster.csv
27. EastWestAirlinesNN.csv
28. eBayAuctions.csv
29. ebayNetwork.csv
30. EbayTreemap.csv
31. email-A-B-test.csv
32. Faceplate.csv
33. farm-ads.csv
34. fashion_mnist_png.zip
35. FlightDelays.csv
36. Fundraising.csv
37. FutureFundraising.csv
38. gdp.csv
39. GermanCredit.csv
40. Hair-Care-Product.csv
41. IMDB-Dataset-10K.xlsx
42. LaptopSales.csv
43. LaptopSalesJanuary2008.csv
44. movies.csv

Machine Learning for Business Analytics: Concepts, Techniques and Applications in RapidMiner, First Edition.
Galit Shmueli, Peter C. Bruce, Amit V. Deokar, and Nitin R. Patel.
© 2023 John Wiley & Sons, Inc. Published 2023 by John Wiley & Sons, Inc.

45. NaturalGasSales.csv
46. NYPD_Motor_Vehicle_Collisions_1000.csv
47. ownerExample.csv
48. Pharmaceuticals.csv
49. ratings.csv
50. RidingMowers.csv
51. SC-US-students-GPS-data-2016.csv
52. ShampooSales.csv
53. Sept11Travel.csv
54. SouvenirSales.csv
55. SP500.csv
56. Spambase.csv
57. SystemAdministrators.csv
58. Taxi-cancellation-case.csv
59. Tayko.csv
60. TextSample.csv
61. TinyData.csv
62. ToyotaCorolla.csv
63. ToysRUsRevenues.csv
64. UniversalBank.csv
65. UniversalBank-Case.xlsx
66. Universities.csv
67. Utilities.csv
68. Veerhoven.csv
69. Voter-Persuasion.csv
70. WalMartStock.csv
71. WestRoxbury.csv
72. WestRoxbury-NewData.csv
73. Wine.csv

Index

Machine Learning for Business Analytics: Concepts, Techniques and Applications in RapidMiner, First Edition.
Galit Shmueli, Peter C. Bruce, Amit V. Deokar, and Nitin R. Patel
© 2023 John Wiley & Sons, Inc. Published 2023 by John Wiley & Sons, Inc.